C000216425

UNELECTED POWER

UNELECTED POWER

The Quest for Legitimacy in Central Banking and the Regulatory State

Paul Tucker

PRINCETON UNIVERSITY PRESS

Princeton & Oxford

Published by Princeton University Press,
41 William Street, Princeton, New Jersey 08540

In the United Kingdom: Princeton University Press,
6 Oxford Street, Woodstock, Oxfordshire OX20 1TR

press.princeton.edu

Jacket design by Faceout Studio
Jacket image courtesy of Shutterstock

ISBN 978-0-691-17673-4
Library of Congress Control Number: 2018935378

British Library Cataloging-in-Publication Data is available

This book has been composed in Minion Pro text with Helvetica Neue LT Std display

Printed on acid-free paper. ∞

Printed and bound by CPI Group (UK) Ltd, Croydon, CR0 4YY

10 9 8 7 6 5 4 3 2 1

CONTENTS

PREFACE

"Of course, if the Bank were ever given monetary independence, you might need to lose bank supervision in case you became an overmighty citizen." Those were the words of the head of the UK Treasury, Terry Burns, to Bank of England Governor Robin Leigh-Pemberton in his London Threadneedle Street office over a quarter of a century ago. I was present as the governor's private secretary, and I have been thinking about them ever since.

Less than a decade later, when Britain's Blair-Brown government was elected in 1997, the Bank of England did regain independence in monetary policy, after an interval of over sixty years, and as predicted it duly lost banking supervision. But within fifteen years, supervision had been transferred back, in the aftermath of the 2007–2009 financial crisis. What's more, supervision came with wider and greater powers than ever before. As those of us then at the Bank worked with government and Parliament to frame the new regime, nothing loomed larger in Bank counsels than a desire to avoid being an overmighty citizen. More positively, we fervently wanted the Bank and its policy makers—independent, powerful, but unelected—to enjoy legitimacy.

This was not just a matter of public virtue, although I like to think that played a part. We were aware of a degree of schizophrenia among the London elite about the transfer of powers to the Bank. Asked whether it was a good thing that the central bank was regaining its historic mission for ensuring the stability of the banking system, the response seemed to be overwhelmingly positive. Asked whether they were comfortable with the concentration of power in the Bank, the same metropolitan figures—not a few of them former senior government officials—were at best lukewarm.

For these reasons, the title of this book was initially "Overmighty Citizens?," recalling the question of whether late-medieval England was destabilized by the overmighty subjects among the nobility whose power and might rivaled or eclipsed that of the king. But even though England's Wars of the Roses have found a vast modern television audience around the world, and even though the problem of overmighty citizens famously preoccupied republican Florence, I found that when explaining what the book is about, I invariably say "unelected power."

The problem—and so the book—is by no means limited to Britain, or to central banking. Concerns about similar delegations exist across the developed world, affecting huge swathes of public life given the extent to which elected politicians have been shedding their powers. Americans call it the administrative state; Europeans, with a slightly narrower focus, the regulatory state. Labels aside, central banks occupy a special place in this constellation. For now at least, their governors have become the poster boys and girls of the technocratic elite. As I discuss, whether in the United States or Europe, that has not met with universal applause, raising questions about the legitimacy and sheer reach of central banks' powers and roles.

This book, then, is about whether and how democratic societies can find their way through these issues. It is about power—unelected power. How to contain it, hold it accountable, legitimize it. But it is also about how to make the power of independent agencies useful, serving society's needs. And it is about the importance of recognizing that formally delegating power in one area sometimes unavoidably entails bestowing de facto power in others.

At a personal level, it amounts to an attempt to make sense of the reservations of three of the Bank of England's biggest post–World War II figures—George Blunden, Eddie George, and Mervyn King—about becoming a powerful independent authority. I came to share that institutional caution over my thirty-odd years at the Bank, a dozen or so of which were spent as a policy maker, finally as deputy governor, and the vast bulk of which happened to be devoted to designing or redesigning regimes for monetary policy, stability policy, or regulation, including in Hong Kong after the 1987 stock market crash.

Holding public office is an enormous privilege. It requires doing, thinking, planning, managing and, perhaps most crucially today, explaining. In that spirit, the first part of the book concludes with the principles that, in my mind at least, guided our contribution to the reconstruction of the UK regime after the 2007–2009 crisis.[1] As well as the economic substance of stability policy, we weighed the acceptable

[1]For example, Tucker, "A New Regulatory Relationship."

limits of unelected power. Among other things, we leaned against suggestions that we take on responsibility for supervising securities exchanges and trading platforms, and that we use our lending policies to steer the allocation of credit. Much of the remainder of the book is an exploration of how those *Principles for Delegation*, as I call them, fit with the deep values and beliefs of mature democratic societies, an exercise I had time for when I took up a fellowship at Harvard in late 2013.

The book takes for granted that institutions matter. While that has become mainstream among economists over the past quarter of a century, and while the institutions of government are increasingly studied by empirical political scientists, it has largely fallen out of fashion among political theorists—the people who map out the moral grounds and goals of public affairs.[2] From the seventeenth to the nineteenth centuries, writers as central to our traditions as Locke, Montesquieu, Hegel, and Mill thought deeply about the structure of the state, and practical state builders as illustrious as Alexander Hamilton and James Madison did likewise. Today, however, with the exception of debates around the EU's governance, discussion of whether the emergence of independent government agencies—and delegation to agencies more generally—represents a profound change in our politics is too frequently confined to lawyers and to academics specializing in regulation or government effectiveness.

The broader discussion ought to be about marrying values to institutions and, thus, to incentives. The book argues that power, welfare, incentives, and values have to be considered together if the institution of delegated unelected power is to be sustainable in our democracies. I hope that it will help to provoke more political theorists and others to join Philip Pettit, Henry Richardson, Pierre Rosanvallon, and Jeremy Waldron in reviving interest in what our values entail for the structure of government, giving legitimacy equal billing with discussions of justice.[3]

The book aims to be practical, offering concrete proposals. Their core was first set out publicly in the 2014 Gordon Lecture, which I was honored to be asked to give by the Harvard Kennedy School. By then I had

[2] For a multidisciplinary review, see Goodin, "Institutions."
[3] Waldron, "*Political* Political Theory."

forgotten, but in the course of writing the book rediscovered, that some of the lecture's underlying concerns had been aired in a speech while I was in office, back in 2007.[4]

In pursuing the questions raised by unelected power, the book draws on political economy, political theory, and some political science and public law, as well as on my own and others' personal experiences. Embarking on trying to weave all that together, I owe enormous thanks to many academics, legislators, officials, and commentators around the world who gave me their time, and in many cases have become good friends.

[4]Tucker, "Central Banking and Political Economy."

UNELECTED POWER

1

Introduction

POWER, WELFARE, INCENTIVES, VALUES

> A press conference is not enough to call it "democracy." I do not expect this illegitimate institution to hear my voice.
>
> —Josephine Witt protesting at the European Central Bank's April 15, 2015, press conference

> It is time to end regulation without representation and restore our faith in the people to make the best decisions for families and businesses.
>
> —US Senator Mike Rounds (R-South Dakota), *The Hill*, May 21, 2015

In the course of 2016, first the UK referendum on membership in the European Union (EU) and then the US presidential election, coming on top of popular discontent and protest in parts of Continental Europe, thrust into public debate issues of populism and technocracy. As models for government, they appear to stand at opposite ends of the spectrum, either embracing or distancing the people. Of course, it is not so clear-cut. Populist leaders typically claim a special alignment or accord with the interests of the People, understood as the True or Authentic members of a political community, allowing them to dispense with the messy business of actual public participation, debate, and disagreement.[1] Technocracy, meanwhile, at least in caricature, claims to have uncovered some kind of scientific method for figuring out what is in the public or common interest—provided, that is, that they, the unelected experts, are left to get on with it, checked only by another group of unelected power holders, the judges. In fact, our technocrats must consult and explain, but still that is not the same as political accountability.

[1]Muller, *What Is Populism?*

Nowhere in our major democracies does either of those systems of government actually exist, but their underlying ideas nevertheless confront each other today as rallying cries in the real world of politics. Those seeking the votes of people feeling let down by and fed up with government over the past quarter century or more find common cause in blaming distant and aloof experts as the enemy. Those on the other side, fearing that (what they see as) basic values or rights will be put aside, warn of the false allure of populist demagogues.

This contest, struggle even, undoubtedly reflects genuine changes in politics and government. The main parties on the Left and the Right are no longer the mass movements they were up until the 1970s, offering distinct *political* programs appealing, in part, to tribal identities.[2] And in government itself, delegation to more or less independent agencies, led by unelected technocrats, has ballooned over recent decades (and earlier in the US).

Those phenomena are related. If there exists sufficient consensus around the goals and the means of public policy that it can be delegated beyond the day-to-day reach of elected politicians, political parties offering rival visions of the good life and how it might be achieved lose some of their point. Protesting at this and, perhaps, a drift toward liberalism, a former deputy leader of Britain's Labour Party complained in 1997 that "Tony Blair is taking the politics out of politics."[3]

But recent socioeconomic disappointment puts the consensus around delegated governance in an uncomfortable light. Economic growth has been subdued since the Great Financial Crisis, and the gaps between the poor, the just-coping, and the rich have widened over recent decades. Hence, it is not complete fantasy to see our democracies as flirting with a peculiar cocktail of *hyper-depoliticized* technocracy and *hyper-politicized* populism, each fueling the other in attempts, respectively, to maintain effective government and to reestablish majoritarian sensibility.[4]

[2] Mair, *Ruling the Void*.

[3] Hattersley, "Pragmatism." Thanks to Jon Davis for alerting me to this.

[4] Flinders and Wood, "When Politics Fails." I use "hyper-depoliticization" to mean lots of it, not merely insulation from both elected branches as in Rubin, "Hyperdepoliticization."

This conjuncture of politics and economics might conceivably end up challenging the basic structures and values of liberal democracy, the dominant model of collective governance since the fall of the Berlin Wall in 1989. That system combines liberalism—broadly, constitutionally constrained government under the rule of law—with representative democracy via some form of free and fair elections. In the years following the demise of the Soviet Empire, there have been growing concerns about *illiberal democracies*, which elect their governments but pay no more than lip service to minority and individual freedoms. The current concerns in the West, by contrast, parse things the other way round: *undemocratic liberalism*, a system of government in which individual rights are entrenched but too little of government is decided by the ballot box or heeds the welfare of the people.

The current upsurge of debate about technocracy and populism can, therefore, make it seem as if we are approaching a point where choices between illiberal democracy and undemocratic liberalism will be hard to avoid.[5] In a way, the purpose of this book is to challenge that pessimism of absolutes. It explores whether it is possible to find a place for technocratic independent agencies in our system of government without jeopardizing democratic legitimacy. Nearly all the discussion will be dry, but in the background is the need to chart a way through a malaise of false choices about government and, thus, about who we are as political communities.

It is not as if unelected power is new. Democratic societies have long found ways of accommodating, and often honoring, the Military, the Judiciary, and, where it existed, an established Church. It is more that there has been a shift in the reach and techniques of unelected power, which now routinely involves writing legally binding rules and regulations. This is nowhere more apparent than in the world where I spent much of my professional life, central banking, which in many countries is today a new third pillar of unelected power alongside the judges and the generals.

[5] Mounk, "Illiberal Democracy."

CENTRAL BANKS AS THE EPITOME OF TECHNOCRATIC POWER

The high tide of central banking came in the mid-1920s—until now, that is. In the words of the League of Nations' prescriptions for economic reconstruction after the First World War: [6]

> [Central banking] should be free from political pressure, and should be conducted solely on lines of prudent finance. In countries where there is no central bank of issue, one should be established.

Within a decade of that proclamation, the 1929 stock market crash, the unraveling of the gold standard, and the Great Depression were enough to see central banks stripped of responsibility, status, and power.

They did not regain preeminence until the 1990s, when the International Monetary Fund and World Bank began prescribing independent central banks and the framework for price stability known as *inflation targeting* to the emerging-market economies rising around the world. But, as though revisiting their past, the Great Moderation they presided over turned nasty, twisting itself into the Great Financial Crisis and years—not yet behind us—of below-par growth.

From Impotence to the Only Game in Town

For the central bankers themselves, however, history has not repeated itself. Indeed, the contrast with the aftermath of the banking crisis, monetary disorder, and economic slump of the 1920s and 1930s could hardly be greater. Then, governments quickly turned away from globalization and central bank–centered macroeconomic policies. Nationalism was the order of the day—autarky, propped up by barriers to trade, controls on capital flows, and financial repression.[7] When at the end of World War II the international economic order was reconstructed at Bretton Woods, New Hampshire, central banks were largely bystanders. In the aftermath, they became backroom advisers and agents as the West was rebuilt and the Cold War negotiated.

[6] Two conferences were convened by the League of Nations, in Brussels in 1920 and later in Genova in 1922. For contemporary commentary, see Hawtrey, "Genoa Resolutions."

[7] James, *End of Globalization*.

How different things are today. Notwithstanding financial disorder and economic stagnation on a grand scale, globalization has hardly been rolled back (as I write); and while the core program for reforming the monetary and financial system was once more forged in international gatherings, this time around central bankers were the leading players. Domestically, they generally emerged from the crisis with more, not fewer, responsibilities and powers. Internationally, recovery seemed to depend on them. They have been, in a popular but deeply troubling phrase, *the Only Game in Town* (chapter 24).

Numerous explanations for this extraordinary contrast with the fate of central banks in the 1930s suggest themselves. Their monetary innovations avoided a repeat of the Great Depression, which is quite a thing; the failure of non-central-bank regulators in the run up to the latest crisis was even more abject; and the central bank–academic economist axis has remained a potent force in shaping post-crisis reform debates. Whichever appeals most, the consolidation of power should make us ponder.

Preexisting Doubts

There were skeptics about monetary independence even before the crisis. For the libertarian Right, the existence of state-backed central banks is an anomalous encroachment on freedom, relieving citizens of the need to be prudent and, in consequence, putting our economies on an inevitable roller-coaster cycle of destructive boom and bust.[8] For parts of the radical Left, central banks are inevitably in cahoots with high finance, repeatedly bailing it out at the expense of taxpayers; and their very existence standing in the way of the emergence of powerful state banks that could be used to pursue wider, redistributive social justice.[9]

In between those political poles lie two broad camps of critics. One, on the social democratic Left, doubts that independent monetary authorities bring economic benefits;[10] fears that central banks are inherently "conservative," and thus unacceptably indifferent to employment and activity; and, even when granting the potential benefits of technocratic

[8] Paul, *End the Fed*.
[9] Epstein, "Central Banks."
[10] Forder, "Central Bank Independence."

expertise, cannot see how it can be squared with democratic legitimacy. They regard monetary independence as a false step, taken as part of an unwarranted crisis of confidence in democratic politics during the inflationary 1970s that followed Vietnam and Watergate and reflecting a wider turn toward delegating "discipline" to autonomous, depoliticized agencies. Driven and, in turn, underpinned by a shift toward international governance and away from domestic democratic control, monetary independence is seen by these critics as symptomatic of a triumphant neoliberalism.[11]

Meanwhile, leading neoliberal thinkers themselves would lament the extent to which today's central banks operate by discretion, echoing Chicago's Henry Simons in the 1930s:[12]

> Deleg[ation] to administrative authorities with substantial discretionary power . . . must be invoked sparingly . . . if democratic institutions are to be preserved; and it is utterly inappropriate in the money field.

More soberly, while the one group seeks to remedy a "democratic deficit," the other wishes to recover the "rule of law" (chapters 8 and 9).

While those critiques flourished at the margins of public policy debate in the years before the crisis, the question of whether our central banks are simply *too* powerful has now become more widespread. That is not surprising given the extraordinary exercise and accumulation of power by central banks since global markets broke down in the summer of 2007. Using their balance sheets like never before, they have intervened in almost every part of the bond and loan markets, initially in order to contain market disorder and later to stimulate economic recovery. Discomfort has been evident on many fronts: in legal challenges against the European Central Bank (ECB) in Europe's constitutional courts, in US litigation around the US bailout of AIG, and in political steps in Congress, from both sides of the aisle, to reform the Federal Reserve.

[11]Krippner, *Capitalizing on Crisis*; Roberts, *Logic of Discipline*; Mazower, *Governing the World*; McNamara, "Rational Fictions." Many papers in this genre pray in aid Stiglitz, "Central Banking."

[12]Simons, "Rules versus Authorities," pp. 2–3.

Even if those challenges come to nothing, they demonstrate a need to think through afresh the degrees of freedom central banks should be granted and, in particular, how far they should be able to venture into what has traditionally been regarded as the preserve of fiscal authorities. So when my friend and former colleague, Bundesbank director Andreas Dombret suggested in the autumn of 2016 that central bank independence is not debatable, my immediate thought was that these institutions are among the last on earth that need "safe spaces" to protect them from criticism or verbal attack.[13]

Central Banking and the Regulatory State: The Issues Become Larger and Deeper

Safe or not, the space they occupy has been enlarged. The earlier criticisms I recalled of central bank independence (CBI) concerned their role as an autonomous part of what I shall term the *fiscal state*, given their ability to change, even transform, the consolidated government's liabilities and assets, and so its risks and income streams (chapters 4 and 22). Now, however, they are more than that.

As the lender of last resort to the financial system—the economic equivalent of the US Cavalry—central banks invariably find themselves at the scene of financial disasters. If ever that was doubted, it has surely been put to rest since markets, firms, and whole economies began to crack in the summer of 2007. No less did those events underline the futility of attempting to insulate the supposedly high-minded pursuit of monetary stability in the interest of general economic prosperity from the altogether more prosaic (but vital) business of keeping the financial system afloat. After a generation during which those two facets of stability policy had drifted apart, even when housed within the same institution, as at the US Federal Reserve, they have once again been harnessed together (chapter 19). Banking supervision has been returned to the Bank of England and granted to the ECB; the Federal Reserve (or Fed) has been supervising nonbank financial groups judged to be systemically significant; and central banks in many jurisdictions have been granted "macroprudential" powers to mitigate threats from credit booms.

[13] Dombret, "Banking Sector."

In terms of the distribution of administrative power, the practical upshot of this reversion to and elaboration of past orthodoxy is that central banks no longer inhabit a rarefied zone in which experts exercise specialized powers in order to smooth macroeconomic fluctuations. In a massive development for modern governance, their newly fortified powers to oversee and set the terms of trade for banking and other parts of finance unambiguously make them part of the "regulatory state"—a distinctive part of the modern state apparatus that developed during the twentieth century, first in the United States and later in Europe, leaving public law playing catch-up (chapters 2, 3, 8, 13, and 15).

This transforms the debate. For the most fervent advocates of monetary independence, it risks taking central banks into more overtly political waters, jeopardizing hard-won achievements of the 1980s and 1990s. For those always uncomfortable with CBI, it increases their unease about a democratic deficit. Concretely, if central banks are to be independent, it must now be on two fronts: from the City of London and Wall Street (what used to be known as the "money interest"), as well as from electoral politics.

In consequence, deliberations on central banking can no longer be bracketed away from what have until now seemed to be largely parallel concerns about a regulatory state empowered to write and issue rules that are legally binding on citizens and businesses.[14] If we must lift our eyes to that broader context in order to meet the challenge of whether society risks central banks and their leaders becoming overmighty citizens, then we need to confront deeper, higher-level questions about the legitimacy of delegating power to unelected officials more generally. In our representative democracies, this places power two steps away from the people, who do not get a chance to vote on the technocratic elite governing much of their lives, and whose elected representatives have voluntarily surrendered much of the day-to-day control they traditionally exercised over the bureaucracy.

With the meteoric rise in the economic might of nondemocratic states in East Asia, this might be met with relief by those, such as politi-

[14]The academic literatures on central banking and the administrative state have long been segmented. Exceptions before the 2007–2009 crisis include Miller, "Independent Agencies," and Lastra, *International Financial*. Since the crisis, legal scholars have become interested in central banking despite the lack of case law that provides their standard raw material.

cal scientist Daniel Bell, who call upon Confucian traditions when advocating government via meritocratic technocracy—Plato's Guardians in modern garb.[15] For them, independent agencies might be in the vanguard of a return to the predemocratic governance of the eighteenth-century's commercial republics (chapter 8). For others, the very same agencies violate the deepest traditions of economic and political liberalism as it developed during the nineteenth and early twentieth centuries. Mirroring their unconscious alignment over central banking, the participatory Left and the constitutionalist Right find common cause in attacking unconstrained delegation.

LEGITIMACY FOR INDEPENDENT AGENCIES

In this book, I try to situate concerns about central banking power within a much broader debate about the role and *legitimacy of independent agencies* and, more generally, of the "administrative state" within our democracies. This is necessary to answer the following questions: Should central bankers be allowed, as regulators, to issue legally binding rules and regulations? Should they have statutory powers to authorize and close banks? Could any such powers decently extend to other parts of the financial system? Should they be free to decide when to provide liquidity assistance to distressed firms? Should monetary policy and other central banking functions be subject to different standards of judicial review? The answers cannot turn purely on what central bankers might be good at. For example, if only elected legislators should set legally binding rules, then central banks should not be regulators (as, for example, they are not in France). Similarly, if only judges should make adjudicatory decisions, as in some jurisdictions' competition policy regimes, then central banks should not make supervisory decisions but instead be restricted to making formal recommendations to the courts. And if, as some argue, combining the writing of regulations with adjudicatory powers violates the separation of powers at the heart of constitutional government, how much worse this becomes when combined with central banks' quasi-fiscal capabilities.

[15] Bell, *China Model.*

For anyone in Europe who doubts these are real issues, they should be aware of pending US legislation making its way through Congress as I write. The REINS Act, which has passed the House of Representatives, would require any material agency regulation to be formally approved by the House and the Senate, meaning political *in*action in one chamber would kill regulatory initiatives in any field (a kind of veto-in-lassitude).[16] And the draft Regulatory Accountability Act (RAA) would, among other things, push agencies toward holding full adversarial-style hearings on proposed rulemakings, and shift the balance of interpretive authority from agencies to courts. More specifically for central banking, another proposal (in the Financial CHOICE Act), which in some versions has cleared the House, would subject the Federal Reserve to *annual* congressional budget approvals for its "nonmonetary policy" functions, removing its formal insulation from politics; narrow its role in emergencies; and require that monetary policy track a rule for the setting of interest rates.

Meanwhile, for any American who thinks these concerns are unique to them, they should be aware that some of the ECB's crisis innovations have been challenged in Europe's constitutional courts; and that debate continues about whether it is acceptable (constitutionally or politically decent) for the ECB to be the banking supervisor. And if anyone thinks the UK might be immune from these various currents, they should know that treasury ministers now have (constrained) powers to order the Bank of England to lend when it doesn't want to during a crisis.

In the course of laying the ground for addressing those issues, the book proposes, develops, defends, and applies a set of *Principles for Delegation* for independent-agency regimes, covering *whether* and *how* elected politicians should confer powers on unelected technocrats shielded from day-to-day politics.

This will require some fairly extensive ground clearing. Notwithstanding concerns about a problematic democratic deficit in the administrative state, rarely is much said about what it means or what democracy entails. To grapple with our problem, we need to look at the

[16] *Regulations from the Executive in Need of Scrutiny*, first tabled in 2009, passed in late 2011, and retabled in 2017.

values associated with the rule of law, separation of powers, and democracy (part II). And before going any further, we need to define two terms.

Independent Agencies

By "independent agency" (IA), I mean, broadly, a public agency that is free to set and deploy its instruments in pursuit of a public policy goal (or goals) insulated from short-term political considerations, influence, or direction. This means insulation from the day-to-day politics of *both* the executive branch and the legislature. Such policy agencies are *trustees.*

True independence in that sense, akin to that enjoyed by the high judiciary in mature democracies although not necessarily as entrenched, requires that policy makers have job security, control over their policy instruments, and some autonomy in determining their budgets (chapter 4).

That is a reasonable description of many modern central banks. But things are not quite so clean when their regulatory peers are examined. On that definition, some US agencies often described as independent, such as the Securities and Exchange Commission (SEC) and other "independent commissions," are not truly independent. By contrast, some of their overseas counterparties, including in the UK, are highly independent, at least de jure. Whether those differences matter depends, in part, on what purpose these agencies serve (chapters 4 and 7).

Legitimacy

By "legitimacy," I mean very broadly that the public—society as a whole—accepts the authority of institutions of the state, including IAs, and their right to deploy the state's powers. Whereas "authority" or "authoritative" are often used descriptively, "legitimacy" is always evaluative, corresponding to the right to govern. To have legitimacy is a good thing, and hence it is important in helping generate voluntary compliance with policies and laws even when people think the specific measures are not sensible or desirable.

As I discuss in part II, I do not mean anything as strong as the community feeling that it is—or, normatively, as its somehow objectively being—under a moral obligation to obey every law. Nor does legitimacy turn on the community *actively* supporting a particular governmental institution or set of policies. But legitimacy grounds and comprises the capacity of an agency to pursue its mandate as part of the broader state apparatus, without relying wholly on coercive power.

The Problem

On both sides of the Atlantic, there have long been vocal pockets of unease about the extent to which the people's elected representatives have handed power to independent agencies of various kinds. Many have vague objectives, with the legislature effectively surrendering high policy. Given that, sooner or later, things go badly wrong for a while in each and every field of government, increasingly handing the big jobs of domestic administration to high-profile technocrats could in slow motion add to already prevalent cynicism about democratic politics. If vast chunks of policy are outsourced, could elected politicians find themselves left with little more than tweeting and foreign policy?[17] Central banks might well be the current epitome of unelected power, but they are part of broader forces that have been reshaping the structure of modern governance. If, drawing inspiration from Britain's 1689 Bill of Rights, "no taxation without representation" was a rallying cry for eighteenth-century Americans, why has "no regulation without representation" not had similarly broad resonance in our own time?

Such are the interdependencies of today's globalized world that those same forces increasingly put agency leaders and staff on planes to all corners of the planet to attend meetings that generate common international policies in almost every imaginable field. Any solution to the domestic potency of technocratic power cannot be blind, therefore, to the coexistence of *international* policy making and *national* democracy. The peaks of the administrative state should not be held by some kind of transnational elite immune from domestic constraint and scrutiny.

[17] Words written well before the 2016 US election.

The good news, as already noted, is that the problem presented by the regulatory state is not novel at its root, only in its specificities. Reflection on two of the most ancient and elemental state functions, the military and the judiciary, suggests that, where society has the benefit of long experience, we have developed deeply embedded norms and conventions about what functions may be delegated and with what degrees of freedom from political oversight and control. In developing the Principles for Delegation to independent agencies, the book draws on both those walks of life (chapters 4, 5, 10, 23, 24, and Conclusion).

PRINCIPLES FOR LEGITIMATE DELEGATION

The Principles carry important lessons for the design of postcrisis central banks and other regulatory regimes. But they gain traction only if they are themselves consistent with sustaining the legitimacy of the democratic state.

While some argue that the legality of an agency's creation and operation is alone sufficient to confer legitimacy, it is thin ground on which to stand, silently assuming that our deepest convictions and norms about democratic politics cannot be violated or threatened by the substantive transfer of powers. Tyrants who seize control of the state have sometimes been careful to wrap themselves in the cloak of formal legality.

Other justifications seem as shaky. In what was uncomfortably close to a longing for Plato's Guardians to run the state, scholars argued for over fifty years, beginning with America's New Deal, that the case for delegation turned on specialist expertise. While that must surely be, alongside legality, a necessary condition—after all, we hardly want our technocratic policy makers to be soothsayers—this cannot be sufficient to warrant delegating policy in a democracy, as independent experts could, instead, publicly advise elected policy makers (chapter 5). That was, indeed, precisely the arrangement for UK monetary policy during most of the 1990s.

Broadly, I argue that the key driver of decisions to delegate should instead be a need for credible commitment, so that government sticks to the people's purposes rather than departing from them for short-term gain, electoral popularity, or sectional interest. For a quarter of a century, that justification has been commonplace among monetary economists when defending the independence of central banks and, in Europe, was seen as warranting the creation of independent utility regulators (chapters 5, 7, and 14).

Once again, however, it cannot be a sufficient condition. "Credible commitment" problems run through so many areas of government that it could warrant almost anything being delegated, as former Federal Reserve Vice Chairman Alan Blinder observed nearly twenty years ago. We know instinctively that would be a travesty. Principled limits on what can be delegated are needed.

At the least, the benefits of delegation should be material. More important, major distributional *choices* should remain in the hands of elected politicians, as only then are prospective losers represented at the decision-making table. Nor should we want unelected experts to have a decisive say in the way we live, as individuals or as members of a political community. In short, they should not be making important value judgments (chapters 5, 9, and 11).

Nevertheless, however tightly constrained, independent agencies are intended to make discretionary decisions *within* their delegated domains. There are no neat, externally given dichotomies separating politics from administration, ends from means, efficiency from equity, adjudication from administration. Societies must instead choose where to draw the lines and then oversee the effects of their choices.

Contrary to what is sometimes implied, then, "legal liberalism"—including wide public consultation on draft rules and challenge via the courts—cannot suffice. Judicial review of administrative action, a solution given priority by many US legal scholars, helps to keep agency regimes within the law (and, perhaps, within the rule of law) by guarding against the arbitrary use of powers. But it is limited to illegal *abuses*, rather than extending to the *misuses* of power that occur when commitments (promises on which people would like to rely) lack credibility. What's more, where oversight is left to the judiciary, the location of the democratic deficit merely shifts from one nonmajoritarian institution to another.

Finding a way through this demands attention to the values that run through democratic representation, participation, deliberation, and responsiveness, the last of which might present itself as the very antithesis of credible commitment (chapters 9 and 10). If delegation-with-insulation is to enjoy democratic legitimacy, the people have to be let in somehow. Where a regime is designed to bind the implementation of policy to the people's purposes, a necessary ingredient is that objectives are framed after public debate and with a high degree of support, over time, across the main political parties. Where the people's preferences are not settled or cannot be encapsulated in a clear and monitorable objective, it is better that policy remain under the control of elected politicians. Today, environmental policy might be just such an example; and, consistent with that, it is typically handled by agencies that bear a partisan stamp (chapters 5, 10, and 11).

In short, delegations need to be structured by the precepts of republican democracy as well as of liberalism. Where the people's representatives release a field from direct electoral accountability, the people themselves need to have a say. The response to "no regulation without representation" has to be for the people's elected representatives to fulfill their own role as higher-level trustees, setting clear objectives and constraints. Only then can independent-agency policy makers themselves be trustees for a delegated public good (chapter 11).

Once established, independent, unelected policy makers need to be deliberative and transparent, so that the people and their politicians can see and debate the results of their handiwork. And there must be accountability for their stewardship of the regime, informing decisions to sustain or amend it.

However tight the drafting of an agency's objective, powers, and constraints, two issues cannot be ducked. Agency policy makers must enunciate the operating principles that guide their exercise of discretion, so that policy is systematic and can be seen to be so. The debates in the US Congress over recent years about whether or not to legislate a "monetary policy rule" for the Federal Reserve are, in essence, about how to achieve that. But this design precept is no less relevant to other regulatory agencies, whose rules should not only be defensible one-by-one but comprise a coherent whole (chapters 6, 11, and 15). Independent agencies should embrace this, by acting as *legitimacy seekers*.

Vitally, but controversially, it should also be clear what happens when an insulated agency reaches the boundaries of its mandate but could help contain a crisis by going into uncharted territory. The merits of systematic policy, on the one hand, and the need for flexibility in a crisis, on the other, can produce an awkward tension during emergencies and their aftermath. How can credible commitment be twinned with the inventiveness inherent in emergency actions? And how could we leave it to unelected officials to determine whether to set aside their statutory constraints? We answer that they should not; but the issue, which has caused no little hand wringing among political theorists, recurs throughout the book (chapters 11, 16, and 23).

Implications

Much of what I've said so far applies across many parts of the administrative state, running well beyond central banking. We will see, for example, that the objectives of competition policy have too often been in the hands of technocrats and judges, who twice in the second half of the twentieth century completely reconstructed high policy without any change in the governing legislation. However effective or grounded in economics, a democratic deficit more than looms here (chapters 3, 7, and 14).

More topically, following the Great Financial Crisis, if securities regulators are to be involved in preserving financial stability, as is almost unavoidable given the importance of capital markets, some of them need greater independence, including somewhat greater budgetary autonomy, so that they are not deterred from trying to contain politically popular but unsustainable booms. Alternatively, their mandates could be narrowed, concentrating on the imperative of ensuring good and honest conduct in financial markets, with jurisdiction over systemic safety and soundness transferred elsewhere (chapters 7 and 21).

RECONFIGURING THE POSTCRISIS MULTIPLE-MISSION CENTRAL BANKS: TRUSTEES, NOT GUARDIANS

The Principles for Delegation are especially important for central banks, which have emerged as institutions standing at the intersection of three crucial manifestations of the modern administrative state. Through balance-sheet operations (quantitative and credit easing) that alter the size and shape of the state's consolidated balance sheet, they are part of the *fiscal state*. Through their role as the lender of last resort, they are part of the *emergency state*. And, as we have seen, they are now unequivocally part of the *regulatory state*. Arguably, no other unelected policy makers occupy a similar position.

Each of their functions—monetary policy, stability policy, bank regulation, emergency liquidity provision—should be shaped and constrained by a regime of the kind already sketched. But, in addition, the regimes cannot be segmented, falling to organizational or cultural silos. And we need to be confident that central bank leaders and their staff take seriously every one of their various functions rather than prioritizing the area that is most salient with the public and politicians or that gives them the greatest personal reward in terms of professional prestige. If that risk were to crystallize, the incentives of ambitious staffers would be to get into the sexiest area, depleting the human capital available to the other functions, even in an emergency. That is, plausibly, what happened at some central banks in the run up to the 2007–2008 crisis, with monetary policy prioritized over regulatory responsibilities.

One part of the solution is to frame the purposes of central banking in a joined-up way, expressing them in terms of a broadly defined *monetary-system stability* that comprises both price stability and banking stability. Rather than anything more micro, such as the quality of services provided to consumers and customers, the primary objective of central banks' involvement in regulation thus becomes system stability, with the desired degree of resilience determined (or, perhaps more realistically, blessed) by elected representatives. That mission has to be part of a *Money-Credit Constitution* that incorporates constraints both on the banking system and on central banks themselves (chapter 20).

Organizationally, multiple responsibilities should be delegated to a single institution only if the agency operates with separate (but overlapping) policy committees. That makes it more likely that each area of responsibility will get the attention and effort it deserves (chapters 6, 11, and 20).

Few central banks would be left untouched by those various precepts. But even the Principles for Delegation cannot easily address the problem of central banks having become the *Only Game in Town*. There exists a strategic tension between central banks and fiscal policy makers, who face few constraints on their powers but carry equally few legal obligations. In consequence, when elected politicians weigh short-term political expediency against taking action themselves to contain a crisis or bring about economic recovery, they can sit on their hands safe in the knowledge that their central bank will be obliged under its mandate to try to provide a solution.

Here, then, is the grand dilemma of central banking. On the one hand, in the interest of democratic legitimacy or, more prosaically, in order to avoid accusations that they have overreached themselves, central bankers need clear regimes, with monitorable objectives for all of their functions. On the other hand, the articulation of such regimes risks exacerbating a perverse strategic interaction with the fiscal authorities, leaving them as the only game in town and thus as potentially overmighty citizens of whom too much is expected (chapter 24).

There is no off-the-shelf solution. A central bank regime for all seasons cannot be designed without a good fiscal constitution existing too: setting boundaries to the authority of central banks needs to take account of what is on the other side of the border. Solving that problem is likely to take a generation. In the meantime, the central bankers themselves need to resist pressures to encroach too far into fiscal territory. To that end, a more explicit *Fiscal Carve-Out,* determined or blessed by legislators, is needed as part of the Money-Credit Constitution that I recommend each advanced-economy democracy develop (chapter 22).

A FOURTH BRANCH OF GOVERNMENT?

At the constitutional level, it is sometimes suggested that independent agencies, and especially central banks, comprise a fourth branch of government coequal with the legislature, elected executive, and high judiciary.[18] I conclude that this is largely a mistake. Even though insulated

[18]Throughout, the terms *elected executive* and *elected executive branch* are used for both presidential and parliamentary systems. Although the executive is not directly elected as such in parliamentary systems, executive government is clearly distinguishable from the legislature. What matters here is that in both systems the heads of the executive were elected by the people (either directly into office or into the legislature on a clear understanding that they would lead the government). That distinguishes them from the unelected leaders of independent agencies.

from day-to-day politics, they are typically subordinate to each of those branches. Agency actions can be challenged in the courts; their rules can be overridden by the legislature; an independence law can be reformed or repealed (chapters 8, 10, and 12).

Typically, that is. One central bank, the ECB, is something of an exception, its independence enshrined in a treaty that can be changed only with unanimity among the European Union's member states, and its balance sheet having been deployed in extremis to preserve the very existence of the currency area. Accusations of "autocratic hegemony," lodged at ECB president Mario Draghi's April 2015 press conference, and quoted at the chapter head, don't often get leveled at independent agencies in functioning democracies. For the moment, the ECB finds itself acting as a *guardian* of the EU project itself. Short of constitutional reform, part of the answer has to be for the European Parliament to do more to enhance the significance of its oversight hearings. Another would be for the ECB to be proactive in seeking broad support from euro-area heads of government when embarking upon truly novel innovations that lie within the legal bounds of its mandate and statutes but beyond familiar conceptions of central banking.

The ECB is sui generis since it serves an incomplete constitutional project. That cannot be said of a different type of agency for which the "fourth branch" label cannot easily be rejected: one directed to underpinning the *institutions of democracy itself.* Electoral commissions, which might, for example, set electoral-district boundaries addressing the gerrymandering problem or bar a prime minister from owning the media or set constraints on campaign finance, are harder to fit underneath the three-branch framework bequeathed by Montesquieu and Madison. They are more prevalent in new democracies than older ones, and bear a family resemblance to the "integrity branch" advocated by Dr. Sun Yat Sen in his model constitution for early-twentieth-century China. They too are, perhaps, better thought of as guardians rather than trustees. Debate about that kind of insulated-agency function has hardly begun in most countries and is no more than encouraged here (chapter 12).

In the meantime, there is much to be done. Whatever the local merits of "technocratic meritocracy" in the East, for us democratic legitimacy is a precious and vital touchstone as the state's structure evolves. The Principles for Delegation are designed to help maintain it. In spirit, they are *constitutionalist*, understood as meaning norms and conventions, sometimes entrenched in a basic law, sometimes deeply embedded in political culture, that set rules of the game for the establishment, structure, and operation of government (chapter 12).

An audit of agencies against the Principles (or something like them) would be no bad thing. The book attempts no more than an initial sketch of such an endeavor. Notwithstanding stark differences among the constitutional conventions and political norms of the major democracies and the contrasting incentives they create around whether and how to delegate, even a brief survey of the administrative state in the United States, Europe, and a handful of other democracies finds nearly all of them wanting to a greater or lesser extent. Either lacking coherence or risking the emergence of unchecked unelected power, words like "expedient" and "ad hoc" variously come to mind (chapter 7 and part III).

Over recent decades, economists have increasingly emphasized the importance of incentive compatibility in designing institutions. If there is a single high-level message in this book, it is that for governmental institutions to be durable, serving the needs of the people over time, their construction must also be *values-compatible*. Where the incentives inscribed into institutional design are at odds with a society's political values, the likely outcome is that in the short-to-medium run incentives dominate, but that in the medium-to-longer run corrosive cynicism and even distrust of government develops. The book is an exploration of what could be done to address the risks that flawed delegations might have been generating in the US, the UK, and parts of Continental Europe. A healthy, legitimate state is *incentives-values-compatible*.

THE RANGE AND STRUCTURE OF THE BOOK

Since the book ranges widely across public policy areas, geographies, and disciplines, it is worth saying that it is *not* about the legitimacy of specific agencies or the merits of their different styles of regulatory intervention. Nor, bigger picture, is it an exploration of whether the modern state is compromised by the way its tentacles reach into so many parts of our everyday lives and how that has gradually transformed who we are, individually and collectively. It does not remotely have the range, let alone ambition, of the work of the Continental European public intellectuals who have taken on that vast subject, perhaps most famously Michel Foucault and Juergen Habermas. Nor is it a broad examination of shortcomings in the modern democratic state of the kind recently pursued by Francis Fukuyama.[19] Rather, it looks at just one corner of the state apparatus and its position in democratic society—independent agencies—albeit one of great importance for understanding the role and legitimacy of the state more generally.

As will become apparent, for my taste too many discussions of the regulatory state, perhaps especially in Europe, are about "independence *versus* accountability" or about combining "accountability *and* control," often stretching the concept of accountability until those supposed antonyms can coexist.[20] To find our way through this, we have to think about what democratic legitimacy entails, but not about whether insulated agencies can help to prop up or restore the ailing authority of a state. So, to add to the earlier self-denials, the book does not engage with whether, for example, the Banca d'Italia, in providing two presidents, two prime ministers, four finance ministers, and a foreign minister for the Italian Republic during difficult periods in the twentieth and early twenty-first centuries, was conferring authority on the Italian state or vice versa. And I am not going to explore whether the transition to democracy in emerging-market and developing countries can depend on a technocratic elite, notably in the judiciary and the central bank. Our concern is whether the legitimacy of a *healthy* democratic state can somehow be bestowed on its central bank and other independent agencies, not whether they can act as some kind of deus ex machina for the state itself.

The book has four parts, covering welfare, values, incentives, and power. The first three parts are about independent agencies in general, illustrated by examples from a range of fields, not only central banking, whereas the fourth is specifically about the postcrisis central banks.

Part I opens with an account of how the general problem of the administrative state manifests itself on either side of the Atlantic, before

[19] Fukuyama, *Origins of Political Order* and *Political Decay*.

[20] For an attempt to puncture a European debate on reconciling independence with accountability, see Busuioc, "Accountability, Control and Independence."

going on to review its purposes, modes of operation, and structure. That provides background to the general design principles for *whether* and *how* to delegate power to "truly" independent agencies, the Principles for Delegation. In a sketch of how they might affect various parts of the administrative state, questions are raised about competition authorities and, in particular, securities market regulators. The style of part I is technocratic, drawing on the economics of market failure and government failure. It is about welfare.

Part II marks a shift in both style and substance. Partly an attempt to stimulate work by others, it explores whether the Principles stack up under different conceptions of our politics (broadly, liberal democracy). This necessitates some examination of the burden of legitimacy, exploring what is entailed by the values associated with the rule of law, constitutional government, the separation of powers, and democracy. The core of this part of the book is what I call a *robustness test* of the Principles: different people place their own weights on our core values, and so expect different things of independent-agency regimes if they are to accept or tolerate them. The result is some elaboration of part I's statement of the Principles, of which probably the most important is the vital need for public debate on purposes and objectives. The discipline most relevant to part II is political theory. It is about values.

Part III takes the Principles back to the real world, looking at how they would or could fit with the different constitutional structures, legal systems, norms, and traditions of the US, the UK, the EU, France, and Germany. I was surprised, but not all readers will be, by the gap between values and incentives-driven reality in nearly all of those jurisdictions. One conclusion is that a jurisdiction should have no more IA regimes than its legislature is capable of overseeing. Part III draws on political science and public law. It is about incentives.

Part IV, which is about power, gets back to the central banks, addressing the big questions posed in this introduction. Has it become too easy for politicians to rely on the central banks to cure or ameliorate the global economy's problems? Led, as they are, by powerful, independent, and unelected policy makers, is their authority tainted by a democratic deficit? Are they, in short, *overmighty citizens,* and what is to be done if they are?

Earlier, in part II, I argue that, in a system of *fiat* money, monetary independence is (normatively) necessary given the separation of powers between executive government and legislature. But that rarely, if ever, explains why central banks were granted independence in practice, so I begin part IV with a brief account of some of the real-world forces behind independence. That leads to a discussion of how, up to the Great Financial Crisis, the desire of central bankers to build credibility through transparency fortuitously helped to underpin their legitimacy.

The ground having been laid, I then assess how practice in the four related spheres delegated to central banks in many jurisdictions—monetary policy, prudential policy, credit policy, and liquidity policy—measures up under the Principles, and what needs to be done. As it turns out, the answers are "not well" and, therefore, "quite a lot." The overall conclusion is that keeping central banks out of these areas is unrealistic, but that their roles should be constrained to go no wider than is necessary to preserve stability in the monetary system. Special care needs to be taken in framing their role in emergencies, given that they are technically capable of doing the job of elected governments but should not do so.

As the book approaches its close, it returns to the judiciary and the military, where our societies rely on virtues of self-restraint and reserve shaped by careful institutional design. We need similar values embedded in an ethic of central banking. If that were to become part of what is expected by peers and public, self-restraint could be self-serving, and so realistic, for unelected power holders seeking public esteem. The concluding chapter includes a summary of the book's proposals for IA regimes in general and central banks in particular.

The book climbs from the practical (part I) to the elevation of our values (part II) and then gradually descends through the jurisdictional comparisons of part III to the central banking specificity of part IV. Some readers might want to jump straight from part I to part IV, others focusing more on either part II or part III. I hope, however, that some will see how the whole fits together and builds, and why the more general questions about values and forms of government are practically relevant to ensuring the durability of some of our core institutions. To hold otherwise would, as I see it, be to put all of our eggs in incentive compatibility alone, trusting in our values—of the rule of law, constitutionalism, and democracy—to evolve and morph with the dictates of expedience. The emerging clash between populist-style politics and technocratic administration suggests that might be a mistake.

The core of the analysis is about domestic policy making in sovereign democratic nations. In fact, however, as already flagged, a good deal of modern policy making is international. I weave in some comments about this as we go, but a robust bridge from the Principles to the legitimacy of international policy making would require further elaboration.

PART I

Welfare

THE PROBLEM, AND A POSSIBLE SOLUTION

It is best to begin by stepping back.

The structure of sovereign power has changed enormously over the centuries. Once upon a time, the king set taxes, dispensed justice, led armies into battle, controlled the propagation of information, and minted the coin of the realm. Gradually, each of those functions was separated from what we now call the executive branch of government. In mature democracies, taxes are set by the elected legislature; judges in the courts dispense justice and adjudicate disputes; a professional military conducts battles; state media, where they exist, are intended to be arm's-length, as with the BBC in the UK; and independent central banks control monetary policy.

Over the course of the twentieth century, this disaggregation of executive government went much further. Administrative agencies now regulate the terms of trade (competitive conditions) in many industries, health and safety at work and in public spaces, the quality of goods and services sold to consumers, social discrimination, the quality of public services, and the integrity of the higher reaches of the state (public appointments, electoral practices, legislators' expenses).

Furthermore, since the 1990s international organizations have been promoting independent agencies as a "good thing." Central bank independence was prominent in the 1990s' "Washington Consensus" on global macroeconomic and financial management. The International Monetary Fund (IMF) advocates independence for financial regulators. The Organisation for Economic Co-operation and Development (OECD) promotes delegated governance across a wider terrain.[1] There

[1]OECD, *Distributed Public Governance*.

is something striking about an official consensus in favor of insulating policy from politics articulated by institutions that are themselves nonmajoritarian, as critics are not slow to point out.

Part I opens with a summary history of how we arrived at this state of affairs on either side of the Atlantic, and follows with a couple of chapters on the purposes and structure of the administrative state, before moving on to identify and apply some principles for when and how to delegate public policy functions to independent agencies insulated from quotidian politics.

2

The Evolution of the Administrative State

A headless fourth branch of government.

—Brownlow Committee to President Roosevelt, 1937[1]

After three decades, the movement to and reinforcement of independent administrative authorities seems uncontrolled.

—Committee of the French Senate, 2015[2]

While we are concerned with a problem—the democratic legitimacy of independent agencies—that is shared across the advanced-economy world, it manifests itself in different ways in different jurisdictions. The purpose of this chapter is to locate debates about the place of agencies in the structure of the state within distinct national or regional regulatory histories.

That there should be differences is hardly surprising given the varying paths taken toward the modern democratic state. During the nineteenth and early twentieth centuries, European nation-states grafted democracy onto a preexisting state that, notably in Britain, had established the rule of law much earlier. If the order in Europe was central state power, then rule of law, and then democracy, in the United States it was closer to rule of law, then democracy, and then central-state building.[3] And in the European Union, only in the past few years have central "federal" regulatory agencies been introduced into a system that initially delegated elaboration and implementation of centrally made laws to member states and their national agencies.

[1]Brownlow Committee, *Report.*

[2]French Senate, *State within the State*. My thanks to Anna Klein, then studying with Thomas Perroud, for help with translation from French.

[3]Fukuyama, *Political Decay.*

THE USA

We will devote most of our discussion to the United States for the simple reason that, with the longest-lived twentieth-century-style regulatory state, its debate about delegation and legitimacy has undergone the most twists and turns.[4] For much of the nineteenth century, including following the Civil War, US politics and policy revolved largely around Congress, political parties, and the courts. Of course there was administrative machinery, but much of it operated at the level of states rather than nationwide. Over time, however, the economic realities of growing interstate commerce and industrialization prompted an acceleration in central-state building.

Although perhaps not strictly accurate, the first step toward a federal administrative state is usually considered to have been taken in 1887, with the creation of the Interstate Commerce Commission to regulate the railways.[5] In that same year, Woodrow Wilson, still a political scientist, published a famous essay on administration, which he urged be improved on scientific lines, occupying a sphere separate from politics.[6] This line of thinking drew support from eroding trust in the courts' capacity to protect the public from big business and growing awareness of the extent to which political-party patronage dominated state administration.[7] A polity of "courts and parties" was reforming itself.

More regulatory agencies and boards were duly established, especially during the "Progressive Era." Under now President Wilson, they included the Federal Trade Commission (FTC) and, after years of debate prompted by the 1907 banking panic, the Federal Reserve System.

The pace remained gradual until the 1930s when, following the stock market crash and in the face of economic depression, the New Deal's institutional reforms shifted power more decisively to the federal center, polarizing opinion and setting the terms of engagement over the administrative state for decades to come. Even eighty years later, the

[4]For a leading summary history of US legal scholarship and doctrine on agencies, see Stewart, "Reformation of American Administrative Law" and "Administrative Law."

[5]The element of myth in this story is brought out in Mashaw, *Creating the Administrative Constitution*.

[6]Wilson, "Study of Administration."

[7]Glaeser and Shleifer, "Regulatory State."

venom of the New Deal debates is extraordinary. President Roosevelt was branded a dictator, taking the country toward, variously, communism or fascism. The feelings were mutual. When, in response to the Supreme Court striking down some of his more adventurous initiatives, Roosevelt pushed a plan to pack the Supreme Court with additional members, his supporters in the Senate branded the Court, in words said largely to have been conjured by White House aides, "a dictator" taking the country toward "a Fascist system of control."[8]

Ironically, the Court had left intact most of the legislation that created a swathe of so-called independent agencies insulated from the president's reach (see below). They included the Fed's new monetary policy committee, the Federal Open Market Committee (FOMC), from which the Treasury secretary was removed, and a raft of regulatory authorities, including the Securities and Exchange Commission (SEC) and the National Labor Relations Board (NLRB). All were headed by multiple-member commissions or boards.

The new structure was soon controversial. As early as 1937, the burgeoning bureaucracy was branded "a headless fourth branch." Dismissing that attack as "somewhat hysterical," James Landis, who had served on the FTC and went on to chair the SEC, responded with what became the canonical case for delegating to agencies: that, compared with leaving policy to politicians, their professional expertise would improve the welfare of the people.[9] But by the early 1960s, advising President-elect Kennedy, Landis himself was advocating moving to agencies with a single policy maker in order to give more drive to their work and more edge to the president's power of appointment.[10]

Over recent decades there have been determined executive branch efforts to get control of the wider government machinery, with executive orders (EOs) increasingly used in the regulatory sphere since Presidents Reagan and Clinton deployed them to advance their rather different regulatory philosophies.[11] This can be represented as bringing democracy

[8]Shesol, *Supreme Power*, chapter 20, p. 350, quoting a 1937 radio address by Senator La Follette.

[9]Landis, *Administrative Process*. Landis was intimately involved in drafting the original securities-regulation statutes.

[10]Landis, "Report on Regulatory Agencies."

[11]Clinton Executive Order 12866 (September 30, 1993). Kagan, "Presidential Administration," published before becoming a Supreme Court Justice but after working for the Clinton administration. For background on presidential EOs, see Chu and Garvey, "Executive Orders."

to agency policy making, entailing changes of course after general elections and leaving the largely exempted "independent agencies" out on a limb.

Confusion about What Counts as an "Independent Agency"

That potted history glosses over a number of vital distinctions. The first is between what are known as "independent agencies" and "executive agencies" (which we shall see are slightly curious terms of art in the US). Lying somewhat beyond day-to-day presidential control, the former are basically immune from executive orders and thus from, for example, a requirement that draft rules be vetted by the president's Office of Management and Budget.[12] Attempts are occasionally made to cajole these "independent agencies" into the elected executive's sphere, most recently by President Obama through an exhortatory order in 2011, leading to a nice exchange of letters between his officials and Fed chairman Ben Bernanke. But those insulated agencies have largely held the ground provided to them by Congress and the Supreme Court.[13]

It clearly matters, therefore, what counts as an "independent agency" in this context. The central test in US law is, crudely, whether Congress has given an agency's top-level decision makers job security. The key case decided by the Court during the 1930s related directly to insulation from politics, as Roosevelt wanted to get rid of an FTC commissioner who did not agree with him.[14]

[12] Such reviews are conducted by the Office of Information and Regulatory Affairs (OIRA), created within the OMB by the Paperwork Reduction Act of 1980. The act exempts "independent regulatory agencies" from various of its provisions and includes a nonexhaustive list of nineteen such agencies, including the Fed, the SEC, the Commodities Futures Trading Commission, and the Federal Deposit Insurance Corporation. As a result, they were excluded from the executive orders mandating that OIRA review drafts of significant government rules and regulations that they conduct formal cost-benefit analysis. Chu and Shedd, "Presidential Review."

[13] Obama Executive Order 13579, saying that independent agencies should (not must or shall) comply with orders binding on executive agencies; and letter of November 8, 2011, from Federal Reserve Board Chairman Ben S. Bernanke to Cass R. Sunstein, Administrator, OIRA.

[14] In *Humphrey's Executor* (1935), the Court concluded that where congressional legislation provides that officers can be fired only "for cause," the president cannot fire them just because of disagreement. This case is widely seen as signaling the acceptability of independent agencies under the US Constitution. On the same day, in *Schechters* case, the Court ruled unconstitutional a delegation in one of the New Deal statutes. Both decisions were unanimous, in contrast to much of what followed.

This test helps distinguish a broad spectrum of agencies from so-called executive agencies (EAs) that lie outside departments headed by Cabinet secretaries but are, nevertheless, within the presidential sphere of control since their policy makers can be removed without cause. Thus, while the Fed, the SEC, the Commodities and Futures Trading Commission (CFTC), and the Federal Deposit Insurance Corporation (FDIC) are independent on this measure, the Environmental Protection Agency (EPA) is not.[15] In a system where Cabinet secretaries are not elected by the people to either their executive office or the legislature, they and EA bosses are alike in being, in democratic terms, essentially helpers to the president. "Independent agencies" are different.

Over the decades, Congress has granted regulatory agencies various other formal protections from presidential leverage, creating a confusingly complex patchwork of bodies with different degrees of separation from the elected executive branch. This tends to obscure the question of how far an agency is insulated from the day-to-day politics of Congress itself, which, in the US system of government, can hardly be ignored.[16] Apart from its role in policy-maker confirmations, oversight, and investigations, Congress has one key instrument of routine leverage or control: annual budget appropriations, which come around with sufficient frequency and can be delivered with sufficient granularity to make the leash as short or long as Congress chooses (as most regulatory commission chairs I have known would confirm, not always protesting it should be said).[17]

Job security, therefore, is not a robust criterion for substantive insulation from short-term politics. Our second vital distinction is, accordingly, between "independent agencies" in the US term-of-art sense and inde-

[15] Interestingly, the founding statute for the Securities and Exchange Commission does not contain an explicit "for cause only" provision but, perhaps because it was established before *Humphrey's* case and reflecting its commission structure, the Court ruled to the effect that its commissioners have job security.

[16] A review of degrees of agency insulation from the president is provided by Datla and Revesz, "Deconstructing Independent Agencies." The paper omits congressional budgetary control from its indices of independence and, therefore, is best seen as a crucial stepping stone toward categorizing US agencies according to their degrees of formal separation from politics. It is striking that while US legal scholarship focuses mainly on insulation from the president (because that occasionally gets litigated), the analytical branch of US political science has tended to focus on insulation from Congress. Terry Moe has long argued for broader political-science engagement; e.g., Moe, "Political Institutions." Also, Kruly, "Self-Funding."

[17] *Harvard Law Review* Notes, "Independence."

pendent agencies in our sense of being insulated from day-to-day politics. Of the "independent agencies" we listed above, Congress controls the budget of the SEC and the CFTC but not those of the Fed or the FDIC.

The overall impression, confirmed by more recent creations discussed in part III, is of little if any principled basis for legislators' choices on how far to insulate agencies from, respectively, the president and Congress.

The Historical Debate about the Legitimacy of the US Administrative State

That confusion has fueled a decades-long, intensely engaged debate about whether delegation to agencies is unconstitutional; whether it violates the values inherent in the US separation of powers; whether it undermines the rule of law; and whether it damages the people's welfare. For some, all of those things and more are true, notably of delegations to the Federal Reserve, against which former Representative Ron Paul devoted much of his professional energy.[18]

The US Constitution says next to nothing about administration. In consequence, at one end of the spectrum of opinion, it is suggested that Congress errs in creating and delegating discretionary powers to agencies at all; it should instead pass statutes with provisions that are sufficiently detailed to be implemented by the executive and judicial branches in a more or less mechanical fashion. This argument has largely been sidelined by the passage of time and Supreme Court reluctance to strike out legislated delegations. But it finds an echo in two other objections.

First, forceful concern is still occasionally expressed about delegation to agencies whose statutory objectives are highly vague, along the lines of "pursue the public interest." Seen by some as a violation of the rule of law, it is central to our inquiry into the demands of democracy (chapters 9–11), leading to a concrete proposal for the United States in part III (chapter 14).[19]

Second, it is protested that a polity supposedly framed around Montesquieu's separation of powers (legislative, executive, judicial) contrives to reassemble all three functions of the state in its regulatory agencies (writing legally binding rules, checking compliance, and adjudicating

[18] Paul, *End the Fed*.

[19] R. Epstein, "Why the Modern Administrative State." Much of the American literature equates the rule of law with the US Constitution.

enforcement measures). This is one manifestation of the "fourth branch" objection: a branch that, if it exists, might flout the state's basic architecture or values enshrined in the US Constitution.[20]

It is associated with worries about the arbitrary exercise of power, fueling a vast and ongoing discussion about the constraints that should be applied to administrative decision making. Since 1946, the cornerstone of the system has been the Administrative Procedures Act (APA), which, after a decade of negotiation, codified norms governing adjudicatory proceedings on particular cases and the making of general policy via legally binding rules. In the succeeding decades, notwithstanding an occasional tap on the brakes by the Supreme Court, federal judges have elaborated those constraints, especially around what is known as notice-and-comment (or "informal") rule making, at times getting into the merits of agency decisions and at times retreating (chapter 15).[21]

These debates remain live. As already noted in chapter 1, among other pending measures the House of Representatives has proposed the REINS Act which, if passed into law, would require all major rules to be positively approved by the House and the Senate, with inaction in either chamber amounting to veto. This would give Congress much greater leverage over rule making than the Congressional Review Act, which until the early months of 2017 had rarely been used since its introduction in 1996.[22] Emblematic of fraught emotions about US government, the REINS bill has inevitably prompted a rash of scholarly discussion about the processes via which Congress is legitimately entitled to intervene in regulatory rule making.[23]

The "Public Interest" versus Interest-Group Liberalism

Meanwhile, since the 1960s US administrative practices have evolved along lines that seemed to embrace some of the values of direct democracy (chapter 9). If the Progressive-Era institutional reforms were

[20] Lawson, "Administrative State."

[21] The brake was applied in *Vermont Yankee Nuclear Power Corp v. NRDC*, 435 US 519 (1978).

[22] CRA provides for expedited cancellation of rules via both houses of Congress passing an explicit resolution that is not vetoed by the president. In the past, congressional efforts to give its individual houses a veto over agency decisions were eventually ruled unconstitutional by the Supreme Court: *Immigration and Naturalization Service v. Chadha*, 462 US 919 (1984).

[23] Siegel, "The REINS Act."

designed to combat the sway or corruption of the robber barons and the New Deal seemed at times to elevate the expert above the elected, by the 1950s political scientists were condemning regulatory commissions as inevitably captured themselves. First, Samuel Huntington documented how the railroad companies ended up dominating the Interstate Commerce Commission, which was eventually abolished. Then, in a blistering attack, Marver Bernstein rationalized capture as part of an inescapable institutional life cycle: early promise, dynamism, and integrity inevitably giving way to torpor and subordination.[24] Ironically, much the same critique was advanced by the Left, who saw the agencies as instruments of corporate liberalism.

These ideational currents reached their apogee in the view that there was no such thing as the "public interest" distinct from individual or sectional interests. Gripped by this doctrine of "interest-group populism," the prescription was to "democratize" agency policy making by opening it up to all sections of society, however underresourced, with agencies performing the role of umpire (chapters 3 and 11).[25]

Beginning in the 1960s the New Left, with roots in the civil rights movement, established "public interest" groups that pressed for regulation across a much broader field, notably the environment.[26] The notion that public policy could and should serve the public interest but that it might not always be secured through incremental negotiation enjoyed something of a renaissance. The ostensible solution, reflected in both Reagan and Clinton executive orders, was a commitment to aggregate cost-benefit analysis, or CBA (chapter 3).

The values of liberal democracy were, accordingly, to be achieved (or salvaged) through a cocktail of scientific inquiry (for Enlightenment-rationalist liberals), public consultation (participatory Left), and challenge in the courts (constitutionalist Right). As we have seen, however, the first part of that package (the EOs requiring CBA) did not apply to the "independent agencies."

[24] Huntington, "Marasmus of the ICC"; Bernstein, *Regulating Business*. For a history of fluctuations in attitudes to capture, from a perspective not hostile to regulation, see Novak, "Revisionist History" in Carpenter and Moss, *Preventing Regulatory Capture*.

[25] Shapiro, *Who Guards the Guardians?*

[26] For the links between the emergence of public-interest lobbying groups and the 1960s' New Left, see Harris and Milkis, *Politics of Regulatory Change*.

Unfinished Business

Clearly, then, the Federal Reserve is not alone in prompting concerns about a "democratic deficit" or the exercise of "arbitrary powers." Ever since constitutional scholar Alexander Bickel changed the weather in the early 1960s by describing the Supreme Court's judicial review of congressional legislation as "a deviant institution in the American democracy," the question of legitimacy has hung over the US's other nonmajoritarian institutions.[27]

Some argue that this concern is most acute at moments of national crisis, such as 9/11 or the 2008 financial collapse, when only the president can provide the leadership and coordination needed to pull the country through to safety. In those conditions, it is suggested, Congress and the courts have little choice but to acquiesce in legal mandates and powers being stretched to, if not beyond, their known limits.[28] But this ignores the incentives for the elected executive to leave it to unelected actors, notably the Fed or the military, to step into the breach. The role of independent agencies in the *emergency state*, as we shall term it in the next chapter, is a major preoccupation of our inquiry, and one that the United States has not resolved.

The current wave of reform initiatives is, however, directed at the normal as much as at the exceptional. Without exaggeration, REINS and other pieces of draft legislation working their way through Congress would transform the American administrative state, giving Congress a much greater say in rule making, formally requiring independent agencies to conduct cost-benefit analysis, and significantly diluting the Federal Reserve's insulation from politics, but with no move toward delegating with clear objectives (chapters 13 and 14).

THE DIFFERENT PATH TO SIMILAR CONCERNS IN EUROPE

While not uniquely American, concerns about the administrative state have taken a similar shape in Europe only relatively recently. Of course, Europeans have been debating the underlying issues since the modern

[27] Bickel, *Least Dangerous Branch*, p. 18. Notable recent reviews include Wallach, "Administrative State's Legitimacy Crisis," and DeMuth, "Can the Administrative State Be Tamed?"

[28] Posner and Vermeule, *Executive Unbound*; Wallach, *To the Edge*.

state began to evolve. In the early nineteenth century, the German philosopher Hegel advocated that government be centered on management by experts in a bureaucratic (rather than democratic) state, whose civil servants, including the judiciary, internalize its values (a new "universal class").[29] More than half a century later, Woodrow Wilson's classic celebration of administration looked back to the same exemplars of executive government: the Prussian and Napoleonic states.[30]

Although England had well-developed state capabilities a thousand years ago, when its new Norman rulers compiled their Domesday Book of property ownership, Britain moved away from patronage and toward a professional civil service only in the mid-nineteenth century. But whereas on the European Continent strong bureaucracy was designed to help hold back the advance of democracy by improving the quality of executive government and control, the British bureaucracy served an executive government that was accountable to an increasingly democratic Parliament.

Despite those differences of motivation and legitimation, neither side of the English Channel developed a modern regulatory state along US lines, comprising specialist agencies intervening in the operation of markets for various goods and services, until really quite lately. "Industrial policy" was tried before "regulatory policy," with the effect that, particularly after World War II, public ownership and control was the prevalent means of state intervention in the economy.

Only since privatization and economic liberalization gradually began to take hold in the 1980s has the "regulatory state" come to the fore, reinforced by diminishing trust in *self-regulation*. Regulation by industry associations, going back decades if not centuries, in fields such as law and medicine became discredited. Statutory bodies were gradually created to fill the void, shifting legitimation from tradition and the overt consent of the regulated to an elected legislature meeting actual or posited demands from customers and others for state protection. Indeed, an apparently pervasive decrease in society's tolerance for what earlier generations might have regarded as the unavoidable risks of day-to-day life seemed to drive regulatory interventions across a wider field than ever before.[31]

[29] Hegel, *Philosophy of Right*, sections 287–297.

[30] Wilson, "Study of Administration."

[31] Majone, *Regulating Europe*, chapter 3; Thatcher, "Delegation"; and Levi-Faur and Gilad, "Transcending the Privatization Debate," an extended review of three books on regulation. The

One political theorist has termed the resulting governance regime "constrained civilian democratic administrative statehood."[32] But that merely poses the questions "Constrained enough?" and "How democratic?"

Those common themes and questions played out differently across European countries according to their political, judicial, and governmental traditions and problems.

THE UNITED KINGDOM

In the UK, during the first part of the twentieth century Parliament increasingly delegated quasi-legislative and quasi-judicial powers, prompting a good deal of concern and public debate along the lines later prominent in the US.[33] But those delegations were to ministers of the elected executive government. It was not until the 1990s that there was a deluge of delegation to arm's-length agencies, under the influence of the New Public Management (NPM) thinking and doctrines that originated in New Zealand.[34]

For Britain, it amounted to nothing less than a shift in the ideology of governance, entailing decentralization or, more to the point, ministers letting go. One strand echoed the politics/administration dichotomy of Woodrow Wilson and his early-twentieth-century followers. In the interest of efficiency, policy (to be preserved for elected ministers) could and should be separated from implementation or "delivery" (to be delegated to agencies).

Another strand, gaining traction after Bank of England independence in 1997, sought improved performance by insulating some (constrained) *policy* choices from politics. This saw the creation of a slew of independent regulators, including those that survive today as the Office of Communications (Ofcom), Office of Gas & Electricity Markets

shift in risk tolerance, together with a preference, novel in the UK, for rules-based regulation and compliance cultures, is the subject of one of those books: Power, *Audit Society*.

32 Muller, "Triumph of What."

33 Chief Justice Hewart's 1929 book *The New Despotism*, a blistering attack on the burgeoning administrative state, led to a government-sponsored review. But government did not implement many of the Donoughmore Committee's proposed reforms: see Bingham, "The Old Despotism," chapter V(2), *Business of Judging*.

34 Hood, "Public Management." Some NPM thinking found adherents in the Clinton administration.

(Ofgem), Competition and Markets Authority (CMA), and Financial Conduct Authority (FCA). Each, among other things, an economic and competition regulator (chapter 3), they have high degrees of formal independence.

Initially, a common thread was that goals would be set by politicians for *single-purpose* agencies, which would deliver under *performance-measurement contracts*: the model used at the end of the 1980s for the Reserve Bank of New Zealand. The framework was very explicitly the principal-agent economics that runs through part I.

There was no *legal* constitutional obstacle to such delegation: Parliament had decided. Nor did it create major challenges for other parts of public law, the English courts having since the 1960s revived and filled out common law constraints on administrative decision making (chapter 15). Under the Westminster system, however, that is not quite the same as saying that there were no *political* constitutional issues, which have largely revolved around accountability.

Complexity and Accountability

Perhaps most prosaically, it is harder for Parliament to hold the elected executive government to account if its members have difficulty understanding the structure of government.

The Institute for Government (IFG), a nonpartisan UK think tank, has documented a bewildering variety of supposedly independent agencies, with ambiguities around just what elected ministers are accountable for to the House of Commons.[35] There are Nonministerial Departments, Nondepartmental Public Bodies, Executive Agencies, and more, without clear principles determining which functions get delegated on what terms to which type of body, an issue raised as long ago as 1946 by the Anderson Committee on nondepartment organizations.[36] Worse, until relatively recently there was not even an authoritative list of bodies with delegated public powers, after an effort in the late 1940s lapsed.

[35] Institute for Government, *Read Before Burning*; followed by Rutter, *Strange Case*. I am grateful to Peter Riddell PC, the Institute's former director, for alerting me to this.

[36] Flinders, *Delegated Governance*, chapter 3.

In the IFG's words, this is an "accountability quagmire." The executive branch Cabinet Office has tried to provide some clarity, and the issues have been examined by the House of Commons Committee on Public Administration.[37] So far, however, these tend to be exercises in classification, whereas what is needed are principled norms that warrant the different degrees of formal insulation from politics. It is almost as if the British have become casual about the distribution of power.

Accountability and Ministerial Control

These are not abstract issues. It turns out that, even for the simplest delivery agencies, the dividing line between policy and implementation was not as clear-cut as it might have been. Any seasoned central banker is familiar with the terrain, known to them as "operational policy," that exists between high policy and detailed implementation. Other fields are surely no different. While rarely in the news, operational policy is not insulated from public interest.

One of a number of examples of incomplete design occurred when a bad backlog in issuing and renewing passports developed in the run up to the 2014 summer holiday season. When it became a national news story and Parliamentary battleground, ministers took the Passport Office back under their direct administrative control. Although on the face of it the function seemed to be pure execution, an operational policy decision had been taken to relieve the backlog by introducing a special fee for urgent cases. Unexpectedly rationing by price did not go down well with the public. Such was the uproar that, in the classic British saying, ministers needed to be seen to do something. Reasserting active control appeared to meet the bill, perhaps because ministers truly were more sensitive to citizens having passports in time for their annual holidays irrespective of their financial circumstances.

[37] Rutter, *Strange Case*. Cabinet Office, *Public Bodies*. As of December 30, 2016, the Cabinet Office website recorded UK government as comprising, among other things, 25 Ministerial Departments, 21 Nonministerial Departments, and 375 agencies and other bodies. Whereas CMA and Ofgem are classified as nonministerial departments, Ofcom is included among agencies and other bodies, as are the Bank of England and the FCA (House of Commons Select Committee on Public Administration, *Who's Accountable?*) Earlier, in 2004, the House of Lords Constitution Committee recommended that a joint committee of the two Houses be established to oversee (the delegated part of) the regulatory state in general.

While there is a general lesson here about clarity when delegating, issues of that kind almost inevitably afflict delivery agencies partly because, formally, ministers are still in charge. Despite the interest it generates among students of public administration, delegation of this kind is simply a matter of the executive government experimenting with organizational structures. That cannot be said when, through Parliament, ministers explicitly relinquish power under the law, as to independent authorities.

Accountability and High Policy

The distinction was evident when, days after winning the 1997 general election, a Labour government announced it would legislate to grant "operational independence" to the Bank of England. Notwithstanding its careful labeling, the measure was opposed by the Tories, whose shadow finance minister Peter Lilley said, "The proposal has obvious attractions in reinforcing the battle against inflation, but it is difficult to square it with our system of parliamentary government."[38]

In a parliamentary democracy, the (executive) government survives only so long as it commands a majority in the elected chamber(s) and can therefore pass its program of legislation. Once it cannot do that, which may be confirmed by a no-confidence vote, a new government must be formed and, if necessary, a general election held. This is a constitutional setup in which, as underlined by the 1918 Haldane Committee report on the machinery of government, ministers need to be accountable to the elected chamber, which formally is in the business of determining whether or not to sustain its delegation to the prime minister and her/his cabinet. Taking public policy out of the hands of ministers sitting in the House is therefore no small thing, unless some other means is found for the legislature to keep under review the acceptability of its delegation.

Ironically, as had been pointed out a few years before the Bank gained independence, Chancellors of the Exchequer had in fact very rarely been asked in Parliament about the government's conduct of monetary pol-

[38] Peter Lilley, Shadow Chancellor of the Exchequer, Hansard, HC Deb, 11 November 1997, vol. 300, cc.725–726.

icy, interest picking up only when one policy framework collapsed and made way for another.[39] That is not surprising. Assuming a workable government majority, parliamentarians have incentives to test ministers only on really big issues. As we discuss in part III, delegation changes their incentives.

Accountability and Crisis Management

The 2007–2008 phase of the financial crisis highlighted another dimension to these issues.

On the one hand, there was not much protest, even when the dust had settled, about the executive government's innovative deployment of antiterrorism legislation to help protect the British people from the implosion of Iceland's banks. On the other hand, legislators were concerned about the division of labor among the key agencies and who they could hold to account for what. "Who's in charge?" was demanded by Parliament as the need for cooperation between government, central bank, prudential supervisors, and securities regulators became apparent in ways hardly envisaged when the prevailing regulatory architecture was established in the mid-to-late 1990s.

In other words, the UK faced its own version of the US's emergency state problem: how agency independence can be squared with a need for coordination, and arguably for political leadership, during a national crisis.

THE EUROPEAN UNION

Of course, the UK is not the only European country to face these issues.

In contrast to the other democracies discussed here, Germany's constitution (or Basic Law), framed after World War II, does make provision for the administrative state, so there is little or no US-style agonizing about the *legality* of agencies as such. Moreover, as we shall see in part III, notions of a dichotomy (deep conceptual and strict separa-

[39] Roll et al., *Independent and Accountable*. The democratic deficit problem was a central focus.

tion) between politics and administration—or between ends and means—were embedded in German conceptions of government by Max Weber's famous early-twentieth-century writings on bureaucracy as the rationalist executor of rules-based policies.[40]

While that has not stood in the way of debate, led by Germany's leading public intellectual, Juergen Habermas, about the broader legitimacy of the state's administrative reach and methods, political insulation has not been a central issue.[41] Most likely, that is because the constitution *expressly* puts administration under the control of ministers (chapter 13).

Compared with Habermas's neighboring work on legitimation conditions for the state's legal monopoly of coercive power, developments in the structure of French governance can appear to have sparked less intellectual engagement. Thus, Michel Foucault's famous explorations of the ubiquity of power, as well as his later emphasis on "governmentality" and the "conduct of conduct," extended so far beyond the conventional state apparatus and its evolving modalities that innovations such as independent agencies must have seemed like so much tinkering.[42]

Any suggestion of French neglect is misleading, however. Political theorists such as Pierre Rosanvallon have specifically explored legitimacy conditions for unelected power holders, such as independent agencies and constitutional courts.[43] And, perhaps more than elsewhere, critical interest has been especially marked within the official sector itself. That seems to be rooted in France's republican institutions and traditions. Like the UK, France has an immensely strong administrative elite. The difference is that it is understood to stand for the public good, posing the problem of how to make sense, politically and constitutionally, of policy that is not carried out by the core civil service under the elected executive's control.

As late as the early 1990s, Christian Noyer, speaking as head of the Tresor (France's Treasury department), and so before his very distinguished reincarnation as a central banker, argued that since the Repub-

[40] Weber, "Bureaucracy."

[41] The issues were famously raised in Habermas, *Legitimation Crisis*, and most extensively treated in his *Between Facts and Norms*.

[42] Foucault, *Birth of Biopolitics*.

[43] Rosanvallon, *Democratic Legitimacy*.

lic was "one and indivisible," monetary policy independence was incompatible with republican traditions.[44] At that stage, the Conseil d'État, France's highest administrative-law court, shared concerns about arm's-length agencies fracturing the unity of the state, becoming somewhat more accepting only a few years later.[45] As the quotes at the chapter head illustrate, however, French politicians still occasionally strike a tone not dissimilar from the 1937 US Brownlow Report.

In each of those European jurisdictions, the structure of the administrative state has been profoundly affected by developments in the confederation of states to which they belong, the European Union (EU). This story and the concerns it has generated are highly distinctive in detail but not in essence. With the central budget always much smaller than national (member state) budgets, public ownership of the means of production, distribution, and exchange was never really part of the EU project even in the heyday of "producer-side" social democracy. Hence a "single market" in goods and services required unified minimum standards: in other words, an EU regulatory state.

Initially, that endeavor was pursued by having designated national agencies apply EU laws that either required local incorporation ("directives") or were directly applicable ("regulations").[46] As time passed, the project was underpinned by requiring that in some fields, notably utility regulation, those national regulators should be formally insulated from political interference. In this way, IA regimes have found a place in all EU member states even when previously alien to their local constitutional traditions (chapter 13).

That, however, is quite a few steps short of pan-EU IAs. While, as in the US, the EU's foundational treaties did not explicitly carve out space for them, in contrast to the US an early European Court of Justice (ECJ) ruling prevented complete delegation of functions that, under the treaties, lie with the European Commission.[47]

[44] Noyer, "A propos du statut."

[45] Conseil D'État, *Rapport*.

[46] It might not be widely understood, at least outside Europe, that, following a ruling of the European Court of Justice in the early 1960s (more than a decade before the UK joined), EU law has been widely accepted as formally trumping national law. *Van Gend & Loos*, 1963: discussed in Van Middelaar, *Passage to Europe*.

[47] *Meroni*, 1957/1958. The case concerned the European Coal and Steel Community's *High Authority*, which was later transposed into the *Commission* of the European Community.

Until recently, the effect was that only "executive" functions, not quasi-legislative functions such as issuing binding rules, were considered capable of being delegated, leading to a population of EU agencies that advised and delivered but did not make policy. That changed following the Great Financial Crisis, which prompted the Council of Ministers, with the agreement of the European Parliament, to convert a set of coordinating bodies into formal regulators: the European Securities and Markets Authority (ESMA) and equivalent authorities for banking and insurance.

Distinctive constraints remain. Notably, the Parliament and Council still enact core (in EU-speak, Level 1) regulatory requirements (e.g., capital requirements for banks); and they have a formal right of veto over certain of the so-called Level 2 rules drawn up by the new regulatory agencies. While that is a fairly gargantuan and technical task for the parliamentarians, it does bring an element of political oversight, involving some member-state governments (including the UK's) more than they would be under their national procedures, and delivering for Europe what some members of Congress have been seeking for US rule writing.

Of course, by far the best-known EU IA combines these various measures. As part of moving to Monetary Union, the participating member states undertook, via treaty, to grant independence to their national central banks, which sit on the policy board of the European Central Bank (ECB). Neither the Council nor the Parliament may instruct the ECB or alter the regime, other than via treaty changes requiring unanimity (and referenda in some states). The regime is, in the language of legal scholars, deeply entrenched (chapters 8 and 11). Even before the Great Financial Crisis prompted the granting of prudential powers over the banking system, that gave rise to rumbling complaints about the ECB, associated with broader concerns about a democratic deficit in the EU itself given, its critics say, the lack of a *demos*, a people with a European political identity.

INTERNATIONAL POLICY MAKING BY GROUPS OF INDEPENDENT REGULATORS

In some ways, the EU is a regional variant of the final element in the evolution of the world of independent agencies that belongs in this scene-setting chapter: collective international policy making by IAs from different jurisdictions.

For all the advanced-economy democracies, a fair slice of public policy is made by international organizations, such as the International Monetary Fund, that are treaty based (but, unlike the EU, do not generate a system of law). Probably rather more policy is made in international fora that have only informal power but lots of it. Some of them involve the core executive branch, others only independent agencies, perhaps most famously the central banks' gathering in Basel.

Since the Great Financial Crisis, the potency of informal international policy cooperation has been plain to see in the high-level reforms agreed at summits of G20 leaders and fleshed out in Basel or by the International Organization of Securities Commissions (IOSCO) under the umbrella of the Basel-based G20 Financial Stability Board (FSB).[48]

That has exposed potential tensions in reconciling international policy making with local self-determination. In response to a mixed peer review by the Basel Supervisors Committee of the EU's implementation of the Basel Capital Accord for banks, the Economic Affairs Committee of the European Parliament, a colegislator for EU directives and regulations, issued the following statement in December 2014:[49]

> A large majority of Members of the European Parliament cannot accept that the Basel Committee puts into question the tools to finance the economy. . . . Even if we are aware of the necessity of international cooperation, the European law is made by the European Parliament and the Council of Ministers. The opinion of a *body that is working without legitimacy and without any transparency* cannot modify the decisions taken democratically by the European institutions. (My emphasis)

Similar sentiments were expressed by the then chair of the US Senate Banking Committee, Richard Shelby:[50]

[48] In the language of international relations theorists, Basel and IOSCO are transgovernmental organizations, a neologism coined by Keohane and Nye, "Transgovernmental Relations," in 1974, as it happens the year the Basel Supervisors Committee was created. They are a special variant as, in contrast to bodies comprising executive-branch delegates, their members are to a greater or lesser extent insulated from day-to-day politics in their home countries.

[49] Econ Committee of the European Parliament, "Reaction to the Opinion." For non-European readers, an EU regulation is the same as a federal statute in the US, whereas a directive is a binding law requiring member states to incorporate its detailed provisions into their national law or regulatory rules.

[50] Shelby, "Trouble with Dodd-Frank."

> We must ask if the influence that the FSB seems to exert over the [US] process is real and whether it is appropriate. [A US] process has little merit if it is merely used to justify an international organization's determination, rather than engage in an independent analysis. . . . In addition, the presence of international regulators in domestic rulemaking only amplifies the challenge of regulatory accountability because it allows decisions to be made beyond the reach of Congressional scrutiny.

This is not completely new. Twenty years ago some members of Congress were concerned when, after more than half a century, the Federal Reserve planned finally to become a formal member of the Bank for International Settlements, taking up its vacant board seat. The then chair of the House of Representatives subcommittee worried "whether this would put the Federal Reserve at some point in time . . . in conflict with the domestic independence they exercise."[51]

This adds another dimension to our problem. Even if power were delegated to independent agencies only in circumstances and on terms that warranted local democratic legitimacy, what happens when those very same independent agencies jet off to international meetings or institutions to agree a common policy for the world (or a large part of it)? In the absence of global or international democratic assemblies representing the people of the world, does a gaping democratic deficit reopen?

That is close to the argument, advanced by Harvard political theorist Dani Rodrik a decade or so ago, that there would prove to be a fateful tension between globalization, autonomous nation-states, and democracy.[52]

THE COMMON PROBLEM: DELEGATION AND DEMOCRACY

To sum up, while there are important differences in these stories, two things stand out. There has been a common dynamic toward regulatory intervention in economic and social life, and a common concern about

[51] Rep. Paul Kanjorski, quoted in Simmons, "Central Bank Cooperation." The Fed did join the BIS.

[52] Summarized in Rodrik, *Globalization Paradox*.

the legitimacy of delegating so much of the state's activity to agencies that are more or less independent from day-to-day democratic control.

The upshot is that democracies pretty much everywhere are struggling, in practice and conceptually, with just how independent agencies fit into a system of accountable government. On its own, this is highly unlikely to cause a "crisis of democracy" of the kind that some got overexcited about during the 1970s.[53] But it is part of the mix that has revived concerns about government by an unaccountable elite under undemocratic liberalism.

To make progress with our inquiry in the legitimation of independent agencies, we therefore need to pause to reflect on ideas, theories, and convictions about the purpose and construction of the administrative state. Those are the subjects of the next two chapters, after which we shall be in a position to try our hand at framing a provisional version of the Principles for Delegation.

[53] Crozier, Huntington, and Watanuki, *Crisis of Democracy.*

3

The Purposes and Functional Modes of the Administrative State

MARKET FAILURE AND GOVERNMENT FAILURE

> There is one and only one social responsibility of business—to use its resources to increase its profits so long as it stays within the rules of the game.
>
> —Milton Friedman, *New York Times*, 1970[1]

> I have insisted on the possibility of separating efficiency and redistributive concerns because such a separation is crucial to the substantive legitimacy of regulatory policies.
>
> —Giandomenico Majone, 1996[2]

The words quoted above of Giandomenico Majone, perhaps Europe's most influential and interesting theorist of the regulatory state, capture what, in Europe, has been the dominant legitimation strategy over the quarter century or so since public ownership of utility services and "strategic" industries was replaced by a regime of "private provision subject to public regulation."

It is a legitimation story that appeals to economic ideas that emerged over the middle of the twentieth century, and so depends on their robustness for its validity. In fact, those ideas were contested. While at the beginning of the century economists were promoting regulation as a fix for problems in markets and as a shield against power, from midcentury onward the concern with power was sidelined, and economists, public intellectuals, and political parties waged a war of ideas around whether "market failure" or "government failure" was the bigger problem.

[1] Friedman, "Social Responsibility."

[2] Majone, *Regulating Europe*, chapter 13, p. 296.

Often, especially in the US and most notably in the field of competition policy, statutory regimes persisted even as ideas and doctrine shifted, leaving technocrats and judges to reconstruct high policy without any obvious democratic imprimatur. We return to that, and what it means for Majone's basic insight, many times through the course of the book. This chapter is about how theories, ideas, and arguments within economics shaped debates on how the business of government should be divided among politicians, technocrats, and courts.[3]

THE CONTOURS OF THE STATE

What were the king or queen, with whom we opened part I, and their political successors up to controlling armies, the mint, and tax collectors; granting monopolies here, denying them there; and establishing codes for trade, standards for some goods and services, and rules of conduct for social life? In other words, what are the purposes of the state, in which independent policy agencies found a place during the twentieth century?

Ideas about all that have evolved as technology, expectations, and beliefs have changed, not least our conception of ourselves as communities and as people (part II). There are, even so, a few common threads from almost the beginning. The state provides security, externally and internally. It provides a mechanism for groups to live by shared rules of conduct where they need to coordinate or wish to cooperate, whether in civil society or in trade. To be binding, those rules (or laws) need to be enforced where a breach offends the community as a whole, or need to be subject to authoritative adjudication where a serious dispute occurs between one person and another that could break the bonds of trust. The commitment to enforce the rules must be credible.

In order to deliver those functions (or provide those services, as some would now say), the state must have a claim on resources (taxation). To avoid having constantly to rely upon coercion and the drain of resources

[3]Thanks to Andrei Shleifer for urging me to stress why the path of twentieth-century welfare economics matters to our inquiry into IAs.

that would entail, the state's role must be treated by the bulk of the population as broadly legitimate. So described, we have an account of the state that draws on a line of thought going back at least to the seventeenth-century English political thinker Thomas Hobbes.

As we move forward to the era of liberalism, the state comes to be seen as framing and enforcing *rights*: initially property rights and gradually—one might say, progressively—claims on other members of the community, treated as basic rights or entitlements (perhaps with some dilution of reciprocal duties). The state begins to guarantee protections for people (and for groups of people) in trade and commerce, whether as employers, workers, or intermediaries. And its role in providing security develops into redistributing resources among different groups, whether to maintain political stability as more people acquire political power (via extensions of the franchise) or in pursuit of ideals of justice, or both. The state emerges, indeed, as the insurer of last resort, there to spread the costs of disaster across the living or forward to future generations, in the interest of preserving welfare and stability today and so that the good things of life, however conceived, can be expected tomorrow.[4]

That familiar account suggests a simple framework for thinking about the modes of operation through which the state affects us, and about its purposes.

Functional Modalities of the State

The state seems to function in four modes or registers:

- a *services state*, which provides, for example, information, education, perhaps health services, and binding adjudication of disputes (private law);
- a *fiscal state*, which intervenes directly in markets (for example, by taxing or subsidizing activities);
- a *regulatory state*, which sets and enforces legally binding rules (including criminal law) on parts or all of the community; and

[4]For an exchange on the role of the state between economists with a very different cast of mind, see Buchanan and Musgrave, *Public Finance*.

- perhaps in a different dimension, an *emergency state*, which might suspend certain laws or norms in extraordinary circumstances in order to preserve or restore order (economic, social or physical).

These functions are not independent: some rely upon others. For example, the service of providing information on the economy and society relies upon regulations to collect the data inputs from private households and businesses, which in turn rely upon a capacity to punish noncompliance. Further, functional modes can be bundled, perhaps most obviously when government steps forward as insurer of last resort via the fiscal-cum-services state.

Throughout this book I use the term *administrative state* to refer to the union of government-agency operations in all four states. Behind it lie the coercive powers and capabilities of the *enforcement state*. Since our concern is the legitimation of the parts of the state most distant from politics, the enforcement state remains in the background of our discussion.

Each of the regular manifestations of the administrative state—services, fiscal, and regulatory—operates via and under the law, exercising powers conferred by a higher law-making authority and with an obligation to stay within the law. That provides some requisite degree of predictability in the sense of nonarbitrary exercise of the conferred powers, which are among the "rule of law" values we discuss in part II (chapter 8).

The regulatory state is distinctive in that it promulgates legally binding rules itself. But that does not mean that its objectives are always distinct. For any given objective, the state might proceed via any of its three administrative modes. If, for example, it wished to promote the provision of credit to a particular part of the economy, it could set up a state bank to do the lending (the services state) or subsidize private sector credit provision via guarantees (the fiscal state) or require banks to set aside little or no equity against such loans (the regulatory state).

Purposes of the State

Those functional categories or manifestations of the administrative state are, therefore, dimensionally distinct from the *purposes* of the state. For that, I follow the public-finance economics of the late Richard Musgrave in distinguishing four broad purposes: physical security, allocative efficiency, distributional justice, and macroeconomic stabilization.[5]

In contemplating the reach and power of the administrative state, we can think, therefore, of a 4 × 4 matrix, with each agency slotting into a cell or cells according to what types of function it undertakes and what broad purposes it serves. For example, the police are in the services-security state; the military is in the emergency-security state; the US government-sponsored enterprises (GSEs) that subsidize mortgages, Fannie Mae and Freddie Mac, are in the fiscal-distributional state; and utility regulators are widely thought of as being in the regulatory-efficiency state (but see chapters 5 and 7).

	Fiscal state	*Regulatory state*	*Services state*	*Emergency state*
Allocative efficiency	Taxing externalities	Competition authorities Utility regulators	National statistical authorities Judicial adjudication of disputes	
Distributional justice	Welfare payments US housing GSEs		Public hospitals	
Intertemporal stability	Monetary policy	Prudential regulators of banks	Banker to the banks	Lender of last resort
Security		Criminal law	Police	Armed forces

Away from the core of elected executive government, most organs of the state fall into only one of its four functional manifestations. For example, securities regulators are part of only the regulatory state; government debt management agencies part of only the fiscal state; and public schools or hospitals part of only the services state, as were Europe's old nationalized industries.

Central banks are different. They feature in every functional manifestation of the state. They conduct financial operations that materially

[5] Musgrave, *Theory of Public Finance*. Musgrave omitted physical security, presumably because he was interested in economic policy.

change the state's consolidated balance sheet, making them part of the fiscal state (chapter 22). Following the 2008/2009 financial crisis, nearly all the major central banks now write rules and policies governing banks and, in some jurisdictions, other parts of the financial system, making them part of the regulatory state (chapter 21). They collect and publish data, in many countries provide banking services to the rest of government, and in some operate the settlement system for bonds or equities, making them part of the services state. And as lenders of last resort, an element in the state's capacity to act as insurer of last resort, they are also part of the emergency state (chapter 23).

Their place within the "purposes" of the state was clear in the past but is now up for grabs. Traditionally, their unequivocal core purpose was macroeconomic stability. But where they have extensive regulatory roles, they might also serve the cause of allocative efficiency. Some commentators and politicians even call for them to intervene in the interest of distributional justice, by, for example, helping to subsidize the supply of credit to regions or sectors.

Thus, central banks appear in at least four, possibly eight, and conceivably twelve cells of our sixteen-cell 4 × 4 matrix. This is remarkable given that most institutions within the administrative state occupy only a single cell. In a nutshell, then, one way of thinking about the problem of "overmighty citizens" is whether central banks or any other independent agencies appear in too many cells of the state matrix for comfort.

WELFARE, MARKET EFFICIENCY, AND DISTRIBUTIONAL JUSTICE

This is where twentieth-century economics makes its entry, claiming to have answers for how to think about what belongs in the public sphere and what in the private sphere, based on conditions for when state intervention in private matters could serve the public good.

The buzzwords were utility, welfare, and, later, efficiency, Pareto improvement, and equity. The lodestar became removing impediments to the efficient allocation of resources in a resource-constrained world (known as allocative efficiency).

Welfare

Economists tend to think of the world in terms of individuals trying rationally to maximize their welfare (a variant of Enlightenment liberalism). For nineteenthth-century political economists, most famously Jeremy Bentham, that meant "utility" in a quite specific sense: the pleasure or pain felt by individual people. Given difficulties in reaching a shared view on how happy or unhappy other people are, however, by the middle of the twentieth century leading economists, partly in the grip of the logical-positivist philosophy briefly fashionable in Vienna and London, held that, as inquirers into efficiency, they did not need to get into whatever might be the *substance* of welfare at all, nor into how one person's welfare compared in absolute terms with other people's. All that mattered was how individuals ranked their preferences.[6] Talk about individuals deriving utility from experiencing (or consuming) something could continue, but it was to be thought of in terms of how they *ordered* their preferences.

To gauge that, economists could observe people's *choices*. On an assumption that people are rational, an individual's choices reflect her or his preferences (and the information available to them): this is the doctrine of *revealed preference*. In a market transaction, they would pay more for A than for B if they preferred A to B, which meant they derived more welfare from A.

Efficiency

Within this setup, the task of economics was to identify the conditions of production, exchange, and consumption under which welfare was generated efficiently in a resource-constrained world. The core concept of efficiency is associated with the name of the late-nineteenth-/early-twentieth-century Italian conservative social scientist Vilfredo Pareto. If a change (say, a regulatory intervention) would improve the well-being

[6]Following London (later Oxford) philosopher Freddie Ayer's version of the Viennese fashion that what we cannot verify is literally meaningless, London School of Economics economist Lionel Robbins forcefully latched onto the view that ethics is just noise and, at the very least, completely separable from the technical science of economics. As it happens, logical positivism had a shorter life in philosophy faculties than in economics.

of at least one person without leaving anyone worse off, it is said to bring about a *Pareto improvement.* If, by contrast, any change would leave at least one person worse off (impaired well-being or welfare), the starting point is said to be *Pareto efficient.*

This conception of efficiency is not especially rich and does not mean that a Pareto-efficient state of affairs is admirable in other senses. For example, if all the wealth in a society were in the hands of a single person, any change that gave everyone else (or, indeed, just one other person) some wealth but depleted the first person's wealth (and well-being) would not be a Pareto improvement because the initially rich person would be worse off: the starting point, however unattractive, was a Pareto-efficient state. The idea of a Pareto improvement is, nevertheless, useful because it captures the thought that if we can make some people better off (improve their well-being) without making anyone worse off, we should.

Over the middle decades of the last century, economists pinned down the circumstances under which Adam Smith's *invisible hand* can bring about efficiency in this sense. In their famous "welfare theorems," Kenneth Arrow, Gerard Debreu, and Lionel McKenzie uncovered the ideal or abstract conditions under which a market economy (the price mechanism) would deliver an efficient allocation of resources, with no gains from trade—no potential Pareto improvements—left unexploited and, therefore, with everyone left with their well-being as high as possible *given* the original distribution of resources. If those initial endowments were redistributed, perfect markets would generate a new Pareto-efficient state of affairs. An even more powerful result, known as the *Second Welfare Theorem,* was that under perfect competition *any* desired Pareto-efficient state could be obtained through an appropriate reshuffling of people's initial endowments.

This breakthrough in technical economics had a massive effect on twentieth-century debates about the functions and structure of the state, and thus on debates about delegation from politicians to technocrats.

Delegating the Pursuit of Pareto Efficiency to the Regulatory State

Most important, it suggested that questions of efficiency can be separated from questions of socioeconomic justice. Pareto efficiency might be a weak test, but it makes us ask whether a society has done as well as it can (absent lump-sum redistributions, which do not affect incentives to trade in the market). If a society is *not* doing as well as it can, we are directed toward removing impediments to market efficiency because markets can in theory take us wherever we want to go. That becomes a central task of the regulatory state. It is the basis for the claim that technocrats can safely be delegated the task of pursuing Pareto efficiency.[7]

Distributional Choices Left Over for Politics: Social Welfare Functions

If, however, we *are* in a Pareto-efficient state but find the results unattractive, that is because we do not like the distribution of welfare across individuals. We can improve upon things only by reshuffling resources, so as to get to another efficient state. Indeed, in theory, we can get to exactly the distribution of welfare we want if only we know exactly how to do the reshuffling.

While no small matter in practice of course (!), this has major implications for politics and government. It assumes, as we do throughout part I, that welfare is the sole guide and goal for public policy: Welfarism, with a capital *W*, as an ethical-political doctrine.[8] In that case, the key is for society to take a view on the (or a) just distribution of welfare.

This entails choosing how to weigh each person's welfare relative to the rest of the community's, known to economists as a *social welfare function* (SWF).[9] That choice is for the world of politics, not technoc-

[7] Gilardi, *Delegation*, pp. 25–26.

[8] Economics has been committed to welfarism but not Welfarism. The former is an explanatory account of human behavior, centered on the view that individuals make rational choices in the pursuit of their welfare, which for some individuals might incorporate weighing the perceived well-being of others or society as a whole (their perception of the common good). This does not commit anyone to evaluating justice or ethical value in terms of welfare. Some people might want, instead, to weigh duties or virtue alongside or even as prior to welfare. Many people do hold, however, that welfare *should*, morally, be *a* criterion of value. Going further, some maintain that it is the *only* criterion. Typically, Welfarism pays no heed to the possibility that people derive welfare from, for example, democracy for its own sake (*intrinsic* value) as distinct from any role that democracy might play in delivering states of the world (*instrumental* value) (Sen, "Utilitarianism and Welfarism"). On the value to some people of (democratic) processes, see Anderson, "Critical Review."

[9] Following Nobel Prize winner Paul Samuelson, a *social welfare function* aggregates the welfare—strictly, the preference orderings—of individuals in some way. In selecting between

racy, and so not our independent agencies. We might even think that such collective choices are the point of democracy conceived of as the General Will, although things are not quite so simple (chapter 9).

The Real World of Public Policy: Compensation Tests, Cost-Benefit Analysis, Money Incomes

That is the theory, focused on obtaining and choosing among Pareto-efficient states of the world. It fits into an essentially liberal worldview, and in its analytical rigor risks obscuring some essentially normative assumptions about the organization of collective life (part II).

Policy is another matter: a world where choices cannot be ducked, where doing nothing is doing something, where implementing any redistributive scheme can be costly, where there are disagreements about the optimum, and where individuals can lose out.

On that last point, it is not obvious that the test of Pareto improvement should be taken literally. If public policy were constrained to pursuing only Pareto improvements, a single loser would have a veto. In the late 1930s, this prompted the British economists John Hicks and Nicholas Kaldor to propose that, instead of actual Pareto improvements, the test should be that, across the population, the net welfare benefits for the winners exceed the net costs for the losers. Provided that condition was met, the beneficiaries could in principle compensate the losers.[10] Whether or not losers were, in fact, compensated was a matter of politics and so, strictly, a separable question.

This is one of the main drivers of the regulatory practice of *cost-benefit analysis* (CBA), which in the previous chapter we saw US presidents demand of regulatory initiatives from agencies they can control.

---

the set of potentially available efficient states (and so its distribution of endowments), society is driven by its *preferred* social welfare function or, put another way, by how it wants to weigh different individuals' well-being. For example, an SWF might give equal weight to each person's preference ordering, through simple adding up, which accords zero weight to distributional issues and so is a relative of the ethical position taken in Bentham's classical utilitarianism. Or an SWF might focus entirely on the welfare of the least-well-off person in the community, which is a relative of late-twentieth-century political philosopher John Rawls's doctrine of "justice as fairness" and, thus, is one way of putting distributional issues first.

[10] Known as *Potential* Pareto Efficiency. There are some technical problems with the Hicks-Kaldor concept, which I won't get into.

CBA can thus be seen as a Welfarist legitimation device: a claim that science, in the hands of technocrats, can and should drive policy choices.

Measuring relative costs and benefits is hard: it requires forecasts, and the well-being of individuals must be weighed somehow. Because economics is very largely about the market exchanges through which people realize their choices, and because money is the numeraire of exchange, it becomes, let's for now say, natural to think of aggregate income or wealth measured in (stable) money terms as a proxy for aggregate welfare.[11] If aggregate incomes rise, a society is better off—or, rather, capable of being better off if it can achieve something approaching the distribution of goods that it wants. The pot of resources is bigger.

Summing up, on the account given here, legitimacy is to be maintained by delegating to technocrats only the pursuit of market efficiency or, practically, the expansion of aggregate income. Where they have options over how to promote efficiency, they should be constrained to choose the course dictated by a social welfare function (objective) given to them by the world of politics. Thus underpinned, off they go, insulated from day-to-day politics.

MARKET FAILURE AND THE REGULATORY STATE

Conceived in those terms, this is a world where, as the chapter head's famous quote from Chicago economist Milton Friedman puts it, business should pursue profits within the rules of the game; and the purpose of government is to generate those rules, with a clear division of labor between politicians and technocrats.

In theory, as well as the integrity of public policy (see below), that nirvana requires (a) complete markets (in the sense that absolutely anything can be traded or insured against) and (b) full information available to and understood by everyone.[12] In practice, the main manifestations of market failure, each inviting a state remedy of some kind, take three broad forms, concerning public goods, spillovers to non-

[11] Okun, *Equality and Efficiency* (chapter 1), argues that not everything is or should be tradable for money (e.g., some rights).

[12] Greenwald and Stiglitz, "Externalities in Economies."

contracting third parties (known as *externalities*), and asymmetric power.[13] Independent agencies are involved in all three, all over the world.

Public Goods

Goods and services tend to be undersupplied by the market if (a) using or consuming them cannot be restricted but is available to all ("nonexcludability") and (b) if use does not deplete availability ("nonrivalry"). Everyone has an incentive to stand back and wait for provision from someone else, so that they can get access for nothing (free riding). Collective-action problems of this kind motivate the state, in its guise as the *services state* and the *security state*. Cutting through the stand-off, the state produces these "public goods" itself.

Lighthouses and national defense are canonical examples.[14] Arguably, so is the macroeconomic stability that central banks exist to preserve, but in fact it is not quite so straightforward. As proves important in part IV, price stability—stability in the value of money—is a public good, but the stability of the financial system is slightly different. In both cases, no one can be excluded from the benefits; but, unlike price stability, financial-system stability is, in the jargon, rivalrous. Like common grazing ground, the resilience of the financial system can be "consumed," leaving it depleted and, thus, reducing the flow of benefits over time. Financial stability is rooted in a "common good" rather than a "public good" and, as such, can sometimes still warrant state intervention, but of a different kind and with different challenges.[15]

At the center of this book, then, central banks are *suppliers* of a public good and *preservers* of a common good, entailing distinct kinds of intervention in the economy.

[13] I do not cover cognitive biases.

[14] Lighthouses could be supplied privately in England, but under local or central-state coordination of various kinds.

[15] On common goods, see Ostrom, *Governing the Commons*.

Externalities

A common resource problem can exist without its being a big deal for society. Overfishing a local pond might be an example. The same can hardly be said of the instability that results when the resilience of the financial system wears thin: the whole of society suffers.

Such spillovers involve a market inefficiency because, as analyzed by the British economist Arthur Pigou a century ago, buyers and sellers will not sufficiently reflect (internalize) those external effects.[16]

Where spillover effects are harmful ("negative externalities"), there tends to be oversupply, most obviously of pollutants. The mid-twentieth-century US public intellectual John Dewey regarded the need to cure these problems as almost definitive of the purpose of the state.[17] This changed the understanding of property rights, because the right, say, to operate a factory does not necessarily create a right to pollute the neighborhood (see below).[18]

As time has passed, efforts to mitigate externalities have by no means been limited to spillovers from ordinary economic transactions but have extended into social life. For example, I could inflict "noise pollution" on my next-door neighbor, ruining the quality of her life, if I play music incredibly loudly all day and night (and without her consent). On both sides of the Atlantic problems of that kind have motivated various forms of social regulation, on the broad grounds that the net cost-benefit can be assessed qualitatively if not quantitatively.[19]

Asymmetric Power, Monopoly, and Antitrust

A slightly different type of problem arises where there is a material imbalance of power between the two parties to a transaction, either because one party is economically dominant (whether as a monopoly seller or buyer) or because of asymmetric information (for example, a borrower knows more about its financial condition than a lender and

[16] Pigou, *Economics of Welfare.*

[17] Dewey, *Public and Its Problems*, p. 12.

[18] This is important to criticisms of the administrative state rooted in the defense of property rights; e.g., Epstein, "Perilous Position."

[19] Sunstein, *After the Rights Revolution*. For the evolution of CBA, see Kessler and Pozen, "Working Themselves Impure," pp. 1859–1868.

might also be sufficiently powerful to decline to open its books). Often those are presented as two distinct problems, but both revolve around asymmetric power.

Problems of asymmetric information drove a lot of early financial regulation, especially after the founding in 1934 of the US Securities and Exchange Commission, which imposed disclosure requirements on issuers and traders of securities (chapter 7).

By contrast, the wave of legislative initiatives in Europe to regulate utilities in the 1980s was prompted by the privatization of suppliers of energy, phone lines, and other such services. No longer under direct "social control," they were instead to be regulated as monopolies. We spend a little longer on this type of market failure, as a step toward highlighting a problem of vagueness in prescribing efficiency as the purpose of IA regimes.

Monopoly risks abuse if the suppliers are able to get away with setting prices too far above their costs (or, what amounts to the same thing, depleting quality) because, in the short-to-medium run, customers have nowhere else to go. Separately, efficiency is lost. A lot has turned on how economists think about this.

In an efficient market, the clearing price—the price at which everyone buys and everyone sells—equates the benefit to consumers of the last unit purchased (the marginal benefit) to the cost of producing that final unit (marginal cost), and similarly for the clearing price for all labor and other inputs for the supplying firms. Both producers and consumers gain from the allocative efficiency, and the total surplus is maximized.[20] Under monopoly conditions, however, the producer is in charge and produces up to the point that maximizes *its* benefit, which is where its marginal costs equal the revenue from selling the extra unit of production (marginal revenue). In the standard cases, this gives the monopolist an incentive to undersupply, with the market price higher than under competition. Consumers lose in two ways relative to competitive efficiency: because some would have made a purchase at the

[20] Assuming that their costs rise with the volume produced, producers enjoy a surplus on the volume generated and sold up to that final unit (broadly, this is profit, and it should be observable). Assuming that benefits decline with each extra unit consumed, consumers enjoy a surplus on the amounts purchased up to the last unit, as they paid less than the purchases were worth to them (this surplus is not readily observable). The "total surplus" is equal to the sum of the "producer surplus" and the "consumer surplus."

lower "competitive" price but did not at the monopolist's price, and because those who did make a purchase paid too much.

Framed that way, the public policy interest is to stand in the way of mergers, cartels, or other agreements among firms that would harm consumers, evidenced by whether or not prices rise or fall. If, however, welfare in the future matters, we care about the incentives of producers to invest in technical improvements that reduce the costs of production in the future (sometimes referred to as *dynamic* efficiency) and so lead to lower prices down the road. It matters, therefore, whether the objective of any antitrust and mergers regime is cast in terms of near-term or longer-term welfare. Either way, however, it is about efficiency and economic welfare.

The Regulatory State Vindicated?

The efficiency-oriented public policy world I have been describing seems to provide a place for central banks, competition authorities, utility regulators, and more. We can stop worrying about the Fed, the Bundeskartellamt (German competition authority), the Autorité des Marchés Financiers (French securities market regulator), Ofgem (British energy-utility regulator), and their many cousins. Their instrumental value is validated by the welfare benefits of efficiency. Their place in the democratic state is warranted by the separability of questions of equity and by the scientific objectivity of cost-benefit analysis. Except that:

- the conditions for efficiency and equity to inhabit completely separate spheres rarely hold,
- the possibility of "government failure" has been neglected, and
- Friedman's assumption that firms take the rules of the game as given has been left unexamined.

The first of those points deprives us of simplicity, the second rescues us from idealism, and the third questions the standard "theory" of the firm. A closer look at each sets up our problem of the place of independent agencies in the structure of the state.

EFFICIENCY VERSUS EQUITY REVISITED

The neatness implicit in positing a technocratic world of efficiency that stands apart, logically as well as organizationally, from a political world of redistribution does not withstand scrutiny. In a metaphor famous among economists, the bucket used to carry resources from rich to poor might be leaky.[21] Redistributive measures (taxes and transfers) can be costly to implement and, more profoundly, they affect incentives.

The deep problem here is that efficiency and distributional justice are strictly separable only assuming that a person's (or firm's) wealth does not (materially) influence how they value the opportunities, choices, or threats they face and, thus, their response to possible government policies. In reality, wealth, and the ability to borrow against future income, frequently *does* affect how someone values opportunities.

This infects CBA somewhat. The underlying spirit of the "potential compensation" test is that, in assessing net benefits to winners and net costs to losers, what should be "aggregated" is each individual's *own* measure of welfare: what the proposed measure means for them by *their* lights. Since that is obviously formidably difficult, economists tend to rely, as we discussed, on the proxy provided by estimated or expected effects on aggregate wealth (or incomes). But that assumes that people's choices (and so implied preferences) are not constrained by their wealth/income. Inferring value is not the same as observing the prices at which voluntary, *unconstrained* transactions would occur in a market exchange. Among other things, this means that CBA cannot unambiguously claim the virtue of context-free "science."

Notwithstanding those niceties, it is argued that even where policy designed to promote allocative efficiency (crudely, to increase total wealth) is tangled up with distributional effects, policy to achieve justice or equity can in practice be set separately, essentially via the tax code.[22] This amounts to saying that politics can mop up any distributional issues after the main "regulatory" course has been charted; and, further, that if politicians wish, they can do so, not regulatory measure

[21]Okun, *Equality and Efficiency.*

[22]Kaplow, "(Ir)Relevance of Distribution."

by regulatory measure, but as part of implementing the outcome of broader debates about distributional justice, taking into account the whole range of regulatory and other policies.

That leaves a good deal hanging in the air. *If* potential Pareto efficiency were to be a warranted goal for independent agencies, does that mean evaluations (whether by cost-benefit analysis or other techniques) of their proposed regulatory or other initiatives should cover only efficiency (aggregate income) considerations? Or should regulatory agencies assess distributional issues themselves, even when their goal is solely efficiency? For example, should they take into account "leaky bucket" costs of redistribution? Remarkably, there seems to be little economic or other social science literature on these issues. More important, as we shall see when discussing real-world state structures in part III (chapter 16), practice in this area is, to say the least, unclear.

INEFFICIENCIES IN GOVERNMENT POLICY MAKING

For many skeptics of regulation, however, the greater problem lies in the pathologies of government institutions themselves.

Inspired by economics, some theories of government—perhaps particularly in the US—conceive of the policy-making process as analogous to a market. Provided the policy marketplace is efficient, the outcomes will be not only explicable but also normatively justified under Welfarist criteria.

The Policy Maker as Auctioneer or Umpire

The role of the state is, on this conception, to help strike the bargain that keeps all interest groups or factions as happy as possible. The bargain might entail supplementing a main, contested legislative act with other measures (known as *side payments*), such as targeted spending commitments or tax cuts, that compensate those groups who would otherwise feel themselves to be losers.

In this way, everybody ends up better off (or no worse off) if the system works. In the metaphor of a market process, the state performs the role of auctioneer. It is a role that any state might play, democratic or not, provided only that people have access to information and are free to "play."[23] Thus, in terms of our central interest, if legislators choose to delegate to an agency, that must have been the efficient outcome of a bargaining process between society's interest groups.

Impediments to Policy-Making Efficiency

We can feel comfortable about the outcomes of that kind of political bargaining process only if the "policy market" is efficient. Thus *all interested parties*, however small they might seem, need to be at the bargaining table; once at the table, all parties need to be able to bargain *on equal terms*; and *enforcing* the resulting bargain has to be feasible.

None of those conditions is easily met. The lobbying industry exists partly in order to tilt the table.[24] The state actor may not be able to make a credible commitment to deliver the promised side payments, either because of an ex ante perceived risk that they will deliberately renege or because ex post they are no longer in power when the time to deliver arrives.[25]

The state umpire may not be neutral and, worse, might be able to conceal from some of the interested parties the advantages it is reaping for itself and/or granting to a favored group. Once the losers wake up to the game having been rigged in some way, cynicism is the only refuge.

This points to a hole in Friedman's view of the sole responsibility of business being profit maximization within *given* "rules of the game" and so, more generally, in the standard economic theory of the firm. Business has incentives to try to tilt the rules, including the processes of government and politics, in their favor. And parts of the business community, especially larger firms, might have the wherewithal to do so. Our need for a theory of the structure of government might have implications for the theory of the firm.[26]

[23] For a model of efficient policy making in conditions of equal lobbying or bargaining power, see Becker, "Theory of Competition."

[24] Olson, *Logic of Collective Action*.

[25] Acemoglu, "Political Coase Theorem?"

[26] Zingales, "Towards a Political Theory."

FROM INEFFICIENCY TO REGULATORY CAPTURE

This has a bearing on the most prevalent critique of regulation and regulatory agencies. As related in chapter 2, not long after World War II a generation of American political scientists argued that, whatever the intent of legislators, agency officials would be captured by the industries they were charged with regulating. The drivers might be the prospect of lucrative jobs after leaving office; the need to recruit technical experts whose mind-set and values have been formed in the industry; or officials finding themselves cognitive inhabitants of an industry's conception of itself. Whatever the combination of causes, capture was plainly a bad thing. Pareto improvements were not to be expected; on the contrary.

By the 1970s Chicago economists were flipping this on its head.[27] Their story was that politicians would "supply" regulatory regimes in response to a "demand" for regulation if they were "paid" enough. That demand might come from the public, who, for example, would desire lower utility prices and who would "pay" in a medium valued and demanded by politicians: votes. But there might also be demand for regulation from the leading firms in an industry, which would desire barriers to entry that entrenched their own position, and which could "pay" the politicians with, for example, campaign finance contributions. The legislator would balance those two sources of demand.

Since, at least historically, members of the public face much greater problems in trying to coordinate a campaign than do incumbent firms in concentrated industries, it was predicted that business interests would often dominate the design of regulatory regimes. The upshot: regulatory agencies that were, by legislative intent, *structurally captured*.

In an important sense, the Chicago theory changed the debate about regulation, at least in the US. From fretting about how industry capture of a regulator's officials or culture could twist policy away from the public's purposes, for a while commentators were encouraged to look upon agency officials as simply and dutifully implementing a regime framed by industry-captured legislators.

[27] Stigler, "Theory of Economic Regulation," and Peltzman, "More General Theory." For a recent survey of the economics literature on capture, see Dal Bo, "Regulatory Capture."

Viewed like that, the action was in lobbying Congress. For others, however, there was not much comfort to be salvaged from contemplating whether capture operated via the legislature or the regulators themselves.

THE ALTERNATIVE MODEL: MORE MARKETS

The legitimation strategy for technocratic delegation with which we began the chapter looks to be in tatters. We cannot be sure that the technocrats would not wade into issues of distributional justice. Worse, they might be programmed or choose to favor some groups in society over others, possibly reflecting a capacity within big business to influence the rules of the game of politics itself.

Economists who opposed the regulatory state offered their own solution: address market failures by taking steps toward more complete markets.

Coase versus Pigou: Property Rights and Transaction Costs

In 1960 Ronald Coase, a British-born economist working in Chicago, explained how regulatory interventions were not warranted where, instead, property rights could be clarified (or created) and where the transaction costs of enforcing those rights were low (theoretically zero). Such legal rights could be traded and hedged via markets, opening up the option of the work of regulation being performed instead by the law of contract and of torts enforced via the courts: as typically put, private choice rather than public choice.

Even better, for allocative efficiency it did not matter how the property rights were initially distributed: the same clearing price would apply whether the polluted victim had to pay the polluter not to exercise rights to pollute or, alternatively, the polluter had to compensate the victim for waiving rights not to be polluted. This is known as Coase's Theorem.[28]

[28] Coase, "Social Cost."

The central point for regulatory policy was *not* that the market always works best unfettered and, thus, that there should never be state regulatory intervention. Rather, it was that the case for regulation turned on the existence of irremediable and material transaction costs standing in the way of efficiency. In other words, it was not sufficient simply to cite an externality to motivate regulatory intervention. There are three things to be said about this.

Creating New Property Rights Can Entail Regulation

First, even where governments choose to address externality problems via creating new property rights, they sometimes opt to regulate the new markets for trading those rights (e.g., pollution permits). Simply invoking "transaction costs" does not seem sufficient to explain or warrant the choice between judicial and regulatory oversight.[29]

Keeping Perspective: The Infeasibility of Committing to Compensate for Financial Instability

Second, some transaction costs can be reduced; others cannot. A classic example of the latter, vital to part IV's exploration of postcrisis central banking, helps to motivate regulatory intervention to preserve the stability of the financial system. In the event of a massive banking collapse pushing the economy onto a persistently lower path of output and employment, the losers are never going to be able to recover their costs from the "financial polluters" because the banks and other intermediaries are bust. More broadly, if the hit to the economy is bad enough, society in aggregate is truly poorer, so it is impossible for transfers to restore all the losers to the wealth (or well-being) they might reasonably have expected had the systemic crisis not occurred. However well property rights were designed and however fairly and efficiently the courts adjudicated conflicts over those rights, they could not be enforced. Stability warrants state intervention to reduce the probability of crises and to limit how bad they are.

[29] A core theme of Shleifer, *Failure of Judges*.

Distributional Justice Is Still Kept Apart

Third, while the allocation of property rights might not affect efficiency, it does have distributional consequences. The victim of pollution is, obviously, out of pocket if polluting rights are granted to perpetrators. As with the chapter's benchmark legitimation model for IA regimes, therefore, the "more complete markets" route assumes that issues of equity can and will be addressed by politicians' redistributive policies, with judges and independent market regulators not having to get their hands dirty.

PATHOLOGIES IN THE STRUCTURE OF GOVERNMENT: WHO SHOULD DO WHAT?

There is an old debate about whether social choices are best left to the market, the impartial reason of the judiciary, or the processes of democratic politics. If regulators are thought of as promoting market efficiency, this can seem to beckon a neat institutional division of labor: aggregate welfare (agencies), legal rights (judges), distributional justice (politicians).

It is hardly so simple, however. In the case of competition policy, for example, efficiency in government requires clarity over whether efficiency in the market is the sole goal; and if so, over *how* the state will go about determining whether, say, a merger or trade agreement among ostensible competitors would promote or impede allocative efficiency. Should the presumption be that mergers are simply a bad thing if they lead to concentrations of economic, and hence potentially political, power; that they should be stopped if they impede competition by reducing the number of participants in a market below some threshold; or that they should be permitted so long as they are likely to generate cost savings, which, prospectively, would reduce prices for consumers? And who should decide?

In the Principles for Delegation introduced in chapters 5 and 6, I will argue that high-level choices about goals should be made by legislators, not by technocrats and not by judges; and in part II I defend that as a principle rooted in our basic political values. We will see in chapter 7, however, that the real world of competition policy regimes does not measure up. Through the middle of the twentieth century, especially in the US, doctrine and practice moved from a broad concern with economic power to focus more particularly on competition; and from a bright-lines approach to an analysis of expected consumer welfare. Each transition was brought about not by an overt change in legislated norms but rather by judges heavily influenced by developments in economics.

On other fronts, by contrast, such as utility regulation and environmental protection, advanced-economy democracies have frequently chosen to entrust the strategies for mitigating "market failure" to administrative agencies rather than relying on the courts to enforce new property rights created by legislative measures. In terms of a Welfarist legitimation, the claim has to be that they will do a better (or less bad) job.

These choices are not immediately explicable since, as we have seen in this and the previous chapter, twentieth-century economists took very different views on how best to promote market efficiency; on the relative reliability of courts, regulators, and elected politicians; and on the separability of efficiency and equity. If institutions, broadly conceived (e.g., private law, a monetary regime, a constitution), are mechanisms for reducing transaction costs across space and time, that doesn't help us much unless we are clear about goals and values.

Away from the academy, economic liberalism permeates policy and political debates about the structure of the state in quite different ways on either side of the Atlantic. In the US, it is deployed by those preferring minimal government to argue against regulation and in favor of private, market-based orderings underpinned by courts enforcing property rights of various kinds; but it is resisted by Left liberals who support regulators under presidential control that pursue efficiency in combination with distributional and other social goals. By contrast, in Europe (on both sides of the Channel), delegation to *independent* agencies has been seen as a means to pursue efficiency without a taint from quotidian politics.

For those readers not interested in economics and economic theory but more interested in politics, political theory, or public law, the takeaways from this chapter should be twofold. First, it must be clear whether the vaunted independence of IA regimes incorporates (and delivers) independence from business and other powerful private sector actors. Second, and more deeply, welfare economics' focus on efficiency does not immediately provide an off-the-shelf legitimating blueprint for the structure of the state; and, in particular, for determining which public policy decisions should be made by politicians, technocrats, or judges.

Making progress with that is going to be difficult so long as we treat "agencies" as a monolith. To this chapter's two-dimensional matrix of the *purposes* and *functional modes* of the administrative state we must add a third dimension, covering its *structure*. That, and in particular the varying degrees to which state agencies are insulated from politics, is the subject of the next chapter.

4

The Structure of the Administrative State

A HIERARCHY FROM SIMPLE AGENTS TO TRUSTEES (AND GUARDIANS)

> When . . . governments . . . pass on their monetary programme to the central banks, it is the same sort of step as is taken . . . in war, when political leaders hand over the task of concerting operations to the military commanders. Broad guidance must be given by the political leaders, but it is only the military commanders who can plan and take practical action.
>
> —R. G. Hawtrey, 1922[1]

In the previous chapter we laid out a 4 × 4 matrix covering the functional modalities and purposes of organs of the state. They were, respectively, whether a body is providing services, writing legally binding rules, using its financial resources and taxing powers to intervene in markets, or coming to the rescue in emergencies, and whether it serves the purpose of security, economic efficiency, distributive justice, or macroeconomic stability. In this chapter, we begin to explore a third dimension, which is at the heart of our investigation: the degree to which an agency is structured to operate independently from day-to-day politics. The range of options is illustrated by the position and norms of the military and the judiciary, which too often get ignored in general discussions of unelected power in the administrative state.

THE BIG CHOICES IN THE DESIGN OF A PUBLIC POLICY REGIME

The architectural choices for a public policy regime are broad. Big picture, the spectrum ranges across two dimensions: whether the legislature sets detailed rules or only broad parameters for policy; and whether it

[1]Hawtrey, "Genoa Resolutions," p. 291.

delegates implementation to an elected executive or to some other part of the machinery of government. This can be thought of as a 3 × 3 matrix: who sets policy (legislature, elected executive, agency) and who implements that policy (court, executive, agency). The cells in the matrix capture the goals and fears of those who care about the structure of the state. For example, the US laissez-faire Right wants to be in the cell (Legislature, Courts) and at all costs to avoid (Agencies, Agencies).

Thus, at one end of the spectrum are laws that are applied case by case through the courts, without any codified elaboration of policy by the executive branch, which is simply responsible for monitoring compliance and taking enforcement actions (typically prosecutions) to the courts. For this model to work, the legislation needs to prescribe mechanically (e.g., a speed limit for driving) or at least in great detail (e.g., some tax codes). It can be thought of as a world of legislators and courts: legislators make policy and courts apply it.

That simple description does not hold where, notwithstanding the same basic legislature-courts structure, legislation sets only vague constraints on private actions. This is a world where judges make high policy through the way they interpret and apply the statutory provisions in particular cases, establishing de facto precedents. It is, for example, the world of competition policy (chapters 3, 7, and 14).

Falling around the middle of the institutional spectrum are regimes where, within the constraints of any legislation, the elected executive is charged with elaborating general policy on an ongoing basis. Implementation may fall to a bureau under the executive's direct and continuous control or to an arm's-length delivery agency.

A little beyond that stand regimes where "policy" is delegated to the executive branch but it relies on an independent agency for the information it needs to elaborate and implement policy. Such "information agencies" include the bodies in many jurisdictions responsible for compiling and publishing official statistics on economic and social conditions; and, increasingly, bodies that produce the macroeconomic forecasts used to help ensure that fiscal policy complies with any mandated or optional constraints.

At the far end of the spectrum is a broad family of agencies that are not under the elected executive's *continuous* control and that determine both general policy and individual cases/actions within their domain of delegated discretion, which may be either tightly or broadly drawn. Such agencies may be subject to varying degrees of ex post influence from the executive branch or legislative committees or both. I call them "policy agencies."

Some are enjoined to fill out the statutory regime with their own detailed rules; some are remitted to apply and flesh out a broad statutory standard through case-by-case decisions and actions (for example, granting and sustaining licenses, setting interest rates); and some are given discretion to choose how to balance their outputs between rule writing and adjudication.

Overstating somewhat the clarity of the categories I have been describing, and oversimplifying some functions, they might be represented thus:

	Policy explicitly set by:	*With elaboration by:*	
	Legislature (without much subordinate codification)	*Executive*	*Agency*
Policy implemented (and fleshed out case by case) by:			
Court	Criminal law		
	Competition policy in US		
Core executive	Welfare payments	EU-Com competition policy	
		US immigration policy	
Arm's-length agency	Administration of national parks	UK delivery agencies	Policy agencies

Legislators and Courts versus Nonlegislative Policy Making

We are interested in a subset of policy agencies: those that are insulated from day-to-day politics. Setting aside unworthy motives, which we discuss briefly in chapter 5, the impulse to delegate a policy role to such arm's-length agencies revolves around views on the capabilities (absolutely and relatively) of legislators, courts, the elected executive branch, and the agencies—on their own and in combination. In other words, the solutions adopted by our societies are telling us something about perceptions of the capacity of the key organs of the state to reduce the transaction costs that run through economic and social relationships.

The argument for delegating regulatory policy to agencies or to courts cannot, for example, be that legislators are congenitally incapable of casting detailed laws, because that is precisely what they do with the tax code. Maybe legislators do not have the capacity to produce detailed laws in as many fields as they want regulated. But then why not make agency-drafted rules subject to legislative veto (as in the EU)? Do we believe that legislators would corrupt the substance of draft rules submitted by expert agencies: that they are more prone to capture?

And where policy is delegated, do we have more faith in one type of *nonmajoritarian institution* (agencies) than another (the courts)? Do we fear, for example, that courts are more likely to substitute their own (inexpert) view of the substance when adjudicating a dispute over private rights created by legislators than when adjudicating a challenge, under administrative law, to a specialist regulatory agency's rules or decisions? Conversely, do opponents of delegation to agencies prefer to rely on judges' preferences because they have more faith in the adversarial process in open court or, quite differently, because they have more leverage over appointments to the judiciary?

Any set of principles for delegating must address those questions. One notable theory (the "enforcement theory of regulation") maintains that, in balancing whether to resolve problems via court litigation or regulation, societies have incentives to gravitate toward structures that maximize the efficiency of enforcement.[2] While that is part of it, efficiency in policy making is another (the focus here in part I), and the values we impose on policy-making processes is yet another (part II). Furthermore, we must avoid treating agencies as though they all have the same structure. Instead, delegation principles must cater for different degrees of insulation from day-to-day politics being appropriate or necessary.

[2] Shleifer, *Failure of Judges*, especially chapter 1, "The Enforcement Theory of Regulation."

Policy Agencies with Degrees of Political Insulation

Policy agencies come in three broad varieties: those that are (or, as a matter of law, can be) effectively controlled by the elected executive branch; those that are (largely) insulated from the executive branch but are subject, through various devices, to material *ongoing* control by members of the legislature, making them sensitive to legislators' evolving wishes and concerns;[3] and those that, subject to legislative reform of their enabling statutes, are largely insulated from *both* the executive branch and the legislature. Our concern is with the legitimacy in democracies of the third set of policy agencies, which includes most advanced-economy central banks.

As I hope is apparent, the spectrum of government institutions is so rich in theory and so complex in practice that it can seem hard to delineate what is going on. As preparation for articulating an independence hierarchy, we can gain some illumination from the contrasting relationships with elected politicians of two of the most essential unelected institutions in any democratic state, institutions that seem too elevated or embedded to carry the "administrative-state" tag: the military and the high judiciary.

THE MILITARY: AGENTS

Economic policy and social policy are not remotely the only areas where important questions arise about degrees of political control. There is a long-standing debate on military/political relations, grappling with the existential question of how a democracy can sustain a military capability sufficient to defend itself (and protect its legitimate interests) without running an unacceptable risk of the military dominating policy, let alone turning on its own citizens or even seizing control of the state.

Much of the debate still revolves around the late conservative theorist Samuel Huntington's advocacy, over fifty years ago, of institutionalizing what he called "objective civilian control." Like Hegel's "universal

[3]Ongoing control is distinct from ex ante control and also from a continuing ability to be heard, which legislators have by virtue of their public platform and legislative power.

class" of civil servants (chapter 2), this drew inspiration from what Prussia had gained by developing a corps of military professionals. With separate spheres of political and military authority, the officer class's operational autonomy could and should be maximized so long as they kept out of politics.[4] This was to be achieved by having ends decided by the legitimate political authority, leaving means to the professionals—the bearers of a distinct military mind-set and culture.

As critics pointed out, echoing Clausewitz's conception of war as a political instrument, that left open how to distinguish between ends and means. Does strategy really begin where politics ends, as Huntington maintained, or does it shade into high policy when goals are vague or evolving, becoming unavoidably political in the face of unexpected losses and costs? Do politicians have a legitimate role in operational tactics when there could be domestic or international political consequences? More generally, how can the relationship between military commanders and their political masters be professionally comfortable, whatever its structural norms? Despite the quibbles, however, the basic precept retains appeal because, in our democracies, it is clear that elected politicians should decide whether or not to go to war and should determine war aims, but also that they should listen to the commanders' advice.

Only a few years after Huntington, US sociologist Morris Janowitz argued that developments in the technology of war (in his time nuclear, today also cyber) had blurred the boundaries between military and civilian skill sets (and, by implication, mind-sets). In a world without sharply defined spheres, necessary conditions for concord and success were the military sharing the values underpinning democratic-civilian control, and reciprocal civilian respect for something like a code of military honor.[5]

Part of what emerges from both lines of thought is the role played by an ethic or norm of self-restraint. When, in recent decades, tension has occurred between US presidents and the military high command, it has been attributed to cultural distance and to an erosion of those older

[4]Huntington, *Soldier and the State*. For reviews of the literature, see the appendix in Cohen, *Supreme Command*, and chapter 1 of Owen, *US Civil-Military Relations*.

[5]Janowitz, *Professional Soldier*, and "Military Elites."

norms, with military leaders stepping out of line to intervene publicly in political or high policy debates.[6]

Nevertheless, whatever their frustrations, US politicians have increasingly looked to the military to take on functions that traditionally belonged elsewhere, partly because it can be easier to get budgetary approval for the armed forces than for the civilian part of government.[7]

The Military as Exemplars for Central Bankers?

As will be apparent, a good deal of that picture is germane to political–central banking relationships. At a surface level, central bankers are also occasionally criticized for making unwelcome public interventions (on fiscal policy or politics more broadly). And they are also sometimes embraced by politicians who would like them to take on more, exploiting a blurred boundary between monetary and fiscal operations (chapters 22–24).

As is evident, however, in the words of early-twentieth-century British economist R. G. Hawtrey quoted at the chapter head, some commentators have seen deeper parallels. Politicians are ultimately in charge. As a monetary Clausewitz might have said, all central banking interventions in markets are an extension of fiscal policy. The central banker has specific operational capabilities but operates under some kind of mandate or guidance. And, it might be added, there is probably something akin to a central banker mind-set.

There are, though, limits to how far the parallels can be pushed. Hawtrey's description is closer to the executive's relationship with a central bank that is *not* independent. The first half of my thirty-odd-year career was spent in just such an institution, with the Bank of England acting more or less as the UK Treasury's agent in implementing policy and as a largely private, behind-the-scenes adviser. Policy goals and guidance were variable; and, despite some acceptance that there were separate high policy and operational spheres, ministers and their officials were sometimes drawn into real-time operational minutiae. In

[6] That this persists is clear from chapter 15, "Reflections," of the memoir of former US defense secretary Robert M. Gates, *Duty*.

[7] Brooks, *Everything Became War.*

equilibrium, there is almost no incentive to relax that kind of ongoing control when goals are being kept under review, and perhaps not much incentive to fix goals as that might lead to arguments for looser control.

An *independent* central bank, by contrast, is very different from the military. Its goal is unchanging rather than fluctuating with political or public sentiment, whereas politicians must keep their war aims and military strategy under review. And independent central bankers have more stable operational autonomy than their military peers. In both cases there is some idea of a dividing line between separate spheres, but it is formidably hard for politicians to observe any line in matters of war and security. In military/political relations, there is a special kind of "equal dialogue but unequal authority," with political restraint a matter of prudential judgment rather than a principled norm, given the value of probing but the hazards in overruling the commanders.[8]

The Military as Pure Agent

These distinctions become clearer by casting them in terms of principal-agent arrangements, as recently applied in more analytical accounts of military/civilian relations.[9]

The starting point is that, as a general matter, when a principal hires an agent to undertake a task, the principal's preferences should prevail. But they cannot be sure that their preferences will in fact prevail, because there are obstacles in the way of monitoring and so controlling what their agent is doing. Thus, a military field commander is liable to face strategic choices without time to consult. This matters because the agent might have different objectives based on their own interests or, even if loyal, a different view as to what is best for their principal. Thus, the political principal (in the US, the commander in chief) cannot even know for sure the character and commitments of the individuals appointed to high command or as key commanders in the field. What's more, even if they could somehow know everything about their generals' prior histories, they still run the risk of a commander seizing the

[8] Betts, "Civil-Military"; Cohen, *Supreme Command*, especially chapters 1 and 7.
[9] Feaver, "Crisis as Shirking."

initiative against their wishes, as General MacArthur, an American World War II hero, was accused of doing during the later Korean War. Although principals can fire their agents, as President Truman eventually did MacArthur, it can sometimes be hard for them to determine whether, guided by their own principles and interests, they should do so until it is too late.

Subject to one important tweak, that principal-agent (P-A) framework seems like a reasonable way of thinking about the structure of military/political relations. The elected politicians should be in charge, even when they change their minds and even when, wisely or unwisely, they interfere in operational detail. It may not be sensible for them to do so, but it is their right. And if dissatisfied with military commanders, they can fire them.[10] The commanders are not formally insulated and, unlike the regulatory policy makers described in chapter 2, do not have job security.

The tweak is that, in contrast to the most pared-down P-A arrangement, where the agent is simply handed a brief that they are expected to deliver, military commanders have a responsibility to furnish their political principal with relevant facts and to provide strategic advice, especially on feasibility and realism, as goals are framed and reviewed. Finding the best or a good practical balance in military/civilian relations amounts, therefore, to individual political leaders reaching a position of enlightened self-interest, under the shadow of their own electoral accountability to the people. Huntington can be viewed as trying to shape public expectations and political-community norms around how politicians should proceed.

That advisory-cum-delivery-agent framework is also a fair representation of the relationship between the executive branch and a *non*independent central bank. The elected executive is free to decide the monetary authority's strategy and tactics, to change its course as and when they choose, and to dig into operational detail, but answers to the electorate. Such central bankers want to maximize their influence and, perhaps, their de facto operational autonomy, guided by and seeking to insert the central banking mind-set where they believe it should prevail.

[10] As documented in Ricks, *Generals*, relieving officers from their command became uncommon for a number of decades in the US. But it was revived by Secretary Gates in his early years at the helm of the Department of Defense.

But those standard P-A accounts do not capture the nature of the relationship when, in choosing to grant independence to the monetary authority or to various regulators, the purpose is formally to insulate policy from shifting political currents. That takes us to our second exemplar state institution: the judiciary.

THE HIGH JUDICIARY: TRUSTEES VERSUS GUARDIANS

If it is the right of democratically elected governments to intervene in military decisions, it is manifestly not their right to intervene in the decisions of an independent judiciary. Indeed, that is the point of judicial independence as a means to underpin the rule of law (chapter 8).

We must distinguish, however, between the courts' roles in ordinary law and codified constitutional law. When applying and upholding ordinary law, judges are bound to implement statutes enacted by the legislature subject only to any constitutional constraints. Ex post, and again within any such constraints, the legislature can undo the *general* effects of judicial determinations and lawmaking by revising an existing statute or introducing a new statute. But there shall be no interference with the judges in their interpretation and application of the law as it stands at the time a specific case comes before them.

We cannot, then, think of them as *simple agents* in the sense of their being *obliged* to be sensitive to the shifting wishes of political principals. A better metaphor would be *trusteeship.* Whether through a written constitution or, as in the UK, a very deeply entrenched early-eighteenth-century ordinary statute, society entrusts judges with the responsibility of determining and administering ordinary laws with a view to the public benefiting collectively from the rule of law (chapter 8). While they are plainly servants of the people in some general sense, they are more clearly *trustees of the law for the benefit of the people.* As the judicial oath in England puts it:[11]

[11]Section 4 of the Promissory Oaths Act 1868. It might be argued that, even when applying ordinary law, judges are simultaneously acting as guardians of the values of the rule of law. This relates to the discussion of codified- versus political- versus common law constitutionalism in chapter 8 and implicitly assumes that rule-of-law values are safeguarded by the judiciary alone.

> I, ———, do swear that I will well and truly serve [the sovereign] —— in the office of ——, and I will do right to all manner of people after the laws and usages of this realm, without fear or favour, affection or ill will. . . . So help me God.

Things are different where the judges rule on the meaning and application of a written constitution and can, with finality, strike out unconstitutional statutes. In effectively setting the rules of the game for politics and government, and in delineating nonpolitical rights, they are sentinels for the constitution conceived of as providing the basic structure and point of origin for a polity's collective existence and way of life. Wearing that hat, they might be thought of as *guardians*. Where rights are codified vaguely or where multiple rights sometimes have to be balanced (that is to say, traded off) against each other, they have an interest, attending to their own legitimacy, in not drifting too far away from the evolving values of the people.[12]

Under this way of thinking, where, as in the US, the top court has the final say on the meaning of the constitution and is also the ultimate court of appeal for ordinary law, it has a split personality (guardian and trustee), its relationship with the legislature varying profoundly according to which hat it is wearing. At least formally, a cleaner separation is maintained in jurisdictions such as France, Germany, Italy, and Spain with specialist constitutional courts modeled on the lines advocated by Austrian jurist Hans Kelsen: a legacy of Austro-Hungary's early-twentieth-century decline that became part of Continental Europe's post–World War II response to the horrors of fascism and of the nearby totalitarian communism.[13] But as time has passed, the ordinary (trustee) courts there have ventured into the territory of constitutional law, blurring the dividing line.[14]

[12] Without getting into judicial balancing of basic rights, this is described as *reflexivity* by Rosanvallon in *Democratic Legitimacy* (chapter 8), the argument being that constitutional courts both structure and reflect society's political and policy debates, a point made in very different language in Graber, *American Constitutionalism*.

[13] Stone Sweet, "Constitutional Courts," argues they are trustees and that courts of ordinary law are regular agents. I see the former as guardians because they are charged with guarding a particular conception of collective political life, and the latter as trustees because, unlike regular agents, they are not at the beck and call of any set of political principals.

[14] Stone Sweet, *Governing with Judges*.

Meanwhile, whether as guardians, trustees, or both, there is no doubting the power of the judiciary. It is not surprising, therefore, that in many jurisdictions judges could be described as living under an ethic or norm of self-restraint, characterized by respecting the institutional competences of the legislature and executive and, in their extrajudicial pronouncements and lives, by a convention of staying out of party politics and conducting themselves discreetly rather than as the celebrities they could all too easily become.[15] While the terms of the respective self-restraining norms differ, in this the judiciary and military have something important in common (a vital point we return to, especially, in the conclusion).

TRUSTEES IN A HIERARCHY OF AGENCIES

The metaphors of principal/agent and trustee help to unpack the substance and significance of different *degrees* of independence of agencies within the administrative state. The least independent of agencies must, when making decisions, either consult their principal or ruminate on what their principal wants (or would want if in possession of the same information and expertise).

By contrast, a trustee must do neither of those things but instead must deliberate on what is required by their mandate: they are insulated from influence and power. Although unusual in the scope of their power, the judiciary is not alone in being in that position. Some agencies of the administrative state, including independent central banks, are too.[16]

Unpacking the metaphor a little, a trust typically has four components that are relevant to us: a settlor, a trustee, one or more beneficiaries, and a trust deed determining what manner of decisions the trustee must or may make in pursuit of what goals (ends) in the interests of those beneficiaries. For an independent agency created via ordinary leg-

[15] Kavanagh, "Judicial Restraint." The classic US account is Bickel, *Least Dangerous Branch*, a rather hopeful account of the "passive virtues" of the Supreme Court. For the UK, see Lord Justice Gross, "Judicial Role Today."

[16] Similar points are made by Rasmusen, "Theory of Trustees," and Driffill, "Central Banks as Trustees," although their focus is not legitimacy.

islation, the settlor is the legislature; the trustee is the agency; in a democracy, the beneficiary is the public as a whole; and the trust deed is the law establishing and setting the terms of the regime, the mandate.[17]

Since I am not the first to resort to the trustee metaphor in discussing regulatory and other government agencies, it is worth underlining that, in contrast to the usage of some authors, it is absolutely *not* a necessary condition that a trustee-agent has unconstrained discretion.[18] The mandate (metaphorically, the trust deed) might in theory be open ended or quite tightly drawn. The key test is that a trustee-agent must consult only the trust deed (their legal mandate) rather than also the settlor (the enacting legislature) or the settlor's successors (today's legislature) in deciding how to use their powers. An important question in what follows, therefore, is whether democracy imposes constraints on how loosely or tightly drawn the "trust deed" for an independent agency might decently be (chapters 6 and 11).

A Hierarchy of Insulation in the Administrative State

We have now encountered the following hierarchy of state agencies, in ascending order of independence (insulation from day-to-day politics):

1. *Delivery agencies*: Bodies under the ongoing control of the executive branch that do not have policy discretion.
2. *Information agencies*: Independent bodies that produce information and give independent expert advice on policy.
3. *Executive agencies*: Policy bodies that are largely under the control of the executive branch.[19]
4. *Semi-independent agencies*: Policy bodies that are not under the control of the executive branch but are subject to substantial leverage from either the legislature or the executive through, for example, frequent conditional budgetary appropriations.[20]

[17] I am grateful to Philip Richards and his former Freshfields colleagues for confirming my understanding of the broad shape of the law of trusts.

[18] The condition I am refuting is assumed in, for example, the survey paper by Stone Sweet and Thatcher, "Theory and Practice," and, in places, in Majone, "Two Logics" and *Dilemmas*.

[19] By calling agencies largely under the control of the elected executive branch "executive agencies," I am closer to US parlance than UK usage, which applies this term to what I am calling "delivery agencies" (category 1). I find the US meaning more natural.

[20] This category may exist only in presidential-style democracies.

5. *Trustee agencies*: Policy institutions that are highly insulated from day-to-day politics.
6. *Guardians*: Institutions that have the final word (or action) on some elemental underpinning or values of the polity.

The military would seem to be the grandest imaginable combination or hybrid of categories 1, 2, and 3. They must do what they are expressly told or what they sincerely believe to be in line with the wishes of their political principals ("delivery"), but they must advise without partiality, fear, or favor. Away from constitutional law, the high judiciary are exemplars of trusteeship. They must decide cases on the basis of their own beliefs about the relevant law and facts.

The question at the very core of our investigation is, What is needed to warrant putting a policy agency in the trustee category rather than in either the third or fourth category? On the way, we will bump into whether an institution within the administrative state could sensibly be a simple agent for one mission but a trustee for another (relevant for the SEC) or, like some courts, combine trusteeship and guardianship (a possible example being the postcrisis ECB).

STRUCTURING TRUSTEE-TYPE INDEPENDENT AGENCIES WITHIN THE ADMINISTRATIVE STATE

Our high-altitude exploration of the place in society of the military and the judiciary has helped separate the concepts of subordinate-agent, trustee, and guardian. But, as was evident from chapter 2's summary history, the real-world administrative state is characterized by agencies with bewildering degrees of independence. We therefore need to say something about four issues:

- the qualities that mark out a truly independent trustee-type agency,
- the hazards faced by political principals in delegating to trustee-type agencies,
- how small design flaws affect incentives to exercise self-restraint, and
- whether it is sensible to try to identify principles for delegating to trustee agencies across the administrative state as a whole.

The Essential Characteristics of Independence

We can, in fact, put some structure around chapter 2's account. Degrees of insulation from the rough-and-tumble of day-to-day politics can be boiled down to questions about three key levers, each of which might be held by the elected executive, the legislature, or both:

1. Do policy makers have control over the use of their instruments (or are their policy outputs subject to approval or veto by politicians)?
2. Do policy makers have job security (or can they be dismissed on the whim of elected politicians)?
3. Do policy makers control their own budget and financing (or do they have to seek *frequent* approval from politicians, and if so, how granular are such budgetary approvals)?

To be a trustee-type agency, the answers must be (yes, yes, yes).[21]

As a matter of fact (not normative evaluation), apparently similar agencies score quite differently under these tests. For example, in their role as rule writers, the EU's financial regulatory bodies (EBA, ESMA, EIOPA) fail the first test, since they must clear draft rules with the Council of Ministers and the European Parliament.

Many US agencies, such as the Environmental Protection Agency, fail the second test. Since Congress confers legal powers on specific officers, the heads of executive agencies can seek to pursue their own course, forcing a president who strongly disapproves to choose whether to incur the costs of obtaining Senate confirmation for a successor. But they are hardly as insulated as agency leaders with job security.

The US regulatory commissions (SEC, CFTC, FTC, and so on) pass the first two tests but fail the third. For budgetary control, it is the frequency that matters. Where an agency has to get political approval for its funding every year, all of its exchanges with legislators and, indeed, all of its external actions take place within the shadow of the impending or live negotiation. The politicians do not necessarily need overtly to deploy their formal power to prescribe or proscribe in order for agency leaders to be sensitive to their wishes. On this test, the Financial

[21] Especially in the US, the third question has often been omitted in studies of the administrative state. But see OECD, *Being an Independent Regulator.*

Conduct Authority (broadly the equivalent of the US's SEC, CFTC, and Consumer Financial Protection Bureau) is more independent, formally, than the Bank of England. Each has instrument independence and each set of policy makers has formal job security, but the Bank of England's budget envelope is set by politicians every five years whereas, subject to public consultation, the FCA sets its own budget (and levies fees from regulated firms to finance itself).[22]

Bringing some of those examples together, the degree of variation across countries becomes apparent. In the area of rule writing for securities market regulation, ESMA is not independent, the FCA is strongly independent de jure, and the SEC is in between. As discussed further in chapter 7, those are striking differences given they have essentially the same purposes and functions, and sit together as equal members of the international authority in this field, IOSCO.

That underlines the importance of normative criteria for *whether* to grant trustee-like independence, the subject of the next chapter. Another set of considerations drives the need for care in *how* to delegate, addressed in the subsequent chapter.

Trustees Are Still Agents: Pathologies, Incentives, and Design

Whatever their formal status, political scientists have long argued that even if not captured by sectional interests, agency officials are liable to pursue their own interests—whether leisure or power—or their own conception of the public good (or welfare) at the expense of pursuing the public purpose as framed and intended by legislators.[23] That is no less true of trustee agents than regular agents, but standard P-A analysis applies in slightly special ways.

As economists have documented, any principal-agent problem has three components: incomplete contracts, adverse selection, and moral hazard. Most elementally, a principal cannot write a fully state-contingent contract that determines what should be done in every possible circum-

[22]The old Financial Service Authority (abolished in the postcrisis shake-up) was in the same position.

[23]For a review of the political science literature, see Gailmard, "Principal-Agent Models."

stance. They are destined to delegate via *incomplete contracts.*[24] Indeed, for trustee agencies the whole point is to delegate some policy discretion: the contract is incomplete by design. The challenge is to confer discretion only where and to the extent intended.

In a simple P-A relationship, the principal might seek to mitigate this problem in a number of ways: choosing an agent whom they trust and believe to share their objectives (an ally, in political scientists' terms); offering corrective guidance when they don't like the agent's choices; requiring advance consultation on big decisions; and regularly updating the contract. Of those, only *a variant of* the first possibility is available for stable trustee-agency regimes.

It is a variant because the trustee's duty is to the trust deed, not the settlor: trustees must be loyal to their mandate, not to their principal. This creates a double-layered problem. First, in the usual way, candidates to take on the role of trustee/policy maker might pose as something they are not in order to get the trappings and/or power of the job. Second, the principal making the appointment has incentives to appoint an ally whose loyalty is to them, not to the mandate. The two hazards are linked, potentially deterring well-qualified candidates from applying at all, in an appointments-process manifestation of what is known as *adverse selection.*[25]

Even where personnel choices are made in good faith and wisely ex ante, they may prove badly flawed ex post because, once again as in a simple P-A arrangement, the principal and the wider public might not be able to observe whether the trustee has walked off the ranch when implementing policy; there might be long lags in detection. This problem of hidden actions is known as *moral hazard.*[26]

For trustee agencies, since ongoing control is ruled out, mitigating these problems depends on the regime's ex ante design and the effec-

[24] Hart, "Incomplete Contracts."

[25] The classic account, giving its title to the *lemons problem*, is Akerlof, "Market for 'Lemons.'" In analyses of delegation, it is commonly assumed that agents know "which type" they are. I doubt that is true in reality: up to a point, policy makers *become* "who they are" while in office, shaped by institutional constraints and culture and by the sequence of events they encounter. Even the idea that their dispositions are already fully formed is a little far-fetched, especially for people new to policy making. The point, rather, is that the principal does not know who the agent/policy maker will become.

[26] The classic reference is Holmstrom, "Moral Hazard in Teams."

tiveness of ex post monitoring. Further, for legitimacy to be achieved and sustained, any structural solution has to combine institutionalized incentives to deliver welfarist objectives (the subject of the coming two chapters) with alignment to our democratic values (part II).

Structure, Power, and Celebrity

While some preliminary illumination of the "whether to delegate" question was provided by contrasting the military and the judiciary, something elemental they have in common sheds light on the depth of the "how" question: their sheer power. While they also each typically embrace an ethic of self-restraint, their incentives to live up to their particular norm are influenced by structure in subtle ways.

For example, US constitutional theorist and commentator Bruce Ackerman has argued that some mid-1980s reforms of the structure of the Joint Chiefs of Staff seemed to create celebrity generals who felt free to campaign openly for their point of view on military strategy and priorities.[27] In a broadly similar vein, during the 2016 US presidential election there were overt interventions by a sitting celebrity Supreme Court justice and a recently retired military chief on the merits of the candidates. Those were circumstances in which structure failed to produce incentives congruent with our values—in the case of US justices, perhaps because with no term limits they seem to plan to retire only when convenient to "their side" of partisan politics; in the case of the retired US military, perhaps because of the low barriers to their being appointed to political office.

We return to the issues of values, culture, and raw power in parts II and IV since, even if some democratic societies can tolerate celebrities in the high judiciary and military, it seems undesirable and unsustainable in more run-of-the-mill parts of the administrative state. But in the next few chapters we concern ourselves mainly with the structure of delegations in welfarist terms.

[27] According to Ackerman, *Decline and Fall*, chapter 2, the key reform was effected by the Goldwater-Nichols Act of 1986, which created a leader of the Joint Chiefs, reducing the others to advisers with impaired rights of access to the National Security Council and the president.

Principles for Delegation to Independent Agencies across the Administrative State?

Finally, then, is it sensible to embark on a quest for general principles of independent-agency regime design that can apply across each of the regulatory state, the services state, and the fiscal state, and thus across agencies with outputs as diverse as rule writing, licensing, setting tariffs, operating directly in markets, and a host of other activities?

It might well be thought odd to undertake such an endeavor given the different issues presented by those various activities of the state. For many opponents of the regulatory state, the central problem is delegating power to make legally binding rules, on the grounds that we the people should elect our lawmakers.[28] For others, however, the quasi-fiscal activity of central banks is more outrageous. There *are* important distinctions here. Whereas people and businesses are placed under a legal obligation to obey regulatory rules, the idea of a duty to obey is completely irrelevant to the interventions of central banks in financial markets: the resulting shifts in asset prices and yields are things that just happen in the world (part II). But our question goes to why (and on what terms) a democratic society should allow unelected technocrats to make discretionary decisions that affect credit conditions and thus prosperity across the economy. At that level, it is similar to asking why we should allow unelected technocrats to write rules to make the world a better place.

Indeed, if the legitimizing conditions for, and so the constraints on, different types of state activity were materially different, perversity could result unless the goals of the regulatory, fiscal, and services states were kept strictly separate. Given that some postcrisis central banks could intervene to preserve financial stability either by adjusting regulatory rules or by intervening directly in the markets, their incentives to do one rather than the other would be tilted if materially different constraints, driven by deeply different legitimizing principles, applied to the two types of state action.

The general issue is by no means limited to central banking. Given many regulatory agencies combine rule making and adjudicatory pow-

[28] Schoenbrod, *Power without Responsibility*.

ers, it matters whether constraints on different administrative-state functions can be drawn up in conformity with common legitimizing principles. That is what we begin to explore in the next two chapters. How it differs from principled delegation to courts or the elected executive, the question posed at the close of chapter 3, is deferred until part II.

5

Principles for Whether to Delegate to Independent Agencies

CREDIBLE COMMITMENT TO SETTLED GOALS

> Americans have decided . . . [to leave] too many policy decisions in the realm of politics and too few in the realm of technocracy. . . . The argument for the Fed's independence applies just as forcefully to many other areas of government policy.
>
> —Alan Blinder, Princeton, and former Fed vice chair, 1997[1]

Having surveyed thinking on the purposes, functional modes, and structure of the administrative state, this chapter strikes out on our construction of Principles for Delegation to trustee-like independent agencies that are highly insulated from day-to-day politics. Sticking with part I's welfarist orientation, we first set out criteria for *whether* to delegate and, in the next chapter, advance precepts for *how* to do so, including constraints on delegating more than one mission.[2] The Principles for Delegation accordingly comprise the following:

- Delegation Criteria
- Design Precepts
- Multiple-Mission Constraints

EXPLANATIONS OF POLICY DELEGATION: SHORT-TERM VERSUS LONG-TERM REALISM

Political scientists would say that, irrespective of the field, a political choice to delegate a policy function reflects little more than a battle of interests. Among plausible explanations, they identify some that seem

[1]Blinder, "Is Government Too Political?"

[2]Thanks to Alberto Alesina for comments on a late draft of chapters 5–6, and to Guido Tabellini for feedback on part of chapter 5.

less than worthy, such as legislators seeking to shift blame for the results of uncertain policies, constraining political opponents, and locking in benefits for particular sectional interests.[3] Which of those and other possible motives dominate depends on the current and prospective balance of political forces among the legislating actors. For example, US agencies are more likely to be insulated from the Administration if they were established when Congress and the presidency were in the hands of rival political parties, known as divided government (part III).[4]

Likewise, the interaction of similar forces determines, within the options available under a country's constitution, how much the delegated regime is pinned down ex ante and to what degree political control is exercised ex post through oversight, budgetary approvals, and so on. If mandates are left underspecified, that is because legislators benefit: they might lack time or expertise to flesh out the mandate, they might have more rewarding priorities, or, again, they might wish to shift blame for policy choices that go wrong onto the bureaucrats. Conversely, where delegation is combined with a specified mandate, that might reflect bipartisan consensus around the value of locking in a "moderate" policy under persistent divided government.[5]

From our perspective, two things are missing from these accounts. First, agencies themselves are taken to be relatively passive; their structure, strategy, and even long-term performance shaped, at inception and thereafter, by the incentives and relative power of their various political principals. That picture does not fit with my experience at all, and is at odds with studies of the occasional influence of, for example, the SEC on congressional policy.[6] Agency leaders and staff can be actors, affecting ideas and, sometimes, the shape of legislation. In the words of one

[3] Fiorina, "Legislative Choice."

[4] Epstein and O'Halloran, *Delegating Powers*. This finding might not be robust. The classic exception to executive agencies being established only under unified government is the EPA, created in 1970 by a Democratic Congress and Republican President Nixon. It matters that the agency was partly formed through the merger of executive branch bureaus and, perhaps, that congressional environmentalists were glad to recruit the president to their cause, giving him some leverage on structure. But my best guess is that the gloss had come off the "independent commissions" in the decades since the New Deal; see Landis, "Report on Regulatory Agencies," for evidence of the shift.

[5] This applies to the institution of delegation the broad findings of Alesina and Rosenthal, "Divided Government." If, however, partisan politicians are rewarded for not comprising, and voters would tolerate not having any policy regime at all in a particular field, the conclusions might not follow.

[6] For the SEC, see Khademian, *Capital Markets Regulation*.

scholar, it is a two-way street.[7] (That being so, in accepting appointment to agencies with vague or incomplete mandates, their leaders must either have personal incentives to take risks or a desire to insert their own (or their sponsors') policy preferences.)

Second and more important for us, the catalog of realist motivations is hardly conducive to producing *enduring* legitimacy. Even if political scientists are correct empirically, that does not mean that the resulting structures are sustainable or conducive to trust in government. There may be only so much cynicism the electors can take from their governors. The guiding assumption of this book is that it would be unsafe to assume otherwise. When it comes to constitutional politics and so to the distribution of government power, realism that does not look beyond the day after tomorrow is a cousin of roulette, as various Western democracies might currently be rediscovering in the reaction against technocracy.

We need, therefore, to turn to justifications for (as opposed to explanations of) delegation to insulated agencies. Before coming to the one that I find most compelling, three other welfare-based cases are reviewed: the value of experts, the separation of policy for efficiency from policy for justice, and the value of technocrats as impartial adjudicators in policy bargaining among competing interest groups. Each is insufficient but suggestive.

Independent Experts as Producers of Reliable Information

The longest-established normative argument for delegation to technocrats—prevalent among legal scholars, political theorists, and students of public administration—has centered on the benefits of harnessing specialist expertise and of creating institutions with incentives to establish and nurture such expertise. With the substance of modern government increasingly complicated, elected politicians would be wise to delegate functions that are beyond them technically. That was the basic case advanced in the late 1930s by the high priest of the New Deal regulatory commissions, James Landis.[8]

[7] Krause, *Two-Way Street*. In the same vein, Carpenter, *Forging of Bureaucratic Autonomy*.
[8] Landis, *Administrative Process*.

More recently, in arguing that independent agencies as a class comprise a fourth branch of government, European political scientist Frank Vibert emphasized the vital role they play in the production, publication, and explanation of complex information in societies otherwise laboring under the problem of whether to trust information generated under close political control.[9]

Rather than making the normative case we are seeking, to my mind Vibert usefully exposes an important distinction that weakens the "expertise" case for independent *policy making.* He rightly says that nonpartisan production and sifting of information can help to engender trust. But that does *not* of itself require nonpolitical *decision making.* It would be possible to combine independent information production and publicly transparent advice with political decision making in the executive branch of government. For roughly half a decade before the Bank of England was made independent in 1997, UK monetary policy was decided via such a structure, with the Bank's analysis published in the minutes of the chancellor/governor meetings and in its quarterly *Inflation Report.*

A more current example would be the independent offices set up in many countries to advise on the economic constraints facing fiscal policy. The US's Congressional Budget Office is widely respected. And the UK's Office of Budget Responsibility is a standing rebuttal of the proposition that pure advisory bodies cannot attract people of sufficient quality and, thus, that decision-making powers need to be granted too if the benefits of expertise are to be secured.

While it would be hard to warrant independent agencies that were not reasonably expert, expertise cannot of itself provide the basic motivation for insulating policy making from politics. Indeed, structures that separate expert advice from decisions might deliver better results wherever the decision maker needs to tap into the shifting currents and values of public opinion.

[9] Vibert, *Rise of the Unelected.*

Efficiency versus Equity or Fairness

That thought brings forth the Welfarist motivation encountered in chapter 3. In bold summary:

1. It is fine for a polity's politicians to delegate the task of making markets more efficient, since that need not leave anyone worse off and so is not within the realm of politics.
2. While society needs a social welfare function to guide its decisions on how to share the gains from enhanced efficiency, that need not trouble the insulated agencies themselves because they are concerned only with technocratic mechanics (science).

The underlying thought is that efficiency can be regarded as objective, scientific, or value-free, in the sense of policy outcomes being assessed against the benchmark (external standard) of a perfectly competitive market. By contrast, justice is a different matter altogether, requiring ongoing debate and choice about how the spoils of growth should be distributed.

The dichotomy between efficiency and equity that lies at the heart of this account broadly mirrors, in more analytical terms, Woodrow Wilson's dichotomy between administration and politics (chapter 2). As we saw, however, it stumbles against the real-world rock of people's wealth affecting the choices they can afford to make (and, probably, the preferences they are capable of expressing). At best, this complicates parceling out different purposes to nonmajoritarian and majoritarian institutions on the basis of an efficiency/equity dichotomy.[10]

The potential separability of efficiency and equity does, however, alert us to the importance of distinguishing between the arguments for and against delegating those two types of public policy goal. The legitimacy conditions for institutions responsible for choices of value or distribu-

[10] In "Regulatory Legitimacy," Majone starts off by making the same point, but concludes that the legitimacy of the architectural split holds on the grounds that it is chosen by governments that are not credit/wealth constrained (Majone, *Regulating Europe*, p. 295). Apart from implicitly (but no doubt largely accurately) assuming that the people are not given a say in the structure of government (see part II), this seems also to assume that independent, efficiency-pursuing agencies can make decisions without taking into account the distribution of resources; for example, that it will not affect the responses they receive to public consultations on proposed efficiency measures.

tional justice are going to be more demanding than the legitimacy conditions for institutions responsible for efficiency. We might just as well say that big distributional choices should not be delegated to insulated technocrats.

That is a constraint on the IA part of the administrative state rather than a driving motivation for delegating policy directed toward efficiency. It does not address whether we should prefer to have "efficiency policy" in the hands of technocrats, the elected executive branch, or courts administering detailed legislative regimes.

Independent Agencies as Neutral Umpires or Auctioneers

Another possible motivation for delegation to insulated technocrats injects a normative turn into the rational-choice theorists' conception of the policy-making process as analogous to a market (chapter 3). When summarizing theories of government failure, we saw how a blithe assumption of legislative efficiency founders on the rocks of imbalances in the political power of citizens and ineradicable uncertainty around whether politicians will deliver on promises to compensate losers.

Paradoxically, the prevalence of such political "transaction costs" opens up the possibility of a case for delegation to agencies based on the prospect of reducing the costs of framing policy in those fields where it needs to be elaborated and implemented over time according to changing conditions. In this kind of setting, delegation might be warranted where (a) the necessary side payments to reach policy bargains are not fiscal but, instead, are adjustments to the regulatory or other policies under an agency's direct control; (b) identifying and making those bargains requires detailed technical expertise; and (c) impartiality and policy stability (i.e., credibility) are enhanced by tying the reputation of the agency heads to a well-defined, transparent mission (reflecting a social welfare function).

The "policy as bargaining" metaphor is maintained. The agency is not seen as forming its own view of the public good. Rather, its role is simply, first, to adopt a sufficiently open process that all interested parties can be heard at the bargaining table; and second, to build a reputation for making credible promises.

What is clear, however, is that of the three conditions for agencies adopting such a role, all the normative work is done by (c). The politicians themselves have all manner of constitutionally permitted side payments available to them, including writing rules; and, as already discussed, they can avail themselves of independent expert advice. Their deepest problem revolves around making promises that carry conviction.

Indeed, the inability to make trusted promises is the ultimate transaction cost in public policy making. The importance of credible commitment is not far short of elemental. And here, at last, we *do* have a genuine motivation for independent agencies, provided delegation to insulated technocrats can be a feasible and effective commitment device.

THE CENTRALITY OF CREDIBLE COMMITMENT

The terms of the debate about delegation were, in consequence, transformed by the work of economists in the late 1970s and early 1980s on the problems faced in areas of public policy that require an ability to make credible commitments (promises that are trusted). A particular variant of this is known as the *time-inconsistency problem*, where even a policy maker whose preferences are stable (the social welfare function is fixed) can find it optimal to deviate from its promised course.[11]

The problem arises where the best policy choice today depends on others' actions and, in particular, their expectations of future policy. Thus, by living in the floodplain, households might force government to break a promise not to build expensive infrastructure preventing floods. More generally, if people act on an expectation that a promise could be broken, it can prove too costly to do otherwise.

A slightly more complex variant arises where belief in a government promise would give government reason to break that promise. For example, if people chose to invest based on a declared policy of low taxation, government could gain (in the short run) by taxing capital after all. If people take policy makers' incentives into account, the policy promise won't be believed.

[11] Kydland and Prescott, "Rules Rather Than Discretion."

These thoughts became foundational within monetary economics (chapter 18). If inflation is high and expected to remain so, government is unlikely to carry through with a policy of low inflation because getting there would create a recession in the short run. Similarly, if a monetary authority were liable to exploit price stability to generate more economic activity, households and firms would not believe the commitment to stability, making it optimal to allow more inflation than declared. In each of these cases, the expectation of a broken promise becomes self-fulfilling.

Away from monetary policy, the centrality of commitment—policy promises being believed and remaining time-consistent—was picked up unevenly and slowly.[12] In fact, however, the core insight has wide application, leading Princeton economist and former Fed vice chairman Alan Blinder to wonder, perhaps somewhat tongue in cheek, why vast areas of government policy were not delegated to independent agencies modeled on central banks.[13]

Blinder's question is designed to unsettle us. While most people would, I think, feel that the thought is wrong-headed, we might struggle to pin down what distinguishes monetary policy from policy domains ill suited to delegation to independent decision makers. What, for example, should we make of a proposal, aired by British education specialists during 2015, that setting a national curriculum for schools should be delegated to an independent agency rather than decided by ministers, on the grounds that stability is vital in this area and so policy should not chop and change with ministries (or even individual ministers)?[14]

The Alesina-Tabellini Model: Delegation Criteria

Over the past decade or so, economists working on political economy have tried to articulate some general normative principles and some predictions of when sectional interests might stand in the way of their being realized. In a pair of papers, Alberto Alesina and Guido Tabellini

[12] In Europe, by the mid-1990s, and at much the same time as the work of his cited earlier, Giandomenico Majone was highlighting commitment as central (Majone, "Temporal Consistency").

[13] Blinder, "Is Government Too Political?"

[14] Personal recollection of BBC report of a speech given by a recently retired official.

analyze the choice politicians face between deciding policy themselves and delegating to insulated technocrats.[15]

Alesina and Tabellini posit that politicians are motivated by wanting to be reelected and technocrats are motivated by professional reputation. For top officials in important agencies, this strikes me as being more realistic than assuming, as others have, that they aim to maximize their agency's budget or size: bluntly, if you have lots of power, you are not very focused on achieving prestige through the size of your workforce.[16]

In this setup, politicians aim to do what is needed to get returned to office, including changing policy course if necessary. Indeed, because they want the people to feel good (modeled as ex post utility or welfare), they are prepared to abandon pursuit of a declared objective. By contrast, since the technocrats' reputation turns on achieving their publicly mandated objective, they aim to do so as well as they can, subject to the effort entailed. As such, they are more likely to stick to a strategic course designed to deliver the objective over time.[17]

In a similar vein, in this model, politicians do only as much as suffices to win the election. Thus, if a policy has sizable distributional effects, their focus is not on maximizing aggregate welfare (the size of the whole cake) but on ensuring that the majority most likely to return them to office (as defined by the voting system) are better off (increasing the majority's part of the cake). The technocrat, meanwhile, again simply

[15] Alesina and Tabellini, "Bureaucrats or Politicians? Part I," and "Bureaucrats or Politicians? Part II." The degree of insulation from politics is assumed to be high, so their results are implicitly about truly independent agencies (our *trustee-type* agencies).

[16] The classic account of bureaucracy with a budget fixation is Niskanen, *Bureaucracy and Public Economics*.

[17] As in any model, the assumptions about motivations, together with assumed constraints, drive the analytical results. So somewhat different results flow in part from assuming that politicians put some weight on legacy as well as on being reelected (Maskin and Tirole, "Politician and the Judge"). I prefer the Alesina-Tabellini setup, as I believe that the big areas where politicians care about legacy (winning wars, building the welfare state, reestablishing a market economy, establishing civil rights, etc.) are not candidates to be delegated to independent agencies. Within domestic policy, those are often areas where the politician is trying to reorient or embed emerging values in society (e.g., the New Deal, the deregulation/privatizations of Reagan and Thatcher), and so do not satisfy Alesina-Tabellini's criterion that society's preferences are settled and stable. Even if politicians do care about their legacy in other areas, they generally need to get reelected to embed their preferred policy, giving them incentives both to trim any legacy-oriented goals that are not popular in the short term and to dissemble about the policies they will pursue (or, if in office, are pursuing).

pursues the mandated objective. Here, assuming the posited motivations, we begin to see the normative case for delegating an "efficiency mandate."

If, however, a policy has sizable distributional effects but its overall effect on aggregate welfare is hard to gauge or negligible (so that it is not a Pareto improvement), the policy is all about making distributional choices. In those circumstances, the performance of the technocrats would not be leashed to the mast of an objective measure, and they would not have the power to make compensating side payments to the losers. While the technocrat would likely execute a prescribed distributional policy more faithfully than the politician (because of the commitment problem), that is the role of a delivery agency rather than the trustee policy agencies we are interested in.

In my words, the Alesina-Tabellini model points toward delegation to insulated technocrats being the better strategy where

- the goal can be specified,
- society's preferences are reasonably stable, as is the underlying environment so that it is fairly clear what society's preferences entail for policy,
- there is a problem of making credible commitments to stick to a policy regime, and (consistent with our earlier discussion of efficiency versus equity)
- there are not significant distributional trade-offs requiring the policy maker to make big distributional choices.

To this could be added, as implicitly assumed by Alesina and Tabellini, that the policy instruments are confidently expected to work. (Where there is radical uncertainty about the costs and benefits of deploying an instrument, having insulated technocrats experiment is less acceptable than politicians taking risks, because the regime can hardly be one of credible commitment and because the technocrat's choices might entail unexpected distributional consequences that they cannot remedy.[18])

[18]This is contrary to the positive political economy of, among others, Huber and Shipan, *Deliberate Discretion*, who predict that uncertainty increases incentives to delegate. Away from their normative results, Alesina and Tabellini find that, where results are uncertain, politicians face a trade-off between shedding blame and extracting higher rents if there is a premium for that uncertainty (e.g., making less effort). By "radical uncertainty," I mean, by contrast, that

Although it might initially seem paradoxical, this warrants two quite different types of delegated regime predicated on the welfare benefits of credible commitment: (1) agencies that are confined to pure delivery of detailed instructions (including redistribution), and (2) insulated agencies with delegated power to pursue a monitorable objective (e.g., monetary policy) or apply a monitorable standard. But it does not provide a warrant for insulating agencies that have discretion to trade off multiple, vague objectives, since they are not solving credible commitment problems. That being so, it leads to the slightly surprising conclusion that at a high level (normative justification), a monetary policy authority such as the Federal Reserve has more in common with a social security office than with, say, the SEC or the EPA![19]

Different Types of Credible Commitment Problem

Although framed in the language of economics, this opens the door to commitment problems extending well beyond measures designed to enhance socioeconomic welfare. Society might have others reason for valuing promises.

Most obviously but also furthest away from the motivation of delegating to a monetary authority, we might want to be assured that the law in general will be applied consistently to different cases in the interest of *fairness*. This too is a question of commitment. It does not turn on the regime itself delivering substantive justice in everyone's eyes, but rather on everyone being confident that, within the terms of the law, they (groups as well as individuals) will be treated in the same way: according to the same criteria, with their particular circumstances having a systematic effect rather than an arbitrary effect on policy choices (chapter 8). This is about *cross-sectional consistency* rather than the

---

neither principal nor agent knows the average (expected) effect of the instrument or the variance of its effects, etc.

[19] Despite a shared stress on commitment problems, this is substantively different from the thrust of Miller and Whitford, *Above Politics*, who seek to justify government bureaucracy in general, even when, implicitly, legislated purposes remain in flux and there is neither a monitorable objective nor a detailed instruction manual. Commitment is also included among the political and administrative transaction costs that drive the themes and results of Horn, *Political Economy*.

dynamic consistency discussed above. It provides a normative justification for delegating the adjudication of legal disputes to an independent judiciary (chapter 4's canonical trustee agency). The judges help to solve the commitment problem because, consistent with the Alesina-Tabellini model, their standing rests, in significant degree, on maintaining a reputation for impartiality.[20]

If the potential scope of commitment problems is wide, so are the underlying drivers. They can be intrinsic to the substance of a public policy field, as in monetary policy or, similarly, the taxation-cum-regulation of capital investment projects. They might lie in the vicissitudes of politics, which can prompt divergence from a declared policy goal in order to prop up or rekindle popularity. Or they might arise from the exercise of private power over policy makers, whether elected or unelected.[21] Broadly, these three manifestations of the problem of commitment can be labeled (1) intrinsic time inconsistency, (2) electoral politics, and (3) sectional capture.

They are each instances of the problem of weakness of the will (*akrasia*, to the ancients).[22] Different elements of the Alesina-Tabellini setup address them. The second and third are mitigated by taking discretionary policy away from politicians who, in the model, need do no more than satisfy a plurality of voters. The first and the technocratic variant of the third (regulatory capture) are mitigated by harnessing unelected policy makers to their reputation for delivering a *monitorable objective*. That does not work unless society knows what it wants, and can frame what it wants in terms that would expose technocrats to reputational hazard if they shirk or pursue a different goal. In an often used meta-

[20] Cross-sectional and dynamic consistency are not divorced. Fairness and impartiality in legal adjudication has instrumental value by increasing predictability, thereby reducing costs of uncertainty for individuals and businesses. These are among the values associated with the rule of law (chapter 8).

[21] The second and third seem to be the drivers formally analyzed in Eggertson and Le Borge, "Political Agency Theory." For example, would a political monetary policy maker have succumbed to pressure from powerful lobbies opposing some of the measures taken over recent years to get inflation back up toward target (chapter 24)?

[22] It is striking that philosophers have long debated whether it is possible for *akrasia* to be rational; see the survey article by Sarah Stroud in the *Stanford Encyclopedia of Philosophy*. Kydland/Prescott, "Rules Rather Than Discretion," identify conditions under which period-by-period optimization can rationally ground departures from a longer-term optimal plan.

phor, society has to want to tie itself to the mast of a policy goal, which it does by tying technocrats to the personal mast of their reputation and standing (chapter 10).

Blinder's Question: So Why Not Delegate Everything?

In essence, the story so far makes a case for delegating any field with tempting but illusory quick wins, any that is highly salient with the voting public, and any that affects powerful vested interests. In that case, why not, as Blinder asked, delegate much larger swathes of public policy to insulated technocrats? The Alesina-Tabellini model delivers an answer in two parts.

The first, to repeat, is that powers should be delegated only if society has broadly settled preferences and those preferences can be specified in an objective that is clear and monitorable. Otherwise, there is nothing to commit to and so to monitor the technocrat against. Alesina and Tabellini cite foreign policy as a field where preferences tend not to be stable. I would add that that is most obviously true of policy on going to war and grand strategy (chapter 4), justifying why the military command can be a pillar of the modern state without being akin to an independent agency.

Judging from the temperature of public debate, the same might still be true of some parts of environmental policy. To insist, as many would, that the science is settled is merely to expose the failure to carry a sufficiently broad part of the politically active public and their representatives for policy to be insulated from day-to-day politics. Thus, unelected environment-agency bosses might care more about their standing with their political sponsors and tribe than about the wider nonpartisan standing that can accrue from delivering a mission that enjoys broad-based support.

The second part of the answer, echoing chapter 3, is that delegation to IAs should not entail their making significant distributional choices, which are center stage in much fiscal policy and many other fields. In the Alesina-Tabellini setup, reserving such issues to politicians is not motivated overtly by political morality or democratic theory, which we come to in part II. Rather, it is a technical constraint given that the measuring rod for non-Pareto-improving policies would be contested; and that only politicians have power to make the side payments required to bring about an efficient policy bargain given the distributional issues at stake.

Implicitly, to the extent that a delegated IA regime has distributional effects, they either are expected to even out over time or, alternatively, were accepted as a by-product of policy when, reflecting society's preferences, the goal was chosen by political principals.

IMPLICATIONS OF THE DELEGATION CRITERIA FOR THE DESIGN OF AGENCIES

The *Delegation Criteria* outlined above have immediate implications for the structure of decision making within independent agencies.

First, the decision-making technocrats pursuing "professional standing" are implicitly senior and visible. This is important: what is *not* contemplated are independent agencies in which decisions are in effect delegated to large groups of junior officials who may give greater weight to job security, leisure, and so on. Even if their diligence and expertise is exemplary, they are not each sufficiently visible to accrue reputational benefits individually, as opposed to collectively doing so from working for a successful institution.

Second, decisions should be made by experts in the relevant field. While that seems obvious, it means that delegation to insulated officials should occur only where society recognizes that there *is* a body of professional, technical knowledge, imperfect though it inevitably will prove, relevant to delivering the regime's purposes. That would rule out some fields, either because there is no recognized body of expertise or because experts are so few that there is not a professional community. Furthermore, formally requiring recognized expertise can reduce the adverse selection problems facing politicians and also constrain the politicians from appointing inexpert allies, since an expert will tend to have a professional reputation already.

Third, the appointed policy makers would desirably also have a reputation for *truly believing* in what they are being asked to do (intrinsic motivation). Otherwise, they might not care about any reputational opprobrium from failing to achieve the mandated objective, freeing them to use their powers to pursue other goals (moral hazard). For example, an in-office professional reputation for making terrific contributions to the economics of competition policy/monetary policy but for mediocre policy choices won't deliver the mandated objective if the incumbent cares only about the former. This most obvious of points in real-world institution building is oddly neglected in many discussions of delegation.[23]

Fourth, decisions should be made by a committee whose members have long but staggered terms. For the decision maker to be independent, long terms are necessary (but not sufficient) to help address the need for credible commitment to a stable policy regime; and to avoid the appointing principal gaining invisible leverage if the policy maker would like another term. A committee is needed because, with a single decision maker, it would be too easy for those making the appointment (the president or prime minister) to choose someone with their own preferences (an ally) rather than society's preferences as framed in the objective. Thus, the committee should not be a rubber stamp for its chair. The members' long terms should, for the same reason, be staggered.

As a concrete example, when faced with the criticism that quantitative easing (QE) was a plot for central banks to finance governments cheaply by buying their bonds, and that independence had willingly but surreptitiously been surrendered, I found that the most persuasive argument, at least in the UK, was to point out that the Monetary Policy Committee contained four "external" members who were not part of the Bank of England's senior executive. It was nearly always accepted that they would not have gone along with any such plot and would indeed have exposed it. The MPC's "externals" underpin the committee's independence, helping to create a culture where each of the "internals" can act independently too.

The case for committees rests, therefore, on more than that in many fields they will make better decisions, or fewer big mistakes, although there is plenty of evidence for that too.[24] Provided each member is em-

[23]For exceptions, see Besley, *Principled Agents*, chapters 1 and 3; Mansbridge, "Selection Model"; and, much earlier, Pratt and Zeckhauser, introduction to *Principals and Agents*.

[24]On committees as monetary policy decision makers, see Blinder, *The Quiet Revolution*, chapter 2.

powered (one person, one vote), they help tie each other to the publicly set objective.

Hazards around Harnessing the Reputation of Independent Agency Policy Makers

Beyond those four inferences from the Alesina-Tabellini criteria about the design of institutions lies a broader, and deeper, issue.

As described, the case for delegation to IAs turns on technocrats being motivated by professional standing and public reputation. In the Alesina-Tabellini model, that sensitivity to reputational standing is an assumption and, like all analytical exercises, the model grinds out the implications of the assumptions. In the real world, this has to be flipped around, the assumption becoming a desideratum of regime design, a normative prescription. Since the posited benefits from delegation are not reaped unless the policy makers *do* prioritize the professional standing that could accrue from persistently achieving the regime's objective, the regime needs to be designed so as to give the policy makers exactly that incentive or priority.

This is taking some important and quite subtle things for granted. Obviously, it is not just about sticks, as assumed in some "contractual" models of delegation. But in emphasizing rewards, a very particular kind of reward is being prioritized. It relies on unelected public policy makers caring about professional, and perhaps broader public, *esteem*. This has to be something that is valued by them in and of itself, not because they can cash it in for wealth following a successful period in office, since that would open the door to interest-group capture through the prospect of lucrative postretirement jobs. Vitally, it is also about gratification from *deferred esteem*, not instant or short-run popularity. The Delegation Criteria rely on such people existing.

They also rely on the culture of a society valuing and conferring regard for successful or dutiful public servants.[25] If society reaches a point where it does not give a damn about public service, then either all bets are off so far as delegation is concerned or agency leaders would have to

[25]Similar points are made, more broadly, in Pettit, "Cunning of Trust." Economists have only recently started to take an interest in culture. For a review, see Alesina and Giuliano, "Culture and Institutions."

care about their reputation only among their narrow peer group. Thus, the feasibility of an incentive-compatible IA regime turns not only on technical questions of design but also on the character of policy makers and the wider society's culture and values.[26]

There is a further twist. Even if our agency leaders are incorruptible, the dark side of policy makers caring about their professional reputation is that a regulated community can seek to tame them by complaining or whispering about them to elected politicians and journalists in order to damage or undermine their reputation. That certainly goes on. Unwarranted but plausible complaints can amount to a capture strategy. The construction of a trustee/independent-agency regime needs, therefore, to allow the policy makers' professional reputation to rest largely on *publicly observable information* rather than clubroom chitchat. In other words, one of the key assumptions driving the Alesina-Tabellini results, and hence our Delegation Criteria, requires transparency about what the agency does and why it does it.

There is, therefore, more to the design of independent agencies than comes directly out of the Alesina-Tabellini model. Indeed, there is a lot more to be said about *how* to delegate.

[26]The notion of "incentive compatibility" was lodged in economics in the early 1970s by Leonid Hurwicz, stimulating interest in incentive constraints alongside the more familiar resource constraints (Myerson, "Perspectives on Mechanism Design"). For our purposes, the question is what is needed for a regime to be *incentives-values-compatible,* because then it can be legitimate on grounds broader than results (see parts II and III).

6

Design Precepts for How to Delegate to Independent Agencies

> Agencies differ in two main respects: Can the activities of their operators be observed? Can the results of those activities be observed?
>
> —James Q. Wilson, 1989[1]

Big picture, the previous chapter's Delegation Criteria might seem to draw a line between ends and means, a distinction to which we return in part II. But delegating only instruments does not mean that implementation of the regime is on autopilot. Trustee agencies exercise discretion over policy. A judge interprets legislation; a central banker chooses this month's interest rate; a competition authority might decide the tests for when market share is too large. It therefore matters for our purposes that the Delegation Criteria do not comprise a complete set of conditions for a delegation to enjoy legitimacy on welfarist grounds. *How* a delegation is structured also matters, delivering a regime of *constrained discretion.*

POLITICAL BALANCE VERSUS INSULATION FROM POLITICS

A deeply flawed starting point would be to think in terms of replicating the pattern of party politics on an independent agency's board or commission. If truly independent trustee-type agencies have anything to be said for them, it is that they might insulate an area amenable to technocratic stewardship from day-to-day politics. There is not much point in taking elected politicians out of decision making only to reinsert partisan politics via *un*elected representatives of political factions. Where that approach is taken, the expertise of nominees is liable to become less

[1]Wilson, *Bureaucracy*, chapter 9, p. 158.

important in the mind of the elected executive and legislators making the appointments than their political allegiance or sponsorship. That can leave technical expertise concentrated among an agency's staff, who find themselves in a contest with "ordinary" board members for influence with the chair, leading to some staffers themselves being selected on the basis of broad political allegiance.

That probably captures something of the reality in at least some of the US regulatory commissions, where party politics *does* seem structurally to be reinserted at board level and where, at least anecdotally, commissioners voting in line with party preferences has become more prevalent as US party politics itself has become more polarized. It is illuminating, for example, that the US Federal Trade Commission's website describes it as "bipartisan" rather than "independent"; and also that a number of senior SEC staffers announced that they were leaving soon after the 2016 presidential election, exposing the extent to which even senior staff appointments have become partisan. But, then, neither agency is a trustee-type independent agency on the broad criteria set out in chapter 4.

FIVE DESIGN PRECEPTS FOR DELEGATING TO TRUSTEE-LIKE INDEPENDENT AGENCIES

Against that background, my suggestion for the *how* part of IA regime delegation has five components. In addition to society concluding that the delegation is substantively warranted and, in particular, does not entail handing over choices on values or high-level objectives, a regime should incorporate the following:

1. A statement of its purpose, objectives, and powers, and a delineation of its boundaries (*Purposes-Powers*)
2. Prescriptions of who should exercise the delegated powers and the procedures to be employed (*Procedures*)
3. Principles for how the agency will conduct policy within its boundaries (*Operating Principles*)
4. Sufficient transparency to enable the delegated policy maker and, very important, the regime itself to be monitored and held to account by elected representatives (*Transparency-Accountability*)

5. Provisions determining what happens when the boundaries of the regime are reached during a crisis, including how democratic accountability works then (*Emergencies*)

We shall come back to these five *Design Precepts* many times, developing them as we widen the perspective from welfare and incentives to values and legitimacy. At first sight they might seem innocuous, but in fact few existing regimes would survive them unscathed.

By delegating to an independent agency, political principals are placing trust in the institution and its sequence of leaders. This cannot sensibly rest solely on believing that the institution and its leaders are naturally virtuous or loyal to its stated objectives (known as *intrinsic motivation*), although that helps. It must also rely on the incentive of the institution sticking to its task on account of the professional and public esteem that it, and its leaders, stand to accrue. Philip Pettit has called this "trust responsiveness," and I think he hits the nail on the head.[2]

The importance of external standing has a bearing on which of the parameters of a regime should be set by legislators, which may be set by the elected executive, and which can be fleshed out by the independent agency itself. While the precise division of labor would inevitably vary across countries/jurisdictions according to the characteristics of their political constitution and customs (part III), some general precepts are compelling. In particular, the highest-level parameters should come in the form of legislation, so that they are hard to change and reflect the assembly's view of the public's settled preferences and purposes.

THE FIRST DESIGN PRECEPT: PURPOSES, OBJECTIVES, POWERS

Thus, the *Purposes-Powers requirement* should be met by setting in legislation the agency's goal (e.g., for a central bank, monetary stability), its independence, and some constraints in the form of boundaries to the delegated regime and, hence, to the domain within which it may exercise discretion. The legislature chooses the high-level goals, not the agency heads who, as unelected technocrats, are not free to impose their

[2] Pettit, "Cunning of Trust."

sense of the public interest. The zone left for discretion is subordinate to those given goals.

As such, this first Design Precept (DP1) goes further than simply hoping to recruit "trust responsiveness" by visibly bestowing power and responsibility in a vague way. It separates the setting of *goals* from the control of *instruments*; that is, an IA should have instrument independence but not goal independence.[3]

The effect is that, in principle, credibility has two sources: *warranted predictability*, derived from consistency in the agency's performance (results), and *normative expectation*, based on the goal being set externally and, crucially, by a higher power invested with legitimacy.[4] Where, by contrast, an agency sets its own objective(s) or target(s), it is asking society to trust it on the basis of its performance alone—or at least to hold it to its own promises. The foundations are thinner. Normative expectation puts some flesh on trust responsiveness. In the metaphor we have used for truly independent agencies, the trustee agency is given a trust deed that is not open ended.

Perhaps the most essential part of this precept concerns the objective an IA is required to pursue or the standard it is required to apply, which acts as a proxy for a social welfare function. The objective/standard should be monitorable, depriving the agency (and any allies in politics or the commentariat) of the ability to assert success on the basis of whatever criteria happen to suit them at the time. An example of a monitorable objective is to achieve inflation of 2 percent. An example of a monitorable standard is to provide liquidity assistance to stricken banks that can provide collateral that meets certain objective criteria but not otherwise.[5] In either case, compliance with the trust deed can be tracked.[6]

[3] The distinction between goal independence and instrument independence has been familiar in monetary economics for nearly three decades (Debelle and Fischer, "How Independent"). Through the first Design Precept, I am advocating that it is relevant to independent agencies in general.

[4] I take this distinction from Hollis, *Trust within Reason*. It is central to Bicchieri, *Norms*.

[5] The latter is equivalent to a provision that an agency *must* act if it determines that the statutory criteria are met. If, instead, the statute provides that it *may* act under those conditions, a monitorable objective is needed to avoid delegating high-policy choices. This is important in part IV, where the constraints on liquidity assistance are multiplied (chapter 23).

[6] In some respects, the nearest to my account is Majone, *Dilemmas*, but there, following one part of the central banking literature (chapter 18), it is assumed that the trustee is more "conservative" than the political principal (giving greater weight to low inflation); whereas I am holding that, rather, they must be incentivized to attach themselves to an objective (or standard) set by their principal.

For the same reasons, if an independent agency is to have multiple objectives, wherever possible they should be hierarchical (what economists call *lexicographic*), so that the highest-ranked objective acts as a constraint on separately pursuing any others, and so on. That helps to deliver clarity and, further, avoids IA policy makers being free to bring to the table their own personal conception of how to weigh equally ranked objectives, making them de facto principals.

This first Design Precept applies equally well to any type of delegated regime, whether it involves writing rules governing the horizontal relationships of firms and households as part of the regulatory state or, as in monetary policy, managing part of the state's own balance sheet as an agency within the fiscal state. In each case, the legislature needs to decide and set down broadly what it wants. For regulatory regimes, the objective might be fleshed out via some kind of quantitative *standard* that illustrates what legislators are after. If, for example, the objective is the stability of the financial system, how resilient does society want the system to be? If the function is environmental protection, what level of emissions is intolerable? Within the fiscal state, how much of various kinds of risk may be taken; and could a least-cost constraint be policed?

By combining lexicographic objectives with a quantified standard for the primary objective, legislators can cater even for possible long-term trade-offs (say, between financial-system stability and growth, as discussed in chapter 21).

None of this calls for legislators to cover every possible circumstance an agency might confront. A regulator could gain material guidance from a quantitative standard in just one area, with a statutory injunction to apply requirements broadly consistent with that standard in other areas after taking into account a range of general considerations specified in the statute. (Again, that is highly relevant to part IV's discussion of financial stability.)

It is worth underlining, therefore, that while specification of the goal and monitorable objective/standard is paramount for independent agencies, it does not entail exhaustive detail. Determining whether a regime satisfies our first Design Precept is not a matter of counting statutory words.[7]

[7] This is a potential flaw in the method of Huber and Shipan, *Deliberate Discretion*.

THE SECOND DESIGN PRECEPT: PROCESSES AND PROCEDURES

The *Procedures requirement* should also to a large extent be met via legislation, along with precedent-based judge-made-law constraints on the manner in which administrative power is exercised. This is about the "who and how" of decision making, in the interests of clarity, fairness, and, in the case of adjudicatory decisions on individual cases, procedural justice.

Appointments

In the first place, therefore, this Design Precept (DP2) covers which group within the agency makes decisions on how to use the delegated statutory powers, how those policy makers are appointed, their terms of office, and high-level parameters on how they should make decisions (one person, one vote; consensus; etc.). If the Delegation Criteria drive some of the substance of these procedural requirements (chapter 5), DP2 provides that they should be part of the law.

That includes a dual key to making appointments and specifying in primary legislation the broad nature of the expertise that members of the policy committee *must* have. Those constraints reduce the capacity of the executive branch to nominate/appoint people (and of the legislature to signal that they will only confirm people) who are personally close to them or share their ideological program but who are inexpert.

Committee Procedures and Reasons

This Design Precept also requires mandatory procedures for consulting on rule making, due process for the exercise of adjudicatory powers, and, more generally, giving reasons for decisions. This makes for better decisions and, provided DP1 is satisfied, can help underpin independence. For the same reasons, the legislature should not prescribe procedures that make an independent trustee agency especially sensitive to particular interest groups.[8] Having to consult widely, hear both sides of a case, and,

[8] The canonical papers on ex ante legislative procedural control in a US-type system are McCubbins, Noll, and Weingast (often collectively known as McNollGast), "Administrative Procedures" and "Structure and Process." Their focus is how legislators can use the prescribed procedures to

crucially, give reasons makes it more obvious if an IA is becoming captured by particular sections of society.

Even where, in line with DP1, the objective and the powers both seem clear, that leaves open whether the powers are used in pursuit of the prescribed objective and only that objective. An easy case would be a central bank with an inflation target of 2 percent and a power, among others, to create money by buying government bonds outright. Imagine that it buys bonds to expand the money supply (lower interest rates) when current inflation is well above target and, vitally, all measures of inflation expectations are for inflation to remain well above target over the medium to long term. That would be a clear misuse of power. But what is to happen in more nuanced cases? The only route through this is for the agency to give reasons for why its measure—its use of particular powers—is warranted to pursue its mandated objective. This is a bridge to our third and fourth Design Precepts on, respectively, operating principles and transparency-accountability.

THE THIRD DESIGN PRECEPT: AGENCY OPERATING PRINCIPLES

The third precept, for the articulation of *Operating Principles*, falls to the agency itself. Because an independent agency is granted some discretion, the higher-level specification of its mandate (*remit* in the UK) is inevitably incomplete. But, as a trustee agency, legislators are trusting it to stick to its mandate. It is not enough for the statutory mandate to be filled out only by agency rules or explanations of its *individual* actions and decisions. An agency should also have high-level principles that bring consistency to its policy decisions, whether its outputs comprise rules, actions (such as monetary policy settings), or enforcement. For example, consistent regulatory policy is not guaranteed by each new set of rules being justified in terms of the statutory objective if each set reflects conflicting ways of assessing risks, costs and benefits, or a different view of how the world works. In similar vein, an independent agency should also be able to explain the principles that guide its interpretation and application of its rule-making powers and of its statutory objectives and constraints.

---

pursue whatever personal, local, or party goals they might have or whatever favors they might need to repay. DP2 puts constraints around this technique.

Such operating principles can underpin the reasons warranting the exercise of discretion permitted by the regime, helping to make policy systematic and comprehensible. Not only does that aid predictability (welfare) and accountability (see DP4), like some of the requirements of DP2 it can also help guard against capture by sectional interests, as biased principles would be exposed to view and public debate.

Even though an independent agency should make policy decisions in committee under one person, one vote (1P-1V), it should endeavor to agree its operating principles by consensus. Where feasible, that would help confine disagreements to differences over the interpretation of facts or the prospective effects of alternative courses of action, reducing the likelihood of higher-level discord. Indeed, it can help balance the centrifugal forces inherent in 1P-1V systems with centripetal forces, encouraging members to agree on broad strategy where they can. Where, however, differences of conceptual framework or strategy occur, minority voters should make clear the alternative principles lying behind their votes.

THE FOURTH DESIGN PRECEPT: TRANSPARENCY AND POLITICAL ACCOUNTABILITY

If, as the Delegation Criteria posit, the purpose of and warrant for IA regimes is harnessing policy makers to a monitorable objective that reflects an agreed public purpose, then, very obviously, *Transparency* and *Accountability* are vital components of regime design.

Transparency

In many fields, including monetary policy, timely transparency is intrinsic to solving the problem of credible commitment, as it helps to demonstrate that policy is stable or systematic (chapter 18). *Warranted predictability* can hardly be achieved if observers cannot see what is going on.

A quarter of a century ago, US social scientist James Q. Wilson put some structure around this in a fascinating treatment of bureaucracy. If his jazzy labels are stripped away, a simple 2 × 2 matrix emerges: whether or not an agency's *outputs* are visible and so monitorable, and whether or not the *outcomes* of its actions are visible and so capable of being evaluated.[9] Only one cell of the matrix is suitable for independent, trustee-type agencies: both outputs and outcomes must be monitorable.

That condition is satisfied less prevalently than might be thought. While, from the mid-to-late 1990s onward, monetary policy (setting interest rates to achieve an inflation target) has scored well in many jurisdictions, the ground has not been so solid when it comes to regulation and supervision of banking (the privately owned and managed part of the monetary system), a problem central to part IV (chapter 21).

Even assuming transparency in outputs and outcomes, more is needed. Getting things right by luck is not the same as getting them right by making broadly good judgments. Hence the reasons and operating principles demanded by, respectively, DP2 and DP3 are subject to DP4's requirements for transparency: they cannot be kept private if a regime is to operate efficiently.

This is as relevant to cross-sectional consistency—and so to capture risk—as it is to time consistency and avoiding short-termism. If, under DP3, an agency has published its operating principles and its actions (policies, rules, enforcement measures), then observers can identify any actions that seem to depart from those principles in the interest of particular groups. The more familiar emphasis, especially among legal scholars, on procedural integrity—an element of DP2—as a bulwark against arbitrary power is insufficient to address capture risk. Even if, as with the courts of law, proceedings and decisions are public, capture can go undetected unless policy is, in addition, set according to articulated principles. That, of course, helps explain why judges give reasons and place weight on precedent in their interpretation and application of the law.

In a nutshell, if the mechanism through which delegation delivers credible policy commitments revolves around harnessing the value technocrats attach to their reputation, then various audiences need enough information to judge whether or not they actually are sticking to their commitments. If they are not, their reputation can suffer through "audience costs" (chapters 9 and 10).

[9] Wilson, *Bureaucracy*. His four classes, for each of the matrix's cells, were termed *production agencies*, *procedural agencies*, *craft agencies*, and *coping agencies*.

As put, the monitors could in principle be everyone and anyone. But care is needed here. In some other fields, real-time transparency might sometimes have to be suspended; for example, it would be perverse to announce that a bank is required urgently to cut back particularly risky exposures if uncontrolled forced sales are likely to bring on disorderly failure with significant social costs. To avoid that without sacrificing monitorability, it becomes important to distinguish transparency from accountability.

Political Accountability

By "accountability," I mean political accountability: to the elected legislature that creates and delegates to the agency. Transparency enriches wider public debate on the regime and its stewardship, and that helps politicians in their oversight function, but the agency is not formally accountable in my view to specific sectional interests or individual regulated firms.[10] At its most basic, this is because, for trustee-type agencies free to make choices in the face of political or sectional opposition, the most important kind of output from the accountability process is *change to the regime itself*, whether amendment or wholesale repeal.[11]

This underlines the need to separate, on the one hand, accountability for the regime itself, lying with politicians, and, on the other hand, accountability for stewardship of the regime, lying with the IA. That, indeed, is entailed by the distinction the Purposes-Powers precept makes between goal independence and instrument independence, driven by the need to harness independent agencies to clear objectives that they cannot change. Unless the goal/instrument distinction is inscribed into an IA regime, when things go wrong the public would face

[10]This is a particular application of the definition of accountability in Bovens, "Analysing and Assessing Accountability." It differs from that in Scott, "Accountability." As I use it, "political accountability" can combine what Jeremy Waldron, in "Accountability," has called "forensic accountability" (but without sanctions) and "agent accountability"; the former because, under DP1, the independent agency is assessed against a monitorable standard and the latter because the accountability is to the legislature that created the IA regime and that sustains its existence. In holding an agent to a monitorable standard, principals are in a position to assess the continued value of the standard that they set.

[11]This implicitly assumes that IA regimes are not constitutionally entrenched or, roughly equivalent, that IAs are not a fourth branch of government. Whether that stands up is examined in part II.

serious problems in knowing who to blame for what—poor design or poor implementation—and in responding to debates on possible lessons. Under DP4, political principals must be accountable for the regime itself (precisely who varying according to the system of government, part III).

For each of those two dimensions of accountability, there are feasibility requirements: the modalities must exist, be used, and be widely understood. Most basically, there need to be fora where oversight by the legislature can be exercised. This is not trivial: as discussed in chapter 2, doubts about how precisely that could be achieved partly drove Tory opposition to Bank of England independence in 1997–1998.

Nor, however, is it enough. Legislators need incentives to do their oversight job in the public interest rather than to suit their own narrow interests and priorities. Here, transparency reenters. If the outputs or outcomes of an IA policy regime are (even with a lag) invisible or if the connection between outputs and outcomes is obscure, legislative overseers are in effect given free license to pursue whatever matters they wish in their public hearings and to claim whatever shortcomings or triumphs suit their own purposes. Just as it is vital to harness the incentives of agency leaders to the public good (in the specific sense of the statutory mandate), so it is likewise necessary to harness the incentives of legislative committee overseers to the public-good task of overseeing IA regimes professionally.

This gives agencies themselves, as legitimacy seekers, incentives to adopt transparency but, whether or not they see that (part II), it warrants the fourth Design Precept on instrumental Welfarist grounds, our focus here in part I.

THE FIFTH DESIGN PRECEPT: EMERGENCIES

The first four Design Precepts might seem exhaustive, but the fifth, *Emergencies,* takes us into different territory. Its importance was put beyond doubt by the protests that met some of the innovations used to contain and subdue the 2008–2009 financial crisis (part IV).

For our purposes, a crisis can be thought of as a state of affairs very damaging to public welfare where the authorities are not equipped to respond, one reason being that they are not empowered to do so. Good (within-regime) contingency planning shifts out the boundary between the normal and the exceptional, and the period following a crisis should be used to fill in gaps in those plans as lessons are learned. But a truly complete contract will never be written down (chapter 4): the world is not about to stop surprising us.

That being so, an IA's political principals should lay down a *process* for decision making in unenvisaged, emergency contingencies. It would in effect be a "pause" or "regime-shift" button that could be pressed when the boundaries of an agency's powers are reached and its contingency plans exhausted but it is latently capable of containing or mitigating the evolving mess.

Few central banks entered 2007–2008 working within regimes that determined what process to follow when they ran out of road, entering unchartered terrain on monetary policy, liquidity policy, and credit policy. That was one source of the subsequent anger, criticism, and worries about their legitimacy. But, among independent agencies, they are not alone in this.

DP5 could, in principle, be satisfied by in-crisis political controls that are either ex ante or ex post. They would be ex post if the political authorities had to approve actions case by case during the crisis, amounting to a suspension of independence. They would be ex ante insofar as the political authorities get to reset the regime in a forward-looking way for the duration of the crisis, leaving its operation to the agency. There should be no ambiguity between which of those approaches is adopted.

A crisis often also requires cooperation and, not infrequently, coordination across different authorities. Whatever arrangements are employed to that end, there should be zero ambiguity as to whether an independent agency's independence remains intact or is suspended. Where the latter, the suspension should be effected under a legal power, and transparently.

Those few remarks do no more than skim the surface of a deeply problematic area, one that preoccupied political theorists through much of the twentieth century: when, if at all, can the state legitimately suspend or set aside the rights of individuals and businesses that prevail in normal times? In part II we discuss the implications of liberal democracy for the exercise by independent agencies of emergency powers (chapter 11); in part III how the details of the problem vary across different constitutional systems (chapter 16); and in part IV how central banks and financial regulators could learn from military/political structures (chapter 23).

CONSTRAINTS ON MULTIPLE-MISSION AGENCIES

Up to this point we have implicitly assumed that an agency has only one mission. But that is not true in the real world. For example, many independent central banks are now responsible for both monetary policy and prudential supervision of the banking system; some economic regulators cover both utilities and broader competition policy; some telecom authorities regulate content as well as the economic terms of trade. The question is under what conditions, if any, this should be allowed.

A case made against multiple-mission agencies is that they are liable to prioritize one mission ahead of the other(s), notably if the effects of one are more easily observed and more highly valued by the public/politicians. The insight is not old: much was made of it in, for example, Wilson's *Bureaucracy*. It has also been investigated by academic economists, who have given structure to the argument by modeling it in two ways: where the technocrat is rewarded with money and, nearer to our interests, where they are motivated by career concerns.[12] However modeled, multiple missions are revealed to be hazardous, and the hazard increases with the fuzziness of each additional mission.

Whether drawing on social scientists' observations or formal economic analysis, in recent decades the solution that gained traction was to allocate each delegated function to a different agency. For a while, indeed, this became a tenet of faith among executive branch policy makers influenced by the New Public Management movement: better to have many agencies each accountable for only one mission.

The precrisis Federal Reserve would be regarded by not a few commentators as emphatically validating the theory and, at some cost to

[12]For a recent study of performance problems, see Carrigan, *Structured to Fail?* On theory, see Holmstrom and Milgrom, "Principal-Agent Analysis"; Tirole, "Internal Organisation"; and Dewatripont, Jewitt, and Tirole, "Economics of Career Concerns." In those papers, the policy maker is implicitly a single person, unlike IAs that comply with the Multiple-Mission Constraints.

society, the pitfalls of combining in one agency functions as apparently disparate as monetary policy and bank supervision. With the top brass selected according to their expertise in monetary economics and/or forecasting the path of the economy, and with the level of interest rates massively salient, the incentive of policy makers to bolster their professional reputation coincided with their personal inclinations to devote their efforts to the subjects that most interested them. Staffers took the message, with supervision of banks becoming a relative backwater for a couple of decades. Or so it is sometimes suggested.

The fate of the UK's post-1997 regulatory architecture offers a different cut on the same set of issues. Consistent with the policy prescriptions drawn from the theory, the regulation and supervision of banks was separated from monetary policy. The Bank of England was still described as contributing to financial stability, but there was no statutory responsibility or objective; nor were any powers conferred (other than its inherent capability to be the lender of last resort once a crisis broke). All financial regulatory functions were located in one agency, the FSA, an "integrated regulator." It is unclear whether UK legislators thought of the FSA as a single-mission agency, but as a matter of fact it had four statutory objectives, in which stability was at best implicit (chapter 7). The following outcomes seem consistent with the theory. FSA neglected stability relative to its more salient consumer protection objectives; and, as is now conventional wisdom, the Bank of England did not give enough attention to financial stability relative to its own more salient, empowered, and monitorable monetary policy function. But somewhat at odds with what is assumed by public administration commentators, it turned out that the various UK authorities did not inhabit hermetically sealed zones but needed to cooperate during the crisis. They initially struggled to do so.

It looks as though the theory fares better than the practical prescription. Yes, there are incentive problems in multiple-mission agencies. But I am unconvinced that single-mission agencies can be a robust solution in all fields. As with any structural model, the theory's results depend upon its assumptions, and so the architects of government structure need to ask whether the assumptions are sufficiently rich or realistic before reorganizing the world in their light.

What the theory potentially neglects are circumstances where one mission cannot succeed without the success of another and, crucially, where each relies on a common information base and analysis. Where those conditions prevail, the case for separation is weakened if incentives impede the smooth flow of information and analysis across institutional borders, as they often do, and/or if one or both of the agencies finds it difficult to build human capital in the field it relies on but is not responsible for.

This leads me to depart from what became, for a while, the reflex prescription for the architecture of the regulatory state. Instead, we need to identify conditions under which an agency might be responsible for more than one function while also seeking to overcome the incentive problems of multiple-mission agencies. The answer lies, I believe, in careful design of internal policy-making structure. We accordingly suggest the following supplementary constraints on legislators creating multiple-mission agencies:

1. An independent agency should be given multiple missions only if (a) they are intrinsically connected, (b) each faces a problem of credible commitment and meets the other Delegation Criteria, and (c) it is judged that housing them under one roof would deliver materially better results.
2. Each mission should have its own objectives and constraints, consistent with the Design Precepts.
3. Each mission should be the responsibility of a distinct policy body within the agency, with a majority of members of each body serving on only that body and a minority serving on all of them.
4. Each such policy committee should be fully informed on the debates and deliberations, as well as the actions, of the others.

The third principle does the work in addressing the standard worries about incentives. It is designed to address the risk of "shirking," since most members of any policy committee (or *chamber*, as they are sometimes termed in adjudicatory agencies) would be responsible and accountable for only that mission. And it is designed to mitigate that risk without vitiating the very case for combining the missions within a single agency, through a minority of members being in a position to weigh, and so air, issues of consistency and, where necessary, coordination.

As the examples of the Fed and the Bank of England have suggested, these *Multiple-Mission Constraints* (MMCs) are very important to part IV's investigation of the postcrisis central banks. They imply, among other things, that independent monetary authorities should not take on discretionary policy functions where their authority is subject to ongoing political control, an issue to which we return more than once.

THE PRINCIPLES FOR DELEGATION AS A PACKAGE

We have now completed our initial account of the Principles for Delegation, comprising the Delegation Criteria, the Design Precepts, and the Multiple-Mission Constraints. Although there is much to come, a few things already merit underlining.

Complementarities and Potential Conflicts

First, the five Design Precepts (and the MMCs) have to be seen as a package: one designed to mitigate both the adverse-selection and moral-hazard problems inherent in any regime of delegation, and to address the inevitable incompleteness of the trust deed. We have seen that there are complementarities. There are also potential conflicts, perhaps especially between DP2 and DP4. In particular, there is a risk that legal duties, under DP2, to consult widely and take proper account of the views of the regulated and wider public could lead to very complicated rule books that defy public comprehension, violating DP4. As it is necessary to comply with both of these Precepts, DP4 should constrain how opaque consultation papers or even rule books themselves may become. That would entail changes in some jurisdictions, as discussed in part III.

The Centrality of Transparency

Second, we have identified a variety of drivers for transparency:

- The political principal (legislature) should demand transparency in order to help tie its trustee agent's policy makers to the mast of their public professional reputation, the fulcrum on which the "politicians versus technocrats" distinction turns.
- The legislature and the agency should desire transparency where it enables the public and businesses to make reasonably informed judg-

ments about the course of policy, aiding efficiency through warranted predictability.

- The public and the legislature should demand transparency from the agency in order to enable public debate on the IA's stewardship.
- The public and the agency have an interest in transparency, as it increases the incentives of legislators to conduct to-the-point oversight of the agency and the regime more generally.

A Regime of Ex Ante Controls: Is Political Override Ruled Out?

Third, if they applied the Principles, politicians would exercise control largely through design, coupled with their ongoing ability to change or repeal an IA-regime. This emphasis on ex ante rather than ex post control is very important. For a trustee-type agency, political control should not be applied ex post through mechanisms such as an annual conditional approval of budgets that set out what the agency may or may not do or, more broadly, giving policy steers. Such measures amount to redrawing the terms of the mandate. And even if legislators never, in fact, go that far, a capability to do so can make—and can be intended to make—an agency sensitive to the shifting preferences of politicians and political parties, which would cut across the purpose of IA regimes being for the legislature to tie society to its desired mast. Such ex post control mechanisms may be optimal for some types of agency regime, most obviously where legislators do not know or cannot agree on a clear objective, but not for IA regimes as presented and motivated here (chapter 10).

This sets up a nice question: do the Principles absolutely rule out statutory provisions enabling political override or special approval of an independent agency's decisions or actions?

I do not think so, in fact. What matters for any *override* is that it be transparent, subject to legislative scrutiny, constrained by clear criteria, and in practice rare. For example, a regime that empowers the elected executive branch to override an IA decision/action on prespecified grounds of "national interest" hardly qualifies independence in normal circumstances. Similarly, for actions requiring *special political approvals*, what matters is that they should be contemplated only where the purpose of a regime could be pursued best by departing from the monitorable standards typically constraining the agency; require a judgment on what degree of social cost is tolerable; and be rare in practice.[13]

SUMMING UP

This and the previous chapter have set out a first statement of Principles for Delegation to trustee-type agencies. The suggestion is that legislators should not create and delegate to truly independent agencies unless the Principles are satisfied.

They are meant to be general, applying to all and any independent-agency regime, whatever the nature of their outputs or field; that is to say, the regulatory state, the services state, and the fiscal state. Wrapping up part I, the next chapter explores what difference that might make in practice.

[13] As such, statutory provision for exceptional approvals is probably more important where an IA regime is framed in terms of monitorable constraints on individual actions/decisions (e.g., least-cost resolution of banks, with the purpose of preserving stability) rather than in terms of a monitorable objective that stands for the purpose (e.g., monetary policy directed to a quantified inflation target). This is relevant to the discussion of the lender of last resort in part IV (chapter 23).

7

Applying the Principles for Delegation

> The current rationale given by most economists . . . is that we regulate for reasons of allocative-efficiency, or to reduce deadweight loss. . . . Most Australians would, of course, be surprised by this. They think we regulate to make sure that the owners of monopoly infrastructure do not take advantage of their position and "gouge" consumers.
>
> —Chair, Australian Competition and Consumer Commission, 2012[1]

There are three big issues concerning the Principles for Delegation to truly independent, trustee-type agencies: their democratic credentials (the subject of part II); whether they could fit with the constitutional structures and political norms of various advanced-economy democracies (part III); and what practical difference they could make to the administrative state, which is the subject of this chapter.

Practically, the Principles pose a series of questions, most notably:

- Are some agencies more independent (insulated from political currents) than they should be, given their mandate or design?
- Are there any agencies that, given their social purpose, might usefully be more independent if they complied with the Design Precepts?

FALLING SHORT OF THE PRINCIPLES FOR DELEGATION

On the first question, an IA agency regime could violate the Principles for Delegation in a number of ways, the gravity of the problem and the availability of remedies depending on how.

Where the policy field satisfied the Delegation Criteria but the institutional structure fell short on some of Design Precepts 2–5, the agency

[1]Quoted in chapter 2 of Decker, *Modern Economic Regulation*, p. 24.

itself could take remedial action, including pressing for more active legislative oversight, as some EU agencies did a few years ago.[2]

A problem with the articulation of goals (DP1) would go deeper, and could be fundamental. Without a clear and monitorable objective, an independent agency's legitimacy would be precarious, since it would be left making high policy, defining its own success criteria. If guided by the Principles, its leaders should highlight and help reduce the problem, as a matter of expedience as well as, if you prefer, political morality. Adopting a strong form of the third Design Precept, the agency would set out how it interprets and plans to apply the statutory mandate. Since it would be substituting for the legislature, it should encourage active public debate on its conception of the mission. For example, when in 2012 the Federal Reserve took the important and welcome step of publishing how it defined "price stability" and "full employment," it would have been better to invite public discussion rather than simply making a declaration of policy.

An order of magnitude worse is where an independent-agency policy regime is unable to meet the Delegation Criteria because society's preferences are in flux, the goal intrinsically indeterminate, or big distributional choices unavoidable. No cure would be available to the agency. The greater the number of such agencies, the greater the risk of a cumulative corrosion of public trust in our elected governors and the system of government more generally. Ideally, expert technocrats would decline to serve. Alternatively, they could subordinate themselves to politicians, putting the law and political morality at cross-purposes.

Using functional examples drawn from the fiscal state and the regulatory state, the next few pages aim to highlight how the Principles might help to clarify the issues around delegated regimes with different degrees of insulation and specificity. The main case study concerns the design of securities regulators, which started out, not quite a century ago, as a mechanism through which politicians could explore how to strike a balance between fairness and efficiency in financial markets. In the postcrisis world they could also help to preserve financial stability, but that might warrant greater insulation from politics in order to make their commitment to stability credible. How this is resolved will affect

[2] Busuioc, *European Agencies*.

the gravity of the problem of potentially overmighty central banks since the less market regulators contribute to preserving stability, the more central bankers will find on their desks and so the more powerful they will be.

THE FISCAL STATE: AGENCIES THAT DIRECTLY AFFECT THE STATE'S BALANCE SHEET

We typically think of fiscal policy as being wholly under the direct control of elected politicians since they decide spending programs and tax policy. In fact, it is not quite so straightforward. The balance sheet of the state—its obligations and claims—is also affected by the structure of the government's debt; by any guarantees provided to households or businesses; and by any loans extended or investments made. In many countries all three of those functions are placed in the hands of agencies, with greater or lesser insulation.

During the past quarter century, the period over which many countries erected their regulatory state, advanced economies have been delegating the management of the government's debt to a specialist, arm's-length debt management agency (DMA). In some countries, famously the US, private sector loans to households to finance the purchase of homes are underwritten by a government agency in order to subsidize home ownership. And many countries have agencies that underwrite the financing of external trade, sometimes through export-import banks.

Each of those delegated functions is exposed to the full gamut of principal-agent problems.

Debt Management: Executive Agencies in the Fiscal State

The goals of government-debt-management agencies are typically purely financial: to minimize (and to control variability in) the cost of servicing the debt *over the medium to long run.* A political principal might, however, favor a pattern of debt issuance that minimizes debt-servicing costs in the short run, in order to create fiscal space for near-term projects helpful to their political base. In case that be thought fanciful, precisely this hazard appeared very briefly in the UK during the mid-1990s, when the public finances were under some pressure. During that period, I ran the Bank of England unit that implemented the government's debt management policy (it was transferred to an agency during the 1997–1998 reforms). I vividly remember a call from my Treasury opposite number to say that another department was floating the idea of issuing zero-coupon bonds. As well as dispensing with the need for cash to pay coupons, the greater attraction was that, under then accounting conventions, the public finances would not register any debt-servicing costs at all. The idea was not taken up, but there was a moment when civil servants plainly wondered whether it would prove irresistible to their political bosses.

In short, elected politicians face a bit of a problem in committing to a stable and prudent debt management strategy because their expected life in office is so much shorter than the life of the debt. But leaving things to an unconstrained independent agent presents different varieties of mischief. At one level, an autonomous debt manager might be captured by the securities dealers that distribute and make a secondary market in their debt, becoming overly sensitive to concerns about short-term market liquidity or to the industry's interest in derivatives being used. At another level, if the agency has discretion to make big strategy decisions on the structure of the debt, they will be making choices on the distribution of the debt burden between today's generation and future generations of taxpayers.

The Principles for Delegation help cut through these hazards. Even though there is a problem of commitment, it is not sufficient to warrant delegation to an independent agency on anything other than very tight terms. Strategic debt management decisions that materially influence the distribution of fiscal costs and risks across generations should not be delegated: strategy belongs to the political principals and should be published so that investors, traders, commentators, and the public can observe changes in course.

Overall, that renders a DMA more like an executive agency–cum–independent adviser than a truly independent trustee-type agency. The Principles identify a reason for that: distributional choices.

Policy Agencies That Are Part of the Fiscal State: Mortgage-Market Support

The second type of fiscal state agency is more challenging because it involves the combination of a public policy mission (e.g., promoting home ownership, exports) with a capability to materially affect the public finances. It is not hard to get more of something in the short run (mortgage lending, say) if the subsidy is big enough. If, however, the subsidy is extended via guarantees (or loans), the costs to the public purse are uncertain because the incidence, severity and circumstances of default cannot be known in advance. Unexpectedly high costs will constrain other projects. If, further, today's targeted subsidies increase the amount of debt incurred by households or firms, they might contribute to a drag on growth or even a systemic crisis in the financial system or across the economy as a whole. The role played in the Great Financial Crisis by state-sponsored US housing agencies (known as Fannie Mae and Freddie Mac) and by the German Landesbanks testifies to those risks.

Standard principal-agent problems infect these functions. Left to elected politicians, it can be attractive to broaden the subsidy during the good times to ensure that as many electors as possible are benefiting or, at least, not feeling left too far behind.[3] But delegating to unelected tenured officials is no solution if they are remunerated on the basis of volumes or some measure of short-term profits. Trying to get reelected, trying to get reappointed, and trying to get rich can induce broadly similar policy choices.

Again, the Principles help. Among other things, any "trust deed" would need to avoid the lure of short-term riches and specify a standard for how much risk can be taken. Something akin to that already prevails in central banking: how much risk should be taken in implementing monetary policy and acting as the lender of last resort (part IV). The same broad approach, of elected politicians determining the risk envelope, should apply to other parts of the fiscal state. The issue cannot simply be handed to unelected independent regulators.

[3]On just such incentives helping to brew the US subprime mortgage crisis, see Rajan, *Fault Lines*, chapter 1.

But something like that occurs in the US, through a remarkable conjunction of regulatory and quasi-fiscal powers. As a result of the crisis, the financial risks taken by Fannie Mae and Freddie Mac in pursuing their mandate are now subject to controls set by and approvals from the Federal Housing Finance Agency, an independent agency formally insulated from both the president ("for cause" protection) and Congress (no annual budget appropriation).[4] The de jure insulation from day-to-day politics might help protect against some of the temptations and excesses of the past. Contrary to the Principles, however, the agency has only a single policy maker and multiple objectives, requiring it to trade off purpose (widening home ownership), fiscal risk (how much Fannie and Freddie might lose in bad states of the world, such as recessions), and the stability of the financial system. Instead, according to the Principles, an insulated regulator should not be free to determine how much risk the public purse incurs via guarantee-and-securitize programs or effectively to decide levels of leverage in household balance sheets without an externally given monitorable standard. Also, it should have ranked objectives: for example, a constraining responsibility for financial stability. None of this is so.

Agencies for Orderly Resolution of Distressed Financial Intermediaries

In some ways a happier example, at least in some jurisdictions, is the institution of the "resolution agency," highly topical since the 2008–2009 phase of the crisis. Having developed in the United States over the past eighty-odd years and now incorporated in the EU and elsewhere as the guarantor of retail deposits and as the agency that can put its own balance sheet behind distressed-bank takeovers in order to maintain the provision of payments services without interruption, resolution agencies plainly inhabit the fiscal state. But, when care is taken, they have come to do so without the taxpayer being exposed.

In the first place, deposit insurance can be backed by a Fund built from the contributions of the intermediaries whose retail liabilities are backed, which ensures that defaulters pay. Of course, the Fund might prove too small, but the agency can recoup any excess payout from sur-

[4] At the time of writing, the FHFA is also the conservator for the GSEs, which collapsed during the Great Financial Crisis.

viving firms. Second, the ability of an agency to opt for reconstruction or managed takeover rather than liquidation can be made conditional on the costs being no higher than the default course of a standard bankruptcy procedure with payout to insured creditors from the Fund. Such statutory criteria (known as *least-cost* (to the insurance fund) and *no creditor worse off*) stand in the way of the agency making big distributional choices. Third, such agencies can be given a duty to act promptly.

If holding the reins, elected politicians might have reason to delay putting abjectly distressed financial firms into resolution—there will be losers, something might turn up—and they might pursue electoral goals when structuring a resolution. That is the basis on which resolution authorities are often highly independent, insulated from both elected branches, as in the US: in order to make credible the policy of resolving failed firms, subject to constraints. In those jurisdictions where politics retains a foothold in resolution, a door is opened to operations that reflect other considerations, such as the welfare of creditors in particular regions or electoral districts. The Principles for Delegation provide a basis for identifying this.

But what if the resolution strategy that satisfied a least-cost constraint would endanger financial stability more than another operationally feasible strategy? If financial instability could be framed in terms of a monitorable objective, that choice could, under the Principles, be delegated to the politically insulated agency. If not, those same Principles suggest some kind of majoritarian sanction is needed. In the US, the FDIC must formally obtain the agreement of the Treasury secretary (and, as fellow technocratic experts, the Fed) before opting for a non-least-cost resolution strategy that would best minimize systemic instability.

Through legislated provisions along those lines, a resolution agency can be within the fiscal state without posing an uncontrolled fiscal risk and without deciding high policy on how much instability society can tolerate.

EXAMPLES FROM THE REGULATORY STATE

Most parts of the regulatory state do not directly affect the state's balance sheet, but they still give rise to plenty of issues, as suggested by the following examples (some of which are picked up in parts III and IV).

Utility Regulators

Away from monetary policy, utility regulation has become the canonical example of insulation being principled, notably in Europe. Independence is held to be warranted on two grounds. First and foremost, by enabling policy makers to commit to a stable regulatory regime, insulating utility regulation can avoid private infrastructure investment being impaired by expectations of policy variability, which would lead to a premium for uncertainty being incorporated into required returns.[5] Second, independent utility regulators might be less likely to be captured than political decision makers.

The second is more controversial (chapter 2), but is important because the social value of commitment would be reduced if the regime, while stable, were bent to the interests of industry incumbents. Drawing on, especially, Design Precepts 1 and 4, sectional capture is arguably less likely where the goal is clear and policy deliberations and actions must be transparent.

What, though, of distributional issues? Plenty of countries require certain services to be subsidized: for example, railway or telephone services to remote, sparsely populated areas. This is plainly distributional; and, as US jurist Richard Posner pointed out decades ago, is effectively taxation via regulation.[6] In terms of our Principles, those choices should be made by elected politicians, either directly or via a clear legislated standard that a regulator effects. As discussed in chapters 13 and 14, however, it is difficult to anticipate all the politically sensitive issues that should be kept out of IA hands.

Competition Authorities: Judges as High Policy Makers

Competition authorities are more interesting in a number of ways. On the account given in chapter 3, they are (or should be) an absolutely vital center of economic policy making in a market economy, ranking in im-

[5] Gilardi, "Same, But Different"; on the path to delegated telecom regulation in Germany, see Gehring, "Consequences," pp. 680–682. Predictability is also stressed in UK Department for Business, *Principles for Economic Regulation*, which seems not to have been an input to the Public Administration Committee's 2014 report on accountability referred to in chapter 2.

[6] Posner, "Taxation by Regulation."

portance with the central bank despite their much lower profile in some countries. They adjudicate merger/takeover proposals and investigate cases of organic monopoly, cartels and other agreements, and abuses of market power. Some jurisdictions delegate this function to an independent agency (e.g., the UK and, subject to some constitutional niceties, Germany). Some have the function spread across the core executive branch and an arm's-length agency, notably the US where both the Antitrust Division of the Justice Department and the Federal Trade Commission are involved. In many jurisdictions, the courts play a major role.

There are, in fact, five broad models, which vary according to where decisions are made or where rights of legal challenge lie. In each, the initial stage of investigation and analysis lies with a dedicated bureaucracy, typically these days in an arm's-length competition authority (CA). Big picture and without getting into differences between merger and antitrust policy, the five models comprise the following:[7]

1. The CA takes a legal enforcement measure to an ordinary court (e.g., matters under the US Department of Justice (DoJ)).
2. The CA decides but with a right of appeal on the merits to a tribunal of judges and experts constituted as a specialist court (UK).
3. The CA decides but with a right of appeal on the merits to a tribunal that is not a court (Australia).
4. The CA decides subject to appeal on the merits to its own top policy makers and to judicial review of due process and fairness by an ordinary court (matters under the US Federal Trade Commission).
5. The CA makes a recommendation to a minister/cabinet member in the elected executive branch.

Except where constrained by constitutional provisions, the fifth is rare today, subject to politicians sometimes retaining "national interest" override powers. Much of the academic literature takes it for granted, in fact, that CAs should be independent in the development of policy (as well as to ensure fair adjudication). Somewhat oddly, however, it does not explain why. A case can be made in terms of credible commitment.

[7]For models 1, 2, and 4, see Trebilcock and Iacobucci, "Designing Competition Law Institutions." The distinction between models 2 and 3 is discussed in chapter 15; and see Cane, *Controlling Administrative Power,* chapter 9.

Where there is a public consensus around the economy being market based, relying on competition and, thus, low barriers to entry, a country might need to embed that consensus in a regime placed at arm's length from elected politicians. Otherwise, elected ministers would be lobbied directly and via media campaigns whenever a takeover bid is launched or new entrants challenge a market's structure. Sometimes, the public outcry at letting a takeover go through might be too much for ministers to take in the short run: not an inherent time consistency problem but the stark reality of electoral politics. This is not just about adjudicatory fairness. Cumulatively, the effect might easily be to ossify incumbents and deter new entrants. In other words, there would be a cost to being unable to commit to the (posited) high-level policy of free markets. Consistent with that, I understand that a desire to commit was a large part of the motivation of the UK Treasury when, just a few years after giving "operational independence" to the Bank of England, they helped usher in reform of Britain's competition authorities, creating a newly independent agency.[8]

Commit, though, to what? The broad purpose of competition policy might be economic efficiency or, rather differently, as in Germany after World War II, preventing overly dominant firms from entering into destructive commercial-political alliances and accommodations.[9] One of the first competition authorities outside the US, the German Bundeskartellamt (cartel office), was designed to provide a clear framework for a *free* market to operate, with a stress on freedom as well as on economic welfare (associated with the *ordo-liberalism* discussed in part II).

Even putting those profound issues to one side, should considerations beyond consumer prices and incomes be weighed? Say a merger of two supermarkets will lead to the combined business having the resources to move out of town into much bigger premises, with lower costs that are passed on to consumers. Should the fact that this could impair social interaction in the town center, potentially reducing civic engagement, be taken into account? In recent decades orthodoxy has held that anything that could be regarded as "distributional" is better pursued via

[8]Thanks to former UK government minister Ed Balls for background. Also, Vickers, "Consequences of Brexit" on the old civil service mergers panel.

[9]On ordo-liberal lessons taken from the Nazi period, see Amato, *Antitrust*. Also, Baeke and Perschau, "Law and Policy," who record the exceptions made for banking and insurance as part of interest-group-sponsored political bargaining in Germany.

other means, such as the tax and benefits code.[10] Thus, in the UK, a ministerial "public interest" override power was removed by Parliament when it created an independent competition authority.

That still leaves big issues hanging in the air. Drawing on chapter 3, what if a merger between rivals would reduce the number of participants in a market but, through production efficiencies, would also reduce prices for consumers? Questions like that, which also arise for anticompetitive agreements and the deployment of market power, prompted one of twentieth-century America's great public policy debates, with the Harvard School's presumption that mergers and competitor agreements were bad (and so per se illegal) eventually giving way, in the 1970s and 1980s, to the Chicago School's insistence that the test should be whether consumer welfare would be enhanced.[11]

This reflected developments in economics, and within a couple of decades was itself adapted to keep up with innovations in game-theoretic analysis of cooperation and collusion and the economics of imperfect information.[12] For us, the significance of these momentous changes is not whether they were grounded in good economics but that each occurred without any amendments to the governing legislation. In other words, high policy changed on the formal say-so of judges and, to some extent, technocrats within the FTC and the antitrust division of the DoJ. The story was only a little better in the EU, where Commission technocrats led the change and the ECJ endorsed it, albeit with some public consultation and elected politicians at least formally blessing the consequent changes in the relevant enforcement regulations.[13]

This gives us a glimpse of why the public might not be clear about the purpose and objectives of antitrust regimes, as illustrated by the quotation from an Australian commissioner at the chapter head. Indeed, anticipating part II, given the significance of the issues—economic, social, political—it is striking how little clarity about objectives is provided by

[10] For example, Kaplow, "Competition Law"; Hovenkamp, "Distributive Justice." This seems to assume that the glue of civil society will hold spontaneously or via other means (Part II).

[11] For Chicago, see Bork, *Antitrust Paradox*. For a survey and synthesis, see Piraino, "New Antitrust Approach."

[12] Kovacic, "Antitrust Policy"; Vickers, "Competition Law and Economics."

[13] On technocratic leadership, see Lowe, "Consumer Welfare." On ongoing EU litigation regarding per se rules on rebates, where there is no statutory policy, see Herbert Smith Freehills, "Advocate General Wahl."

the legislated regimes themselves. And it is astonishing that much of the debate, perhaps especially among US legal scholars, is conducted on the basis that the defining choices will be made by judges through the resolution of specific cases; and that the way to bring about regime change is, therefore, to change the doctrinal oxygen in the judges' chambers, law schools, and agency boardrooms. Judged against our Principles, too much high policy is being left to agency policy makers and judges as if there is no room for politics at any level.[14]

These issues are not separable from the structural choices enumerated earlier. While agency policy makers, however insulated, have to give an account of the exercise of their delegated sphere of discretion to elected legislatures, judges do not. We return to these issues in parts II and III (especially chapter 15).

Prudential Regulators

Turning to a field at the heart of part IV, it is widely asserted, by central banks and the IMF among others, that prudential supervision of banks and other financial institutions should be delegated to independent agencies.[15] Principled reasons are rarely given. It is, I think, taken for granted that elected politicians should not be allowed into this area given the temptations of their somehow getting banks to direct credit toward their favored causes and local projects.[16]

Curing one problem is not, however, enough. Such agencies typically have multiple vague statutory objectives (in some cases requiring them to construe and trade off things like consumer protection, stability, access to high-quality services, and efficiency); their inputs are hard for outsiders (legislators and the public) to identify; their supervisory outputs are typically confidential as a matter of doctrine; and the results of their policies and decisions are hard to assess. In a nutshell, they make general policy on how safe and sound (or not) the banking system should be, and yet it is very difficult for anyone to monitor how well the regime works until it is too late. Whatever the imperative of putting clear water

[14] A similar point is made, for different reasons, in Pitofsky, "Political Content."

[15] For example, see Basel Committee, *Core Principles*, Principle 2.

[16] Miller and Whitford, *Above Politics*, opens with a striking story that illustrates the value of insulation. More generally, see Quintyn, "Independent Agencies."

between politicians and banking regulation, how could near total opacity be tolerable? That, at least, is the question pressed by the Principles.

By today's standards, it is discomforting to look back on decades during which the role of independent agencies in prudential supervision relied so heavily on unverifiable trust. Where, as traditionally in the UK and perhaps some other parliamentary democracies, ministers were confidentially briefed on key issues and cases, up to a point the locus of trust shifted to the elected executive. Insulation from politics was compromised, but perhaps defensibly so as long as bank failures were liable to lead to bailouts. Executive-branch ministers would offer an account to the legislature and the public after failures but typically only then, when inevitably they would seek to shed blame. For the supervisors themselves, the upshot was a degree of institutional schizophrenia: independent or not?

I argue in part IV that, through a series of innovations sparked by the 2007–2009 crisis, it is now feasible for the Principles to be satisfied. It has become somewhat easier for legislators to specify what they want from prudential supervisors; to avoid taxpayer bailouts; and for both legislators and outside commentators to monitor an agency's supervision before it is too late. What matters for us, however, is that, had anything like the Principles existed beforehand, they would have helped identify the need for reform even without a crisis.

SECURITIES REGULATORS AND STABILITY: A PROBLEM OF VAGUE OBJECTIVES

The functional examples above illustrate various ways in which the Principles can help clarify the issues around the structure of delegation:

- Debt management: whether commitment can be achieved without releasing policy from majoritarian control
- Housing market subsidies: ranking objectives and constraining fiscal risk
- Resolution of distressed financial intermediaries: using constraints to limit discretionary choice
- Utility regulation: whether distributional choices are properly settled in the mandate

- Competition policy: whether technocrats, judges, or legislators determine the objective
- Prudential supervision: whether secrecy invalidates whatever case exists for insulation

The case of securities market regulators is in many ways richer, as the variance across jurisdictions (chapter 4) invites us to ask whether some are excessively and others insufficiently insulated. The underlying question is what these agencies are for.

Although international bodies, including the IMF and IOSCO, have long maintained that they should be independent, principled reasons have not been offered beyond the importance of keeping individual cases away from politicians and the need for expertise. The historical and present roles of securities regulators illustrate, in fact, how a combination of vague objectives and residual political control can make sense when elected politicians cannot decide what they want, but becomes problematic once there is a welfare-depleting problem of credible commitment. The kernel of the story is that securities regulators moved from being peripheral to being essential to the preservation of financial stability without anyone seeming fully to grasp the implications.

Disclosure-Enforcement as the Traditional Core of Securities Regulation

For many decades the central mission of securities regulators, in those jurisdictions where they existed, was to help make markets fair and to deter fraud. In the country that led the way, the United States, the core policy, arrived at after extensive public debate, was *disclosure-enforcement*: legislators would require extensive disclosure by issuers of securities and by stockbrokers, and the regulator would enforce those standards. The case for insulating that enforcement role from day-to-day politics has always been widely accepted, and was fortified by the attempts of the Nixon administration to interfere with some SEC investigations.[17]

Over time, however, in many jurisdictions securities regulators became overt policy makers, writing legally binding rules.

[17] Khademian, *Politics of Expertise.*

Vague and Multiple Objectives

It is hard to avoid concluding that the agency itself is making high policy if its statutory objectives are vague or indeterminate. In the paraphrase of its mission statement, the SEC is responsible for protecting investors; maintaining fair, orderly, and efficient markets; and facilitating capital formation. (As I write, the Trump administration has appointed a chair who plans to shift the emphasis to the last of those, in an effort to reinvigorate the economy.)

Jumping forward in time and across an ocean, the UK's Financial Conduct Authority has a strategic objective of ensuring that financial markets function well, and three operational objectives:[18]

- Securing an appropriate degree of protection for consumers
- Protecting and enhancing the integrity of the UK financial system
- Promoting effective competition in the interest of consumers

As with the SEC, no monitorable standard is set and no weighting is given for the three operational objectives, so the agency's policy makers have to decide, taking into account eight statutory principles of good regulation.

Interpreting and Applying Powers When Objectives Are Multiple and Vague

An example illustrates the kind of issues this lack of clarity can generate. Following the 2007–2008 part of the crisis, the old FSA concluded that it should start regulating financial products rather than relying on rules governing marketing and distribution, in effect banning some retail products rather than relying on disclosures. It was, moreover, concluded that the extant legislation permitted this and that therefore, strictly, political approval was not needed. At the board, some, including myself as an ex officio member from the Bank of England, felt that as the

[18]Financial Services and Markets Act, as amended in 2012. The objectives of the old FSA, which was also the prudential supervisor of banks, were market confidence, public awareness, consumer protection, and reducing financial crime. It also had to have regard to the competitiveness of UK financial services, which some believe gave politicians a lever in pressing for "light touch" regulation. Safety and soundness were not mentioned.

agency's powers had not been used in this way before, that as it raised questions about ends as well as means, and that as (so far as we knew) Parliament had not debated banning products when the legislation was introduced, this might amount to a de facto regime change, meriting public debate and political scrutiny in order to be legitimate.[19] After discussion, the FSA went ahead, but with the chairman, Adair Turner, writing to Treasury ministers and to the chair of the House of Commons Treasury Select Committee to explain what was happening, effectively giving them an opportunity to object.

That story highlights one route through which regulatory policy can evolve: an agency construes existing powers in a way that supports or permits novel interventions in the market. The much longer history of the SEC underlines another mechanism: that as markets develop or new public concerns emerge, legislators extend, refine, or transform an agency's powers and even, implicitly at least, its purposes. As they do so, the relationship between legislators and the agency becomes complex. Reform might be legislator led, designed to rein in or steer the agency, or it might be actively solicited by the agency itself.[20] This is hardly surprising. There is rarely, if ever, consensus on what is wanted so each vintage is tailored to the specificities of current preoccupations (hedge funds, mutual funds, etc.).

In that the SEC and FSA (and its successor, the Financial Conduct Authority) are the same. But in another sense, they could hardly be more different. As we saw in chapter 4, whereas formally the FCA is highly independent, more so de jure than the Bank of England, the SEC is not fully insulated from day-to-day politics. As well as being subject to congressional control through annual budget appropriations, the executive branch has periodic control through what seems to be an informal convention that the chairs of regulatory commissions offer their resignations (qua chair) to an incoming president. If accepted, this shifts

[19] While deputy governor, I was ex officio a nonexecutive director of the FSA. The board was not involved in individual cases.

[20] On congressional influence over SEC policy through incremental legislation, see Weingast, "Congressional-Bureaucratic System," which reviews how liberalization of equity-market trading platforms depended on Congress. But that is hardly surprising if the law needed changing, the bigger question being who generated the ideas. Khademian, *Politics of Expertise*, documents the opinions of numerous former SEC and congressional officers and staff that on various occasions Congress has found it difficult to legislate without the SEC's public expert support.

the balance of power in the agency, given the chair's control of the agenda and work priorities; and it might give the majority to supporters of the president's program and goals (if the outgoing chair opts to surrender his or her tenured position as an ordinary member).

So, broadly speaking, the market regulators in the the world's two biggest capital markets have more or less the same purpose and mission but completely different degrees of formal insulation from politics.

One way of caricaturing the thinking in the US, where a similar combination of vague objectives and partial political insulation prevails in other fields, runs along the following lines: something must be done; politicians do not know (or cannot agree) quite what should be done, so they hand the matter over to an agency with vague statutory objectives but broad powers (chapter 13); but that is thought not to matter much insofar as the issues at stake can reasonably be battled out among different interest groups, with the agency holding the ring and striking a bargain, and with further iteration available via the courts; and politicians from both branches can formally intervene to steer the ship or get their proteges or allies appointed if they (or their backers) do not like what they see.

One crude way of caricaturing the UK, where many independent regulatory agencies have been established over the past quarter century, would be: something must be done; nobody trusts politicians, so an arm's-length agency should be set up; no one knows exactly what should be done, so the agency's statutory objectives should be plentiful; if general policy goes off track, politicians can probably bend the agency to their will through the media or direct pressure—as appeared to happen when the tenured CEO of the FCA abruptly resigned during 2015.

These caricatures, which are unfair to many independent-minded regulators and to politicians, are offered because they help to illustrate how our Principles offer a clear, normative steer in choosing between the two models. If the objectives are vague because society's purposes are not clear or settled, full independence is a step too far: the US setup is preferable to the UK's because the element of political control is overt and rooted in law (part III).

Contrary to the position of various international organizations, therefore, unless progress is made in framing monitorable objectives, the normative criteria I am advocating seem to warrant independence in securities regulators' adjudicatory role but not, wholly, in their rule-writing role. They are not trustees for a settled goal. The problem today is that part of what we need from securities regulators *is* now reasonably clear and *does* suffer from a serious commitment problem.

Securities Regulation and Financial Stability

Into my caricature of the US I slipped the vital assumption that the policy issues at stake could reasonably be determined through a process of agency-mediated bargaining among interest groups; in other words, something like the tenets of "interest-group populism" have to hold.[21] But that assumption isn't remotely valid when there are major social costs at stake that no actors in the private sector will internalize. In consequence, day-to-day political sensitivity among securities (and derivatives) regulators becomes less defensible the more they become involved in making policy to preserve the stability of the financial system, as inevitably they have following the Great Financial Crisis.

That role faces a major commitment problem, affecting both preferences/objectives and policy choices. Crudely, it might suit politicians to allow exuberance in asset markets if that improves the feel-good factor and eases the supply of credit to voters and donors. Those are conditions in which, consistent with the Principles, delegation to a truly independent agency with a clear objective is warranted (chapter 20). For legitimacy, political control needs to come through the articulation of a regime that does not involve forms of back-seat political driving or front-seat technocratic intervention in distributional justice.

I am arguing that in the *past* the case for the "independent" status of securities regulators was not well articulated, and the reality arguably misdescribed when international authorities suggested that they were generally independent. Looking to the *future*, however, the current position, allowing a substantial degree of de facto political leverage over rule writing in key centers (the US and EU), might not be warranted if the regulation of capital markets is to contribute to financial stability. The structure of our argument can be cast as follows:

[21] For an account of its potency in 1960s and 1970s America, see Shapiro, *Who Guards the Guardians*.

- If monetary authorities are independent so as to help solve society's problem of making credible commitments to maintain stability . . .
- And if, at least in the wake of the financial crisis, securities regulators are integral to maintaining financial stability . . .
- Then securities regulators need, in their stability role, the same degree of independence as monetary authorities, subject to the same kind of constraints.

Lack of insulation is a problem for welfare when a policy field trying to contain major social costs is afflicted by a genuine problem of credible commitment. But vague objectives are a problem for legitimacy when an agency is delegated powers with insulation from day-to-day politics. We may be facing an incipient crisis in securities regulation through a lack of analysis of how agencies bearing the burden of sustaining stability in the public interest should be designed.[22]

SUMMING UP

This chapter, rounding out part I, has done no more than scratch the surface of the difference that could be made by a more principled approach to delegation to agencies insulated from day-to-day politics. Even a cursory review has pointed to a problem with who sets competition policy and an awkwardness at the center of financial-markets policy.

A thorough examination ought to be undertaken of how regulators in different jurisdictions stand under the Principles. I suspect it would show that a principled case for delegation has sometimes been advanced but often has not, even where one was potentially available. It would also reveal that few delegated IA regimes have been articulated clearly, leaving some independent agencies with vague goals and fuzzy constraints. Finally, it would probably suggest that some agency functions might warrant more insulation from politics in order to help cure commitment problems.

Part I's conclusion, then, is that we might simultaneously be leaving both too much and too little to technocrats and judges. Too much where

[22] For an elaboration, see Tucker, "Fundamental Challenges."

debates about goals are unresolved or where insulated agencies are inadequately constrained and incentivized to deliver the welfare benefits of credible commitment. Too little where the people's welfare could be improved by setting aside day-to-day politics. We return to these issues in part III but must first confront a deeper challenge to our inquiry.

While the focus of part I has been welfare, it is by now clear that we might also face legitimacy shortfalls not rooted in welfarist costs. The Principles for Delegation stand on solid ground, helping us to think about the division of labor among elected politicians, judges, and technocrats in various parts of the administrative state, only if their demands square with and reflect the deep values underpinning our democratic politics. The central question lurking in the background is whether the Principles for Delegation are consistent with legitimate state power in our democracies. That is the subject of part II.

PART II

Values

DEMOCRATIC LEGITIMACY FOR INDEPENDENT AGENCIES

> The "first" political question . . . securing . . . order, protection, safety, trust, and the conditions of cooperation . . . is the condition of solving, indeed posing, any others. . . . The Basic Legitimation Demand implies . . . the state . . . hav[ing] to offer a justification of its power to each subject.
>
> —Bernard Williams, *In the Beginning*[1]

Critics of independent agencies see them as a plague infecting modern representative democracy. Part II examines whether the Principles for Delegation can help to remove the specter of a democratic deficit opening up whenever significant power is handed to technocrats insulated from day-to-day politics.

Although it takes us away from the quotidian substance of central banking and the regulatory state, this means saying something about legitimacy: what it signifies, and what it requires.[2] We argue that it does not go as far as entailing a moral obligation to obey the state but means, broadly put, that citizens accept that they should not resist or undermine the system of government. To share in this, legitimate IA regimes need to accord with the deep values and beliefs held by significant parts of a political community about constitutional democracy. Since those values and beliefs are not monolithic, the Principles must pass what I call a *robustness test* (conducted in chapter 11). That necessarily draws on different views of politics, government, and democracy, so these introductory remarks conclude with a summary of four distinct streams

[1] Williams, *In the Beginning*, chapter 1, pp. 3 and 4.

[2] Thanks to Paul Sagar for discussions on these issues.

of democratic politics. As well as preparing for what is to come, that helps to highlight the distinct virtues that those different traditions see in "price stability," the core goal of central banks.

THE LEGITIMACY OF THE ADMINISTRATIVE STATE: DERIVATIVE LEGITIMACY

In the Introduction, *legitimacy* was defined as meaning, very broadly, that the public accepts the authority of the institutions of the state and their right to govern, so that they are not wholly reliant upon coercive power.[3] Legitimacy reduces the resource costs of government and so, other things being equal, enhances its performance.

For the agencies that concern us, the implication is that a delegated regime's legitimacy amounts to the public accepting that the coercive power of the state lies in the background and may reasonably be used to force compliance with agency policy or rules in certain circumstances, but with such enforced compliance being rare. The higher-level state is, thus, not only the creator but also the backstop to the institutions of the administrative state. The legitimacy of an agency is, in consequence, in part at least, *derivative* of the legitimacy of the state and, thus, that of the system of government itself (see below).

One important question, therefore, is whether the conditions for the legitimacy of the state and system of government itself carry over to independent agencies (*transitivity*). Trivially, in democracies one condition cannot carry across: that the agency's policy makers be elected. (Or, rather, if that condition were transitive, independent agencies could not be legitimate in democracies.) Our inquiry addresses whether other conditions for the legitimacy of the democratic state are transitive, and also whether they are sufficient to legitimize independent agencies. Conversely, do the ways in which independent-agency regimes are established, substantively framed, and operated jeopardize the legitimacy of the higher levels of the state?

[3] In liberal democratic republics, we do better to think of a right to govern rather than a "right to rule," the term widely used by theorists. "Right to govern" is also preferred by Coicaud, *Legitimacy*, but he puts greater weight on consent than I do.

Related to that, if any agencies enjoy authority somewhat independently from the source of their legitimacy, should they subordinate their authority, accepting that their democratic legitimacy is more important to the overall health of the polity? That has emerged as a major issue for independent central banks in mature democracies, especially in emergencies, and requires careful delineation of their legitimation.

To pursue those issues, we need to expand a little upon the significance of legitimate political authority and the conditions for its obtaining in the real world.

LEGITIMACY AND REASONS TO OBEY THE STATE

Political theory in the West, especially since the seventeenth and eighteenth centuries, has often made a three-way equation of political legitimacy, authority, and a moral obligation to obey the law. Various reasons have been offered for this, mainly rooted in the writings of Thomas Hobbes, John Locke, and Immanuel Kant. While these intellectual traditions have departed in many ways from the ideas of their founders, they might crudely be summarized as follows:

- *Hobbesian*: Political legitimacy, authority, and reciprocal obligations to the state are sourced in the *rational interests* of people in obtaining security, stability, and solutions to collective-action problems.
- *Lockean*: Political legitimacy, authority, and reciprocal obligations to the state are sourced in actions of *voluntary consent* by individuals.
- *Kantian:* Political legitimacy, authority, and reciprocal obligations to the state are sourced in the *moral obligations* that people owe each other to cooperate in collective governance.

Those three traditions share the view that citizens have a moral and political obligation to obey the law based on the idea of some kind of contract between rulers and the ruled. Very different notions of contract are involved, however.

The most famous, following Locke, appeals to a strong intuition that we would have to agree *voluntarily* to have a moral (as opposed to merely legal) obligation to obey each and every law. It stumbles on the lack of actual explicit consent to modern government, and on the tenuous notion that signals of only tacit (implied) consent, such as voting in elections, could be enough to entail moral obligations with such telling consequences.[4]

By contrast, for other traditions, the supposed contract is no more than a metaphor for conveying how the members of a political community ought to conduct themselves: for Kantians by the dictates of justice, and in the Hobbesian tradition by the light of instrumental rationality.[5] Each faces difficulties in grounding an obligation to obey in the real world.

Kant and his modern followers, perhaps preeminently twentieth-century political theorist John Rawls, hold that enlightened reason will lead us to a cooperative equilibrium that recognizes and reflects each person's inalienable right to autonomy and dignity: others are *ends* in themselves, not *means* to our respective self-centered interests. We thus have duties to each other as well as an interest in our own welfare or well-being, entailing a rich catalog of reciprocal rights. Government exists to articulate and enforce those rights, and as such should be obeyed. But left hanging in the air is how an Olympian justification of the state can frame the practical design of institutions that would work tolerably well in societies plagued by disagreement at every level of politics and prone to bad government.

By contrast, Hobbesian political theory brandishes a kind of realism. In its prescription of instrumental rationality, it bears more than a family resemblance to the economic theories of the market and government surveyed in chapter 3, the world of *homo economicus*: individuals who make rational choices in maximizing their welfare. For the pursuit of our goals to be feasible, we need a state to provide security, an infrastructure for markets to work, and a means for resolving problems of coordination and cooperation. Such *contractarian* agreements about the structure of the state or the "rules of the game" need not be the product of once-and-for-all constitutional conventions but could amount to a cumulative series of bargains, negotiations, or evolutionary practices, perhaps initially among different parts of the elite but in modern times,

[4]The classic modern account of the need for consent and the difficulties of obtaining it is Simmons, *Justification and Legitimacy*, chapter 7.

[5]For a summary from one point of view of Hobbesian *contractarianism* and Kantian *contractualism*, see Hamlin, "Contractarianism."

to some extent, between the elite and the people.[6] Because the state helps to solve otherwise unresolvable problems of living together in a community, Hobbesians hold that it is rationally in our interests to obey a state constructed for that purpose and, therefore, we *should* do so. But they are left with the problem of why people would stick to rules grounded in no more than instrumental expedience. If we could not be confident of the state holding together through adversity and (the inevitability of) poor performance, when expedience wilts, why should its laws bind today? A polity built on Welfarism alone may be fragile.

Part of the problem with these three stories, relying respectively on consent, a constructed ideal, and posited rational self-interest, is their sheer ambition in yoking legitimacy and obligation together. This matters because the public plainly do not expressly consent to IA regimes, and it is not obvious how a putative arbiter of political morality is entitled to say that IAs can be justified by some abstract standard if the consequence is an obligation to obey. We argue that each school strives for more than is needed for IA legitimacy.

THE SIGNIFICANCE OF LEGITIMACY: UNBUNDLING AUTHORITY AND OBLIGATIONS TO OBEY

To see this, a little more precision is needed, distinguishing four things:[7]

1. An institution having *pragmatic authority*, in that people think it makes good sense as a general matter for everyone in the relevant community, including themselves, to follow the institution's policies, rules, and leadership simply because they generally provide good or tolerable solutions to coordination and cooperative problems.

[6] This finds descendants in game-theoretic accounts of bargaining in high-level politics. Hobbes himself saw men and women as often in the grip of passions and so seems closer to a view that communities would learn the hard way that it was best for them carefully to weigh their interests. On Hobbes's pessimism about passions, see Holmes, *Passions and Constraint*, chapter 3.

[7] This is somewhat similar to the categorization in Buchanan, "Political Legitimacy and Democracy." Given our focus on the *derivative* legitimacy of subordinate agencies, my approach to the grounding of legitimacy is different from Buchanan's: internal rather than external; local rather than timeless; sociological rather than morally normative. Distinctions between authority, obligation, and legitimacy are explored in Green, *Authority of the State*.

2. The *legitimacy* of the state and its institutions, in the sense of (a) their having a recognized and accepted monopoly right to resort to the state's coercive powers to back their policies, laws, and rules; and (b) the people living by a norm of not resisting or undermining the system of government on the grounds that it is recognized as having the right to pass laws that seek to establish binding norms that influence or constrain conduct and behavior.
3. *Political obligation* (a strong reciprocal of legitimate authority), in the sense that people are (viewed as being) under a presumptive moral obligation to obey each of the state's laws simply because it has the requisite legitimate authority.
4. Accepting a *moral obligation to obey specific laws* or to go along with specific policies irrespective of whether the state and its institutions are legitimate, authoritative, or owed an obligation to obey under 1–3. (For example, a tyrannous regime might have a law banning murder to which people feel morally committed.)

For our purposes, it is 1 and 2, pragmatic authority and legitimacy, that matter.

Central Banking as Pragmatic Authority

Authority is not an attribute confined to the highest levels of the state. In the history of the Bank of England, its governor enjoyed great authority in the City of London's community of financiers and merchants during much of the nineteenth and twentieth centuries. Despite diversity in the backgrounds of the partners of the major firms, more or less all came to accept that in times of collective difficulty, the authority of the Bank could and should be both accepted and relied upon. This stemmed from (a) the Bank being recognized by the banking community as having private information and networks unavailable to others by virtue of being the operational *pivot* of the system (part IV), (b) the governor being drawn from that community, and (c) the community judging that it benefited from vesting the Bank with authority to use its information and its position at the center of the payments system to provide leadership in the interests of the system as a whole.[8]

[8] See Kynaston, *City of London*, and Giannini, *Age of Central Banks*. Giannini, one of the finest writers on central banking, passed away at a tragically young age.

That authority was emergent, in the sense that it evolved through custom and practice, after initial minority resistance from some private banks.[9] Up to a point, it held within those parts of the City that came to rely on the Bank's banking facilities, and, in origin at least, involved a degree of community consent in the choice of governor. But those sources of authority were localized, not extending to the non-City financial community, let alone to the wider population of the UK. Where the Bank's power extended to the affairs of the nation, notably its early-nineteenth-century monopoly over the note issue, that came from statutes passed in the Westminster Parliament. Thus, while its pragmatic authority relied on the rational self-interest of City barons in there being solutions for collective-action problems, the legitimacy of its formal powers relied on the legitimacy of parliamentary government.

For a while the central banks of a number of jurisdictions managed to combine organic authority with derivative legitimacy and have been seeking to do so again after the topsy-turvy changes of the late 1990s and 2000s (chapters 18 and 19).

By contrast, today few regulatory functions call upon an organic source of authority, as evidenced by the decline of self-regulatory bodies. But they might still rely upon pragmatic authority where the goal is to solve coordination problems. For example, the participants in a market need rules of the game to guide and constrain their conduct, and up to a point will be indifferent to the details, valuing clarity over uncertainty, disorder, and conflict. Such situations bear a family resemblance to pure coordination games, such as which side of the road to drive on, where the solutions are largely self-enforcing. Most cooperative endeavors and so most regulatory interventions, however, are exposed to the risk of defection (free-riding on others' compliance). The costs of defection therefore matter.

Those costs are higher where communities choose to adopt and enforce such cooperative endeavors via the body that underpins the solutions to pure coordination problems and that provides basic needs such

[9]Including Hoares, a seventeenth-century private bank that petitioned against the Bank's charter, reflecting a struggle between the political economy worldviews of Whigs (the Bank's backers) and Tories (its initial opponents). See Pincus, *1688*, chapter 12. Even in the late twentieth century, one British merchant bank held out against a possible market solution to the Barings crisis, just as it is said that, on Wall Street in 1998, Bear Stearns held out against a collective private sector solution for the problems of (the splendidly named) Long-Term Capital Management facilitated by the Federal Reserve Bank of New York.

as security: the government of the state. That way, if people attempt *wholesale defection* from regulatory regimes, they are liable to undermine the whole system of government, entailing serious costs for themselves and others. This exploits the pragmatic authority (usefulness) of basic government. But the bundling of functions also increases the capacity of the state to extend well beyond the provision of basic services. If it relies on pragmatic authority alone, the system is stable only so long as the value of its (assumed) provision of basic needs and solutions to cooperative problems is not outweighed by the costs and unpopularity of poorly chosen or implemented initiatives plus the costs of transitioning to a new constitutional regime.[10] As the nonbasic initiatives multiply, likely bringing increased variability in the quality of government, the more important the legitimacy of the system becomes as it acts as insulation against disappointment and failure.

The regulatory and other regimes of government derive their legitimacy—but not their own pragmatic authority, which might be negligible if they are incompetently delivered or their purpose is not valued—from that of the system as a whole. Legitimacy is their backstop.

Legitimacy Underpins Authority

We are, then, concerned with the legitimacy of laws that confer power on administrative agencies and other organs of the state.[11] People do not obey such laws; they accept them (or not). Of course, some of those laws confer law-making power on agencies, and there the question of

[10] The implicit thought experiment concerns the costs of separate governance for (a) basic needs and pure coordination problems and (b) cooperative ventures. This has some things in common with Hardin, *Liberalism*, which explains constitutional stability in terms of the costs of change.

[11] Four kinds of *legal* right (and correlating duty) are often associated with, among other contexts, a "right to rule": a claim right to impose obligations, a power right to create liabilities, a right to immunities, a permissive right to a monopoly of coercion (Hohfeld, *Fundamental Legal Conceptions).* But from a claim right to impose legal duties, it is quite a leap to infer political or moral obligations to obey every law. The problem seems to me to arise because here we are dealing with a claim right of government in respect of a whole political community rather than, say, bilateral rights/duties. If the law writer was only ever going to write one law and the population accepted its right to do so, it would be odd to think that they didn't also accept a duty to obey that law. But where a law giver is a government writing many laws (some unknown number of which turn out to be flawed and so revised or repealed), the duty is plausibly of a different kind (or so I maintain).

compliance does arise, but it is not the defining feature of the administrative state. When an independent central bank sets its interest rate, people do not obey—there is nothing to obey; the resulting configuration of asset prices just is. Rather, they go along with the decisions and with the right of the central bank to make them.

Even if it were argued (some parts of the community believe) that citizens do have a moral obligation to obey laws passed by a representative assembly (say, because of moral authority conferred by democratic elections) but have no such obligation to comply with legally binding rules issued by independent regulatory agencies, that would not be fatal to the operation of the administrative state. It would, perhaps, substantively constrain what could be delegated to IAs. For example, such agencies might need to stay away from passing rules that stake out materially new norms with overtly moral content. But, as chapters 9–11 argue, the values of democracy impose that constraint anyway, irrespective of whether there is a moral obligation to obey laws passed by the legislature.

Instead, what matters for IAs (and other parts of the administrative state) is people accepting that, as a general matter, the state has a right to create agencies and enforce agency rules; and that they (citizens) should not systematically get in the way of the implementation of agency policy or obstruct fellow citizens from helping agencies, or otherwise seek to undermine the prevailing system of government.

Under those conditions, dissent is channeled through routes acceptable under the polity's norms and conventions, with people understanding that they may be punished if they break the law in the course of their protest. While civil disobedience could occur without comprising revolution, those responsible would accept that the state could apply and enforce the law against them.

This account leaves people free to reach their own views of the justice of laws and, therefore, helps separate questions of justice from those of legitimate government.[12] While a case can decently be made that citizens are under an obligation to each other to comply with laws that solve the most basic coordination problems—the kind of laws that would characterize a minimalist state, and most likely enjoy pragmatic authority

[12] Philip Pettit makes a similar point, and I suspect it was this shared view that sparked our friendship shortly after I arrived at Harvard (Pettit, *On the People's Terms*, chapter 3).

anyway—there is no such simple grounding for obeying rules that meet with *continuing* disagreement and are not singly integral to the system's survival.

Summing up, while not entailing a moral obligation to obey, this conception of legitimacy is not thin. Not only would it put insurrection beyond bounds, it would preclude pervasive and sustained passive resistance, which would surely impair the efficiency of government and so, in time, welfare, security, and stability. But it allows for civil disobedience over particular laws or policies.

The idea of civil disobedience of a legitimate government jars somewhat with the Hobbesian, Lockean, and Kantian ideas with which we began, but not with our societies' ideas of liberal democracy. The meaning or significance of legitimacy is not completely separable from the grounds of legitimacy—the particular values associated with *our* particular form of politics. Although this high-level point might seem distant from the real world of IA power, it is absolutely fundamental to the legitimacy test we apply in part II to the Principles for Delegation.

THE CONDITIONS FOR LEGITIMACY: AN INTERNAL, REALIST ACCOUNT

If the problem with the Hobbesian account of the state is lack of glue, the attachment is provided partly by our values, beliefs, and commitments. They shape how we evaluate results (and vice versa) and mean legitimacy amounts to more than expedience, more than simply that "it seems to work for now."

In spirit, this appeals to the strain in our intellectual history, going back to Scottish philosopher David Hume, that sees social institutions, including the structure and role of the state and government, developing through efforts and initiatives fashioned by need, the ebb and flow of power, experience, and the evolution of ideas via debate and attempted justification.[13] By simultaneously forging and reflecting our

[13] Hume, *Treatise*, Book III, e.g., pp. 539–567. Sagar, "State without Sovereignty." What, following Hume, Sagar refers to, in quotation marks, as "natural" and "moral" obligations map broadly into what I describe in later chapters as instrumental and intrinsic grounds or justifications.

values, the development and performance of government can leave political communities exhibiting, in Hume's own terms, "allegiance" to the state. Rather than the thin relations of convention, we have the thicker relations of a shared way of life that inform how a political community thinks (normatively) of itself.

In other words, values are part of the fabric of a political community. While it is prudent to think about the performance of office-holding *individuals* as being shaped by incentives, as assumed in part I's construction of the Principles for Delegation, it would be reckless to think about institutional design without bringing in values, because societies tend to evaluate institutions partly through their values. Our first response to poor government performance is not, "Well, that's OK. With such incentives, no wonder." It is often closer to, "They should and could have done better," "They have let us down," or "Why have the people we elected let this happen?" Once we come to think about institutions solely in terms of incentives, cynicism sets in, undermining legitimacy. On this view of political life, incentives need to be aligned with values, and legitimacy matters.[14] The legitimacy of IA regimes, therefore, depends on *incentives-values compatibility.*

On this account, the significance of and conditions for legitimacy become endogenous and simultaneously determined. Not only might the conditions for legitimacy vary across time and place, there might be variations, at least of emphases, *within* a political community. As such, a system of government can be legitimized without each and every person's allegiance being explicable in identical terms.

Our inquiry into independent-agency regime legitimacy is, then, normative in the sense of prescribing what is likely to be needed in our democracies, but without seeking to establish timeless high-level criteria for the *moral* justification of the administrative state. In terms that have become popular among political theorists, this is a "realist" rather than "ideal" exploration of independent-agency legitimacy. It is legitimacy "for us" or, as Bernard Williams put it, "now and around here" given our particular convictions about, commitments to, and ways of

[14] This amounts to saying that only half the story is captured in, for example, Hardin, "Institutional Commitment."

living with democratic governance. In other words, legitimacy given *our* history.[15]

The Importance of Opinion: Evolving Conceptions of Central Banking Legitimacy

This departs somewhat from, without I think wholly sacrificing, the famous descriptive account of legitimacy given by the early-twentieth-century sociologist Max Weber. For him, the legitimacy of an institution or organization rested simply on the beliefs of the relevant group, with three contrasting sources of belief: tradition, charisma, and, in the conditions of modernity, rational-legal.[16] That captures something important about the predicament of central banking.

Its twentieth-century history could be told in terms of a bumpy transformation from a compound tradition-charismatic legitimacy, embodied by the Bank of England's "mesmeric" Montagu Norman at the beginning of the century, to rational-legal legitimacy at its close.[17] As already discussed, well after Norman's time, perhaps into the 1990s, central banks were still widely perceived as having *authority*, testifying to the abiding relevance of tradition, and helping to provide a reservoir of trust on which they could draw when things went wrong.

By the late 1990s, however, all that seemed less relevant, if not horribly antiquated. As we discuss in part IV, society was demanding well-articulated statutory regimes—the embodiment of legal-rational legitimacy—for independent monetary authorities. Instead of drawing on authority among financial intermediaries sourced in function, discretion, and private information, central banks found themselves reliant on standards of legitimation that required them to reveal information

[15] Williams, *In the Beginning*, chapter 1, "Realism and Moralism in Political Theory," and Hall, "Basic Legitimation Demand." This is distinct from the theories of legitimacy surveyed in Peter, *Democratic Legitimacy.*

[16] Weber, *Social and Economic Organisation*. For a review of the sociological literature, Suchman, "Managing Legitimacy." While largely about private sector organizations, some of its points carry across to the state.

[17] Norman was described as mesmeric by Sir Jasper Hollam, who started his career as a clerk in Norman's time and retired in the late 1970s as deputy governor (source: transcripts of interviews for Forrest Capie's history of the Bank of England). Hollam, who was central to the Bank's efforts to contain the UK's Secondary Banking Crisis in the mid-1970s, passed away while I was beginning this project.

and publicly explain their decisions in the cause of transparency and accountability (part I's fourth Design Precept). In other words, they found themselves navigating their way from a world in which they occupied a position grounded in authority and practical know-how (knowledge of the markets) to a world of legitimacy and scientific achievement (knowledge of economics). Grasping this, many became leaders—borrowing a term, *norm-shifting trendsetters*—in calling for this transformation or, as many preferred, "modernization."[18]

What had changed was what Hume called *opinion*. It is not enough that people simply *believe* that an institution or form of government is legitimate. To live by a norm that they should not passively resist or actively seek to undermine the system, and for that norm to endure in the face of shocks and disappointments, the institutions of government need to square with the people's deep values.

Three Criteria for Legitimacy: Conformity with Our Perception of Our Values

This was put well a quarter of a century ago by the British social scientist David Beetham:[19]

> A given power relationship is not legitimate because people believe in its legitimacy, but because it can be *justified in terms of* their beliefs. This may seem a fine distinction, but it is a fundamental one. (Emphasis in original)

Beetham argued that in practice legitimate power depends on three conditions being satisfied: it needs to be established and exercised (1) by legally valid means, (2) under laws, norms, and conventions that conform to a society's deep values and normative beliefs about governance, and (3) with expressions of de facto recognition, acknowledgment, or engagement through the actions and cooperation of the people.[20]

[18] Bicchieri, *Norms*.

[19] Beetham, *Legitimation of Power*, p. 11.

[20] In the second edition (pp. 266–268), Beetham argues for avoiding the term *consent* for the third condition, preferring something like the formula I have used in the main text, on the grounds that "consent" would cover the second criterion's test of beliefs-cum-values whereas, for a society as a whole, beliefs can be inferred but not directly observed. That approximates to Hume's criticism of Locke's concept of tacit consent.

For our inquiry, one can think of the first condition as being whether a delegation to an independent agency has occurred at all in law: a test of brute fact. Validation needs to come from agents whose voice is accepted as final by some wider group, which always includes the core officials of the state but can shift with time and circumstances.[21] For us, the actors are typically the judges and, given full-franchise democracy, the wider public, as illustrated by the US Supreme Court's role in resolving the outcome of the 2000 presidential election between George W. Bush and Al Gore.

But narrow legal validity is insufficient, because members of that wider group will have views on how legally valid power should be conferred and exercised.[22] The second condition is, thus, about the opinions of members of the political community drawing on their deep beliefs and standards: are the laws and conventions under which the delegated powers are established and exercised legitimate given those values? If not, a deficit opens up. Among other things, this condition covers who can make the laws, how they should be made, and what their objective should be, all of which takes us back to the political philosophers, not now as seekers of universal truths but as contributors to a society's debates and pervasive beliefs about legitimate government. The sociological and philosophical conceptions of legitimacy blur: the normative standpoint is inside the political community.

The third condition is about whether and how society lives those beliefs and standards, which determines whether there is something like "collective acceptance." If not, there would be passive or active resistance. In principle that is an empirical matter, but it might be hard to measure or assess to an objective standard (meaning a standard that would escape dissent).

For the second and third tests, there is a question of who counts. In today's world, with full-franchise democracy, everyone with a vote (today or tomorrow) plainly matters to legitimation. It is not a matter of

[21]For example, after England's break from Rome, legitimate succession of monarchs rested more heavily on Parliament, as sanction from the bishops was worth less once the monarch was the head of the church (Greif and Rubin, "Endogenous Political Legitimacy").

[22]Again, this is not new. England's Richard II was deposed despite being the legitimate king under the principle of primogeniture, as he lost the confidence of some of his magnates. But his successor, Henry IV, could not escape a sense of invalid rule among at least part of the political community (Sabl, *Hume's Politics*).

finding a representative agent or dominant tendency in public opinion and practice. In a free, pluralist society, different people and different groups place different weights on different elements of agency design and performance, and different weights on the various elements of their society's beliefs and norms. That means that, in today's liberal democracies, legitimacy has multiple sources or grounds: there are many *legitimacy audiences*. Some prioritize results or, specifically, their socioeconomic welfare, others what they regard as political rights, others conformity to constitutional provisions, others public participation, and others how far a regime is embedded as a familiar, even taken-for-granted, feature of their environment (chapters 8 and 9). It also means that legitimacy comes in degrees rather than being binary and, furthermore, that it is being continually renewed, squandered, eroded, or even enhanced.

The upshot is that independent agencies are actors, not just passive carriers of legitimacy or illegitimacy. Particularly when discussing central banks in part IV, I therefore have something to say about the need for these institutions to be self-conscious *legitimacy seekers among multiple audiences*. Losing just one significant audience can be problematic.

THE POLITICAL-VALUES ROBUSTNESS TEST OF THE PRINCIPLES FOR DELEGATION

That provides the background to the tests we will be applying to our Principles for Delegation to see whether they can safeguard the legitimacy of delegation in our democratic republics. The starting point is that not everybody in a democracy holds to precisely the same set of values and beliefs about politics and political structures. What might be termed the *legitimating ideology* or *legitimation principle* is not a monolith. Beetham's second condition needs to be revised to: X is legitimate because it can be justified to people in terms of each of their particular core beliefs about government.[23]

[23] Williams, *In the Beginning*, sets up his "Basic Legitimation Demand" as an obligation to justify to each citizen-subject the coercive nature of the state. Framing this as an obligation to *each* citizen draws on the values of liberalism, consistent with his broader point that we legitimize from within the system we inhabit.

A regime for delegating extensive power to unelected, independent officials needs, therefore, to enjoy legitimacy under different conceptions of democratic governance that prevail among reasonable people living in representative democracies.[24] What I am embarking on in this and the next few chapters can therefore be thought of as a *robustness test*.[25] It has big consequences for IA regimes because it multiplies the constraints they must satisfy (and so will require us to add to the Principles).

In this, I am assuming that different strands of mainstream political and democratic theory are reflected, to varying degrees, in the values and beliefs that people would apply in assessing the legitimacy of delegated governmental regimes. This is not to suggest that people in general express their views about democracy and government in the language of the political theories on which I draw in the next few chapters. Rather, the assumption is that those ideas run through popular discourse and play a role in shaping the way that people think, perhaps in headline terms, about politics and their relationship with the state; for example, that they are entitled to vote, to have a say, to be told what is going on, to dissent, to equality before the law, to some rights.

Rather than being cut off in some hermetically sealed philosophical tower, political, legal, and constitutional theorists are actors in the world, even if only at a distance and via intermediaries. However rarefied their theories, many eventually percolate into opinions and values, becoming reflected in the norms and conventions of political life, the living of which helps, reciprocally, to shape those values.

Politicians themselves—through their occasional and sometimes unexpected role as state builders, reformers, and defenders—generate and

[24] How to delineate reasonableness is fraught with difficulty, but for my purposes it excludes people who hold to political beliefs, values, programs, or practices that embrace, foster, or aim for tyranny or widespread oppression. For us, reasonableness is cast within our liberal democratic values and traditions. Subject to that, on a sociological or "internal" test of legitimacy, delegation needs to square with normative conceptions of politics/government held by significant parts of a community that is at peace, without their being coerced and with those views making a material difference to the community's collective life.

[25] The idea of a robustness test could be applied to the legitimacy of other institutions or practices. A general theory of such tests lies well beyond the scope of this book. It is distinct from the Rawlsian *overlapping consensus* because people do not need to find a common set of reasons on which they can agree but only to acquiesce in the institution itself (viz., democracy in its particular forms in particular states). But nor is it a shallow-rooted modus vivendi, because the reasons people have for acquiescing in the institution are sourced in their particular values and beliefs on politics and government. See Rawls, *Political Liberalism*, chapter 13.

transmit some of the basic ideas and principles that form part of our public political life, employing rhetoric that can be elevated or demotic, and sometimes both. Some of it rings down the ages. The ancients aside, think of America's founding fathers in their Declaration of Independence and, vitally, in the Federalist Papers written, largely, by Alexander Hamilton and James Madison;[26] or Abraham Lincoln at Gettysburg, in the midst of war, "Government of the people, by the people, for the people"; Churchill, "Democracy . . . the worst form of government, except all the others"; or the famous saying, attributed to English Lord Chief Justice Hewart, "not only must Justice be done; it must *be seen to be done*";[27] or, finally, *liberté, égalité, fraternité*, words whose deep and particular meaning for the French people has resonated again since the wave of terrorist attacks in France.

Those particularities and variations are important, and we return to them in part III since distinctive national versions of our democratic stories and institutions shape local debates about the legitimacy and operation of the administrative state. For the moment, however, we stick with the core ideas about the nature and justification of our liberal democratic republics.

DIFFERENT CONCEPTIONS OF DEMOCRATIC POLITICS

In particular, I assume that public attitudes to government draw on and are reflected in different normative and positive schools of thought within liberalism (whether progressive or conservative), republicanism, social democracy, and those strains of conservatism that are distinguishable from liberalism. As I employ them, those categorizations are broad.

Liberalism and Republicanism

I am taking *liberalism* to be largely value neutral, with instead an emphasis on procedural fairness and on individuals being largely free to pursue their preferences, projects, and goals. Each is to be treated with

[26] Under the pseudonym *Publius*, of the people, after Publius Valerius Publicola, a legendary founder of the Roman Republic.

[27] *R. v. Sussex Justices, ex parte McCarthy*, 1924 1 KB 256.

equal respect in the sense of toleration rather than approbation.[28] The private and public spheres are separate.

Liberalism seems to help us cope with pluralism, at least as a matter of *our* history. The procedures and constraints regarded as necessary to deliver fairness and equal respect are often associated with "rights" of varying kinds.[29] How those rights are conceived varies across different strands of liberalism, leaving room for very different views on where the lines barring state intervention should lie. This is sometimes associated with different conceptions of liberty. *Classical liberalism*, for example, emphasizes property rights, the rule of law, and freedom from interference. In terms of the distinction made famous by British historian of ideas Isiah Berlin, this is "negative liberty" (with thin rights) as opposed to "positive liberty" (with thick rights).[30] The tenets of German *ordo-liberalism*, meanwhile, which developed before but flourished after World War II, prioritize clear rules of the game for economic life, with government institutions maintaining compliance in the interests of a healthy society and social justice.[31]

If liberalism revolves around a right to pursue personal projects, I take *republicanism* to emphasize citizenship and self-government. Drawing in different degrees on traditions associated with Athens and Rome, it comes in various shades.

Civic republicanism harks back to ideas of Athenian democracy, inclining toward prioritizing the formation, forging even, of shared values and collectively agreed policies among an active citizenry.[32] It

[28] For the emergence in the modern world of this kind of toleration (tolerance without approbation), see Shorto, *Amsterdam*. Shorto's explanation of how mutual toleration emerged in Amsterdam does, however, have a distinctly republican flavor: the community working together to address the collective-action problem of reclaiming land, from which more or less everyone stood to benefit.

[29] "Rights" is in quotes because ordinary laws create legally enforceable rights (and duties), but liberals hold that some rights are or must be deemed so basic or fundamental that they ought to be beyond choice and trump other objectives, while being traded off (or balanced) against each other by someone. People and societies disagree about what those "rights" might be. Quotes are not used where the context makes the meaning clear.

[30] Berlin, *Four Essays on Liberty*, chapter 3. For a distinction with republican freedom, see Pettit, *On the People's Terms*, chapter 1.

[31] This doctrine-cum-tradition is not confined to Germans. Early ordo-liberals associated with Freiburg included Luigi Einaudi, later governor of the Banca d'Italia and president of Italy.

[32] Today this is often associated with the work of political theorists Alastair McIntyre, Charles Taylor, and Michael Sandel.

typically stresses the existence of substantive virtues and public (or community) interests over and above individual interests (thus, *civic virtue*). This tradition sometimes values "self-realization" as a member of a political community, with a nod to Aristotle's good life. Because of its apparent attachment to the civic strengths of small, homogeneous political communities, it is perhaps better referred to as *communitarianism*, the label I employ henceforth. There is no substantive distinction between public and private spheres. (The basis of legitimacy is collective self-government.)

What is generally referred to by political theorists as *neorepublicanism,* which I call simply *republicanism*, finds its inspiration less in Athens than in Rome, the late-medieval Italian city-states, English seventeenth-century debates, and America's founding fathers. As the basis for government being a public matter, it typically prioritizes freedom from domination: not being under the control of a master or mistress.[33] Life under a benign despot does not count as free, and so more than freedom from interference is at stake. This conception of politics accordingly stresses the importance of people, as individuals and as groups, being able to shape and challenge (or contest) public policy. Power is to be dispersed, office held temporarily, and officeholders accountable. But, in contrast to communitarianism, universally active participation in the political life of the republic (or commonwealth), let alone unanimous agreement, is not required: the public and private spheres are blurred but not coterminous.

As such, this might be thought of as liberal republicanism: what matters is the ability and capacity of each person to participate in collective self-government if they wish—as citizens rather than as chapter 3's consumers, workers, and investors.[34]

Conservatism

Conservatism (in its variants distinguishable from free-market liberalism) values stability in social institutions and does not take atomistic rational individuals as its point of departure. It often presents itself as

[33] Pettit, *On the People's Terms*. Skinner, "Liberty." For emphasis on government being the public's business, see Waldron, "Accountability."

[34] Pettit, *Just Freedom*, chapter 5.

eschewing ideology in favor of tradition and evolutionary or organic change, prioritizing reforms that preserve the roots of things, however remotely.[35] As such, conservatism is not, in essence, in opposition to modern democracy established through gradual reform and embedded by the passage of time, as in Britain's gradual moves toward full-franchise elections to a representative assembly.

The public and private spheres are rooted in a natural order of things; and, similarly, legitimacy lies in established practices that form part of a community's way of life. The eighteenth-century British parliamentarian Edmund Burke called this *prescriptive legitimacy*.[36]

Social Democracy

Social democracy is perhaps more rarely articulated explicitly as a political theory than as a program for action within politics itself.[37] It places overt weight on positive liberty and less weight than classical liberalism on the preeminent importance of property rights. The two points are connected because, as one commentator puts it:[38]

> To safeguard the negative liberty of all citizens, liberal theory restricts positive liberty to only some of them, the owners of property.

Social democracy looks to the state as an active agent in enhancing the prospect of people and communities being able to realize their capabilities or entitlements. Initially associated with the idea of an economic Plan in the hands of an earlier technocracy, today it might come through state provision of services or, under legal constitutionalism (chapter 8), the enumeration of socioeconomic rights.

For social democracy, the legitimacy of the state turns on whether it delivers or is tending toward a certain substantive conception of justice. The public sphere exists to transform relations of social or economic inequality within the private sphere, whose autonomy is restored only teleologically. It is inherently redistributive.

[35] This is broadly the approach of Burke. Also, Huntington, "Conservatism as an Ideology," and Scruton, *Meaning of Conservatism*.

[36] Thanks to Jesse Norman, MP, for discussions on Burke.

[37] A recent exception might be Meyer, *Theory of Social Democracy*.

[38] Meyer, *Theory of Social Democracy*, p. 15.

Because social democracy incorporates democracy, it values the individual and so, in contrast to socialism and communism, can sometimes be hard to distinguish from Left liberalism. Similarly, after World War II, Western European Christian democracy blended a liberal approach to economic affairs with moderate conservatism in social values, a stress on social solidarity, and antinationalism.[39] More generally, the boundaries between the various political traditions covered here are blurred.[40] In the modern world, liberalism and republicanism in particular are intertwined, one bringing an emphasis on rights, the other a stress on participation and challenge, and both wanting to guard against abuses of power. I return frequently to what those traditions entail for IA regime legitimacy in the following chapters.

I rarely call upon communitarianism, since it speaks more to active participation in the politics of local (municipal) government and the case for power being delegated to towns and villages than it does to the structure of national-level government.[41] I also devote less space to social democracy, given the Principles' insistence that big distributional choices be made by elected politicians.

Social democracy is not alone, however, in bearing on the substance of public policy regimes. Liberalism and republicanism also do so, sometimes pointing in rather different directions, sometimes broadly aligned. Since I say less in the following chapters about substantive policy, as opposed to how regimes are established and maintained, I therefore close this introduction to part II with a few observations on what the values associated with various political traditions imply for the

[39] Muller, *Contesting Democracy*, pp. 132–143.

[40] For example, some variants of republicanism shade into social democracy by arguing for an active state in forging values and creating conditions for people to live lives that are fulfilling or, more restrictively, free from domination. But some forms of "communitarian" civic republicanism shade into conservatism by prioritizing the values of cohesive, organic, and so historic communities. Perhaps more important, liberalism and republicanism have been intertwined in the political history of many states, notably the US, as discussed in Kloppenberg, *Virtues of Liberalism*, especially chapter 4, "Premature Requiem: Republicanism in American History." It can also be confusing that in some countries, again including the US, social democrats call themselves liberals, perhaps because they see the state's role in terms of regulatory and constitutional (rights) intervention rather than in public ownership or control of part of the means of production, distribution, and exchange.

[41] For example, in Sandel, *Democracy's Discontent*, an acid test of freedom is "to share in governing a political community that controls its own fate." This leaves open how far into day-to-day government "controlling one's own fate" goes.

purpose of, first, antitrust policy and, second, monetary policy. Broadly, the conclusion is that for antitrust policy legitimate delegation-with-insulation would have to overcome a basic political question about goals, whereas for monetary policy the legitimation problem revolves more around whether, notwithstanding fairly broad agreement on purpose, discretion can be adequately constrained by a monitorable objective or standard.

Mergers and Antitrust Policy under Different Political Traditions

The prevailing ethos of contemporary mergers and antitrust policy is, at its root, liberal and Welfarist: we should each be free to pursue our personal welfare without interfering with others. Inefficient markets sacrifice aggregate welfare. Policy should maximize the size of the cake (chapter 3).

In chapter 7, we recalled, however, that after the War, the early ordo-liberals in Germany were focused just as much on the role that anticartel policy could play in avoiding concentrations of private political power. On the American side of the Atlantic, similar concerns ran through Woodrow Wilson's "New Freedom" campaign and the thinking of his supporter, collaborator, and Supreme Court appointee Justice Brandeis, one of the architects of the Federal Trade Commission. As the decades passed, this strain of antitrust thinking gradually disappeared, including within ordo-liberal circles. But in the 1990s, former Italian competition chief and prime minister Giuliano Amato returned to it, asking whether containing the political-social risks of dominant economic power should rank alongside or, even, ahead of the desirability of falling consumer prices (marginal costs).[42] This is a quintessentially republican sentiment, almost exactly echoing the focus of Philip Pettit and others on whether anyone, private or public, can decently have the power to dominate their fellow citizens.

[42]Wilson, *New Freedom*, VIII–XI; Amato, *Antitrust*. Within ordo-liberalism, there was a switch in emphasis from the generation of Eucken to that of Bohm. Hayek approached market dominance with benign neglect, perhaps believing that evolutionary forces would act as a safeguard. (With thanks to Lars Feld.)

Prompted by the political upheavals triggered by the Great Financial Crisis and the excesses that accompanied and fueled the credit bubble, this idea has lately begun to resurface in debates about competition policy.[43] To give only one example, a republican twist to competition policy would, perhaps, take a different line on private vendors of information, news, and advertising.

My point is not to take a position on whether liberal or republican values should prevail. Rather, it is that questions of purpose run deep in this field, placing a burden on elected legislators, especially if they seek to put policy beyond their own day-to-day reach (an issue we return to in chapter 11).

Price Stability under Different Political Creeds

Price stability, the traditional core purpose of central banking, is different. Although independent central banks are often seen as the embodiment of liberalism, or even neoliberalism, I want to argue that price stability can be seen as a legitimate goal for the state under both liberal and republican conceptions of politics and, subject to one qualification, under social democracy too.

For *liberals* (progressive as well as conservative), the definition of price stability favored by former Fed chair Alan Greenspan seems to warrant its legitimacy: that it obtains when "economic agents no longer take account of the prospective change in the general price level in their economic decision-making."[44] That is almost the canonical liberal case for any measure or regime: that it helps to leave autonomous people (and businesses) free to pursue their private projects and well-being without interference (in this case from noise in the value of money).

For *republicans*, a means of embedding price stability should be attractive because it helps protect the people from the *possibility* of an arbitrary imposition of taxation through (unexpected) inflation. Republicans

[43]First and Waller, "Antitrust's Democratic Deficit"; Davies, *Limits,* chapter 3; Khan, "New Tools"; Rahman, "Domination."

[44]Greenspan, "Transparency in Monetary Policy," echoing Volcker, "Can We Survive Prosperity?" from nearly twenty years earlier: I am obliged to Ed Nelson for pointing this out to me. For a contextual account, see Orphanides, "Road to Price Stability."

would want this to reflect the people's wishes for stability as a collective good, rather than the outcome of a battle between competing interests. They would also desire an arrangement—an institution in the broad sense—that constrains the state from reneging on promises of price stability: insulation from domination by the state. On this view, price stability helps—is even necessary—to underpin the legitimacy of the state itself.

Social democrats would probably pause to ask whether the state faced a trade-off between an objective of price stability and, broadly, jobs. Since the 1960s and 1970s, their view has probably shifted to accepting that if medium-term inflation expectations can remain anchored, the state has considerably more latitude to use monetary policy to stimulate demand to offset the effects on activity and jobs of adverse shocks to the economy's cost structure (part IV). In other words, many social democrats would see the pursuit of price stability as a *means* to enabling state-controlled monetary policy to provide society with insurance against difficult macroeconomic circumstances, protecting people and communities from hardship. While insufficient on its own, they would not regard price stability as inconsistent with their values and goals; they would not be seeking price instability.

In chapter 17, we will see that both they and liberal conservatives can look for more, but suffice to say now that all the great traditions of Western democracy can find something of value in price stability. The legitimacy challenge is whether we can get beyond a broadly settled purpose and frame a regime for delegation that meets our values in other respects.

WHAT LIES AHEAD

Under any of the conceptions of politics we have been sketching, effective governance combines at least three broad attributes: a capacity to govern through state machinery or bureaucracy, accountability, and rule of law.[45] Different political traditions balance them in different ways. Our inquiry is about how one part of the state apparatus—independent

[45] Fukuyama, *Origins of Political Order.*

agencies—fits into the way this is managed under democracy, the modern realization (and enrichment) of political accountability.

Before reaching our robustness test, we begin, then, in the next couple of chapters, with the values of the rule of law, constitutionalism, and democracy.

8

Independent Agencies and Our Political Values and Beliefs (1)

RULE OF LAW AND CONSTITUTIONALISM

> Hostility to law, expressed in the principle of broad and unguided delegation of power, is the weakest timber in the shaky structure of the new public philosophy. . . . The question of standards disappeared as the need for them increased.
>
> —Theodore J. Lowi, *The End of Liberalism*[1]

Applying the approach to legitimacy outlined in the introductory remarks to part II, this chapter focuses on the values of the rule of law and constitutionalism. Together, they add up to the idea, articulated forcefully by John Locke, of limited (constrained) government. They are effected via norms concerning the structure of a state's governing institutions (the famous separation of powers); and via laws or conventions limiting what the state can do, perhaps stating what it must do, and constraining the exercise of its powers. Both sets of values predate but run through today's *constitutional democracies*. Notably, they drive some current policy debates in the United States. For example, calls for the Fed to follow a rule for setting interest rates appeal to the "rule of law"; and objections to regulators, including the Fed, issuing legally binding rules appeal to the "separation of powers." It matters, therefore, whether these political values are clear and unambiguous, and whether our Delegation Criteria and Design Precepts live up to them. In exploring what this entails, some of the context for contemporary debates on monetary policy and financial regulation becomes clearer.

The burden of the argument, reinforced in subsequent chapters, is that while these values entail material constraints on the operation of

[1]Lowi, *End of Liberalism*, pp. 93 and 97.

the administrative state, they are not sufficient to guarantee *democratic* legitimacy for IA regimes. Put crudely, oversight by the courts simply is not enough.[2]

THE RULE OF LAW: GOVERNMENT VIA AND UNDER THE LAW

When introducing the different modalities and purposes of the administrative state in chapter 3, agencies of all kinds were described as acting *via and under* the law. The expression *rule of law* stands for what our values and norms demand of the law (legality), driving some of the Design Precepts incorporated into our Principles for Delegation. The roots of the idea are not modern: in medieval England, the king was said to be subject to the law. The rule of law is not, however, a monolithic, uncontested concept, and so what it demands needs unpacking.[3]

The purpose here is not to grapple with what law *is* but, rather, following part II's general approach to legitimacy, to sketch various mainstream accounts of the values of rule *of* law so as to see how they frame conditions for rule *by* law to enjoy sustained legitimacy in our constitutional democracies.

Many such accounts try to abstract from the substance of the public policies that law instantiates and effects. Perhaps most famously among modern writers, the late Harvard law professor Lon Fuller enumerated the following qualities demanded of law by rule-of-law values: generality, being publicly announced, being prospective rather than retroactive, clarity, internal consistency, being reasonably stable over time rather than subject to unpredictable or capricious change, compliance being realistic, and the promulgated law actually being the law enforced and applied by the executive branch and the courts.[4]

The formal rule-like qualities of law emphasized by Fuller provide people with the (degree of) certainty and clarity needed to plan their affairs and to make their cooperative endeavors sustainable. For prosper-

[2] My thanks to Kevin Stack for pressing me to cover the rule of law before the values of democracy. He is not to blame for the substance.

[3] Waldron, "Rule of Law."

[4] Fuller, *Morality of Law*.

ity, economists can argue—and did argue to the post-1989 countries transitioning from communism—that the rule of law should have priority over democracy as it guards property rights against the volatility and excesses of majoritarian policy making.[5] That is the classic liberal view of a law of rules, associated in modern times with Hayek:[6]

> Stripped of all technicalities, this means that government in all its actions is bound by rules fixed and announced beforehand—rules which make it possible to foresee with fair certainty how the authority will use its coercive powers in given circumstances and to plan one's individual affairs on the basis of this knowledge.

The deeper values here are freedom from interference and the Hobbesian goal of stability.

From Rules to Fair Adjudication

This sentiment is by no means confined to classical liberals. Thus the social-democratic liberal political philosopher John Rawls:[7]

> A legal system is a coercive order of public rules addressed to rational persons for the purpose of regulating their conduct and providing the framework for social cooperation. When these rules are just [and so should be accepted] they establish a basis for legitimate expectations. (My interpolation)

While Rawls and Hayek are left to disagree on the substance of public policy, they share the conception of law as rules. To eliminate discretion, however, the rules would have to be mechanical, in the sense of everyone readily agreeing—indeed, finding obvious—how each and every rule must be applied in every conceivable circumstance. Where the law cannot be administered as a mechanical rule, as very often it cannot, it is subject to interpretation and judgment-based application.

This opens up a somewhat different, overlapping conception centered on the processes and institutions of the law. It finds its most famous

[5] Barro, "Rule of Law."
[6] Hayek, *Road to Serfdom*, p. 80.
[7] Rawls, *Theory of Justice*, p. 235.

expression in the precepts of the late-nineteenth-century British constitutionalist Albert Venn Dicey:[8]

> No man [*sic*] is punishable or can be lawfully made to suffer in body or goods except for a distinct breach of law established in the ordinary legal manner. . . .
>
> Not only . . . with us no man is above the law, but (what is a different thing) . . . here every man, whatever be his rank or condition, is subject to the ordinary law of the realm and amenable to the jurisdiction of the ordinary tribunals.

Abstracting from the details of the common law system that framed Dicey's view of the world, here we have it that government must operate via and under the law; and implicitly a call upon the integrity of the courts, amounting to a demand that, whatever the matter, people who go to law or are taken to law should, on both sides, have a fair hearing under an impartial, expert judge insulated from the rest of government.

What counts as "fair" shifts over time, but a fair hearing is today typically held to entail either a balanced and open investigation by the judge (civil law systems) or, broadly, reliance on evidence and arguments available to and challengeable by specialist professionals on both sides, a capacity to contest the applicability of the relevant laws, and judges giving reasons for their findings so that, in turn, they can be challenged in a higher court.

The justification for this conception of the rule of law might be fairness for its own sake, rooted in valuing the dignity of each and every member of the community: equality before the law. Like one of the warrants for democracy discussed in the next chapter, fair and open processes also have epistemic value: when applying the general provisions of the law to specific cases in all their particularity, debate in court is likely to lead to a better decision (according to the standards by which such decisions are judged by the professional community and the wider public). And by allowing challenge, they embrace the republican value of contestation: that people should be able to have their day in court, as the saying goes.

[8]Dicey, *Law of the Constitution* (and discussion in Bingham, *Rule of Law*, pp. 3–4).

Taken together, fair procedures are necessary for courts to provide adjudication with *finality*, meaning that the outcomes are accepted as bringing closure to a dispute even where, on the merits, disagreement might persist. This condition for legitimacy finds a strong echo in the research of social psychologists into what members of the public demand of the administration of law: in a word, fairness, at every stage of the process, from policing to courtroom.[9]

Those two conceptions—of formal norms and of fair process—are often combined to some degree, which is hardly surprising since both feature prominently in the values of democratic societies.[10] Some jurists and commentators also seek to incorporate particular substantive values into a conception of law on the grounds that they are (or should be) universally supported, but I largely set those aside here since we are concerned with the legitimate *structure and processes* of democratic governance.[11]

We seem, then, to have bumped into a need for compromise between a purist norm that the rule of law is a law of rules and the value of fair hearings that include debating points of law and how the law should be applied to contested facts.

Under the former conception, the rule of law might seem to have been sacrificed—we are under the rule not of law but of men (*sic*).[12] After the Second World War, Hayek was concerned that the pursuit of social justice, via the discretionary administration of the welfare state, was having just that effect.[13]

The counterargument maintains that the terrain amenable to *mechanical* rules does not exhaust the scope of legitimate government. Neither Hayek nor Rawls has much to say about democracy, but in democracies we accept laws/regimes that are not entirely mechanical if duly passed through a properly elected assembly (and not violating any constitutional constraints). Indeed, in a democracy, it would be odd to deprive the people of the right to pass nonmechanical laws: to do so

[9] Tyler, *Why People Obey.*

[10] For example, "Rule of Law and Its Virtues," included in Raz, *Essays on Law.*

[11] Perhaps the most significant such account in recent years is Bingham, *Rule of Law*, with eight precepts that include respect for substantive human rights.

[12] Scalia, "Law of Rules."

[13] Hayek, *Political Ideal*, quoted in Tamanaha, *Rule of Law.*

would be the tyranny of a particular conception of the "rule of law," which therefore cannot be *ours* (chapters 9 and 10).

This amounts to ditching an imaginary metaphysics of the "rule of law" as something external to ourselves. Just as economists are fond of saying, "There are only households," looking through the (distorting) veil of companies and investment vehicles to the ultimate investors, workers, and consumers, so we cannot take flesh-and-blood people out of the application of the law. Legal rules do not apply themselves.

Rules versus Standards: Contemporary Debates in Postcrisis Central Banking

That does not make the underlying issues go away, of course, as the question becomes how best law can be framed and its interpretation-cum-application constrained so as to be consistent with our values. For the administrative state, including IAs, this manifests itself partly in a debate about the relative merits of "rules" and "standards (a cousin of part I's discussion of rules versus discretion)."[14] The difference can be illustrated with an example from prudential policy for a stable financial system (the focus of part IV):

- *Rule*: "Licensed banks must maintain tangible common equity (as defined) of at least X percent of total assets (as defined)."
- *Standard*: "Licensed banks must manage their affairs prudently and maintain capital adequate to remain safe and sound in stressed states of the world."

Of course, the terms of any rule may require interpretation and judgment (see above), so the distinction is one of degree rather than of absolutes.[15] But, unless its terms are drafted very loosely, the rule imposes a somewhat tighter constraint.

[14] For its relevance to antitrust policy, see Crane, "Rules versus Standards." Here, in part II, following legal terminology, the term *standard* might briefly seem to be used in a slightly different way from in the welfarist discussion of part I. There (chapters 5 and 6) a standard could be part of an objective or part of a binding constraint, and the question was whether the objective/constraint was monitorable. The apparent difference dissolves because a monitorable standard is rule-like (see main text).

[15] See Schauer, *Playing by the Rules*.

This is no less relevant to monetary policy, but here the analysis can be pushed a step further by reintroducing part I's distinction between goals and instruments:

- *Rule for Objective*: "Monetary policy shall be set so as to achieve an annual rate of inflation (as defined) of Y percent."
- *Standard*: "Monetary policy shall be set so as to maintain price stability and full employment over the medium-to-long term."
- *Rule for Instrument*: "The policy interest rate (as defined) shall be set according to the formula F."

Hayek's choice between rules and (vague) standards is clear enough:[16]

> When we obey laws, in the sense of general abstract rules laid down irrespective of their application to us, we are not subject to another man's will and are therefore free. It is because the lawgiver does not know the particular cases to which his rules will apply, and it is because the judge who applies them has no choice in drawing the conclusions that follow from the existing body of rules and the particular facts of the case, that it can be said that laws and not men rule.

Unsurprisingly, therefore, those who place great weight on that conception of the rule of law espouse instrument rules for monetary policy and rule-based banking regulation, as reflected in various draft laws that have passed the US House of Representatives in recent years.[17]

Monetary history is replete with examples of almost every type of rule imaginable. Perhaps the most famous is the nineteenth-century gold standard, which was legislated, observable to the public, and, relatively speaking, simple.[18] While the rule purported to be binding, on a number of occasions it was suspended by the Westminster Parliament, always with a promise to return once the immediate exigencies had passed. In a deep sense, therefore, the real "rule" governed the various circumstances in which a country would suspend and return to the standard. That higher-level rule could only be inferred from practice, a

[16] Hayek, *Constitution of Liberty*, p. 153, quoted in Tamanaha, *Rule of Law*.

[17] Taylor, "Legislating a Rule."

[18] Unlike, say, a "rule" for money growth or the path of a short-term nominal interest rate, which requires continuous judgments about shifts in the demand for money or in the equilibrium rate of interest.

practice that was finally broken in the early 1930s. Policy rules are, in other words, complex things.

Partly for that reason, on the other side of contemporary debates, standards (or a rule for an objective) are preferred by those who regard the state of economic knowledge as insufficient for society to harness itself to an interest-rate rule, let alone a mechanical one; and, in the regulatory sphere, by those who place weight on the avoidance strategies likely to be adopted by regulated industries (as discussed in chapter 21). Even though interpretation and discretionary judgment are, then, unavoidable, rule-of-law values nevertheless push in the direction of those judgments being consistent over time (in other words, principled), any exceptions being carefully explained, and any change in the underlying principles being signaled in advance. This is a world where policy makers are expected to furnish their choices with *reasons*, enabling challenge and incentivizing consistency and clarity. It goes for agencies' application of the law just as much as for the courts (and helps to underpin our third Design Precept, as discussed below).

In the same spirit, formalist rule-of-law values mean that room for discretionary judgment should be constrained by laws that incorporate a *clear* standard (or objective) and that avoid unnecessary vagueness. Hayek might not get his mechanic, but he should be spared an artist. We should do the best we can. Our first Design Precept demands just that: while not precluding instrument rules, it requires that objectives and standards operating as the front line constraint should be monitorable—and, so rule-like.

In summary, a rule-of-law standard comprises values and norms that a society wants to shape the constraints that bind people who (unavoidably) make, enforce, and interpret the law. This is *constrained discretion,* exactly the concept invoked in chapter 6 to motivate the Design Precepts for how to structure IA regimes; except now the need for constraints is no longer a matter of expedience and efficiency but is rooted in some of our deepest values.

Debates about the operation of postcrisis central banking should be seen in that light. They are not simply about economics. The same goes for the broader question of how central banks fit into the structure of the state, since that is similarly constrained by rule-of-law values.

CONSTITUTIONALISM AND THE STRUCTURE OF THE STATE: SEPARATION OF POWERS

From ancient and medieval times, the design of the state has been continuously debated, with core precepts ranging from spreading and sharing power across different groups in the political community to delineating the functional purpose and powers of distinct government institutions.

The idea of a "mixed constitution," balancing power across different groups, goes back to Aristotle: the one (monarch), the few (aristocracy), and the many (people). In Republican Rome it was manifest in the fragmentation of power across the Senate, the People's Assembly, the veto rights of the Tribunes of the People, and the Consuls.

A group-based structure prevailed in parts of medieval and early-modern Europe. England had a bicameral parliament, giving both the aristocracy and regional representatives (gentry and burghers) some kind of check on the monarch's law-making, tax-raising, and executive powers, which proved central to the political struggles of the seventeenth century. Prerevolutionary France, meanwhile, emphasized the three Estates of church, nobility, and the rest (the people!), who alone lacked privileges and political rights.[19]

From the Enlightenment onward, the stress shifted, in theory if not always in practice, to a functional distribution of powers across three canonical branches: legislature, executive, and independent judiciary. This is the *separation of powers* that the French liberal political scientist Montesquieu thought he saw, and admired, in eighteenth-century Britain.[20]

While this model came to be reflected in almost every advanced-economy democracy, its realization and evolution varied considerably.

[19] In England, the princes of the church (cardinals and bishops) sat in the House of Lords. So did the abbots of the great pre-Reformation monasteries but as landed magnates rather than officers of the church.

[20] Montesquieu, *Spirit of the Laws*. In fact, over this period, partly through the efforts of Sir Robert Walpole, often referred to as Britain's first prime minister, the executive branch embedded itself in Parliament through the granting of offices. Montesquieu might have been misled by the Tory and sometime exile Viscount Bolingbroke, who would have preferred more degrees of separation between the Crown (executive) and Parliament (Tombs, *English and Their History*, p. 318).

Whereas in England the ordinary courts were to be a check on a latently mighty executive, the imperative in postrevolutionary France was to protect the People's Assembly from potentially reactionary courts.[21] Hence Napoleon molded the old King's Council into what today still serves as the *Conseil d'État*, France's highest court of administrative law.

The variation is not surprising. A monolithic prescription for the structure of the state does not flow from the deeper values that are today associated with the separation of powers, which include (1) "no man being a judge in his own cause," motivating a judiciary that stands independent of the lawmakers; (2) the benefits to efficiency and effectiveness, and thus to the people's welfare, of a division of institutional labor into functional competences; and (3) avoiding concentrations of power, for the reasons famously urged by American founding father James Madison:[22]

> The accumulation of all powers, legislative, executive and judiciary, in the same hands . . . may justly be pronounced the very definition of tyranny.

Even taken together, this bundle of purposes is consistent with either hermetically sealed functional spheres or, alternatively, degrees of overlap where, in Montesquieu's words "power [is] a check to power", as realized in the US system of checks and balances.[23]

Although the precise structure of the state is left underdetermined, the standard tripartite "separation of powers" leaves the executive government bridging between a legislature that promulgates general forward-looking rules binding the public and a judiciary that interprets and applies the law, with finality, in particular cases. At one end of the spectrum, the legislature delivers, subject to constitutional constraints, most of the rules of the game (the laws of the land) for our collective life together, while at the other end the courts apply the law through fair procedures that respect our equality before the law. One is in essence political, while the other is meant to be the opposite.

[21] For a recent succinct summary of the contrasting histories and conceptions in France, Germany, UK, and US, see Mollers, *Three Branches*, chapter 1.1. For a broader conceptual genealogy, see Vile, *Constitutionalism*.

[22] Hamilton, Madison, and Jay, *Federalist*, No. 47.

[23] Montesquieu, *Spirit of the Laws*, which combines the value of balance (a descendant of mixed government) with partial separation, as discussed in Vile, *Constitutionalism*.

As the only 24/7 branch, the executive sits in between, administering the law in all the many millions of actions and choices that never end up in a courtroom; deciding which cases to take to court and subsequently enforcing the courts' decisions; increasingly through the twentieth century, fleshing out the law through regulations and ordinances; and, drawing on that rich experience, proposing initiatives or amendments to the legislature. Far from being mechanical, this catalog of functions entails discretionary choices and so policy making. In practice, even where not in concept, the executive is everywhere a hierarchy, with a boss (president or prime minister) at the top, whose general policy directs, steers, and maintains coherence across the executive branch as a whole, whether via direct decision, consultation, or the power of appointment/removal and therefore of patronage.

In terms of the received eighteenth- and nineteenth-century norms of constitutionalism, therefore, the most obvious thing about independent agencies is that they lie outside the executive hierarchy. That fragments power (good in terms of Madisonian values) but reduces the scope for executive coordination (bad in terms of welfarist efficiency).

Second, unlike noninsulated agencies, they cannot comfortably turn to elected politicians for day-to-day guidance on how to interpret or apply their mandate. Our Delegation Criteria and first Design Precept mitigate that by prescribing clear, monitorable objectives.

Third, in common with other parts of the administrative state, where they span legislative, executive, and adjudicatory functions they seem to challenge the Montesquieu-Madisonian value that control of all three should never lie in the same hands. As one leading scholar on the administrative state puts it:[24]

> Below the very apex of the governmental structure, the rigid . . . [doctrine] should be abandoned in favor of analysis in terms of separation of functions and checks and balances.

But there is a further thought, associating the separation of powers with the values of the rule of law by demanding:[25]

[24] Strauss, "Place of Agencies," p. 578.
[25] Waldron, "Separation of Powers in Thought," p. 467.

articulated government through successive phases of governance each of which maintains its own integrity.

For us, the idea is that citizens should be assured (and able to see) that each of the different steps in governance via independent agencies has integrity in its own right and also when taken together.[26] Chapter 11's robustness test of our Design Precepts must check whether they can deliver that.

THE RULE OF LAW AND INDEPENDENT-AGENCY REGIMES

In the introduction to part II, we argued that the derivative legitimacy of independent agencies would call upon a principle of transitivity: the values and beliefs that underpin the legitimacy of constitutional government cannot be violated by the delegation. Those values include the rule of law and, in some form, a separation of powers. It is striking that few attempts have been made to assess the administrative state as a whole against those values.[27]

One such value was a demand for rules that are legally binding only if generally applicable, transparent, and reasonably predictable in their application. While the laws that establish agencies are not general but specific, the underlying values plainly are transitive. We should want an IA's general policy making to be, in Fuller's terms, general (over the relevant domain), transparent, forward looking, as clear as possible, consistent, stable, and practicable.

When we turn to the fair-process conception of the rule of law, we need to pause because the very purpose of delegation is to change the institutional setting in which policy making, rule writing, and decision making occur. One possible starting point would be to stipulate that if

[26] The value accorded to, for example, the de facto separation of evidence gathering from prosecutorial decisions was apparent in the surprise of US commentators when, during the 2016 presidential election, the FBI seemed to preempt decisions formally belonging to the US Department of Justice.

[27] A notable exception is Kevin Stack, who, taking the work of Peter Strauss as a benchmark, has outlined what amounts to an audit of US administrative law against five precepts of the rule of law: authorization, notice, justification, coherence, and procedural fairness (Stack, "Administrative Jurisprudence"). The differences in my approach revolve, as discussed below, around (1) adding the demands of democracy and, in consequence, (2) distinguishing truly independent agencies from other organs of the administrative state. Also on the rule of law and the administrative state, see Dyzenhaus, *Constitution*, chapter 3.

an agency's functions are quasi-judicial, then its processes should be modeled closely on those of the courts; and if quasi-legislative, through the writing of legally binding rules, then its processes should be modeled on those of the legislature. But that line would seem to undermine the purpose of delegation: if the processes are to be substantively identical, why not leave the functions with the courts and legislature? Nevertheless, such reasoning goes some way to explain why, early in the twentieth century, US courts pushed administrative agencies to use court-like hearings when determining particular cases; and why, through the 1946 Administrative Procedures Act, Congress required "formal rule-making" to be conducted through hearings open to the public. But the very same Act's enabling provisions for (the unfortunately labeled) "informal" adjudication and "informal" rule making more than genuflected toward allowing departures from, respectively, court-like and parliamentary-like procedures (chapter 15).

Once that mental door is opened, it becomes apparent that it is the higher-level value of fair procedures that must be transitive; hence a century's worth of judicial and legislative lawmaking on standards for agency decision making and on the circumstances under which aggrieved parties can resort to the courts for redress or protection.

Administrative Law

That is the realm of administrative law, a vital part of public law and so of constitutionalism.[28] One of Dicey's core precepts was that government must be subject to the law. As has been said many times, by famously insisting that this be effected by the "ordinary courts," he muddled up the basic norm with its institutional form; other jurisdictions, most famously France, have separate court systems for private law and for public law given their particular histories. Elsewhere, Dicey focuses on his substantive precept that the rule of law is at odds with "the existence of arbitrariness, of prerogative, or even of wider discretionary authority on the part of government."[29]

[28] On the place of administrative law within constitutionalism, see Bremer, "Unwritten Administrative Constitution."

[29] Dicey, *Law of the Constitution*. The 1914 edition marks a changed view of the French system: quoted in Endicott, p. 480.

Modern formations discard the element of innocence in denying discretion in government (and the courts). As the late Lord Bingham put it shortly after stepping down from the UK's highest court, the elected executive branch and agencies "must exercise the powers conferred on them in good faith, fairly, for the purpose for which the powers were conferred, without exceeding the limits of such powers and not unreasonably."[30]

In most advanced-economy constitutional democracies, an aggrieved party might, as a broad generalization, be able to resort to the courts with a challenge to executive or administrative action based on any or all of the following:

- that the purported exercise of power lay beyond the boundaries of the delegated power (vires),
- that the power had been exercised in a way that did not comply with prescribed and fair procedures (natural justice or, in terms more familiar in the US, due process),
- that not all relevant or some irrelevant considerations had been taken into account, and
- that the power had been exercised in a deeply unfair or biased or unreasonable or irrational or disproportionate way.

At different times and speeds, the twentieth century saw a massive development of administrative law across the developed world and beyond. Of course there are variations and idiosyncrasies, some of which are important in part III, but taken as a whole rights of challenge along the lines listed above are widely regarded as essential to avoid the arbitrary exercise of administrative power. Furthermore, mobilizing one of the values of the separation of powers—checks and balances—judges or legislators have typically insisted upon a degree of separation between an agency's rule-making, general policy function, and its adjudicatory responsibilities.

[30]Bingham, *Rule of Law*, chapter 6, p. 60. Before heading the UK's highest court, then the Law Lords, Bingham was Master of the Rolls and then Lord Chief Justice, the only judge to have held all three positions. He was once described to me by a former judge as one of the two greatest British public officials since World War II; the other was the late Bank of England governor Eddie George.

Delegation-plus-Insulation under the Rule of Law

All that applies, however, to the parts of the elected executive and to agencies that are *not* fully insulated from day-to-day politics. We are concerned with *delegation-plus-insulation*.[31] This drives some requirements that do not typically feature in the administrative law of the major jurisdictions. In particular, our third Design Precept demands that an independent agency publish the *operating principles* that guide its exercise of delegated discretion, among other things making clear where (and why) it plans to implement policy through rules or case-by-case application of a standard. That matters when an agency is insulated from day-to-day politics and, furthermore, is likely to be accorded respect by the courts by virtue of the gravity or socioeconomic significance of its mandate. Most significantly, the Principles for Delegation demand that an IA regime operate with a clear purpose and a monitorable objective (or standard), consistent with the formalist version of rule-of-law values with which we began. Clearly, however, that requirement is not addressed to the agency itself but to legislators.

When it comes to insulated IA regimes, therefore, due process and other administrative law constraints on *how* an agency operates cannot suffice. Administrative law can at best mitigate flaws in the design or operation of delegations that flout or stretch our values. On the more basic issue, we are into the realm of higher law and constitutional conventions, facing questions of whether powers may be delegated to agencies at all, may (or even must) be delegated only on certain conditions, and who decides.

SUBSTANTIVE CONSTITUTIONAL PROVISION FOR IA REGIMES

As we explore in part III, very few jurisdictions make express provision for the administrative state in their basic law or conventions; and where (as in Germany) they do, administration is sometimes put under ministerial control, apparently precluding IA regimes (chapter 13). Typically, therefore, the permissibility of the regulatory state and degrees of insulation have become matters of interpretation and interpolation.

[31] Thanks to Kevin Stack for urging me to emphasize this.

What, though, of the underlying values of constitutionalism? In particular, should citizens have any rights that could be delivered or safeguarded only through delegation to arm's-length decision makers? That, of course, generates wildly different answers.

Buchanan on the Need for a Monetary Constitution

The late US public-choice theorist James Buchanan called for a polity's monetary regime to have constitutional status. Viewing day-to-day politics as mired in a battle of interests and normal administrative policy making as polluted by the self-interest of bureaucrats and their clients, Buchanan argued that priority should rationally be given to constitutional entrenchment of property rights and similarly embedded rules-based fiscal regimes. He accordingly held that stability in the value of money should be incorporated into the Hobbesian concept of "security" provided by a sovereign state, enabling efficient economic transactions.[32] For not dissimilar reasons, but with more of an eye to political freedoms, European ordo-liberals demanded embedded rules of the game to frame the market economy and thus for an insulated competition authority. This line of thought is central to part IV (chapter 20).

Late in his life, Buchanan conceded his position was instrumental, motivated by a conviction that people would be better off if certain rules of economic life could be put beyond the reach of normal politics.[33] Much the same applies on the other side of the debate. Whereas Buchanan, and before him Hayek, prioritize rights designed to prevent the state from interfering in market-based choices, progressive liberals advocate rights intended to protect individuals from each other and, thus, from what they might refer to as untrammeled market forces, with the state as agent in administering those protections.[34]

[32]Buchanan, "Constitutionalization of Money." This is a cleaner statement of similar views expressed in earlier papers. Hobbes is explicitly recruited to the constitutionalist liberal cause. For Buchanan, the written constitution seems to play the role of Hobbes's unitary "sovereign," even though the constitution constrains the laws rather than delivers them.

[33]Buchanan and Musgrave, *Public Finance*.

[34]In the British literature, Harlow and Rawlings, *Law and Administration*, distinguish between "red light" and "green light" variants of public law, the former constraining the state in the spirit of classical liberalism, the latter enabling it in the spirit of mid-twentieth-century social democracy. By contrast, US progressive liberals have tended to focus on civil rights rather

Once that is clear, disagreements about the catalog of entrenched rights and practices take on their true complexion: as battles to lock substantive conceptions of politics—of the good life and justice—into constitutional law or conventions. The significance for us, exploring whether there is a place for IA regimes without committing ourselves to a substantive creed, is (a) where the order of things gets determined, since that will fix who (judges or elected politicians) settles the place of agencies in the state structure; and, as we proceed to part III, (b) whether the incentives ingrained in institutional structures are aligned with political values.

LEGAL VERSUS POLITICAL CONSTITUTIONALISM: ADMINISTRATION UNDER JUDGES OR POLITICS?

A parting of the ways seems to come in whether constraints on the state, whatever their substance, are codified in a written constitution, find expression in common law, or are embedded in conventions of political life. The first is the dominant form of *legal constitutionalism*, the last a form of *political constitutionalism* through which the people's representatives exercise restraint under soft law and a watchful people.[35]

Formally, the vital distinction is that under both variants of legal constitutionalism, but not under political constitutionalism, the judges are empowered to strike out legislation that violates a higher law.[36] That is not to say, however, that legislators have free rein in polities without judicial review of legislation, since courts might construe statutes so as

than socioeconomic welfare, which might leave them closer to classical liberals once the rights they seek became embedded.

[35] Bellamy, *Political Constitutionalism*.

[36] Long before the new constitutionalism, England's common law acted as a check on English government without formally having the final word on legislation. "Common law constitutionalism," a recent movement distinctive to England and a few similar jurisdictions, holds broadly that the courts could strike out legislation that violated ancient rights, on the basis of the somewhat controversial doctrine that parliamentary supremacy is sourced in the common law and, thus, a gift of the judges. Where people stand on this bizarre but, for Britain, possibly important debate seems often to turn on which end of England's ghastly seventeenth century one prefers. I say less in the main text about common law constitutionalism as its academic and judicial proponents have generally had little to say about the structure of delegation within the administrative state. See Laws, *Common Law Constitution*, and, on the other side, Goldsworthy, *Parliamentary Sovereignty*.

to be consistent with embedded rule-of-law values. Nor is the only constraint in polities with a written constitution the basic law itself.

This is sometimes articulated in the proposition that our societies' legal systems amount to more than a combination of overtly constitutional provisions and ordinary statutes. Rather, it is suggested that, in addition to some uncontroversial but uncodified legal norms, there are some *super-statutes* that are quasi-constitutional insofar as the fabric of the society's way of life would be fundamentally changed were they to be repealed.[37]

There is something to this. Even where, as in the UK, a supreme parliament could in theory repeal any statute, that does not mean the legislature could get away with it. It would be really quite something to try to repeal, for example, those parts of the 1701 Act of Settlement, which, after nearly a century of struggle, enshrined judicial independence by protecting the top judges from being sacked at the king's pleasure. And, in the US, repealing the Federal Reserve Act *without putting anything in its place* would be a constitutional adventure, leaving the country's monetary regime adrift (chapter 12).

Addressing the narrower question of when common law courts might be able to strike out legislation, Lord Justice Laws, quoted with approval extrajudicially by Lord Phillips when president of the UK's Supreme Court, described a "constitutional statute" as one that[38]

> (a) conditions the legal relationship between citizen and state in some general, overarching, manner, or (b) enlarges or diminishes the scope of what we would now regard as fundamental constitutional rights.

Irrespective of the context of those remarks and of whether the English judges do have that power, these seem like good tests for whether a *long-lived* statute is likely to be deeply embedded in public beliefs about decent government, with a high de facto barrier to repeal. All of which is to say that, under political constitutionalism, the legislature is not unconstrained; and that, under legal constitutionalism, the courts are liable to err if inattentive to deeply embedded public values and associated

[37] Eskridge and Ferejohn, "Super-Statutes." For criticism of a later book version, see Vermeule, "Super-Statutes."

[38] Lord Phillips, president of the Supreme Court, quoting Lord Justice Laws in *Thorburn v. Sunderland City Council*, a judgment from 2003 (Phillips, "Art of the Possible").

expectations. No polity manifests a pure form of legal or political constitutionalism: some deeply embedded statutory regimes are akin to the constitutional conventions or norms that inhabit a space between politics and law (and some of which can in practice become incorporated into law over time). Legislators need to be attentive to the values of the law, and public law is part of politics.[39]

Contemplating the administrative state, and IAs in particular, through the lens of constitutionalism ends up, therefore, taking us to questions about the role of judges in democracies.

Judges as Guardians of Constitutional Integrity: The Problem of the Infinite Regress

The separation of powers in a constitutional democracy gives the independent judiciary a central role in the life of its citizens under the administrative state. For some, this is absolutely consistent with our deepest political values. Accepting and embracing the inevitability of judicial interpretation, the late US- and UK-based legal philosopher Ronald Dworkin argued—somewhat clumsily unless he really meant it—for "those with better views, or who can argue more cogently, [having] more influence."[40] In a similar spirit, Rawls identifies the US Supreme Court as the exemplar of "public reason," the only means through which legitimate law and public policy could be made.[41] While others argue that handing judges (some of) the most important and, probably, contentious value judgments confronting society is a violation of the spirit of democracy, the fact is that in many constitutional democracies—perhaps most notably Germany and the US—that is exactly their role.[42]

[39]For a particular version of that thesis, centered on underpinning the state, see Loughlin, *Idea of Public Law*; more generally, Elliot and Feldman, *Cambridge Companion*. On conventions, see Barber, *Constitutional State*, chapters 5 and 6.

[40]Dworkin, *Freedom's Law*, p. 27.

[41]Rawls, *Political Liberalism*. It is, for me, a truly remarkable view given the opaque insider-code language that a constitutional court must often use when it decides moral issues.

[42]The greater the scope of constitutional rights (e.g., socioeconomic welfare), the more they have to be balanced against each other, potentially leaving the courts making trade-offs among public policy objectives typically associated with the democratic assembly. Critics of judicial power over legislatures include Bellamy, *Political Constitutionalism*, and most notably Waldron, "Case against Judicial Review."

As we said in chapter 4, this makes judges into *guardians*, standing far higher than trustees for laws that the legislative assembly may change.

But creating independent agencies, insulated from day-to-day politics, is an act of politics. The political community needs some way of monitoring whether its delegated monitor (the judiciary) is conducting itself as intended. The conduct of the judges in adjudicating cases against the delegation of power or its exercise must itself meet standards of legitimacy. But who is to say whether they rise to that? In the question famously posed by the Roman satirical poet Juvenal sometime around the reign of the emperor Adriano (Hadrian): who guards the guardians?

This appears to be an infinite regress. It reminds us that in democracies all institutions hang in the air unless they have public support or acceptance.

LEGALITY DOES NOT SUFFICE FOR LEGITIMACY

We can now pull together the threads running through this chapter.

If the application of our rule-of-law values were in practice limited to questions of due process (fairness), prioritizing openness, and petitioning by interested parties, something precious would be lost. This was exactly the complaint half a century ago of Theodore Lowi, quoted at the head of this chapter, when he lamented that US judges were underpinning a form of interest-group bargaining that abandoned the need for a legislated standard or objective. In democracies, that is especially problematic for agency regimes insulated from day-to-day political control (chapter 11).

The New Few: Central Bankers, Regulators, and Judges

At other times and places, the judges go further, either openly getting into substance or using procedural diktat to push agencies toward their preferred positions on public policy.[43]

Where the public and the judges acquiesce in shirking by the legislative assembly (see part III on the US), technocrats or judges become the

[43] Shapiro, *Who Guards the Guardians?*

policy makers in a new version of Aristotle's mixed constitution: the one, in the form of a powerful president or prime minister (and his or her narrow circle of helpers); the many, being the people and their relatively passive representatives in the legislature; and, in Ferdinand Mount's words, a *new few*, in the form of leaders of the administrative state.[44]

If that is indeed how things stand today, all that has changed over the centuries since the Enlightenment is a shift in unelected state power from a hereditary aristocracy to a meritocratic and technocratic judicial, central banking, and regulatory class. Rather than late-nineteenth-century America's system of parties and courts, this would be a system of agencies and courts: precisely the problem of technocracy posed in the book's introduction.

Central Banks Need the Delegation Criteria

Our quest for legitimation conditions can arrive at essentially the same place by asking whether legality suffices. Plainly, the rule of law and constitutionalism demand that the machinery of government—such as independent agencies—must comply with any basic law and constitutional conventions, codified or not. Some—perhaps in the US, many—scholars and commentators would stop there: if government structure X is OK under the constitution, then it is legitimate. I reject that view, and the rather narrow conception of the authority of democratic governance that it draws upon and fosters.

It merely relocates the legitimacy issue to whether a constitution's provisions, as construed and applied by a constitutional court (and other actors), are in accord with society's values. A written constitution does, of course, play a significant role in shaping, structuring, and sustaining beliefs and values.[45] But it would be far-fetched to claim that the direction of causation never runs the other way. The norms and beliefs that underpin society's conception of legitimate government quietly

[44] Mount, *New Few.* His new elite includes business and elected politicians. I refer more narrowly to unelected holders of de jure state power.

[45] Graber, *American Constitutionalism.* Some authors (e.g., Dyzenhaus) use "legality" to connote lawfulness that squares with rule-of-law values. I use the term more narrowly, as the values are better seen as informing or comprising conditions for legitimacy, which in our societies include but are not limited to the rule of law.

change over time, with the more important changes gradually reflected in constitutional interpretation and/or amendments. That is no less true for legitimate state structures, which must somehow both respect the law and track evolving values and expectations.[46] Our inquiry must, then, engage with the values that have come down to us from constitutional government as conceived in the eighteenth-century's commercial liberal (but not democratic) republics.[47]

Our Delegation Criteria are partly the result of such engagement. By demanding that any IA regime be framed with a clear purpose and monitorable objective, they more than genuflect toward the rule-of-law values of generality, predictability, transparency, and comprehensibility. The people need to know what they are meant to be getting and to have reasonable assurance that that is what they will, in fact, get. Some of the Design Precepts then come in behind to underpin a demand for fair processes. In language familiar to American readers, this amounts to a nondelegation doctrine (chapter 14).

But that cannot be enough *for us*, citizens of democracies. The rule of law and constitutionalism do not exhaust our political values. While central banks and their regulatory cousins can be challenged in the courts, they must pass a greater test. Constitutional *democracy* requires us to contemplate what democracy is and means, and whether its distinctive values can accommodate insulated policy making.

[46] I take that to be the central message about former US Supreme Court Chief Justice Hughes in Ernst, *Toqueville's Nightmare*.

[47] Sagar, "Istvan Hont."

9

Independent Agencies and Our Political Values and Beliefs (2)

THE CHALLENGES TO DELEGATION-WITH-INSULATION PRESENTED BY DEMOCRACY

> A representative democracy, where the right of election is well secured and regulated & the exercise of the legislative, executive and judiciary authorities, is vested in select persons, chosen really and not nominally by the people, will in my opinion be most likely to be happy, regular and durable.
>
> —Alexander Hamilton to Gouverneur Morris, May 19, 1777[1]

> No government by experts in which the masses do not have the chance to inform the experts of their needs can be anything but an oligarchy managed in the interests of the few.
>
> —John Dewey, *The Public and Its Problems*[2]

As history shows, liberals were not always quick to embrace franchise reform, and their misgivings persist even today.[3] Some see in democracy the shadow of unconstrained *populism*. The majority might oppress a structural minority, today's citizens might make choices that impoverish future generations, or they might undermine or revoke essential political and civil "rights." Hayek was open about this, explicitly rejecting "current majority opinion as the only criterion of the legitimacy of the powers of government".[4] On the other side of liberal politics, echoes can sometimes be found in the followers of Rawls. Democracy

[1]Letter from Alexander Hamilton to Gouverneur Morris, May, 19, 1777, US National Archives, *Founders Online*.

[2]Dewey, *Public and Its Problems*, p. 208.

[3]"Political Democracy: Liberal Resistance to Suffrage Extension," chapter 6.i of Fawcett, *Liberalism*; and, from a different perspective, Muller, *Contesting Democracy*, chapter 1.

[4]Hayek, "Liberalism," p. 143.

becomes a means for individuals to exercise their sovereignty in the political arena as citizens, through the formation of law, but only *within limits*. This is a worldview into which expert independent agencies, insulated from the popular swirl, can find a comfortable and valued place. For others, however, it raises the risk of a technocracy-led undemocratic liberalism. This chapter begins the process of exploring whether IA regimes can be squared with our democratic traditions and values.

DEMOCRACY AND THE AUTHORITY OF LAW

The previous chapter's exploration of what distinguishes rule *of* law from rule *by* law, and how it constrains IA regimes, did not offer an account of the resilience of law's authority. If it relies upon people believing in the legitimacy of the laws in general (in the source of lawmaking), democracy shifts the grounds for such beliefs.

Democracy can make the law *our* law in some sense. Approaching legitimacy as a property of institutions that turns on standards internal to our way of life—legitimacy *for us*—the sustained authority of law, including any basic law, notwithstanding occasional and sometimes persistent government failure, is partly derivative of the legitimacy of democracy.[5]

Marking a departure from predemocratic constitutional liberalism, this poses different demands on independent-agency regimes. For liberalism, legislation (or state action more broadly) is illegitimately coercive if it crosses the boundaries of our rights: rights that might be conceived as lying in the natural order of things, as rooted in our inherent worth, or merely as whatever are stipulated under constitutional norms. For modern republicanism, by contrast, the coercive and normative state can be justified only if we, the people, can somehow control the making of laws, so that legitimate force can be used only to enforce *our* laws and policies: liberty lies in being our own legislators.[6] For many, those thoughts lie deep in our convictions about democracy.

[5]This is quite different from accounts of authority that rest on its instrumental value alone (that it seems to work). Having discovered he took a similar view, I am grateful to Scott Hershovitz for exchanges during a visit to Michigan University and since. See Hershovitz, "Legitimacy, Democracy," which was responding to Joseph Raz's view of authority as, for example, in Raz, *Morality of Freedom*.

[6]For this ideal in republican Rome, see Beard, *SPQR*, chapter 4.

The Central Banking and Independent Regulator Challenge to Democracy's Value

This helps to resolve the age-old problem of "Who guards the guardians?" which runs wider and deeper than the previous chapter's question of how we monitor the quality of judicial "oversight" of the administrative state. Not all misuses of power are illegal. If agency leaders bluff their way into office or later wander off the ranch, exploiting ambiguities in the law (chapter 4), somebody needs to check what's what. Our elected representatives! But then who checks up on the political checkers, since they might shirk too? Is the only solution to the infinite regress the virtue of our leaders, as Plato has Socrates and Glaucon argue over in *The Republic*?

The general answer is that a political community is its own watchdog. For a predemocratic state, the solution lies in the mutualized monitoring of an oligarchic elite that stands to gain from the stability and prosperity that staying faithful to the "rules of the game" is expected to bring; for that reason, even a king had to carry his courtiers.[7] That hardly works once the whole adult population are enfranchised as citizens, since their interests might diverge from those of a governing elite. Democracy creates a world in which the people themselves can monitor and hold accountable their governors.[8]

The central question of this book, then, is whether central banks and other insulated, truly independent agencies escape that precious process, perhaps even being designed to do so. If that were so, how could delegation square with our democratic values?

In clearing the path toward an answer, this chapter unpacks democracy's different modes, justifications, and values, emphasizing public debate and challenge as well as competitive elections. Independent-agency regimes depart from our societies' usual standards of responsiveness, participation, and representation, leaving central banks and other IAs facing the possibility of a "democratic deficit" with many facets. Reflecting that, the chapter piles up the concerns that the Principles for Delegation need to meet. It argues that, in prioritizing the values of direct

[7] For an essay on the evolution of self-monitoring, see Greif, "Impact of Administrative Power."

[8] For discussions of this by "mechanism design" economists, see Hurwicz, "Guard the Guardians?," and Myerson, "Fundamental Theory."

democracy, something is missing in those solutions focused on public participation in rule making and other policy choices. Representative democracy demands more.

CONCEPTIONS OF DEMOCRACY

Although there are different conceptions of democracy, they invariably share the view that democracy is fundamentally about each member of a political community having, in some sense, an equal say in its governance and equal opportunities to exercise that say. Flipping coins to decide political questions might be fair (in a different sense), but it does not give people a say. An important source of the concerns around the legitimacy of independent-agency regimes is, then, how people can be said to have an "equal say" in those parts of government.

I start with the most basic elements of democracy before turning to the specificities of *representative* democracy.[9]

Democracy as Voting

The most familiar *conception* of democracy is centered on making political decisions via a system of voting: each person has one vote with which to register or express their preferences (whether as electors or legislators), and the result is determined by aggregating the votes in some way. A person's vote might reflect a sense of their own individual interests or those of a group with which they identify, or it might reflect their beliefs about the common good. Different people might be motivated differently, but the essence is that collective decisions are made by voting.

There are two variants of this first conception. The first drills down into the idea, going back at least to Rousseau, that democracy is a means for *aggregating* preferences or views on the political choices facing a

[9] Some of the discussion has elements in common with Ober, *Demopolis*, which came out as my book was going into production, except that he is engaged in a thought experiment about the conditions under which a group wishing to avoid autocracy would embark upon and be able to sustain basic democracy. By contrast, I am interested in what can be inferred about legitimation conditions from the opinions citizens might hold given how, in actual advanced-economy democracies, we talk and write about democracy, whether it arose from singular historical events (Germany) or evolved step by step (Britain).

community. If this can be accomplished in a way that reveals *the General Will*, all is well. More prosaically, if administrative power is to be delegated, we need a rigorous mechanism for determining a social welfare function that everyone can accept (chapter 3).

In the middle of the twentieth century, however, Kenneth Arrow demonstrated that, analytically, it is impossible to square democracy, as opposed to dictatorship, with a series of apparently innocuous prerequisites for collective decision making, including consistency, the contemplation of all conceivable options, and a person's choice between two options being unaffected by other options.[10] This generalized a phenomenon identified two hundred years earlier by French political economist Nicolas de Condorcet: that individual preferences can be such that there is a majority for A over B and B over C, but also for C over A, leaving the electorate locked into a never-ending cycle.

Fortified by a battery of further analytical "impossibility results" on collective decision making, this intellectual juncture caused degrees of panic and delight in different parts of the academy, as it seemed to show that democracy cannot be relied upon to track the people's collective purposes. Here, it was said, was the basis for preferring constrained liberal democracy over democratic populism, and also for prioritizing choice via competitive markets over choice via politics given Kenneth Arrow's parallel welfare theorems (chapter 3).

Needless to say, democracy carried on oblivious. Maybe that was because we do not expect to have *all* conceivable options on the table when choices are made. Democracies try things out in the firm expectation that experience will reveal options that had been obscured or ignored.[11]

[10] Arrow, "Concept of Social Welfare." Arrow approached the question by stipulating a set of conditions (axioms) that any legitimate procedure of social choice would need to meet. Loosely, these amounted to some "democratic" conditions, such as that if every citizen prefers x to y, then so does society, and that the SWF is not determined by an umpire or "dictator"; together with some "logical" or informational constraints, such as preferences being formed over all possible states (completeness) and preferences between (fully specified) states x and y not depending on anything else (independence). Arrow demonstrated that, on those *apparently* benign assumptions about prerequisites for legitimate, rational social choice, it cannot be done: the ranked preferences of a set of individuals cannot reliably be translated into ranked aggregate social preferences.

[11] A broader point is that fixing the axioms of any preference aggregation procedure is itself properly a matter of social choice, reflecting how we think about democracy. The axiomatic enterprise would work to ground legitimacy only if a choice procedure were feasible and also em-

In that spirit, the less analytical variant of the voting conception of democracy sees it as a way of making fallible, for-the-time-being choices in the face of disagreement, with the prospect of those choices being revisited down the road in light of experience or swings in public opinion. There is no General Will, just a way of living together. Faced with persistent, frustrated disagreement due to conflicting values, which political theorist Jeremy Waldron calls *the circumstances of politics*, we hold elections and accept the outcome, until next time. [12]

The implication for our inquiry is that resorting to IA regimes as commitment devices could look like an illegitimate way of permanently side-stepping disagreement (chapter 10).

Democracy as Talking: Public Reason versus Debate

Over the past few decades, responding to prevalent tensions among the deeply held values of different communities in "pluralist" developed economies, some writers have articulated an alternative, *deliberative* conception of democracy. According to this view, the essence of democracy lies not in voting but in reasoned debate among members of the political community. Compared with the preference-aggregation conception of democracy, here the "equal say" comes via a capacity for any citizen to contribute equally to the outcome of talking together.

An idealized version of this account holds that, in a properly democratic society, each member has an opportunity to participate in deliberation and that everyone puts aside the deep issues, beliefs, doctrines, or interests that divide them, giving each other's reasons equal respect in striving to find common ground when making political choices. Under those conditions, political decisions would be grounded in reasons that all *could* accept (or that none could reject) as opposed to agree with. Following John Rawls, this has become known as the *liberal principle of legitimacy*.[13]

---

ployed, recursively, to select its own axioms: that is, the decision procedure stipulated by a constitution was used to select itself.

[12] Waldron, *Law and Disagreement*, chapter 5.

[13] For example, Joshua Cohen, a leading deliberative democracy theorist, stipulated that "outcomes are democratically legitimate if and only if they *could* be the object of free and reasoned agreement among equals" (Cohen, "Deliberation and Democratic Legitimacy," p. 73. (Later in the same piece Cohen observes that consensus will not always be reached even under

Whereas Rawls seems to restrict the precept to the rules of the game for politics (constitutional norms), his European counterpart Juergen Habermas goes further, extending essentially the same requirement to regular laws: "only those statutes may claim legitimacy that can meet with the assent of all citizens in a discursive process of legislation."[14] Habermas has a point insofar as there is no nicely principled dividing line between constitutional and ordinary politics: on which side does a decision to delegate powers to our independent agencies lie? His argument might, furthermore, have force if we were to equate legitimacy with an "obligation to obey" each and every law rather than, as posited in the introduction to part II, with accepting the right of the state to enforce the law and an obligation not to undermine the edifice as a whole. Instead, however, the effect of his extension is to alert us to the test's fragility. In any *actual* public policy debate there *are* people who disagree; for example, as we know from part I, some people oppose delegation to independent agencies in general and others oppose specific delegations.

But the proposed test is not about actual consent or agreement. It is hypothetical; the consent or agreement that *ought* to be given, as the basis for an ethical politics, according to the light of reason. The "General Will" reborn as the "General Ought," the deliberative turn takes the Kantian umpire to be an idealized standard for public debate.

This is not going to get us far with the question of IA regime legitimacy. Who is to say whether the opponents of such regimes "could" have agreed if only there had been free and reasoned deliberation in which rival conceptions of life had been put to one side? "The Federal Reserve is legitimate because you would have agreed if only you had been 'reasonable'": try that on former congressman Ron Paul!

Indeed, far from helping us, this is uncomfortably close to the perceived ethic of elite technocracy that comprises one of the core criticisms of IA regimes: a strain of liberalism for sure, but with democracy diluted. Nevertheless, the value of deliberation, in the sense of rich and open public debate, is part of *our* idea of a healthy democracy. Giving

"ideal conditions" and so voting might be entailed.) This puts into "deliberative space" Rawls's legitimacy test: "political power is fully proper only when it is exercised in accordance with a constitution the essentials of which all citizens as free and equal may reasonably be expected to endorse in the light of principles and ideals acceptable to their common human reason" (Rawls, *Political Liberalism*, p. 137).

[14] Habermas, *Between Facts and Norms*, p. 110.

people a decent say—by identifying, explaining, and, where we can, setting aside irrelevant deep differences—can help to get better results and, hence, to sustain us as a political community.[15] Not hypothetically but in reality, this is how views on political institutions and norms are forged, refined, and challenged. It is associated with our demand for reasons to justify public policy and the value to us of debating those reasons.[16]

This suggests that where technocratic institutions, such as IA regimes, are designed to solve commitment problems, the reasons of different parties for going along with them need not be the same but cannot materially conflict, since otherwise a functioning institutional design would not be feasible: precisely the spirit of our robustness test of the Principles for Delegation. In addition, however, since disagreement in some things will persist, periodic reviews of delegated regimes are useful to check that support for or acquiescence in our particular institutions of government are not taken for granted.[17]

This view of reasoned, respectful debate accords with the value of votes being used to resolve important political differences and disagreements for the time being. If agreement or consensus, whether reasoned or not, cannot be reached, democracies still have to make decisions, and voting makes that possible.[18] What's more, whereas a voting system can be enshrined in law, it is not so easy to make fair and reasoned deliberation an enforceable right. But debate—publicly and within political parties—is vital to determining and framing the propositions to be voted upon, making consistent choices easier to reach. These points are missing from part I's initial articulation of the Principles, and so we return to them below (chapter 11).

[15] This is distinct from the nonideal conditions approach, in Gutmann and Thompson's *Democracy and Disagreement*, of seeking consensus in reasons espoused by participants.

[16] Some radical theorists on the Left have embraced something like this, arguing that there is not a pristine, interests-free "rationality" out there to frame reasoned debate and that power relations suffuse and partly construct all social relations and conventions; they seek to reground and reenergize ideological politics within a shared culture of toleration—adversaries rather than enemies. See Mouffe, "Deliberative Democracy," which, interestingly, draws on the English conservative political theorist Michael Oakeshott.

[17] This fits with the broad alignment of our approach to legitimacy with that of Bernard Williams. Periodic debate about our institutions contributes to meeting his *Critical Theory Principle*: that the reasons people offer themselves and each other for our constitutional/institutional setup are reasons they are free to examine critically, at least from time to time (Williams, *In the Beginning*).

[18] As recognized in Habermas, *Facts and Norms*, p. 306.

Democracy as Challenge, and as Watching

For *participatory democrats* on the Left, however, no deliberative version of democracy involves the people enough, in practice leaving public policy to a self-sustaining elite, subject only to an occasional vote on which party governs. Where this leads is unclear. Simply advocating ground-level civic or economic democracy leaves hanging in the air how any national policy making is to be delivered and consistency achieved (the Party?).[19] While participatory democrats press an important point about public life, in the context of the administrative state it could amount to seeing *participation* as a substitute for *representation* (see below).

More generally, however, a conception of democracy as "debate and vote" does risk missing something important: *challenge*. With neither an unchallengeable General Will nor General Ought available, accountability becomes vital. As argued in the introduction to part II, we must distinguish between challenges *within* the norms of a polity (and so accepting enforcement of the laws) and extralegal challenges *to* those norms. Republican theorists place great weight on the former kind of contestability. Certainly, any conception of democracy would be thin without conventions and avenues of challenge to government measures, politically and legally.[20]

The resulting package—voting, debating, and challenging—gets us closer to how democracy provides its own solution to the infinite regress of "who guards the guardians?" Everyone can watch and, having watched, complain, protest, mobilize, and vote. This is *democracy as watchfulness*: contingently active watchfulness. It is what is going on when we say anything along the lines of, "Hey, you're not bothering to implement law Y," or, more topically for us, "Hey, you [an IA] are meant to think and act independently."

[19] For an account of the radical aims of some "participatory democrats," see Zolo, *Democratic Complexity*, chapter 3.

[20] Jumping ahead a bit, this avoids concluding that if democracy is warranted by equal political respect, then a person would fail to respect her peers if she refused to obey some laws, a view that seems to be espoused in Christiano, *Constitution of Equality*, chapter 6. On the view adopted here, disrespect of fellow citizens *would* be entailed by resisting or, more broadly, not cooperating generally with a democratic state legitimized by citizens' opinions and conduct.

It is absolutely vital to legitimating the administrative state. Making the institutions of democracy *incentive-compatible* demands that independent (and other) agencies be transparent, so that groups and individuals can see what is going on without being drowned in noise.

JUSTIFICATIONS OF DEMOCRACY

That brief survey of different conceptions of democracy tells us something important about our quest. Unless we can find a role for voting, public debate, challenge, and watchful accountability in our account of central banking and other IA regimes, we shall have fallen short of what we need for legitimation. But there is something even more pressing: that the *justification for democracy itself* should not be undermined by delegation to trustee-like agencies. Exploring this begins to reveal the core of our problem.

We have seen that neither of the two main conceptions of democracy—voting and deliberation—can be self-legitimating, through the exercise of rational calculus or higher reason alone. We might think this refreshing: legitimacy cannot come from the schoolroom, whether economics (chapter 3) or philosophy, but only from us. The basis for legitimation must be found in the actual values and beliefs embedded in our liberal democratic republics.

There are two quite different kinds of justification for democracy: intrinsic and instrumental.[21] It does not seem much to venture that each is given weight among members of the community, especially as they are not as neatly compartmentalized as they might at first seem.

The Intrinsic Warrant for Democracy

The intrinsic justification is that, for some people, support for democracy and the source of its resilient authority lies in its expressing and constituting values they hold dear, such as political freedom and/or po-

[21]For example, Anderson, "Democracy," and Arneson, "Supposed Right," both contained in Christiano and Christman, *Contemporary Debates.*

litical equality. This would tend to put procedural fairness in the foreground: democracy as what gives meaning to our being politically free (or equal) in the sense of together making laws and rules for living together.

Lest it seem fanciful that anyone would hold to such a view, imagine two worlds, with different political systems but in which all socioeconomic outcomes are always identical. A Hobbesian Welfarist would rank them equally: we should support whichever one we happen to be in. But now it is revealed that one is a democracy, and the other a benign dictatorship. Perhaps some people remain indifferent, but I would hazard that some do not. It matters to some people how the political choices that generate the resulting outcomes are reached. If they reject the perfect benign dictatorship, they are affirming something about the value to them of some combination of participating, choosing, rejecting, changing minds, and learning alongside or in trusting competition with citizen peers. People who place great weight on this justification might well look askance at independent central banks and regulators.

Instrumental Justification

The other type of justification is *instrumental*, turning on the practical results that democratic government does or can over time realistically deliver. On this view, relative to other ways of organizing politics, such as monarchy or oligarchy, democracy is warranted if it provides the best means for obtaining society's most basic goals (Churchill's point). On the assumptions implicit in chapter 3, the relevant goal would be socioeconomic welfare, but an instrumental justification for democracy need not be limited to that. Whatever the conception of the "good" that people carry around, democracy is justified because, in their view, it is best at delivering or promoting that good.

Thus, even if intrinsic justifications of democracy do not make sense to some people, they may nevertheless see democracy's warrant as lying in its promotion of political freedom or political respect for all. As for those who prioritize socioeconomic welfare, the key thing is that the idea of what is good is independent of democracy's procedures and qualities.

Time horizons might be quite long. Someone might believe that their family, group, class, or society as a whole will be better off in the longer run by virtue of the way a democratic republic can combine basic stability with a capacity for altering the course of public policy in the light of results. For that reason, occasional and even, up to a point, persistent poor government performance would not rob the system of government of its authority.

Views on the source of those instrumental merits might vary according to which broad conception of democracy someone holds. Thus, a deliberative democratist might hold that democracy works because of its "epistemic" qualities, for example, via bringing many voices and perspectives to debates, helping to avoid "groupthink" and overreliance on technical experts, and so on.[22] An alternative view, most famously associated with the mid-twentieth-century political economist Joseph Schumpeter, might see democracy's instrumental edge as based on electoral competition between parties, factions, and points of view, the contest turning on who does best at detaching floating voters from their habits or group loyalties.[23] These two schools would apply very different legitimation standards to IA regimes, as chapter 11 lays bare.

More generally, democracy's instrumental worth might lie in its capacity for government by "trial and error": being able to change course relatively easily when something seems not to be working. This is a characteristic of democratic governance that, to my mind, is not stressed enough. It points to flaws in the story of democracy's warrant lying in its delivery of procedure-independent goals, and presents a particular challenge to delegation-with-insulation.

The notion that our goals are independent of democracy's processes pretty obviously has a lot going for it when it comes to the biggest tasks of government summarized in chapter 3, such as avoiding or containing the great disasters that can afflict us: war, famine, political collapse, complete economic collapse. Indeed, some maintain that democracy is justified and widely supported precisely because of its record, relative to nondemocratic societies, on exactly those fronts.[24]

[22] That, broadly, is the view advanced in Estlund, *Democratic Authority*.

[23] Schumpeter, *Capitalism, Socialism & Democracy*.

[24] Amartya Sen has famously said that no established democracy has ever suffered a major famine (Sen, *Development as Freedom*). The broader point is also made in Estlund, *Democratic Authority*.

But the last example in that list should give us a jab in the ribs given the circumstances in which this book is being written and read: the aftermath of a financial crisis in which economic collapse was, in 2008–2009, only just averted and following which economic performance has been staggeringly weak by modern standards. Recurrent episodes of financial instability of greater or lesser gravity suggest that even the most mature democracies are as capable of conjuring up some kinds of crisis as they are at improvising to get themselves out of the mess before it undermines constitutional government itself.[25] Perhaps that predilection lies in democracy's capacity to satisfy a desire for pleasure today, while hoping for the best for tomorrow.

For our purposes, that points toward two related issues: first, whether democracy can on some fronts best pursue our ends through binding itself to a particular goal or course (the subject of the next chapter); and second, the importance of distinguishing the great issues of security, stability, and famine from other things. For much of what governments, and especially administrative-state agencies, do day to day, the activity and projects take shape only through the democratic process and remain the subject of ongoing public and political discussion.

In thinking of democracy as proceeding by trial and error, this amounts not only to testing out the *means* of achieving fixed or given ends but also to exploring, reviewing, and revising those ends, objectives, goals. It takes us away from an instrumental justification of democracy thought of exclusively in terms of its epistemic qualities: how well democracy does at delivering laws and other policies that match an external (objective or procedure-independent) standard. This is not analogous to the jury system in criminal trials tending to get things right on average over time. It is instead about, for *some* areas of public policy, *producing* our standards of "goodness" or "rightness" through a democratic process of continuing debate and periodic voting.[26]

For those, like John Dewey, quoted at the chapter head, who see democracy's value as lying in those kinds of value-generating processes, the whole point is to decide together through debate and procedures for resolving disagreements what government should try to do (and not do).

[25] A theme of Runciman, *Confidence Trap*. On democracy's possible susceptibility to financial crises, see Lipsey, "Democracy and Financial Crisis."

[26] A similar point is made in Richardson, *Democratic Autonomy*.

As such, from this perspective, democracy is seen as a decent way of forging, articulating, and revisiting our goals, alongside pro tem means for achieving them. It is *democracy as exploration*: finding out about ourselves and remaking ourselves as political communities in the process. The intrinsic and instrumentalist justifications blur.

If that goes for much of run-of-the-mill executive government, including in the administrative state, it could *not* carry across easily to our trustee-type independent agencies. Since they are billed as solutions to problems of credible commitment, the object of the commitment cannot be part of a process of ongoing Deweyan discovery. If continuous exploration were democracy's sole or main warrant, independent central banks would seem to be ruled out unless we were prepared to dilute the place of democracy itself in our system of government (chapter 10).

Justificatory Conceptions of Democracy and the Robustness Test of IA-Regime Legitimacy

Whether one tends toward an intrinsic or instrumental view of democracy's warrant, we are clearly well beyond the purely socioeconomic welfarist considerations that drove the initial articulation of the Principles for Delegation in chapters 5 and 6. But we are not faced with an irreconcilable clash. *For us*, governance by *Plato's guardians*, however wise and expert it might prove in delivering results for the citizenry, would be at odds with the commitment of many in our societies to individual autonomy or freedom in political affairs and with our attachment to public debate and some kind of collective decision making, and so would be hard to sustain without force given pervasive disagreement about public policy goals.[27] On the other side, a democratic state of such wide-ranging and enduring incompetence that its citizens were impoverished or lacked basic security would be unlikely to sustain popular support or even acquiescence. In terms of how, following David Beetham, I specified the general conditions for legitimacy, the former problem would violate the need for governing structures to square with

[27] Viehoff, "Authority and Expertise."

our basic values and beliefs, whereas the latter would undermine the prospect of expressive (or performative) acceptance.

If that discussion broadly captures the various ways in which people would justify or explain the right of the state to enforce the law in the democracy in which they live, then it sets the terms for our inquiry.

Most obviously, it becomes vital to the legitimacy of independent agencies that any delegation should not violate—and, ideally, would further—the grounds regarded by people as underpinning the legitimacy of the higher-level, democratic powers. Thus, for those who see the (primary) justification for democracy as being that it reflects or is necessary to underpin political freedom, then any delegation to an independent agency should not violate the conditions for liberty (under its different conceptions). For those who see the justification as reflecting or promoting equal political respect for individuals, then delegation to agencies should not violate or undermine equal respect or standing in the political sphere. If democracy is viewed as warranted because it comes closest among political systems to guaranteeing basic rights, then the role and powers of independent agencies should not violate those rights.[28] If it is warranted for some because it tends to make people better off socioeconomically, then the delegation to agencies must not make them worse off. And so on. Hence the Principles for Delegation must be robust to each of those warrants for our system of government.

THE EXTRA DEMANDS OF REPRESENTATIVE DEMOCRACY

That list of demands was cataloged without getting into the particular form of democracy under which we live: *representative democracy*, an expression perhaps first used by US founding father Alexander Hamilton in the letter quoted at the chapter head.[29] Doing so reveals our problem

[28] Allen Buchanan, "Political Legitimacy and Democracy," for a statement of the view that democracy is warranted because it promotes the attainment of basic rights (however conceived).

[29] The concept of "representation" is fairly elastic: Pitkin, *Concept of Representation*, and Runciman, "Paradox of Representation."

as being the legitimacy of *commitment under double delegation*, and shifts the focus to the value of electoral competition, representation, and participation.

IA Regimes as Double Delegation under Representative Democracy

Two hundred years ago the Swiss-French writer Benjamin Constant, an admirer of Britain's commercial liberal state, drew his famous contrast between the *liberties of the ancients* (the right to republican self-government) and the *liberties of the moderns* (the right to be left alone).[30] Unlike the city-states of ancient Greece or late-medieval Italy, modern nations have large populations, spread in some cases over vast territories. It is unrealistic for all citizens to debate and vote on all matters of significance to the community. There has to be delegation if government is to be tolerably efficient, consistent, and effective.

While that is consistent with government by officials who are unelected or elected on a restricted franchise, over the course of the nineteenth and early twentieth centuries the people demanded and secured a right to elect their governments and hold them accountable via the ballot box. This has a number of virtues:

- Individual citizens are not in a position where they are heard only if they turn up in person to the legislative assembly. They are represented.
- It is easier for individuals to continue challenging and opposing measures they do not support, as they are freed from social pressures (perhaps evident after some referendums) to be silent after the People have spoken.
- The polity has the resilience that flows from being able to use elections to sack the government without questioning the system of government itself.[31]

That catalog of qualities—space for liberal (negative) freedom without nonparticipants being disfranchised, government consistency, policy contestability, and political-system resilience—should not be sacrificed

[30] Constant, "Liberty of the Ancients" (1819).

[31] For a report on survey evidence in nascent democracies, see Beetham, *Legitimation*, pp. 260–261.

in delegating to IA regimes. Those risks arise, however, because IA regimes involve *double delegation*: from the people to their elected representatives, and from those representatives to the independent agencies.[32] With central bankers and other IA policy makers unelected and enjoying job security, their policy making can be largely deaf to challenge and opposition. So if much of government ends up in IA hands, the people are more likely to respond to (the inevitability of) poor performance by questioning the system of government. In other words, extensive delegation of government to IAs risks creating a brittle form of undemocratic liberalism.

Burkean Trustees and Experts: How IAs Differ from Elected Representatives

To make sense of this, we need to look more closely at the first level of delegation. What kind of agents are the people's representatives?

Political scientists have offered rival, but not mutually exclusive, accounts of how elections might induce representatives to serve the public's purposes or interests.[33] At one end of the spectrum, the people elect their government on the basis of a *mandate* covering what each political party promises. This is *forward looking.*

But in most systems elected representatives are not legally obliged to deliver a specific mandate, and are not subject to recall if their electors get fed up with them. At least formally, elected politicians have some independence of conscience as trustees of the public interest.

That was the view articulated, before the age of full-franchise democracy, by Edmund Burke, a supporter of American independence but critic of the French Revolution, when he famously declared

[32]Executive-agency regimes do not involve double delegation in the same sense. Legally, there is a double delegation: from people to legislator and on to the executive. But politically, it is more like a transfer of power between elected politicians directly accountable to the public. When either the president or prime minister has de facto control or levers over policy, the people retain greater traction over the day-to-day stewardship of the regime. For the same reason, the regime is unlikely to be able to make credible commitments, as we see when strategy on, say, environmental policy shifts after a general election.

[33]For a survey, see chapters 1 and 2 of Przeworski, Stokes, and Manin, *Democracy, Accountability and Representation.*

independence in a speech to his Bristol constituents (after he had been elected!):[34]

> [The representative's constituents'] wishes ought to have great weight with him; their opinion, high respect. . . . It is his duty . . . above all, ever, and all cases, to prefer their interests to his own. But his unbiased opinion, his mature judgment, his enlightened conscience, he ought not to sacrifice to you . . . or to any set of men living. Your representative owes you . . . his judgment; and he betrays, instead of serving you, if he sacrifices it to your opinion. . . . Parliament is not a *congress* of ambassadors from different and hostile interests; . . . but parliament is a *deliberative* assembly of *one* nation, with *one* interest, that of the whole. (My emphasis)

On that account, as US political theorist Henry Richardson has observed, the system relies for its effectiveness and warrant in part on elected representatives being better than the general public at framing, conducting, and resolving debates on public policy ends and means.[35] As trustees, politicians seem to write their own trust deed, and choose to leave it vague and subject to ongoing revision.

Under another account, however, the system is *backward looking.* The people vote out governments that have not performed well irrespective of what, if anything, they initially promised. Constrained by their desire to be reelected (and by the law), the people's elected representatives accordingly lie somewhere between "trustees" and "delegates." They must be alive to, and sometimes *responsive to,* the expressed or apparent wishes of their electors and are incentivized to make judgments about what will enhance their electors' welfare and so will be valued after the fact.[36] That is pretty much the assumption about politicians' objectives made in chapter 5 when we described the Alesina-Tabellini model of whether to delegate to politicians or insulated technocrats.

The significance for us is that this standard view of representative democracy does not translate at all comfortably into a world of independent agencies whose leaders are never exposed to the rigors of personal

[34] Burke, 1854 [1774], pp. 446–448.

[35] Richardson, *Democratic Autonomy.*

[36] As in Madison, *Federalist Papers*, No. 57, p. 294.

election and whose whole purpose is to be insulated rather than responsive. Unlike elected representatives, they really are trustees.

Certainly, the terms of legitimacy are altered. Most obviously, of the three headline institutional-design features that help warrant the first-step delegation to elected representatives—*voting* on the basis of a *forward-looking mandate* and a *backward-looking record*—only "mandate" survives when the people indirectly grant power to an independent agency. In that sense, while they might be trustees, independent-agency policy makers are not *Burkean*, free to substitute their view of the public good for the public's own conception. Rather, IA policy makers are trustees who are duty bound to stay faithful to the public's prescribed purposes and goals. The mandate (trust deed) of an IA regime accordingly carries an awful lot of weight in generating legitimacy. A regime of double delegation comprising a people's trustee with a vague trust deed (elected politicians) overseeing an IA trustee with a similarly vague or open-ended trust deed would be seriously problematic.

This matters all the more given the way *representative* democracy broadens and exacerbates the problem of commitment that IA regimes are designed to solve.

Credible Commitment Redux

When the Principles for Delegation were introduced in chapter 5, three variants of the credible commitment problem were identified: inherent time inconsistency, politicians having private incentives to depart from an agreed objective in order to get reelected, and societal factions having a private interest in getting policy makers to diverge. The system of government affects how they arise.

The first can arise under any system of democracy, popular or representative. That is because in some fields the optimal course for policy, *if* chosen period by period, really does diverge from the optimal longer-run course. Even a wholly virtuous social planner faces the problem.

The second and, in some ways, third variants are, by contrast, largely a product of the agency structure of representative democracy, which as discussed makes elected politicians somewhat responsive to their electors' shifting wishes and their backers' interests. Whether thought of as Burkean trustees, delegates of local districts (*constituencies* as they are called in the UK), or clients of specific interest groups, politicians have incentives to tack, disguising their true course and its possible costs from the wider electorate. Whereas a monitorable mandate might constrain an IA, it does not stand in the way of political policy makers.

Whether in the legislature or executive branch, they are acutely sensitive to emerging views on salient issues that affect their election prospects. Indeed, far from retreating into an elite cocoon between elections, if anything today's politicians can sometimes be more like the political equivalent of financial market "day traders," acting as though their political fortunes are highly path dependent. Each morning there is news, good or bad. If good, they and their team spend the day trying to hold onto their gains. If bad, the day is spent in rebuttal and deflection, in a desperate bid to square the political slate before the end of the day, going to bed having avoided a setback and ready to go around the course again the following day.

Here we see the other side of the coin of representative government. In the balance with system resilience, contestability, policy consistency, and liberal freedom, we must put the risk of responsiveness morphing into an endemic short-termism that depletes the people's welfare. IA regimes are, then, offered as a mitigant to some of the problems generated by political myopia. Delegating to IAs is a mechanism for elected representatives to safeguard those areas of policy where they would themselves wish to act as trustees but recognize they cannot commit to doing so: the Burkean trustees fulfil the trust placed in them by appointing an unelected trustee with a monitorable mandate that can foster normative expectations.

Trial-and-Error Democracy Redux: A Challenge for Commitment Regimes

As observed earlier, however, under democracy public policy proceeds by trial and error. Economists call this *error correction*: as lessons are learned, legislation is repealed or amended; institutions are reformed, abolished, or created; and with varying degrees of difficulty, even constitutions can be changed.

This acquires particular features under representative democracy through the periodic electoral competition between candidates from competing political parties. In this "repeated game," the people can try out not only specific policies but also political parties, policy platforms, even ideologies, and see whether they fit. In other words, the trial-and-error aspect of democracy is intensified and broadened, applying at the level of entire programs of government, not just individual policies. If representative democracy delivers the goods—the instrumental warrant for democracy in general—this aspect of accountability is plausibly a large part of the explanation.

It means, however, that opposing political parties might be committed to repealing each other's legislation even when a policy has worked tolerably well: because it was not their policy. That is a world where the "trial" can continue irrespective of whether material "error" is manifest.

Looked at thus, the flip-flopping pathology of electoral competition might both make the case for commitment devices and impede their realization. The next chapter looks at whether the instrumental value of commitment technology can in principle be squared with the intrinsic values of democratic policy making. Part III turns to how in the real world incentives to delegate are shaped by specific constitutional structures.

The Continuing Allure of Direct Democracy: Participation in Agency Policy Making

Before summing up the democratic deficit problem presented by IA regimes, we should return to direct democracy's continuing hold over the political imagination. Its defining characteristic is, of course, that all citizens can vote on all legislative measures and major public policy choices, such as whether to go to war or enter into a treaty or undertake a major public project or redistribute wealth or provide social insurance of any kind, and so on.

While that does not preclude creating an executive to implement policy, there is no deep distinction between delegating to an elected executive or to unelected agencies. Instead, there is a distinction between delegating to citizen-members of the assembly and delegating specialist functions to outsiders, as ancient and medieval states did when they hired mercenaries to lead and recruit armies. Any executive or agency drawn from the citizenry is directly accountable to their peers in an assembly where all (enfranchised) interests are represented. Thus we read of the Athenians holding citizen-admirals and others to account, whereas under representative government their successors—and today's central bankers and other IA leaders—are accountable in some way via the people's representatives rather than directly to the people themselves.

But with administrative-state agency leaders unelected and IAs insulated from the day-to-day wishes of elected representatives, the attractions of more direct forms of democracy reassert themselves for some citizens. Thus, a good deal of commentary sees potential redemption in agencies consulting widely on their proposed policies. Perhaps especially in the US, the value of participation acts as a warrant for fairly demanding rule-making procedures, which have been described as[37]

> not only designed to produce better executive decisions but also to give citizens assurance of the democratic legitimacy of executive policymaking.

Another US scholar sees the prospect of salvation for the administrative state in something like our third Design Precept: that agencies explain how they plan to exercise their delegated powers, construing them narrowly:[38]

> (This) does not ask who ought to make the law . . . (but) how (or how well) the law is being made. . . . In so doing, it reinforces a certain conception of democracy. By requiring agencies to articulate limiting standards, it ensures that agencies exercise their delegated authority in a manner that promotes the rule of law, accountability, public responsiveness, and individual liberty.

If left at that, the legitimacy of delegated regimes would turn on a simulacrum of direct democracy under the umbrella of the rule of law. While necessary, it seems unlikely to satisfy those citizens who value the representative element in our system of government. While elected assemblies fall short of the stipulation of US founding father and second president John Adams that they "should be an exact portrait, in miniature, of the people at large, as it should think, feel, reason, and act like

[37] Rose-Ackerman and Perroud, "Policymaking and Public Law," p. 302.
[38] Bressman, "Schechter Poultry," p. 1402.

them," they surely come closer than the average independent agency's policy board.[39]

Such citizens would, I suggest, be looking for their elected legislators to take responsibility for the purposes and direction of a delegated regime insulated from day-to-day politics, not merely its formal existence. As one of the preeminent writers on the separation of powers puts it:[40]

> The history of Western constitutionalism has been the history of [how] to maintain the . . . authority of the legislature.

Somehow the trade-off between welfare and responsiveness needs to be struck in a way that satisfies the values of both representation and participation.[41]

DEMOCRACY AND INDEPENDENT AGENCIES: A MULTIFACETED DEMOCRATIC DEFICIT

In chapter 1, we suggested that some critics of independent central banks and regulators are vague about the "democratic deficit" that bothers them. That turns out to be unsurprising because the worries are multiple and varying.

The issue certainly goes beyond the questions of rule of law and constitutionalism discussed in the previous chapter. Revolving around rule-like lawmaking, vires, fair procedures, and separation of powers, the demands of those political values on the modern state, although vital, would be prerequisites for legitimate delegation under *nondemocratic* constitutional government.

Nor, under our robustness test, can "better results" suffice as the extra ingredient. Judging by the deep values running through our

[39] John Adams, quoted in Pitkin, *Concept of Representation*, p. 60. Here I am departing from the line in Rohr, *Run a Constitution*, that the legitimacy of the administrative state could be secured by having a workforce that was a mirror of the electorate. While that might be feasible for delivery agencies administering, for example, social security, it is not yet realistic for policy agencies.

[40] Vile, *Constitutionalism*, p. 352.

[41] Urbinati, *Representative Democracy*, argues that political theorists neglected the compatibility and even mutual dependence of representation and participation because they were in the grip of categories inherited from Montesquieu and, especially, Rousseau: particularly that of the sovereignty of the people as general will, which cannot be represented but just *is*.

public debates and bequeathed by our history, some people value democracy in and of itself as a way for living together in a political community. This seems to be missed by those who argue that even if an agency's democratic pedigree is thin, a decision by legislators to delegate—and, likewise, a decision by an agency to pursue a particular course of action—can be justified (morally or, in sociological terms, to the public) if it is the best available choice in welfare terms, taking into account all the particular circumstances.[42] Even within its Welfarist framework, this argument is rendered vulnerable by its implicit assumption that each decision—by the assembly, by agencies—stands to be justified alone, on the basis of its particular outcomes, whereas in fact it is surely broader. Decisions and results have cumulative and complicated effects on trust in, and so the resilience of, the high-level political institutions under which specific policy choices are made and government operates. Too much delegation takes us toward a form of undemocratic liberalism that can survive only so long as it is lucky enough to deliver the goods.

Changes in the structure of the state are rarely salient with the public and can, over time, become a familiar part of the face of government. When things go wrong, however, and the public discovers that large swathes of the state lie beyond their reach, the reaction might not be pretty if it infects trust in our system of government.

How can government engage the public sufficiently to ground proposed reforms of the state's architecture? If "no taxation without representation," going back to Simon de Montfort's challenge to royal authority in the thirteenth century, is embedded in modern constitutional government, why does "no regulation without representation" not have quite the same resonance?[43]

[42] That is argued in an interesting paper by Adler, "Justification, Legitimacy." The point was independently put to me in a stimulating conversation with political theorist Daniel Viehoff at Yale during the early summer of 2015. The idea runs through Majone's analysis of delegation within the EU.

[43] When I googled this expression, I found that it had been used twenty years ago in Scheuerman, *Between the Norm*. It has recently been asserted by some US Republican Party politicians (see quote at the head of chapter 1). I do not intend any party-political partisan sentiment.

The Many Sides of the Democratic Deficit

The argument of this chapter is that when we ask *what features* of representative democracy matter to us and thus *why we care* about delegation-with-insulation, the answer is anything but monolithic.

After reviewing the various tangled strands of our democratic values, we can see why people might object to IAs: because they reduce public participation; or because their policy boards are even less representative of the makeup of the community than the elected assembly; or because they unavoidably delegate choices on values and objectives; or because they are vulnerable to "expert" groupthink; or because, where their objectives are fixed, they reduce government's flexibility to respond to events in the interests of the people; or because they reduce the capacity of the electorate to register discontent via the orderly means of an election; or because they restrict debate to an in-crowd of cognoscenti who lack the ability and incentives of elected politicians to communicate with a broad public in comprehensible terms; or because the members of the technocracy are part of a transnational (Davos) elite that has bootstrapped itself into power in pursuit of their own interests and view of how the world should be organized; or, more simply, because the spread of unelected power is alien to who we are, who we struggled to be.

If that range of views (and more) is widely reflected in society, then the legitimacy of IA regimes is going to need somehow to satisfy each of them. There is not one monolithic democratic deficit that hangs over independent agencies: there are potentially *as many IA-regime democratic deficits as there are prevalent views of why democracy matters to us.*

The point of the chapter might, then, be summarized as follows. Within the liberal tradition, as Montesquieu said, "liberty is a right to do whatever the laws permit."[44] To which republican democrats add: only if we somehow control the making of the laws or, through representative democracy, the lawmakers.

Taken together, the past two chapters have attempted to enumerate the challenges to central banking, and to IA-regime legitimacy more generally,

[44] Montesquieu, *Spirit of the Laws*, p. 161, Book XI, s. 3.

presented by the values of the rule of law, constitutionalism, and full-franchise representative democracy. The next three chapters set out our response on, respectively, whether commitment regimes can be squared with democracy, whether the Principles for Delegation can suffice to legitimate independent agencies, and how the Principles and the agencies they govern fit into constitutionalism.

10

Credible Commitment versus Democracy

AGENCIES VERSUS JUDGES

> The power of the Legislative being derived from the People by a positive voluntary Grant and Institution, can be no other, than what the positive Grant conveyed, which being only to make Laws, and not to make Legislators, the Legislative can have no power to transfer their Authority of making laws, and place it in other hands.
>
> —John Locke, *Second Treatise on Government*, 1690[1]

> Accountability is administrative law's central obsession, which it furthers through mechanisms for public participation, Congressional oversight, centralized White House regulatory review, and judicial review. . . . A very different model dominates in the world of financial regulation. There the defining structural precept is not accountability but independence."
>
> —Gillian E. Metzger, *Through the Looking Glass*, 2015[2]

The democratic deficit that some argue contaminates delegation to independent agencies, and therefore their authority, is typically seen as arising because policy making is removed from the people's accountable elected representatives. This is reflected in the quotations that head this chapter, which taken together say that financial regulation by rule-writing independent agencies is an abomination, a sentiment the postcrisis central bankers would do well to tune into.

On the account of delegation to independent technocrats espoused by this book, however, the problem arguably runs deeper. I have maintained that delegation to a truly independent agency can be warranted only in order to solve a problem of making credible commitments in

[1]Locke, *Two Treatises of Government*, Second Treatise, chapter XI, s. 141, pp. 362–363.
[2]Metzger, *Through the Looking Glass*, p. 130.

those policy areas where a lot is at stake and credibility is essential to success. But a central characteristic of democracy is the right of the people to change their minds: about what they want (ends) and about how to go about obtaining what they want (means). On that basis, any *deeply* entrenched solution to a problem of credible commitment violates the people's democratic rights. If, as I have suggested, "trial and error" is central to the operation of democracy, then there has to be scope for the public to conclude that their commitment device was an error. Put another way, if responsiveness is part of the essence of democracy, commitment devices would seem to be antidemocratic or, as Americans might put it, countermajoritarian.

There appears to be a paradox here. On the one hand, delegation is designed to help the democratic state deliver better results by sticking to the people's purposes: in that sense credible commitment is enabling of democratically generated purposes. On the other hand, the people have to remain free to change their purposes. The resolution has to be either that there are some commitment problems where democracy, as ordinarily understood, should be suspended or, alternatively, that an institution designed to enable credible commitment cannot be absolute.[3]

To make sense of this, it helps to unpack the problem a bit. There are three separable issues:

- whether the values of democracy are violated by one generation making commitments that *seek* to bind the future (their future selves and subsequent generations);
- whether democracy's values are at odds with making any such commitments *inviolable* (so that untying the knots would be revolution, at least technically); and
- whether democracy's values point to commitment technology in different parts of our political life having different degrees of entrenchment.

This chapter addresses the first of those issues, finding instruction in the independent judiciary's role as both impartial adjudicators and un-

[3]The former is the course taken where constitutionally entrenched provisions are (almost) impossible to change—the approach advocated by Buchanan and fellow conservative public-choice theorists such as the late Gordon Tullock, who prescribe a unanimity requirement at the constitutional level; that is, everyone has a veto and so majoritarian democracy is constrained (Buchanan and Tullock, *Calculus of Consent*).

elected lawmakers. That also helps to offer an answer to a question posed in chapter 4 concerning criteria for when a public policy regime might be delegated, consistent with our democratic values, to the courts, elected politicians (or their partisan allies), or insulated IAs. Chapter 12 returns to the question of whether any IAs should be more deeply entrenched than others, ranking with the three canonical branches of government.

CREDIBLE COMMITMENT AND DEMOCRACY: TENSION OR ENABLING?

Devices to make our pledges or commitments credible are a form of self-binding (personal or communal). In the social sciences literature, the paradigm of self-binding is Odysseus's famous order to his shipmates, while they meandered home from the Trojan beaches, that he be tied to the mast but their ears be plugged so that he could listen to the music of the sirens without yielding to their calls to approach.[4] It is, regrettably, a thin metaphor for our issue. The tricksy traveler and philanderer was interested in *his* consumption *today* rather than guarding against the longer-term perils of succumbing tomorrow to instant gratification. He was able to succeed only by *ordering* his crew. They did not, in the spirit of democracy, draw lots to determine who among them would get to hear the music. And the conduct of third parties is not meant to be affected by Odysseus's self-binding, whereas that is exactly the purpose of IA regimes.

A somewhat more apt exemplar of political self-binding appears in the same story, but stuck back at home on Ithaca. Penelope created an elaborate device to shield herself from the short-term rewards of taking a new husband during Odysseus's long absence, thereby preserving the integrity of the kingdom and the longer-run welfare of its people.

The story of constraining commitments in the politics of the West is a journey from Odysseus's self-indulgence to Penelope's self-denial. It begins with the late-medieval French political theorist Jean Bodin, famous for his advocacy of a strong sovereign but less so for his views on

[4] Elster, *Ulysses and the Sirens*.

constraints. Bodin advised that wise sovereigns would buttress and enhance their powers by tying their hands in various ways, such as ruling within the law and in line with established custom.[5] Here we see a forerunner of the language of constitutionalism but for the benefit of a personal sovereign ruler.

Once we get to constitutional representative democracy, things become more symmetric. Viewed as separate actors, the people might want to constrain their representatives, and the governors might want to constrain their people. Like Bodin's sovereign, the politicians (government) enhance their power by embracing arrangements that tie their hands somewhat. But, unlike that older sovereign, this is not just self-interested prudence but a condition for being granted power at all, in the interests of the people themselves. Meanwhile, the people allow themselves to be bound by acquiescing in general elections being held only infrequently, reducing popular power. The distribution of power, and the ideas, values, and incentives underpinning and reflecting it, are reshaped together.

Left intact across that leap of time is a distinction between the "rules of the game" *for* politics (constitutional norms and conventions) and public policies determined *by* or *within* politics. The former cannot be subject to continuous or capricious change without the consequent uncertainty undermining the practice of politics as a means of addressing the problems and challenges of living together in political communities. A degree of collective self-binding around the modalities of government is necessary for democracy to have any meaning, including preserving it for tomorrow. This was a point powerfully made by Madison in response to Thomas Jefferson's hankering after a new constitutional convention every twenty years or so, one for each new generation.[6]

Even within the metarules of political procedure and conduct, there is a distinction between mechanical rules and rules requiring interpretation (chapters 4 and 8). While there are certainly examples of the former, such as the US constitutional provisions that a presidential term

[5]Holmes, *Passions and Constraint*, chapter 4.

[6]Although it seems doubtful that Jefferson would have thought it legitimate for a future US generation to reintroduce monarchy. Madison's debates with Jefferson, Thomas Paine, and others on constitutional commitments are summarized in chapter 5 of Holmes, *Passions*, "Precommitment and the Paradox of Democracy."

last four years and that no person serve more than two terms, many rules of democratic and legislative procedure involve interpretation or judgment in their application, requiring a second-order rule determining, mechanically, who has the final say. The overriding goal and norm is that those interpretations-cum-applications remain highly stable.

The arguments for stability are different when we turn to what is decided *within* politics, such as, for example, some substantive legal rights and the outputs of the security, services, fiscal, and regulatory states. If one purpose of democratic politics is to allow for collective *choice,* that includes making choices on what, if anything, to put beyond simple majoritarian processes and what to leave as part of ordinary politics.[7] A polity might want to entrench the right to a fair trial presided over by an impartial judge, which would bar retrospective legislation and perhaps some nonpolitical rights, but not those public policy regimes it wants exposed to trial and error.

On that conventional line of thought, there is the following hierarchy of candidates for binding commitment:

1. Mechanical rules on the structure/procedures of politics
2. Institutions for applying interpretative rules on the structure/procedures of democratic politics and government
3. Institutions for applying interpretative rules on any "fundamental" or "basic" rights beyond democratic political rights
4. Institutions for adjudicating legal cases under (and with the final word on the meaning of) ordinary law
5. Public policy commitments

Together, the first four categories show that embedding institutions as a commitment device is not alien to democracy. Political communities seek stability in the first and second because they structure politics itself; in the third as a commitment to certain liberal values; and in the fourth as part of a commitment to fair adjudication in the application of the law. All four categories seem fundamentally different *in kind* from the fifth, concerning, as they do, the institutionalization of constraints on democratic power according to the values of the rule of law and constitutionalism (chapter 8). For some, this would make the case *against*

[7] Similar points are made by Waldron, *Law and Disagreement*, chapter 12.

independent agencies. That, however, rests on a flawed assumption and also misses something important.

We need to escape the common assumption that abuses of power in representative democracy are either (a) extralegal measures that can be cured by the courts or (b) policy failures that can be remedied via the ballot box. Those conditions do not hold where all parties competing to govern share temptations/incentives to renege on some substantive promises and, further, the social costs of their doing so, and of being expected to do so, are material. In the language of democratic values, breaking some pledges may not be illegal, but it can breach the people's trust in very serious ways. It is a *misuse* of power.

Seen thus, the key question about public policy regimes might seem to be whether or not goods such as price stability, financial stability, the protection of investors, or environmental protection should be regarded as unqualified rights ranking with, for example, the right to vote in free and fair elections or any right to free speech. That is how the matter was seen by James Buchanan who, as we flagged in chapter 8, effectively wanted price stability to be put beyond the reach of legislators.

But framing the issue as "constitutional" falls into the trap of thinking that commitment technology is all or nothing. Legislated law—and, up to a point, law more generally—is a commitment device, open to change only via formal amendment or repeal, and so exposed to attendant audience costs (chapter 6).[8] Since those costs come in degrees, the de facto embeddedness of a law depends on how far it is woven into the fabric of the polity's beliefs and ways of life: this creates the possibility of chapter 8's "super-statutes" but via political, not uniquely legal, constitutionalism.

In other words, elected legislators can use ordinary legislation to retain ultimate control of a policy regime while putting obstacles in their own path: exposing themselves to the political costs of overriding or repealing an IA regime that enjoys broad support or acceptance and that they made a public fuss about insulating.

[8] For judge-made law, the demands of precedent and giving reasons create such costs among the community of lawyers.

ADJUDICATORY VERSUS RULE-WRITING AUTHORITIES: SUSTAINING RULE-OF-LAW VALUES

That way of thinking about delegation to IAs sheds light on another way of approaching our problem. It is sometimes suggested that administrative-state agencies of all kinds should be confined to adjudicating the application of laws and rules passed by elected legislators, and so should not themselves be able to write legally binding rules.[9] The argument is that society has very clear values demanding impartial adjudication of how laws/rules should be applied in particular cases, and therefore any adjudicatory body needs to be independent of political and other irrelevant influences so as to be assured of taking each case on its merits. But, so the argument proceeds, the writing of legally binding rules is a legislative function that requires not independence but the active involvement of or oversight by elected representatives (or, perhaps, political participation of some other kind).[10]

On this model, IAs would be akin to specialist courts, posing the question of which of our values determine when a field should be delegated to an insulated agency rather than to regular judges.

Adjudication as Policy Making

But is the starting point robust? In answering that, we do well to remember that not all laws come through legislation. In adjudicating legal disputes amongst citizens, the judiciary, acting as part of the services state, establishes principles along the way. And in applying statutory law, the judiciary has to interpret and construe: it decides what legislation means and/or the boundaries of its reasonable application. In one

[9]These issues are discussed in Verkuil, "Purposes and Limits," and in Stack, "Agency Independence," which draws implications for US "independent-agency" functions from the Supreme Court's judgment in *Free Enterprise Fund v. Public Company Accounting Oversight Board*. The PCAOB was established, by the Sarbanes-Oxley legislation in the wake of the Enron and WorldCom scandals, as a kind of subagency under the SEC to oversee accounting and auditing. The case concerned whether Congress could give tenure to its policy board members.

[10]I cast the argument in terms of general values rather than the specific US Constitution provisions around presidential oversight that concerned Stack, "Agency Independence," p. 2417.

sense, this reveals the obvious point that judges make law. Lawmaking is not a monopoly of the legislature.[11]

For our purposes, the crucial point is that, in order to maintain consistency and generality, adjudication, whether in the hands of courts or specialist agencies, entails an accretion of principles. A series of adjudicatory decisions generates something like an implicit rule or general policy.

By the early 1960s, prominent US legal scholars and justices were making just this point. Judge Henry J. Friendly prominently expressed concern that the standards applied via agencies' adjudicatory decisions were not "sufficiently definite to permit decisions to be fairly predictable and the reasons for them understood" and prescribed that "the case-by-case method should . . . be supplemented by greater use of . . . policy statements and rulemaking."[12]

The argument that, for legitimacy's sake, IAs should be delegated only adjudicatory functions seems, therefore, to pose a riddle:

- agency adjudicators should be independent, as it is a quasi-judicial function or, put another way, the rule-of-law values of natural justice (due process) apply, including an impartial and independent adjudicator
- adjudicatory decisions should be consistent across time and cases
- the principles underpinning consistent adjudication amount to policy making
- given the rule-of-law norms of predictability and clarity, those policies should wherever feasible be articulated ex ante, as rules
- rule makers should not be independent of elected politicians as they are acting as legislators

Courts versus IAs: Incrementalism versus Participation

Exposing the riddle does not demolish the case for adjudicatory-only IAs. Perhaps we could have a system that combines adjudication by officials insulated from politics with occasional catch-up lawmaking by

[11] This is not just true of the common law system of binding precedent. In civil law systems, precedent operates as "soft law" under a principle of *jurisprudence constante*, that is, an interpretation or doctrine clearly determinative of a series of core cases. This may be especially prevalent in public law (Fon and Parisi, "Judicial Precedents").

[12] Friendly, *Federal Administrative Agencies*. The effect was to introduce more formal codification into the regulatory policy of common law jurisdictions.

the legislature codifying into rules the agencies' underlying principles and policies, as amended in the light of public debate. But, then, why not delegate to the courts rather than regulatory agencies? To benefit from technical expertise, the administrative state's adjudicators could be specialist judges, subject to judicial review by generalist courts.

By revealed preference, however, there are fields where we want regulation to proceed via the open promulgation and debate of policy rather than the accretion of adjudicatory precedent. The reasons, I suggest, are rooted in the democratic values discussed in the previous chapter. Agencies (and elected legislators) can consult on their planned policies, whereas (a) courts do not consult the public on their principles and precedents and (b) periodic legislative law reform is not a simple palliative since it can impose unpalatable adjustment costs on the public. Moreover, we want our regulatory policy makers to explain and defend their policies publicly and to the legislature, whereas we do not want our judges to be compelled to explain themselves to legislators (a point important to chapter 15). We want regulatory policy and monetary policy to be debated in the cockpit of politics, even where we want an agency in a particular field to be free to make an independent decision in light of public consultation and debate. These are the values of participation and accountability.

What could account for these distinctions between insulated agencies and insulated judges? I suggest that they turn on the difference between fields where we do and do not know how to frame a monitorable objective. Judicial lawmaking, very obviously in the common law tradition but also in the role of nonbinding precedent in civil law jurisdictions, is in its essence incrementalist, developing and refining principles through a stream of individual cases, each with their own specific circumstances but linked by common threads that are gradually discerned and enunciated by judges. Agency policy making is, given our democratic values, preferable where society knows broadly what it wants (the settled purpose of the Delegation Criteria and the monitorable objective of our first Design Precept), desires wide consultation on any rules that effect the regime (delivering some kind of "equal say"), and wants to keep both the regime and the exercise of delegated power under public review.[13]

[13] At a high level of generality, this might fit broadly with the principled limits on lawmaking by judges advanced in Bingham, "Judge as Lawmaker," chapter I(2), *Business of Judging*: in particular, "(2) where . . . amendment calls for . . . research and consultation . . . [and] (5) where the

IAs as Rule Writers: Legislative Self-Binding

The adjudication-only IA proposal seems, therefore, to begin at the wrong end of the issue, inviting the question of why we would bother to have IAs at all. The big underlying question is not whether adjudication of particular cases is special; it is whether other functions of the administrative state can legitimately be insulated day to day from elected politicians.

The grounds for credibly committing to impartial adjudication of disputes via the institution of an independent judiciary are provided by the fundamental value of avoiding abuses of power. I have suggested in this chapter that, in democracies, we also want to guard against *misuses* of power, by which I mean the deployment of power in ways that are not illegal but profoundly let down the public, leaving them less well off and exposed to more risks than if their settled purposes were respected.

This matters most where the expectation that promises will be broken leads to the very behavior that leaves people worse off. While the classic cases might be price stability and utility regulation (chapters 5 and 7), this problem can infect the legislative process itself.

Imagine, as if we need to, that there has been a major financial crisis and, further, that there is very broad support for a major overhaul of the regulatory regime. Imagine too that this is going to take some years to develop: not because legislators have other current priorities but rather because, even though the broad direction of and standard for policy has been determined, a huge amount of thinking is needed on the detail. The expected length of the process is not driven by legislators' incentives or their lack of technical expertise but by the underlying substance. It would take anybody years (as indeed it has). Because it will take years, legislators worry about whether their resolve, and that of their backers or the public at large, will hold as memories of crisis fade and the short-term lure of easy credit and asset-price inflation reasserts itself. Con-

issue arises in a field far removed from ordinary judicial experience" [a principle of interinstitutional respect], pp. 31–32. Aimed at the question of judges versus elected policy makers, Bingham also includes "(3) where . . . there is no consensus within the community." Where ends are at stake, that would preclude IAs as well as judges. My thanks to Lord Justice Gross for pointing me to this essay.

scious of that risk—that their preferences will buckle and bend—the legislators decide to bind themselves to the mast by delegating to an independent agency the job of filling in the detail of the reformed regime.

Compared with standard explanations offered by political scientists, this is not a case of legislators seeking to shift blame or being inexpert, lazy, or time constrained. It is a case of legislators trying to commit to their *own* high policy.

Crucially, they have not absolutely bound their successors (or their future selves), because they cannot. But they have established a structure that makes any such backtracking more visible—to commentators, the public, and the world. Under the delegated structure, future legislators must pass legislation to override the independent agency's rules, amend its mandate, or abolish it altogether. Each requires only ordinary legislation, and is well within their constitutional rights, but each is highly visible and so can increase the political costs of bending to special interests or yielding to transient temptations.

Proportionality in IA Rule Writing

For such delegated lawmaking to survive our tests of democratic legitimacy, IA rule writing must, among other things, do no more than is needed to achieve its legislated purpose, including not interfering with liberal freedoms (individual rights) more than needed. This echoes the efficiency mind-set of chapter 3, is akin to the Continental European (originally German) public law doctrine of *proportionality*, and needs to be incorporated into our first Design Precept.

It is a cousin of chapter 5's bar on delegating big distributional choices but acts as a constraint on the exercise of powers that have been delegated. It is addressed to individual rights rather than to collective interests and rights, and might be applied more tightly to unelected IAs than to elected policy makers (chapter 11). An example would be not restricting people's right to choose between utility service providers, in the cause of ensuring the resilience of the relevant infrastructure, unless really necessary. Considerations akin to that play a significant role in part IV's assessment of the "macroprudential" powers that might decently be conferred on independent central banks (chapter 21).

THE ELECTED EXECUTIVE VERSUS INSULATED AGENCIES VERSUS COURTS

The role I have been describing for IAs as a form of nonabsolute commitment technology in a healthy democracy is quite distinct from two other sets of circumstances that can confront our elected representatives:

1. A nation faces a serious and pressing problem, and legislators agree that something must be done and soon but are not at all clear what to do.
2. Legislators know broadly what they want to do but are not able to articulate a detailed regime and, further, cannot agree upon a monitorable objective. Instead, legislators converge on a number of equally ranked objectives with no clear or principled (let alone deterministic) rule for how they should be weighed and traded off against each other.

Those circumstances can warrant delegation-*without*-insulation. In the first case, legislators might delegate rule-writing powers to the elected executive (or an executive agency under its control) for a limited period of time. The executive would be placed under a duty to explore how to address the problem *and* to report back to the legislature with proposals for a more definite standard and regime.[14] In terms of legitimacy, delegation of this kind would rest on a combination of the democratic credentials of the elected executive plus the time-limited nature of the mandate.

In the second case, the legislature might want the regime to be fleshed out through a process that combines technical expertise with partisan political debate. It therefore wants the process insulated from an elected

[14] Roberta Romano has advocated a structure similar to this when the US Congress does not know what it wants to do but concludes it cannot do nothing (Romano, "Regulating in the Dark"). There are examples of this. In the US, the first radio regulator, the Federal Radio Commission, was created for one year in 1927 and annually renewed for seven years until a permanent agency, the Federal Communications Commission, was created by legislation in 1934. In the UK, the Bank of England was created in 1694 under a time-limited charter. Charter renewal was a crunch moment for decades. If government finances were under pressure, the Bank would seek renewal years in advance of rollover dates.

executive controlled by a single political party. Those might be circumstances under which the solution would be an agency whose policy-making body broadly mirrors the political composition of the group of legislators themselves and is subject to frequent control via, say, budgetary approvals and directives (for example, the US's regulatory commissions). So, inverting chapter 6's discussion of partisan commissions, the whole point would be that the agency's policy makers were party-political animals, with clear allegiances and lines into particular legislators. In terms of legitimacy, delegation of this kind rests entirely on politicized policy making: creating a specialist miniature version of the population of legislators and veto players.

We have arrived, therefore, at some general principles for a division of labor, in a constitutional democracy, between courts, the political executive, and insulated agencies:

- Delegate to independent courts where a credible commitment to fair adjudication is imperative and the nature of the issues is such that general principles will best emerge and can be maintained only incrementally through application to particular cases.
- Delegate to politicians (or to agencies under continuing strategic control of the elected executive or the legislature) where goals and objectives are fuzzy, so that questions of credible commitment to a settled policy do not arise and/or high level trade-offs have to be made.
- Delegate to IAs where commitment to a declared policy is socially valuable and is feasible if insulated from day-to-day politics, and where the agency's discretionary general policy should be exposed to public debate and accountability.

The striking thing about this is that what distinguishes IA regimes from delegations to the elected executive and the courts turns in each case on values associated with democracy: respectively, the welfare of the people, and formalizing public participation in debating the exercise of discretion.

DEMOCRACY AS WATCHFULNESS AS A SOLUTION TO CREDIBLE COMMITMENT

In concluding this chapter, I want to deploy another feature of representative democracy, flipping on its head the "commitment versus democracy" challenge with which it opened. Not only can democracy be squared with attempts at binding commitment, it can be the key ingredient in making the commitment technology credible.

We maintained, in part I, that unless IA regimes can be designed in ways that harness their policy makers to their mission, the desired benefits would not be secured, which part II has argued would deprive them of legitimacy. Policy-maker virtue being insufficient, incentives matter too. In part I we worried only about the incentives of a trustee agency's leaders. But an IA regime is also vulnerable to legislators repealing an agency's independence or overriding its policy decisions for reasons of short-term or sectional gain. In other words, maintaining an IA regime has to be *incentive-compatible* for the politicians as well.

That sounds tough, but chapter 9 argued that democracy is its own solution to the infinite-regress problem of "who guards the guardians?" The importance of this to our project of legitimizing IAs is immense. Democracy creates or comprises an actor-audience that can observe the words and deeds of elected policy makers, with some actions more visible than others. This is the source and basis of part I's "audience costs."

Even where policy is rule-like, in many fields expert observers disagree about when there have been systematic shifts in policy. In consequence, when policy instruments are in the hands of political principals, it is not easy to be sure whether they are reneging on the regime (cheating) or merely making judgments that not all experts share. Things are quite different if the only instrument in politicians' hands is formal repeal or override, since they must take that to their parliament (or at least make an announcement) and expose to public scrutiny a deliberate repudiation of the regime they said they were committed to. The costs to elected representatives of reneging on their promise to stick to a policy regime are raised, since they are much more likely to be spotted. The incentives of elected politicians are shifted, therefore, by concentrating their power in the public use of legal instruments rather than in the day-to-day exercise of executive discretion.

When it comes to making credible commitments, *democracy as watchfulness* gets more traction through formal delegation to agencies that are formally insulated.

If this chapter has established that institutions designed to make settled policy commitments credible are not intrinsically anathema to democracy, even when writing legally binding rules, it has left open how independent agencies should be designed and constrained. Our Design Precepts purport to answer that. We are now ready, then, to undertake our robustness test of the Principles for Delegation.

11

The Political-Values-and-Norms Robustness Test of the Principles for Delegation

> The [elected political] principal can transfer his or her powers, but not legitimacy, to the delegate; hence the latter must find ways of establishing his or her own legitimacy.
>
> —Giandomenico Majone, 2005[1]

The dispersion of views on democracy and government is central to our inquiry into the legitimacy of independent-agency regimes. Assuming, as we do, that citizens accept the legitimacy of representative democracy, they plausibly do so for different reasons, each of which needs to remain standing once independent-agency regimes are introduced. Those reasons either carry across to IA regimes under a principle of transitivity or at least must not be undermined by delegation-cum-insulation. Majone's prescription is an important but only partial truth: although IAs would rationally be legitimacy seekers, boot-strapped self-legitimation is a fool's errand in healthy democracies.

This chapter accordingly conducts a *robustness test* of the Principles for Delegation: are they robust to the different reasons people have for going along with the legitimacy of democracy, as reflected in public debate and discourse? The test is structured around various real-world approximations of the political theories encountered in the previous chapters: elite-majoritarian democracy, interest-group liberalism, conservatism, republican democracy, and deliberative democracy. Each generates its own set of requirements, which we check against our Principles for Delegation, identifying gaps and refinements. The proper roles of IAs in emergencies, in defining crimes, and in public debate emerge as big issues.

[1]Majone, *Dilemmas*, section 4.4, p. 74.

ELITE-MAJORITARIAN DEMOCRACY

At one end of the spectrum are strict and simple "majoritarians." Following Schumpeter, who served in government in Vienna before World War I and later found a home in the Harvard economics department, they would set no higher test than that an agency's independence is favored by a majority of a legislative assembly that was itself freely and fairly elected under full-franchise voting in elections held every few years.[2]

That is so thin that it hardly requires, as a normative matter, any of the criteria for double delegation set out in the Principles for Delegation. In terms of our transitivity test, there is not much to be transitive: democracy as voting is legitimate (and so survives) if it delivers whatever the voters happen to care about most at the time (basically, socioeconomic welfare). This supposedly realist version of "elite" democracy would find it hard to object to pretty much any key area of government being put in the hands of insulated experts if that was what the legislature concluded. What happens is, simply, what happens. Schumpeter was fairly explicit about this, citing the judges, the Bank of England, and the US Interstate Commerce Commission as just three attempts to separate the sphere of public authority from politics.[3]

Schumpeterian delegation by a democratically elected assembly does meet the first of the tests of legitimacy we adopted following Beetham: a legal measure taken under a society's constitutional process for creating laws. It implicitly embraces an instrumentalist warrant, and formally leaves power with the people (albeit only periodically) insofar as a future legislature would be free to reverse course or overrule IA measures.

But if that were all there was to it, delegation-cum-insulation would not amount to much more than one part of the elite passing the policy parcel to another part. To the extent that some people believe this is what real-world electoral democracy amounts to, it fuels the view, advanced by some "radical democrats," that the administrative state is little more than a techno-oligarchy.[4]

[2]Schumpeter, *Capitalism, Socialism & Democracy*, chapters 22 and 23.

[3]Ibid., pp. 292–293.

[4]Zolo, "Democracy and Complexity." A recent instance of arguments for elite management of the state comes in Worsthorne, *Aristocracy*. Worsthorne, who was Bank of England governor

CONSTITUTIONAL LIBERALISM

Perhaps the most pared-down intermediate conception of democracy incorporates richer attributes than the simple right of all adults periodically to vote for the members of the legislature. To give the people a say, it adds freedom of conscience, free speech and association, and plural sources of information, so that members of the public are not condemned to cast their votes in a state of ignorance, shaped only by the declarations of competing elite subgroups.[5] With a right of free speech and association comes a right to protest. The people are able to object peacefully to what is being done in their name by their representatives. The idea of "representation" starts to get some grit.

Going further, liberals add constraints of various kinds on majoritarian government to protect political minorities, including the essential need for the rule of law administered by an independent judiciary. Perceived abuses of power can be challenged and individuals enjoy some rights (varying according to the polity's views on justice). This is democracy combined with public law of the kind described in chapter 8, and it starts to put flesh on and principles behind part I's second Design Precept.

Such constraints are, of course, intrinsic to the actual democratic order in today's liberal, market economies: *liberal democracy.* To enjoy legitimacy, agencies need to be subject to constraints and checks and balances that are broadly equivalent in their effect to those that help underpin the majoritarian institutions themselves. Thus, legal limits on the legislature and elected executive cascade down to IAs.

Such a system of government could, in brute reality, amount simply to constrained, orderly competition among rival lobby groups. We briefly review its two main forms—*pluralism* and *corporatism*, typically associated with the US and Continental Europe—before seeing how this bears on the Principles.

Montagu Norman's stepson, advocates an "aristocratic" governing elite formed slowly but meritocratically and nurtured to exercise power.

[5]This is, in essence, Robert Dahl's concept of *polyarchy*, the term he introduced to distinguish real-life representative democracies from ideals of democracy: rule by the many through the "aggregation" of the preferences of competing minorities, interest groups, and so on (Dahl, *Preface*, and *Democracy and Its Critics*, chapter 15).

Interest-Group Pluralism under the Rule of Law

Under this cousin of Schumpeterian democracy, factions compete for power and, for a while, grab the electoral spoils. Once elected, they *and* their appointed agency leaders generate policy by striking bargains among those interest groups with the resources and incentives to be active (known to us as lobbies). Within their respective delegated domains, agencies hold the ring. The "techno-oligarchy" critique is, perhaps, softened as the electors can get involved via "public interest" groups, but it is hardly vanquished since only a weak conception of agency impartiality is at work (chapters 3 and 5). These agencies are not independent in our sense of being insulated from day-to-day politics. Rather, their purpose is to replicate and manage the politics of fields too detailed or insufficiently salient for elected legislators to make the effort.

Half a century ago, Yale political scientist Robert Dahl celebrated this view of democracy as providing, perhaps, the only realistic means for bringing the people into government in a pluralist society. If the confluence of forces produces a delegation with only the vaguest mandate or entailing big distributional choices, that must be the efficient outcome, not only in the short run but, since even moderately rational political actors would be forward looking, in the longer run too.[6] On the other side, it was excoriated by Theodore Lowi in *The End of Liberalism*, summed up thus:[7]

> Any group, representing anything at all, is dealt with and judged according to the political resources it brings to the table and not for the moral or rationalist strength of its interest.

Interest-Group Corporatism: Consensus-Based Coalition Democracy

The other variant of interest-group bargaining is found in countries that reject "winner-take-all" elections in favor of more consensual systems of government. This is characteristic of those polities that moved to democracy recognizing the challenges posed by regional, ethnic, social, or

[6] Dahl, *Democracy and Its Critics.*
[7] Woolley and Papa, *American Politics*, p. 174.

religious cleavages.[8] They typically have proportional-representation electoral systems, intended to deliver an assembly and government that reflect the combustible makeup of the people and their identity-bound interests.[9] They are also characterized by corporatism: government via consultation and cooperation with large established and organized groups that "represent" different groups in society. Examples include the "social partners" in wage negotiations, and networks of industry and consumer associations in regulatory policy.[10] Where the groups have organic roots, sustained meaning for their members, and cover the key bases of society, this can draw on the republican tradition of "mixed government," balancing the force of different communities. Where, instead, the groups are newly constructed or have drifted away from their roots, it is a system that can involve public policy being thrashed out among nominated insiders.

Either way, as under pluralist bargaining, consensus-building negotiation requires agency policy makers in such systems to be transparent with the "partners" about emerging policy plans in order to consult.

INTEREST-GROUP LIBERALISM AND THE PRINCIPLES

Compared with part I's essentially welfarist statement of the Principles for Delegation, therefore, some of their constraints have become clearer and some now rest on firmer ground. Notably, the second Design Precept's demand for mandated processes gains content. The processes must live up to rule-of-law values (chapter 8), such as avoiding irrationality or unreasonableness, and should deliver proportionality where legal rights are compromised, with less leeway than might be given to elected policy makers to strike the trade-off among rights or between rights and other public policy objectives.

In a similar vein, IAs were originally precluded from making big distributional choices, in chapter 5, because, by definition, they do not

[8] The classic text is Lijphart, *Patterns of Democracy*. Arguably, the US has such cleavages, but they were not recognized as such by the Framers.

[9] Kelsen, "Foundations of Democracy."

[10] Lijphart, *Patterns of Democracy*, particularly Table 9.1, chapter 9. On corporatism in, especially, economic policy, see Schmitter, "Century of Corporatism."

have the technical capacity to award the fiscal side payments necessary to compensate losers. We now see that that is not just some historical curiosity but is rooted in our values: no taxation without representation. Since regulatory interventions can sometimes operate like a redistributive tax (chapter 7), the same applies to them.

Finally, if in the real world democracy involves bargaining or consensus building, IAs must consult because, by transitivity, they should not be more opaque than agencies that operate as an adjunct of politics.

Even, then, on a still somewhat pared down version of constitutional democracy, we can find grounds in our political practices and values for various elements of the Principles:

- IAs being established and operating under delegating statutes passed by a properly elected legislature (Delegation Criteria)
- The deeply entrenched right of the legislature to rescind the delegation or to override an IA's rules or general policies via forward-looking ordinary legislation
- Some kind of accountability to the legislature (Design Precept 4), so that it can decide whether to exercise those powers
- Minority rights being protected by, among other things, reserving big distributional choices to the legislature (Delegation Criteria)
- Rights to a fair process in administrative adjudication (Design Precept 2)
- Broad rights to judicial review of particular decisions (DP2)
- Individual liberal rights being protected by a principle of proportionality in rule writing and application (DP1)
- Transparency in general policy making so as to allow interested parties and interest groups to make rational decisions, participate in negotiations/consensus building, and challenge IA decisions (DP2 and DP4)

That catalog of constraints on delegation-cum-insulation is, nevertheless, fairly thin. Other than its prohibition on big distributional choices, it says little or nothing about the special circumstances of insulation from day-to-day politics: (1) what to do if IAs have latitude to flesh out their own goals, (2) emergencies, and (3) concentrations of power in unelected hands. The first and the third open the door to our republican values.

Vague Goals and the Insufficiency of Legal Liberalism

On the first, liberal democracy does require an agency's exercise of discretion to be limited *in some way* since, otherwise, protection against abuse of power would be in the eye of the beholder. Where, however, a statutory mandate is highly vague, mainstream liberalism responds by looking to the courts to clamp down on the "arbitrary" exercise of power, stipulating procedural safeguards and consultation with interested parties. This is legal liberalism.[11] It was not good enough for Lowi, whose apocalyptic sentiments plainly extended to the administrative state:[12]

> A government of statutes without standards may produce pluralism, but it is pluralism of privilege and tight access.

Perhaps for some citizens, the democratic value of "participation" in agency policy making, if open enough, might offset the sacrifice of the formalist values of the rule of law: predictability and clarity via a promulgated standard (chapter 8). But that cannot suffice for a regime whose very purpose is to lend credibility to policy commitments: commitment to what?

Courts might seek to remedy the hole, pushing agencies to articulate a clear and consistent goal for policy or, alternatively, gradually developing their own high policy in the light of pleadings by interested parties in order to embed the objective in law. Whether under pluralist or corporatist liberalism, this amounts to the objective or standard for policy being articulated via a process of interest-group bargaining umpired by either unelected technocrats or judges. Some members of the community might, however, want high policy (the standard or objective) to be determined via the core institutions of representative democracy. For them, judicial sanction might bestow legality but cannot get far in underpinning a regime's legitimacy more deeply, as the courts themselves are nonmajoritarian.

Similarly, for IA regimes insulated from day-to-day politics, the legislature ensuring that it rather than the court establishes the basic

[11] US authors typically refer to liberal legalism, but I think this is misleading as most democratic states, notably the US, cannot call upon preliberal legalism.

[12] Lowi, *End of Liberalism*, p. 125.

tenets of procedural fairness and effectiveness, as in the US's 1946 Administrative Procedures Act, can help but does not plug the substantive vacuum.[13] When it comes to credible commitment, trading participation, due process, and judicial oversight against a legislated standard is a setback for democracy, not an act of prudent expedience, if anything like Lowi's views are held by significant parts of the community. This points us toward our republican values (see below).

Emergencies, Contingencies, and Liberal Democracy

If so far there seems to be a hole around what parts of government can decently be insulated from politics, the values of liberal democracy have more to say about emergencies and power, the subject of our fifth Design Precept.

Chapter 6's essentially operational discussion was clear that *within-regime* contingency planning should be as rich as possible given prevailing knowledge and experience. But the unenvisaged or unplanned-for does and will happen. What then? The question is pressing because even away from war, terrorism, and law and order, some types of crisis—for example, in the financial system or the environment—could be so grave as to threaten the stability of the state or society itself.

This raises big issues. Among legal and political theorists, there is great debate about whether, faced with the gravest disasters and threats, the executive can or even must act beyond the law, some arguing that it is inevitable, necessary, and tolerable, but others holding that there must be some kind of accountability.[14] Under the most extreme variant of the "executive-will-act" view, the constitutionalism discussed in chapter 8 is a sham, waived aside when the chips are down: the true power of

[13]Thus, a values robustness test does not permit me to share the conclusion of John Freedman, in *Crisis and Legitimacy*, that the solution to the riddle lies principally in adopting APA-like statutes. (See part III for considerations bearing on Westminster-style democracies.)

[14]For example, in rejecting "liberal legalism," Posner and Vermeule, *Executive Unbound*, argue that in practice legal constraints do not get applied when things are sufficiently dire and that legislators step back, leaving the way open for the executive to do what only it can do, on the basis of a political judgment about whether they will have public support. For a view that liberal democracy *can* be sustained even under emergencies, see Lazar, "Exceptionalism," and *States of Emergency*. Lazar does not see liberalism as exhausted by its legal procedures but as drawing as well on ex post public accountability, including via parliaments. Perhaps because the president is not formally accountable to Congress, Posner and Vermeule go further.

the state (sovereignty) lies with whoever wields the power to act in emergencies.[15] If, then, in an emergency the elected executive steps aside, leaving an independent agency (say, the Federal Reserve or the ECB) to act alone, the agency is revealed as the true sovereign. Heady, and deeply disturbing, stuff!

Fortunately, the values of liberal democracy impose constraints on how all this applies to IA regimes. We must distinguish between elected and unelected policy makers. It is hard to see how any conception of democracy can ex ante warrant unelected, insulated IA officials being free to improvise to save the economy or society beyond what is within their mandate. After that point, elected officials need to be involved, even if only minimally, to frame, via some kind of legal instrument, an extension of the mandate and so, in effect, to bless what the agency does next. Under liberal democracy, the plan must be that *elected* officials will always be involved when an independent agency runs out of road.

That partly (not completely) ducks the big background question of whether the elected executive is itself constrained in the exercise of emergency powers only by politics and not by our values.[16] In consequence, it leaves open just how free elected politicians should be to make an in-crisis extension of an IA's discretionary powers.

It seems to me that liberal values dictate that if there is a question of people's legal rights being violated, decisions on the *exercise* of those new powers should not be delegated to an IA, however convenient that might be for the elected executive or legislators. Rather, elected politicians should formally make the big decisions, if necessary giving directions where implementation is handled by an agency. In that kind of case, the agency would no longer be independent in respect of the instruments/powers concerned: their independence would be suspended, which ought to be clear to the public. In other words, the norm should be that if politicians want to take a gamble on public support, they should control the instruments themselves rather than look for a proxy agent.

Where that kind of moral question does not arise, however, an independent agency might be given new discretionary powers. Even then,

[15]This is associated with the Nazi political theorist Carl Schmitt. Anyone flirting with detaching the thoughts from the man might usefully read Lilla, *Reckless Mind*, chapter 2.

[16]Silverstein, "Constitutional Democracies," which reviews Lazar's book, and Ramraj, *Emergencies*.

the leaders of a *legitimacy-preserving* IA will want to satisfy themselves that what elected politicians seek is both within their legal powers and, further, does not violate society's deep beliefs and norms about legitimate government. They should also focus on whether the extension is natural given their core purposes and the nature of the unprovided-for crisis. Thus, politicians giving a central bank legal authority to lend to nonbank financial intermediaries is not the same kind of thing as seeking to authorize them to lend to fundamentally insolvent firms or to pursue policies for overtly distributional (say, regional or sectoral) ends (part IV).

This, I believe, reveals that some of our core values lie behind the fifth Design Precept. To the supposedly uber-realist response that "norms apply only in normal times," it may be countered that even if true, that is yet another reason for DP5: proper regime design shapes the limits of the normal. A crisis is, in essence, a state of affairs for which there is no substantive or procedural provision (chapter 6). An independent agency should, therefore, be eager to cover as many scenarios as possible under ex ante contingency planning, as that shifts outward the boundary at which a crisis in the regime itself (as opposed to the emergency in the world) is reached. An IA should also positively want politicians to specify in law up front what process will be adopted once the boundary, however distant, is reached. That way norms for nonnormal times can be developed or forged under democratic political authority during the normality of "peacetime." In short, our fifth Design Precept withstands values-based scrutiny.

POWER AND REPUBLICAN LIBERALISM: AVOIDING "OVERMIGHTY CITIZENS"

The third gap in liberal democracy's constraints on delegation listed above concerns concentrations of power. While an ethos of "constraints on power" lies at the heart of constitutional liberalism, it is reinforced by those variants of republicanism that draw inspiration from Rome before the Emperors and from Northern Italy's late-medieval city-states: safeguarding against domination. In the modern period, the *dispersion of power* was absolutely central to James Madison's vision for the new

American Republic. This drives some important reinforcements to, as well as glosses on, the procedural and substantive demands of the Principles for Delegation.

Committees, Not Sole Decision Makers

Those values underpin the Principles' requirement that IA policy should be made in one person, one vote (1P-1V) committees. It is not just a matter, implicitly assumed in part I, of underpinning independence and enhancing the quality of decision making—both instrumental, welfarist considerations. It also avoids concentrating power in the hands of one person. That is exactly why, in hearing appeals within the judicial system, the highest courts sit as panels or committees. Protecting against the kind of constitutional betrayal perpetrated by Weimar's Hindenberg would hardly have been delivered by substituting a constitutional court comprising a single supreme judge for a supreme president.[17] No more, at a lower level, should a single central banker control instruments that affect the people's economic freedom (introduction to part II).

The Multiple-Mission Constraints and Power

The same imperative underlines the importance of the Multiple-Mission Constraints (MMCs) for agencies given more than one set of responsibilities by their legislature. It is not only about enhancing results by structuring agencies in ways that provide incentives for them to take each mission seriously (chapter 6). Once we bring in our political values, it becomes apparent that the MMCs serve a wider purpose. They avoid conferring undue power on any one independent agency and its leaders by (a) setting a fairly high bar for combining missions at all, which is about fragmenting power *across* agencies; and (b) requiring different policy committees for an agency's different missions, which is about diluting power *within* agencies.

The core of the MMCs is demanded, therefore, by one of our *nonwelfarist* constitutionalist values: dispersed power.

[17] Muller, *Contesting Democracy*, p. 146.

Combining Rule Writing and Adjudication: Separation of Functions

As well as reinforcing the grounds for IAs making decisions in specialist committees, the republican take on liberal values also demands some additions to the Principles. In particular, they were largely silent on what is entailed by the values variously associated with the *separation of powers* (chapter 8).

For those who emphasize dispersing power, delegation to independent agencies could be a positively good thing since it fragments the power of the administrative state and of government more generally. But that is not enough for those who see the central value of the "separation" as lying in no one person or group taking on all three broad *functions* of government—writing the laws, checking compliance with and enforcing the laws, and adjudicating particular cases.[18]

If this tenet of constitutional government under the rule of law is transitive, and it is hard to see why it would not be, the upshot is that any agency granted all three functions should have clear structures for disaggregating them. Thus, if the governing body formally approves the rules, it should not be the final adjudicator of individual cases: there should be either a right of appeal or internal separation. Similarly, the people who investigate compliance should not have the final say on merits in the adjudication of particular cases, and so on. This amounts to putting more flesh on our second Design Precept, which now requires constraints on internal organization and division of labor.

Crime and Punishment: A No-Go Area for Independent Agencies

I also want to argue that republican-liberal values would put one area of rule making beyond the reach of IAs. While the Principles bar the delegation of major distributional choices to insulated agencies, at least as initially framed they leave open the possibility of IAs writing rules that create or specify criminal offenses.

Breaches of rules written by the regulatory state meet with sanctions that range from an injunction to stop doing something, via the with-

[18] Waldron, "Separation of Powers or Division of Power."

drawal or qualification of a license to operate in a particular market, to a fine or imprisonment. It seems to me clear that imprisonment goes to a person's basic liberties, and furthermore that noncustodial sentences can be intended to carry a social stigma going well beyond sanctions that resonate only within a regulated community. It follows that only elected legislators, as representatives of the people, should be able to create criminal offenses.

This would rule out the legislature delegating to agencies a power to fill in the details of a criminal offense, as occurs in the US (chapter 13). If agencies are lawmakers by virtue of writing legally binding rules, they should not be criminal-law makers. That needs to be added to the Principles for Delegation.[19]

One could go further. Should an independent regulatory agency be able to ruin (bankrupt or bar work of any kind to) a person or business? While, in the area of economic regulation, it must be reasonable for a regulatory agency to be able to bar a person or firm from the relevant industry or line of business, it arguably goes too far for agencies to be empowered to ruin them to the point where they cannot operate in other parts of the life of society. To do so would be to encroach on their liberties beyond what is necessary to achieve the agency's mandate (proportionality).

That implies that the authority delegated to them by legislators should not include the levying of ruinous fines. If nonruinous fines and a bar from the industry do not deliver a sufficient deterrent, legislators could empower the elected executive branch to pursue criminal sanctions, including heavier fines, via the courts. Thus, it is not uncommon to make it a criminal offense to practice a regulated trade without an agency-granted license. The Principles need to be enriched with this proposition too.

It follows that agencies should not be able to decide themselves to bring criminal prosecutions. Those decisions should be made within the core executive branch headed by elected representatives. That fits with a rule-of-law value emphasizing the importance of integrity in each distinct phase of a governmental measure (chapter 8). And it reflects the

[19] A similar conclusion was reached by the UK Law Commission, "Criminal Liability." They also recommended that Parliament should not delegate to executive branch ministers a right to create criminal offenses via the UK's system of secondary legislation.

democratic value of both ends of the criminal process—oversight of prosecution policy and determination of guilt/innocence by juries of peers—involving representatives of the people.

Beyond Socioeconomic Welfare: Avoiding Choices Materially Affecting Political Power

We can now see that if the republican element in our democratic values is taken seriously, there is a problem with the view outlined in chapters 3 and 5, and emphasized by scholars in Europe, that delegation to insulated technocrats is acceptable and sensible where policy need not leave anyone worse off: that IA regimes are legitimate when limited to the pursuit of Pareto efficiency.

Imagine that, relative to a policy of doing nothing, a sequence of within-regime policy choices gradually makes one group in society hugely better off, but leaves the other group's welfare unchanged in an absolute sense. While apparently a Pareto improvement, it might deliver a very marked shift in the distribution of economic and, critically, political power, which could destabilize the political order. In the language of liberalism, minority (or even majority) *political rights* could be jeopardized by material changes in the socioeconomic balance of power within society. More clearly in the language of republicanism, unelected officials should not make choices that lead to some citizens being able to dominate others.

This is the principled objection to judges and technocrats being given license to make the major changes in mergers and antitrust policy (chapter 7) that permitted the reemergence of business empires whose leaders have unparalleled access to heads of government and legislators across the world. The point here is not about whether this was good economics. Nor, clearly, since the big formal choices were made by judges, is it about whether the changes were lawful. It is about the constraints that should apply to IA policy makers and judges if delegated regimes are to square with our values. The big shift in high policy on antitrust and mergers should have been made through the institutions of representative democracy.

This, too, needs to be incorporated into the post-robustness-test revision of the Principles.

Summing Up the Implications of Constitutional Liberal Democracy for the Principles

To sum up so far, many of the components of our Principles for Delegation to independent agencies can be seen as being driven not only by Welfarism (part I) but also by one or the other or both of the two elemental features of constitutional democracy: majoritarian institutions (crudely, democracy on its "preference aggregation" conception) and a set of embedded liberal constraints (crudely, constitutionalism and rule of law).

The first and arguably most important Design Precept—that the mandate must be conferred by the legislature—is driven by the values of both democracy and liberalism: elected politicians should define the basic mandate and constraints that determine the purpose and boundaries of the regime. The second Precept—stipulated procedures for normal times—is driven by the need to avoid abuses of power: that is the essence of constitutionalist constraints and the rule of law. The fourth Precept—transparency and political accountability—is driven principally by democracy: accountability to the people via their elected representatives, who must compete for office. The fifth—emergencies—is driven, like the first, by both: democratically elected representatives should be in control of any regime extensions in emergencies, in order to constrain the powers of officials and to make sure that elected politicians remain accountable for the regime itself.

This catalog of liberal demands barely touches, however, on two of the Principles' other requirements: that an IA's objective be clear and monitorable and that it should articulate its *operating principles* (the first and third of the Design Precepts). Arguably, they simply support effective delivery and accountability by promoting systematic and proportionate policy making, and as such find a place under the umbrella of a Welfarist liberal democracy. But they also provide something richer. Combined with DP4 (transparency in actions and reasons), DP3 gestures toward the value of public debate about a regime and its operation, which is better motivated by republicanism and those conceptions of democracy that give center stage to talking (deliberation) and to watchfulness rather than to voting and legal challenge.

Even more fundamentally, democracy in the alternative base sense of participation in politics has slipped from view. The *Schumpeterian realist* and the *consensus* views of democracy bizarrely converge in seeking to deliver *responsiveness via representation*. One explicitly revolves around the election of competing elite factions, the other around pooling and dispersing government power across a proportionally representative and partially unelected elite. Despite their massive differences in dynamics and aspirations, they have in common a relatively small space for public participation and debate.

Without such participation, either system might be less responsive than some citizens wish. The former would fall short if competing parties have a shared interest in flawed policy regimes: exactly the problem of credible commitment. The latter could do so where the processes of compromise and veto characteristic of proportional systems serve insiders. In either case, the elected elite could, for a while, drift away from the represented (unless barriers to the entry of new parties were low).

In those circumstances, IA regimes might not create a deficit of liberalism or of constitutionalism, but they would still leave a democratic deficit (for some). In one sense, that is hardly surprising since liberalism and ideals of constitutional government prevailed in predemocratic countries. Once the values of full-franchise democracy are taken seriously, however, neglecting them risks infecting the warrant for a regime of delegated-cum-insulated policy making on both instrumental and intrinsic grounds. To see this, we need to turn to other political traditions that influence our values: conservatism and, especially, republicanism.

CONSERVATISM AND PRESCRIPTIVE LEGITIMACY: DURABILITY AS A PRECONDITION FOR EFFECTIVENESS

Liberal bases for IA legitimacy—valid legislation, compliance with rule-of-law values, avoiding concentrations of power, not delegating big choices about the distribution of power—do not say anything about the conditions for the *durability* of delegated regimes, implicitly assuming that good results suffice. Since any good regime goes through bad patches, that will not do. Something important is missing.

If, as we have held, a necessary condition for delegating to an independent agency is the instrumental value of credible commitment, it is hardly worth the bother unless the regime is expected to endure. But if it is not expected to endure and its efficacy is thereby seriously compromised, how could it be legitimate?

In a parliamentary democracy it is perfectly feasible for legislated regimes to flip-flop as the executive government changes, as evidenced by the British nationalization, "privatization," and renationalization of some supposedly strategic industries, such as steel, in the decades after World War II.[20] In US-type systems, by contrast, poorly performing policy regimes might survive given the formidable obstacles to repealing legislation, but at a price paid in attitudes to the system as a whole (chapter 13).

The Bank of England Example

Monetary policy is an excellent example of a field requiring a stable regime, as its efficacy turns partly on the public's formation of expectations of *future* policy decisions. Thus, after the then Labour government of Tony Blair and Gordon Brown introduced operational independence for the Bank of England in 1997, Governor Eddie George, a deeply serious man, stressed to me more than once that it would not be secure until there was eventually a change of government and they too supported independence. (That took nearly fifteen years, long past the point at which the Tories had publicly reversed their initial opposition to independence.)

The striking thing about George's view is that, although I doubt he would have put it this way, it implied that the legitimacy of the 1997–1998 regime change initially rested only on a law having been properly passed by a properly elected legislature. Whether it accorded with the UK's deep values and beliefs about proper government could be challenged so long as the Tories maintained their opposition on the grounds of a "democratic deficit." In other words, the regime needed to grow

[20] The British steel industry was nationalized in 1946, privatized in 1952, renationalized in 1967, and reprivatized during the 1980s.

roots, including ways for the Bank's policy makers to account for their stewardship.

This emphasis on durability, and thus on bipartisan sanction, fits with those schools of conservative political thought that put great weight on the organic evolution of institutions, captured in Burke's conception of "prescriptive legitimacy." While explicit political authorization and accountability for the regime would be paramount, as evidenced by Burke's own forthright opposition to the privately controlled East India Company, they could not in themselves be sufficient.[21]

Our Design Precepts seem broadly to live up to those demands but, we can now see, only when supplemented by the additional ongoing test that the regime's continuing legitimacy turns on *enduring* acceptance: becoming embedded in the life of the society it serves. That could describe the evolution of judicial independence in Britain after the struggles of the seventeenth century, which helped set the stage for its becoming a universally shared value enshrined in the US Constitution toward the close of the eighteenth.[22]

REPUBLICAN DEMOCRACY: THE NECESSITY OF PUBLIC SUPPORT FOR INSULATED REGIMES

A stress on durability would appear also to chime with at least those variants of republicanism that, in crude summary, require broad cross-sectional support in society for key policy regimes, delivered not only through representative legislators but also, crucially, through broad and ideally active participation in public life.

Of course, once put like that it becomes apparent that there is more going on here than the instrumental success of a delegated regime. Liberalism—certainly in political theory, whether Hayekian or Rawlsian—has an undercurrent of government happening *to* the voting public, whose legitimizing consent is inferred or deducted from "first principles" and whose wilder populist urges need to be guarded against.

[21] I am grateful to Westminster parliamentarian Jesse Norman, MP, for conversations on Burke (Norman, *Edmund Burke*).

[22] Sorabji, principal legal adviser to the lord chief justice and the master of the rolls, "Constitutional Status."

The republican tradition, by contrast, is based on the tenet, coming down to us from the early Romans, that the people controlling and challenging government is the essence of liberty. Democratic citizenship is added to constitutional government, equality before the law, and individuals being free to pursue their personal projects. For members of the community who place weight on this value, the legitimacy of a particular delegation is going to turn on public support and continuing opportunities for challenge.

Settled Preferences and the People's Purposes

This goes directly to the unease we expressed about how little liberalism, as we construed it, says about the problem of vague mandates.

Most obviously, if the instrumental purpose of delegation to trustee agencies is to help the democratic state deliver better results by sticking to the people's purposes, then *the people's* purposes had better be known or, rather, determined by some process that has deep legitimacy. That is exactly the role of democracy's procedures.

Under republican conceptions of democratic politics, it requires rather more than a whipped vote in the assembly. Put another way, if democracy constitutes or promotes the capacity of citizens to realize political freedom through some form of self-government, then citizens need to be able to participate in public debate designed to reveal whether there *is* broad consensus favoring a proposed delegation.

This is captured in the one vital part of the Principles omitted from our discussion of the demands of liberal democracy: the Delegation Criteria's emphasis on *stable societal preferences* as a necessary precondition for double delegation. Preferences are unlikely to be stable unless they are broadly shared; and, with the exception of basic needs, they are unlikely to be broadly shared unless publicly debated over an extended period.

Public Debate: Values

Those themes resonate with the realistic variant of the "deliberative" school of democracy described in chapter 9: doing the best we can to generate open debate in which interests and preconceptions are on display and so partly diluted.

For a proposal to create an IA regime, this would cover debating the nature of the problem, what the objective might be, and why delegation might help. Official sector advocates of delegation would give *reasons*, including evidence of different kinds and from different sources, presented at different levels of technical detail. Further, they would need to address whether an independent agency's decisions would be observable, and whether outcomes could be evaluated against a standard fixed in advance. The public would need to be told if the success of the proposed regime might be hard to track. And all of that would need to be open to challenge and revision in an iterative process.

In terms of some of today's most potent Continental European traditions of political thought, this seems to bring about something of a reconciliation between the Freiburg ordo-liberal desire for rules of the game for socioeconomic life and the Frankfurt Habermasian prescription of political choices being made through rich and reasoned debate. It amounts to marrying instrumental and intrinsic legitimation norms but with our republican values demanding that the debate be real, not hypothetical.

Most important, debate would be needed around whether delegation would take elected politicians out of decisions the public would prefer them to make. In chapter 5's initial articulation of the Principles, this was about whether significant distributional choices would be handed to the independent agency. But the language of economics employed in part I obscures the underlying value at stake here.

From the perspective of republican conceptions of democratic politics, we simply do not want unelected technocrats deciding or shaping the kind of society we live in. For example, it is not for an independent competition authority to determine that we should live in a market economy, whether we wish to restrict market power at the expense of consumer welfare, or whether we should tolerate economically efficient market power even when it brings concentrated political power. Rather, the agency's purpose follows from those choices having been made in our version of the democratic forum. Similarly, we do not want regulators to decide that drugs in general should be legalized but to apply a democratically agreed standard to particular drugs. We do not want a media regulator deciding that there should be a public service broadcaster but rather to apply a standard across the industry that takes its cue from a higher-level public choice. In other words, we do not want

IAs making big choices about society's values. We do not want them to act as modern-day *founders*.

We would similarly hesitate before choices with such wide-ranging implications were determined via interest-group bargaining presided over by a technocratic or impartial umpire. As one of the current English Supreme Court justices has put it:[23]

> Single-interest pressure groups, who stand behind a great deal of public law litigation in the United Kingdom and the United States, have no interest in policy areas other than their own. The court [and, I add, the IA] . . . is likely to have no special understanding of other areas [than the ones before it].

This might seem like a circular rewriting of the Delegation Criteria to say that political choices are for politicians, not for technocrats. If chapter 5 left open what counts as a "big distributional choice," now the issue is what choices count as "political."

Views on what features of a person's life are relevant to redistributional policy vary over time and across societies.[24] What's more, given that, as discussed in chapter 9, there is no analytically robust process for determining a social welfare function incorporating distributional weights, those social choices are always intrinsically contestable. This, then, is politics. Given the circumstances of our *democratic* politics, legitimacy requires that the boundary to the forbidden zone for IAs be drawn by the representative legislative assembly after public debate. Yes, the assembly *is* in effect determining what counts, for the time being, as Political, with a capital *P*.

Thus, the pitfalls in Majone's principle of delegating "efficiency" but not "justice" (chapter 3) are to be navigated within politics itself. This is not the politics/administration dichotomy that, we saw in chapter 2, structured the advocacy of Woodrow Wilson and his contemporaries, but a set of distinctions forged via ordinary politics and constrained by the slower-moving politics of constitutional conventions. Given the val-

[23] Sumption, "Limits of Law." In terms of part II's discussion, this amounts to saying that such litigation does not give a wide enough group an "equal say" in the requisite sense in representative democracies.

[24] Questions of gender, race, or age have not always been thought of as relevant to distributional politics. Maybe other things that differentiate people will be by future generations.

ues of representative democracy, elected legislators stand accountable to the people for the choices they make about the boundaries of IA power.

Since the costs of getting it "wrong" are cumulatively damaging to the democratic system of government itself, the official sector must be under a burden to get the issues out in the open. The questions for public debate are not anything as abstract as "What counts as a big distributional choice?" but can be framed more prosaically as, "Are you [citizens] comfortable with this particular independent agency deciding X so long as they are barred from getting into Y and Z? And if not, would delegating just X be OK?"

Public Debate: Realism

This all begs the question of whether it is realistic to expect public debates of this kind. In the middle of the twentieth century, two of America's leading public intellectuals locked horns on just that. Center-Left liberal John Dewey, whom we have already met, argued that public reason and participation were integral to democracy. Centre-Right liberal Walter Lippmann, a central figure at the 1938 Paris *Colloque Lippmann*, a forerunner of the neoliberal Mont Pelerin Society, argued that looking for rich public debate was utterly unrealistic and naïve: most people would choose an evening watching television or a sporting event over debating public affairs.[25] Both seem wrong. On the one hand, people of all kinds do sometimes discuss events and politics with their friends, colleagues, and family, even if they prefer watching or playing sports. On the other hand, Lippmann's apparent condescension aside, he was obviously correct that it is not remotely realistic to assume that everybody is tuned in to all or many significant public issues.

That, however, is hardly the point. The deliberative republican precept is that the state apparatus, political parties, and a free media should remove obstacles to debate and encourage debate on big political choices, including, in particular, decisions about the distribution of the state's

[25] Dewey, *Public and Its Problems*; Lippmann, *Phantom Public*. For a brief account of the debate, see chapter 26 of Ryan, *On Politics*. Attendees at the Paris Colloque included Hayek, French liberal Raymond Aron, Austro-Hungarian liberal Michael Polyani, and Freiburg ordo-liberals Wilhelm Ropke and Alexander Rustow.

powers. It is realistic for government to seek a wide spectrum of views through public consultation, using the media to reach out and so not relying mainly on lobby groups and aligned think tanks.

This does not mean that everyone must be a technical expert or even literate in the subject matter. In free, advanced societies, commentators, interest groups, and proselytizers provide *translation services*, building epistemic bridges between technical specialists and the public, exposing gaps, flaws, inconsistencies, and choices in official proposals and plans.[26]

Ultimately, in *representative* democracies, "broad public support" means support across the main political parties, informed by those opportunities for challenge and debate. In the case of regimes that would be completely new, and so with newly created agencies, the responsibility for and interest in generating debate falls squarely to the promoters of any legislative proposal. The formality of standard parliamentary procedures does not preclude wider participation, however. While practice varies across jurisdictions, draft bills can be published for public comment, alongside or prior to parliamentary processing; legislative committees might invite public participation in hearings, perhaps selected by ballot, or solicit questions the public would like them to ask technocratic witnesses.

The new technology has a bearing on this, eroding the gulf between the ancient world and modernity. The Athenians had a right to speak at the Assembly, but few exercised it (or so historians think). In a similar spirit, today's technology provides a means to participate but not an obligation. The reality of the ancient liberties lay, perhaps, in nagging, pressuring, or moaning at prominent citizens on their way to or from the assembly, or perhaps petitioning via an intermediary with private access to the leading citizens and orators. Today, it might mean mailing elected representatives, joining an electronic petition, blogging, or debating on social networks. But it also means trying to disentangle facts,

[26] An emphasis on translation services, inspired I suspect by reading philosopher Donald Davidson nearly forty years ago, was central to my view of how multidiscipline organizations, such as the Bank of England, needed to function, with mutual respect across specialisms: see Tett, *Silo Effect*, pp. 248–249. A similar idea of a division of labor in public deliberation is discussed in Christiano, "Rational Deliberation."

grounded (tested) opinions, rumors, and lies given the blurring of boundaries between expert, serious, inquiring, mendacious, and frivolous commentary and criticism.[27]

An Example from Central Banking

When a proposal involves granting new powers to an already existing independent institution, there is also a strong case for expecting the agency itself to contribute to the public debate by explaining, provisionally, how it would expect to deploy the proposed powers. That amounts to anticipatory delivery of the operating principles required by DP3.

It is exactly what the Bank of England did in 2011 when, well ahead of the Westminster Parliament's crucial Second Reading of the Bill making the Bank responsible for financial stability and banking supervision, it published a document setting out how it would plan to pursue those responsibilities, holding a webcast conference to help initiate and broaden access to its contribution to public debate.[28] Since the planned new approach was going to mark a very big break with the previous regime, we wanted that factored in to the public discussion, Parliament's decision whether to go ahead, and the drafting of the legislation itself. Our aim was to help meet the necessary conditions for public debate without strongly advocating that the responsibilities in question be transferred to us.

REPUBLICAN ACCOUNTABILITY AND CONTESTABILITY

Public debate cannot end with enactment of an IA regime. Accountability is common to all modern conceptions of democracy. Enjoying insulation from day-to-day political pressures does not shield independent agency leaders from debate and challenge of various kinds. It makes them all the more important. Our values entail three channels:

[27] Nichols, *The Death of Expertise.*
[28] Bank of England, *Prudential Supervision Authority.*

- An ability to challenge the legality of an agency's decisions in impartial and independent courts whose proceedings are, routinely, open to public view
- An ability to participate in broad public debate on an agency's general policy proposals, decisions, and operations
- Public explanation of an agency's performance before committees of the delegating legislature

We have seen that the first—the liberal demand for due process and judicial "oversight"—cannot substitute for the second and third given our republican values. On its own, judicial review of administrative action would merely shift the location of the democratic deficit from one nonmajoritarian institution to another. For example, where an IA regime lacks a clear legislated purpose and monitorable objective, the requirement that rule making be proportionate, not intruding unnecessarily on liberal freedoms (chapter 10), becomes an invitation to the judiciary to construe an IA's vague purposes or to trade off (balance) its multiple objectives in ways that reflect the judges' own values. This becomes obvious when we think about whether high court justices, the subset of the educated elite who studied law, could cure any democratic deficit in my former central banking colleagues, the subset who studied economics. For delegation to enjoy democratic legitimacy, the people have to be let in, all the more so where the regimes purposefully tie their elected representatives' hands, as well as their own, for the time being.

Under republican values, the exercise of discretionary powers, however constrained, must then also be overseen more broadly, politically. Our five Design Precepts for delegated regimes seem to square with that. Without something like them, it is hard to see how reasoned public debate on the regime could take place. With them, the public is able to know the goals of the regime, the principles that guide the IA's exercise of its discretionary powers, what it has actually done, the general policies (e.g., rules) it is proposing and applying, and its reasons for those proposals, decisions, and actions.

Something more is needed, however, than initially contemplated in chapters 5 and 6. An IA's policy decisions will not always work as expected, so its policy makers need to be able to explain why, even with hindsight, their choices were reasonable, opening themselves up to challenge and rebuttal. Whether or not formally framed as cost-benefit analysis, those choices implicitly or explicitly rest partly on probabilistic forecasts of their policy's effects. Given our republican values, IAs need to publish information that provides a basis for debating whether their forecasts—of benefits, of costs—were broadly borne out and, if not, were nevertheless reasonable. In a nutshell, IAs should engage in ex post review.[29] That has become common among monetary policy makers but seems to be rare among regulatory agencies.

Limits to Participation: The Example of Central Banking

Participation faces big hurdles, however, as a universal solution to IA legitimacy.

While feasible for rule writing, it is neither feasible nor desirable for adjudicatory decisions, including a central bank's regular decisions on the level of the short-term risk-free interest rate. Indeed, the burden of this book is that where the purpose of a delegated regime is to secure credible commitment to a stable policy, insulating policy makers from the vicissitudes of public sentiment may be vital precisely so that they can stay constant to a publicly willed objective.[30]

Even in the arena of IA rule making, it is slightly misleading to draw on the spirit of direct democracy when advocating public participation. There are circumstances where opposition to a draft rule from across all points of society is not of itself sufficient for an independent agency to change course. Imagine, for example, that an IA charged with preserving financial stability proposes a rule in order to contain a credit and asset-price bubble that the agency believes is likely, when it bursts, to bring down the financial system and throw the economy into deep recession, with millions of jobs lost. That everyone—the public, bankers, elected politicians—enjoys booms might have been the very purpose of

[29] Thanks to Ricky Revesz for alerting me to a formally specific version of this in Institute for Policy Integrity, *Strengthening*.

[30] This counts out the solution offered in the stimulating essay by Kelly, "Unlocking the Iron Cage." Like Rohr nearly twenty years earlier, Kelly's solution might work for welfare delivery agencies, the case he explicitly discusses, but would not work for policy institutions.

delegating the rule-making power to an insulated agency (chapter 20). What would matter in that case would not be the weight of current boom-time opinion but the clarity of the agency's purpose and the richness of the public debate when the delegated regime was established. Both republican and participatory values meet instrumentality most vitally, therefore, in the framing of independent-agency goals.[31]

It would be unsafe, however, to rely on an airtight boundary between goals and implementation. However carefully framed, choices around ends can inadvertently be placed in the hands of IAs. Public participation in IA policy making accordingly carries special weight when an agency is embarking on a course that concerns not only means but ends too. In chapter 7, we cited the example of the UK Financial Services Authority moving to ban products after the 2007–2009 crisis. Implicitly, this was reducing the freedom of citizens to make their own choices, and so raised questions about ends even though the proposed course was within the agency's legal powers. As with politics/administration, there is not a clean ends/means dichotomy, only lines drawn by legislators for the time being. When ends or completely unexpected means are in view, public debate is essential.[32]

Legislative Oversight

While the Design Precepts rightly provide a basis for healthy public debate, an IA cannot generate (or synthesize) its own legitimacy through wide participation alone. Participation and public debate are necessary but not sufficient.[33]

[31] In emphasizing statutory goals, I strike a slightly different note from the otherwise similar set of concerns in Rose-Ackerman, "Citizens and Technocrats," which is addressed to the administrative state as a whole.

[32] Richardson, *Democratic Autonomy,* offers a grounded analysis of the unavoidable role of agency policy making in determining ends, not just means, upending the Weberian tradition.

[33] Imagine an IA with a very vague mandate ("pursue the public interest") that is desperately keen to obtain public consent for its core general policies, including its own proposals for monitorable objectives. To that end, it organizes an electronic plebiscite, which attracts massive participation and generates a clear majority in support of its proposals. The IA has, in effect, set up a shadow electronic parliament (single-issue direct democracy). But, under representative democracy, something vital is missing: the agency of the people's elected representatives in, for example, generating consistency across policy regimes and maintaining accountability over time (chapter 9).

Consistent with that, under representative democracy, the central forum is provided by committee hearings in the legislature. Independent agencies, not being "majoritarian" themselves, must account to the legislative assembly, the cockpit of representative democracy, for their stewardship of the regimes entrusted to them. It is the democratic legitimacy of the assembly that delivers, through a properly enacted statute, some of the preconditions for an IA's own derivative legitimacy. And it is the legislature that can take away the IA's powers and position. Debates with and among legislators are different in kind from other discussions and deliberations because they are *actors*, and uniquely so.[34]

For the IAs themselves, therefore, parliamentary hearings provide the single most important channel of communication *with* the public. They are televised, widely reported, and revolve around exchanges with the people's elected representatives. They give IA policy makers an opportunity to cast aside the jargon of their technocratic tribe in order to communicate in language that lets in the public, without competing with elected politicians for public recognition or popularity. Reciprocally, questions and confusions of concern to the public can be raised and pressed by legislators, in what amounts to a form of *discursive accountability*.[35] And the legislators themselves need to exhibit understanding of the delegated regime, in particular the objective and any instrument rule they have laid down: otherwise, how can they ask pertinent questions about the regime's operation and stewardship? They can be "held to account" by the media if they fall down on the job. This is the 360-degree *democracy as watchfulness* described in chapters 9 and 10.

Hearings also provide IA leaders with a public forum for highlighting problems in the design or construction of the regimes entrusted to them. Where an IA needs, in its view, more or different powers to fulfill an existing mandate, I suggest that the values of democracy are inconsistent with its staying silent on such matters at legislative hearings; they might even give it a *duty* to make their concerns clear to legislators. It would be irresponsible for IA policy makers to stay silent if they believe they cannot deliver the mission and, especially, the specific objective

[34] For a concerted attempt to raise interest in the importance of legislative processes for realizing our values, see Waldron, *Law and Disagreement*, part I.

[35] There is a flavor of that view in Gehring, "Consequences."

delegated to them. In a similar spirit, republican democratic values imply, I suggest, a responsibility for IA leaders to highlight gaps between their powers and vague mandates. Often it is assumed that vague mandates enhance an agency's power, but that need not be so: the broad terms of a mandate might imply to politicians and the public that an independent agency will deliver goods that, in fact, lie beyond its capabilities. IA leaders have an interest in getting these problems out of the shadows and into the glare of public debate.

THE VALUES OF DELIBERATIVE DEMOCRACY APPLIED TO IAS' DECISION-MAKING PROCESSES

What about decision making by the IAs themselves? Here something close to the ideal advocated by deliberative democracy theorists is apposite and realistic: equal respect among policy makers, using only those reasons that are likely to resonate with fellow policy makers and expert reviewers, setting aside personal preferences, being open to persuasion. In a word, deliberation.

By stipulating that a clear, ideally lexicographic objective be set by elected representatives, the Principles for Delegation aim to make it difficult for individual IA policy makers to bring to the table their personal preferences on the big issues. Beyond that, the value of deliberation obviously reinforces the precept that IAs' delegated powers should be conferred on committees, with debates designed to help individual members reach their own decisions rather than to influence a chair-cum-leader.

The epistemic strength of committees lies, on this view, not only in the benefit of aggregating the votes of members with different views of the facts but also, crucially, on exploring arguments with fellow experts *before* voting. That was certainly my own experience in the UK's monetary policy committee, where not infrequently members changed their minds in the light of debate.[36] On this basis, some central bank

[36]The benefits of deliberation are not especially emphasized in the otherwise compelling discussion of committees in Blinder, *Quiet Revolution*.

committees, including the US Federal Open Markets Committee and the ECB's Governing Council, are too large.[37]

Since IAs make judgments, there will be disagreement (just as among members of judicial panels). Our fourth Design Precept demands that the inevitability of disagreement be manifest and public, avoiding the risk of a single IA policy maker trying to argue that theirs was, in the circumstances, the only decision that any reasonable person could make. Transparent disagreement among committee members helps to insulate an independent agency against attacks that its purported authority rests on an omniscience that can never be achieved. It also helps make clear, consistent with the democratic value of publicity, that discretion to make (fallible) judgments is being granted by the legislature. And, more practically, minority votes help legislative committees identify the salient issues on which they should examine policy makers when IA committee members testify (chapter 15).

In substance, part I's original statement of the Principles imposes those demands on IA policy making, but mainly on the ground that they underpin an agency's independence by diluting the ability of elected politicians to determine policy through their choice of its head. In the course of part II, we have identified four other distinct reasons why IAs should decide policy in committees:

- To disperse power, rather than concentrating it in the hands of one person who might pursue a personal agenda (*constitutionalism*)
- To mitigate, via collective monitoring of each other, the risk of individual policy makers substituting their values for the legislated objective and purpose (*republican democracy*)
- To create an environment where policy is more likely to be deliberative (*instrumental warrant*)

[37] The Fed is also constrained by statutory requirements for transparency when three or more governors discuss something. I was once asked by a Fed governor whether, at the Bank of England, we ever discussed substance outside of the formal meetings. My answer, which I think might have prompted something between admiration and puzzlement, was that that was the point of working there, but that we almost never had bilateral discussions, and that our discussions were not about where to set monetary policy. It is possible that the US Sunshine Act might have had perverse effects, impeding analysis and deliberation, at least among policy makers nominated and confirmed by elected representatives.

- To reveal disagreement and, thus, expose to scrutiny the committee's key deliberations (*republican contestation and deliberative democracy)*

Quite demanding specifics flow from this. For example, the chair should not dominate the setting of the agenda; and where the terms of delegation encourage consensus, members must nevertheless be free to cast their vote as they wish where genuine consensus cannot be reached.

Deliberative Committees versus Instrument Rules

This emphasis on the value of committees makes it harder to adopt a binding rule for an IA's policy instrument (for example, a monetary policy interest rate). Chapter 8 argued that it is likely that the "real" rule would end up being about when the stipulated instrument rule is followed, when put aside, and when readopted. We can now see that instrument rules do not sit comfortably with committee-based decision making.

If the rule were mechanical, there would be no point in having a policy committee. If, instead, the inputs to the rule (sticking with the monetary example, the state of the economy and the posited value of variables on its equilibrium path) require interpretation and judgment, it is possible that majorities could exist for each one of the inputs without a majority existing for the decision on the instrument setting they produced.[38] Policy making by committee is, surely, about outputs; and its justifications are, to repeat, not just about results but also, consistent with our political values, about avoiding concentrations of power.[39]

[38] This is known as the *Discursive Dilemma*. The standard example involves a university committee of three people deciding whether to offer someone a job. Each member rates candidates on two criteria (research and teaching) and also overall. The three members' views are (Pass, Fail, No), (Fail, Pass, No), (Pass, Pass, Yes). A majority passes the candidate on each input, implying they should get the job. But a majority also concludes that they should not be offered a job (List and Pettit, "Aggregating Sets").

[39] Maybe advocates of legislatively mandated instrument rules assume that a committee would adopt instrument calibrations recommended by staff, but I have no idea why a policy maker would commit to do that when they, not the staff, would be accountable for their votes. Plus, de facto delegation to staff might, under some conditions, risk loosening the harness that delivers credibility (chapter 5).

SUMMING UP THE POLITICAL VALUES ROBUSTNESS TEST OF THE PRINCIPLES

Our exploration of political and democratic values has piled up the prerequisites for legitimate delegation to trustee-style independent agencies. In the spirit of the robustness test, neither participatory democrats on the Left nor rule-of-law constitutionalists on the Right turn out to have a monopoly over the standards that delegation to IAs must satisfy (because they do not have a monopoly over the values of democracy and constitutionalism). In addition to their concerns, others have to be weighed, including results and the elemental role of elected representatives in shaping high-level policy regimes.

In consequence, the Principles do not answer society's need for legitimacy if there is a strong demand for *active* public participation in *all* government decision making (including, for example, monthly interest-rate decisions). Such levels of participation cannot be squared with the purpose of a trustee-agency regime being to address a problem of time inconsistency or credible commitment. Society simply cannot have both. But the Principles do demand that public participation in debates on goals (or ends) and on big shifts in policy (means) should be facilitated.

A "Pass" plus Some Enhancements

That being said, overall the Principles come out of this exercise pretty well. Compared to their initial statement in part I (chapters 5 and 6), however, there were some important clarifications, elaborations, and enhancements:

- Wide public debate, with participation as broad as possible, is needed before an IA regime should be established.
- Opportunities to challenge and debate the regime must be sustained once it is up and running.
- An independent agency should contribute to those public debates with information and research on how it evaluates the effectiveness of its instruments and the social costs of the ills it is mandated to mitigate; and it should make available data for independent research.

- An IA should publish data that enables ex post evaluation of its cost-benefit and other forecasts.
- An independent agency should not be delegated power to make big choices on society's values or that materially shift the distribution of political power.
- An IA's rule making should not interfere with individual liberal rights more than necessary to achieve the legislated purpose and objective (proportionality).
- An IA should not be able to create or frame criminal laws or to bring criminal prosecutions.
- Its sanctions should not include ruinous fines.
- The processes demanded by the second Design Precept must help to deliver the values of the rule of law in IA rule making, adjudications, and other actions.
- Within a rule-writing IA, the structure for determining (adjudicating) individual cases should have degrees of separation, and each distinct phase of policy making should have its own integrity.
- Undue concentrations of power within IAs should be avoided.
- An independent agency's policy-making body should be deliberative, with a voting committee of equal members.
- Its mandated objective, standard, or instrument rule must be understood by legislators and broadly comprehensible to the public.

The final version of the Principles for Delegation, which are put to a different kind of test in part III, is set out in the appendix to the book. The most important elaboration is the need for rich public debate. Debate cannot go on forever, however, and a clear consensus is not always achieved. That the Principles might not deliver the ideal universal consensus stipulated by strong versions of deliberative democracy strikes me as no bad thing if it means, consistent with the "trial-and-error" features of democratic politics stressed in chapter 9, that a fringe minority of skeptics or even opponents exist to sustain debate on a particular regime's merits.

REVISITING DELEGATION-WITH-INSULATION UNDER THE VALUES OF CONSTITUTIONAL DEMOCRACY

The introduction to part II outlined a variety of traditions that run through democratic politics. We can now see how they might view the Principles for Delegation. It looks as though liberal democrats, republican democrats, social democrats, and conservative democrats could all find things in the Principles that accord with their deep convictions about politics and government, while continuing to disagree about policy itself.

Liberals, of whatever complexion, place most weight on the procedural constraints required by the Design Precepts. In particular, they would, I think, emphasize judicial review and the requirement of DP5 that what happens, procedurally or substantively, in an emergency should be clear. It seems to me that, provided a regime is Principles-compliant, liberals ought to be able in general to *tolerate* delegation to trustee agencies so long as they believe that state intervention of the kind concerned is warranted and legitimate.

On the substance of a regime, liberals of different stripes would part company. Regulation especially, but not uniquely, entails *interference* with members of the public in their private lives. Libertarian liberals will set a high bar for state intervention. Social democratic liberals (oddly, a rarely used label in the US) will set a low bar if they believe the hazards of state intervention are more than offset by the capacity of the state to prevent or mitigate interference *between* citizens due to uneven power relations. The point for our inquiry is that the merits/demerits of the substance of a public policy regime can be separated from the question of whether, if adopted, it could decently be delegated to an independent agency insulated from day-to-day politics.

Conservatives would emphasize the importance of time demonstrating that a regime was achieving better results, together with accountability to an ultimately responsible elected legislature and delegating only within the grain of a polity's traditions and values.

Republicans could probably go further. Indeed, some see positive virtue in independent agencies such as central banks (and, as discussed in the next chapter, electoral commissions), precisely because they can be expected to stick to the public's agreed purposes when an elected executive government might be overwhelmingly tempted to substitute its private, short-term goal of getting reelected.[40] On this view, a regime of delegation-with-insulation can be legitimate if, but only if, as demanded by the Principles, it can be understood, monitored, and challenged *by the public* for whether it does in reality deliver the desired degree of independence and the agreed-upon public (or common) good.

The 1980s Bank of England Attitude to Monetary Independence

That value, which has dominated this chapter's discussion, is captured in some valedictory reflections by one of my former bosses and mentors. Looking back to the 1980s' debates about central bank independence in the UK, I am struck that an earlier generation of leaders at the Bank of England did not want monetary independence, despite lamenting the costs of inflation, until and unless there was broad-based support in society for price stability. As Deputy Governor George Blunden put it in the closing words of his final speech in 1990, after more than forty years in central banking:[41]

> My ideal is a publicly responsible central bank entrusted with effectively maintaining the stability of the currency but in a society where such stability is generally desired, where inflation is recognized as a deadly sin, and where government is dedicated to price stability.

Blunden was talking about more than a broad-based belief in the *effectiveness* of monetary independence; he meant that public consent or support was a condition for *legitimacy* too.[42] It is exactly the theme of

[40] Pettit, *On the People's Terms*, summary points 19 and 20, p. 306; and, earlier, Pettit, "Depoliticizing Democracy." This is distinct from advocacy of delegation to agencies in general solely on grounds of promoting deliberative policy making (e.g., Seidenfeld, "Civic Republican Justification," which does not distinguish between agencies with different degrees of insulation from political currents).

[41] Blunden, Julian Hodge Annual Lecture. Blunden was the first chair of both the Basel Committee on Banking Supervision and the Basel Committee on Payment Systems. My eulogy at the memorial service for him is in the Bank of England archive.

[42] A little later, a candidate for the leadership of the Conservative Party called Governor Leigh-Pemberton in substantively the following terms: "Robin, thought I'd let you know that today I will call for Bank independence"; "I should rather you didn't"; "Why not?"; "Time not ripe."

this book, and the motivation for the Principles for Delegation that I have tested and defended in this chapter.

On this view, duly passed legislation is necessary but not sufficient. Embedded, stable preferences, generated by experience and shaped through debate, are also needed—in a democracy.

12

Insulated Agencies and Constitutionalism

CENTRAL BANK INDEPENDENCE DRIVEN BY THE SEPARATION OF POWERS BUT NOT A FOURTH BRANCH

> Should there be a truly "independent" monetary authority? A fourth branch of the constitutional structure coordinate with the legislature, the executive, and the judiciary?
>
> —Milton Friedman, testimony to US House of Representatives Banking Committee, 1964[1]

Throughout part II we have been exploring whether the Principles for Delegation stack up under the deep values and beliefs prevalent in our democratic societies about politics and government: the rule of law, constrained government, and, most vitally, representative democracy itself. We have concluded that, suitably enriched, the Principles can, as a general matter, legitimize the transfer in democracies of limited policy-making powers to truly independent agencies insulated from day-to-day politics.

Against that background, this chapter addresses how the Principles and independent agencies fit into constitutionalism. It considers the following:

- Whether the administrative state invalidates or is invalidated by the canonical three-branch separation of powers
- Whether the Principles (or something like them) should amount to a constitutional convention
- Whether the Principles can accomodate the role of IAs in international policy making
- Whether all truly independent agencies should be treated alike in the constitutional setup

[1]Friedman, "Statement, Testimony, and Comments."

- Whether any particular IA regimes should definitely exist, given the basic tenets of constitutionalism or our broader political values
- Whether independent agencies—all of them, some of them, and in particular central banks—comprise a coequal or independent "fourth branch" of government

Whereas part III turns to the practical realities of US, Westminster, and EU statecraft, for now we maintain a stripped-down conception of the state, assuming only that there is a degree of separation between an elected legislature and an elected executive and that the integrity of the law is entrusted to an independent judiciary (without distinguishing between civil law and common law traditions). Even that will prove enough to disinter some important constitutional distinctions between independent agencies according to their functions, including between electoral commissions and monetary authorities.[2]

THE ADMINISTRATIVE STATE, CONSTITUTIONALISM, AND THE BRANCHES OF THE STATE

The basic geometry of government is not inscribed in stone. At least in its operation, the familiar triangular structure that became embedded over the long eighteenth and nineteenth centuries *was* transformed by the development of the regulatory state over the course of the twentieth century. Structures, norms, and expectations have been adaptive, shaped not only by legal frameworks and the ideas of constitutional authors but also by the dynamics of government responding to what the public demands or expects. The changes are material, but are they elemental?

On the one hand, public law has had to evolve in order to keep proper checks on the exercise of delegated power. The legislature has had to tack to its own creations, developing processes and protocols for constraining agencies and overseeing them via specialist committees. And the elected executive branch has needed to learn to coordinate across the multitude of government functions without violating

[2]Thanks to Nick Barber for comments on an early draft of this chapter.

the integrity of those agencies granted formal independence by the legislature.

On the other hand, it is unclear whether any of that fundamentally challenges the basic structures of constitutional democracy.

From Political Theory to Political Values

Part of the problem is that neither of the two dominant strands of modern political theory have had much to say about this. Modern Hobbesians *do* emphasize that, to meet the welfarist diktats of instrumental logic, the state will rationally incorporate limits on government in order to guard against abuses of power. And, since there is no analogue to Adam Smith's "invisible hand" guiding government toward efficient policies, they hold that discretionary regulation is likely to substitute incurable government failure for curable market imperfections. A polity would, therefore, rationally seek to remedy impediments to efficient markets by creating new property rights; and should as far as possible look to rules rather than governmental discretion when addressing important collective-action problems that cannot be left to the market (chapters 3 and 8).[3] In other words, Hobbesians typically carry a lot of prescriptive baggage on what the state should and should not do but relatively little on how things should be structured below the "constitutional" level.

By contrast, modern Kantians imply that the state needs to do a lot to safeguard people's autonomy and dignity. They place greater faith (not a word they would use) in approximating the economist's social planner through the agency of constitutionally constrained government. For markets to function decently, not only does the state need to provide an infrastructure and rules of the game, but it *should* address distributional outcomes that offend against society's sense of justice (or, more idiomatically, what is right given each person's intrinsic value and entitlement to autonomy). But, again, Kantians do not say much about state structure or delegation, beyond the implication that government should have whatever powers and structure are necessary to deliver justice, as determined through high-level constitutional arrangements that ensure fair and reasoned debate among free citizens (chapter 9).

[3] Brennan and Buchanan, *Reason of Rules*.

Rather splendidly, albeit with some exceptions, the Hobbesian cynics are typically found on the political Right and the Kantian idealists on the social democratic (or progressive) Left. When, rarely, they meet in debates about the administrative state, they tend to pass as ships in the night: one arguing for a limited state in the cause of "liberty," the other for whatever policy prescription might further "equality." This signifies the extent to which much political theory has lost interest in government.

In thinking about the structure of government, we can, however, turn instead to our diverse values and beliefs about the exercise of state power.[4] Part II has drawn on the following precepts:

- The importance of avoiding concentrations of power
- The need for constraints and checks to avoid abuses of power
- The vital importance of impartial adjudication to ensure fair enforcement of rules (laws) backed by the coercive power of the state
- The value of citizens being able to comprehend and rely upon the integrity of each substantive link in the chain of a government process
- The value (to citizens' welfare) of avoiding structures that cannot be expected to deliver the people's purposes as determined through a representative democratic assembly (systematic but legal misuses of power)

Those precepts plainly rule out some institutional innovations, notably transferring all legislative power to the executive branch with the former "legislature" becoming an oversight body of some kind.[5] But they do not uniquely demand Montesquieu's three-branch standard, which if understood mechanically could in practice leave elected politicians delivering inferior policy in some fields for want of an ability to make credible commitments.

One possible response to this would be to jettison the architecture bequeathed by eighteenth-century Europe's history and thought. In early-twentieth-century China, for example, Sun Yat-Sen articulated a five-branch state, adding an *examinations branch* to vet and nurture a

[4] For an account of how different traditions of political thought drawing on, respectively, freedom and efficiency motivate a separation of powers, see Barber, "Prelude."

[5] As aired in Zolo, *Democratic Complexity*, p. 184: "The need should be recognised for a new division of powers to take account of the functional decline of legislative assemblies. The function of promulgating ordinary laws could be given to the executive power while elected organs could receive wider powers of inspection and control over the activities of the administration."

meritocratic bureaucracy and an *integrity branch* charged with keeping the other branches straight and honest.[6] That kind of structure exists in Taiwan, and did so in Thailand until political disturbances during the mid-2000s. With the possible exception of France's system of *grandes écoles* (and especially the super-elite École Nationale Administration), the examinations branch seems remote from Western democracies, but not so the idea of an integrity branch. It is manifest in the various independent ombudsmen (*sic*) that have sprung up across parliamentary democracies in recent decades,[7] and perhaps in bodies like the Public Appointments Commission established by the UK a decade or so ago. This seems to have prompted constitutional debate in only a few countries even though, as the current chief justice of Western Australia has argued, we need "to carefully think through any departures from the traditional constitutional structure."[8]

A Regulatory Branch?

Central to the concerns of this book, similar critical examination needs to be applied to the suggestion of US constitutional theorist Bruce Ackerman that we add to our conception of the legitimate Western state not only an integrity branch but also a *regulatory branch*.[9] He argues, in effect, that it already exists de facto, so we would do well to face up to it. This would entail accepting that it would be decent for a polity not merely to delegate regulation under ordinary legislation but, more strongly, might alienate (that's to say, irrevocably transfer) the power to write legally binding rules to agencies of various kinds.

This book does not go that far. Constrained by democratic values, we argue (chapter 10) for the more modest proposition that, in order to guard against *misuses* of power, a legislature might in certain limited circumstances seek to raise the political costs (for both its current mem-

[6] For example, Ip, "Building Constitutional Democracy." I am grateful to John Braithwaite, of the Australian National University, for alerting me to this Chinese tradition and its manifestations in parts of East Asia.

[7] The term *ombudsman* is still generally used by states that employ this institution.

[8] Martin, "Reflections," and "Forewarned and Four-Armed," expressing reservations about integrity agencies' immunity to legal challenge. Also from Australia, Field, "Fourth Branch of Government," and Wheeler, "A Response."

[9] Ackerman, "New Separation of Powers."

bers and their successors) of later reneging on a policy. The legislature would set a clear standard or objective that establishes and frames the direction of travel. Where the nature of the field/problem is such that it would take years to flesh out the regulatory regime, by which time legislators themselves might find it hard to stick to the course they had charted, they would delegate to a trustee-type agency the responsibility of *completing the job*, governed by a monitorable objective. The legislature would remain free, constitutionally, to repeal or reform the regime and similarly free to pass laws to override any or all of the agency's rules. Delegation-cum-insulation via an IA regulatory regime is a device for legislators to hold to the public purposes framed *by them* when the issues were most salient.

On this view, much of the regulatory state does not warrant such insulation. Delegation to an agency with a bare mandate to "pursue the public interest" is not the same thing at all: it abdicates the legislature's responsibility to frame high policy, violating our democratic values (chapters 11 and 14). Nor do the other types of delegated rule-making authority outlined in chapter 10: for example, a temporary, time-limited mandate to the elected executive branch to experiment with a view to generating proposals for a more permanent, legislated regime; and delegation to a formally politicized agency charged with trading off different objectives and held on a leash by elected politicians. The Principles for Delegation are not designed for any of those circumstances.

The Constitutional Place of Trustee Agencies

Nevertheless, even though more insulated, and so more powerful, than other agencies, trustee agents so conceived are not generally part of a "fourth branch" ranking equally with the familiar three branches of the high-level state. They are plainly subordinate, albeit insulated day to day. Powers are delegated and constrained, not alienated. The legislature can repeal or reform the scope and terms of the delegation, and can override any IA measures through normal legislative processes.[10] The courts can determine the meaning of the delegating law.

[10] For a discussion in a US context, see Strauss, "Place of Agencies."

Since such trustee-type independent agencies exist as a means to commit to a well-articulated public policy purpose and objective, their statutory powers should be interpreted, by the courts (and so by IAs themselves), purposively; and where an ostensibly clear objective leaves ambiguity, with the overall grain of the statutory scheme. That is because the legitimacy of the delegation depends on the intention of credibly committing to a legislated purpose and on constraints that, accordingly, bind the agency to that purpose.[11]

This norm of statutory interpretation would mean an IA should desist if a proposed measure might at a stretch be within the law on a textualist analysis of the statute but could not reasonably be viewed as aimed at pursuing the agency's statutory purpose.

Further, within the spirit of political constitutionalism (chapter 8), where a measure is legal but there is good reason to believe that nothing remotely like it had been contemplated as serving the mandated purpose when the legislation was passed, our democratic values would put the agency under a duty to seek some kind of blessing from current elected government officers.[12] As an example, this would have entailed the ECB gaining support from the heads of government collectively when it introduced measures to stop the euro area itself from falling apart a few years ago: the question being, "do your governments want the monetary union to survive?" (chapter 23).

In summary, the Principles for Delegation fit into a constitutional setup where, at the margin, the three canonical branches retain their core roles in respect of Principles-compliant IAs.

[11] I have in mind something like the following. Say a statute empowers an agency to make rules requiring "prudent conduct" of banks and that the overall purpose of the statute is financial stability, defined as conditions under which the supply of core financial services will be preserved in the face of a shock up to a specified size (see part IV). Then when issuing rules defining prudent conduct, "prudent conduct" should be interpreted to mean conduct material to preserving stability as defined, not conduct that would help to protect investors or make the economy dynamic or deliver a rationally assessed risk-adjusted return. This approach echoes the 1950s' US Legal Process School of Hart and Sacks, but distinguishing between different kinds of administrative-agency regime according to their general purpose (commitment, exploration/experimentation, delegated politicized decision making) (Hart and Sacks, *Legal Process).* My thanks to Jeremy Waldron for alerting me to this. See also Stack, "Purposivism."

[12] This precept has helped me make sense of my discomfort, relayed in chapter 7, when the UK's former Financial Services Authority planned to move from basing the protection of retail investors on the regulation of distribution to the regulation of products.

THE PRINCIPLES AS CONSTITUTIONALIST SOCIAL NORMS

It is now easier to see how the Principles for Delegation fit into the general scheme of constitutionalism. If it is defined as establishing "a set of rules that determine how a practice or institution is organized and run," the Principles are plainly in that spirit.[13] They are putative *norms* guiding the structure of part of the administrative state, offering themselves as a standard against which legislative efforts can be assessed and held accountable. By regulating the distribution of day-to-day power between elected politicians and unelected state technocrats, they equally plainly—echoing the words of the British jurists cited in chapter 8—condition the legal relationship between citizen and state in a general, overarching manner.

In short, constitutionalism can (and, on the view I am advancing, should) make room for arrangements that help the democratic state to make credible commitments, while placing constraints on the institutional means for doing so. In that way, consistent with the value of constitutionalism (chapters 8 and 10), the enduring stability of democratic republics is pursued by enhancing their delivery of widely valued goods.

This does not mean that, to gain traction, the Principles must always and everywhere be incorporated into a legal constitution (whether codified or not) so that they are justiciable. They might amount to a convention, living in the space between law and quotidian politics, at first underpinned by political and social sanctions rather than the courts (but possibly later partly by being respected by legal doctrine). In other words, to make a difference they would at least need to amount to a "political norm," accepted by and hence commanding allegiance among the core officers of the main branches of the state, and supported and informally enforced by a critical mass of outside commentators.[14]

[13] Bellamy, "Constitutional Democracy."

[14] This is akin to the explication of Westminster supremacy in Goldsworthy, *Parliamentary Sovereignty*.

Reaching a Metaconsensus through Public Debate

The Principles can serve as a *norm* in that way only if embedded in public practice and opinion. Since, however, they in effect pile up requirements driven by different conceptions of democratic politics, it is hard to think of them as representing an "overlapping consensus," in the sense of being common to—the intersection of—competing viewpoints.[15] Such a lowest common denominator would be thin, whereas the Principles are anything but that (or so it seems to me).

Instead, agreement on the Principles could be reached only if people with different degrees of attachment to various of their society's values and beliefs about politics could go along with those of the Principles' requirements they themselves thought unnecessary but that others valued. That would be feasible only if each point of view accepted the *institutional consequences* of others' beliefs and values.

This would *not* be an agreement that entailed universal accord around delegation in specific cases. People might disagree about whether the conditions were or could be met, case by case. Agreement around the Principles would therefore amount to a *metaconsensus* about part of the structure of government.[16] Getting there would require public debate.

This is important in addressing a possible challenge, up to now glossed over, to chapter 11's robustness test of the Principles. Since I selected the conceptions and values of democratic politics and governance that were deployed in earlier chapters, how could it be any better than the *liberal principle of legitimacy* test of "no reasonable objection" that I summarily dismissed in chapter 9 on the grounds that it effectively imposes the values of the umpire? The response is that surviving this

[15] As explained in the introduction to part II, our robustness test does not seek an "overlapping consensus" in reasons/justifications. In Rawls's earlier writings, what was at stake was a political conception that could provide an agreed basis for organizing politics (Rawls, "Overlapping Consensus"). What I have in mind is that everyone could agree on an institutional realization of, say, democracy, but without the motivating values being monolithic. So in a three-person state, A, B, and C might share values only as pairs, but each of them would be able to live with the institutional consequences entailed by the, to them, odd belief held by the other two. This meets the arguments in Estlund, "Jeremy Waldron on *Law and Disagreement*," which implicitly posits that the legitimacy of majoritarian democracy must have monolithic grounds. A community going along with or showing allegiance to their political institutions is not the same as the community's members each assenting to a single justificatory proposition or principle.

[16] For a similar point but cast in terms of debates about specific policies rather than the structure of government, see Dryzek and Niemeyer, "Reconciling Pluralism."

book's robustness test amounts to no more than suggesting that the Principles warrant serious consideration via public debate. That is, *real* public debate, which has slipped the Kantian moorings sought by the normative deliberative democrats—not reasoning in an imaginary seminar room but genuine debate, disagreement, and compromise.

Such debate might plausibly involve what would look like a contest among different values. If, for example, one part of a political community places weight on only those elements of the Design Precepts that serve the needs of procedural fairness, they would want—and, more narrowly, it might serve their professional interests to push for—ever more exacting processes. That being so, the equilibrium may be one where the marginal benefit of the added processes to that group is equal to their marginal cost to another group that weighs only the instrumental welfarist consequences of a regime. In that case, society would in theory end up being indifferent about whether or not it realized the benefits of credible commitment via delegation-with-insulation. (If this seems far-fetched, imagine US administrative law scholars and professional economists.)

There might also be trade-offs *among* the "procedural" requirements themselves. For example, there could be tension between those processes that shed public light on policy makers' deliberations and those that equalize power among the members of an agency's policy committee, the former giving the public the wherewithal to debate how the regime works and the latter protecting the public against excessive concentrations of power in committee chairs. Concretely, the publication of the transcripts of all policy meetings provides daylight, which is valuable for public debate, but risks pushing the real deliberations out of collective committee meetings into bilateral side meetings with the chair (or his or her emissaries). Again, views could differ on the balance of costs and benefits.[17]

There is unlikely to be a resolution of those issues that is both detailed and general, applying equally across all fields or to all potential IA regimes. Rich public debate about regime design is needed *case by case*. It is likely that in some cases the trade-offs for public debate would inherently be about where to strike the balance between the "instrumental" and "intrinsic" warrants for democracy.

[17] Warsh, *Transparency*, pp. 36–39.

The Principles and Incentives for IA Policy Makers

What about the IA policy makers? Against the line of some modern Hobbesians, we have accepted that not all problems of credible commitment can be solved by mechanical rules. Delegation to IAs entails some exercise of constrained discretion.

Nevertheless, the Principles *are* Hobbesian in spirit, insofar as they rely on tethering the *interests* of agency leaders to a mandated goal. They assume that trust in institutions, and trust responsiveness (chapter 6), require well-designed incentives (and that it would be reckless to proceed otherwise).

More than that is going on, however. As discussed when the Delegation Criteria were introduced in part I, if the interest we seek to harness is a desire amongst IA leaders for prestige and standing, the society must be one that, as a matter of fact, values dutiful public servants and is prepared to "bestow" esteem on them. If that is no more than a cynical ploy, conferring empty honors, it would hold no value for the prestige-seeking technocratic policy makers and thus, more significantly, no utility for society. Our approach appeals, therefore, to conceptions or practices of "public virtue" even as it seeks to avoid relying on individual policy makers' private virtue. That is one precondition for incentives-values compatibility in this area.

The Principles as a Social Norm for IA Policy Makers: Inducing Self-Restraint

If embedded as a political and social norm, the Principles might help to create incentives for self-restraint.

Given their high status within our societies, IA policy makers have opportunities to act as thought leaders beyond their field or delegated duties. Judges and military leaders have long faced those temptations, giving rise to the ethic of reserve described in chapter 4. As presented there, this might have seemed to be a matter of virtue. But, of course, it is part of the rich set of public expectations, sometimes informally codified, that frame the position in society of military commanders and judges. Embedding something like the Principles as conditions restricting the incidence of delegation-with-insulation might similarly help to induce a norm or ethic of self-restraint among central bankers and other IA policy makers (a precondition for legitimacy returned to in chapter 16 and the book's conclusion).

All this would, of course, be something of a change: that is the point. Which groups might have incentives to help shift healthy constitutional democracies toward such a political norm (what Cristina Bicchieri calls the "trendsetters")?[18] Perhaps, a few legislators here and there. Maybe IA leaders themselves, to the extent they perceive the need to act as legitimacy seekers.

Potent advocates for the Principles (or something like them) would include the international institutions (IMF, World Bank, OECD, and sector standard setters such as Basel and IOSCO), whose whole purpose is to establish common international policies and norms. Here, however, we bump into a problem. In the past those institutions have often advocated delegation-with-insulation without always setting out principled grounds (chapter 7) or sensitivity to local political values. Indeed, acting as the insulated high priests of international liberalism, they would proselytize IAs, wouldn't they!

INDEPENDENT AGENCIES ABROAD: IMPLICATIONS FOR INTERNATIONAL POLICY MAKING

We need, therefore, to confront an elephant in the room: how the norms codified in the Principles for Delegation can be sustained when IAs are acting not within their domestic environment but, instead, with their foreign peers as part of an international policy-making community.

Time has passed but not a great deal has changed since Harvard political scientist Dani Rodrik famously argued that globalization, autonomous nation-states, and democracy comprise an impossible trilemma.[19] Democratic nations continue to participate in international agreements and accords. IAs, and central banks especially, are very much part of this. It is a world where democratically elected assemblies first delegate policy to domestic independent agencies, and the agencies of different

[18] Bicchieri, *Norms*.

[19] Rodrik, *Globalization Paradox*.

countries then gather together to coordinate or even to set common standards, which they undertake to abide by faithfully.[20]

Like IAs themselves, collective international policy making has its roots in problems of credible commitment. In fields where countries' policies or problems have material effects (spillovers) on others, they care about each other's actions. Each country wants credibly to promise its peers that there is no need to worry about it in order to receive a reciprocal promise. International policy-making machinery is, in that sense, collective hand-holding in front of one another and the world, and so tracks the most basic reason for the existence of the state itself (democratic or not): *mitigating collective-action problems* (chapter 3).

Consistent with that, national policy makers can sometimes find it easier at the international table than in a purely domestic setting to escape the reach of those powerful national lobby groups whose domestic clout would otherwise threaten the overall national interest. And, perhaps particularly in highly technical areas, it can sometimes be easier for domestic authorities to commit to sticking to a regime they would like to adopt if part of the "policing" lies in the hands of their expert international peers. I am fairly sure that I observed all of those forces at work during my time as a central banker.

Even so, this state of affairs could threaten to undo the work of legitimizing IAs within the norms of national constitutionalism. The product of IAs' collective international gatherings and deliberations must, somehow, enjoy legitimacy too. I suggest that there are four necessary conditions for this:[21]

1. Locating policy making in international machinery should promise, and ex post actually deliver, better outcomes than could be achieved by national political policy makers (*instrumental warrant*).
2. There should be democratic endorsement of the high-level policy regime (purpose) *and* of either the international machinery itself (treaties) or those of its substantive policies that are intended to be binding (local law-making) (*democratic procedure*).

[20] Here I address only the informal international machinery utilized by IAs, as the elected executive typically participates in treaty organizations whose rules are directly binding.

[21] The four tests can, I believe, be mapped into those in the "complex standard for legitimacy" set out in Buchanan and Keohane, "Global Governance Institutions." Similarly, there exists a broad mapping into the Principles for Delegation for domestic independent agencies.

3. The institution should conduct itself in line with the values of the rule of law, so that, among other things, arbitrary power is constrained and abuses of rights are protected against (*rule of law*).
4. Policy formation and outputs should each be sufficiently transparent to benefit from public debate and scrutiny, so that society/countries can decide whether to maintain the regime and can contest its outputs and modalities (*Design Precept 4*).

Our domestically legitimized IAs should participate in international policy making on that basis, which becomes a supplementary provision of the Principles.

The last of those precepts warrants a bit of fleshing out. First, international standard setters should consult openly, encouraging responses from far and wide. Second, the chairs of the key groups and subgroups of those international bodies should give speeches, explicitly wearing their international hats, explaining the evolution of their group's thinking. Third, IAs themselves should do what they can to ensure there is broad domestic knowledge and understanding of the international deliberations they are party to, conveying the extent to which their agency's domestic policies are being framed in light of those international discussions, agreements, or standards.

Taking those steps together, this amounts to coming clean about the reality of international coordination, exposing it to debate and criticism.

THE SEPARATION OF POWERS AND SPECIFIC IA REGIMES

We can get so far, but no further, without engaging with particular regimes. Drawing part II to a close, two contrasting case studies—electoral commissions and monetary authorities—reveal that an IA's specific purposes can make a difference to its place in the constitutional scheme.

Electoral Commissions: Guardians of Democracy?

Electoral commissions are bodies that in some states determine, variously, the boundaries of electoral districts, the amounts that may be spent on elections, rules on conflicts of interest, advertising, and so on. Their purpose is to underpin the integrity of the democratic state by setting and implementing the rules of the game for representative democracy itself.

They are sometimes bracketed with ombudsmen (*sic*) and anticorruption bodies as "integrity agencies." That is potentially misleading.[22] In principle, each of the three main branches of the state could contain bureaus that police the integrity of the others. But that does not work if a polity wishes to get away from, say, elected representatives determining the boundaries of their districts (in the UK, constituencies) and, further, wishes to shield sitting judges from involvement in something so elementally political.

The electoral commission function is by no means always housed within independent agencies. It is perhaps more commonly insulated in newer democracies, sometimes by a written constitution. But older democracies are hardly immune from concerns about the gerrymandering of districts, campaign finance, and electoral integrity: familiarity with democracy is not in itself insulation against its erosion.

Whatever their current formal status in particular jurisdictions, as a device for committing to electoral integrity they could in principle be established in two quite different ways.

Under the first, the legislature would establish the commission under an ordinary statute and make it a trustee-type agency. The elected legislators would in effect be saying, "We mean to be good but we need to bind ourselves, and for that reason we are setting up an independent agency that is highly insulated from day-to-day politics." The legislature would be free to amend or repeal its delegating act or to override the commission's decisions, but doing so would be a highly visible step.

The de facto independence of an electoral commission established in this way would turn, therefore, on public and political opinion and, thus, partly on its performance. In a striking example of the contingencies of independence, it is widely thought that an electoral commission bled power, standing, and, due to recruitment difficulties, eventually capability after problems (lost ballots) with the administration of an election in the state of Western Australia in 2013.[23]

[22] The distinction between integrity agencies and electoral commissions is also made in Ackerman, "New Separation of Powers." He allocates electoral commissions to a *democracy branch*.

[23] "Inquiry into the 2013 WA Senate Election," www.aec.gov.au.

Under the second approach, the electoral commission would be more deeply embedded, most obviously through establishment in the "basic law" or constitution. Not only would elected legislators be barred from interfering, they would *not* be free to repeal or amend the institution through ordinary legislation. While design questions arise about how the commission would itself be appointed and account to the public, this is plainly a step beyond the domain of our Principles.

Indeed, a combination of deep entrenchment, whether by law or convention, with their role of protecting the integrity of the democratic process gives some electoral commissions the status of guardians, ranking higher in the order of things than normal IAs and perhaps constituting a genuine fourth branch.

Where Do Central Banks Stand in the Constitutional Order?

Our other case study, monetary authorities, leads to a different conclusion, one that is in some respects more interesting. We spend more time on it, as a precursor to part IV and because central banks are, today, the epitome of unelected power.

In the introduction to part II, we argued for the legitimacy of price stability as a public policy objective in a democratic polity—boldly, that it is a condition for liberty. Does that imply, as Milton Friedman clearly meant to imply (and lament) in the statement quoted at the chapter head marking the Fed's fiftieth jubilee, that central banks comprise a "fourth branch" of government?

This thought has animated others. As observed in chapter 8, for James Buchanan it meant policy should be heavily constrained:

> Something analogous to the independent judiciary . . . seems required, but . . . bound by the parameters set out in the constitution.[24]

Whether or not he thought it a good thing, Robert Dahl would also have included central banks among his "quasi guardians" (quasi because "they would not possess the moral and epistemological justification that

[24] Buchanan, "Constitutionalization of Money," p. 256. He comes close to saying that this is achievable only in a polity where a written constitution is the ultimate sovereign authority rather than parliament. That simply shifts the locus of the highest level of politics, including partisanship, to the members of the Supreme Court, who interpret the constitution.

Plato . . . claimed for true guardianship").[25] More recently, British public law theorist Martin Loughlin included them among a group of *ephors*, in homage to the group of Spartans charged with supervising the fundamental welfare of the state and so in some respects standing above their kings.[26]

To try to make sense of these suggestions that central banks are not regular IAs, let's go back to the king we met at the start of part I, holding fiscal, judicial, informational, and military power close in his chamber. One of the earliest steps toward our modern state was the demand of medieval parliaments to approve the king's desire to levy extra taxes. It remains at the heart of the separation of powers. That separation would be undermined if the executive government could use a power to print money as a substitute for legalized taxation. If the executive branch controlled the money creation power, it would at the very least be able to defer its need to go to the legislature for extra "supply," and at worst could inflate away the real burden of its debts to reduce the amount of taxation requiring parliamentary or congressional sanction. In other words, it could usurp the legislature's prerogatives.

There are only two solutions to this. One is to pass a law tying money to a binding, mechanical rule, most obviously some physical standard, such as gold. The other, where a society has accepted fiat money, is to delegate the management of the currency's value to an agency designed to be immune from the necessities and temptations of short-term popularity.

The choice between a commodity standard and an independent central bank-managed, fiat-money regime must be made by the legislature. While views differ, a return to gold is unlikely to be the choice of today's full-franchise democracies. The purpose of the old gold standard was to deliver external convertibility and stability of the currency, which served the interests of those for whom trade and international exchange mattered a lot. The consequent volatility in domestic output and employment would probably not be politically sustainable in the modern world; the public wants price stability to come in harness with measures to smooth the business cycle (macroeconomic stabilization

[25] Dahl, *Democracy and Its Critics*, p. 337.

[26] Loughlin, *Foundations of Public Law*, chapter 15. For the broader view of IAs comprising a fourth branch, Vibert, *Rise of the Unelected*, treats central banks as canonical.

policy). This is a facet of what has become known as *embedded liberalism*, comprising a system that incorporates measures to mitigate the costs to individuals or groups of free-market capitalism.[27]

CENTRAL BANK INDEPENDENCE AS A COROLLARY OF THE HIGH-LEVEL SEPARATION OF POWERS

On this view, an independent monetary authority is a *means* to underpinning the separation of powers once the step to adopt fiat money has been taken. The regime is *derivative* of the higher-level constitutional structure and the values behind it.

This is a substantively different kind of warrant for central bank independence from the welfarist and democratic tests incorporated into our Delegation Criteria.[28] They are *permissive*, placing constraints on how much may legitimately be delegated to an IA (credible commitment, no big value judgments), whereas now we have a reason why monetary policy *should* be delegated.

BARRING MONETARY FINANCING OF GOVERNMENT: A REPUBLICAN VALUE

This view provides a double-headed constitutional basis for a rule that the central bank should not provide "monetary financing" to government. On the one hand, if the government could demand central bank financing, it would have access to the inflation tax by the back door, and the commitment to stability would lack credibility. A bar on such demands can be thought of as a central bank's *Fiscal Shield*.[29] On the other hand, if the central bank could lend directly to government on its own discretion, unconstrained by its stability objective, it would be able to choose whether or not a financially stretched government survives, making it a master rather than a trustee. Both elements of a "no monetary financing" rule draw on the republican value of nondomination.

CONSTITUTIONALLY NECESSARY BUT NOT AN EQUAL FOURTH BRANCH

We are now in a position to sum up where central banks, as monetary authorities, stand in the order of things:

27 Ruggie, "International Regimes." Ruggie himself focused on the welfare state rather than on macroeconomic stabilization policy.

28 As, for example, in Blinder, *Central Banking*, and Drazen, "Central Bank Independence."

29 In part IV, when discussing concerns that have arisen with central bank liquidity and credit policies, we introduce the concept of a *Fiscal Carve-Out*, supplementing the *Shield*.

- Monetary independence is *permissible* (can in principle achieve legitimacy) because, via commitment, it can prospectively achieve better results and help to protect people's liberty, while (or so part IV argues) being amenable to constraints in line with the Principles.
- Further, it can be *normatively warranted* as a means of underpinning the higher-level constitutional separation of powers. That is not a consequence of the time-inconsistency welfare problem inherent in monetary policy as such but, rather, arises because monetary policy could otherwise be used as an instrument of general taxation by the elected executive.
- But, in contrast to the legislature taking on, say, the court's functions of adjudicating individual disputes, it would not be an abomination if the people left the legislature with a power to employ the inflation tax via ordinary legislation.
- In consequence, in a fiat-money system, independence is a corollary of the constitutional separation of powers but does not need to be embedded in the basic law.
- Where not deeply entrenched via a basic law, not only can the agency's decisions be overruled by the legislature but, in addition, the regime may be reformed or repealed. In order to reap the benefits of credible commitment, a central bank statute needs, therefore, to be embedded via broad public support.
- A "no monetary financing" rule is necessary to avoid the central bank having powers similar to that of the legislature itself. If it could choose whether or not to fund government, it would be a very mighty citizen: indeed, in some circumstances a dominating superior.

A HIERARCHY OF TRULY INDEPENDENT AGENCIES: TRUSTEES AND GUARDIANS

The two case studies, of electoral commissions and monetary authorities, presented in the preceding section enrich our conception of truly independent agencies. Compared with the single category of trustee-like agencies introduced in chapter 4, we now have a richer picture of a hierarchy of independent-agency regimes:

1. *Trustee-type* independent agencies that are established in ordinary statutes to deliver credible commitment to a public policy purpose for purely consequentialist reasons (for example, a regulator established to write rules to flesh out a standard for financial system resilience).
2. *Trustee-type* independent agencies that are not established by the constitution but are a corollary of the higher-level separation of powers (for example, independent monetary authorities).
3. *Guardian-type* agencies that are established by the constitution to preserve democracy and the rule of law generally (canonically, constitutional courts and, perhaps, some electoral commissions).

To underline our earlier conclusion, it seems hard to argue that trustee-type independent agencies in either the first or second category can comprise an equal "fourth branch" of government alongside the canonical branches. Those three branches have powers over the agencies—creation, purposes and powers (legislature), appointments (executive), and compliance with law (courts)—but *not* vice versa. This is a world where, under the Principles for Delegation, the rules of the game are set, can be amended, and are monitored by the three familiar high-level branches.

By contrast, truly independent agencies that fall into the third category might constitute a distinct fourth branch. They are, in essence, *guardians of the democratic process and the rule of law.* The high judiciary and, perhaps, independent electoral commissions meet that description. As a general matter, central banks do not.

Might Central Banks Still Be Overmighty?

As part II comes to a close, we have an answer to Friedman's question of whether, in a democratic constitutional republic, independent central banks do or should comprise a fourth branch: no. We must, however, enter two qualifications.

First, what about those central banks, notably the ECB, that are established by treaty, are beyond the reach of the democratically elected powers, and have acted to underpin the system they serve?

Second, even if not properly regarded as a fourth branch, is it not still possible that central banks could be *overmighty citizens*? As the problems with the "robber barons" in early-twentieth-century America showed, private people and organizations can wield too much political power. Is that not a bigger risk when great government agencies have the fiscal and coercive power of the state behind them? Do our Principles provide sufficient reassurance that they will not wield power politically? Do we end up relying on an ethic of self-restraint?

To address those questions we need to move from part II's focus on values to look more carefully at incentives. Our goal is IA regimes that are incentives-values-compatible. In part III we look at the real-world state structures in which central banks and other independent agencies find themselves, nationally and internationally. Then, in part IV we examine more closely the powers of the postcrisis central banks and how to ensure that legitimacy is not undermined by their being overmighty citizens in practice.

PART III

Incentives

THE ADMINISTRATIVE STATE IN THE REAL WORLD: INCENTIVES AND VALUES UNDER DIFFERENT CONSTITUTIONAL STRUCTURES

> Dangerous ambition more often lurks behind the specious mask of zeal for the rights of the people than under the forbidding appearance of zeal for the firmness and efficiency of government.
>
> —Alexander Hamilton

> You must first enable the government to control the governed; and in the next place, oblige it to control itself.
>
> —James Madison[1]

The first two parts of this book, setting out the Principles for Delegation and then examining them against our general notions of constitutional democracy, have abstracted from actual state structures. It is time to get closer to the real world. The next few chapters offer a more granular exploration of the capability of different national political constitutions to frame, oversee, and hold to account independent agencies. In deciding whether and how to put policy at arm's length from day-to-day politics, how do they navigate the apparent tension between the values pressed by two of the West's most towering state builders, Hamilton and Madison?

If there are varieties of capitalism, there are also very obviously varieties of constitutional democracy.[2] The focus in this inevitably reductive survey will be the US, the UK, and, to a lesser extent, France, Germany,

[1]From Hamilton, Madison, and Jay, *The Federalist,* Nos. 1 and 51, pp. 3 and 266.

[2]On the former, see Hall and Soskice, *Varieties of Capitalism.*

and the EU, with a few examples drawn from other advanced-economy democracies.

Our underlying question is whether, across those different systems, independent agencies constructed according to the Principles for Delegation would violate the constitutional setup or be a natural elaboration of the order of things. If the Principles are not at odds normatively with a jurisdiction's constitutional order, the issue is whether different state structures and political conventions can *in practice* accommodate them. One of the big issues that emerges is whether the values underpinning particular constitutional structures are always consistent with the incentives those structures generate. We begin, therefore, with how a country's constitutional and political geometry affects the incentives of their elected legislators.

THE INFLUENCE OF THE CONSTITUTIONAL STRUCTURE ON POLITICS

In the "political values" robustness test of the Principles that occupied part II, we assumed little more than representative democracy incorporating a separation of powers between executive government and the legislature, with the integrity of law in the hands, partly, of an independent judiciary. In the real world, constitutional structures are much richer, and legal systems draw on different traditions.

Many, but not all, polities dilute elected legislative power across different assemblies. The degree of separation between the executive and the legislature varies from high (US, EU) to low (UK). Some states are unitary, others federal, with the latter exhibiting large variations in the division of power between the center and the provinces.

Representative democracy's most basic institution, the system of voting, also comes in different shapes. Democracies are typically made up of districts (or *constituencies* as they are known in the UK), with elections to choose either a single candidate or multiple candidates to represent each district. Some have a first-past-the-post (plurality) decision rule; others have proportional elections, which can involve voting for party lists rather than individual candidates.

In some countries, the whole state-structure package, including the electoral system, is formally enshrined in a written constitution or "basic law," of greater or lesser length and prescription, subject to higher or lower hurdles for amendment, and whose meaning emerges and evolves through practice and interpretation. In other countries, notably the UK, the constitution comprises an accretion of laws, practices, and conventions that is not codified in one place.[3] Whether or not formally codified, the constitutional setup influences various dimensions of politics, including the structure of political parties (whether few or many, whether characterized by strong or loose discipline among their elected representatives); whether or not coalition government is the norm; whether the laws on campaign finance are tight (UK) or relaxed (US); and whether claims to social and economic rights are justiciable.

The construction of governments and the independence of individual legislators relative to party bosses depend on these high-level rules and conventions. And the same underlying incentives and constraints have a powerful influence on the structure of the administrative state and how it is overseen.

Two First-Past-the-Post (Plurality) Systems: The UK versus the US

While profoundly different in other respects, the US and UK lie at one end of the spectrum of electoral systems. Their legislative assemblies comprise single-member-district representatives elected on a plurality of votes and with the public having no legal obligation to vote. Often termed *majoritarian*, a common shorthand for modern representative democracy, in neither country does government in fact require a majority of the popular vote, let alone of those entitled to vote. A UK versus US comparison illustrates, however, how things can differ even across first-past-the-post (plurality) systems.

In the UK, the election (or reelection) prospects of individual candidates typically depend heavily on the popularity of their party, and in particular their party leaders, as voters know they are very likely to be choosing a single-party executive government that will be able to legislate

[3]That does not preclude the package being summarized informally in one place. Under the initiative of former cabinet secretary Gus O'Donnell, and following the example of New Zealand, the UK published such a summary in December 2010: *Cabinet Manual: A Guide to Laws, Conventions and Rules on the Operation of Government*. The manual carries no formal legal authority and is not static.

its program. This makes both party leaders and regular members of Parliament highly sensitive to *national* public opinion. And it generates a high degree of parliamentary-party discipline, except when backbenchers conclude that they will not get reelected without a change in party leadership.

By contrast, in the US, where a party platform struggles to prevail given the need for alignment between Senate, House, and Administration, voters are more attentive to candidates' sensitivity to local interests and values. Party discipline is typically loose. The upshot is that legislative outcomes reflect bargains among many competing positions and views.[4]

Taken together, these high-level constitutional structures and party-political systems influence the role and clout of committees in the legislature. In the US, congressional leaders and committees hold the keys to the legislative process, including a right to table and, in effect, veto draft statutes. Members are incentivized to allow their peers to serve on those committees that are most relevant to the local interests of their constituents (and where, according to proponents of interest-group pluralism (chapter 11), they might have an informational advantage).[5] Given relatively loose party discipline, committee members are typically free to pursue those local interests, as well as the national interest as they perceive it. In consequence, US Bills are complicated things, filled with special measures necessary to carry a majority of votes in committee and/or on the floor of each house.

In the UK, by contrast, parliamentary select committees do not have a formal role in legislation. Rather, it is the executive branch that has a de facto monopoly over the tabling of legislation. Party discipline is strong on the floor of the House of Commons and in the (distinct) bill committees that process draft legislation. The House of Lords can delay and amend, often today acting as a "liberal amendment chamber," with the executive sometimes loathe to overturn its measures in the Commons if that means using up capital with their backbenchers. Nevertheless, legislation basically gets passed, and the technical integrity of statutes is largely underpinned by the specialist Office of the Parliamentary Coun-

[4] Pettit, "Varieties of Public Representation," appendix.
[5] Shepsle, *Analyzing Politics*.

sel, which can make technical improvements to draft Opposition or Second Chamber amendments that the executive government decides to accept.

Crucially for our purposes (chapter 15), members of the House of Commons are typically less partisan—that is, party discipline is less strong—when sitting in the select committees that oversee independent (and other) agencies, which for many backbenchers has arguably become their main source of political leverage and prestige. As such, they have gained informal influence over regulatory legislation through their joined-up interventions on public policy substance.

Perhaps the best way of summing up the differences between these two "majoritarian" systems is in terms of *decisiveness*.[6] In the UK, governments can govern: as soon as they cannot get their program through Parliament, they cease being the government. By contrast, the majoritarian elements of the US political structure are counterbalanced by the fragmentation of legislative power across House, Senate, President (and Court). In the language of political scientists, this creates many "veto points."[7] When a party holds all three points of the legislative triangle, more bills may pass than under "divided government." The opposition might wait many years for an opportunity to repeal those measures. In other words, partly by design, the US legislative system is rarely decisive, and is in a desperate dash when it is. This is very important to the structure of the administrative state.

Consensus Systems and Continental Europe

The US system's reliance on compromise to get things done has some things in common with those Continental European democracies that rely on consensus and corporatism (chapter 11). Observing that power is more likely to be shared in countries characterized by "deep cleavages" of, for example, religious faith or ethnicity, Arend Lijphart contrasts the institutional implications of the "consensus" and "Westminster" models of democracy.[8] Among the former are the obvious list of proportional

[6]Cox and McCubbins, "Political Structure."

[7]Tsebelis, *Veto Players*. For background on veto powers in the US Congress, see McCarty, Poole, and Rosenthal, *Political Bubbles*.

[8]Lijphart, *Patterns of Democracy*. His characterization of the UK system has become a caricature, underplaying the role of the courts, the second chamber, and, as time has passed, the

representation, multiple political parties, and coalition government, including "grand coalitions" of the main parties, which, by contrast, have occurred in the UK only during periods of national disaster or major war (and would be viewed as risking extremism gaining critical mass outside the coalition parties).[9]

In addition to liberal checks and balances, underpinned by specialist constitutional courts, such systems tend to disperse power to bureaucratic agencies. Together, corporatism and delegation are seen as reducing the incidence of conflicts that could prove intractable for elected politicians representing different parts of fractured communities. And the insulated courts are seen as deterring technocratic trespasses against socioeconomic and civil rights, the Continental European lodestar since World War II and its aftermath. Indeed, this system of government often positively embraces nonmajoritarian institutions, since they help to avoid concentrations of power and might produce unbiased information that helps foster public consensus. Independent central banks fall squarely within this way of thinking.[10]

Among the nations discussed in part III, Germany, while monolingual, has many of the characteristics of a consensual polity. Like the US, it is a federal state, with a written constitution and a powerful constitutional court: the culture is of a rules-based *Rechtsstaat*. But it is also a parliamentary democracy, with MPs elected under proportional representation, leading to coalition governments.

Our other Continental European example is France, which has a semipresidential system of government that can lead to periods of cohabitation between a president and a parliamentary majority from different parties.[11] It has fairly strong short-term party discipline but a tradition of party splits and reconfigurations (perhaps induced by two-round elections). Overall, this can push France toward the indecisive end of the spectrum, except where a strong president is backed by a supportive parliamentary majority. In marked contrast with the US, however, administrative coherence is generally maintained by the highly

---

select committees. But big picture his contrast stands. Also, Dahl, *Democracy and Its Critics*, chapter 18.

[9] Words written maybe two years before the 2017 German elections.

[10] Cama and Pittaluga, "Central Banks and Democracy."

[11] Elgie, "Semi-Presidentialism."

homogeneous technocratic inner elite, trained and formed at the famous *École Nationale d'Administration* (ENA). This group spans all branches of the state, including the constitutional court, as well as key pillars of the private sector, and has traditionally seen itself as devoted to (if not embodying) the values of the Republic.

The Special Case of the EU: Confederal Governance

Both France and Germany, and for the moment the UK, are members of the EU. As briefly described in chapter 2, the EU is, approximately, a confederation of sovereign states, which, through a series of treaties, suspend or pool elements of national sovereignty in a way that has created a corpus of EU law. Its legal directives must be implemented nationally, and some of its laws, including rules drawn up by some agencies, have direct effect. Within its machinery, the European Commission has a monopoly on formally proposing legislative acts, and the Council of Ministers and Parliament decide. For some kinds of measure, including much of the regulatory state, the Council decides by supermajority (qualified-majority voting) rather than unanimity.

In practice, policy making inhabits a space that oscillates between the legal institutions of the EU and intergovernmental agreements among the member states. At crucial moments, including during the 2008–2009 phase of the financial crisis, the latter mode has tended to dominate. As Germany's Chancellor Merkel has often commented, Europe operates by consensus within the constraints of the law.

This is reinforced by the character of the Parliament (EP), whose members are determined via separate elections in each member state, largely via party-list proportional representation. There are no EU-wide political parties but instead various groupings of center Right, center Left national-party representatives. As overt coalitions, these groupings generate a further layer of compromise.

The Parliament is large (over 700 members), with its committees similarly large: as of late 2016, the ECON committee that oversees the ECB and financial regulation had sixty-one members. In consequence, speaking time during legislative debates and agency hearings is heavily rationed. On legislation, the Parliament is represented in what are known as *trialogue* negotiations with the Council and Commission by the chair of the relevant committee and a dedicated *rapporteur* elected by that committee's members. The effect is to confer power on relevant specialists, under the shadow of the floor vote necessary for legislation to pass.

A very important feature of the EU system, distinguishing it from national democracies, is that the broad trajectory of policy tends not to change after EP elections, even though the Parliament must approve the composition of the Commission (as a block).

POLITICAL INCENTIVES, VALUES, AND THE DESIGN OF THE ADMINISTRATIVE STATE

Those varying formal state arrangements create incentives and norms that pervade the political culture, with profound consequences for the shape of the administrative state—for *whether* to delegate, *how* to do so, and for *oversight* arrangements.

The Power of Incentives

So how might the underlying political structures of different jurisdictions be expected to affect delegation-with-insulation? This introduction to part III offers an outline that we will fill out over the next few chapters.

Leading UK politicians have historically been used to being in control of policy when in office and, as such, we would expect them to approach delegation with a jaundiced eye, as indeed historically they did (see chapters 2 and 17). In the words of one political scientist, they (and their civil servants) are naturally "power hoarders."[12] For subtly different reasons, we might similarly expect the French elite, spanning politics and administration, to be leery of delegating power to independent agencies (evidenced by the quote from Christian Noyer in chapter 2); and if pursued, to be very careful to ensure that its ethos is reflected in the choice of agency leaders.

[12] Matthew Flinders, in written evidence submitted to the Political and Constitutional Reform Committee of the House of Commons, May 2012.

Under their quite different, typically highly divided form of government, US politicians, in either the executive or legislative branch, are not especially used to being in control of policy. This would leave them liable to scrap among themselves for institutional and personal influence, including blocking or hemming in the power of their opponents.

Whereas in the US, delegation to independent agencies could be a means for politicians of a particular stripe to lock in a policy they happen to favor during a brief period of legislative power, in consensus democracies delegation to nonpoliticians can be a structural solution to a historical problem of conflicting societal values or perspectives among different "national" groups within the polity. In other words, the ongoing bargaining process characteristic of US-style interest-group pluralism might be predicated on the "pluralism" being only skin deep (and so might erode, or become sclerotic, if ideological differences were ever to evolve into deeper social cleavages, as perhaps they have).

Meanwhile in the EU, the Commission has incentives (and arguably a duty) to promote legislative initiatives that centralize regulatory power at Community level.[13] Individual member-state politicians have incentives to resist, in order to hold onto power themselves, except where an EU initiative enables them to lock in a policy that their national rivals oppose or to escape blame by moving a field out of national politics.

Whether that is how things turn out depends on whether the incentives to delegate generated by particular systems of democratic governance sit comfortably with the values that supposedly underpin them. This turns out to be hugely important for making sense of national debates about the administrative state.

Accountability: The UK Focus

In the UK, with legislative power concentrated, there is rarely much doubt about who, ultimately, is responsible for determining the terms of a piece of legislation and the quality of its subsequent execution: the executive government of the day.

The corollary of this is the central role of *accountability* in British public life. With no ambiguity around who was responsible, there was

[13] A similar point is made in Majone, "Two Logics."

traditionally no doubt about who should be held accountable: the executive government, in the House of Commons, to the country, and in the courts. Incentives and beliefs about government were aligned: the two main political parties had little incentive to delegate, which squared with deep norms of executive branch accountability.

Writing half a century ago, before the explosion of delegated governance, one leading commentator captured how, historically, parliamentary supremacy reconciled the twin pillars of the British system: government under the control of Parliament and executive actions under control of the law:[14]

> Ministerial responsibility [became] the crux of the English system. Whilst it remained a reality the whole edifice of constitutionalism could be maintained; should it cease to be a workable concept the process of disintegration between the legal basis and the operation of government would begin.

The advent of independent agencies (and, separately, EU membership) threatened to alter that delicate balance, potentially upturning it. This explains why the issue of accountability has been so central to British debates about independent agencies.[15]

Contrast that with the US, where any number of actors might have a de facto veto over legislation or executive branch implementation. It is hard to be clear who should be held accountable for a piece of legislation when it is so difficult to unravel the contributions, red-line points, and compromises of the Administration, the House, and the Senate and their committees and individual members, and the later role of litigants and the courts in determining what the legislation means. "Accountability" seems to play a smaller role in American political culture than across the Atlantic because, by design, responsibility is fractured and, therefore, shared.[16]

This is a world in which it is commonplace to talk about agencies being accountable to courts as judicial overseers, a notion that would seem slightly odd to the British.

[14] Vile, *Constitutionalism*, p. 254.

[15] Wright, "Politics of Accountability."

[16] It is striking how few US books on democratic theory mention accountability; for example, barely in Dahl, *Democracy and Its Critics*.

The Right to Pass Laws under the Constitution: A US Focus

Conversely, many Americans would, I suspect, be surprised at how relaxed Brits and some other Europeans have become with administrative agencies making laws (in the form of legally binding regulations) and, more generally, exercising discretion. These concerns drive proposals for fundamentally reforming the US administrative state, and similarly those calling for Congress to give the Fed a rule for setting interest rates.

The root of the issue is that the Constitution clears the way for a legislative program only when one of the political parties, with popular and dynamic leadership, wins all three points of the electoral triangle—President, House, and Senate. If, further, the unified government is responding to a widely felt national need, perhaps in an emergency, and both the policy and the president enjoy support across the country, the courts may lean toward allowing the heart of even constitutionally adventurous measures to stand.[17]

When the typically brief period of unified government passes, the opposing party might not get a realistic opportunity to repeal a measure they heartily dislike until they manage to gain hold of all three points of the triangle. If that takes many years, perhaps decades, the measure's institutional reforms will have become part of national life. The structure of government, the role of the state or the people's legislated entitlements are altered. This is how the constitution can evolve without formal amendments to the document itself. The very existence of the modern administrative state is arguably an example.[18]

Ironically, therefore, if Burke's prescriptive legitimacy operates in his homeland via successive governments *choosing* not to repeal an inherited measure, a less happy version of informal entrenchment seems to operate in the US. There time does not necessarily heal wounds. Indeed, some might be scratched forever when, as during the New Deal reforms of the administrative state, one side's leaders prove able to alter the institutional fabric, and so constitutional reality, of the nation's government.

[17] That is the story told by Ernst, *Toqueville's Nightmare*, of Chief Justice Hughes's retreat during the 1930s from substantively constraining to requiring procedural integrity in the administrative state.

[18] The somewhat controversial idea of constitutional turning points (or "moments") is advanced in Ackerman, *We the People*.

Incentives and values can be at odds in other ways in the US. As we shall see, given congressional incentives to shed blame, rule-making power can land wherever it is taken by the balance of bargaining power rather than being guided by values-compatible principles about the structure of government (chapter 13). Arguably, the US system struggles to achieve *incentives-values compatibility* as opposed to the narrower incentives-compatibility emphasized by economists. This might go some way to explain the vexed and tortured tone of much US commentary on the administrative state: given the structure of legislators' incentives, it is tough for the system of government to live up to its own values.

Output Legitimacy: A Solution for the EU?

Things are different again in the EU. In order to propel and to maintain their Project, the member states had incentives to give the unelected Commission monopoly rights to initiate legislation; and to delegate various regulatory functions to the Commission and, later, to independent agencies. Given the lack of a demos and the paucity of active continent-wide public debate and participation in EU affairs, that structure of unelected power prompted the argument that the values of democracy are regarded as being realized via "output legitimacy" (an essentially consequentialist legitimation strategy).[19] This sits on shaky ground, however, as it relies on regulation being validated by "procedure-independent standards" that do not need the imprimatur of a prior democratic process and, put starkly, on continuously successful outcomes.

The gap cannot be remedied by the supplementary idea of "institutional throughput" legitimacy, vital though that is (broadly corresponding to rule-of-law values plus varieties of participation, and thus to our second and fourth Design Precepts).[20] That is because this legitimation strategy—output-plus-throughput credentials—cannot delineate substantive no-go areas for unelected technocrats by recourse to processes that embody democratic values. As such, it draws implicitly

[19] Although he introduced the ideas much earlier, an English language version is in Scharpf, *Governing in Europe*, by which point he had become pessimistic about the adequacy of EU outputs.

[20] Schmidt, "Democracy and Legitimacy," which distinguishes "institutional" from "constructive" throughputs.

on an insistence that, since the EU has almost no redistributional capacity, its regulatory interventions are, almost by definition, directed at values-neutral efficiency improvements. But, as discussed in chapters 3 and 5, in the real world there are not neat lines between efficiency and equity, which matters all the more given Commission incentives to push the EU's regulatory reach.[21] So elected politicians are needed after all.

If democratic sanction comes largely from the Council of Ministers and the prime-minister-level European Council, the implication is that it falls to them to generate the public debate needed on measures to establish EU independent-agency regimes. That values-driven prescription might well clash, however, with their incentives to negotiate behind closed doors, compromising on delegating values choices to unelected technocrats (violating our Delegation Criteria, which go beyond "output," "throughput," and procedural "input" legitimation tests). It would seem that a leap is needed to a more transparent system (for example, the Council meeting in public when debating and passing legislation), if the incentives of participating ministers are to be brought more nearly into line with the democratic values, and hence the public debate, upon which the legitimacy of their own national power relies.[22]

WHAT LIES AHEAD

It is my hope that those examples of how beliefs and norms can be shaped, or put into flux, by particular institutional structures for democratic government help to demonstrate how debates about the legitimacy of the administrative state in the real world are unavoidably complex. While any polity's institutions are shaped by the deep beliefs forged through its particular history, those beliefs and values are themselves partly shaped by inherited institutional structures and the incentives they generate.

Since what we are dealing with here is power—who has it, for what purposes, and on what terms—the interconnectedness of events, beliefs, values, norms, laws, and institutions is no small matter. It is hard enough

[21] Majone, *Dilemmas*, chapter 7.2.

[22] Article 15(2) of the Treaty on the Functioning of the EU (TFEU) seems to require this already, but we do not see televised debates in the Council.

to make public policy incentives-compatible. It might be even harder to make it incentives-values-compatible, especially when it comes to innovations in the structure of government.

We explore this in the next few chapters, starting with how local incentives and values affect whether to delegate at all to independent agencies, and going on to how the challenges of vague objectives, accountability, and emergencies vary across the West's advanced-economy democracies. On the way, we revisit the special challenge of IAs as collective international policy makers.

13

States' Capacity for Principled Delegation to Deliver Credible Commitment

> Successful long-run economic performance requires appropriate incentives not only for economic actors but for political actors as well. . . . The constitution must be self-enforcing in the sense that the major parties . . . must have an incentive to abide by [it].
>
> —Douglas North and Barry Weingast, 1989[1]

The core of the normative case for delegation to trustee-type, truly independent agencies is that, in some fields, the people's welfare can be improved by materially reducing problems of credible commitment, without violating the deep values of constitutional democracy. Whether such agencies do or can exist in practice depends on whether legislatures are capable of framing appropriately constrained commitment regimes. The outcomes can be represented in a two-dimensional matrix, spanning, in one dimension, whether or not the Principles for Delegation (or something like them) are satisfied or could be satisfied and, in the other, whether or not a regime is delegated to a truly independent agency. There are five types of outcomes:

	Satisfy Principles	*Don't but could satisfy Principles*	*Cannot satisfy Principles*
Delegated to an IA	Democratically legitimate welfare enhancement	Remediable legitimacy problem	Unremediable legitimacy problem
Under political control	N/A	Welfare opportunity cost	Sensible

[1]North and Weingast, "Constitutions and Commitment," p. 806. Ironically, the paper is about the value to Britain of the Bank of England being created in 1694 so as to make credible the government's promises to repay debt, whereas today orthodoxy holds that central banks should be barred from monetary financing of government so as to make credible a commitment to low inflation (part IV).

Three of the cells are of particular interest because they amount to legislators making a mistake, either leaving people worse off than they need be (insufficient delegation to IAs) or taking undue risks with support for the system of government (excessive delegation to unelected officials). A country might be more prone to one or the other of those "mistakes" depending on the incentives generated by its constitutional structure and norms.

In this chapter, we look at whether our main jurisdictions are realistically capable of tying themselves (and their public) to a mast without delegating inappropriate powers (such as distributional choices or creating criminal offenses). It turns out that commitment capability does not turn on whether a jurisdiction's legal system is based on civil law or common law but more on the incentives generated by its constitutional structure and conventions. Crudely, our provisional conclusions are that the US is more likely to suffer opportunity costs but is also exposed to legitimacy risks; that the UK might incur legitimacy risks; and that Germany might have more de facto than de jure independent agencies, posing the question of whether its legal norms have kept up with its values and beliefs about effective administration. In each of those cases, however, and also in France and the EU, there is no insuperable obstacle to delegation policy being more principled if only something like the Principles became embedded as a norm.

We start with the US and then go on to the UK, France, Germany, and the EU, in each case examining constitutional capability and veto points.

THE UNITED STATES

In the US, the capacity to delegate at all to insulated agencies is subject to unending debate. While no one doubts that Congress can excuse an agency from annual budget appropriations, its capability to legislate insulation from the president is contested.

During the middle of the twentieth century, rule making by agencies was often described as *quasi-legislative*. But today, mainstream US legal scholars are more inclined to maintain that, irrespective of whether it *looks* quasi-legislative, as a matter of law it must be conducted under the executive power since the Constitution (Article 1) stipulates that "All legislative powers [are] vested in Congress":[2]

> These activities take "legislative" and "judicial" forms, but they are exercises of—indeed, under our constitutional structure, they must be exercises of—the "executive" Power.

To an outsider this could come close to redefining the meaning of words in the manner of Lewis Carroll's Queen of Hearts. But *legality* is one of the three components of *legitimacy*, and no one seriously doubts the Supreme Court's power to have the final say on legality.

The argument that such delegations are permissible runs, essentially, that while the Constitution gives Congress a monopoly on legislation, it permits the executive to "fill in the details" of statutory provisions; and, further, that agencies may perform that filling-out function because the Constitution does not require the president directly to control the executive machine as opposed to exercise broad oversight of it. Opposition to delegation framed in terms of the Constitution accordingly takes one of two forms: either that agencies are left with excessive latitude to fill in the details (the subject of the next chapter, and of our Delegation Criteria and first Design Precept) or that both IAs (as we define them) and the semi-independent regulatory commissions are insufficiently amenable to presidential control.

The Effect of Multiple Veto Points

Those issues are inevitably entangled with the structure of the incentives created by the US system of government, which is well known for having legions of veto points standing in the way of institutional change of any kind. Indeed, that was part of founding father James Madison's aim: "The weight of the legislative authority requires that it should be . . . divided." [3] Here is a characterization of how this works out (with elaboration to come in the next two chapters). It is hard to pass laws; once

[2] *City of Arlington v. Federal Communications Commission*, 2013, quoted in Vermeule, "Review of Philip Hamburger." This view can seem to maintain that every organ of US government must be in one and only one of the three branches specified in the Constitution, a view challenged in, for example, Strauss, "Place of Agencies."

[3] Madison, No. 51, in Hamilton, Madison, and Jay, *Federalist*, p. 267.

passed, it is hard to change or repeal laws; Congress finds it hard to settle upon clear objectives; even when controlled by the same party, the Senate can constrain the president's choice of appointments to agency policy boards; congressional committees face weak incentives to oversee agencies, except when prompted by constituents or powerful interest groups, but have the option of exerting significant "control" over those agencies where they have retained a statutory grip on the purse strings (appropriations);[4] and the courts face both worthy incentives and less worthy temptations to fill any perceived vacuum in constraining agencies, acting as unelected policy monitors and makers.

Presidential versus Congressional "Control"

The upshot is a complex patchwork of executive agencies, semi-autonomous commissions, and truly independent agencies (such as the Fed). In any particular case, the chosen structure depends on the alignment of the political stars, with very material consequences for which, if any, set of political actors can exercise ongoing "control."

For executive agencies, *the president* has considerable powers: to sack the policy makers, to have the White House machine vet draft rules, to issue executive orders on how they approach their mission.[5] While former executive agency staff have stressed to me that such agencies can enjoy considerable de facto independence, such accounts typically highlight the quality of an agency head's relationship with the president or his/her immediate circle. By contrast, for independent agencies (such as the Fed) and regulatory commissions (e.g., the SEC), presidents can dismiss policy makers only "for cause" (which, although often undefined, might include gross incompetence, negligence, or dishonesty).

Of the instruments of *congressional leverage* over agencies, this book has particularly emphasized *annual* budget approvals (with the stress on frequency). Combined with the associated capacity to prescribe and proscribe courses of action by agencies, this can amount to an expedited procedure for amending an agency's founding legislation, overcoming the veto points that characterize more normal legislative reform (given

[4] Tollestrup and Saturno, "Congressional Appropriations Process."

[5] Kagan, "Presidential Administration"; Bressman and Vandenburgh, "Inside the Administrative State"; Lewis, *Presidents*.

the Court's ban on line-item presidential vetoes).[6] Conversations over the years have left me with the clear impression that the heads of such agencies, which include the regulatory commissions, often lead their lives navigating the shifting preferences and concerns of congressional committee members. As a knock-on effect, agency leaders may become more sensitive to the wishes of the president if they believe his/her support may help them with Congress (or the opposite if they believe it would exacerbate their relationship with Congress). The direction of policy is, then, inevitably sensitive to changes in the balance of political opinion and to the interest groups that fund (and so might defund) key committee members.

Combined with the various actors' veto powers, that menu of political control instruments provides the backdrop to the competition between the two elected branches of government over the structure of the US administrative state. The game's outcomes turn partly on whether the US is in a phase of divided or unified government. During the former, congressional opposition often (but not always) seeks agencies that are insulated from day-to-day presidential control.[7]

By contrast, during the typically brief spells of united government, an administration will (rationally) want either an executive agency, where the president can sack the policy makers on a whim, or an independent agency with only one policy maker, leaving the Senate minority trying to constrain the appointment to the "least bad" of the president's allies.

On this account, a truly independent agency with a policy committee should be a rare outcome. It is. Of the thirteen agencies identified in one important study as highly independent from the president, a ma-

[6] *Clinton v. City of New York*, 1998. There had been presidential attempts to veto specific provisions of bills well before the 1998 case, going back at least to President Lincoln, and in the mid-2000s a bill cleared the House but not the Senate and so did not get tested in the Court.

[7] Horn, *Political Economy*; Epstein and O'Halloran, *Delegating Powers*; Huber and Shipan, *Deliberate Discretion*; Lewis, *Presidents*. For reviews covering both legal scholarship and, respectively, public choice theory and political science, see Gersen, "Designing Agencies," and Moe, "Delegation, Control." Given our earlier discussion of the US rule-writing commissions as akin to specialist, full-time committees of the legislature with a 3/2 party split (chapters 6 and 10), there is a question as to why the incumbent president's party gets to hold the majority of seats even under divided government. The answer, I think, is that the enacting president would otherwise have had a strong incentive to veto legislation that did not give his party a structural majority. The politicization of the commissions observed today was the almost inevitable equilibrium.

jority are, by my reckoning, subject to the annual political appropriations process.[8] But, equally, when an IA (or regulatory commission) is created, it is very likely to survive.[9] That being so, if an administration and its senatorial allies wish to dilute or undermine an IA's de jure insulation, their best bet is through appointments. In the US expression, personnel is policy (which, given IAs' warrant (chapters 5 and 11), underlines the importance of long, staggered terms being served).

In summary, the complex process of bargaining set up by the multiplicity of institutional and personal veto points in the US can lead to the following outcomes that cut across our Principles for Delegation:

1. Under united government, an agency may be made truly independent even if clearly settled public preferences do not exist.
2. Some agencies are subject to regular congressional control, in particular via annual spending controls, even though some of their functions compellingly warrant greater insulation from day-to-day politics.
3. De facto independence can be undermined even where de jure independence persists.

As I write, a topical example of the first issue is the Consumer Financial Protection Bureau (CFPB). Rather than being subject to congressional budgetary appropriations, very unusually it is funded out of Federal Reserve profits (which in effect turns the Fed into a passive conduit for a hypothecated tax determined by the agency itself).[10] It has only one policy maker, who has job security ("for cause" protection). And the elected executive cannot direct its policies. Whatever the substantive merits of the social cause the agency serves, in terms of the Principles for Delegation the key points for our inquiry are that (to put it mildly judging from partisan commentary) it is not clear that US society has settled preferences for how much consumer protection it wants or how, broadly, any

[8] Datla and Revesz, "Deconstructing Independent Agencies." Some agencies have budgetary independence without scoring highly on Datla and Revesz's tests of formal insulation from the president (e.g., the FDIC). A recent paper going beyond insulation from the president is Selin, "Agency Independent."

[9] Research on the US administrative state finds that US "independent-agency" regimes are more durable there than policy regimes delegated to the executive branch (including executive agencies) (Lewis, "Policy Durability").

[10] The difference in political contexts and cultures makes it hard for me to understand why the Fed did not say publicly that this was wrong: that seigniorage should go to the central federal coffers for Congress to dispose of.

degree of protection should be delivered. Nor is it clear how a single-policy-maker structure can ensure that a steady policy course is maintained through different political administrations. When a new party commands enough veto points, they will be able to install an ally who takes a different approach. For that very reason, agency incumbents have incentives to embed their worldview so deeply that it would be very hard for the other side to dismantle over any reasonable time period. In one sense, this is simply the game of politics, but for legitimacy to be sustained "game" is quite the wrong metaphor in a field where there is anything but a consensus on ends and means.[11]

We argued in chapter 7 that the Securities and Exchange Commission (SEC) is an instance of the second issue. It could make a very substantial continuing contribution to preserving financial stability, but it is hard for it to commit to that so long as its budget is under annual political control. The problem is, in part, that the SEC is also responsible for areas of policy where the preferences of the people are less obviously settled and where it has to make trade-offs among equally ranked statutory objectives. As currently designed, greater insulation from politics would, therefore, be inappropriate, the question being whether the welfare costs for the American people warrant some recasting of objectives and structure.

Perhaps the most important historical instance of the third issue is the on-off de facto independence of the Federal Reserve from its founding in 1913 until Paul Volcker's stewardship in the 1980s (chapter 17). According to the Principles, it would have been preferable for Fed independence to be formally suspended during the long years of political monetary policy.

A Step Too Far: Agencies Creating Criminal Offenses

Separately, judged against the Principles, the US is too relaxed about some of the powers it delegates. Notably, many US agencies are empowered to create criminal offenses, as a former attorney general pointed out to Congress a few years ago:[12]

[11] As I write, some of these issues are heading to the Supreme Court, and a new acting head has been appointed.

[12] Thornborough, "Overcriminalisation."

> Regulatory agencies routinely promulgate rules that impose criminal penalties that are not enacted by Congress. Indeed, criminalization of new regulatory provisions has become seemingly mechanical. One estimate is there are a staggering 300,000 criminal regulatory offenses created by agencies without Congressional review.

A key example is the way an SEC rule criminalized insider trading some thirty to forty years after the governing statute had passed into law.[13] While the SEC is not fully insulated from politics, the example is highlighted here because US doctrine on delegation does not distinguish between degrees of insulation. An IA so endowed would be too powerful.

Principled Delegation to Achieve Credible Commitment

Summing up, if the Court were ever to conclude that presidents could exercise close control over agencies of all kinds, insulation from day-to-day politics and so the possibility of credible commitment would be dead in the water in the US (beyond entrusting constrained policy discretion to the insulated judges). Furthermore, if that included the Federal Reserve, powers of taxation (via surprise inflation) would effectively be granted to an elected officer outside the legislature—the president—who has incentives to deploy them (chapter 12 and part IV).

Meanwhile, the US currently has the technology to entrench independent-agency regimes, but the tangled forces and incentives embedded in its legislative structure are such that it rarely does so. This matters. Case study research suggests that US agencies' insulation from political pressure on policy making *does* increase with the degree of formal independence.[14]

All told, some problems of credible commitment are probably left unaddressed, leaving the American people worse off than they might be

[13] The Securities and Exchange Act of 1934 creates a criminal offense of financial fraud but does not define it. In the early 1940s, the SEC issued rules fleshing out that crime but did not apply them to insider trading until the 1960s (as a civil offense) and the 1970s (as a criminal offense). In the UK, although there had long existed a criminal offense of fraud, insider trading did not become a crime until Parliament made it one in the 1980s, after a good deal of public deliberation.

[14] For example, Wood and Waterman, "Dynamics of Political Control."

as the SEC example illustrates. But nor is the US free of the legitimacy risk of overinsulating agencies when societal preferences are not broadly settled, as the CFPB example shows. In the latter case, the best solution might be to move to a commission structure under budgetary control so that groups of partisan technocrats have to navigate each other and Congress until consensus around objectives emerges. Some of the specific reforms proposed by the House of Representatives would push things in that direction.

But some of them, notably the REINS Act, which is still making its way through Congress as I write, would exacerbate the problem of commitment. If, as we argued in part II, the constrained delegation of rule writing to a trustee-type independent agency can be warranted and squared with democratic values where elected legislators wish to commit to a clear standard, it would be perverse for a later Congress to have an *expedited and simple* means of abandoning such commitments. By effectively (although not formally) turning agency rule making into a process for generating proposals for laws, REINS would leave legislators exposed to the temptation of undoing their own best intentions to commit to a policy under the imperative of getting reelected, raising funds from vested interests, and so on. For policy commitments to be credible and for legislative processes to live up to our values, Congress needs to constrain itself to holding a vote to override IA rules, so that resiling from their promise to delegate incurs the "audience costs" that act as a commitment technology under *democracy as watchfulness*.[15]

Whatever its merits for executive agencies and for the semipolitical commissions pursuing vague or multiple objectives, therefore, a *passive* veto does not make sense where the Delegation Criteria and first Design Precept are (or could be) satisfied. For those regimes, the solution to the democratic deficit is, primarily, to avoid vague objectives (next chapter).

As with so much in US government, REINS would, moreover, create perverse incentives. Agencies would likely oscillate between, on the one hand, reliance on adjudication (avoiding the passive veto) and, on the other hand, high-profile rule making where the blame for any

[15]On the values of legislative processes, see Waldron, *Law and Disagreement*, Part I, and *Dignity of Legislation*.

inaction could be pinned on Congress. In the latter case, IA leaders would have incentives to ensure, partly through extensive consultation, that the general public understood the stakes. All that is the fair game of politics when the public's purposes are unsettled or unclear, but reintroducing short-run politics when the public's purposes are settled elevates the interests of elected representatives over those they represent (part II).

THE UNITED KINGDOM

At quite another point of the constitutional compass, the UK's politics is characterized by strong party discipline but a weaker separation of powers. As suggested in the introduction to part III, so long as a government has a working majority in the House of Commons, it can get laws through Parliament and repeal or amend laws fairly easily; it can get its nominations through any de facto Parliament confirmation hearing; and the courts have traditionally largely confined themselves to the law in a narrow sense (chapter 15). This setup leaves the executive prey to fashion in the design and operation of the administrative state.

The problem of credible commitment is, in fact, intrinsic to the system. Since it is easy to change laws (and since the judiciary will not strike out legislation), no legislated public policy regime or institutional structure is born with deep roots.[16] Historically, UK government has indeed struggled to achieve a stable course, with flip-flops in both broad policy and the structure of administration.

Burkean Prescriptive Legitimacy

Hence our earlier suggestion that, under the UK's political constitutionalism, all legitimacy has a Burkean flavor. Arguably, the defining feature of the British system is not what any particular government does but what it chooses *not* to do: which inherited statutes and regimes it does not repeal or amend. Bipartisan support or acceptance of public

[16]This is an overstatement of how the English courts work since they can formally declare a statute incompatible with the Human Rights Act. That pushes ministers toward embracing multiple procedural safeguards when preparing legislation, but it is largely irrelevant to their ability to commit.

policy regimes accrues via abstention. (These are *intertemporal checks and balances* rather than the more familiar US system of contemporaneous veto points.[17])

Put another way, the deep problem of commitment facing a Westminster-style Parliament means that the installation of commitment technology in a particular field, such as monetary policy independence, cannot itself be credible until custom and practice bestows upon it the requisite aura of authority (as discussed for financial regulation in chapter 19).

That, however, does nothing to explain why, since the 1990s, British politicians have seemed positively to embrace independent agencies, particularly economic regulators. More formally insulated IAs were established in the UK over the past twenty-five years than, perhaps, over a full century in the US.

One possible explanation for this architectural change in the British state might be that it suited the interests of parts of one political party (Labour) to put various functions at arm's length, anticipating that it would be costly for the other party to undo reforms they would not have initiated (see chapter 17 on Bank of England independence). It is also possible that there was a broadly based ideational shift among civil servants and policy analysts toward mitigating the UK system's inherent problems of commitment, with the regime change from public ownership to public regulation of privatized utilities providing both the opportunity and, arguably, the need.

While offering possible welfare-based explanations, that story does not address the values-based obstacle to delegation presented by the UK's deep attachment to the doctrine of parliamentary accountability. The solution came through the combination of a revolution in Westminster's select committee system (chapter 15) and a creative use of Parliament's capacity to delegate some parts of regime design and maintenance to the elected executive.

[17]This is an important part of the answer to Ralf Dahrendorf's question of how the British system of government can enjoy legitimacy when it produces "innovative minority rule" (powerful governments elected, via plurality, with only 40 percent or so of the vote). Answer: We, British citizens, know that legislative mistakes can be repealed (Dahrendorf, "Politics in Industrial Society," footnote 7).

One part of this is picked up in the next chapter: the executive being charged by Parliament with fleshing out the objective laid down in primary legislation. Combined with its de facto legislative powers, this helps underline that ministers are responsible, and so accountable, to Parliament for the regime itself (as opposed to its stewardship).

Other elements of the UK system also maintain a residue of ongoing political control and so address concerns about accountability; but they do so in ways that, in different degrees, might temper the achievement of credibility.

Override Powers: Trimmed Independence as a Solution to Distributional Choices

Among those other techniques, the UK's IA regimes typically grant an override power to the executive.

For some utility regulators, this has the effect of putting big distributional choices in the hands of accountable politicians, helping to overcome the problem of the fuzzy boundary between efficiency and equity. Some regimes include "national interest," "national security," or "foreign policy" grounds for executive branch override (e.g., Ofcom), although their reach is constrained by EU law in the telecom and energy fields. By contrast, a more open-ended provision exists for the Treasury publicly to override Bank of England monetary policy decisions.

In the not wholly dissimilar Australian and Canadian constitutional systems, the executive government can give directions to the bodies responsible for the prudential supervision of the financial system. In the UK, however, the government did not have such a power over the old Financial Services Authority before the Great Financial Crisis and does not have it over either of Britain's postcrisis microregulators, including the prudential agency embedded in the Bank of England.

In terms of delivering credible commitment (and, thus, compliance with the Delegation Criteria), what matters here is that any such executive branch powers have to be exercised transparently, with public reporting to Parliament, and that they are exercisable only in specific and rare circumstances. Otherwise, agency leaders would be sensitive to the politicians' finger twitching over the trigger, the shadow of political power infecting agency policy even when not formally exercised.

Single-Boss IAs: An Obstacle to Credible Commitment

Another risk to effective commitment arises from the UK practice of structuring IAs with a single policy boss.

Parts I and II press the case for IAs making decisions in committees on the grounds (among others discussed in chapter 11) that that helps to underpin independence and so credibility. While that is exactly how the Bank of England's Monetary Policy Committee is constituted, as well as, of course, the Appeal Court and Supreme Court, many of the UK's economic regulators (e.g., Ofcom, Ofgem) have a single director general in whom power is solely vested, subject to oversight by a part-time board (chapter 15). At the least, this reduces the probability of policy being stable when the boss changes, and thereby dilutes the effectiveness of the attempt to commit. It also increases the probability of the elected executive appointing allies to head these agencies, so the structure may be incentives-compatible for legislators even as it cuts across the purpose of delegation-with-insulation.

This matters because an intrinsic challenge in the Westminster system, given the executive's extensive powers of patronage and communication, is the possibility of a gap existing between an independent agency's de jure and de facto standing. Chatter around London about practice over the past couple of decades or so suggests that the degree of de facto independence of various IAs has varied according to the personality of the director general and the relevant minister. That risk is greater the less clear the reasons for making an agency independent in the first place, the thinner the public debate that preceded the legislation, and the vaguer its objectives. Those are circumstances where parliamentary oversight is harder to channel in ways that can counterbalance executive power. They underline the potential value of something like the Principles for Delegation where credible commitment is desired.

Reordering the Legislated Constraints as Circumstances Change

The bigger challenge in the UK, however, is sustaining the *political* commitment to policy commitments in a polity where the public expects ministers to legislate to address new challenges and circumstances. Thus, the statutory objectives of the energy utility regulator (Ofgem) have been amended a few times "to bring them more explicitly into line with government policy, not least in respect of delivering government targets for renewable energy."[18] This affected costs.

To some extent, that example might be driven by genuine shifts in what British society wants from energy regulation, giving rise to trade-offs we revisit in the next chapter. But, plausibly, more was going on than a rethink on purposes, given awkward trade-offs. So long as wholesale energy prices were low, utility regulation was a political backwater. As prices rose and energy bills came to account for a material share of household spending, the political focus changed. In one sense, understandably, ministers wanted the independent regulator to protect struggling households. That could amount, however, to grafting distributional choices onto a policy regime originally designed to foster economic efficiency.

Whether the insulation of regulators is intended to hold even in adverse circumstances should be part of deciding whether or not to delegate to IA regimes at all. In a highly salient area, such as one directly determining household bills, the exercise of a legislative override for essentially short-term reasons might be popular even when understood as regime change, so that the posited "audience costs" of reneging on the policy promise do not materialize. In other words, it is not easy to sustain a promise to commit in a Westminster-style system unless an understanding of the value of sticking to a course in uncomfortable circumstances is embedded across society. Big picture, this underlines part I's discussion of the need to think through the machinery for reconciling the politics of distributional equity with a desire to make credible commitments to market efficiency. That seems to be unfinished business in the UK. My guess is that part of the problem is the lack of rich public debate about delegating utility regulation a couple of decades ago.

Too Relaxed about Delegated Power?

The same might be said of the way power is concentrated in some British IAs. More generally, the UK might have become too relaxed about delegation. It is striking, for example, that Ofcom is responsible for the

[18] Tutton, "The Future."

regulation not only of the economics of the media but also of the *content* of media output. On the face of it, this is a remarkable concentration of power in the hands of an agency with a single head. With the addition in 2016 of responsibility for overseeing BBC output, which presumably includes public goods of a different type from privately provided competitive media services, our Multiple-Mission Constraints would press the question of whether the agency's design falls short of what our values demand.[19] Even if, as some argue, technological change is blurring the boundary between platforms and publishers and so between economic regulation and the regulation of content, that would at most make the case for housing both under one roof, not delegating them to identical policy makers.[20] The MMCs would demand formally separate "chambers" within the agency for its different responsibilities, with powers conferred on distinct multiple-member committees directly by Parliament and members individually accountable for their specific delegated responsibilities.

Summing up, the UK has overcome the biggest obstacle in the way of making policy regime commitments (political accountability) but, having done so, might have become casual about the location of power.

TWO VERY DIFFERENT CONTINENTAL EUROPEAN COUNTRIES

If the structure of the US regulatory state can reasonably be described as expedient and the UK's approach as prone to shifts in fashionable ideas, the broad landscape of delegation in each is not a total surprise given the incentives created by their constitutional conventions and political structures. When we turn to France and Germany, however, the

[19] This question was barely addressed in the Clementi Report on BBC governance or the UK executive government's response. Public debate focused on whether or not the BBC should self-regulate rather than also on whether Ofcom was well designed for its new (or existing) responsibilities. Ofcom's main board is required by statute to have a committee dedicated to content, called the Content Board, but (1) the big decisions are reserved to the main board; (2) the Content Board's individual members do not have to explain their votes and decisions to parliamentary committees or via speeches; and (3) power is in reality concentrated in the director general, giving the elected executive government incentives to appoint an ally (chapter 6).

[20] It is possible that the categories *platform* and *publisher* are inadequate for the new world. If so, the question of this book is, Who, formally, should determine a new framework: elected legislators or unelected judges and technocrats?

mapping from "political constitution" to the structure of the administrative state seems to lose its way—at least if they are taken to be paradigmatic examples of, respectively, "executive-led" and "consensus" democratic states. In truth, the formal reality is almost the opposite of the formulaic expectation, and so we say more here about each than hitherto in this book.

France

A unitary state with a strong executive, France has much in common with the UK. Hence the shared reluctance we have described among the political class to embrace delegation to independent agencies—but grounded in aversion to diluting core executive branch competence rather than British-like worries about impaired parliamentary accountability. Those reservations eventually gave way, however, to global trends, dynamics created by EU initiatives, and evolution in its own deeply embedded values. From today's vantage point, this amounted to incentives-values compatibility being restored by incorporating the value of "Europe" alongside the values constituted in the idea of the Republic.

France is also very different from the UK. It has a codified constitution under a constitutional court, which, perhaps consistent with guardianship, comprises former top politicians as well as career jurists. The constitution establishes an executive; puts the civil service under its control (Article 20); confers on the prime minister a power to issue legally binding "regulations" and to delegate that power to ministers (Article 21); and gives the president powers to issue decrees in a state of emergency, constrained by parliamentary impeachment powers (Articles 16 and 68).[21] Therefore, independent agencies had to find a place within French constitutional constraints and doctrines (rather than, as

[21] On the rule-making and decree powers, see Huber, "Executive Decree Authority." *La Constitution* of the Fifth Republic was passed in 1958. Major amendments were made in 2008, with just one vote over the supermajority required in the two elected chambers. Notable for our purposes were amendments narrowing the executive's power to pass legislation without parliament; giving parliament a veto over presidential appointments to the constitutional court; and authorizing, subject to some hurdles, ex post judicial review of legislation on grounds of infringement of basic liberties (which, following a court decision of the 1970s, are taken to include the values inherent in the 1789 Declaration of Rights).

in the UK, just happening because a supreme parliament willed it). The Constitutional Council has held that the provisions for the president and prime minister to issue decrees and ordinances[22]

> are not an obstacle to the legislature's conferring to a public authority other than the Prime Minister the responsibility to make rules allowing for the implementation of a law on the condition that this authorization concerns only measures of limited scope as to their field of application and their content.

The practical effect, broadly, seems to be to confine agencies to adjudication of various kinds, subject in only a few areas to (rarely used) ministerial veto or override. In contrast to our two North Atlantic examples, legally binding regulations are mainly issued under the authority of ministers, consistent with France's tradition of executive branch unity.[23] Most French regulatory agencies promulgate general policy, within the constraints of their statutory mandates, by issuing guidance on the criteria they will apply in fulfilling their adjudicatory responsibilities (in line with our third Design Precept).

French exceptionalism is manifest in another way too. While *autorités administratives indépendantes* (AAIs) have become a familiar part of French governance, they do not all share the same inspiration of mitigating straightforward time-consistency problems and do not even each fall squarely within our category of trustee-type agencies. Some might more obviously be candidates for the class of *guardians*. This is notably so of the Commission Nationale de l'Informatique et des Libertés, established in the 1970s to protect the integrity of data held by the state on citizens.[24] In the same broad territory of institutions designed to protect citizens from risk of state abuse, the Conseil Supérieur de l'Audiovisuel (CSA), an ex post regulator of media content, was established in the 1980s as another of France's earliest arm's-length agencies. Extensive public debate led to the conclusion that it needed to be strongly insulated from elected politicians, given the vital role of a

[22]Decision No. 96–378 DC of July 23, 1996, paragraph 11. Thanks to Martin Rogoff.

[23]This might explain why the key criterion for IA legitimacy in part two of Rosanvallon, *Democratic Legitimacy*, is impartiality, since that would fit with thinking of insulated agencies as providing fair adjudication rather than legally binding norms.

[24]Halberstam, "Comparative Administrative Law."

free media in a democracy. Perhaps because of the sequencing, perhaps because of sensitivity to concentrations of power outside the core executive, in contrast to Britain (see above) the CSA is separate from the telecommunications economic regulator.

As the population of AAIs grew, including the Autorité de la concurrence (competition authority) and the standard set of utility regulators, the Conseil d'État defined them in a wide-ranging 2001 study as[25]

> act[ing] on behalf of the State without being subordinate to the Government and . . . act[ing] with complete autonomy, such that their actions may not be influenced or sanctioned except by the courts.

In other words, in the assessment of France's highest court for administrative law, this is full insulation, capable of mitigating a wide variety of credibility problems. While the Conseil is, perhaps, not a massive fan of the concept, it is committed to the view that where AAIs exist, they should be properly independent. In contrast to the UK, where norms of IA design are underdeveloped, this French judicial conceptualization largely precludes elected executive branch override powers.[26]

Consistent with that, the Conseil has occasionally, in its prevetting of laws, queried whether a planned new agency really needed to be independent. That theme, among others, was taken up forcefully in 2015 by a committee of the Senate, which expressed concern that while some AAIs had been created in response to international and EU imperatives, others were simply a "symptom of distrust toward political bodies"; that some lacked a clear rational; that they were too often populated by former officials of the Conseil d'État and similar bodies; and that they were not in any case securely insulated, citing government's capacity to close the Consumer Safety Commission by declining to appoint a quorum of members.[27] Two years later, in early 2017, reflecting a more moderate tone in the Assembly (the lower house), France enacted two statutes on AAIs. Their number was reduced from around forty to around twenty-five; and elements of a common statutory framework were established, including provisions on appointments, tenure, and officeholder conflicts.[28]

[25] Conseil d'État, *Rapport*: English translation from Elgie, "Quasi-Autonomous Agencies."

[26] There are some override powers, but I was informed by some high-ranking French officials that, compared with the UK and other countries, they are very rarely used.

[27] French Senate, *State within the State*.

[28] Source: Interviews with French officials. In contrast to the AAIs whose independence is rooted in domestic legislation, the Banque de France is independent as a condition of France's

Germany

In many ways, Germany meets the criteria for a model *Lijphartian* consensual state, with federalism and coalition governments formed after proportional representation elections, under a Basic Law guarded by a powerful constitutional court. It does not, however, really fit the thesis of rampant formal delegation to independent agencies associated with such polities.

As noted in chapter 2, unusually for a major democracy, Germany's Basic Law does make explicit provision for the administrative state, including delegation by the parliament to the elected executive branch and delegation by ministers to agencies. As a general matter, every decision by a public authority must be traceable to the public through a "chain of legitimacy," with legislation having to lay down the "content, purpose and scope" of any powers conferred on the executive (Article 80.1).[29]

Crucially, however, the Basic Law also makes clear that, perhaps with the sole exception of the Bundesbank, agencies are subordinate to the relevant ministry.[30] More specifically, in common with the core civil service, each agency is formally subject to one or both types of ministerial oversight and override: *Rechtsaufsicht* and *Fachaufsicht*, which are broadly equivalent to the English-American vires and substantive merits.[31] The financial regulator (BaFin) is subject to both; the famous cartel office (Bundeskartellamt) only to Rechtsaufsicht.

Accordingly, drafts of regulatory rules are often submitted to ministries for vetting before being finalized and issued in the name of the agency itself. Parliament and its committees do not have to approve proposed rules. Nor, as discussed in chapter 15, do they actively oversee the work of agencies, apparently on the grounds that it (simply) comprises implementing a clear policy set down in law under the

---

participation in the European monetary union. Technically, therefore, its prudential supervision authority is also exempt from ministerial involvement in budgeting for AAI resources.

[29] Puender, "Democratic Legitimation."

[30] In fact, Germany's first post–World War II Chancellor, Adenauer, was leery about monetary independence (Marsh, *Bundesbank*, chapter 6). Views differ on the Bundesbank's constitutional status prior to European monetary union: a monetary institution was specifically contemplated by the Basic Law, but its independence was made explicit only in the ordinary legislation that created the Bundesbank.

[31] For example, Bach and Jann, "Administrative Zoo."

control of the designated ministers.[32] In other words, in Germany the politics/administration dichotomy, which we spent much of part II dismantling, seems to be alive and well, drawing on the spirit of Weber if not also the Prussians.

That might seem to be the end of it: except for monetary policy and the adjudication of particular cases, no commitment devices based on nonpolitical policy making and no question of a democratic deficit. A system liable, perhaps, to incur some welfare opportunity costs but not exposed to legitimacy issues.

The question, however, is whether that is how it actually works in practice. An agency's de facto political insulation depends on how actively incumbent ministers and their leading civil servants intervene (or signal their readiness to intervene) in the organization, conduct, and substance of its business. That in turn depends on the appetite *and* capability of ministries to be active overseers. Their incentives are, perhaps, dampened by parliament itself not actively overseeing the exercise of ministerial power over agencies. Where, for that or any other reason, a ministry is not active and where the governing legislation does not pin down everything important, the result could in principle be greater de facto than de jure independence.[33]

In a possible real-world instance of this, academic analysts concluded that Germany's financial regulator, *BaFin*, enjoyed considerable autonomy before and during the early phases of the 2007–2009 financial crisis because, they say, the Ministry of Finance did not have the resources to fulfill its de jure role. Consistent with that, I do not recall the ministry taking responsibility for the crisis. But, the same researchers report, eventually the ministry responded by exercising its right to reorganize the regulator, diluting the power of its head, and by strengthening its own capabilities.[34] Certainly, my experience was of competent and ac-

[32] Ministerial powers are specific and, so far as the law is concerned (Article 65), to be exercised independently by the relevant ministry rather than under specific instruction from the chancellor or cabinet. In the UK, by contrast, legislation typically grants power to the "secretary of state," a venerable but generic term covering a number of departmental ministers carrying that title. Among other things, this makes it easier to reallocate responsibilities in Whitehall. The prime minister, as First Lord of the Treasury, is legally a secretary of state.

[33] Doehler, "Institutional Choice."

[34] Handke, "Problem."

tive German finance ministry involvement in the post-2009 work to reform the global system.

It obviously matters to our inquiry whether those academic studies are robust. On the one hand, if ministries are always in control, then it is possible that too few German agencies are insulated from politics, risking welfare losses through impaired credibility. If, on the other hand, ministries are *not* really in control, with de facto autonomy outstripping de jure insulation, the effect might be to improve welfare in some areas (competition policy is a possibility) but to violate deep values in others.

It is important here to distinguish two possibilities. One is that ministries sometimes neglect their responsibilities and, in consequence, agencies are let off an intended leash. The other, quite different, is that an embedded attachment, on the center Left as well as the center Right, to the tenets of ordo-liberalism acts to constrain the agencies, and that this is understood by the ministries.

Put another way, *have the facts of administrative life outstripped the law*? If so, was that driven by society's expectations and values evolving beyond the terms of the law, but with facts and informal soft norms remaining aligned; or was it a matter of the facts slipping the leash of society's norms (informal and formal)? At the least, it looks as though the long-standing Habermasian discourse on state structure, democracy, and the rule of law (facts and norms) invites concrete institutional analysis of which of Germany's regulatory and administrative agencies should be seen as a solution to commitment problems.

Civil Law Nations within the EU

Broadly, then, it seems that, after initial hesitations, Europe's two great historical unitary states, Britain and France, have taken the largest leap toward delegating authority to formally insulated agencies, but that France is more aligned with Germany in retaining ministerial involvement in most rule making.

Any impression that civil law jurisdictions face stricter limitations on delegating rule writing to unelected officials than common law countries would be, I believe, misleading. Bank supervisors have historically issued legally binding regulations in Italy, Mexico, and Spain; and, prior to European monetary union, the Bundesbank set reserve requirements via delegated rule-writing powers.

More important than legal traditions for our Continental European case studies (and as I write, still for the UK) are the effects of EU membership. In some fields, such as telecommunications and energy, EU law requires that national regulators be independent from national politics, prompting a certain amount of constitutional head scratching in Germany (since, among other things, it is deprived of discretion to require ministerial Fachaufsicht). Moreover, regulatory policy and law have increasingly been set at EU level.

THE EUROPEAN UNION

We turn finally, therefore, to the broader structure of European law and the EU's own "independent" agencies (in quotes because, as chapter 2 describes, with the notable exception of the ECB, most EU agencies enjoy only partial insulation).

Changed Incentives, Evolving Doctrine

For decades following the *Meroni* judgment of the European Court of Justice (ECJ) in the late 1950s, it was absolute doctrine—not only legally but, in Brussels, politically—that the European Commission's executive powers could not and must not be delegated. Commissioners and their permanent staff, the veritable vanguard of the "European project," protected this with vigor, perhaps never more so than during the ultimately inconclusive convention held in the early 2000s to draw up a European constitution.

Nevertheless, they have occasionally had to give ground, notably in the aftermath of a crisis in the late 1980s that saw the commissioners resigning en masse following problems of fraud and inefficiency. The new Commission president, Romano Prodi, fostered agencies in order to disperse power geographically across Europe and to enable an overstretched central bureaucracy in Brussels to refocus on its core mission. A degree of delegation became, under duress, an instrument of relegitimation for the Commission itself.

Since then, EU agencies have multiplied and their roles gradually deepened. After long being delegated only advisory or narrow delivery roles (the bottom two tiers in chapter 4's hierarchy), the more recently created bodies approximate policy agencies elsewhere, drafting rules and taking adjudicatory decisions.

On the way, legal gymnastics have been employed to put agencies on solid constitutional ground. After years of relying on a *unanimity* provision of the Treaty (enabling the European Council to take measures, after consulting the Parliament, *necessary* to pursue the objectives of the common market as a whole), the powers that be moved to utilize articles devoted to specific parts of the Internal Market (enabling the Council, on a *majority* vote, but with the Parliament now as a colegislator, to establish agencies as "instruments" for pursuing *specific* policies).[35] In other words, assuming the European Parliament is disposed to favor the creation of EU agencies, the number of veto points was reduced.

Helpfully for the architects of these subtle reforms, ECJ doctrine also evolved. In an important case brought by the UK challenging the crisis management powers of the EU securities market regulator (ESMA) on the grounds that they contravened *Meroni*, the Court ruled in 2014 that ESMA's power to ban short selling was acceptable given that it was hedged about with constraints, including a duty to consult member states.[36]

All this occurred without the formal core of the Court's nondelegation doctrine being jettisoned. In consequence, the "Level 2" rules drawn up by the European Supervisory Authorities (ESAs) are, once finalized, formally issued by the Commission. In other words, an unelected body issues legally binding rules drawn up by other unelected bodies *but* only after vetting by the nationally elected members of the Council and Parliament.

[35] Andoura and Timmerman, "Governance of the EU." A UK challenge against the new route failed in the ECJ in 2004: Case c-217/04, *UK v. European Parliament and Council of the EU*, May 2, 2006.

[36] Nicolaides and Preziosi, "Discretion and Accountability."

Agencies, the Commission, and Legitimacy

For our inquiry into the feasibility and legitimacy of credible commitment devices, at one level it might seem that there is little or no difference between regulatory powers being held by an agency or by the Commission, both being bodies under unelected leadership. But that would be wrong.

EU agencies are created to serve a specific purpose and, *if* properly designed, the standing of their technocrat leaders might be yoked to their professional reputation for delivering that purpose as reflected in a monitorable objective (chapters 5 and 11). By contrast, the Commission exists to further the European project; and its leaders, while unelected, are typically former national politicians. In other words, it is a political body, with the reputation of the members of its leadership group among their peers (our harness) turning on their success in pursuing a teleological goal.

An important question, therefore, is whether steps toward commitment via technocratic agencies are undermined by the various review and approval mechanisms incorporated into the EU's processes.

Commission Oversight of EU Agencies

The first of those instruments concerns the Commission itself. As well as formally issuing rules and regulations, it sits on agency boards and exercises budgetary power. Might its de facto monitoring of an agency's alignment with the Project ever conflict with its de jure oversight of the technocratic delivery of their delegated tasks; and if so, would that be transparent to other actors?

My impression, albeit drawing from only financial regulation, is that the Commission's substantive authority on agency boards depends, as it should, on the quality of its representatives relative to an agency's executive and the various national representatives.

But substance is not all in matters of the bureaucratic balance of power. Researchers have assembled fairly compelling anecdotal evidence attesting to the power of the Commission in agency deliberations.[37] Perhaps most obviously, this operates through the budgetary process:[38]

> First of all, the Governing Board can decide something, that's what we want. But then the Commission can still say this is not what we are going to give any money for. This is not our priority. So they steer a lot with money to get things through or to hold it up.

Of course, that sounds remarkably like the US Congress's annual appropriations process. We are back full circle, suggesting that EU independent agencies are closer to the US semi-independent commissions than to the world's independent central banks, potentially compromising their ability to commit. Except the analogy with the US is inexact because, in contrast to the members of congressional committees, EU commissioners are not elected but nominated by national governments and appointed by the Council (subject to veto by the Commission president and, for the College of Commissioners as a whole, the Parliament).

Commitment versus Political Override of EU Agencies

The Commission's levers and incentives must be taken alongside the powers of, first, the Council and Parliament. If either exercises its right of veto over agency rules, that would be transparent, raising the stakes in doing so, and inducing reliance on informal influence. Members of the Council or the Parliament might also sometimes wish to protect agencies from the Commission, just as in parliamentary democracies the parliament sometimes protects an IA from the executive branch (and vice versa). For that protection to be available, however, the Commission's own use of informal leverage would have to be visible, as MEPs have (with a degree of concern) pointed out to me.[39]

[37] Busuioc, "Accountability, Control and Independence"; and Egeberg and Trondol, "EU-Level Agencies," which reports interviews suggesting that agencies are more sensitive to national regulators on their boards and to the Commission than to national ministers and officials. These case studies are not focused on the independent ESAs.

[38] Quoted in Busuioc, "Accountability, Control and Independence," p. 611.

[39] Somewhat ironically, this is analogous to the incentives of members of the European Parliament and Council to exercise informal influence over the Commission's own exercise of del-

The second set of non-Commission power holders are the national regulatory agencies, which as I write typically hold a majority of the voting power on EU agency boards. Some of them are fully independent domestically, while others are subordinate to the executive branch. Even where EU law requires national agencies to be completely independent in their EU functions, they are liable to be amenable to political influence at home if, in breach of our Multiple Mission Constraints, they retain other politically subordinate functions or if their leaders' desire for standing and prestige is focused on their national community. There is plenty of anecdotal evidence of this concerning the ESAs (and the ECB's prudential supervision arm).[40] For commitment to a regime's policy purpose to be credible, the votes at both agency boards and Council would need to be published, so that commentators and the public could observe such divergences. This is yet another case of a regime's design needing to become incentives-compatible via "audience costs."

In summary, while the legality of delegation-with-more-insulation has been managed in the EU, these issues leave open whether EU regulatory agencies can, in fact, credibly commit.

SUMMARY

This chapter has offered illustrations of how the forces inherent in particular constitutional conventions and traditions drive diversity in the structure of the regulatory state across countries. In consequence, they are exposed in quite different degrees to the opportunity costs of inferior policy performance and to the political risks of fragile legitimacy. This poses the big question of whether jurisdictions generally could do better by following the Principles for Delegation to independent agencies (or something like them).

We examine that in two parts. The next chapter addresses the extent to which advanced-economy democratic states do (or could) give their

egated authority rather than their incurring the costs of deploying their formal veto (Kaeding and Stack, "Legislative Scrutiny?").

[40] On September 20, 2017, the EU Commission published outline proposals that might mitigate this problem at the ESAs.

independent agencies a clear statutory purpose, objective, and standard—the demand of our first Design Precept. Without a clear objective, it is not clear what "credible commitment" could mean. The subsequent chapter considers practices in relation to the Design Precepts' requirements for processes, transparency, and accountability.

14

The Problem of Vague Objectives

A NONDELEGATION DOCTRINE FOR IAS

> The only question for the courts is whether the agency has acted within the scope of its discretion—i.e., whether the resolution of the ambiguity is reasonable.
>
> —US Justice Antonin Scalia, 1989[1]

That truly independent agencies need clear objectives flows from the central argument of this book that, under certain conditions, delegation-with-insulation can be squared with our deepest political values. Vague, indeterminate, or incoherent objectives break the circle of a commitment to the people's democratically agreed purposes that shields IA policy makers and their staff from both day-to-day politics and the risk of capture by industries and other sectional interests.[2]

We now look at how two jurisdictions, the US and the UK, representing the traditions of legal constitutionalism and political constitutionalism (chapter 8), measure up to this requirement of our first Design Precept.

OBJECTIVES AND STANDARDS FOR INDEPENDENT AGENCIES IN THE US: A REVIVED NONDELEGATION DOCTRINE TO IMPLEMENT THE FIRST DESIGN PRECEPT

We start with the US, where the multiplicity of obstacles in the way of Congress framing clear objectives might explain the relative rarity of truly independent agencies insulated not only from presidential politics but from day-to-day congressional currents too.

[1] Scalia, "Judicial Deference," p. 516.

[2] The Principles therefore seek to address the issues raised in Barkow, "Insulating Agencies."

In the previous chapter we saw that agency rule making is currently regarded as being, under the Constitution, an exercise of the executive power, filling in the details of congressional legislation. Never mind if, because the enacting statute covers only the high ground, the agency finds itself filling in more or less all the substance. Never mind even if, because that legislated high ground does not include a clear objective and/or standard, the agency finds itself making high policy. The very idea of "detail" is slipping away, and "filling in" hardly seems the most apposite verb. Maybe "legislating" would be closer.

The issue here, highlighted throughout this book, is the importance of distinguishing between *legality*, which of course the court can determine, and *legitimacy*, necessary to sustain a system of government through thick and thin.

Vagueness and Indeterminacy in Delegations to Agencies and to Judges

The question of whether Congress can delegate without laying down a clear objective is hardly unknown to US jurisprudence. Something akin to our first Design Precept used to be known as the court's *nondelegation doctrine*. From the late 1920s that has required, broadly, that delegation to an agency—any agency, independent or under the president's control—should not occur without an "intelligible principle" being laid down to guide and constrain the agency.[3]

Since there are many US agencies, the delegating statutes must surely be deemed to meet that test (somehow or other), a point made to me most emphatically by some US legal scholars. Indeed, the nondelegation doctrine's last serious outing was in 1935. But maybe, rather like "filling in the details," the meaning of the expression "intelligible principle" has become peculiar to a high priesthood, slipping the moorings of the language used by the people over whom they preside.

In practice, seen from the perspective of technocrats who run agencies (my tribe), the doctrine has been honored at the cost of breaching

[3] *J. W. Hampton, Jr., & Co. v. United States* 276 US 394, 409 (1928). The key holding is, "If Congress shall lay down by legislative act an intelligible principle to which the person or body . . . is directed to conform, such legislative act is not a forbidden delegation of legislative power."

our values: the test should be not whether an agency is "legislating" as a term of art but whether it is effectively choosing society's high policies and balancing its values. On that test, it is striking that US regulators with quite different degrees of insulation often share a problem of somewhat vague mandates, as a few examples illustrate:

- Federal Communications Commission: To serve in "the public convenience, interest, or necessity" and "so as to provide a fair, efficient, and equitable distribution [of radio services]"[4]
- Federal Energy Regulatory Commission: To ensure that utility-type charges are "just and reasonable"[5]
- Environmental Protection Agency : To set a policy for air pollutants "requisite to protect the public health" with an "adequate margin of safety," and with a secondary requirement to deliver policies "requisite to protect the public welfare"[6]
- Securities and Exchange Commission: To deliver a combination of investor protection; fair, orderly, and efficient markets; and capital formation (chapter 7)
- Federal Reserve: To maintain the safety and soundness of banking groups (chapter 21)

I maintain that, in each case, this lack of clarity leaves the agency determining (and, in some cases, trading off) ends, not merely means, as has been apparent over the decades when a new president secures the appointment of an EPA boss or SEC commissioners devoted to major shifts in policy.

Whatever the jurisprudential niceties, the prevailing state of affairs is fairly clear: some agencies get to set high policy. "Contested" hardly does justice to the scholarly response. Some seek to bury the nondelegation doctrine, shedding no tears as they dig; others suggest it has been succeeded by nondelegation "canons" that proscribe agencies from entering certain areas of public policy; and others still lament that its "evisceration . . . has left a void in the constitutional structure."[7]

[4] *National Broadcasting Co. v. United States*, 321 US 190, 215 (1943).

[5] Federal Power Act.

[6] Clean Air Act.

[7] Posner and Vermeule, "Nondelegation Doctrine"; Sunstein, "Nondelegation Canons"; and Ginsburg and Menashi, "Our Illiberal Administrative Law," from where the quote comes (p. 492).

Most critics of vague delegations level their guns at the agencies of the administrative state. Few observe that, under some circumstances, vague statutes can yield as much political policy power to unelected judges. As we saw in chapter 7, US judges made truly massive changes in mergers and antitrust policy during the final quarter of the twentieth century, possibly enhancing economic welfare but also possibly shifting the balance of political power toward big business. This was feasible only because the relevant statutes set radically indeterminate objectives and standards. The judges hardly erred in applying their best understanding of developments in economics that enjoyed widespread endorsement. They did, though, treat themselves differently from agencies when they switched economic theory horses without wide consultation of the kind regulators are expected to undertake when revising rules (chapter 15).[8]

Further, according to the Principles, legislators erred in leaving unelected judicial officials free to make high policy, at odds with the republican element in American values. The thesis of this book is that by doing so, they endangered confidence in the system of government, on a slow-motion fuse to be sure, but one which has been throwing off sparks in recent years. The judges might have taken a different course, sticking to precedents that reflected outdated economic doctrine and so calling for Congress to review the statutory regime. That they did not do so plausibly owes something to the difficulties of legislating in the United States.

The Democratic Muddle That Occurs When an Empty Nondelegation Doctrine Meets Deference to Agency Statutory Interpretation

This problem of vague or indeterminate objectives is, arguably, exacerbated by another US judicial practice: deferring to agencies' interpretation of the law. In 1984, in a somewhat remarkable decision, the Supreme Court determined, again in broad summary, that where an agency's governing legislation is vague, the courts should defer to an agency's own interpretation of its provisions provided that interpretation is not

[8] Lemos, "The Other Delegate." And contrary to the Bingham principles of judicial lawmaking noted in chapter 10.

unconscionable.[9] At first blush, this is extraordinary. Like civil law judges, an English judge would regard it as the role and duty of the courts to determine the correct meaning of laws, as emphatically stated by Lord Diplock in 1983.[10]

Different traditions aside, the effect would seem to be to maximize the zone of discretion granted to US agencies by vague or ambiguous statutes. *Normatively*, allowing bureaucrats to decide their own powers is an odd state of affairs in a democracy. But *positively*, it plausibly reflects the incentives of the Court and Congress. Given the impediments to passing laws in the US, if the courts frequently overruled agency understandings of their purposes and powers, the judicial interpretations would very likely persist even where many elected legislators and the balance of public opinion supported the agencies. In other words, alongside their largely irreversible determinations of constitutional law, the courts would find themselves de facto writing the laws delegated to agencies through their interpretation of statutes under administrative law. One can see why judges would shrink from this. In the UK, by contrast, if the courts determine that a law means something materially at odds with what elected policy makers thought they had intended or contrary to current policy, Parliament would sooner or later amend the law. The *Chevron* doctrine of interpretative deference can, therefore, be thought of as part of a more general equilibrium determined by, inter alia, the capabilities and practices of other parts of the high-level US state. Put another way, it marks an attempt by the Supreme Court to check the enthusiasm or willingness of lower courts to turn themselves into legislative organs given indecisiveness in the legislature itself.[11]

[9] *Chevron USA Inc. v. Natural Resources Defense Council Inc.*, 467 US 837 (1984). The Court's newest member, Justice Gorsuch, expressed doubts about *Chevron* when sitting in a lower court: *Gutierrez-Brizuela v. Lynch*, (2016). Strictly, the APA expressly requires courts to determine all relevant questions of law (section 706).

[10] *Energy Conversion Devices Inc.'s Applications* [1983] RPC 231: quoted in Hallam-Eames, "*Chevron* Doctrine," arguing that it is possible to overstate the US/UK difference given the discretion of UK agencies to apply the law reasonably (see below). On a lack of constitutionalist roots for but practical sense of the British approach, see Endicott, *Administrative Law*, chapter 9, which among other things points out that a single "correct" interpretation can admit a number of different applications of the law.

[11] The same institutional constraints and incentives help to explain the low formalism of US courts (and much legal theory) compared to England: Atiyah and Summers, *Form and Substance* (on differences in antitrust law, pp. 323–324).

Understanding something, however, does not make it a decent basis for sustained legitimacy. Again, incentives-values compatibility seems hard to reach here. To pin down the core of that awkwardness, we have to look at things a little bit more closely. A useful insight is provided by the rationalization of the deference doctrine offered by the late US Supreme Court justice Antonin Scalia, who joined the Court after *Chevron*:[12]

> An ambiguity in a statute committed to agency implementation can be attributed to either of two congressional desires: (1) Congress intended a particular result, but was not clear about it; (2) Congress had no intent on a particular subject, but meant to leave its resolution to the agency. When the former is the case, what we have is genuinely a question of law, properly to be resolved by the courts. When the latter is the case, what we have is the conferral of discretion upon the agency.

Accepting Justice Scalia's twofold distinction, it seems to me that in his second case it is important to distinguish between three types of ambiguity in the detailed provisions of a statute delegating a regime to an agency:

1. The ambiguous provision is part of a statute that sets the agency a clear purpose and objective.
2. The ambiguity is in a statute that sets only vague purposes and/or objectives.
3. It is in a statute that sets multiple unweighted purposes and/or objectives and so is indeterminate (when there are enduring trade-offs).

In the first case, one obvious course is for the ambiguous statutory provision to be interpreted and applied purposively (as advocated in chapter 12 for IA regimes on the grounds that, for them, purpose is all). But that hardly works for resolving the second or third types of ambiguity. Thus, ambiguity in specific provisions is more serious when it occurs in a delegating statute with vague or indeterminate objectives.

It is not clear that simply dropping the *Chevron* doctrine would help live up to the values of constitutional democracy. If the courts did not

[12] Scalia, "Judicial Deference," p. 516.

defer to agency interpretation in cases 2 and 3, they, rather than the agency, would become the de facto legislators, as occurred in competition policy: hardly an advance in terms of democratic legitimacy.

Alternatively, it might be argued that given the difficulty Congress faces in amending and repealing laws, it would be against the spirit of democracy for Congress to pass detailed statutes. Preferable, given the real-world constraints, for the job to fall to agencies that are under degrees of congressional and/or presidential control and that are required by law to consult widely and freely and to explain the reasons for their decisions. But this is merely to say that incentives-values compatibility lies beyond reach: that values must tack (or bend) to incentives if institutions themselves are impervious to reform. Crucially for us, it also fails to engage with those independent agencies that are highly insulated from both elected branches.

The core of a solution begins to emerge once the "democratic deficit" problem here is pinpointed. The Court could, I want to suggest, maintain a more targeted version of the nondelegation doctrine.

Toward a Nondelegation Doctrine for Trustee-Style IA Regimes

Even if US courts have to date been satisfied with statutes that enjoin agencies to "pursue the public interest," such vague purposes are, in the normal sense of the words, neither intelligible nor principled, straining the deep values of democracy. It is a mistake, however, to treat all agencies as more or less alike, irrespective of how they fit into the structure of the state.[13] It should be possible, within the constraints and incentives of the US system, to distinguish between different agency *types*, taking into account their varying degrees of insulation from day-to-day politics and the principled purpose of their delegated powers.

Where that purpose is credible commitment, such agencies need to be insulated from day-to-day politics, but they are not meant de facto to be granted the authority of primary legislators since they are a device for tying government to the people's settled purposes (Delegation

[13]Nor are those distinctions regularly made in the canonical political science literature (e.g., the survey in McCubbins, "Abdication or Delegation").

Criteria, and chapter 11). A revised nondelegation doctrine would, I suggest, focus on them.

Reflecting our first Design Precept, I am therefore airing the possibility of a version of the nondelegation doctrine that distinguishes truly independent trustee-type agencies from other forms of delegation (those without full day-to-day insulation). The requirement for an "intelligible principle" would be revived in substance but only for them, since they lack the majoritarian proximity of the executive agencies.[14] There would then be little question of politically insulated agencies being free to determine their own powers, because reasonable interpretation would be disciplined by the statutory purpose and objective.[15]

For polities with legal constitutionalism, something along those lines would help to recognize the values of democracy by constraining the representative assembly to frame high policy before allowing unelected, insulated technocrats (and judges) to deploy the state's powers.[16]

Beyond the United States

This is not relevant only for the United States. A judicial check of the broad kind described above could operate in, for example, France, where many AAIs have multiple unprioritized objectives notwithstanding the Constitutional Council's stipulation that delegations should be limited.[17]

Policing this version of a nondelegation doctrine for IAs would naturally fall to the Conseil d'État, whose role involves offering an opinion on a draft statute's constitutionality, including the sufficiency of purposes.

[14] The same might, perhaps, go for the courts themselves, who as argued in chapter 4 are, when applying ordinary legislation, canonical independent trustees. Under the principles espoused in chapter 10, wearing their constitutional hats, they should lean against their judicial kin being delegated the role of "filling in" the high policy omitted from a vague or indeterminate statute. As with IAs covered by our Principles, discretionary general policy delegated by statute to the independent judiciary should be constrained by a monitorable standard.

[15] For illustration, see footnote 11, chapter 12.

[16] In this my argument overlaps a little with Ely, *Democracy and Distrust*. The point is not that democracy is the dominating principle encoded into the US Constitution itself but, rather, that it is the constitution of a representative democracy. A similar point is made in Dorf, "Democracy and Distrust." But, perhaps in contrast to Ely, I want to say here only that it has implications for the distribution of power across the state.

[17] Source: High French officials.

While not formally binding on legislators, the Conseil's view tends to prevail as it is given great weight by judges presiding over subsequent judicial review cases. It therefore has the tools to apply the Principles in France.

Of course, the burden of avoiding delegation with vague or indeterminate objectives does not rest solely with the courts. In the US, the president could veto vague statutes, and arguably should feel compelled to do so.[18] Failing those formal routes, experts could decline to serve as IA policy makers, the media could protest, and public opinion could assert itself if a norm of "clear delegation" is breached. All of those forces are just as relevant in other democracies, including those without a written constitution and thus reliant on political and popular scrutiny of legislation, such as Britain.

FRAMING IA OBJECTIVES AND REMITS IN THE WESTMINSTER SYSTEM

Turning, then, to the UK, the position is in many respects quite different, as government has more degrees of freedom in a Westminster-style parliamentary democracy.

Most obviously, the executive government keeps tight control over the detailed language of statutes, even when it bows to the broad substance of Opposition or Second Chamber amendments. But there is more to it than that. The menu of mechanisms for setting ex ante objectives is rich.

Secondary Legislation

One route is "secondary legislation," under which the primary legislation establishing the regime (the "enabling Act") permits the executive government to flesh out the detail via "statutory instruments" subject to expedited parliamentary procedures (of positive approval or veto). While it can be used controversially to grant profound powers to the

[18] A point made some decades ago in Lowi, *End of Liberalism*.

elected executive, as recently argued by former lord chief justice Igor Judge, it can in principle also be used benignly to fill out high policy, and so constrain the purpose and scope of the "tertiary legislation" effected by regulators' rules.[19]

A topical contemporary example is the regime for ring-fencing the domestic UK retail banking operations of large financial groups, which is intended to make them more resilient. Partly due to Bank of England advocacy, key parameters concerning which activities must, may, and may not be conducted within a ring-fenced bank were set out in government secondary legislation rather than in rules of the regulatory agency (a Bank of England body), as had initially been proposed by government officials. The then Bank leadership believed that it should not be allowed to decide something so architectural; elected politicians should do so.

Back in the 1930s, when debate raged about the New Deal agencies, James Landis floated the possibility of secondary legislation being used in the US.[20] Generally speaking, it has not been, except in a relatively low-profile but important way. Under the 1934 Rules Enabling Act, Congress established machinery and processes for setting the rules for federal court procedure. In broad summary, the recommendations of a mixed committee of judges and lay experts are, once approved by parts of the judiciary, submitted to Congress and take effect as law if not vetoed or remitted back within seven months.[21] This compromise process cuts through uncertainty about whether the court has inherent constitutional authority to set its own rules of procedure.

Perhaps the elected branches of the US state could find ways of filling out the statutory remits of agencies if they developed this technique, an approach that would pursue the underlying spirit of the (pending, as

[19] Judge, "Ceding Power" and *Safest Shield*, pp. 99–106. For a history of the New Zealand Parliament's oversight of secondary legislation, see Morris and Malone, "Regulations Review."

[20] Landis, *Administrative Process*, pp. 77–78.

[21] The proposed rules are drawn up by the Committee of Rules of Practice and Procedure, whose members are appointed by the Supreme Court chief justice under the Act. Draft rules are vetted first by the Judicial Conference of the United States and then by the Supreme Court before being submitted to Congress. My thanks to Daniel Coquillette, the current reporter to the Standing Committee on Rules, for explaining the facts to me. Needless to say, he should not be blamed for the broader inferences I draw in the main text.

I write) REINS Act but focused on providing monitorable objectives rather than rule-by-rule scrutiny (and so without creating as much work for stretched legislators).

Statutorily Required Remits from the Executive

In Britain, statutory instruments are not the only mechanism available for fleshing out a delegated regime. A statute can require (or provide for) the elected executive to flesh out the regime in a nonstatutory remit, with more informal parliamentary oversight of how it does so. Although the high-level goal *must*, on the view I have set out in the Principles, be in statute, Parliament can be spared the need to enshrine all the detail in primary legislation, allowing for slow-motion learning as the regime is applied.

Some remits cover a whole Parliament, often with provision for mid-term review (e.g., competition authority, water utility regulator, energy utility regulator). These *Strategic Policy Statements* (colloquially, the "strategic steer") seem to have been introduced by the Cameron government to redraw the boundary between high policy and regulatory discretion. But, consistent with anecdotal evidence that these documents can develop into shopping lists as drafts are circulated around Whitehall, some are so detailed that "strategy" is not quite the right term.[22]

Others, such as the remits for Bank of England's monetary policy and financial stability committees, are issued annually. For example, for monetary policy, the Bank of England has a lexicographic objective established in primary legislation plus a remit via which the elected executive defines price stability (since the regime's inception, an inflation target) and provides guidance on how the Monetary Policy Committee (MPC) should manage short-term trade-offs between inflation and economic activity. Bank watchers sensibly scrutinize this carefully each year, whereas the competition authority remit seems to get less attention (and is typically signed at a lower level in the elected executive government).

[22]They were gradually introduced following the UK Department for Business, Innovation, and Skills' *Principles for Economic Regulation*, mentioned in chapter 7, and as I write are being extended to cover Ofcom's economic regulatory function. Some data are included in Stern, "British Utility Regulation Model."

It should be said that this technique does have hazards and is not available in all executive-dominated political systems; for example, as discussed in the previous chapter, French ministers are *not* empowered to expand on an agency's statutory remit. Where it is available, to be incentives-compatible, the executive must be constrained from reframing a regime to its own ends. In the case of the Bank of England, the Westminster Parliament having specified "price stability" as the primary objective, the executive government could not set a target for inflation that is unreasonably high without risking challenge in the courts. But some of my former colleagues were concerned about subtle backseat driving when, in 2013, the remit was amended to push the MPC toward employing "forward guidance" on the future path of interest rates (which, it should be said, the incoming governor was committed to). As provided for by the fourth Design Precept, the executive government needs to be monitored and held accountable by the legislature for its part in the determination of IA regimes.

Constitutionally, the remit mechanism can work in the UK because ministers, including the prime minister, are subject to the law and are accountable to Parliament. By contrast, in the US the president is not accountable to Congress and, as I understand it, presidential prerogative powers are not judicially reviewable. Whereas secondary legislation might conceivably be workable in the US, it is hard to imagine Congress allowing the president to set *nonstatutory* remits for the Fed, FDIC, or other insulated agencies.[23]

Multiple Objectives and "Have Regards" Requirements

If all this sounds too good to be true, the sting in the tail comes in a UK predilection for giving IAs multiple statutory objectives that rank equally. Even if each were clear and incorporated a quantitative standard, which they rarely are or do, this would leave the agency having to make trade-offs among their various duties. Despite having the wherewithal to frame regimes in line with the Principles, the UK often lets agencies into high policy by this back door, as illustrated in chapter 7's

[23] Of course, US cabinet officers can be accountable to Congress; but I cannot see how, say, the US Treasury secretary setting a remit for the Federal Reserve would bring even a veneer of democratic pedigree, since the officeholder is no more elected than the Fed chair.

discussion of financial regulation and the previous chapter's account of Ofgem having objectives to promote both low consumer prices and investment in renewable energy.

This is compounded by Parliament's habit, developed over the past decade or so, of including in regulatory legislation a series of social goods, factors, or considerations to which an agency should, in the jargon, "have regard." The UK's new Prudential Regulation Authority has around thirty such factors to weigh somehow, the Financial Conduct Authority around fifty.[24] Absent case law, agency leaders and legal counsel have to decide, implicitly or explicitly, what this amounts to: are they subordinate objectives, nonbinding constraints, or what? Whatever turns out to be the correct legal construction, they can certainly make a difference.[25] The old FSA was required by its mid-1990s statute to have regard to the competitiveness of the financial services industry, a harbinger for the "light-touch" regulation that was part of London's contribution to the financial crisis a decade later.

As David Currie, drawing on extensive experience of chairing UK-IA oversight boards, has commented:[26]

> The tradition in UK regulation has been to postulate a range of duties (and 'have regard to's) and to place on the regulator the onus of balancing those duties. In my experience, there is considerable advantage in having a clear primary duty, such as the Ofcom one, sitting above these.

The problem was stressed in a report from Westminster's Second Chamber in 2007 and seems to have been part of the drive behind getting sponsoring ministries to offer a strategic steer on trade-offs.[27] There is some skepticism in London, however, about whether that may prove a passing fad. There is no legislated obligation for ministers to issue guid-

[24] Source: The respective chief executives.

[25] Case law provides that, where an agency is required to have regard to a code or guidance, it must provide proper reasons for departing therefrom: summarized in Coleman, "The Future." Arguably, that is distinguishable from having to have regard to a set of broad statutory considerations that are not elaborated anywhere.

[26] Currie, "Regulatory Capture." Ofcom is the UK's independent regulator and a competition authority for the communications industries. As of early 2017, Currie chairs the board of the UK's Competition and Markets Authority, having previously chaired the board of Ofcom. See the next chapter for issues concerning UK-IA "oversight boards."

[27] House of Lords, *UK Economic Regulators*.

ance; and even if there were, it is not clear that the utility regulators' statutory objectives are specific enough, as a matter of law, to constrain ministers to a role consistent with our Principles for Delegation.

A MONITORABLE STANDARD IN HIERARCHICAL OBJECTIVES

Some readers might be thinking: it is all very well advocating a revived nondelegation doctrine for IAs, but how are judges, commentators, and citizens to know when an objective is "too vague," "too indeterminate"; don't we just end up in the same place as now?

To answer this, we have to go back to the Principles for Delegation and, in particular, to the criteria for whether to delegate at all to an insulated, trustee-type agency. The Principles make it a prerequisite that the objective be *monitorable* (and not just by a tiny band of experts hoping to serve at the agency). In terms of our values, part II argues that this is necessary to ensure the benefits of credible commitment are directed toward the people's purposes. In terms of incentives, part I argues that it is necessary to harness IA leaders to their mission, distinguishing them from elected politicians, who, in their drive to be reelected, tend to focus on short-term utility. If those are the reasons for requiring a monitorable objective, the point here is that whether or not a statutory objective is monitorable is, almost by definition, observable, so the courts would not have to draw arbitrary lines. Our proposed course should not be vulnerable to the "when is vague too vague?" problem.

This has important implications when the legislature wants to give an IA multiple objectives. Unless it is given up-front guidance on which objective to prioritize in different circumstances, there is room for disagreement between the agency and society (or between different sectional interests) about the extent to which the agency is fulfilling its objectives. Monitorability is jeopardized, if not sacrificed. The solution is that either weights should be put on different objectives or they must be hierarchical (lexicographic, as economists put it).

In principle, that should be easier to achieve in a parliamentary system than in the US. Experience suggests otherwise, however. If the US risks combining under- and overdelegation, perhaps the key hazard in the UK has become *overdetermined* delegation, which an agency can break through only by implicitly ranking society's goals itself.

The conclusion of this chapter, therefore, is that, under both legal constitutionalism and political constitutionalism, something like our Principles of Delegation could help legislators do a better job in framing IA regimes and so in underpinning the legitimacy of unelected power in our democracies.

15

Processes, Transparency, and Accountability

LEGAL CONSTRAINTS VERSUS POLITICAL OVERSIGHT

The courts will "inquire into minute details of methodology, data sufficiency and test procedure and will send the regulations back if these are lacking."

—US agency attorney, 1970s[1]

I'm afraid that there simply is not time for select committees to look at each and every one of the [agencies] within their remit . . . select committees simply do not have the time and resources to do what they already do, never mind having their burdens added to.

—Chairman of the House of Commons Agriculture Committee, 1999[2]

Even where an independent agency is set a clear statutory purpose and a monitorable objective, under our Principles for Delegation that is insufficient to deliver legitimacy for politically insulated, unelected power in today's constitutional democracies. Other necessary elements include policy decisions being made by committee, constraints on life after leaving office, fair decision making, and effective public accountability.

A full review of compliance with Design Precepts 2–4 is beyond the scope of this book. Instead, after a few examples of the structures and personal constraints under which IA policy makers work, this chapter is mainly about transparency, judicial review, and political accountability. While details vary greatly across countries, most seem to face problems with the potential tension, identified in chapter 11, between judicial and political oversight, as the quotes above bring into focus.

[1]Quoted in Strauss, "Rule-Making," footnote 15.

[2]House of Commons Select Committee on Public Administration, *Quangos*, quoted in Flinders, "Distributed Public Governance," p. 900.

DESIGN PRECEPT 2: COMMITTEES, APPOINTMENTS, AND SEPARATION OF FUNCTIONS

In many jurisdictions, IA policy decisions are made by committee. Within the monetary policy world, that is true of the US, the euro area, Japan, and the UK (although some committees in effect decide via chair-led consensus). In the regulatory world, it is true of the EU's financial regulatory agencies (although their boards have the character of specialist mini-assemblies of national representative experts). Similarly, the EU Competition Commissioner must obtain the agreement of fellow members of the College of Commissioners, which I understand from personal conversations is a reality, not a fiction.

Committee decision making is not, however, an embedded international norm. Across central banking, Canada and New Zealand are exceptions; and there are many more in other fields, including, as we have seen, the US Consumer Finance Protection Bureau (led by a director) and many of the UK's economic regulators (directors general). By the values reflected in the Principles, these regimes are problematic.

The Insufficiency of Oversight Boards

That issue cannot be solved by the kind of boards employed in the UK, which mix executive experts and "independents" and, as such, are modeled on private sector public company boards, a symptom of the New Public Management's enthusiasm for modeling the state on for-profit institutions operating in competitive markets.[3] These boards typically combine, in varying degrees, "oversight" with some "general policy" responsibilities. If they are purely for oversight but are not expert, they probably cannot penetrate what is going on, and so cannot dilute their director general's CEO-like power. If, by contrast, as in some cases, they are formally responsible for signing off and issuing legally binding rules or other substantive policy measures, it is hard to see how they could decently be anything other than independent experts, with each and

[3]The prevalent regulatory agency governance structure in the UK comprises a "chief executive" policy maker overseen by a statutory board of part-time "independent members" and a small handful of executives.

every one of them able to defend and explain the rules or measures they approve.

Further, if, as in the UK, only the chair and director general are typically subject to parliamentary confirmation hearings, a nasty paradox results. Either board members have equal authority despite their different degrees of democratic sanction or, alternatively, the playing field of power tilts toward the chair and DG, leaving them as overmighty citizens. According to the Principles, neither sits comfortably with durable legitimacy.

Effective internal oversight is, of course, absolutely vital, with an independent element helping to insulate IAs from political involvement in matters of internal structure and processes. But it is not a surrogate for fragmenting discretionary power or for political accountability for the exercise of policy discretion. At least in Britain, this is an unresolved problem in the governance of governance.

Independence from Capture Risk: Entry and Exit Constraints

For an IA regime to deliver credible commitment, each and every one of its policy committee members needs to be not only insulated from day-to-day politics but also immunized against capture by private interests, including, obviously, regulated industries.

Policy on entry and on exit/retirement is vitally important for this.[4] Yet there appear to be no established norms, across countries or fields. For example, the major jurisdictions do not uniformly bar from central bank policy making those who owe duties to financial intermediaries or who have been active, as participants or donors, in partisan politics.

Similarly, regulators leave to join trade associations, lobby groups, and firms they regulated. And whereas former Fed policy makers cannot work for a regulated bank for two years, they seem to be free to speak on monetary policy almost immediately. Elsewhere, the constraints vary in different ways.

[4]Where, as in the UK, some policy makers are part-time, clear restrictions on conflicts of interest while holding office are essential. After a few years during which the Bank of England leadership favored a more restrictive policy than the Treasury, which carries the burden of finding qualified people who are prepared to serve, an agreed accord was published. It has since been replaced by codes mandated by Parliament (paragraph 13B(2) of the Bank of England Act 1998, as amended by the Bank of England and Financial Services Act 2016).

Given the amount of policy that is now framed or coordinated in international fora, countries could benefit from exchanging information on their policies and practices in this area, not least so that they know the postoffice constraints on others around the table.

For us, the big question is whether tougher requirements should apply to IAs than to less politically insulated agencies. So far as I know, no jurisdiction singles out IAs for special treatment at present. We return to this issue at the close of part IV's examination of whether the multiple-mission postcrisis central banks risk being overmighty citizens.

Separation of Functions

There is rather more convergence among jurisdictions toward norms on the integrity and openness of decision making. For example, in line with the Principles, there is typically some separation of functions where an IA both writes and enforces rules. In France, that was made a requirement by the Constitutional Council (for agencies but not yet for ministerial adjudications). In the US, it is stipulated by the Administrative Procedures Act (APA).[5] In the UK, it is not an absolutely binding general precept, but is required by some regime-specific statutes and, in any case, is observed by many agencies in order to reduce the risks of successful challenges via judicial review. In the EU, it is not required or, as I understand it, practiced by the Commission in its regulatory roles, except to the extent that all commissioners are formally involved in, for example, antitrust decisions.[6]

DESIGN PRECEPTS 2–4: CONSULTATION AND PUBLIC DEBATE

There is also convergence toward facilitating public debate in various ways, including via advisory committees and public consultation on rules and regulations. Each, however, occupies only part of an uncomfortable space between judicial review and political accountability.

[5] The US Constitution incorporates overlapping powers and checks and balances but not a pure or "abstract generalization" of separation of powers: *Buckley v. Valeo*, 424 US 1, 124 (1976); Manning, "Separation"; and Strauss "Place of Agencies." On the history and lingering appeal in the US of pure separation, see Vile, *Constitutionalism*, chapter 6.

[6] Asimov, "Five Models."

Advisory Committees

In many countries, especially those with corporatist traditions, legislation requires agencies to set up advisory committees, but they often leave policy makers walking a narrow path between capture and banality.

In the US, Congress has provided a general statutory framework for such committees. That seems eminently sensible. But, at least anecdotally, the effect is said to have rendered their deliberations quite sterile.

In the UK, many independent regulatory agencies are mandated by their governing legislation to establish consumer and practitioner committees, which are obliged to publish reports on how the agency is doing. The regulators are not accountable to such committees, but that can become obscured. I once found the chief executive of a regulatory agency sitting outside a room waiting to be invited in to take questions from the practitioner committee: the mise-en-scène felt wrong.

Nor can such committees claim to represent the whole of the community reflected in their titles. As a former senior UK minister once commented to me, many MPs are better tuned into public and consumer opinion than consumer panel members. Consistent with that, an anecdote doing the rounds in London some years ago had it that a few members of the Financial Services Authority's early consumer panels had formerly been members of the Trotskyist Socialist Workers Party. I don't know whether that was true, but if so, I doubt whether they represented strong strands of public opinion.

The underlying need is to be clear about what these panels are for. A former chair of the UK's communications regulator, Ofcom, has described how he persuaded their consumer panel to focus on the broad approach the agency was taking to analyze consumer issues rather than lobbying on specific issues, which they could do via other channels.[7]

Statutory requirements to engage with committees drawn from particular interest groups cannot substitute for decent public debate.

[7] Currie, "Regulatory Capture."

Consulting on Draft Rules: The Risk of Labyrinthine Complexity

The principal formal means of enabling that wider debate is consultation on rules and policies.

In the US, all agencies must consult widely on legally binding rules (but not on guidance covering, for example, how they interpret their powers). The relatively light demands of the APA have been transformed by judicial lawmaking in this area, with regulators having to publish their response to each material point.[8]

In Britain, IA-specific statutes now routinely lay down requirements for consulting interested parties, and agencies must typically publish a *general* account of the representations they receive and their response to them. The general obligation is to "tell [potentially interested parties] enough (which may be a good deal) to enable them to make an intelligent response." In France and Germany, consultation is neither a general legal obligation nor a common feature of specific statutory regimes, although in practice agencies have been moving toward using it.[9]

In not a few countries, however, consultation documents risk being so dense that they are accessible to members of the public only when mediated by interest-group trade associations and sectional lobbyists. Where there is a risk of either the legality (vires) or specific application of a rule being challenged in the courts, the agency prudently caters for that in its formal documentation and statements. In other words, the consultation and explanatory documents are, to a greater or lesser extent in different jurisdictions, written for lawyers by lawyers seeking to protect their agency.

Operating Principles

The same considerations could deter or dilute the articulation of the *operating principles* called for by the third Design Precept. Technically, issuing such guidance is feasible under almost any structure of demo-

[8] As I write, the pending Regulatory Accountability Act would require much more, trial-like formality in public consultations (see chapter 1).

[9] On Britain: then master of the rolls Lord Wolf, quoted in Endicott, *Administrative Law*, p. 35 (also commenting that "consultation is not litigation," in *R v. North and East Devon* [2000]). On France: Rose-Ackerman and Perroud, "Policymaking and Public Law." On Germany: regulatory officials and Puender, "German Administrative Procedure."

cratic governance. For example, although the US Supreme Court has held that an agency cannot render its actions constitutional through self-interpretation of its governing statute, it has not ruled out agencies publicly articulating their broad interpretation and planned application of their powers.[10]

In reality, however, away from monetary policy (part IV), operating principles are hardly conspicuous—with notable exceptions, such as US and EU guidance on horizontal mergers, explained by the imperative of particular cases being determined speedily. Among financial regulators, in the 1980s the Bank of England explained how it thought about the statutory requirement that each person running or controlling a bank should be "fit and proper." But that kind of thing has slipped out of fashion in many jurisdictions, possibly because of the risks of litigation. If such documents are construed literally or ideologically by the courts, they would probably end up being incomprehensible as agency lawyers sought to dodge future bullets.

I mentioned in chapter 11 that, consistent with republican values, the Bank of England published a document in 2011 explaining in broad terms how it would approach the proposed new responsibilities for prudential supervision being debated in Parliament. It is worth adding here that the first instinct of very experienced and high-quality staff was that this would need to be a meaty, nuanced document of considerable length. Our response was that it should be short so that people other than lawyers, consultants, and lobbyists could read it. And that was not even about a legally binding rule!

Solving this general problem matters. Providing a reasoned justification of each rule or decision is not the same as having consistent principles that guide and underpin an agency's policies. The courts cannot be expected to fix that. Given legal challenges tend, inevitably, to be about one particular rule or adjudicatory decision, the broad consistency and credibility of policy is not easily justiciable. If judges do fix it, they become the policy makers, which is problematic in itself.

[10] Bressman, "Schechter Poultry" and "Disciplining Delegation."

DESIGN PRECEPT 2: RULE-OF-LAW VALUES VIA JUDICIAL REVIEW

The apparent intractability of that issue emerges when comparing how the judicial review systems of different jurisdictions contribute to compliance with the Principles.

On the one hand, our democratic values point toward constraints on IA processes being laid down by the elected legislature, reflecting how a particular society wants to balance decisiveness, participation, and due process. On the other hand, those values vie for priority with entrusting an independent judiciary with overseeing the administrative state's compliance with rule-of-law values, whether embedded in a codified constitution or the ancient traditions of the common law.

Which institution dominates depends on incentives. Thus, while civil (Roman) law systems might seem to lend themselves naturally to procedural codification with a legislative stamp, codifying public law relies heavily on governments being prepared to promulgate constraints on themselves. Germany did not formally codify administrative procedures until 1977, after nearly two decades of work, and even then covered only adjudicatory decisions, not rule making. It took France until 2015 for the National Assembly to pass a statute codifying standards implicit in decades of judicial decisions.[11] In the EU, while the Treaty provides for judicial review by the European Court of Justice (ECJ) and lays out four broad grounds, they are vague, leaving the judges to develop many of the procedural requirements and substantive constraints binding EU agencies and the Commission.[12]

Among common law jurisdictions, the UK's 2006 Legislative and Regulatory Reform Act requires regulators to be "transparent, accountable, proportionate and consistent" and provides for executive government to issue guidance on agency rule-writing processes. But given executive dominance (for so long as licensed by Parliament to govern) and an uncodified constitution, it is no surprise that canons of procedural integrity were developed by the judiciary through the common law.[13]

[11] Puender, "German Administrative Procedure," and Custos, "2015 French Code."

[12] Articles 263 and 267 of Treaty on the Functioning of the European Union (TFEU).

[13] The heavy lifting was led in the 1960s and 1970s by, notably but not exclusively, Law Lords Reid, Wilberforce, and Diplock. Two highlights worth mentioning here include the judges re-

By contrast, in the US the high degree of separation between the legislature and the executive branch gives the former a strong interest in imposing codified procedural constraints on the administrative state. In contrast to whether to delegate with a clear objective (chapter 14), this is a rare instance of incentives-values compatibility in the US system of government, the 1946 Administrative Procedures Act (APA) still providing the core of its administrative law (chapters 2 and 8).

Incentives and the Judges: Fairness and Vires versus Substantive Rationality

Of course, whatever the degree of codification, in all jurisdictions individual cases give the judiciary opportunities to elaborate administrative law in light of their system's constraints, incentives, and values. For us, the great question is how far they get into merits and, thus, develop general policy without being subject to political oversight and public debate.

Normatively, the discussion of part II might point toward the intensity of judicial review of IA decisions increasing with the extent to which the IA regime falls short of the Principles (entailing a democratic deficit) and with how far the challenged actions cut across liberal freedoms. This would not distinguish between different types of IA activity per se—for example, between the monetary policy decisions and prudential stability decisions of a multiple-mission central bank (part IV)—but only between their pedigree and effects. The thought is reflected in the following matrix.

	Principles-compliant	*Principles deficit*
No "basic rights" at stake	Thin review (e.g., not unreasonable)	Less thin review (e.g., clearly reasonable)
"Basic rights" at stake	Thicker review (e.g., proportionality)	Thick review (e.g., proportionality and merits)

jecting statutory provisions designed to preclude judicial review of executive action (*Anisminic*, 1969, a case stemming from the 1958 Suez Crisis); and a series of later cases which, step by step, brought executive/Crown prerogative powers within scope. One standard textbook treatment is Wade and Forsyth, *Administrative Law*.

A Principles-compliant IA with multiple instruments would (a) be constrained by the law (courts) to choose the instrument least invasive of individuals' freedoms (taking into account any legal rights furthered by the action), but would (b) face a lower test (unreasonableness or irrationality) in determining that action was needed to achieve its statutory objective and in calibrating the instrument employed. While the former amounts to a "check" (and could give courts an incentive to unearth new rights), the latter reflects the value of institutional "balance," with the courts respecting the mandate given to the Principles-compliant IA (and not judges) by democratically elected legislators (and perhaps respecting the IA itself if it was an equally ranking branch of government). Meanwhile, for a noncompliant IA, enjoying insulation from politics without appropriate constraints coded into the delegated regime, more intense judicial review would give them (and conceivably legislators) incentives to mitigate (or remedy) the regime's flaws.

How far the intensity of real-world judicial scrutiny varies with the identity of the decision maker and the nature of the decision is not entirely clear or consistent across the major democracies, and in some cases has ebbed and flowed over time. In part, differences across jurisdictions reflect variations in the extent to which constitutional traditions incorporate and codify civic, social, and economic "rights."

It is hardly surprising, therefore, that in Germany, a lot of the work is done by the Basic Law, with many challenges to administrative action centered on whether a delegating statute (1) specifies the requisite content, purpose, and scope (i.e., a constitutional vires test: chapter 13) or (2) cuts across the values of democracy or other constitutional rights, which have been construed as extending to the social-cum-economic sphere.[14] Beyond that, German administrative law incorporates the doctrine of proportionality, developed by judges in nineteenth-century Prussia, before the advent of democracy, to constrain the autocratic-liberal state's policing of society, and elevated during the late twentieth century to the widely diffused constitutional principle under which

[14] Puender, "German Administrative Procedure," and Bignami, "Regulation and the Courts." Where the realm of rights is discovered-cum-determined by judges to extend more broadly than previously thought, under legal constitutionalism (chapter 8) the effects include shifting the final voice and arbiter in the area concerned from the democratic assembly to the courts. That partly explains why I occasionally put "rights" in quotation marks.

legal rights must be appropriately balanced.[15] The specialist administrative court will, further, overrule the bureaucracy where power has not been exercised when it should be or where relevant considerations have been ignored or balanced incorrectly, the latter most obviously entailing more than merely deciding reasonably.[16] Overall, the effect is that the courts can get into the substantive merits of administrative-agency decisions.[17] Thus, in terms of our second and fourth Design Precepts, Germany's "chain of legitimacy" for delegation relies on judicial—and, where it really exists, ministerial—oversight rather than on public participation in rule making or, as discussed below, parliamentary accountability for the policy regime.

The European Court of Justice has both drawn on and, perhaps given the circumstances of confederation, departed somewhat from those German conventions. In applying the four Treaty grounds for review and policing freedoms incorporated into the treaties, central tests are proportionality and "manifest error" in questions of fact or discretion, which in recent decades has been applied with greater intensity in areas where the Court has found substantive rights inscribed into the law.[18] But the apparent borrowings from German jurisprudence have not stood in the way of differences between the German Constitutional Court and the ECJ when it comes to whether the intensity of review should be sensitive to the identity of the decision maker, notably in the challenge, recounted in the next chapter, to some ECB crisis innovations.

Among Anglo-Saxon countries, in the US legitimation can seem to rely heavily on judicial policing even though its constitution specifies relatively few categorical rights. The contrast with the UK is striking given what are apparently similar abstract standards of review. Under the APA, a key test in the US is whether an action is "arbitrary or capricious" (highly pejorative language in ordinary speech, which seems to darken American debates about the bureaucracy). In the UK there are tests of good faith, reasonableness, and, more recently reflecting EU experience, proportionality. Also, compared with France, both systems

[15] Mathews, "Proportionality"; Schlink, "Proportionality"; and on the high theory, Alexy, "Constitutional Rights."

[16] *Ermessensausfall, Ermessensfehlgebrauch,* and *Ermessensuberschreitung.*

[17] Bignami, "Formal versus Functional Method."

[18] For a comparison of different jurisdictions from about a decade ago, see Craig, "Law, Fact and Discretion."

grant standing to challenge an administrative agency in the courts to a fairly specific range of parties, which is more consistent with protecting liberal "rights" and rule-of-law values (chapter 8) than with *republican contestability* (chapters 9 and 11).[19]

Notwithstanding those similarities, however, US judicial review of agency decisions is, in many respects, more intrusive or exacting (depending on one's point of view) than review by the English high court.

Away from "human rights" cases, there is a marked reluctance among the UK's senior judiciary to substitute their own view of policy when requirements of vires, procedure, and natural justice are met.[20] By contrast, during the 1970s US appeals court judges developed the doctrine of "hard look" review, encapsulated in the words quoted at the chapter head and, in effect, enabling judges to substitute their view of the facts or of how the law should be applied to the facts. While the Supreme Court eventually reined back the activism of lower courts, a test of "rationality" remains, entailing a focus on whether an agency's decisions are warranted by its reasons and the facts, not "running counter to the evidence before [it]."[21]

The two systems also differ in their approach to challenges to regulatory rules *before* they are applied. The English courts do not take such cases, essentially on the grounds that court procedures deliver integrity in surfacing the particular circumstances of specific disputes and challenges but are less well suited to general policy making (see chapter 10's

[19] Under a UK statutory provision that it is for the courts to determine whether an applicant has "sufficient interest" in an executive action for a case to be heard, English judges have established broad standards for adjudicating a person's *standing* to bring a challenge against government. In 2013–2014, HMG retreated from a consultative proposal to introduce a statutory restriction of standing to "direct" interests. It had met with widespread opposition from the legal community, including retired judges.

[20] Reasonableness and proportionality are typically seen either as being appropriate for different types of case or, alternatively, as lying on a spectrum where the threshold for state intervention (and the intensity of judicial review) increases with the seriousness of the liberties or rights potentially jeopardized (e.g., Carnwath, "From Rationality to Proportionality").

[21] The key modern case is *Motor Vehicle Manufacturers Association of the United States v. State Farm Mutual Automobile Insurance Co.*, 463 US 29, 43–44 (1983), summarized in the section "Domestic Hard Look Review" of Sitaraman, "Foreign Hard Look Review," p. 520. Adrian Vermeule, in *Law's Abnegation*, especially chapter 5, argues that the courts apply only a thin test of rationality, but focuses on Supreme Court doctrine rather than what goes on in the appeals and lower courts and their effect on agencies. Even at the level of the Supreme Court, the practices and procedures of some regulatory commissions, notably the SEC, have been transformed by recent judicial interventions (Kraus and Raso, "Rational boundaries," and SEC, "Operating Procedures").

reference to Bingham's criteria for judicial lawmaking). By contrast, in the US rules are regularly challenged hot off the press, essentially on the grounds that policy makers violated general (i.e., APA) or regime-specific statutory provisions governing their production.[22] As with particular cases, these lapses can include flaws in substantive reasoning, such as inadequate cost-benefit analysis (even where CBA is not formally required by statute).

So far as I understand it, these American doctrines do not distinguish between independent authorities, semipolitical regulatory commissions, and executive agencies closer to politics. Taken together with "deference" to an agency's interpretation of ambiguous provisions in the statutes it applies (chapter 14) and, in a broadly similar vein, of its own rules, they seem to lead to the curious state of affairs where, putting it too starkly, US judges might step back from questions of law while stepping into questions of fact, reasoning, and policy. Big picture, things seem to be the other way around in Britain where, shortly into the post–World War II era, the courts laid down that statutory powers must be used to promote the policy and objectives of the legislation and that those statutory provisions were for the courts themselves to determine as a matter of law.[23]

The explanation lies, as ever, in the incentives and interests created by the specifics of the separation of powers and, in particular, the prevalence of legislative veto points. Broadly, primary legislation being a massive endeavor of uncertain quality in the US, the courts find themselves the "masters" of the administrative state, with varying degrees of relish, whereas English courts can exercise restraint knowing that systematic flaws in the substance of a policy regime will be fixed by Parliament if public opinion or elected-executive-branch interests so demand.[24]

In broad summary, then, the equilibrium under the US Constitution is one of judges as backstop general policy makers. While one can marvel at the training US judges must get in probability theory and statistics

[22]For comparisons of substantive versus process review across the US, Canada, France, and Italy, see Rose-Ackerman, "Judicial Review."

[23]*Padfield v. Minister of Agriculture* [1968], a case about no delegation being unfettered.

[24]What I take to be an essentially similar starting point informs the fascinating comparative analysis (also covering Australia) in Cane, *Controlling Administrative Power.* I am grateful to Peter Cane for exchanges on our overlapping topics. For comparisons with the EU, see Craig, *Global Administrative Law.*

to fulfill this role, the issue for us is of a democratic deficit opening via a peculiar route. On the one hand, it fits with (and might warrant?) the overt politicization of the American judiciary. On the other hand, there is an accountability lacuna (Design Precept 4). If Congress delegates degrees of discretion to IAs (and to other agencies), it can expect them to explain and defend their general policy. If, instead, the *substance of policy* is in effect determined by the courts, there is no such accounting, in the language of the public, to their representatives, helping them to decide whether to sustain the policy regime.

Review versus Appeal: US Administrative Judges and UK Tribunals

When, however, we turn to dedicated machinery for appeal on merits, the potential dilemmas for how to balance the values reflected in our second and fourth Design Precepts are more acute in Britain.[25]

The US establishes, by statute, administrative law judges *within* agencies such as the SEC, so that, consonant with separation-of-powers values, there is a degree of functional distance in enforcement decisions. Appeal, on merits, tends to lie to the commissioners themselves, who were of course the rule makers. The risk of conflict in lawmakers determining the application of their own rules is ameliorated by the right to challenge the integrity of the process via judicial review in the Article III courts (the administrative law judges themselves being emanations of the Article 1 legislators). All told, this is not a bad setup, since the commissioners can account for their general policy to Congress (see below) and the courts can invigilate their procedural integrity.

In the UK, appeals on merits from agency decisions in particular cases are to special tribunals established by statute, and now operated as a coherent system covering the whole of the administrative state, ranging from "mass administrative justice" to the slightly more rarefied world of independent regulatory authorities. The wrinkle is that, in contrast to Australia, which after deliberation made exactly the opposite choice, UK tribunals are technically courts presided over by judges. Consistent with that, the highest courts entertain challenges against tri-

[25]For a comparison of different structures for adjudicatory decisions, appeals, and review, see Asimov, "Five Models."

bunal decisions on only narrow grounds but have also underlined that tribunals themselves may substitute their own view of the correct substantive decision.[26] Indeed, doctrine seems to be, broadly, that[27]

> expediency requires that, where Parliament has established such a specialist appellate tribunal in a particular field, its expertise should be used to best effect, to shape and direct the development of law and practice in that field.

As a package, this makes sense in terms of self-restraint by the highest courts; and might stack up if, as maintained in the 1957 Franks Report, tribunals should be treated as simply "machinery . . . for adjudication rather than . . . of administration."[28] But that imports an adjudication/administration dichotomy that is no better grounded than the politics/administration dichotomy we dismissed in chapter 11, and is in any case hardly apt for policy agencies applying nonmechanical statutes. A political community could still choose to draw a line between the two as a matter of convention, but in that case it is not clear that the UK's line sits comfortably with our values.

That is because, for a former policy maker, defining the role as *shaping and directing the development of practice* marks the upper tribunal as a body of fellow policy makers. Yet, partly due to their being judges, tribunal chairs do not testify to House of Commons committees to explain and defend the principles and, thus, the de facto general policies they develop in the course of their work. If, as anecdotally seems to be the case, agency policy makers pragmatically accept those tribunal policy principles as having the force of (nonlegal) precedent—because it would be irrational to be overturned twice on essentially the same substantive point—a democratic deficit opens up through tribunal policy makers not being exposed to the public scrutiny and debate that is the value of parliamentary accountability.

[26] Elliot, "Ombudsmen, Tribunals, Inquiries," puts this in context of the juridification of agency accountability (as well as using the "mass administrative justice" tag); see also Rose and Richards, "Appeal and Review." On a 2014 case in which the Supreme Court overruled the Court of Appeal on a matter disputed between the Tribunal and Ofcom, see Richards, "Dogma in Telecoms."

[27] Carnwath, "Tribunal Justice," p. 9.

[28] Quoted in Carnwath, "Tribunal Justice," p. 3.

It is ironic that the US variant of this challenge arises because regular judges are tempted into policy, whereas the UK's arises because tribunal-based policy makers have been designated as judges. It is similarly ironic that, only a little more than a century after Dicey's strictures (chapter 8), the UK's tribunal system has evolved into something like France's Conseil d'État, similarly organized into separate "chambers" but formally housed in the judiciary rather than the executive branch.

The French Conseil d'État

The Conseil is, indeed, the paradigmatic appeal tribunal. It takes challenges against rules and regulations issued by agencies, and appeals against their adjudicatory decisions.[29] In line with French republican values, access to the Conseil is wide, and policy is required to respect the 1789 Revolution's value of equality.[30] Over recent years, challenges have been allowed against "soft law" statements, such as press releases, where, for example, through market behavior they could materially affect economic (or potentially social) welfare.[31]

Consistent with judicial norms, the Conseil reaches determinations after public hearings. Consistent with administrative norms, it effectively conducts de novo reviews, perhaps without the seesawing variations in doctrine characterizing the ordinary courts of judicial review in the US.

As such, the Conseil occupies, by long history and design, territory in between the Anglo-Saxon spheres of judiciary and high officialdom. By virtue of reviewing on merits, members of the Conseil contribute materially to the articulation of general policy. By virtue of being judges, members of the Conseil do not testify to parliament to explain their general policies.

[29] This does not preclude some legal challenges via the ordinary courts; for example, against competition authority decisions on cartels. Jurisdiction is often specified in the delegating statute. Source: High French officials.

[30] Bignami, "Formal versus Functional Method."

[31] This is of interest for the US given policy makers' use of tweeting.

A Central Banking Example

The issues for our inquiry can be illustrated by a central banking story from thirty-odd years ago.

Under the UK's 1979 Banking Act, there was a system for banks to appeal against the Bank of England's banking supervisory actions. During my first few years there, I attended a meeting of the most senior prudential supervisors to decide whether to close a small bank. One of the big bosses, I cannot remember who, asked whether a decision to close the bank was likely to be overturned on appeal (to a tribunal). I have never forgotten the response of Brian Gent, a usually undemonstrative man who was, by general recognition, one of the finest-ever bank supervisors. Swinging his arm, Gent said, "Then it will be the tribunal's fault when this bank fails." Then and later the Bank would have taken a quite different view of being overturned by the courts on the integrity or fairness of its processes.

While the merits/process divide is not sharp, the distinction can and should be made. If judges get into substance, subtly or not so subtly shaping general policy, it is much harder for agencies to account for general policy and for representatives to debate the workings of the regime. While that might not matter so much for agencies under political control, the structure of merits review does affect the capacity of IA regimes to enjoy democratic legitimacy.

IAs Testifying to Parliament on Disagreements with Judicial/Tribunal Policy

Short of the parliament insisting that tribunal (or, in France, Conseil chamber) chairs should testify regularly on their general policies (which, I suppose, they might deny having), the solution is for agency leaders to make clear in their own testimony where general policy has, in effect, been set by the tribunal and where they disagree with those policies. Otherwise, contrary to our fourth Design Precept, accountability for policy slips into a vacuum, with the risk of elected legislators being in a weak position to judge whether an IA regime is working or needs reform.

This is reminiscent of chapter 12's solution to the problem posed by an IA transnational elite, requiring them to testify domestically on emerging international policies. It places burdens on legislative oversight committees and technocrats alike. It is not easy for testifying officials to volunteer answers to questions they have not been asked.

In order to avoid alienating, respectively, the judiciary and domestic legislators, it might seem expedient for national executive branch and agency officials to avoid drawing attention to their policy disagreements with tribunals and, separately, the extent of their international work. But just think about what such silence would mean. The public can be misled by sins of omission just as easily as by sins of commission, but only for so long.

DESIGN PRECEPT 4: POLITICAL OVERSIGHT OF IA REGIMES

It matters hugely, therefore, whether, in line with the fourth Design Precept, political accountability can really be achieved via testimony to legislative committees, remembering that this means distinguishing between accountability for a regime's design and for its stewardship.

Democratic Accountability for Design of IA Regimes

There can be no doubting elected politicians are in the firing line when a regime abjectly fails. Across Western democracies, the political parties controlling executive government took a hit at the ballot box for the Great Financial Crisis. In the US, UK, and France, the Republicans, Labour, and UMP were voted out of office. Only German Chancellor Merkel's CDU survived in government, but even they had to go into a grand coalition with the Social Democrats. Insofar as executive governments had a responsibility to ensure that the regulatory regime was fit for purpose—or, even more important and most basically, that, in line with Design Precept 1, the regime had a clear purpose—that accountability was fair enough.

In parliamentary systems, this is relatively straightforward. The executive branch, the main initiator of laws, needs to keep each major regime under review; and the legislative committees need to ensure that they do so.

It is a more complex and delicate matter in US-style presidential systems. On the one hand, the executive branch is not formally responsible for an IA regime. On the other hand, as the Republicans found, the incumbent party can pay the costs for poorly constructed policy. This gives the elected executive powerful incentives to publish reviews of policy regimes and put proposals to Congress when it is concerned about their foundations. Treasury Secretary Paulson did just that when he published proposals for reconfiguring the US financial-regulatory architecture, with a view to, as he saw it, better aligning formal responsibilities with capabilities and reducing fragmentation.[32]

Under any system of government, however, what legislators and the public know about a regime relies heavily on IA testimony. Hence, it is absolutely vital that the modalities of accountability to the elected legislature be both feasible and trusted by the people. As in other areas, the variation is quite marked.

Feasibility of Political Oversight: The United States

As a general matter, the mechanics of political oversight are, on the face of it, straightforward in the US where both houses of Congress have long worked through committees.[33] Indeed, many US agencies are overseen by *many* congressional committees. While that can lead to a barrage of requests, investigations, and edicts, sometimes sacrificing consistency and impairing administrative efficiency, no one has any doubt that Congress will do some oversight of agencies via its committee system.

Similarly, with the exception of the presidents of the Federal Reserve's twelve regional banks, all IA office-holders are among the vast number of presidential appointments subject to Senate confirmation.[34]

[32] US Department of Treasury, *Blueprint*.

[33] The qualification "as a general matter" is added only because, in the case of the Federal Reserve, the presidents of the twelve regional Federal Reserve Banks are not legally officers of the federal government, although that need not stop Congress from calling them to testify and explain their policy positions.

[34] Impressionistically at least, the number of former Senate staffers serving on regulatory commissions has increased. If that were to extend to the more insulated agencies, their independence could be compromised.

Feasibility of Political Oversight—the United Kingdom: Transformation via the Select Committee System

The position in the UK was historically more complicated given the convention that government should be accountable "on the Floor of the House." It is therefore hard to overemphasize the importance of the emergence, over the past thirty-five years, of powerful House of Commons select committees, in what amounts to an important constitutional evolution. It started with reforms led by Norman St. John Stevas in the early 1980s under Mrs. Thatcher's prime ministership, although she herself was apparently a skeptic.[35] In the intervening decades, a series of incremental (and understudied) reforms has strengthened the select committee system; since the latest major change, in 2010, the chairs are elected by the House of Commons rather than selected by party managers. Service on a major committee has become a source of prestige and publicity for individual members.

When acting on a cross-party basis through unanimous reports, the committees have gained some leverage over appointments and, perhaps more evidently, in the legislative process—not through formal, procedural power, but through the weight that their views carry in the House.[36]

Big picture, these developments made agency accountability feasible. Indeed, it would not be an exaggeration to say that the growth of the UK's regulatory state and of the standing of parliamentary committees has been symbiotic. This is how a semblance of incentives-values compatibility was restored.[37]

[35] Based on an exchange with Charles Moore, Mrs. Thatcher's authorized biographer.

[36] Formally, appointments are made by the elected executive under what are known as the Nolan Principles: jobs advertised, a public statement of the nature of and qualities needed for the job, and an interview conducted by senior/top civil servants who submit a short list to the deciding minister. For some independent agencies, including the Bank of England's monetary policy and financial stability committees, there are informal parliamentary hearings before a term of office begins, with the select committee publishing its conclusion on whether the "candidate" is fit for office against the statutory criteria.

[37] A "semblance" because, where the UK has adopted an IA regime as part of an EU initiative, the values of parliamentary supremacy and accountability are maintained only on the views, respectively, that the UK could leave the EU and that the national regulators could be summoned to give an account. This extends beyond this book, but Brexit can be thought of as the result of incentives-values incompatibility unless, like France, the UK were to embrace the value of Europe. Remainers broadly did, Leavers did not.

Feasibility of Political Oversight: France and Germany

Across the brief stretch of water separating the UK from Continental Europe, our other unity state, France, subjects its independent agencies to checks that are distinctive of the French state apparatus. The finances and operations of all agencies may be inspected by the super-elite *Inspection générale des finances* (staffed by officials graduating highest from ENA); and their management and spending are reviewed by the powerful and independent *Cours des comptes* (court of auditors), which safeguards the integrity of public funds. But while appointment hearings are now held for at least some AAIs, my impression is that public oversight by the assembly plays a somewhat smaller part in the life of French agencies than, perhaps, for their British counterparts.

Similarly, in Germany, regulators are typically called to testify to Bundestag committees mainly when draft legislation in their field is under consideration. Rather than routinely overseeing their stewardship of the existing regimes, such hearings tend to be ad hoc. So, although German agencies might elaborate general policy through adjudicatory decisions, there is little or no public accounting, as opposed to judicial oversight. Also, as far as I can tell, appointment hearings are not held in Germany, presumably on the ground that agency policy makers are under ministerial control (chapter 13).

Central-Bank versus Financial-Regulator Testimony across the Wider World

Such variations are by no means limited to Continental Europe. In Canada, the prudential supervisor, the Office of the Superintendent of Financial Institutions (OSFI), is obliged to publish its internal audit reports, but, as in Continental Europe, its head is typically asked to testify before Parliament only when something has gone wrong or is otherwise preoccupying politicians. By contrast, the Australian Prudential Regulation Authority (APRA) testifies twice a year on its stewardship of the prudential regime and the soundness of the financial system. That is about the same frequency as in the UK, in a normal year, for prudential and utility regulators.

Most, but not all, central bankers appear much more frequently (part IV). At one end of the spectrum is Japan, where Bank of Japan governors might testify at least fortnightly to the Diet, compared with the Bank of England governor appearing six to eight times before the Commons' Treasury Committee during "peacetime," now that there are regular hearings on stability as well as monetary policy. At the other end of the spectrum, their German counterpart may testify on economic policy generally but never on monetary policy to the Bundestag, on a widely held view that to do so would compromise the central bank's independence. Somewhere in between, the ECB president appears twice a year before the European Parliament's ECON Committee for a "dialogue" on monetary policy, the choice of language presumably signaling the central bank's constitutional elevation (part IV).

This dispersion in routine legislative oversight practices and norms ranks, to my mind, with vague mandates as symptomatic of a lack of consensus about the prerequisites of democratic legitimacy for unelected power.

IMPEDIMENTS TO EFFECTIVE POLITICAL OVERSIGHT

Even where hearings are routine, they do not always live up to the significance we are giving them. This is for a number of reasons.

Iron Triangles and the Political Entertainment Business

Perhaps the deepest skepticism about legislative oversight is sourced in what political scientists call *iron triangles,* an expression used to capture the potentially incestuous relationship between a regulator, the relevant legislative committee, and the regulated industry. In the US context, the concern is that members of the oversight committees often represent districts or states in which the regulated industry is particularly important for jobs and taxes, making them highly sensitive to the industry's interests; and that the industry goes out of its way to help fund the members' reelection campaigns, to release staff to serve in the agencies, and to provide a home for retiring committee members when they leave office. At its most cynical, everyone is regarded as wholly captured, and any other take on the public interest is lucky to get a look in.

In both Westminster-style and proportional representation systems, where politicians' reelection prospects depend more heavily on the relative standing of their party and where campaign finance is more constrained, those US-style dynamics are typically weaker. But that is not to say that the incentives in such systems give rise to unalloyed virtue. There is in all systems a different kind of triangle: between an oversight committee, the media, and the public. What could easily be regarded in a jaundiced way as the *politics-as-entertainment business* is, in truth, intrinsic to the complex communications between politicians and the public they represent. It need not undermine the value of testimony, and indeed can help give agency leaders an invaluable public platform.

In practice, however, congressional and Westminster committees *do* seem to approach their oversight functions quite differently, again most likely for reasons rooted in legislators' powers and incentives.

Police-Patrol versus Fire-Alarm Oversight: Alarms Are Too Late When It Matters Most

Political scientists often distinguish between "police-patrol" and "fire-alarm" oversight: the former being ongoing, more or less comprehensive scrutiny, the latter highly case-specific in response to public or interest-group complaints or alerts. In groundbreaking work, US researchers argued in the 1980s that an apparent preference among congressional committees for the less resource-intensive fire-alarm mode of operation does not free US agencies to do whatever they wish: they will still be found out and held to account.[38] In consequence, it was argued, the hand of oversight might be largely invisible so long as things were are going tolerably well.

Even so, what might just as well be termed "ambulance-chasing" oversight of agency policy and actions is hopelessly inadequate if a serious crisis ensues, since it is of essence ex post. Fire-alarm oversight suffices only for those areas of public policy where failure is not horribly

[38] McCubbins and Schwartz, "Congressional Oversight Overlooked."

costly for society as a whole. The failure to ensure that US financial regulators and supervisors were focused on the resilience of the US financial system in the years up to the 2007–2008 crisis illustrates that all too graphically and tragically.

It is therefore striking that, at least for the *major agencies*, Westminster committees seem on the whole to try to conduct police-patrol oversight, as well as following up on scandals, crises, and complaints.[39] Arguably, the limited *formal* leverage of Westminster committees in the legislative process increases the incentive of committee chairs and members to oversee, and be seen to oversee, the conduct of independent agencies.

Indeed, it is plausible to think that UK parliamentary scrutiny of a policy area is more intense when delegated to an independent agency than if the levers are held by the executive government, as government backbench supporters would then be likely to leave the heavy lifting to the opposition parties, making the oversight process more partisan and so easier for ministers to deflect.[40] As a provision for IA regimes, Design Precept 4 seems to be incentives-values-compatible in the UK.

Beyond "Police Patrols" to Public Debate: Implications for Oversight of IAs

There is, however, another problem with framing oversight practices in terms of police patrols and fire alarms. They are metaphors associated with identifying failings and, as such, betray an impoverished conception of the role that hearings can and do play in democratic societies. They miss the dimension of hearings stressed in part II: providing an occasion for public debate about an IA's mandate and stewardship. Testimony is not just about exposing flaws in the work of unelected officials; it is also about communication with the public via their elected representatives, a form of discursive accountability (chapter 11).

That entails putting on display the kaleidoscopic range of opinion prevailing on an IA's policy committee. Each and every voting member should be called to testify over the course of, say, a year. They should do

[39] Flinders, *Delegated Governance*, chapter 6, "External Accountability."

[40] Research bearing this out is planned for inclusion in a forthcoming book by Cheryl Schonhardt-Bailey tentatively titled *Accountability, Oversight and Deliberation of Economic Policy in UK Parliamentary Committees.*

so in the interest of public accountability; and they should be given an *opportunity* to do so in the interest of ensuring the public debate is rich and relevant.

Within the world of central banking and financial regulation, some jurisdictions satisfy that condition more nearly than others. For example, Fed and ECB testimony on monetary policy is centered on the chair, with other committee members not testifying routinely or at all.

None of this is easy when a committee operates by consensus, with voting of "true preferences" held in reserve. That mode of operation can be necessary when a committee is too big. It can also help to constrain the scope for agenda manipulation in those fields where, at each meeting, the policy committee has to prioritize among numerous threats to its objective, select which of a number of instruments to employ, and then calibrate the chosen instrument. That is why the UK 2012 legislation mandated the Bank of England's Financial Policy Committee to try to reach decisions by consensus, with voting held in reserve.

Whatever the motivation, however, if consensus is always achieved, so that minority votes never occur, there is an observational equivalence between consensus and leadership. Persistent unanimity outside of a crisis would be odd. Legislative overseers must conduct hearings so as to tease out differences in view if they are to gauge the effectiveness of the process they have enacted and delegated.

Comparing US and UK Legislative Oversight of Monetary Policy Makers

Our argument is that independent agencies, not being "majoritarian" themselves, must account to the legislative assembly, the cockpit of representative democracy, for their stewardship of the regimes entrusted to them. To recap part II, it is the democratic legitimacy of the assembly that confers, through a properly enacted statute, the *procedural* component of the agency's own legitimacy. And it is the legislature that can take powers away. For those precise reasons, such hearings, when conducted in jargon-free language, are also the single most important channel of communication with the public.

How such hearings are conducted therefore matters a lot. Are they discursive or adversarial? Do they stick to the delegated field or wander off into areas that are of interest to legislators but beyond the agency's responsibilities? Do legislators from different parties, or factions within parties, conduct themselves in a partisan way, or does the committee as a whole "hunt as a pack"? In all these respects, it seems likely that the reality of hearings varies considerably across countries.

In a fascinating comparative study, based on quantified textual analysis, of US and UK hearings to oversee the Federal Reserve and the Bank of England, Cheryl Schonhardt-Bailey finds that the Westminster hearings are more interactive and discursive than the Washington hearings. Comparatively, there is less grandstanding, less process, and more continuity in lines of questioning from member to member.[41]

That accords with my own experience and, as Schonhardt-Bailey suggests, may have something to do with the fact that, in the UK, typically four or five members of the Bank of England policy committee attend a hearing. This is not "testimony" in the sense of an occasion for the chair to read out a long essay, which would often be unwelcome as Treasury Committee members and commentators want to use the time to ask the Bank about material (e.g., an *Inflation Report*) that is already in the public domain. To be clear, it is not always comfortable for the central bankers on parade: the "hunting as a pack" metaphor can be apposite. But the hearings are almost invariably occasions when the UK central bankers find an opportunity, if they wish, to raise their own questions and ideas about the regime.

As with the issues we covered earlier in part III, these differences likely flow from the disparate incentives created for legislative committee members by the countries' constitutional and political structures. Without a formal role in legislating, Westminster select committee members can seek to maximize their informal power by acting collectively. The hearings are a repeated "game" where, over time, the prestige of committee members, not only of agency policy makers, is at stake. As such, UK hearings constitute the substantive as well as the procedural pivot around which public accountability and debate about an IA regime revolves: incentives-values compatibility.

By contrast, with party discipline weaker in the US and committee members having an effective veto over legislation, congressional over-

[41]Schonhardt-Bailey, "Monetary Policy Oversight." I should declare that Schonhardt-Bailey is married to my former colleague Andrew Bailey.

sight hearings plausibly matter less to the standing of individual members than their capacity to initiate and promote reforming legislation or formal investigations. Over the decades, committee members have tabled scores of bills for reform of the Fed.[42] While few get close to making it onto the statute book, the exercise provides an opportunity for a member to stake out a position: an approach that seems to be more rewarding than asking questions at routine oversight hearings. It seems possible, therefore, that a vital normative contribution to the legitimacy of delegation-with-insulation is impaired.

Faced with this, the leaders of a legitimacy-seeking independent agency would rationally put forward proposals for how the sessions could be improved.[43] They would also seek out other ways of communicating and interacting with the public, without competing head on, in style or substance, with elected politicians. Federal Reserve chairman Ben Bernanke embarked on something like that during the financial crisis, although the argument I am making is not remotely crisis-specific. Central bankers everywhere are active in giving speeches and media interviews. Some other independent-agency leaders do likewise, but it is perhaps not as widespread as it should be.

Feasibility Redux: Legislative Committee Overload

The role for legislative committees that I have been describing is plainly demanding: in time, resources, and expertise, as evidenced by the words quoted at the chapter head from a former Westminster committee chair, who added "This [is] disappointing but an acceptance of reality."[44]

Unless things have changed greatly, an important conclusion would follow given our Principles for Delegation. If there are any truly independent government agencies, highly insulated from day-to-day politics, that cannot be subject to proper legislative committee oversight because of resource constraints, then in terms of democratic legitimacy, it would be better if those agencies did not exist in their current form and, instead, were subject to control by the elected executive government. In

[42] Binder and Spindel, "Independence and Accountability."

[43] For precisely that from the most experienced former Federal Reserve policy maker of recent times and an equally seasoned Fed watcher, see Kohn and Wessel, *Fed's Accountability*.

[44] House of Commons Committee on Public Administration, *Quangos*.

other words, if the committee system can do a thorough job only for "major agencies," then the purpose of any truly independent agency must really matter to social welfare. That is probably the single most important addition to the Principles that emerges from part III. It gives a practical edge to the audit of IA regimes that we are advocating.

Where a legislative committee is too stretched or its hearings otherwise less than wholly effective, an independent agency must somehow find other routes to explain itself to the public. But the agency's policy makers must also never give up on the forum, the elected legislature, where their duty to explain and account begins and ends: fail, try again, fail better.

SUMMING UP: TENSIONS BETWEEN RULE-OF-LAW VALUES AND REPRESENTATIVE DEMOCRACY UNDER THE ADMINISTRATIVE STATE

One of this book's central themes is that, for IAs, the key channel of political accountability is to the people *via their elected representatives*. Legal contestability, while vital, cannot engage with the overall value of a delegated, politically insulated policy regime; it does not deliver even a simulacrum of the people having an "equal say" over general policy or policy makers. It is as if we are confronting an IA regime manifestation of the tension our societies seem to be facing between liberal values (chapter 8), instantiated today in judges balancing (trading off) multiple basic rights, and democratic republican values (chapters 9 and 11).

In consequence, whatever the differences in systems of judicial review and merits appeal, the upshot is that each jurisdiction struggles to combine keeping agencies within the law and leaving agencies properly accountable for their general policies in the public forum. Achieving that combination is, we hold, especially important for IAs insulated from day-to-day politics.

For Principles-compliant IAs, our political values suggest the solution is to focus judicial review on promoting the integrity and openness of processes rather than on judicial policy making, as that would help to underpin the democratic element of liberal democracy.[45]

[45] A similar approach is advocated, but for the administrative state as a whole, in Rose-Ackerman, "Judicial Review."

The Burden of Process as a Driver of Delegation: The Dilemma of the Administrative State

The dilemma generated by searching substantive review and exacting procedural norms becomes almost a paradox once the incentives they set up are contemplated. The greater the incidence of delegation to arm's-length agencies, the greater the incentives of the judiciary to impose demanding standards of fairness, due process, and substantive rationality. But unless, as in France, administrative law distinguishes between administrative decision makers according to their democratic pedigree or proximity, the more demanding the general standards, the greater the incentives of executive branch politicians to have policy regimes delegated beyond their day-to-day control.

This dynamic might go some way to explain the enthusiasm for delegation-cum-insulation in the UK. The forces are subtly different in the US where, apart from the president, no one in the executive branch is personally elected. But a wish to distance the political center from the burden of routine judicial scrutiny might still help to explain the prevalence of regulatory and administrative powers in executive agencies, outside the ring of a president's most public cabinet allies.

For the administrative state as a whole, this creates a democratic no-man's-land of appointed officials who did not knock on doors appealing to people to get themselves elected, and so it reinforces demands for contestability via the courts and for wide consultation. Overall, the underlying legitimation principle relies on the combined allure of public participation (whether grounded in the values of interest-group liberalism or direct democracy), an appeal to science (technocracy), and due process.

In this book, we hold that even if that state of affairs were sustainable for executive agencies and semi-independent agencies held on a more or less tight political leash, it is not sufficient for fully independent agencies. Where insulation is strong, the values of participation and public reason cannot substitute entirely for the modalities and burdens of representative democracy (chapters 9 and 11). Above all, elected representatives must set clear objectives and, through regular hearings, help to ensure ongoing public debate *(*Design Precepts 1 and 4*)*. We have seen in the previous chapter that few jurisdictions live up to this. That can be especially problematic in emergencies, to which we now turn in rounding off part III.

16

The Limits of Design

POWER, EMERGENCIES, AND SELF-RESTRAINT

> Two problems bedevil liberal legalism: delegation and emergencies. . . . In emergencies, only the executive can supply new policies and real-world action with sufficient speed to manage events.
>
> —Eric Posner and Adrian Vermeule, 2010[1]

In part II we saw that it is possible to identify general criteria, the *Principles for Delegation*, for conferring power on truly independent agencies that can be squared with broad notions of democratic legitimacy. In the past few chapters we have been surveying whether that conclusion survives contact with the real world. It turns out that only some elements of the Principles are close to being reflected in the actual regulatory- or administrative-state structures of the major Western advanced economics.

The constitutional position of agencies in these democracies ranges from precise to indeterminate. The legal framework for agency processes ranges from general to ad hoc. The practices for accountability to the legislature range from intense to occasional. And the alignment of agencies' de jure and de facto independence looks to be variable—across countries, within jurisdictions, and over time.

That variety challenges the central assumption of this book that conditions for the democratic legitimacy of IAs are about legitimacy for *us*, measured against *our* societies' beliefs and values. The past few chapters might throw into question just who "us" is.

Thus, on our account, the US system struggles to achieve incentives-values compatibility; the UK has partly restored it only through the innovation of parliamentary committee oversight and residual elected-

[1]Posner and Vermeule, *Executive Unbound*, p. 7.

executive control; France has in effect sought to maintain it by placing the value of Europe alongside that of the Republic; and Germany faces the quite different issue of whether its Basic Law accords with the capacity to commit to policies that can enhance the people's welfare. In other words, we seem to have encountered quite different core legitimation criteria for the administrative state:

- *United States*: due process, with participatory rights, invigilated by the courts
- *United Kingdom*: parliamentary accountability (balanced with the rule of law)
- *Germany*: a "chain of legitimacy" from a clear delegating statute via formal ministerial oversight of proportionate exercise of bureaucratic discretion, all policed by a constitutional court (democratic *Rechtsstaat,* embodied today in ordo-liberalism)
- *France*: the orientation to public service of an elite cadre of administrators and judges, for the Republic-within-Europe
- *European Union*: perhaps, welfare enhancement via policies subject to European Council and Parliament veto of rules and to judicial oversight of adjudication, directed toward the teleological goal of ever closer union

If quite different principles, with varying mixes of legal and political constitutionalism (chapter 8), really are needed to ground the administrative state in specific advanced-economy democracies, our project would appear to lose traction because the background assumption of shared democratic values would be thin. But I think the conundrum is greatest when we fail to distinguish between truly independent authorities and other agencies.

For the latter, where political leverage of some kind is an intended reality, it is not surprising that local norms should differ somewhat, since the capability and incentives of political actors to exercise those controls vary so much. By contrast, authorities truly insulated from day-to-day politics present a common challenge to representative democracies. Surely one basic shared belief and value is that fairly elected representatives of the people should, after public debate and within constitutional constraints, set the objectives of public policy and the powers for pursuing them in primary legislation; should oversee the exercise of those duties and powers so as to decide whether to sustain them; and should be accountable to the people for doing so.

If that is even close to being right, then our democracies also share the challenge of how to frame and oversee the roles and responsibilities of trustee-type independent agencies. Despite the shortfalls and variances, the past few chapters did not uncover insuperable formal constitutional obstacles to applying something like the Principles in any of the jurisdictions, and identified reasons for doing so in each of them.

It is my thesis that this matters to the health of our democracies, although perhaps only in slow motion. Drifting toward a system of insulated unelected power is liable to create political fragility unless by some miracle IA performance is uniformly and persistently exemplary. Politics is, perhaps, the least likely domain for divine intervention.

To round off part III's survey of the Principles' feasibility, this chapter accordingly revisits two political challenges, so far passed over, that are common across healthy democracies: keeping IAs away from big distributional or values choices; and, at slightly greater length, properly constraining the role of IAs in emergencies. With examples drawn from the financial crisis, this discussion brings us back to the nagging question of self-restraint, and so sets the stage for part IV's examination of postcrisis central banking.

DELEGATING CHOICES ON DISTRIBUTIONAL EQUITY AND VALUES: A DELEGATION CRITERION

In order to embed a norm that IAs should not make big distributional choices (or otherwise determine the shape of the societies they serve), it is necessary to be able to detect where such questions arise.

Big unexpected distributional *effects* from IA policy are more easily identified if they come in sizable discrete lumps or with sustained costs to particular groups, as central bankers have been discovering since they embarked on quantitative easing (chapter 24). But things are not so straightforward where the distributional effects of a series of regulatory measures are modest individually but material cumulatively. This points up an awkward question that gets scant treatment in the voluminous literature and commentary on regulation. Should independent agencies themselves assess the likely distributional effects of their policies even where, under regimes compliant with our Principles, those effects should not be weighed in their own decisions? Or should the executive branch or legislative committees make such assessments, and could they do so without encroaching on an IA's independence? As a general matter, it is not obvious that this is even recognized as an issue in many jurisdictions, whether or not agencies are politically insulated.

In principle, it *is* reflected in the regime for executive agencies (EAs) in the US. With the force of executive order, President Clinton introduced (and Presidents Bush and Obama maintained) a requirement that EAs include an assessment of distributional effects in the cost-benefit analysis (CBA) underpinning rule writing.[2] The implication is that they might make distributional choices, calling upon the majoritarian pedigree of the president. Even though not subject to presidential orders, some "independent commissions" have covered distributional issues in their own published guidance to staff on how to apply CBA.[3] Perhaps they too could call upon the implied democratic quality of their partisan commissioners. For the truly independent agencies that concern us, things would be more delicate, but they could, perhaps, alert Congress and the executive branch of any unexpected material distributional effects of their policy choices.

Whatever the formal powers and constraints of agencies, there are some discomforting facts at ground level. In case study research published in 2014, Harvard political economist Richard Zeckhauser and coauthors found little sign of distributional issues being examined.[4] If that is commonplace and the effect is to keep nonmajoritarian bodies out of inextricably political issues, that may be all well and good as far as it goes. But it might also signify a failure of politicians to address whether or not they want the distributional effects of regulatory policies exposed and debated.

[2]Executive Order 13563, *Improving Regulation and Regulatory Review*, January 18, 2011, Section 1(b): "Each agency must . . . (3) select, in choosing among alternative regulatory approaches, those approaches that maximize net benefits (including potential economic, environmental, public health and safety, and other advantages; *distributive impacts; and equity*)" (my emphasis). There is also an exhortation to "scientific integrity."

[3]For example, Securities and Exchange Commission, *Current Guidance*.

[4]Robinson, Hammitt, and Zeckhauser, "Attention to Distribution."

Things elsewhere might be even less clear. I have, for example, not been able to find guidance on how to handle distributional issues in the UK framework for regulation. We are, therefore, left not really knowing what, if any, framework is truly employed by jurisdictions to maintain a de facto separation between the delegated Technocratic pursuit of economic efficiency/aggregate welfare and Political choice on distributional justice. Precisely that issue has arisen in monetary policy since the 2008–2009 crisis (chapter 24), so for central bankers it overlaps with the question of the proper limits on emergency powers.

EMERGENCIES: DESIGN PRECEPT 5

As suggested in chapters 6 and 11, it is useful, under almost any form of constitutional government, to think of a *crisis* as being highly adverse circumstances for which the machinery of the state is not *formally* prepared, lacking the powers or capabilities to cope.[5] Government is forced to innovate: taking new powers, using existing powers imaginatively, or declaring an emergency in order to activate some latent powers. In a constitutional *democracy*, the question is who may do so, legally and without violating our values.

The fifth Design Precept (*Emergencies*) addresses the place of IAs in such situations. It underlines the importance of mandating extensive *within-regime* contingency planning and, most of all, the imperative of planning for *elected* policy makers to be involved in any resets of IA regimes during a crisis. While part II concluded that this squares with our core liberal-republican values, how things play out in practice seems to be highly sensitive to constitutional structures and contingent political conventions.

The United States

In the US, the need for the elected executive to handle emergencies is advanced by advocates of "presidential control," and even as demonstrating the illegitimacy of independent agencies, period.

[5]Of course, even when it is not a crisis in that constitutionalist sense, very bad events would still be experienced (and might be described) as a crisis by those directly affected. I hope the intended meaning of the word *crisis* at various points of this chapter is clear from the context. I sometimes use *disaster* to mean a crisis for those affected.

The president is enjoined by the Constitution, it is argued, to provide a "unitary executive"; and when is joined-up government more needed than in a crisis? It is precisely then that the president's democratic legitimacy is greater than that of any other elected actor, since only the president has received a *national* mandate from the people. Being the commander in chief has metaphorical resonance and symbolic significance: when it matters most, isn't it clear that the president should take charge?

On the other side of the debate, skeptics of the president being the nation's all-purpose commander are wont to point out that presidential *oversight* of executive government is not the same thing as *deciding* everything; that the Constitution is ambiguous on which of the previous paragraph's implied roles is conferred on the president; and that the only unambiguous power is to seek an opinion from anyone exercising the executive power. Advocates of independent agencies are likely to add that they can cooperate with the elected executive branch and other parts of the administrative state without being commanded, just so long as their legislated zone of insulation is not violated. And advocates of congressional primacy in lawmaking are liable to oppose the capacity of the president to reshape independent-agency mandates in a crisis except with congressional blessing.

While something like that standoff characterizes more general debates about the organization of the US government, it becomes particularly pointed for the role of arm's-length agencies in emergencies. Two positions are advanced by supporters of activism:

- that the country is served best if *independent agencies* have the flexibility to come to the nation's rescue, as they are perceived as less partisan than the president and, therefore, the public and/or Congress are more likely to acquiesce in any exceptional measures they take to protect the nation and its people; or
- that the core executive branch, supported by agencies of all kinds, including IAs, should take charge in an emergency, under the authoritative guidance, if not control, of the president.

The first entails maximum flexibility for IAs. Contrary to what I have been arguing throughout this book, on this view it is unhelpful for agency goals and powers to be too precisely specified ex ante, since that could constrain them in an emergency, potentially leaving the country and the people's well-being at the mercy of the capacity of the president and Congress to cooperate in expeditious law reform. In other words, holders of this view would reject our first Design Precept (specification of clear purposes, objectives, and powers) because it creates the need for the fifth Design Precept (involving elected politicians in resetting an agency's de jure regime or approving its actions when it has run out of road but could, given its intrinsic capabilities, help solve the crisis). Better, on this view, to embrace statutory vagueness so as to leave the nation and the American people better protected during crises.

This is by no means a hypothetical position. In discussions with former US federal government officials from both parties, I have repeatedly been reminded, forcefully and eloquently, of the contrast between bicameral-presidential systems and parliamentary systems of government, and how agencies simply need to be able to act in the public good given the impediments to decisive responses in a US-type system. At its root, this is an argument that the legitimacy and life of the state would be in greater jeopardy if agencies had to stand by and let the people suffer.

It seems, however, that members of Congress tend to see things differently, at least after the event. A recent example is the way the 2010 Dodd-Frank Act trimmed the Federal Reserve's lender-of-last-resort powers only a couple of years after its exceptional actions at the height of the crisis. In other words, even applying only pragmatic, outcomes-based criteria, there is a choice between, on the one hand, agencies acting to "save the world" once but not necessarily being able to do so again and, on the other hand, agencies deferring to political authority when they are at the boundaries of their remit and powers (as widely understood).

This is not just—as if "just" could be apposite—about a potential tension between the welfare of the people during a crisis today and how to discount the welfare of their children and grandchildren during future crises. The line that agency mandates should be so vague that they can stay within the law while being substantively free from constraint, allowing them to act as the US Cavalry without ex ante political blessing, comes uncomfortably close to diluting rule-of-law values and to setting aside normal democratic processes when things are bad enough.

If we mean to hold to those values, then consistent with Design Precept 5, the original remit from the legislature should, at the very least, seek to anticipate what might be needed during disasters, with updates as lessons are learned from one crisis to the next. This might sound obvious but, since the Great Financial Crisis, there has probably been less general interest in lessons for managing and containing financial disorder than in lessons for preventing it.[6]

The alternative view is, as flagged, that the US president, as the single personally elected member in the executive branch, should be free to shape emergency policy and thus to provide political direction to and democratic cover for agencies, including IAs and regulatory commissions, venturing into the unknown. This, in effect, is the line taken by Eric Posner and Adrian Vermeule in their stimulating exploration of the inevitability and, as they see it, acceptability of executive branch dominance during national emergencies, with the constraints on any presidential violation of rights coming from ex post political accountability to the people rather than from law.[7]

It is hard to doubt Posner and Vermeule's argument that in a crisis Congress cannot move as quickly or as specifically as the executive, or their evidence that the US Supreme Court has a revealed preference for allowing the executive to act. But it does not follow that this state of affairs is "good" or, more to our theme, sustainable. Since their work was published in 2010, we have seen the legislature of more than one country stand in the way of military action in Syria following earlier executive-led adventures; and tension over presidential initiatives to address the US's immigration issues via executive order (a sentence written well before the 2016 election, I should perhaps add). In other words, the boundaries of executive power are constantly being negotiated. Given this book's concerns, IA leaders would do well to inscribe on their hearts the following: the president cannot be guaranteed to provide effective air cover for cavalry charges.

That was more or less exactly the conclusion reached in chapter 11's more abstract examination of how our deep political values bear on the

[6] An exception is former Treasury secretary Timothy Geithner, who very much continues to focus on the inevitability of extemporizing in the face of unimagined disasters. Geithner, *Stress Test*, and "Are We Safer?" (As I define *crisis*, regimes for resolving distressed intermediaries in a more or less orderly way count as crisis prevention from a constitutionalist perspective. In that sense, crisis management begins where the charts end and government powers are improvised.)

[7] Posner and Vermeule, *Executive Unbound*.

role of IAs in emergencies. Their policy makers, as custodians of their institutions' legitimacy, should want support from the president if they venture into the unknown at the edge of their legal powers; but they should also ask themselves whether their putative course is at odds with the standards, beliefs, values, or clear wishes of the people and the society. That leaves me affirming the spirit of Design Precept 5: *legitimacy-seeking* agency leaders should strive for ex ante arrangements, ideally underpinned in legislation, covering the procedural rules of the game for crises.

Two European Cases

The euro area provides a striking instance of the costly uncertainty that can arise when the script is incomplete. The ECB's announcement in autumn 2012 that it stood ready, in certain circumstances and subject to specific conditions, to purchase the government bonds of struggling member states was challenged in the German Constitutional Court, which sought formal guidance from the European Court of Justice (ECJ). During a period of existential risk for the euro area, this could have exacerbated market uncertainty, entailing severe costs for the people. That did not materialize, but some observers do believe that the public clamor in some countries around the German legal challenge had the effect of delaying the ECB's decision to launch quantitative easing for the quite different, and unequivocally core, purpose of stimulating euro areawide aggregate spending and output in order to keep inflation in line with its target over the medium term. Eventually, more than a year later, the ECJ concluded that the ECB's support operation policy was *intra vires*, with the German court following.

It can reasonably be argued that the episode splendidly demonstrates that even the most independent of independent central banks is subject to the law and that, accordingly, the courts determine the meaning of their statutory powers. It could also be argued, however, as the German court did, that the ECJ should have applied a more demanding test to the ECB's reasoning, effectively conducting the kind of de novo review discussed in the previous chapter.[8] In hard reality, however, the

[8]Drawing on the Basic Law's "democracy clause," the German court's final judgment contains what, to a layperson, reads like a protest at the ECJ's not having undertaken a deeper substantive analysis of the ECB's plans given its high degree of political insulation. BVerfG, Judgment of the

judicial guardians found themselves faced with choosing whether to ground an economic guardian in ways that might have jeopardized their own existence. For us, the lesson is how much better it would have been if the reach of the ECB's powers had been clearer in advance.

This is illustrated by the ESMA crisis-powers court case cited in chapter 13. It shows how uncertainty can be reduced where (1) legislators think ahead about whether, in a disaster, anyone might need a particular power, who should hold it, and under what terms it can be exercised; and (2) any legal challenge is made when the power is created rather than when it is used in the midst of disaster. That way, a crisis for those affected by a disaster can be mitigated as it need not be a *crisis* in constitutionalist terms.

Westminster

Under the UK's parliamentary system, by contrast, the concern has been less to do with the completeness of substantive crisis management regimes than with whether politicians ultimately call the shots, as evidenced by the "Who is in charge?" debate following the 2007–2008 phase of the Great Financial Crisis (chapter 2). Significantly, there was an emphatic and bipartisan call by the key parliamentary committee overseeing economic and financial policy—the House of Commons Treasury Committee—for clarity that the chancellor of the exchequer would in future be firmly in control of any risks to the public purse during a crisis and, further, could ensure a joined-up strategy across agencies, independent or not. In other words, in contrast to the US, Parliament and executive government tend to be aligned in their views of disaster management structures, provided ministers keep the House or its committees informed.

That is not quite what it might seem at first glance, however. Yes, Parliament was more openly comfortable than Congress might admit to being with the executive government holding the reins. But Parliament was certainly not writing the executive a blank check, metaphorically or literally. The House wanted to know that the necessary substantive and procedural arrangements *were* being put in place (chapters 22 and 23).

Second Senate of 21 June 2016—2 BvR 2728/13—paras. 181–189. http://www.bverfg.de/e/rs20160621_2bvr272813en.html.

THE IMPERATIVE OF SELF-RESTRAINT AMONG THE MIGHTY: JUDGES, GENERALS, AND CENTRAL BANKERS

As we bring part III to a close, two things will be apparent: a heady mix of unease, alacrity, and confusion prevailing among legislators about delegation-with-insulation; and the letter of even the most carefully constructed (Principles-compliant) regime being insufficient to guarantee that unelected power holders will stay within bounds.

Today, both are apparent in attitudes to the central banks. The very embodiment of modern unelected power, they span, as chapter 3 observed, the fiscal state, the regulatory state, and the services state. And given their financial capabilities, they can find themselves at the front line of the emergency state too.

To critics, proclamations of high principle in central bank design seem to be at odds with reality. This is no recent thing. As long ago as the 1950s, Texas congressman Wright Patman, when chairing a committee looking into the Fed, declared, "[the Fed is] an arm of Congress, but . . . not responsible to Congress, in any meaningful sense."[9] In fact, of course, the Fed's objectives, powers, and boundaries stem entirely from congressional acts and persist only through congressional choice. The committee's critique should, rather, have been that Congress could not exercise its constitutional right and democratic duty to oversee the Fed, and so decide whether or not to sustain the regime, *without transparency.*

That insight, incorporated into our fourth Design Precept, needed a few decades to take hold but is consistent with another lesson from the past few chapters. Given the complex, even contradictory, incentives of elected politicians, it is vital that independent agencies be *legitimacy seekers*. In the couple of decades or so before the Great Financial Crisis, central banks were, in the main, active seekers of legitimacy for their monetary policy role, becoming more transparent and somewhat more systematic (chapter 18). The accumulation of powers during and in the wake of the crisis requires those efforts to be redoubled, and the principles for central bank design and legitimacy to be reexamined.

[9]Committee on Banking and Currency, *Primer on Money.* Quote from Rep. Patman, chair of House Committee on the Federal Reserve.

This is a necessary condition for a norm of self-restraint, the importance of which we flagged in part II (chapter 12), to make any sense. While familiar enough for generals and judges, today it surely applies with as much force to the new third pillar of unelected power, central bankers.

If their formal mandates are open, expectations exaggerated, and history a blur, it will be even harder for society to expect central bankers (and other IA officeholders) to observe any informal lines: the spirit behind the formalism of clear mandates makes it easier to infer where the unwritten boundaries lie. Part IV accordingly seeks to frame formal constraints for postcrisis central banking in a way that helps, in the book's conclusion, to locate the zone for self-restraint.

PART IV

Power: Overmighty Citizens?

THE POLITICAL ECONOMY OF CENTRAL BANKING: POWER, LEGITIMACY, AND RECONSTRUCTION

> The centre or pivot, for the purpose of enabling every part of the [monetary and credit] machine to move.
>
> —Francis Baring, the founder of the English banking dynasty, on the Bank of England, 1796[1]

We are concerned with power: the unelected power of the central bankers. A historical example is Montagu Norman of the Bank of England, whom we met earlier in the book. Monarch of the City of London, guardian of the international gold standard, enforcer of domestic budgetary discipline, his powers, but not his office, were stripped away in the early 1930s. Born in 1871 and formed in the world left behind by World War I, Norman's mistake was not to grasp the profoundly changed expectations of public policy brought about by full-franchise democracy: recessions mattered, and opacity bordering on obscurantism was alienating unless policy was magnificently effective. Even had he wanted to be a legitimacy seeker, he had lost his bearings. A man desperately devoted to trying to do the right thing, he is a reminder that, where legitimacy is fragile and jealousies about relative power abound, costly mistakes—contributing to crises—can prompt profound institutional reform.

While observers differ on whether central banks and their leaders emerged from the latest crisis as heroes or villains, no one doubts their

[1] Baring, "Observations," p. 6.

increased power, responsibilities, profile, even celebrity. In this final section of the book, we examine whether their new roles and standing can be squared with the Principles for Delegation.

CONSTITUTIONAL CENTRAL BANKING

Part IV builds on a series of findings (in part II especially) particular to central banking itself. We have argued that there is no question of anyone *having consented to obey* the central bank, but on our account of legitimacy people would need to accept its right (a) to reshape the state's balance sheet toward certain ends and (b) to write rules and make regulatory decisions that the democratic core of the state may choose to enforce via independent courts. What, then, warrants the central bank's exercise of those rights being insulated from day-to-day politics? In short, we have concluded the following:

- The objective of price stability fits with some of our deepest values since it contributes to preserving freedom and, in particular, aims to protect people from the state abusing its monopoly powers over the issuance of money.
- Under fiat money, independence for the monetary authority is a corollary of the higher-level separation of powers between the fiscal authority of the legislature and the elected executive government: if the elected executive were to control the monetary levers, it would have the power to tax (through unexpected bursts of inflation).
- Central bank independence is, therefore, grounded in the values of constitutional government.
- Central banks are not, however, inherently a new fourth branch of government since they are subordinate, in different ways, to each of the higher-level branches of the state: delegation of statutory powers (legislature), nomination or appointment of agency leadership (executive), and adjudication of disputes under the law (courts).

As such, we are clear that, intrinsically, central banks are *not guardians* of either the high values or integrity of the democratic rule-of-law state.

Constitutional Variation: The ECB Is Simultaneously More and, Perhaps, Less Than a Regular Central Bank

That general characterization applies with equal force to presidential, Westminster-style, and consensus-based coalition government democracies, despite their profound differences.[2] But it stumbles, and the argument is transformed, when we come to the ECB.

Unlike most democracies, the euro area's central bank does not work alongside a counterpart fiscal authority elected by the people.[3] Since a bank of issue has *latent* fiscal capability, establishing a common money entailed creating a fiscal instrument in a confederal polity *without* the familiar fiscal constitution of nation-states. As if recognizing this, the architects of the monetary union sought to constrain the ECB via an entrenched constitutional duty, enshrined in Treaty, to maintain price stability. On this view, ECB independence is still, normatively, a corollary of a higher-level constitution: not, like the Fed or the Bank of England, in order to avoid a violation of the separation of powers but rather to avoid inadvertently creating a monetary-fiscal authority with many degrees of freedom (for which, as yet, there is no constitutional sanction). Consistent with that, the ECB was not established under the same Treaty provision (Article 7) as the Council, Parliament, and Commission, signaling its different status.

In parallel, substituting discipline for discretion, the Treaty enshrined a principle of "no bailouts" for member states participating in the monetary union. When it came to pass, however, that stumbled against incentives-values incompatibility. Members had short-term incentives to sign up to "discipline" but not more enduring incentives to abide by or enforce their agreement. Moreover, for many parts of the European Union the fiscal constraints were not even values-compatible. So when the euro area faced an existential crisis, the lack of confederal fiscal capabilities left the ECB as the only institution that could keep the currency union from shattering. It became the guarantor of the European project

[2]For the US, that challenges those exponents of a "unitary executive," who maintain that the president at least has to be able to fire and hire at will any officer of the executive machinery. If that were so, the president would have a tax lever.

[3]Trichet, "Building Europe."

itself. Not only a mighty citizen, but *the* essential citizen: a *guardian*, so *more* than a normal central bank. Politically, its greatest challenge is to navigate itself to the more modest and proper role of trustee.

In doing so, it needs to confront another challenge. If it is true that many governing Council members systematically vote in line with perceived national interests rather than in line with the outlook for the euro area as a whole, the ECB might be *less* than a normal central bank. The two points are related. The more the ECB is cornered into being a guardian, the harder it is for the members of the policy board to put aside their different perspectives on the existential problems they confront.

AN INCOMPLETE STORY

In consequence, the ECB's embarking on particular initiatives, such as buying corporate bonds and steering credit, cannot presumptively legitimatize similar actions taken by other central banks functioning in regular constitutional democracies. Even for them, however, the story told so far about constitutional central banking is incomplete or flawed in three respects: politics, regulatory roles, and internationalism. We say a little about each here to pave the way into part IV.

Politics and Central Banking

It might seem, first of all, that we are taking for granted that since central banks should be independent authorities, they are or will be. But that does not remotely follow. None of our discussion of agency independence in general or our advocacy of a constitutional basis for monetary policy independence in particular is sufficient to explain why, in the real world, central bank independence is granted and sustained *in practice*. Politics intrudes, and must be brought into our story.

In actual fact, two quite different models of central banking have prevailed over the past couple of hundred years. One sees a country's central bank as the operational arm of government financial policy, occupying a distinct sphere of expertise and authority. The other regards them as independent authorities delegated *specific* responsibilities and *formally* insulated from day-to-day politics.

Both models rely on expertise but call upon it in markedly different ways. Under the first, the central bank's functions are determined by technocratic comparative advantage rooted, as Francis Baring observed two hundred years ago, in its being the pivot of the payments system, an elemental part of the services state, generating relationships across the banking community and imbuing a distinctive central banking "know-how" mind-set (see chapter 4 for the military analogy). Under the second, the central bank does only those things that have been formally delegated, irrespective of whether, across the state's overall machinery, it might be best equipped to handle others.

Those modes of existence are so different, and associated with such contrasting legitimation canons, that the passage from political control to independence is complex and often difficult. In emerging market economies, even after formal independence central banks are sometimes expected (and occasionally want) to continue to perform a very wide range of functions due to operational comparative advantage. Examples include involvement in economic development measures, such as promoting financial inclusion and steering credit to priority sectors. The effect can be to leave the central bank occupying two worlds: that of insulated policy making and that of political choice.

In the advanced-economy democracies, by contrast, the transition from subordinate agent to independent trustee has typically raised questions of power and its boundaries, sometimes at the cost of welfare. For example, as it sought to make itself tolerably fit for monetary independence, the Bank of England, on its own initiative, dropped its involvement in industrial finance, corporate rescues, corporate governance, some non-core banking services, and all securities settlement services.[4] Upon independence, banking supervision and government debt management were transferred elsewhere. In a strikingly un-Humean moment, the history of Britain's monetary system was set aside in the interest of legitimating the insulation of monetary policy from politicians.

[4]Some of this amounted to rethinking central banking's place in the services state but without an articulated framework.

These frictions were not purely a product of local circumstances. Central banks typically come to formal independence already endowed with what, in part II, we termed pragmatic authority. With the core of the banking community, that is precisely what flows from their being the pivot of the monetary system, the bankers' bank. With the general public, something more is going on, a touch of magic even. Here central bank authority arises, as a source of *symbolic power*, from their physical bank notes being held and used as money (making top central bankers highly sensitive to questions of bank note design, integrity, and circulation). Given the role of symbolic power in state power generally, this is no small thing.[5]

Already an authoritative and powerful citizen, statutory independence confers modernized legitimacy on trustee-like insulation at the core of macroeconomic policy. The result is a mighty citizen.

It is of no surprise, then, that moves to independence often involve debates about the central bank giving up some historically established functions. But nor should we be startled that underlying tensions remain latent when the zone of naturally endowed authority is broader than the mandated zone of formal legitimacy.

The long-standing debate about whether central banks can or should be bank supervisors should be seen in that light. Its roots lie in questions of power, not only in what structure will deliver the best results (chapters 19–21).

Monetary Authorities in the Regulatory State

Second, the constitutional argument for central bank independence (CBI) applies only to monetary policy, with its latent power of taxation. It does not apply to the other responsibilities a central bank may have, notably regulatory policy and prudential supervision.

Parts I and III highlight the complexity and variety of regulatory agencies, across countries and even within jurisdictions. Some are truly independent, some insulated from the executive but not the legislature, some under the control of the executive. While that is explicable in

[5]Bourdieu, "Social Space," and Bourdieu, Wacquant, and Farage, "Rethinking the State."

terms of the incentives and constraints facing politicians under different constitutional systems, the structure of the administrative state seems not to be grounded in any set of principles based on the purposes and functions of regulatory agencies in a democratic republic.

This raises an obvious but troubling point for postcrisis central banking, which combines monetary policy with bank supervision and, in some cases, other functions. Unless a compelling case can be made for the insulation of such functions, then either they should not be conferred upon central banks or, against the grain of our Principles for Delegation, central banks would somehow have to house a noninsulated function alongside their insulated monetary responsibilities.

Historically, the central banking mind-set incorporated a concern for banking-system stability. But that was gradually displaced during the 1990s as Germany, which had always been committed to formal separation, came to be viewed as the model of an inflation-fighting monetary authority. Ironically, to put it mildly, this emergent rival orthodoxy overlooked the specificities of Germany's constitutional setup (chapter 13). Since the Bundesbank (Buba) is, more or less alone among German agencies, exempt from the Basic Law's stipulation of ministerial control over executive policy making and implementation, there is reluctance in Germany to give the central bank de jure responsibility for banking supervision. To do so would mean that the central bank was not fully insulated from politics in *all* of its functions.

That is a good, perhaps even decisive, argument for not putting supervision under Bundesbank control. It is, however, quite different from arguing that supervision should not be combined with monetary policy in any jurisdiction, whatever the constitutional circumstances. Indeed, stepping across the Atlantic, Mexico's constitution also singles out the central bank for entrenched independence but in quite different terms. Whereas in Germany the Buba's legal insulation applies only to monetary policy, the Mexican central bank's independence covers all its functions, so it could take on prudential supervision only if the country's politicians and the public were content for supervision to become insulated.[6]

[6] My thanks to Luis Urritia Corral at the Banco de Mexico.

To argue that central banks must never be responsible for prudential supervision, as German officials are wont to do, would be to maintain that the German constitutional arrangements are optimal for all. That basic driver of the German position could usefully be brought into the open, since it affects ongoing debates about whether the ECB should continue to be the prudential supervisor of euro area banking stability.

The question of the ECB's role in prudential supervision has a further twist. Since in its monetary function it is, for now, a guardian, undertaking supervision means that it combines guardian and trustee functions: its general policies can be overruled by legislation on one front but not the other. As with some supreme courts that rule on both constitutional and ordinary law, there is a question whether we can make sense of this given the profound differences entailed for accountability and the application of our fourth Design Precept.

Internationalism: A Transnational Elite

Third, it is not easy to identify a group within government (broadly defined) that comes closer to fitting the description of a transnational elite than the central bankers. Our judges occasionally meet informally at conferences and seminars to exchange views, and some even cite foreign cases or principles when grappling with difficult issues. Regulators in various fields meet not only to exchange views but to forge common policy approaches. Central bankers have, however, long taken this to a different level. The Bank for International Settlements in Basel, established in the aftermath of World War I, does all of those things but is much more: a veritable home away from home for central bankers, whatever their roles, seniority, or institutional independence. It provides a forum for exchanges of views, training, standard setting, policy cooperation, and occasionally policy coordination, as well as an emotional refuge for battered or bewildered governors.

To be clear, my own experience of this was never anything other than hugely positive. I am confident that the "Basel experience" makes for more open-minded central bankers, by exposing them to the different ideas, practices, problems, and contexts of their peers. The patina of revealed truth or natural law running through national positions on technical issues rarely survives contact with equally compelling doctrines or better results elsewhere.[7]

But the social gains to the people from international policy networks are not the point here. Whether the state is in reality run by Plato's guardians might not always and everywhere be in the gift of the people. The gradual and cumulative internationalization of policy making could unobtrusively hand the reality of power, if not its formal accoutrements, to a new transnational meritocratic elite.

Rodrik's trilemma of internationalism, described in chapter 12, was not news to international economists and policy makers. It had long been recognized that a country could not combine national control over domestic monetary policy, a fixed exchange rate, and liberalized capital flows. Each country had to choose two out of three. After World War II, most countries more or less surrendered domestic monetary autonomy, tying themselves to a de facto dollar standard. To police the rules of the game agreed at the famous Bretton Woods conference in New Hampshire's White Mountains, the International Monetary Fund (IMF) and the World Bank were created. At its heart, the system relied on the dollar holding its value against gold, but the US authorities proved unable to square that with their foreign and domestic policy priorities.

The Bretton Woods framework collapsed in the early 1970s under the weight of US fiscal profligacy and inflationary incontinence. Since then, most countries have opted for a floating exchange rate with domestic (or, as in the euro area, regional) control of monetary policy. Technically, each jurisdiction is free under IMF treaty rules to adopt capital controls, but the strong norm has been that they do not do so. This was a world, most thought, in which the effects of one country's monetary policy on others would be confined to shifts in exchange rates, leaving national economies to manage their own domestic monetary course in the interests of their own citizens. It was, moreover, a world decisively chosen and maintained by elected governments.

Soon enough, however, countries discovered that they had a stake in each other's stability policies and practices. In 1974, Bankhauss Herstatt

[7] Disclosure: In the aftermath of the crisis, I chaired one of the Basel standard-setting bodies and also one of the FSB groups working on "too big to fail" financial intermediaries.

failed in Germany. It had no physical presence, indeed no meaningful commercial business, in the US, the UK, or elsewhere, but it changed the face of banking policy throughout the world. When Herstatt defaulted on the dollar leg of foreign exchange transactions, the costs of its failure leaped across the ocean, just as when the Viennese CreditAnstalt had collapsed in the early 1930s. The international response was to create a shared framework for banking stability. G10 central bank governors created the Basel Supervisors Committee, setting in motion a process of convergence in bank regulatory standards and supervision that continues to this day.

Fast-forward a couple of generations, and another ratchet in the process of policy internationalization came when the disorderly collapse of Lehman in late 2008 exposed, glaringly and painfully for people across the world, fault lines in the global regime. As in the 1970s, the substantive initiative and drive behind the core reforms came from international meetings and debate—reflecting a view that no nation, not even the US, can act alone to make its financial system safe.

Under the new global dispensation, banks must carry more capital and liquidity, with minimum requirements ratcheting up for banks whose failure would unambiguously have systemic consequences; standards and protocols have been agreed for the resolution of cross-border financial institutions by putting losses onto bondholders rather than taxpayers; derivatives have to be centrally cleared or, for nonstandard contracts, subject to minimum collateral requirements; information on derivative transactions is held in a new kind of infrastructure, trade repositories; and there is ongoing monitoring of risks from "shadow banking" (but without agreed substantive general policies).[8] The reader does not need any technical expertise to see how extensive the collective exercise was. Crucially, many of the resulting standards have been drawn up largely in Basel, by the International Organization of Securities Commissions (IOSCO), or through the G20 Financial Stability Board. Further, perhaps in anticipation of countries seeking autonomy in divergent local initiatives, the various international standard setters have taken steps to monitor compliance, for the first time publishing

[8]Tucker, "Regulatory Reform." These issues do not just fall to central banks and banking supervisors but must involve securities regulators too, as evidenced by White, "Enhancing Risk Monitoring."

assessments of the degree to which their member jurisdictions are faithfully implementing the agreements.

In summary, the extant regime can be cast as follows:

- Unless there were to be a shift to financial autarky, stability policy must in large degree be made internationally, given the extent and social costs of spillovers in the international financial system.
- International standards are drawn up very largely by *unelected* officials from agencies that are largely *independent* in their home jurisdiction.
- Those standards are pointless unless compliance is faithful and consistent across the world.
- International criticisms of incomplete domestic implementation are sometimes regarded as an intrusion on democratic authority and autonomy, as reported in the Introduction (chapter 1).

In other words, the lessons from the great financial crisis (and, indeed, from the 1990s' Asian crisis before it) collide with Rodrik's critique of modernity in what Dirk Schoenmaker has termed the *financial trilemma*.[9] Complete national control over the minimum standards of financial-system policy, international financial integration, and domestic financial stability cannot be combined. The bridge to Rodrik's megatheorem is clear: if the world opts for financial integration and financial stability, then democratic nations will not have autonomy over policies on the financial system. Since it is hard to imagine people opting to embrace recurrent financial *in*stability, the apparent choices are (1) to give up financial globalization and thereby regain domestic control, (2) to retain financial integration and relocate democracy to the global plane (the dream of cosmopolitan democrats), and (3) to maintain international financial integration, set financial policy globally, and accept the dilution of democracy!

The international policy–augmented version of the Principles articulated in chapter 12 aims to break out of this unappealing trilemma, essentially by restricting international policy making to *informal* agreements that must be subjected to transparent domestic processes before being translated into legally binding norms. The upshot is that if we are to

[9] Schoenmaker, *Governance of International Banking.*

avoid our central bankers being *overmighty citizens*, their efforts as *legitimacy seekers* cannot be confined to domestically salient issues.

WHAT LIES AHEAD

Part IV tries to find a way through these various issues, guided by our Principles for Delegation.[10]

It opens by briefly recalling a few especially egregious examples of political involvement in monetary policy and the explanations offered by political scientists for the wave of CBI measures in the 1980s and 1990s. That leads to the story of how monetary policy makers seized on a revolution in ideas within economics to make a principled case for independence. Partly by chance, the same insights laid the basis for designing institutions that could achieve legitimacy through transparency, a buzzword of the period.

The model that evolved appeared, for a while, to deliver both credibility and legitimacy. But it was found badly wanting by the Great Financial Crisis, which prompted a wave of previously unimagined emergency operations and, later, an expansion of powers and functions. It is those circumstances that have posed the big question of just *how much* power and *how many* functions can be delegated with legitimacy to these institutions.

We consider their roles in supervision, credit policy, and crisis management, seeking to frame each as part of a joined-up *Money-Credit Constitution* (MCC) that incorporates constraints on their financial operations via the terms of a *Fiscal Carve-Out*. Throughout, the underlying questions are whether central banks are now overmighty; and whether, over time, the extraordinary position of these new, reluctant masters of the universe will erode or undermine not only their own legitimacy but even that of our democratic system of governance.

In chapter 3, we argued that central banks might occupy eight or even an alarming twelve cells of a 4 × 4 matrix mapping the four modes of operation of the administrative state (fiscal, regulatory, services,

[10] My thanks for comments on part IV to Bill English at Yale, former director for monetary affairs at the Fed Board.

emergency) into its four purposes (security, allocative efficiency, distributive justice, and macroeconomic stability). Using the Principles for Delegation, in this final part of the book we attempt to squeeze postcrisis central banking back into the three, perhaps four, cells devoted to macroeconomic stability.

17

Central Banking and the Politics of Monetary Policy

Time is getting short. We want to get this economy going.
—Fed chairman Arthur Burns to President Nixon, December 1971[1]

Why would executive government ever table and mobilize its party behind a central bank independence law? Virtue is not absent from politics, but nor are interests! Further, why would de jure independence deliver de facto independence? And why should even a robustly independent central bank be capable of making credible commitments? Constitutional arguments and higher-level principles, while necessary to making the case for legitimacy, don't answer any of those questions. Positive analysis is needed alongside the normative.

The story of central bank independence revolves around a potent mix of interests and ideas, told in this and the following chapter. For us, the striking thing is that the role of central banks as lenders of last resort and overseers of monetary system stability barely features in the 1980s and 1990s debates about independence.

POLITICAL CONTROL OF MACROECONOMIC DEMAND MANAGEMENT

Especially in fiat-money systems, the elected executive branch has powerful incentives to hold onto the monetary reins, while paying lip service to the value of stability.[2] This is more than apparent in key episodes of modern British and American monetary history.

From the mid-1970s, when the UK went bust and had to turn to the IMF for help, the last G7 country to do so, leading Westminster politi-

[1]Abrams, "How Richard Nixon," Conversation No. 16-82, December 10, 1971.
[2]Ferguson, *Cash Nexus*, especially chapters 5 and 8.

cians on both sides stressed the priority of defeating inflation. Yet, notwithstanding a series of failed experiments with monetary regimes during the 1980s and into the 1990s, prime ministers declined to loosen their grip. Thus, when then finance minister Nigel Lawson proposed independence for the Bank of England, Prime Minister Thatcher responded, "to hand over the responsibility for monetary policy, and thus for the fight against inflation, to an independent Bank . . . would look as if the Government were admitting that, after all, it was unable to bring inflation down itself, which would be highly damaging politically."[3]

A few years later when, in 1992, sterling fell out of the European Exchange Rate Mechanism and desperately needed a new nominal anchor, finance minister Norman Lamont attempted to shackle himself and his colleagues by committing to publishing the Bank's advice and announcing a target for inflation, thereby shifting everyone's incentives somewhat.[4]

Those stories are somewhat at odds with researchers having struggled to find compelling evidence of a "political business cycle," which would be an example of the second type of commitment problem identified in chapter 5. But they might have been looking in the wrong place. They tend to start from an assumption that political monetary policy aims to boost economic activity to coincide with a general election, whereas, from what I saw in the late 1980s and early 1990s, the goal can be less concrete and more immediate. A surprise easing of policy would sometimes be targeted at improving near-term opinion poll ratings, political popularity being heavily path dependent; in a system with floating-rate mortgages, as in the UK, the effect on households' pockets of an interest-rate cut is almost instant. Lamont's reforms helped deter at least that variant of politicized monetary policy.

They were not, however, the end of the story. After leaving office, Lamont became concerned by his successor's public rejection of Bank advice to tighten policy in the run up to the 1997 general election, concluding that transparency was insufficient to depoliticize monetary pol-

[3]Lawson, *The View*, p. 870. At the time, I was private secretary to then governor of the Bank of England Robin Leigh Pemberton, and was given the same account by an official who was in a key meeting between Thatcher and Lawson.

[4]Governor Leigh Pemberton had seen ERM membership as a proxy for the central bank independence the government was not prepared to grant. He had first aired the possibility of inflation targeting with Bank colleagues a few years earlier.

icy when the stakes were high enough. He became an open advocate of Bank independence.[5]

Those were momentous years within the Bank itself. On the first occasion that Eddie George, the then governor and a lifelong central banker, realized the Bank's advice to raise interest rates would almost certainly be set aside, he went around the table asking each of us to give our individual view before he put the Bank on a course where it would be in open disagreement with the government. Perhaps especially for those of us in the middle ranks, this remains a special moment, not so much because of the political frisson but, looking back, because, in effectively pooling some of the responsibility that, at the time, formally belonged to the governor alone, George was taking a step toward the culture necessary for making monetary decisions by committee.

If in the UK reality tracked the legal arrangements for monetary decisions, driving a debate about whether politicians should cede control, in the US the Fed was always formally insulated, but appearances were sometimes misleading. Indeed, the decades following World War II amount to a monetary morality tale. During the War, the regime was informally but overtly changed to prioritize cheap financing for the ballooning public debt. Afterward, trapped as the operational arm of government financial policy, the Fed increasingly sought to escape its role as the agent of financial repression and monetary financing, leading chair Marriner Eccles to wage a war of his own: one that saw him displaced from the chair, notes leaked revealing presidential deception, and culminating in the administration feeling betrayed when the Fed applied the letter of the famous 1951 Treasury-Fed Accord.[6] It is said that former president Harry Truman once crossed the road to avoid William McChesney Martin, the man he had moved from the Treasury to the Fed chair in the firm expectation of retaining political control—only to find, like Henry II seven hundred years before, that his Thomas à Becket had changed sides.

Politically, Martin's achievement was to restore a degree of Fed autonomy, albeit within a framework incorporating close cooperation with the fiscal authorities in the cause of activist aggregate demand management.

[5]Lamont, *In Office*, pp. 322–327; and for frustrations with the continued politicization of interest-rate decisions, pp. 337–340. Lamont has never received sufficient credit for the 1992 monetary reforms, which broke with the past and were a precondition for what came later.

[6]Hetzel and Leach, "Treasury-Fed Accord" and "After the Accord."

Seeking to exploit a trade-off between jobs and inflation, this setup was sensitive to whichever goal politicians thought was the more salient for the time being. It could not survive the 1970s. An institution that had not completely buckled under the power-charged politics of Lyndon Johnson's administration, voluntarily surrendered to President Nixon, and for the worst of reasons: party-political alignment.[7]

The moment, during the run-up to President Nixon's 1972 reelection campaign, is caught on the infamous Nixon tapes. During conversations that rarely stayed within appropriate bounds, Fed chairman Arthur Burns utters the stomach-churning words quoted at the chapter head.[8]

This was faux independence: ostensibly detached central bankers suborned by politics. What is so shocking is not simply the use of monetary policy for party-political ends, which might be expected to disturb a former central banker, but that Burns meanwhile masqueraded as the leader of an independent agency. For our political values, that is especially serious, as it amounts to conspiring against the public in a violation of the separation of powers.

In fairness, Burns occasionally wriggled free, and he was personally put under sustained, and sometimes deeply unpleasant, public pressure via the media.[9] Well might his valedictory lecture to his international peers have been titled "The Anguish of Central Banking."[10]

POLITICAL SCIENCE EXPLANATIONS OF INDEPENDENCE: INTERESTS AND VETO POINTS

Whatever the moral qualities on display in those various episodes, they underline one thing: the surprise of governments embracing central bank independence. Indeed, if the point of CBI is to take interests out of monetary policy, why should politicians agree?

[7] For a brief summary of Chair Martin's relations with Presidents Eisenhower and Johnson and with Congressman Patman, see Conti-Brown, *Power and Independence*, pp. 48–51 and 201–203. On the 1960s, see Fessenden, "1965."

[8] Abrams, "How Richard Nixon." On the Nixon-Burns relationship more generally, see Conti-Brown, *Power and Independence*, pp. 192–195. Whereas Conti-Brown concludes that presidents can dominate the Fed if they wish *and* find themselves with a soulmate chair, I argue that the Principles' provisions would help to make this obvious and so deter both parties.

[9] Abrams, "How Richard Nixon"; and, for a striking account involving Alan Greenspan, Mallaby, *Man Who Knew*, pp. 139–144.

[10] Burns, "Anguish of Central Banking."

As a general matter, that depends on who gains from the reform, who stands to lose, how much traction those different groups have with legislators, how the legislators themselves perceive their own interests (or those of the cause, ideology, or groups in society they serve), and the number of constitutional or de facto veto points that have to be overcome.[11] Within that realpolitik framework, political scientists have identified a wide range of possible forces, from both the "demand side" (those actively wanting independence) and the "supply side" (legislators being willing to provide it).[12]

On the *demand side*, it is suggested that the financial sector likes and presses for low inflation or, more generally, that creditors favor independence because of a lower likelihood of their (nominal) claims being inflated away. This interest is often identified with banks, but in fact the constituency varies with the structure of a country's financial system.[13] For example, banks are less important to the story where, as in the UK, loans typically carry a floating rate of interest and so, broadly, adjust for inflation. There the financial sector advocates of low inflation during the 1970s and 1980s were mainly long-term investment institutions (life insurance companies and pension funds) and the stockbrokers who served them.[14] That is because, on behalf of households, they were the major investors in long-term nominal bonds.

Another demand-side force was the community of central bankers and monetary economists. Of course, CBI would increase their power and influence, but they did have arguments. Even under the Bretton Woods regime, under which most countries pegged their currency to

[11] On veto points and CBI, Moser, "Checks and Balances"; Keefer and Stasavage, "Improve Credibility"; and Hallerberg, "Veto Players."

[12] Surveyed in Bernhard, Broz, and Clark, "Monetary Institutions." For a critical review, see Forder, "Central Bank Independence."

[13] Posen, "Central Bank Independence" and "Declarations Are Not Enough." In subsequent papers, Posen asked whether societal preferences were the key to improved inflation performance, which is only a few steps away from this book's thesis that credibility depends on durability, which depends on (and underpins) legitimacy, which depends on, among other things, stable social preferences (chapter 11).

[14] Many leading advocates of the UK's version of monetarism were economic analysts at stockbrokers (e.g., Tim Congden, Patrick Minford) or journalists (Sam Brittan and a young Nigel Lawson, who went on to become a leading politician). My guess is that they were highly exposed to the long-term investment institutions. That certainly applied to John Fforde, Eddie George, and others at the Bank, who had a different attitude to inflation from, say, 1970s chief economist Christopher Dow. The former group ran government debt management and so faced the problems that lack of monetary credibility presented to funding the deficit.

the dollar, itself pegged to gold, Chicago economist Milton Friedman and others were making the case that floating exchange rates would permit smoother adjustment to international current account imbalances. But precisely because that would restore domestic monetary sovereignty, it posed the question of how politicians could be deterred from abusing the monetary power. After Bretton Woods collapsed, those issues could not be ducked, prompting a quarter-century-long debate about rules versus discretion (as told in the next chapter).

On the *supply side* (i.e., within the legislative system), political scientists suggest that government politicians may wish to: bind their successors (begging the question of whose interest that serves); or transfer blame for macroeconomic underperformance to the central bank (although that plainly does not work for the ministry that introduces independence); or, in polities characterized by multiparty governments, to prevent any single coalition partner or faction from getting control of the monetary power by holding the finance ministry portfolio.[15]

Each of these factors obviously has some force, but what matters is how they combine in particular circumstances, giving rise to the variety of CBI stories. For example, in the UK the vociferous asset management/stockbroker lobby for monetary discipline had to wait nearly a quarter of a century before Bank of England independence was restored. The explanation might lie in an inversion of the argument that a government can reward its supporters by binding its successors. To be clear, that account is not empty. For example, as argued by Delia Doylan in research on Latin America, where a government is implementing large-scale *political regime* change in the transition to democracy, embedding some of its own values via CBI might be attractive for the incumbents.[16] But if "normal politics" typically involves power alternating between two main parties, a government might sometimes prefer to gamble on the opposing party making a (bigger) mess of monetary policy.

Indeed, if a political party believes it is (and is expected to be) *less* prone to monetary laxity than the opposition and also that inflationary problems are politically salient, it has fairly strong incentives *not* to bind

[15]This is the application to central banking of the broader argument that consensus-based polities naturally favor delegation to arm's-length technocrats (introduction to part III). See Bernhard, "Political Explanation" and *Banking on Reform*.

[16]Doylan, "Holding Democracy Hostage" and *Defusing Democracy*.

its successors. Knowing that sooner or later, the opposition will replace them, leaving monetary temptation on the table might accelerate their own return to government. It seems to me plausible that this is how the British Tory party thought about Labour, which generally favors a larger state and so higher deficits or taxes.

If that is broadly right, it becomes less of a surprise that it was Labour that, eventually, introduced Bank of England independence. On this account, they were trying to bind themselves and so remove from the table an economic lever perceived to help the Tories. Further, learning the lessons of the Lawson-Thatcher episode recounted above, they took the plunge on their first weekend in office in May 1997, so that no one could doubt they were acting from a position of strength rather than in retreat.

That is not dissimilar from the Italian communist party having favored moves toward CBI in Italy.[17] Bizarrely, though, taken at face value, it seems to have Labour delivering benefits for natural Tory supporters in order to keep themselves in office longer. Together with some other reforms, it led to accusations that New Labour was simply adopting Tory clothes in a search for personal power that amounted to ideological betrayal.[18]

The picture is, however, more complex. Especially in jurisdictions with few veto points, such as the UK, whatever motivates the introduction of CBI, the delegation-with-insulation could be reversed when the other side gains legislative power. And even in countries with many veto points, such as the US, politicians could seek to pack the policy board with allies dedicated to softening the commitment to price stability. It matters, therefore, whether CBI can work for the economy as a whole.

SAVING THE INFLATION RISK PREMIUM: A POLITICALLY NEUTRAL FACTOR FOR CBI?

The most persuasive account of CBI in the political science literature concerns emerging market economies (EMEs). Sylvia Maxfield argues that once they liberalize the capital account, EMEs find it prudent to

[17] Goodman, "Politics of Central Bank Independence."
[18] For a view of the UK story, see King, "Epistemic Communities."

adopt CBI in order to protect themselves against skittish, skeptical international investors.[19] This is often presented as countries subordinating themselves to international capital markets, creating a domestic democratic deficit as they surrender economic sovereignty. But that construction misses something important, which applies beyond EMEs.

The most compelling reason for CBI is to enable governments to save paying an inflation risk premium on their debt; not the compensation for expected inflation, but the premium charged for the risk that higher average rates of inflation tend to be associated with more volatile inflation. This amounts to saying that there is a *real* cost from suspicions of monetary indiscipline. It has nothing to do with international capital markets; a premium for inflation risk gets charged by both domestic and foreign investors in longer-term nominal bonds.[20]

Techniques exist to measure the effect of monetary regime changes on debt financing costs. At the time we thought Bank of England independence might have taken around fifty basis points off the cost of servicing UK government nominal debt. Recent research suggests that a good portion of that might represent a fall in risk premia.[21] If so, the impact on debt servicing costs would be quite something given that risk-free real rates of interest averaged around 2½ to 3 percent at the time.

Even bearing in mind uncertainty, a reduction of between 5 and 10 percent of the real rate of interest paid on nominal bonds would be a lot. Big picture, it would explain why the Tories did not reverse Labour's CBI measure when they got back into office. Had they done so, they would have caused bond yields to rise, hurting their natural constituencies.

More important, on this explanation of CBI, while there are different ex ante incentives to be the reformer, there is *not* an asymmetry in

[19] Maxfield, *Gatekeepers of Growth*.

[20] This "instability premium" story should be distinguished from the "seesaw effect" discussed in Acemoglu, Johnson, Querubin, and Robinson, "Policy Reform." Their argument is that since prudent monetary policy constrains government, politicians try to wriggle free. In polities with weak institutional constraints, deprived of the capacity to misuse monetary policy to pursue short-term ends, politicians are likely to resort to other instruments, including fiscal policy. On my argument, there is a true saving to be distributed somehow, and so prudent monetary policy is not necessarily constraining for government. Of course, the two phenomena could shade into each other if governments exaggerate the scale of the savings, pursuing a fiscal policy that puts the monetary anchor in jeopardy.

[21] Joyce, Lilholdt, and Sorensen, "Extracting Inflation." For a summary, see Guimares, "Government Bond Yields?"

Right/Left partisan interests ex post. If CBI does reduce risk premia, a government of the Right would be free to deploy saved debt servicing costs in lower tax rates for their favored groups, while a government of the Left could deploy the the savings in higher public spending directed toward their favored groups.

This account breaks down only if a political faction actively wanted their country to pay a risk premium in order to force government to shrink. One could imagine that being true of parts of the US Right. In practice, however, that would turn on its head the dynamic between the Volcker Fed and the Reagan administration, which pressed Volcker to ease up on monetary restraint (and the higher debt-servicing costs entailed pro tem) so that they could avoid cutting expenditures.[22]

This account of CBI has traveled some distance from the usual balance-of-lobbying forces favored by political scientists. It has not jettisoned interests, retaining a realist edge, but has introduced a benefit that is in the broad public interest: not paying a premium for avoidable risks. It gets traction, however, only if political actors come to believe there is, more or less, a free lunch from central bank independence. That brings us to a revolution in ideas.

[22] Silber, *Volcker.*

18
The Shift in Ideas

CREDIBILITY AS A SURPRISING DOOR TO LEGITIMACY

> Institutions [can] do the work of rules, and monetary rules should be avoided; instead, institutions should be drafted to solve time-inconsistency problems.
>
> —Larry Summers, 1991[1]

Throughout the Western world, the lamentably high and variable inflation of the 1970s, continuing in some advanced economies well into the 1980s and beyond, fueled calls for monetary reform. A profound shift in economic analysis and ideas, beginning in the mid-1960s and taking twenty-odd years to gain traction, ended up driving technocratic reforms that quite fortuitously also created conditions for legitimacy.

During the two decades or so leading up to the wave of formal CBI measures in the late 1980s and 1990s, economists documented the importance of expectations of future inflation in the determination of prices and wages; and the apparent lack of a *long-run* trade-off between unemployment and inflation, with an associated "natural" rate of unemployment prevailing on average, given structural features of a country's *real* economy.[2] Since, on this evidence, there were no longer thought to be permanent and awkward values-based trade-offs to be struck between jobs and price stability, it was not essential for politicians to maintain day-to-day control of the monetary levers.

For some, that absolutely did not mean handing the reins over to the central bankers. As Milton Friedman, one of the leaders of the revolution, emphatically put it, "the two most important variables in their loss function are avoiding accountability on the one hand and achieving

[1]Summers, "Price Stability," p. 625.

[2]Mankiw and Reiss, "Friedman's Presidential Address."

prestige on the other."[3] As a prediction of the future, this was hopelessly wrong, with central bankers eventually harnessing accountability as a public self-disciplining device. Friedman's take on the world was, indeed, full of ironies. Having done as much as anyone to advocate the withdrawal of politics from economic policy, for which he was awarded the Nobel Prize in 1976, when much of the West was gripped by stagflation, his specific monetary prescriptions undid themselves.

His preferred approach, manifest in sustained and prickly criticism of the Volcker Fed during the 1980s, was for strictly "rules-based" regimes, with the authorities having no discretion to waiver. This was in the spirit of Hayek: rules, not men (*sic*), were needed for government under the rule of law (chapter 8). The first irony, therefore, was that the viability of Friedman's favored rule—a target for the growth rate of (some measure of) the stock of money—was undermined by the very market liberalizations that formed part of the same ideological project as "monetarism." Financial innovations and freedoms made the demand for money (however measured) highly unpredictable, leaving the authorities struggling to know where to set their targets, how to interpret the data outturns, and how to explain to the public the changes to targets made from year to year or, sometimes, in the course of a year. Even if the longer-run demand was stable, so that the policy would eventually work (on which views differ), it could not survive the challenge of political accountability in jurisdictions where people wanted to have a vague sense of what on earth was going on. Friedman's Chicago colleague, Henry Simons, had anticipated that decades earlier, when he aired the possibility of targeting the path of the price level itself (or, in today's version, the inflation rate).[4]

So, after a brief interlude in the early 1980s when a few countries did, more or less, put policy on a money-based autopilot, judgment reentered in order to combine a nominal anchor with stabilization of fluctuations in demand and activity. That second purpose reflected the dictates of modern democracy but also constituted the Achilles' heel of discretionary policy.

[3]Letter from Milton Friedman to Stan Fischer, quoted in Fischer, "Rules versus Discretion," p. 1181. Also, Friedman, "Independent Monetary Authority."

[4]Simons, "Rules versus Authorities." For a review of how monetary targeting unraveled in the UK, see Goodhart, *Monetary Theory and Practice*, chapters II and III.

The relevant feature of the world was (and is) a certain amount of stickiness in nominal wages and prices: not everything reacts instantly to monetary announcements. On the one hand, this means that policy makers can help the economy recover from recessions or can contain unsustainable booms in aggregate spending. On the other hand, it means that, even without a meaningful trade-off between inflation and growth in the longer run, policy makers could be tempted to exploit the *short-term* trade-off to generate a burst of growth that, for a while, would be popular with the people, even though not sustained. But businesses and households would anticipate that in their wage bargaining and price setting, so in steady state inflation would end up higher than promised without anything durably gained in activity or jobs.[5] This is the time-inconsistency problem we met in part I (chapter 5). Why, then, should central bankers be trusted to keep inflation low?

In the real world, meanwhile, central bank independence did seem to make a difference. Most notably, underpinned by the famous "stability culture," which comprised part of Germany's reinvention of itself after World War II, the Bundesbank was widely recognized to have done better than any other major Western monetary authority at containing inflation in the face of the 1970s/1980s oil-price shocks, without the German economy suffering more than elsewhere. On the other side of the Atlantic, in the face of concerted efforts by the Reagan administration to pack the Federal Reserve Board against him, Paul Volcker had enjoyed sufficient public support (just) to take the decisive steps in conquering inflation in the world's reserve currency, a job consolidated during Alan Greenspan's early years at the helm, and which seemed to have laid the foundations for an exceptional period of growth.[6] By the early 1990s, economists were compiling evidence that central bank independence could improve inflation performance without exacerbating volatility in output and jobs: an apparent free lunch.[7]

[5] Barro and Gordon, "Model of Monetary Policy."

[6] Silber, *Volcker*.

[7] Alesina and Summers, "Macroeconomic Performance." Later studies suggested a weaker effect of independence, but hypothesized that the performance of the earliest independent central banks had helped bring about a sea change in attitudes to inflation in countries with different systems (e.g., Crowe and Mead, "Central Bank Governance"). It is plausible that convergence of inflation performance would be delivered by a wish to avoid continuous nominal depreciation against low-inflation currencies with independent central banks.

Something seemed to be going very well if only the right policy regime existed. That fueled interest in analytical models that "solved" the inflation-bias problem. The two main formal explanations were Ken Rogoff's *conservative central banker*, who was more anti-inflationary than society and so less inclined to exploit the short-term trade-off; and, later, Carl Walsh's *contract* under which central bankers were incentivized to resist temptation by the ability of politicians to "punish" their agent for missing a target.[8] It is easy to see Rogoff's inspiration in the inflationary hatred of the Bundesbank and the disinflation wrought by Paul Volcker, dependent respectively upon epoch-altering history and one man's convictions. Walsh's, by contrast, was to be found in the apparently more mundane inflation-targeting "contract" introduced in the late 1980s by New Zealand. The Reserve Bank became, in effect, a norm-shifting trendsetter for the design of modern monetary institutions—demonstrating, as Keynes must surely have known, that economists and political theorists are not infrequently unknowing publicists for worlds constructed by practical men and women.

For central bankers around the world had, of course, seized on the, for them, happy conjunction of abstract analysis, empirical research, and real-world comparative performance. Events and conferences were held, at which the various strands of thinking on the costs of inflation, the lack of a long-term trade-off between inflation and jobs, the importance of credibility, the transmission mechanism of monetary policy (without much mention of banks), and, not least, the track record of existing independent central banks were brought together with force. Stanley Fischer, recently vice chairman of the Federal Reserve but then still at MIT, the de facto intellectual headquarters of everything that followed, produced what became the standard account for the conference that marked the Bank of England's tercentenary in 1994.[9]

For critics, this represented the skillful pursuit of group interests by a strong "epistemic community" drawn from academia and policy circles. It was, indeed, true that many of the leading academics contribut-

[8] Rogoff, "Optimal Degree," and Walsh, "Optimal Contracts."

[9] Fischer, "Modern Central Banking." The importance of MIT for the story of part IV cannot be overemphasized. Not only did they bring Chicago's rational expectations revolution back to Keynesian business cycles, they produced an extraordinary number of the people who went on to become top policy makers.

ing to this literature later landed plum policy jobs. But, for good or ill, there is also no doubting that an important shift in ideas *had* occurred. As the quote from Larry Summers at the chapter head illustrates, by the early to mid-1990s, many policy makers had reached the view that experimentation with monetary instrument rules needed to give way to delegation to carefully designed monetary institutions.

This was concrete but incomplete. On the one hand, the substantive point was clear enough. In seeking to balance aggregate demand with aggregate supply (the economy's productive capacity), policy was to focus on the outlook for inflation over the medium term and was to be *systematic*, since that would harness expectations to its delivery.[10] The era of flexible inflation targeting, as it came to be known, was beginning.

On the other hand, no one had pinned down how it was possible to design institutions that, in Summers's terms, would solve time-inconsistency problems.

SUSTAINING CBI VIA CHECKS AND BALANCES

Indeed, the purpose of retelling that history, which will be overly familiar to readers from the economics profession, is that it does not quite work. Even if it helps to explain how independence came to be granted or, in the Fed's case, reactivated, it does not explain why CBI should be sufficiently successful to be sustained in law and in practice. After all, lots of other components of the machinery of government get ripped up as fashions change and as inevitable disappointments occur.

If politicians are victim to time-inconsistency problems and short-termist political temptations when they hold the monetary instruments themselves, why, if it suited them, wouldn't they overturn or undermine any delegation when that's what they control? Why wouldn't a conservative central banker be replaced by an "accommodating" central banker when the going gets tough? Similarly, why should government be relied on to enforce a contract against a central banker if the deviation from target is actually useful to the politician's purposes, helping

[10] Taylor, "Discretion."

them to recover popularity or get reelected? As was pointed out twenty years ago, the time-inconsistency problem is simply relocated.[11]

This might seem to amount to a devastating critique of the so-called Italian school of political economy on which we relied in part I when drawing on Alesina and Tabellini to propose credible commitment as the positive warrant for delegation to trustee-like independent agencies.[12] The big question is, If institutions take the place of rules, why should they be any better?

These concerns are not imaginary. While central bank policy makers did not themselves subscribe wholeheartedly to the time-inconsistency inflation-bias models of academia, they *did* think there was a commitment problem and they *were* worried about the sustainability, and so credibility, of monetary independence. In other words, many central bankers were more focused on political short-termism.[13] But for both communities, the solution lay in regime design, so that people could see whether what was going on was what was promised.

Building Institutions: Mandates, Incentives, and the Mast of Public Reputation

As the 1990s progressed, orthodoxy became that the monetary objective should be observable and central banks' actions comprehensible (in line with our Principles for Delegation). Targeting inflation by setting an interest rate fitted the bill because it made sense in terms of the day-to-day lives of households and businesses, whereas targeting a monetary aggregate had been incomprehensible to anyone other than the cognoscenti. Emphasizing that policy would be set according to the

[11] McCallum, "Two Fallacies."

[12] Posen, "Do Better Institutions," a book review of, among others, Alesina, Roubini, and Cohen, *Political Cycles*.

[13] As a tribe, central bankers did not have much truck with academic models suggesting they would themselves renege on commitments in order to generate a temporary boom in output and employment beyond a sustainable path. Credibility would come only with deeds, but was not technically infeasible because monetary policy was not the series of one-period games deployed in formal models (Goodhart, "Game Theory," and Blinder, *Central Banking*). (In many of the inflation-bias models, the policy maker is effectively given an objective of driving unemployment below its sustainable level, so of course they fall into the trap.) On central bankers' views of credibility, see Blinder, "Central Bank Credibility."

outlook for inflation, many central banks moved toward publishing forecasts for growth and inflation and tried to explain, broadly, how they would respond to different kinds of economic shock.

If one word, again stemming from the revolution in ideas, sums this up, it is *transparency*.

The guiding concepts were *expectations* and *incentives*. If inflation in the short term is powerfully influenced by expectations of inflation over the medium term, then households and firms need information to help them form those expectations. If the traction of policy comes through expectations of the path of the central bank's month-by-month decisions, as reflected in the bond-market yield curve, then the markets need information on the central bank's approach to policy (in the jargon, its *reaction function*).

If, then, the central bank is to be incentivized to stick to its mandate, its target and actions and the results all have to be visible. That way, it is hoist on its own *reputation* for competence and reliability. The complex processes through which that reputation is produced depend, crucially, on the transparency and comprehensibility of a central bank's outputs and outcomes, on the extent to which its mandate provides for exceptional circumstances, and on the multiplicity of channels for scrutinizing it and for *publicly debating* its conduct and performance.[14] Do not think only of the "conservative" central banker but of the "scrutinized" central banker.

As for concerns about de facto independence, if government is to be incentivized to leave the central bank alone, any override or interference has to be highly visible. The integrity of a monetary regime depends on the range of actors who can observe and influence, directly or indirectly, the conduct of the political principal. The goal is to raise the *political* costs of political short-termism: it is easier to spot and so publicly debate whether politicians have "cheated" when they deploy a rarely used high-profile statutory power to override an independent central bank than when, in a regime *without* CBI, they choose to keep the policy rate of interest at, say, 3.5 percent for a prolonged period rather than raising it to, say, 4 percent.

[14] The stress on the visibility of outputs and outcomes exactly captures the dimensions used by James Q. Wilson to categorize agencies, as discussed in chapter 6 (Wilson, *Bureaucracy*).

This is a system of checks and balances. To be credible, modern monetary regimes rely on many people in different capacities—many audiences—watching what is going on in a 360-degree equilibrium.[15]

Although only groups of elite specialists may grasp all the details of a monetary regime and its operation, the instrumental value of the basic setup being comprehensible is that it makes it possible for those experts to intermediate with the wider public via newspapers, blogs, and social media. Hence central banks learn to invest in comprehension and monitoring by a wide range of intermediaries: the press, commentators, academics, business economists, trade unions, financial market analysts and traders, and the general public. This is not a matter of segmenting audiences; or rather if it is, it will backfire. Messages to different parts of society need to be consistent. Some "watchers" consume so much of central banks' output that inconsistencies would be spotted and publicized.[16] Nor is it a mandate for deploying demotic language that might resonate with public emotions, which lies within the realm of electoral politics, not technocratic trusteeship.

Preferences, Contracts, and Reputation

What I have been describing does not rely on any one economic theory of credible commitment but calls upon each of them. Mandates are akin to contracts, but with enforcement via public reputation rather than relying on a potentially conflicted executive branch or legislative majority. That depends in turn on central bankers truly caring about their reputation for delivering the mandate; so it matters that the society is capable of bestowing esteem and that the central bankers should truly believe in the regime: not "conservative" central bankers in that they prefer lower inflation than anyone else, but "conservative" in that they would regard departing from a formally delegated mandate as a bad thing. This is a triple lock of preferences, incentives, and reputation, almost exactly as posited in chapter 5.

[15] For arguments along these lines, see Susanne Lohmann, "Reputational" and "Why Do Institutions Matter?," which seem to me to get close to how many central bankers conceive of modern monetary regimes. The "audience theory" is subjected to some empirical testing in Broz, "Political System Transparency."

[16] For an anthropological view of central bank communication, see Holmes, *Economy of Words*.

LEGITIMACY AS A CONDITION FOR CREDIBILITY

The greater irony in Friedman's condemnation of central bankers' values and character, therefore, is that being seen to fulfill a monitorable mandate could be the source of the personal prestige he held central bankers to crave.

Here the riddle at the heart of this book resolves itself. If accountability is the route to the prestige that helps anchor the system instrumentally, then we are also in the territory of legitimacy. More than simply part of a mechanism for incentives-compatibility, 360-degree monitoring is, reprising part II, *democracy as watchfulness.*

For CBI to be sustainable, society must support it. As stressed in part II, that requires debate, and so scrutiny; it depends on performance, but also on reasons. Whether we think of them as wise and virtuous or as purely self-interested, sensible central bankers will want to invest in *reasoned* debate and criticism of their policies.

A comparison can be drawn with the judiciary. We know that before judicial independence was embedded in the US Constitution, it had been fought for in the UK and theorized over on the continent of Europe from the seventeenth century onward.[17] We are also keenly aware that in parts of the world that struggle continues, buttressed by United Nations and Commonwealth principles.[18] But today many of us in the established democracies probably take judicial independence for granted. It might, therefore, come as a surprise to discover that across the developed world, top judges are active in explaining, and sometimes defending, how they fit into their particular jurisdiction's constitutional setup. With reason. To give just one example: only a decade or so ago, British judges had to struggle with the executive government over how the budget for the administration of the courts would be set and controlled.[19]

The same goes for central bankers. A society's constitutional norms and institutional structures need continuous explanation and underpinning. For central bankers, their interest in trying to influence the

[17] For the perspective of a judge, see Lord Justice Brooke, "Judicial Independence."

[18] United Nations, "Basic Principles," and Commonwealth (Latimer House), *Principles.*

[19] For example, Lord Justice Leveson, "Dicey Revisited."

shape of the regimes they administer is linked to their proper role in explaining those regimes.

Thus, in Britain from the late 1980s onward the Bank of England's leaders gave lots of speeches on the costs of inflation and on monetary stability being a precondition (but not a sufficient condition) for prosperity, enabling market signals to work more cleanly in allocating resources. After independence was granted, there was massive determination to avoid being painted as "inflation nutters." Eddie George, the Bank's governor during the early years, repeated those points again and again, including into his retirement.[20]

Dual-Purpose Transparency

The economic literature on the virtues of transparency in generating *effective* monetary policy turned out, therefore, to be coterminous with thinking that sees transparency as essential to ensure the accountability of *both* the central bank for their stewardship of the regime *and* their political principals for its formal construction.[21] For *effectiveness*, transparency enables and so harnesses informed expectations about the course of policy and, thus, the path of nominal variables. For *legitimacy*, transparency enables informed public debate about the regime and its operation, through a process of *discursive accountability* (chapters 11 and 15).

Looked at this way, credibility, the preoccupation of central bankers and economists, and legitimacy, the preoccupation of their critics, are not, after all, in separate registers. If society truly wants price stability and that is reflected in a legislative act, the legitimacy conferred frees the central bank to make compelling commitments.[22] Without the act

[20] On not being inflation nutters, George, Speech at the TUC. On stability's value, George, "Approach to Macroeconomic Management."

[21] For a literature review that discusses the credibility effects with little or no mention of the significance for legitimacy, see Blinder, Ermann, Fratzcher, de Haan, and Jansen, "Central Bank Communication." Blinder has, of course, written about central banking and democracy elsewhere.

[22] This is at odds with the perception of those scholars who conclude that CBI was erected entirely on formal legal conditions (e.g., Roberts, *Logic of Discipline).* It *is* consistent with skepticism about the explanatory power of formulaic indexes of CBI, and with the view that the broader political and social context matters, as in Acemoglu, Johnson, Querubin, and Robinson, "Policy Reform."

of institution creation by the legislature, the central bank will not feel able to impose on society short-term costs that might sometimes be necessary to keep longer-term inflation expectations anchored in the face of shocks such as oil-price hikes that temporarily push inflation up but demand and output down. But *with* (operational) independence *and* a clear goal from elected representatives, the central bankers can properly regard society as having tied itself to the mast of its own preferences. They are free to proceed on the basis of stable preferences rather than preferences that shift with circumstances. So, again, the central banker does not have to be more conservative than society but rather needs to be dutiful—the "dutiful and legitimate central banker." Credibility through legitimacy, and legitimacy through credibility.

That, of course, was the message of part II's exploration of our political values. I have been describing an approach to framing monetary regimes that, more or less, accords with the Principles for Delegation—a clearly articulated regime, simple instruments, principles for the exercise of discretion, transparency that is not deceptive, engagement with multiple audiences, and, most crucially, testimony to legislative committees; all directed at establishing and maintaining a reputation for reliable, legitimate authority.

WHY INSTITUTIONS MIGHT BE ABLE TO DO THE WORK OF RULES

In summary, the answer to the question of why institutions can do the work of instrument rules is that *institutions are devices for reconfiguring incentives.*

By shifting the balance of interests, they produce new incentives for generating expertise and producing information; conjure checks where none previously existed; and can even procure stewards for values a society would like to attach itself to. Many individual central bankers really do believe in the value of price stability, which is less surprising when one grasps that independent central banks are devices designed to manifest and embed that value.

The institutions of democratic governance are distinctive for two reasons. They draw on the checks and balances of 360-degree monitoring, solving the infinite-regress problem. But to be sustainable over the long run, the incentives they embody and reinforce must be aligned with (or reshape) our values (parts II and III). The revolution in economic ideas that promoted transparency as an instrument of policy efficiency had the invaluable side effect of helping to align central bank practices with the values of democracy.

Of course, that was too good to be true . . .

19

Tempting the Gods

MONETARY REGIME ORTHODOXY BEFORE THE CRISIS

> We [the UK Treasury] have neither claim to be consulted nor power to enforce our views [on the Bank]; . . . it would be generally recognized that in order to avoid political influence on [monetary] matters it is not desirable that we should have any such claim.
>
> —Advice to Winston Churchill, 1925, only a few years before the Bank was stripped of power[1]

The previous chapters' account of modern monetary regimes lies at the confluence of four separate streams of thought: the economics of credibility, political science on sectional interests, political theories of legitimacy, and the sociology of trust. By embracing transparency, the central banking community and their political principals constructed regimes that seemed capable of delivering better policy and, with hindsight, of meeting the conditions for legitimacy reflected in our Principles for Delegation. Oh happy day . . .

WHAT A HAPPY STORY!

In varying degrees, monetary policy regimes really did live up to that description.

In the UK, the regime of "operational independence" established in 1997 includes a hierarchy of statutory objectives, with price stability given primacy; and a requirement for the executive government to produce an annual remit, which defines "price stability" and gives the

[1]Memo from Otto Niemeyer to then chancellor of the exchequer Churchill, quoted in Kynaston, *City of London*, p. 316. Churchill commissioned two reviews of Treasury/Bank relations during this period.

Bank's policy makers time to bring inflation back to target after cost shocks (e.g., oil-price collapses or spikes) in order to avoid undesirable volatility in output and employment. Decisions are made on a one person, one vote basis in a statutory Monetary Policy Committee (MPC) that includes "external" members, who were intended by the executive government to bring fresh air into the central bank's career bureaucracy. The Bank is required by statute to publish minutes of its policy meetings and its analysis of inflation trends, which it does via probabilistic "fan charts" that emphasize uncertainty and risk.[2] Because it is impossible to tell what crises the country might face, Parliament gave the executive government a power to override the MPC, but it must be used transparently and only in exceptional circumstances. Public accountability is centered on separate hearings of Bank and Treasury officials in front of a House of Commons select committee, which was being newly energized at much the same time (chapter 15).

That package went some way toward addressing concerns about central bank independence. Assessed against Joseph Stiglitz's general critique, the inspiration for many of the critics of CBI cited in the book's introduction (chapter 1), the UK system does not confer goal independence; it is based on a committee that disperses power and helps to expose genuine uncertainty and disagreement to public view and scrutiny; and it requires transparency.[3] Within the "post-Keynesian" community, one author recalled that a similar balance of democracy and technocratic know-how had been advocated by Keynes himself in a report on the Indian monetary system.[4]

It is perhaps encouraging, then, that some features of the UK regime were controversial within the central banking community. In private encounters, Governor Eddie George fiercely defended the UK's rejection of "goal independence" as undesirable and unnecessary, in the face of criticism from Bundesbank president Hans Tietmeyer, who regarded the UK's "operational independence" as a flawed half measure.[5]

[2]Mervyn King liked to stress at the *Inflation Report* press conferences that the probability of the MPC's central projection turning out to be correct was 0 percent! Point forecasts are not very interesting.

[3]Elgie, "Democratic Accountability," and Stiglitz, "Central Banking."

[4]Bibow, "Keynes" and "Reflections."

[5]Recollections of these previously unreported conversations were passed on to me by Andrew Bailey, the head of George's office at the time and present for some of the exchanges. By

That is very far from saying that the British setup is perfect. There is, for example, no domestic statutory bar on direct monetary financing of the government—any legal constraint current coming from EU treaties.[6] Its interest lies, rather, in Britain having been late to the CBI party and, hence, in its being able to draw on extensive domestic debate, the academic literature, and experience elsewhere. It is not surprising, therefore, that broadly similar precepts guided the evolution of other national regimes.

Everywhere, transparency increased massively.[7] Even in the US, where legislation gives equal weight to "stable prices" and "maximum employment," the Fed eventually published its view of what is meant by those components of its statutory purpose.[8] More or less everywhere, both the outputs (a short-term interest rate) and the outcomes (inflation) of policy became hugely more visible and comprehensible to the public and their legislators. With hindsight, the narrow monetarists dented their claims to serve democracy and the rule of law by wrapping the technology of central banking in a cloak of mystery. In the new world, the techniques employed aided legitimacy.

Whether for those reasons or others, independent monetary authorities became the rage. As CBI spread, it became harder to buck the trend, via what some have termed *mimesis*.[9] Eventually, this was institutionalized in canons of orthodoxy. In Europe, that came through the Delors Report's strong recommendation that any monetary union be founded upon an independent central bank. In the wider world, it worked through IMF advocacy and, in specific cases, conditions attached to support packages, as part of the so-called Washington Consensus.[10]

---

virtue of being free to define their own nominal targets (today, inflation targets) consistent with their statutory mandate for price stability, both the ECB and the Fed have some goal independence, not only instrument independence. On this, I seem to differ from Bernanke, "Monetary Policy."

[6] Lawyers may differ on whether monetary financing is banned in the UK under Article 123 of the Maastricht Treaty establishing a monetary union within the EU.

[7] Geraats, "Central Bank Transparency" and "Monetary Policy Transparency."

[8] There is a peculiarly undebated question of how the Fed's statutory mandate should be parsed into a purpose and an objective. The legislated language is "shall maintain long run growth of the monetary and credit aggregates commensurate with the economy's long run potential to increase production, so as to promote effectively the goals of maximum employment, stable prices, and moderate long-term interest rates." Arguably, it is natural to read the first clause as an objective (albeit one that, in terms of the Principles, is hard to monitor) and the second as the purpose (Fisher, "Financial Stability," and Tucker, "Monetary Policy").

[9] McNamara, "Rational Fictions."

[10] Williamson, "Washington"; and a retrospective, distinguishing between earlier and later versions of the package, in Fischer, "The Washington Consensus."

Pristine and Parsimonious

For a couple of decades, the monetary policy conducted under this global standard was fairly simple and straightforward.

Compared with much of the administrative state, central banks did not rely on a plethora of "key performance indicators," which are useful for managing projects and for delivery functions but not for facilitating public debate on achieving a public purpose. With quite simple goals, central banks relied on public explanation of what was going on in the economy, probabilistic forecasts of its future evolution, and providing enough information to enable analysis, debate, and criticism. Many experts see that kind of approach as necessary for social or political trust.[11]

Deploying their position as the monopoly supplier of the economy's final settlement asset (their money) and exploiting short-term stickiness in prices and wages, central banks set a very short-term interest rate to steer—*rough*-tune, not fine-tune—spending in the economy, aiming to keep it broadly in line with the economy's productive capacity and, hence, inflation at target. Since the effect of any one day's *overnight* rate of interest on its own would be negligible, central banks aimed to pursue a *systematic* policy that would shape *expectations* of the future path of the policy rate. It was recognized that the principles underpinning policy might need to be updated from time to time as lessons were learned about the workings of the economy, but the metaprinciple was to remain principled.[12]

In its instruments, monetary policy was, in short, highly *parsimonious*.

Although it influenced asset prices and bank-lending conditions—and, to be clear, was expressly recognized as *relying* in part on doing so—there was no *direct* intervention in the allocation of credit. That job was performed by capital markets and private sector banks. Anything else would have seemed at odds with a market economy.

Further, the central bank's exposure to risk was low; either by virtue of operating in low-risk Treasury bills or by lending against (in the

[11] O'Neill, *A Question of Trust* and "Perverting Trust."

[12] Woodford, "Principles and Public Policy," makes similar points. As it happens, I do not share the enthusiasm for some of the specific substantive principles Woodford advances, which I think mix up practicable policy in a world of wobbly rationality with ideal metastandards for evaluating earthly economic life.

jargon, *repo-ing*, for "sale and repurchase") a wider class of securities but with *excess* collateral. In consequence, the distance from fiscal policy was marked (although not zero, as I discuss).

Policy might, therefore, have been described as *pristine* as well as *parsimonious*: desirable qualities for an IA regime.

Staying Close to Base: Abstemious

Finally, contrary to what much of the political science literature and some wider commentary would predict, on the whole the central bankers did not seek more powers or responsibilities than, they believed, were needed to preserve price stability. They were not empire builders, targeting budgets or ever greater reach as a measure of prestige. Many wanted, in particular, to avoid being the banking supervisor, fearing that would draw them into the politically charged territory of consumer protection. They were conscious of their power, and, whether by conviction, principle, or expedience, many did not want to jeopardize it by extending into unwarranted areas—into other agencies' turf.

So, not only pristine and parsimonious, *abstemious* too. It was an age of innocence.

THE GODS EXIST

Looking back, this was eerily reminiscent of the international consensus following World War I. At much the same time as the League of Nations conferences upheld the principle of central bank independence (chapter 1), Churchill received the unequivocal advice quoted at the chapter head. That moment proved to be the high-water mark for Montagu Norman and his generation, who had forged an international model that collapsed as the gold exchange standard unraveled.

Such was the backlash that, as we saw, even a quarter of a century later the Fed faced demands from President Truman to hold down long-term bond yields to help fund the Korean War, wriggling free only after winning support from Congress.[13] Meanwhile, in the UK, the Bank of

[13] Hetzel and Leach, "Treasury-Fed Accord."

England was known as the "operational arm of the Treasury" until at least the late 1970s.

As, a quarter of a century on, central bankers strode the world, they might have asked themselves whether history would repeat itself. If nothing else, would books like *Maestro*, Bob Woodward's celebration of long-term Federal Reserve chairman Alan Greenspan, the most famous central banker since Norman, summon the gods from their slumber?[14]

Tragically, vigilance *had* been urged. Just a decade after Arthur Burns had ended his career with a cry of anguish, Paul Volcker, the towering figure of twentieth-century central banking, had taken to the stage in 1990 to share his own valedictory thoughts with his peers. Highlighting not only the virtues of price stability but also (vigorously asserting an older mind-set) the vital role of central banks in overseeing the stability of the banking system, Volcker presciently posed the big issue in his title: "The Triumph of Central Banking?" with an emphatic question mark.[15] Was no one listening?

WHAT AN UNHAPPY STORY!

No sooner had the leading central bankers alerted the world to the wonders of the *Great Moderation* in the early 2000s than the international economic and monetary system fell apart in the *Great Financial Crisis*.

Monetary regimes, apparently so carefully designed, were found wanting. And having become, by doctrine, inclination, and expertise, overly detached from the system's stability, there was nothing short of a reawakening among central banks to the significance of most monetary liabilities being issued by private businesses (banks). Inflation targeting had no more heralded the End of Monetary History than, twenty years earlier, the collapse of the Berlin Wall had marked the End of History (as Francis Fukuyama had wondered in his paean to Hegel).

As the financial and economic crisis broke and deepened, there was unscripted innovation on a grand scale. In addition to finding themselves acting in their institutions' traditional role as lenders of last

[14] Woodward, *Maestro*.

[15] Volcker, "Triumph of Central Banking?" The question mark was underlined by Volcker during the Q&A.

resort to the banking system, central banks provided liquidity to "shadow" banks, such as money market funds and finance companies. With the banking system on its knees, they stepped in as "market makers of last resort" to keep key capital markets open. And while details and timing varied across currency areas, after their short-term policy rates hit the "zero lower bound" in early 2009, they turned to providing macroeconomic stimulus by acting *directly* on the whole battery of risk factors incorporated into asset prices—term premia, liquidity premia, and credit-risk premia. To do so, they intervened with overwhelming force in the markets for long-term government bonds, corporate bonds, and mortgage bonds, and subsidized some kinds of bank lending relative to others. In the process, they have come much closer to steering the allocation of credit in the economy and have taken more risk onto their balance sheets than in many decades.

"Parsimonious" and "pristine"—hallmarks of the 1990s and early 2000s—are hardly suitable epithets. A brief age of innocence, during which monetary policy legitimacy had eclipsed central banking authority, passed as the community bumped into some of the world's complex realities.[16]

Legitimacy Crisis?

The consequent challenges were not only to efficiency and effectiveness but to legitimacy too. A system that, judging by our Principles for Delegation, seemed more or less satisfactory around the middle of 2007 was stretching the bounds of acceptability only a couple of years later.

In terms of the Delegation Criteria, questions were being asked about whether the central banks were, after all, making big distributional choices. Processes were under strain or not as well constructed as had been thought (Design Precept 2). For example, in the UK it turned out that decisions on liquidity assistance to the system as a whole and to individual firms were insulated from politics (good) but were not made by committee (not so good; a governance position that, bizarrely, in terms of our democratic values, is under the control of the lay Court of Directors, and might still exist).

[16] For a robust assessment, see Wolf, *Shifts and the Shocks*.

Almost no central bank had articulated operating principles for its lender-of-last-resort policies or for how it would operate monetary policy at the effective (or "zero") lower bound for interest rates (DP3). Few had thought through how to ensure political accountability for operations that could not be immediately transparent without sparking panic, exposing the people to even greater risk and hardship (DP4). Perhaps most problematic of all, no jurisdiction had clear rules of the game for determining how central banks could come to the rescue in unforeseen circumstances or, put from another perspective, when they should stop (DP5). That alone proved not far short of explosive in the US when a series of nonbanks were rescued (AIG) or allowed to fail (Lehman).

In other words, a harsh examiner would probably issue a Fail on central banks' compliance with the Principles during the crisis, having happily issued Passes (with varying degrees of distinction) only a few years before.

Yet More Power!

And yet central banks accumulated *more* power in the wake of the crisis! This is particularly true of regulation and supervision, where they had previously been most abstemious (or relaxed).

There are many possible explanations for this. First, whatever the shortfalls in monetary regime design, through their innovations the monetary authorities helped to avoid a repeat of the 1930s Great Depression, which was no small thing. Second, the failures at other agencies in the run-up to the crisis were, arguably, even more obviously abject. Third, the crisis prompted a shift in ideas about the purpose of central banks, implying that if the biggest problems were with regime design rather than stewardship, then responsibility lay partly at the door of elected politicians.

The second and third explanations were potent in the UK, where the Bank of England and others argued that, as a central bank with no regulatory powers prior to the crisis, it faced a problem of "missing instruments" if society expected it to maintain financial stability as well as price stability.[17] In an overhaul by a new executive government elected

[17] Mervyn King, then governor of the Bank of England, Speech (2009).

in 2010, the precrisis regulator was abolished by Parliament. As a body created only in 1997/1998, the Financial Services Authority (FSA) had not put down roots deep enough to protect it against the backlash. If the Bank of England benefited from some *Burkean* prescriptive legitimacy through its three centuries of existence, the FSA did not. Instead, for prospective prime minister David Cameron prudential supervision belonged with the Bank because the role required "authority and . . . respect," but an expanded Bank was seen to be in need of reform if its latent authority in the banking sphere was to be endowed with legitimacy.[18]

In the euro area, the ECB and others argued that the monetary union was incomplete and fragile without a banking union: the transmission of a monetary policy intended for the currency area as a whole was being impeded by banking collapse or fragility in some member states. The ECB got the job of banking supervision for the euro area as a whole, not least to overcome perceptions that national authorities were captured by their local banking systems (but see chapter 13).

By contrast, the Federal Reserve *was* a bank supervisor before the crisis, and this, combined with controversy around some of its emergency operations, put its functions in play while the Dodd-Frank bill was negotiated on Capitol Hill through 2009 and into 2010. Political currents were such that the Fed ended up with an expanded supervisory role, but perhaps with narrower so-called macroprudential responsibilities—the capacity temporarily to recalibrate regulatory requirements to protect against booms—than some of its European and Asian counterparts, and with debates about its governance and accountability left unresolved.

Those differences are details, however. Big picture, the contrast with the 1930s could hardly be greater, with the new concentration of power concerning many former and some serving central bankers.[19]

[18] Interview with Patience Wheatcroft, *Wall Street Journal* (European edition), December 14, 2009, six months before the 2010 general election.

[19] Although not always framed in terms of legitimacy, see Goodhart, "Changing Role"; Shirakawa, "Future of Central Banks"; Eichengren et al, *Rethinking Central Banking*; Issing, "Paradise Lost"; Cecchetti, "Central Bank Independence"; Volcker, "Central Banking"; and Buiter, "Central Banks." And from seasoned observers: Middleton, Marsh et al., *Challenges*.

ASSESSING TODAY'S CENTRAL BANK REGIMES: LEGITIMACY VIA PRINCIPLED BOUNDARIES

It is finally time, therefore, to take the reflections in this book, and in particular our Principles on *whether* and *how* to delegate, to the four connected fields in which today's central banks find themselves center stage: monetary policy, liquidity policy, regulatory and supervisory policy, and credit policy.

We seem to face a nasty tension, rooted in central banks performing two quite different *types* of function (chapter 23). On the one hand, they are expected to operate monetary policy in a *systematic* manner in order to smooth fluctuations in economic activity without jeopardizing the economy's nominal anchor. Seen thus, they are institutions designed for normal circumstances. On the other hand, in their role as the lender of last resort (LOLR), they are expected to operate with the *flexibility* of the economy's equivalent of the US Cavalry—an institution for economic and financial emergencies.

If a central bank succeeds in building a reputation for operating a systematic monetary policy, won't that reputation be jeopardized when it reveals its normally hidden innovative side during a crisis? Conversely, might a reputation for rule-like behavior in normal times sap confidence in its ability to ride to the rescue in a crisis? In other words, do central banks need to sustain a rich, multipurpose reputation that, Janus-like, faces in two directions?

Certainly, that kind of double-think has characterized debates about central banking over the years. In fact, however, the discussion in parts I and II reveals it to be a false starting point. For democratic legitimacy, the LOLR function *must* be framed by a Principles-compliant regime no less than the standard monetary policy function. The same goes, moreover, for wider balance-sheet policy and for the central bank's involvement in regulation and supervision.

Further, since we are dealing here with multiple-mission central banks, the regimes cannot be segmented, falling to organizational silos, but must be joined up. Otherwise, there is not much point in housing them together.[20] As already indicated, the following chapters argue that

[20] Tett, *Silo Effect*.

we need something like a *Money-Credit Constitution* (MCC), covering both central banking and constraints on the private banking parts of the monetary system.

If the initial systematic policy versus flexible policy dichotomy dissolves on closer inspection, two other problems rise to take its place. The first is what happens at the boundaries of the regime in circumstances where, by going further, the central bank could avert or ameliorate a major crisis. This is no less of an issue for monetary policy than for LOLR policy, as we saw in 2009 when central banks reached the effective "zero" bound for their interest rate. How should our fifth Design Precept—Emergencies—be operationalized for central banking?

In the background lurks the big issue discussed in abstract and more general terms in parts II and III (chapters 11 and 16). Is society better off giving central banks extensive de facto freedom to "do the right thing" to save the nation in emergencies, leaving them to take the heat from angry legislators and members of the public in the aftermath of having "saved the world"?

Consistent with DP5, I argue for the importance of the central banking "trust deed" being as clear as possible, substantively and procedurally. Where, despite those best efforts, unenvisaged operations are exceptionally sanctioned by political principals, they should remain within a reasonable definition of central banking. The implicit blurred boundary between central banking and fiscal policy needs, therefore, to be made explicit, in a *Fiscal Carve-Out* that forms part of an economy's Money-Credit Constitution.

The most important constraint is that elected politicians should not be able, in effect, to delegate fiscal policy to the central bank simply because they cannot agree or act themselves. Absent that stricture, we would all too likely find ourselves in an equilibrium where elected representatives leave the heavy lifting to the central bank. Arguably, that has happened on both sides of the Atlantic (chapter 24).

Here, then, is the second problem that emerges in our exploration of postcrisis central banking: the *grand dilemma* signaled in the book's introduction (chapter 1). The more central banks can do, the less the elected fiscal authority will be incentivized to do, creating a tension with our deepest political values. In short, determining the boundaries for central banking is harder when it is unclear what lies beyond that line, under the control of elected policy makers.

Those are among the biggest issues that we encounter in what follows. They concern our liberty and our democratic system of government.

20

A Money-Credit Constitution

CENTRAL BANKS AND BANKING STABILITY

> I can perceive none of those modifications of the bank charter which are necessary, in my opinion, to make it compatible with justice, with sound policy, or with the Constitution of our country.
>
> —President Andrew Jackson's message of veto of the privately owned Bank of the United States, July 10, 1832

> The Government should take away from the banks all control over money, but should leave the lending of money to bankers.
>
> —Irving Fisher, espousing the Chicago Plan for "narrow banking," 1936[1]

> I insist that neither monetary policy nor the financial system will be well served if a central bank loses interest in, or influence over, the financial system.
>
> —Paul Volcker, 1990[2]

The 2007–2009 phase of the Great Financial Crisis cruelly exposed the standard monetary policy regime as insufficient to preserve stability. If, as I have suggested, orthodoxy on the design of monetary regimes was the happy product of an evolution in ideas and an accumulation of experience, the ideas turned out to be incomplete and the experience misremembered.

As confidence in the soundness of banks first ebbed in 2007 and then evaporated in the autumn of 2008, their balance sheets cratered, financial markets closed, and the supply of credit to households and firms in the real economy atrophied. The combination of a collapse in the financial system and in sentiment hit economic activity and jobs hard. This met

[1] Fisher, "100% Money," p. 413.
[2] Volcker, "Triumph of Central Banking?"

with determined action by the world's major central banks to ease monetary and credit conditions. But with a broken banking system, confidence weak, and a debt overhang in the household sector of some economies, the transmission of monetary policy into spending was impaired.

For some students of twentieth-century monetary politics, this course of events would have confirmed the deep flaws they had long seen in the monetary constitution. James Buchanan, whom we first met in part II, advocated not only rules-based control of the supply of money but also a ban on leveraged private sector banking, which served no monetary purpose once an economy had migrated from a commodity (gold) standard to fiat money and so had autonomy in avoiding monetary shortages. He wanted the power of money creation to be reserved entirely for the state.[3] Others, by contrast, positively embraced private money creation but wanted to keep the state out of it, allowing the normal rules of commercial life to operate without any safety net, described by Buchanan as "anarchy."[4] The real world in which we live involves both state money creation and private money creation, with the state underpinning the private system via deposit insurance and the lender of last resort.

Whether a principled case exists for the involvement of *independent* central banks in that complicated world is exactly the kind of question that our *Multiple-Mission Constraints* (MMCs) are meant to help address. The first substantive constraint poses three conditions for combining functions at all within a trustee-type independent agency:

> An independent agency should be given multiple missions only if
> (a) they are intrinsically connected,
> (b) each mission faces a problem of credible commitment but does not entail making big distributional choices, and
> (c) it is judged that the combination will deliver materially better results.

With those tests in view, this chapter starts by exploring why, in the words of Paul Volcker quoted above, central banks have a clear *interest* in the financial system and, further, a need for some *influence* over it. It

[3]Buchanan, "Constitutionalization of Money," p. 255.

[4]Smith, *Rationale of Central Banking*; Hayek, *Denationalisation of Money*; and Dowd, *Private Money*, which contains a short section entitled "Abolishing the Bank of England," possibly explaining why Eddie George asked for a summary (Buchanan, "Constitutionalization").

goes on to argue that stability policy relies heavily on credibility, making part of the case, under our Delegation Criteria, for insulation from day-to-day politics; and it explores whether better results are likely to be achieved through delegation to the monetary authority.[5]

WHY MONETARY STABILITY AND FINANCIAL STABILITY ARE INTRINSICALLY CONNECTED

Volcker's two concerns are obviously distinct. One (interest) is descriptive, while the other (influence) is normative. It does not follow that a public authority should have a formal role, meaning powers of direction or restraint, in a field merely because it has an interest. Monetary policy makers have a very clear interest in the structure of labor markets and, more generally, the supply side of the economy: broadly, the more flexible an economy's product and labor markets, the less central banks have to do to steer aggregate demand in the face of nasty shocks to the economy.[6] But no one argues that central banks should have a formal role in supply-side policy. So Volcker's normative stipulation must rest on something special about the nature of their interest in the financial system, which stems, essentially, from the place of banking in the monetary system and that of central banks in the banking system.

Fractional-Reserve Banking: Private Liquidity Insurance and Money Creation

An economy's banking system provides liquidity insurance to the rest of the economy (to households and businesses). Banks do this by allowing customers to withdraw deposits on demand and to draw down committed lines of credit on demand. Their capability to provide this liquidity insurance stems from their deposit liabilities being treated by us (people and businesses) as money. When a bank makes a loan, it simply credits

[5]With thanks to Nellie Liang, Brookings Institution and former director for financial stability at the Fed Board, for comments on late drafts of this and the next chapter, which discusses whether a stability regime can meet the Design Precepts.

[6]George, "Approach to Macroeconomic Management," makes clear that the 1990s' Bank of England leadership felt much more comfortable gaining operational independence *after* supply-side reforms in the 1980s had made the real economy more flexible, as that reduced the burden on demand management in accommodating shocks to the economy.

its customer's deposit account, expanding the supply of money. Resources are created with the stroke of a pen—in the past literally, today figuratively. Even if the deposit is immediately transferred to another bank, the monetary liabilities of the system as a whole expand. *Banks are monetary institutions.* In fact, most of the money in today's economies is the deposit money issued by private banks, known as *broad money* (or, because it is created by their own lending activities, *inside money*).

This is not a riskless business. It is known to economists as *fractional-reserve banking* (FRB) and, for once, the jargon conveys something important. While commercial banks undertake to repay deposits on demand, they employ *only a small fraction* of those deposits in low-risk, liquid assets (of which the lowest-risk and most liquid are balances with the central bank, known as *reserves*). Most of their assets comprise illiquid loans to risky borrowers. The resulting balance-sheet structure—demand deposits backed by illiquid risky asset portfolios—is inherently fragile.

If a bank is faced with a surge of withdrawals, it may have to sell assets at discounted prices—either because it is straining the liquidity of the markets for those instruments or because it is treated as a forced seller. Suffering a loss on the sale impairs the bank's net worth (solvency), reducing the security of its remaining liabilities. There is, in consequence, a first-come, first-served incentive for customers to draw on their liquidity insurance before it is too late. Such runs tend to afflict not only unsound banks but also any sound bank that is liable to be rendered insolvent ex post by the fire sales made to meet withdrawals, in what amounts to a self-fulfilling panic.[7]

Liquidity crises have been a feature of modern capitalism. As well as hurting those depositors who get stuck when the doors close, they have much wider social costs. Since the private money system is based on credit money, the afflicted part of the banking system loses its capacity to make loans to businesses and households once its deposits are no longer accepted as money. If the crisis is widespread, other parts of the banking system might not be able to substitute seamlessly, or may even be pulled into the vortex themselves through direct losses and contagion. As credit supply tightens, the economy deteriorates, causing more people to default on loans and, thus, fueling the incentive to run on banks.

[7] That story is broadly captured in Diamond and Dybvig, "Bank Runs."

All of which is to say that we live in a world in which payments and loans—and, therefore, the *monetary system* and the *credit system*—are inextricably intertwined, surviving or falling together. Enter the central banks: elementally, as part of the *services state*.

Banks settle claims among themselves across the central bank's books, in its money, the economy's final settlement asset. Echoing Francis Baring's words at the beginning of part IV, this is the pivot: the liquidity backstop—the liquidity *re*insurer—for the banking system and, thus, for the economy as a whole.

When, in the early phases of the Great Financial Crisis, the central banks lent to banks against a wide range of collateral, they were seeking to avoid a contraction in individual bank balance sheets (microinsurance). When, later, the banking system as a whole teetered on the edge of total collapse, central banks eased credit conditions by buying assets from nonbank financial institutions. That massively increased the supply of (narrow) central bank money, offsetting shrinkage in the banking system's supply of (broad) deposit money (macroinsurance).[8] They did this to help prevent widespread economic seizure.

As with any kind of insurance, the known availability of this liquidity reinsurance gives banks (and others) incentives to take more risk than otherwise since it shields them from some of the costs of their own actions and choices. This "moral hazard" problem (chapter 4) makes crises more likely through the very efforts of the state to contain their social costs.

For these reasons, as previewed, crises prompt renewed debate about whether banks and banking should be allowed at all, to which some respond that it is central banking itself that should be banned.

Banning Central Banking

In the 1830s, President Andrew Jackson's conviction that a national bank would threaten the country's welfare prompted him to veto renewal of the charter of the Second Bank of the United States, the de-

[8]This is how Mervyn King persuaded the UK that quantitative easing was not inherently inflationary: we were addressing a problem of "not enough money" threatening deflation. By contrast, the Fed tends not to highlight the monetary part of quantitative easing (or of monetary policy more generally), which left it exposed to accusations that it risked runaway inflation by creating too much money.

scendant of Alexander Hamilton's First Bank. Ever since, this has provided inspiration for the "free banking" movement, which wants to abolish central banking, not banking. Deprived of their backstop and forced to compete, bankers would be driven to prudence, it is maintained, and so the economy could operate without the social costs of boom and bust. There are three pitfalls here.

First, this argument assumes that the legislature and the elected executive are somehow themselves deprived of the right to bail out ailing banks: by the middle of the nineteenth century, the US federal government was effectively guaranteeing privately issued bank notes, giving depositors an incentive to switch into notes at the first sign of trouble. Second, it assumes that banks are sufficiently homogeneous and monitorable for an improvident note issuer to be spotted and excluded from the "clearinghouse" via which they would settle their obligations to each other. But, in contrast to such a club-like world, which perhaps existed when the Bank of England governor's pragmatic authority was at its zenith, today's banks are so complex and heterogeneous that the dynamic might just as likely be toward a collective slide into overissuance. Third, it assumes that full-franchise democracies would tolerate the volatile swings in economic activity and jobs that accompanied the nineteenth-century gold standard (where, as is occasionally advocated, gold was adopted as the new monetary anchor).[9]

In a different register, free-banking advocates also implicitly assume that society could accept even more power in the hands of private bankers. Quite apart from the irony of Jackson's own preoccupations having been with the untrammeled power of bankers, I doubt it is worth creating more private political-financial power in order to obtain competitive money issuance.[10]

But none of that is to deny force in the central point about moral hazard, to which we return when discussing principles for the postcrisis LOLR (chapter 23).

[9] Under the Hayek proposal, there would be competition between different standards chosen by the issuing banks themselves. For a (former) Bundesbanker's view, see Issing, "Hayek, Currency Competition."

[10] Jackson's veto hinged on monopoly rights and tax exemptions for a bank serving a public purpose but owned and largely controlled by private (including foreign) shareholders, which at the time was still the model for the Bank of England in London.

To Ban or Permit Fractional-Reserve Banking?

Around a century after Jackson's presidency, Chicago economists launched the other line of attack on the place of banking within a monetary system. Under the "Chicago Plan," fractional-reserve banking itself would be banned, leaving only what are today known as *narrow banks* wholly invested in government bonds or central bank reserves (with central banks in turn invested in government bonds).

Personally, I doubt whether this would be wise. The liquidity insurance provided by banks, including through committed credit lines, reduces the need for households, businesses, and other financial intermediaries to self-insure against liquidity risk by holding stocks of liquid securities. That releases resources for use in the risky enterprises that can help generate growth and prosperity.[11] In other words, banking has social value, which needs to be placed alongside the social costs of failure. Regulatory regimes are designed to reduce those *gross* costs, leaving *net* social costs below social benefits.

Advocates of narrow banking believe that enterprise is doomed to failure. They want to separate the economic institutions of money and credit. To have any chance of success, any such regime could not be confined to businesses falling under the legal description of "bank." There would not be much point in requiring de jure banks to hold 100 percent of their assets in government bonds if the economic substance of their current liquidity creation and liquidity insurance services could be replicated elsewhere, as they surely would be in a world of endemic regulatory arbitrage. The policy would need to extend to any form of intermediation that had the economic substance of banking, known today as *shadow banking* in its myriad shapes and sizes.[12]

It is worth pausing to absorb how radical this is. It rules out *open-end* mutual funds replacing banks as the economy's core lenders to households and small businesses. Since they redeem on a first-come, first-served basis, the opacity of the underlying assets would expose

[11] If the likelihood of deposit withdrawals and credit facility drawdowns are not highly correlated, the aggregate benefits increase (Kashyap, Rajan, and Stein, "Banks as Liquidity Providers").

[12] For recent advocacy of this, see Cochrane, "Towards a Run Free Financial System." On the other side, see Cecchetti and Schoenholtz, "Narrow Banking."

them to runs. *Closed-end* unlevered credit funds with no short-term debt liabilities are immune to runs and so would not be banned. But some investors would no doubt want their holdings to be tradable in a liquid market, driving a segmentation between "riskless" and risky funds, the latter becoming the new mainstay of credit supply.[13]

Given the difficulty of valuing their portfolios and the lack of a redemption discipline on their management, there would be some uncertainty about the strength of demand to invest in the risky funds, and thus about the adequacy of credit supply to the economy as a whole. That sounds like a question of economics, but could all too easily become one of politics. If the supply of credit to the economy were materially impaired, there would likely be calls for the state to fill the gap. Indeed, rather amazingly, some of the strongest political support for the 1930s Chicago Plan came from advocates of government deciding how to allocate *credit* in the economy. As Senator Bronson Cutting put it at the time, "private financiers are not entitled to any profit on credit."[14] A project that academics saw as immunizing money from credit was, in some political eyes, a means of getting the price mechanism out of credit allocation, converting the central bank from a monetary institution into a state-credit bank. It is something to ponder: credit creation in the hands of politicians—pandering to popularity, doing favors for friends, or approximating a planned economy.

Arguments aside, the narrow banking question is for elected politicians. In the wake of the 2008–2009 phase of the Great Financial Crisis, the issues were debated, to different degrees in different countries.[15] Rightly or wrongly, the universal decision was not to make what would have amounted to a massive change in the constitution of money. The costs of transitioning from one setup to a radically different one were too unknowable for it to be taken seriously by those in office, elected

[13] Kotlikoff, *Jimmy Stewart*.

[14] Phillips, "Chicago Plan," pp. 17–25.

[15] In the UK it was given oxygen when central bank governor Mervyn King expressed interest in his old friend John Kay's *Narrow Banking*. This led the government to establish a review chaired by John Vickers, which came down against narrow banking (and against Glass-Steagall separation of "commercial" and "investment" banking), but recommended ring-fencing any material retail banks within wider banking groups, after which the narrow banking debate subsided (UK Independent Commission on Banking, *Interim Report*, pp. 97–100).

politicians and technocrats alike.[16] For better or worse, the world has persevered with fractional-reserve banking, subject to redesigned regulatory constraints.

The Two Components of Monetary Stability

That being so, I venture that Buchanan would, no doubt with regret, today join with many in regarding *banking stability as integral to monetary stability.* The public policy objective of preserving a stable financial system, able to provide the core services of payments, credit, and risk insurance in all weather, is not completely separable from monetary stability, because it is largely the stability of the private part of an economy's monetary system, the banks, that is at stake.

I suggest, then, that we should think of "monetary system stability" in this broad sense as having two components:[17]

1. Stability in the value of central bank money in terms of goods and services
2. Stability of private banking-system deposit money in terms of central bank money

To be clear, and this is very important for where we are going, the second leg absolutely does not entail that no banking institutions can be allowed to fail; only that the monetary liabilities of distressed firms must be transferable into claims on other, healthy deposit-taking firms or otherwise mutualized so that payment services are not interrupted.

That view of the importance of the banking system used to be orthodoxy at the summit of central banking, integral to its distinctive mind-set, as reflected in Paul Volcker's stark insistence that monetary authorities be involved in stability policy. It is now being restored after becoming sidelined during the cultural revolution of the 1990s (chapter 18).[18]

[16] On transitional costs of constitutional change, Hardin, *Liberalism*.

[17] Advocated in the introductory section of Tucker, "*Turner Review* Conference."

[18] At the Bank of England's 1994 tercentenary conference, banking supervision was stressed only by former governors Larosiere, Richardson, and Volcker and former BIS head Lamfalussy (Capie et al., *Future of Central Banking*, "The Philosophy of Central Banking" and "Central Banking in Transition"). Similar sentiments to Volcker's had been expressed the previous year

FROM INTEREST TO INFLUENCE

Establishing that society has an interest in monetary stability being defined broadly is insufficient to carry us as far as Volcker's institutional conclusion. A monetary policy maker might think it can rely on an arms-length regulator to ensure banking-system stability and money market efficiency. In fact, however, as the system's pivot, central banks can hardly avoid a broader role of the kind Volcker prescribed.

The Inalienable Interest in Influence: The LOLR at the Scene of Financial Disasters

The issuer of an economy's money can do something that no one else can do: create money at will. When there are sudden shifts in the demand for its money, it must accommodate those demands if it is to avoid inadvertent restraint on economic activity. Runs on the banking system—people demanding that their deposits be redeemed in cash, now—amount to increases in demand for a central bank's money. If banks do not hold sufficient central bank money (or assets that can be converted into central bank money via the market) to meet their customers' demand for cash, they will fail if they cannot go to the central bank and exchange illiquid assets for cash. Assuming the central bank agrees, it is doing two things at the same time: it is stabilizing banking by acting as a lender of last resort, and it is ensuring that the liquidity crunch does not interfere with the course of monetary policy. The missions of preserving banking stability and price stability are intimately intertwined not only for society but for the central banks themselves in their most elemental function: creating money.

This has dramatic effects on where and when the central bank crops up in a country's economic life. The monetary authority cannot credibly deny that it will ensure that "the clearings go through," their jargon for a day's payments across the economy being completed. In a nutshell, the LOLR is pretty well certain to find itself at the scene of a financial

---

by Eddie George, in "Pursuit of Financial Stability," a speech given just a few months after George became governor.

disaster. Unsurprisingly, therefore, societies typically expect their central bank to give an account of how things could have come to such a pretty pass. After the collapse of Northern Rock in 2007, the front cover of the British edition of the *Economist* showed a photograph of the then governor of the Bank of England under the headline "The Bank That Failed."[19] Not a tryptich of central banker, regulator, and finance minister—the members of the UK's then Tripartite Committee for Stability—but the first only. My point is not that the Bank did not carry its share of responsibility. It is that a setup where supervision and regulation were formally and practically at arm's length from the central bank could not, when it mattered most, insulate the reputation of the monetary authority from prudential problems, as some in the UK and elsewhere had hoped. Responsibility without power is as unattractive—and can be almost as bad for society—as the converse.

If that is so, central banks, as lenders of last resort, have an interest in being able to influence the system's regulation and supervision. At the most basic level, when they lend, they want to get their money back! They need to be able to judge which banks (and possibly near-banks) should get access to liquidity, and on what terms: the source of their historical pragmatic authority over banking. Even opponents of "broad central banking" generally accept that, as the lender of last resort, the central bank cannot avoid inspecting banks that want to borrow. Events in the UK in 2007 demonstrated that doing so from a standing start is hazardous for society. A central bank must be in a position to track the health of individual banks during peacetime if it is to be equipped to act as the liquidity cavalry (and if it is to be able to judge how its monetary decisions will be transmitted to the economy).

Formalizing Official Sector Power in Today's Constitutional Democracies

In some jurisdictions (for example, Germany and Japan), this is reflected in arrangements where the central bank conducts inspections of banks but does not make *formal* regulatory decisions. There might be cultural specificities here. Sitting next to him at dinner, I once asked former

[19] *Economist*, September 20, 2007.

Bundesbank president Helmut Schlesinger why he publically maintained that central banks should not be the bank supervisor when, as a matter of fact, many Buba staff were engaged in bank supervision. The response was that the central bank was not formally responsible or accountable, so banking problems would not infect the Bundesbank's reputation and standing as a monetary authority.[20]

In my own country, and I would guess the United States, the central bank could not escape censure over a banking crisis by saying that it was only one of a number of de facto supervisors, not the de jure regulator. (As reported above, the Bank of England could not escape responsibility for a banking crisis even when it had no role in supervising banks and markets.)

To be clear, the position of this book is that *if* central banks are to be involved materially in supervision, whether alongside other agencies or not, our democratic values demand that their role should be formalized for all the reasons explored in part II.

FROM INFLUENCE TO INSULATION: TRUSTEES FOR MONETARY-SYSTEM STABILITY

Arguing that central banks warrant some kind of formal role in stability policy is not sufficient for their to be insulated from day-to-day politics in pursuing those responsibilities. It is sometimes argued, in fact, including occasionally by central bankers, that a multiple-mission central bank could be granted different degrees of independence in their different fields.[21]

[20] On BaFin's routine reliance on Buba supervision: section 7(2) of Banking Act. Anticipating the influence of the Buba myth, its extensive role in supervision is underlined in Quinn, "The Bank of England's Role." For a recent account of Buba's contribution and engagement, see Dombret, "What Is 'Good Regulation'?"

[21] Stan Fischer has used the metaphor of a marriage, where each partner might lead on different parts of their life together (press conference, April 18, 2013, reported by Pedro da Costa, Reuters). But marriage partners are free to give and take as they please; they are not trustees for some mandated "public good," they are not seeking public esteem, and one of them does not have greater inherent legitimacy. Bernanke, "Central Bank Independence," argues that, in its regulatory/supervisory functions, the Fed has and should have no more independence than other regulators, and thus less than in its monetary policy functions, including the discount window and LOLR. On my argument, that might be the wrong way around. In fact, however, the Fed has pretty much the same political insulation in supervision and regulation as it does in

While obviously technically feasible, a mixed model would put monetary independence at risk. The public, commentators, executive branch politicians, and legislators are likely to think of their central bank as a monolith. Within stability policy, I doubt a central bank could maintain independence in its LOLR decisions if it was subject to political control in its supervisory role. And if politicians held formal levers over some areas of policy, they would be sorely tempted to use them as informal bargaining chips over monetary policy. That's just how the world works.

Separately, nor would a mixed model be conducive to successful institution building. The technical benefits of bringing missions together would likely be squandered if staff perceived a pecking order of importance or status: the curse of the Greenspan Fed, visited on the American people and the wider world, was its supervisors being regarded as a lower form of life than its monetary researchers (chapter 6).

If that is broadly right, central banks should not have a material role in stability policy unless a good case can be made for insulation from day-to-day politics. This is where our Delegation Criteria come in.

Stability Is Generally Valued

There is, I contend, a widely shared sentiment, across democracies, that the collapse of the financial system is a bad thing. By that, I mean that people seem likely to agree that the core financial services of payments, credit supply, and risk insurance should be sustained in almost all circumstances. Society's basic preferences in this area are broadly settled (although whether they can be manifested in a clear objective is deferred until the next chapter).

Credible Commitment

It is probably also uncontentious that booms in the supply of credit, in house prices, and in financial asset prices more generally can be deeply alluring once under way. In this sense, stability policy shares some of

---

monetary policy, and a lot closer to that than to, say, the EPA or SEC: job security, budgetary autonomy, instrument autonomy (chapter 4).

the characteristics of monetary policy. Political decision makers would be tempted to substitute their own interests (reelection, popularity) for the country's interests. That might involve allowing a potentially destabilizing credit boom to persist in order to harness the "feel-good factor" or, more subtly, shading policy to favor backers and particular constituencies. And it might be effected obscurely through, for example, policy on excess collateral requirements ("haircuts") for central bank market operations or more overtly through reducing headline capital requirements.

In other words, there is a classic problem of credible commitment here: society would ideally like to tie itself to the mast of "stability" but finds it difficult to do so.

That, of course, is the essence of the case, under our Delegation Criteria, for handing the ropes over to a truly independent *trustee-type* agency. At the least, there is almost as good a case for independence in haircut policy as in monetary policy. But further, subject to the constraints discussed in the next chapter, a pretty compelling case can also be made for insulating the officials who flesh out the regulatory regime for stability.

The Curse of Taxpayer Bailouts: Fiscal Risks Must Be Bracketed Away

What, though, of the historical prevalence of taxpayer solvency bailouts, an unambiguous fiscal measure, when preventive measures have failed and all that remains is a choice between the abyss and capitulation? This gives the elected executive (and their civil service protectors) an ongoing interest in the conduct of prudential supervision, wanting to know when any firm might be ailing. And once assured a seat at the table, at other moments they are liable to espouse the merits of an easier policy.

That being so, necessary conditions for insulation might be the following:

1. The regulator is satisfied that firms could be resolved individually in a tolerably orderly way without taxpayer solvency support.
2. Any insurance scheme is funded up front by the industry, with any ex post shortfalls made good by a hypothecated tax on the surviving parts of the industry.

3. The executive branch is granted a power to override the regulator's actions if they believe there is a tangible *direct* threat to the public finances, subject to any such use being contemporaneously transparent to the leading members of the relevant legislative committee and to the full assembly after a suitable delay (if immediate public disclosure would be destabilizing). (This condition would replicate the monetary policy override power that exists in some countries.)

If those conditions could not be satisfied, the lead supervisor might be placed at a short arm's length from central government but ultimately under executive branch political control (a US-style executive agency), with the central bank sitting awkwardly as a detached LOLR. A legitimacy-seeking central bank would, then, have a huge incentive to promote the development of regimes for resolving distressed intermediaries without public money being at risk.

Given the reforms to resolution regimes over recent years, I assume here that they are sufficiently credible for independent central banks not to be ruled out as supervisors.[22]

WILL MULTIPLE-MISSION CENTRAL BANKS DELIVER BETTER RESULTS?

Even if, as we have argued, independent central banks *could* have a role in stability policy, that does not demonstrate that they *should* be the sole or even the main stability authority. They might, for example, play a limited role, with another body in the lead. The final step, therefore, is whether a case can be made that stability is more likely to be achieved under the stewardship of the central bank (the third of the MMC tests). There are three types of arguments, concerning feasibility, cooperation, and incentives.

Harnessing the Authority of the Central Bank

Delegating stability policy to the central bank avoids the formidable challenge of establishing another body with the authority and independence needed to "take away the punchbowl," as Fed chair William McChesney Martin put it, in the face of political and public pressure. *If*

[22]Tucker, "Resolution of Financial Institutions."

an economy's central bank is already endowed with both authority and legitimacy, giving it responsibility for stability might be preferable to the uncertainties in starting afresh. In particular, the risks of industry capture might be reduced, as monetary policy makers' standing in the community does not depend on bankers.

Cooperation and Information Exchange

If, however, the central bank and the lead stability authority are separate, they need to cooperate—indeed, coordinate—to an unusually high degree. Information flows need to be frictionless. That is more easily stipulated and promised than secured. For individual bureaucrats, clashes that can be painted as "turf wars" can be highly damaging, leaving underlap as an institutional equilibrium that suits the private interests of those concerned. For society, however, underlap can be a lot more damaging than overlap. The world discovered exactly that when it bore the costs of the distance between central bankers and regulators in the two main international financial centers over the decade or so leading up to 2007/2008.[23]

The case *for* independent central banks taking on the stability role is, therefore, essentially to combine credible commitment with reduced barriers to policy coordination. The argument *against* such a role rests on the possibility of conflicts of interest.

Moral Hazard from Insuring Liquidity and Macrostability

People, businesses, and financial intermediaries plausibly take more risk than otherwise, including taking on too much debt, due to central banks' role as the LOLR to the financial system and as the authority that seeks to smooth the economy's ups and downs.[24] While this has attracted attention since talk of the "Greenspan put" during the 1990s, it is not obvious that it should knock central banks out of contention for formal regulatory and supervisory responsibilities. After all, these various moral hazard risks are no smaller when a separate body is the regulator.

[23] In the UK, confidence that information would flow smoothly was strongly, but naively and damagingly, asserted (Roll et al., *Independent and Accountable*, pp. 44 and 68).

[24] Miller, Weller, and Zhang, "Moral Hazard," and Farhi and Tirole, "Collective Moral Hazard."

Indeed, there is a case for allocating control of the regulatory mitigants to the generator of the monetary moral hazard problem. Because the behavioral response to central banks' expected LOLR and monetary policy actions increases their exposure to financial risk and to falling short on their objectives, they have incentives to be tough regulators. By contrast, especially if under pressure from politicians or industry to soften the regime, a third-party regulator might be tempted to rely partly on the prospect of monetary bailout if things turn out badly, as it does not itself incur the costs of the central banks' ex post interventions.

The same cannot be said of the forbearance argument. It comes in two forms.

Forbearance In Monetary Policy Induced by Prudential Responsibilities

The first forbearance hazard is that a monetary policy maker will defer a needed tightening of monetary conditions if it would tip some banks over the edge into failure. As summarized by Steve Cecchetti as the 2007 phase of the Great Financial Crisis was unfolding:[25]

> The most compelling argument for separation is the potential for conflict of interest. . . . The central bank will protect banks rather than the public interest. Making banks look bad makes supervisors look bad. So, allowing banks to fail would affect the central banker-supervisor's reputation.

Since our argument for delegation-with-insulation rests on harnessing IAs to their preoccupations with reputation, this obviously matters. It underlines the massive importance of the point made above about effective resolution regimes: they must be used to liberate supervisors from fear of failing banks, and monetary policy makers from any temptation to soften policy merely to bail out their supervisory colleagues.

[25] Cecchetti, "Financial Supervisors." Also, Copelovitch and Singer, "Financial Regulation," which appeals to a structural explanation from Dewatripont, Jewitt, and Tirole, "Economics of Career Concerns." The central difference with this book is that, under the Multiple-Mission Constraints, each mission is delegated to a distinct committee, whereas Dewatripont et al. have a unitary policy maker.

Forbearance in Prudential Policy Induced by Constrained Monetary Capabilities

The other form of the forbearance problem might, I suspect, be less tractable for policy makers. It could occur where a central bank avoided tightening prudential limits on banks because it feared that it did not have the monetary ammunition (say, because interest rates are close to zero) to offset any temporary hit to economic growth if, as a result, credit supply contracted. Of course, deferral merely raises the probability of a banking crisis further down the line. If by then the monetary arm had restored its ammunition (interest rates have risen), forbearance might have paid off. If not, forbearance made things worse. This accusation has been leveled over recent years at the authorities in Continental Europe, where banking fragilities have lingered longer than elsewhere.

Under the Principles for Delegation, there are two mitigants. The first, discussed in the next chapter, is a monitorable objective, so that a forbearing supervisor finds it hard to hide. The second lies in the separate policy committees demanded by the Multiple-Mission Constraints: the prudential committee must do what is right under its mandate, outvoting its central bank chair if necessary. If that would bring disaster upon the economy, the problem should be taken to elected politicians since the overall monetary regime would be in a corner.

SUMMING UP

Overall, this canter around the long-standing issue of whether central banks should be banking supervisors points toward a healthy conclusion: that by virtue of their (if only latent) pragmatic authority as the monetary system's pivot, they cannot sensibly be excluded (or exclude themselves) from regulation and supervision of the financial system, but nor can they make a unique claim that only they should regulate or supervise in the cause of system stability. Our interest, however, is not whether central banks *must* be the financial stability authority but, rather, whether their being granted that role would violate our democratic values and norms. So far, it would seem not.

A Shift Away from Cruder Forms of New Public Management

This chapter has, then, put flesh on the assertion in the preface that formally delegating power in one area sometimes unavoidably entails bestowing de facto power in others. On the view presented in this book (part II), it is much better, given the values of constitutional democracy, to formalize, circumscribe, and structure that involvement.

Clearly, this does not fit at all with one of the core precepts of New Public Management (NPM), which advocated *one function per agency* in order to enhance accountability.[26] In the UK, I suspect that NPM was a subtle (and baleful) influence on the 1997 decision to transfer prudential supervision away from the Bank of England. That mattered beyond Britain's shores. Given London's position as a global financial center and given that various other countries, including China and Korea, followed the UK, at least in some cases probably encouraged by the IMF, the UK contrived to put the world onto a false, even delusional, path. Administrative fashions come unstuck eventually, and this one did so spectacularly.

While one could despair at the mechanical application of NPM doctrine, that would miss the bigger picture, because there should be no doubting the hazards this multiple-mission project entails. They are substantive, cultural, and political.

A Money-Credit Constitution

First, we need a way of joining up the central banking regimes necessary for monetary-system stability: not so much a "monetary constitution" of the kind advocated by James Buchanan but, instead, a *Money-Credit Constitution* (MCC).

By that, I mean rules of the game for banking and central banking designed to ensure broad monetary-system stability. An MCC would cover the constraints on the business and risks in banking and what central banks must do (their mandate), may do, and may not do—all grounded in shared principles so as to generate a coherent whole. A polity's MCC would operate as a political norm, not necessarily formally

[26] Hood, "Public Management."

entrenched but, at least, embedded as a convention inhabiting the space, discussed in chapters 8 and 12, between politics and law.

This idea would have been familiar to our nineteenth- and early-twentieth-century predecessors. Their Money-Credit Constitution comprised the gold standard, a reserves requirement for private banks (an indirect claim on the central bank's gold pool), and the lender-of-last-resort function celebrated by the mid-nineteenth-century British journalist Walter Bagehot.[27] That package was deficient insofar as it did not provide explicitly for solvency crises as opposed to liquidity crises. Worse, as our economies moved to embrace fiat money during the twentieth century, policy makers relaxed the connection between the nominal anchor and the binding constraint on bank balance sheets so comprehensively that it became nonexistent.

At a schematic level, a Money-Credit Constitution for today might have five components: a target for inflation (or some other nominal magnitude), a requirement to hold reserves (or assets readily exchanged for reserves) that increases with a bank's leverage/riskiness and social significance, a liquidity reinsurance regime for fundamentally solvent banks, a resolution regime for bankrupt banks, and constraints on how far the central bank is free to pursue its mandate and structure its balance sheet.

While for the time being leaving open the key policy decisions on how resilient the private part of the monetary system should be (chapter 21), this structural benchmark makes clear that constraints on and, thus, supervision of banking soundness are integral to an economy's Money-Credit Constitution.[28] Both are indeed conditions for the legiti-

[27] Bagehot, *Lombard Street.*

[28] On a broad point of substance, the constraints on banking would take the following general shape: X percent of the face value of short-term liabilities (S) to be "covered" by holdings of liquid assets, discounted to the value attributed to them by the central bank (d.LA); residual assets ((1-d).LA plus assets ineligible at the central bank) to be funded in prescribed minimum proportions by common equity (K) and debt that can be converted into equity without disruption (known as bail in-able debt, B), plus any "uncovered" short-term liabilities ((1-x).S). K and B could be higher, the riskier or lumpier the asset portfolio. Where X is set at 100 percent, this delivers full liquid assets cover for short-term liabilities, an idea first floated in the Bank of England by David Rule when, before the Great Financial Crisis, we were thinking about contingency plans for a 9/11-type disaster. A permanent version, structured as a public facility, is advocated in King, *End of Alchemy.* Under such a scheme, ongoing industry lobbying (and associated political pressure) would be directed at the definition of short-term liabilities, the population of eligible instruments, and the level of haircuts.

macy of private banking itself, given the privilege of access to the lender of last resort and officially imposed barriers to entry. But, compared with twentieth-century doctrine, and given endemic regulatory arbitrage and legion financial-system interconnections, the focus would be on the economic substance of *banking* (maturity transformation, leverage, and credit intermediation) rather than solely on intermediaries having the legal form of "banks."

Challenges for Multiple-Mission Central Banks: Culture

Quite apart from whether satisfactorily constrained purposes, objectives, and powers can be framed, a multiple-mission central bank entrusted with such a Money-Credit Constitution faces serious cultural and political challenges.

A central bank involved in preserving stability must know many things. Whereas a monetary policy maker needs to know about the real economy and about how interest rates are transmitted via the money markets, a stability policy maker must also have deep knowledge, practical as well as theoretical, about financial institutions and about financial markets and infrastructure that they do not themselves routinely operate in or use. A multiple-mission central bank must be, in an overworked metaphor, a fox as well as a hedgehog.[29] It cannot be the sole preserve or domain of macroeconomics PhDs.

This partial resurrection of an older central banking mind-set, allying eclecticism with formal analysis, can be reconciled with the demands of legitimacy only by, following the Multiple-Mission Constraints, fracturing formal power across separate policy committees served by a unitary staff.

Challenges: Politics

Up to a point, central bank leaders can shape their organization's culture. But they cannot shape or control politics, and a multiple-mission central bank touches politics in hazardous ways. The credit system in-

[29] For a comparison between hedgehog-like monetary institutions and fox-like competition authorities, see Vickers, "Central Banks." Viewed with hindsight, Vickers's essay can be read, perhaps, as an unintentionally elegant account of what was set to go wrong in the preservation of broad monetary stability (as defined in the main text).

volves the allocation of resources within the economy; regulation entails writing rules and being subject to legal challenge; and supervision (backed by regulatory powers) entails making judgments on and taking action with respect to individual firms. Any and all of those activities can politicize central banks, whereas the whole point of independent monetary authorities is insulation from the political fray.

In particular, involvement in regulation and supervision creates incentives for the regulated industry (and its political sponsors) to "capture" the central bank, if only via cognitive dependence on technical input in a complex field.[30] Alternatively, if the central bank is tough with the banks, it creates an "official opposition," which lobbies both the elected executive and legislative arms of government against the supervisor, politicizing the regime.

In navigating this terrain, a central bank regulator must, like any regulator, strike a balance between interventionism and benign neglect. Given that prudential regimes are directed at market failure, a regulator/supervisor cannot be a fully signed-up disciple of "laissez faire" without failing in its duties to the people. The neoliberal world-view that critics from the Left sometimes associate with monetary authorities is not sustainable in multiple-mission central banks. But that gives rise to a corresponding worry on the Right that central banks might develop an interventionist, even dirigiste, temperament, with the costs of government failure amplified by central banks' insulation from day-to-day political direction.

For each and all of these reasons, there are voices within central banking who oppose taking on any role beyond maintaining price stability. I have argued that this amounts to mythmaking: the myth that they are not involved when, in reality, they are.

LOOKING FORWARD: CENTRAL BANK DESIGN

In the following chapters, therefore, guided by the Principles for Delegation to independent agencies developed in parts I–III, we sketch the options for operationalizing a Money-Credit Constitution.[31] This

[30] Carpenter and Moss, *Preventing Regulatory Capture*; and, in particular, the chapter by James Kwak, "Cultural Capture and the Financial Crisis."

[31] Among other recent similar exercises: Balls et al., "Central Bank Independence."

entails examining stability-oriented prudential policy (chapter 21), using the central bank's balance sheet as an instrument of credit policy (chapter 22), and fashioning emergency LOLR policy (chapter 23), which, respectively, correspond to central banking's place in the regulatory state, the fiscal state, and the emergency state. The purpose is not to arrive at definitive answers, which might reasonably differ to some degree across jurisdictions, but rather to help inform public debate by putting bounds around the decently available options given the political values underpinning the Principles.

21

Central Banking and the Regulatory State

STABILITY POLICY

> If society wanted a largely risk-free financial system, [the authorities] could indeed produce one. But this would only be at enormous cost . . . [in terms] of the services to industry and commerce.
>
> —Eddie George, shortly after becoming Bank of England governor, 1993[1]

The previous chapter argued that since society is clearly averse to financial crises and that since there is a problem of credibly committing to a policy designed to keep crisis at bay, stability policy might be delegated to a trustee-type independent agency. Those, however, are only some of the prerequisites. Under our Principles for Delegation, any such regime would need to set the agency clear goals, avoid conferring powers to make big distributional choices, sanction only necessary interferences with individual freedoms, require publication of the *operating principles* that guide the exercise of regulatory discretion, and compel transparency in the service of contestability, public debate, and political accountability. In short, the outputs and outcomes of policy would need to be sufficiently visible.

This chapter is about how to confine and structure the regulatory role of central banks to achieve that. As a step toward marking out the broad outline of a monitorable objective, we begin with the nature of the problem that an independent stability authority could decently address.

[1]George, "Pursuit," p. 61.

A LIMITED STABILITY MANDATE FOR INDEPENDENT CENTRAL BANKS

The various pathologies or frictions in the financial system give rise to two distinguishable types of social cost:[2]

- *Boom*: A misallocation of resources and, in particular, overaccumulation of debt, which matter whether or not booms end in busts.[3]
- *Bust*: A collapse in asset values and a withdrawal of or severe tightening in the supply of essential financial services following a crisis at some intermediaries, bringing about a macroeconomic downturn and social distress.

Both are products of negative externalities (chapter 3). Society cannot sit back and rely on private virtue, prudence, or incentives to ensure allocative efficiency or intertemporal stability, because the private benefits of socially destructive behavior within the financial system exceed the private costs.

The drivers of the first type of social cost—misallocated resources and overindebtedness—include myopia and incentives to herd: the problem of a financial-system party that has slipped into drunkenness. They are grasped in only broad or qualitative terms, typically involve some violation of "rationality," and so, today, are hard to predict or model. That being so, a system designed to *fine-tune* credit and asset-price dynamics would be too ambitious for delegation-with-insulation, as we do not know how to frame a monitorable objective that would, if achieved, deliver an agreed purpose. While the ratio of outstanding credit to aggregate national income (or a ratio of their growth rates) could be set as an objective, it is not yet clear how well that connects to things we care about, nor whether available policy instruments could steer it reliably or predictably. Political policy makers might take on that mission but, under the Principles, not insulated technocrats.

[2]This chapter draws on Tucker, *Financial Stability Regimes*. For international variety in stability regimes, see Liang and Edge, "New Financial Stability Governance Structures."

[3]Borio et al., "Labour Reallocation and Productivity Dynamics."

The second type of social cost—chaos followed by severe economic downturn—is both more salient with the public and better understood by technocrats. It is driven by fire sales of assets, contagion, and the dislocations entailed by intermediaries entering bankruptcy, when the shutters come down and liquidators look after the private interests of creditors, not the wider economy and society. The remedy is a resilient financial system that can continue functioning in the event of bankruptcies and distress. In this case, the instruments are relatively straightforward: when banking institutions are required to increase their equity, most likely there is a proportionate increase in the scale of losses it would take to push a bank over the edge in most states of the world. I argue, furthermore, that a regime for system resilience *can* be given a monitorable objective. The effect is to sidestep the imponderable difficulty of defining, and hence of measuring and monitoring, *financial stability* or *financial instability*.[4]

Institutionally, this fits with the previous chapter's articulation of the central banking mission as *broad monetary-system stability*. Thus, a Principles-compliant Money-Credit Constitution would preclude central banks from intervening in market malfunctions, including some asset-price booms, that jeopardize the efficient allocation of resources in the economy but not the financial system's resilience. Nor would it be a regime directed toward actively managing credit conditions for different sectors or regions, since that would violate the Delegation Criteria's bar on distributional choices and on objectives that cannot be monitored.

Regulatory Mandates That Independent Central Banks Should Not Be Given

Further, following the Principles and our definition of *monetary-system stability*, central banks should *not* be responsible for

- competition policy, which would make them more powerful than they need to be, and therefore too powerful;

[4]Chapter 23's discussion of central banks' role in crisis management offers a different but complementary solution.

- the structure of the financial services industry, as it involves high-level trade-offs between efficiency and resilience;
- its external competitiveness, as that invites political pressure to relax resilience standards and adopt "light-touch regulation";
- sponsoring the industry's interests in government or in society, which would be liable to lead to capture by sectoral interests and so to lower resilience than desired;
- consumer protection, which would confuse the public about the nature of a broader "stability" mandate, as well as taking most central bankers beyond their comfort zone and vocational drive; and
- market regulation, as it unavoidably incorporates consumer protection and, separately, would make central banks too powerful (the Fed plus SEC!).

This catalog is not insignificant looking across the world of central banking today, some of whose powers could be delegated elsewhere.[5]

More to the point, it also invites the question, How resilient should the system be, and who should decide?

FRAMING A STANDARD FOR SYSTEM RESILIENCE: POLITICS, TRADE-OFFS, AND PUBLIC DEBATE

If the public policy purpose of a central banking stability mandate should be continuity of services from the system as a whole, thus avoiding the worst costs of "bust," the core of the regime must be a monitorable *standard of resilience*. That much is entailed by the first Design Precept, cast as a revived "nondelegation doctrine" in part III (chapter 14). The big questions are what it means in principle and in practice.

Roughly speaking, policy makers need to determine the severity of shock that the system should be able to withstand. In principle, that would be driven by three things:

[5] It would, therefore, be good for the Fed to lose its residual consumer protection functions. If, nevertheless, the legislature does delegate any of those, or other, tasks, it is the central bank's democratic duty to pursue those responsibilities with as much vigor and professionalism as it brings to its monetary stability functions. The legitimacy of the central bank regime would, however, be fragile.

1. A view of the underlying (stochastic) process generating the first-round losses from end borrowers that hit the system
2. A picture (or model) of the structure of the financial system through which those losses and other shocks are transmitted around the system
3. A tolerance for systemic crisis

The first and second are properly objects of scientific inquiry by technocrats and researchers. The third is different. Whereas the central belief of monetary economics relevant to the design of policy institutions is that there is no *long-run* trade-off to speak of between economic activity and inflation, we do not yet know enough to judge whether prosperity would be damaged by totally eliminating the risk-taking structures that can threaten periodic bouts of instability.[6] As I recollect former UK Treasury secretary George Osborne putting it, no one wants the stability of the graveyard. How much residual systemic risk to permit is, in democratic societies, properly a matter for democratic debate and choice, as Eddie George had signaled a generation earlier in the remarks quoted at the chapter head.

The "tolerance for crisis" that, in principle, elected politicians would bless needs unpacking. Crisis/noncrisis is not binary but more akin to Dante's Circles of Hell: there are degrees of awfulness. In 2008/2009, policy makers avoided a repeat of the 1930s Great Depression. The next generation must (and can) improve on that: the improvements to, for example, resolution regimes drawn on in the previous chapter will not eliminate banking system distress but can contain its social costs better than in the past.

In consequence, we should think in terms of society's tolerance for different bad states of the world. The spectrum ranges from, at one end, all core services ceasing to be provided to, at the other end, severe impairment of only one broad type of service. Abstractly, we could conceive of a vector specifying, for a series of core financial services, that society would not tolerate a probability of greater than p of there being a reduction of x percent or more in the provision of service i. Thus, we might plausibly impose a probability of very close to 0 percent on a seizure of the payments system causing us to have to resort to bar-

[6] Ranciere et al., "Systemic Crises."

ter (as happened in parts of the United States during the 1930s) but a slightly higher probability of a temporary interruption in bank lending or insurance.

In practice, politicians need to decide (or bless) a basic resilience requirement for core intermediaries (constraints on their balance sheets and interconnectedness). That cannot come out of the sky but must reflect judgments on (1) and (2) above and also on the effectiveness of other policies and instruments, including how far the provision of core services could be maintained (a) by resolving or transferring the functions of failed intermediaries and (b) via replacement capacity entering the market.

Even armed with those judgments, however, it would hardly be realistic to ask politicians or the public a question as raw as, "What is your tolerance for financial crisis?" Nevertheless, technocratic policy makers can help frame debate about what scenarios financial systems should be able to withstand, offering estimates of how likely they are. I doubt, for example, that European policy makers believe their banking system should be unscathed if an asteroid completely destroyed the United States (and its economy). But it seems likely that the public wants the kind of banking-system implosion that destabilized the world in 2008/2009 to occur less frequently than every seventy-five years. The advent of public stress testing of banks and others, discussed below, can help to inform that badly needed debate.

An International Standard of Resilience Already Exists

However ethereal this might seem, I want to insist that something like a tolerance for crisis is already, and unavoidably, implicit in existing regulatory standards, such as the Basel III Accord for banks. When it was blessed by G20 leaders and, in Europe, formally passed into EU law by the Council and Parliament, politicians surely understood that they could have chosen a much tougher or much lighter standard.[7] I want to argue that, under the Principles for Delegation, in the interests of effectiveness and legitimacy, what the standard means (the accepted re-

[7] Paragraph 29 of the communique of the Seoul G20 Summit, November 2010.

sidual tolerance for crisis) should become as explicit as possible, if only by way of illustrative examples.

It is no accident that these are international minimum standards. Given the spillovers from problems in one country's financial system to other economies, a state of affairs where each jurisdiction unilaterally chooses its own resilience standard would not be sustainable. Either the world shifts toward financial autarky or reconciles itself to the existence of a global commons (see below) that demands a shared minimum standard for resilience. Its collective endorsement by national democratic leaders needs, therefore, to be underpinned by national consultation and challenge, in line with the Delegation Criteria, if further articulation and implementation is to be delegated.

IMPLEMENTING THE RESILIENCE STANDARD: INSULATED TECHNOCRATS

Having chosen (or blessed) a high-level resilience standard or benchmark in the light of such public debate, on the argument of the previous chapter elected politicians would desirably delegate its implementation to a highly insulated agency, given their own incentives to relax constraints on finance for short-term benefit. The chosen long-term trade-off would, thereby, be nailed to a mast, subject to override/amendment only through overt, formal steps that the public could observe, consistent with our "audience costs" theory of delegation under "democracy as watchfulness" (part II).[8]

Thus, independent agencies, including potentially a multiple-mission central bank, would be mandated to

1. Apply the resilience standard as formally specified to a particular well-defined domain of intermediaries (e.g., banks)[9]

[8]Thanks to Riccardo Reiss for exchanges on how the combination of a long-run trade-off with short-term trade-offs can strengthen the case for delegation-with-insulation if the people's representatives wish to commit to striking the trade-off in a particular way.

[9]Strictly, this ought to reflect the circumstances of particular jurisdictions. Where, as currently in parts of the euro area, an economy is less flexible and so less able to absorb nasty shocks without loss of activity and jobs or where an economy has a weak fiscal regime so that government does not have the option of supporting aggregate demand in a downturn, individual finan-

2. Apply the same underlying tolerance for crisis to other sectors and activities, adapting the regulatory standard's form and substance to take account of the nature and degree of the threat they pose to systemwide resilience (Design Precept 1)
3. Explain publicly and consult formally on how those sector or activity characteristics have been taken into account (Design Precepts 2 and 4)

In that way, the articulation and application of the resilience standard across the financial system would have democratic credentials without legislators having to work out all the details themselves, consistent with chapter 10's conditions for delegated rule writing.

That is not the end of it, however. Any set of regulatory requirements calibrated to deliver the desired standard for resilience in more or less normal conditions might prove insufficient in the face of extraordinarily strong booms or changes in the structures through which losses are transmitted around the financial system. In what has become known as *macroprudential* policy, the stability authority would, accordingly, also be mandated to make dynamic adjustments to regulatory requirements where warranted to sustain the desired degree of system resilience.[10]

While all that is a formidable endeavor, the IA's job is not exhausted by regulatory rule writing and adjustment. There is another layer of complexity with major implications for the monitorability of a resilience standard, and so for the feasibility of democratic oversight of the post-crisis central banks.

System Resilience as a Common Good Plagued by Hidden-Action Problems

The resilience of individual financial intermediaries is not akin to the resilience of individual airplanes. Some aircraft share common components, but each one is not invariably put in jeopardy by problems in other models. In the financial system, intermediaries are so interconnected that a serious problem almost anywhere can bring down the ceiling.

---

cial intermediaries need to be stronger in order to meet the desired system-wide standard for resilience.

[10]Too often described as *macroprudential instruments*, they are standard prudential regulatory measures used in pursuit of macroprudential (or systemwide) goals.

Those direct and indirect exposures and dependencies are almost impossible to avoid. As customers, we do not all use the same intermediary, so they have to meet on our behalf via settlement systems and the money markets through which an economy's financial transactions are effected and the intermediaries' books are balanced. Smaller intermediaries depend on larger firms for what amount to infrastructural services, such as clearing, custody, and liquidity insurance. Efficiency is served through the competition that the interdependencies permit.

Making good an assertion in chapter 3, this means that the financial system's resilience can be thought of as a *common good*: the benefits accrue to everyone but can be eroded by individual members of the system. Each has incentives to take more risks than they would willingly incur if the system were not believed to be resilient. So as long as they are not spotted, they will be undercharged for risk by their customers and market counterparts. Since firms seem to care about relative short-term performance, it is hard for them to stay virtuous. If, however, many firms succumb, in aggregate some of the resilience of the system as a whole is eroded, invalidating the assumption upon which their private risk appetites were predicated. This is an example of the *problem of the commons*, where historically individuals would overuse the common grazing land, leaving everybody worse off.[11]

Unlike a local, physical commons, the erosion of the financial system's resilience creeps up on us, because firms are able to disguise their true condition via what economists call *hidden actions*. The financial community is now too diverse and scattered to self-police. When, instead, the state writes rules to constrain intermediaries' balance-sheet choices, regulated firms find ways of taking more risk than contemplated in the calibration of those rules; and unregulated intermediaries structure themselves so as to stay outside the scope of the rules even though the economic substance of their business is essentially the same. In other words, finance is a shape-shifter. Regulatory arbitrage is endemic, and the rule writers can end up chasing their tails.

On this way of thinking, the Great Financial Crisis was waiting to happen. That it was triggered by the relatively small US subprime mortgage market reveals that the system's resilience was wafer thin. It had

[11] Ostrom, *Governing the Commons*.

been eaten away over the preceding years by the dynamics of the system itself.

Microprudential supervision, focused on hidden actions, is called into existence to break this problem. It occupies a distinct space between financial stability policy making and the enforcement of the rule books in which headline capital, liquidity, and other requirements are enshrined.

To sum up so far, unlike price stability, the authorities cannot "produce" financial stability by their own efforts but must stop or deter private intermediaries from eroding the system's resilience.

Micro- and Macroprudential Supervision Don't Really Exist (on Their Own)

That cannot be delivered by looking at intermediaries one by one because the financial system is just that—a *system*, with component parts connected within sectors, across sectors and markets, via interactions with the real economy, and across countries. As the first chairman of the Basel Supervisors Committee, George Blunden, whom we met in chapter 11, said in the mid-1980s: [12]

> It is part of the [supervisor's] job to take [a] wider systemic view and sometimes to curb practices which even prudent banks might, if left to themselves, regard as safe.

Somehow that fundamental insight got lost over the following two decades. While some regulatory actions and some supervisory activities are directed at "atoms" and others at aggregates, they serve a common purpose. In consequence:

- The standard microprudential statutory objective of ensuring the "safety and soundness" of individual intermediaries should be framed explicitly in terms of system resilience and stability (as in the UK's 2012 legislation).[13]
- That means not trying to achieve zero failures.

[12]George Blunden, "Supervision and Central Banking," pp. 380–385. Blunden had by then retired as chair of the Basel Committee but had returned to office as deputy governor of the Bank of England.

[13]Cast in terms of ensuring intermediaries carry on business in ways that avoid adverse effects on stability, and minimizing the expected effect of their failure on stability.

- It is hard, but not impossible, completely to separate responsibility for system stability from microprudential supervision.[14]
- But, following the Multiple-Mission Constraints, where combined in the central bank, microprudential supervision should be delegated to a distinct committee given the adjudicatory nature of its outputs.

In what has amounted to a macroprudential reorientation of banking and financial policy, this is a world where independent stability authorities are more than writers of legally binding rules and regulations. Alone, or together with similarly insulated sector-specialist agencies, they monitor intermediaries, infrastructure, and markets, making adjudicatory judgments.

Given this is a problem of the commons, their chances of deterring resilience-depleting regulatory arbitrage and stability-threatening recovery strategies are likely to be improved somewhat if they enjoy some pragmatic authority among members of the financial community as well as the derivative legitimacy available to well-designed IAs (the important distinction made in the introduction to part II). Such pragmatic authority is less likely to prevail in countries, such as the US, that set up agencies with overlapping jurisdictions. Any benefits from regulatory competition are liable to be outweighed, in the field of stability policy, by a retreat to measures that depend on the credibility of formal enforcement.

Rules versus Standards: Judgment-Based Supervision

Stability policy therefore confronts the issue around rules versus standards discussed in chapter 8. As we described there, today most parts of the regulatory state adopt a rules-based approach in order to guard against the exercise of arbitrary power: everybody knows what is being demanded of the regulated community, and proposed rules can be exposed to consultation and challenge. We have argued in this chapter, however, that rules provide a shaky foundation for stability policy given endemic avoidance and evasion. Policy makers are left in a game of

[14]Germany has an interesting system where the Bundesbank makes microprudential inputs to BaFin and macroprudential recommendations to the ministry without being formally responsible for decisions in either sphere.

catch-up—one they are bound to lose. A compliance-based approach of identifying and punishing rule breaches after the financial system has imploded, creating economic havoc, does not exactly rise to the seriousness of the stability mission.

Instead, the microsupervisor has to be ready and able to make judgments of the following kind: "Firm X is managed so imprudently that there is no reasonable prospect of its meeting the required standard of resilience in the states of the world it is likely to confront." Where that judgment is reached, the microsupervisor needs to be ready (and legally empowered) to revoke the firm's license or place (monitorable and enforceable) constraints on its risk taking.

The basic criteria (standards) underpinning the supervisor's findings—for example, prudence, competent management, a separation of powers within the intermediary—have to be established in statute and interpreted in light of the regime's purpose. When applying them to individual firms, the microsupervisor is called upon to comply with the canons of procedural fairness and reason summarized in parts II and III.

THE POTENTIAL FUNCTIONS AND STRUCTURE OF A MULTIPLE-MISSION CENTRAL BANK

The potential functions of the postcrisis central banks are now clearer. While the core standard of resilience should carry some kind of political sanction, a central bank trustee of broad monetary-system stability could in principle play a role in

1. Calibrating how that standard is applied to the banking system (broadly defined) and, conceivably, to other parts of the financial system
2. Microprudential supervision of banking intermediaries at or toward the core of the payments system (chapter 20)
3. Microprudential supervision to detect and deter hidden actions of other individual firms, funds, structures, and so on, that might need liquidity reinsurance to maintain the provision of core services to the economy

4. Surveillance of the system as a whole to identify vulnerabilities
5. Dynamic "macroprudential" adjustment of regulatory requirements to maintain the desired degree of resilience in exuberant conditions
6. Deploying crisis management tools and policies, notably as the lender of last resort (chapter 23)

It hardly needs saying that such a central bank's stability arm would be very powerful. It would also face being unpopular whenever regulatory requirements were temporarily tightened to maintain the resilience of the system in the face of a boom. Bankers, financiers, elected politicians, and great swathes of the public would then likely find common cause in complaining about central bankers spoiling the party on the basis of their supposedly higher wisdom.

This is not theoretical. Among the advanced-democracy central banks, the Bank of England unambiguously has all six roles (not exclusively in every one of them), with the Fed and ECB differing only in having, respectively, slightly more limited or informal macroprudential responsibilities and powers.

We have already discussed the importance, if legitimacy is not to be sacrificed, of a democratic imprimatur for the resilience standard itself, and we identified missions that a central bank should *not* be granted. Drawing on the Principles for Delegation, the remainder of this chapter turns to constraints on powers, structure, operating principles, and political accountability.

Limited Powers: No Disproportionality or Big Redistributional Choices

The Principles for Delegation stipulate that big distributional choices are precluded and that rule making must be proportionate to the regime's purpose. This means that each and every potential regulatory (or "macroprudential") instrument must be assessed for whether it would take central banks into the arena of political choice or unnecessarily interfere in liberal freedoms (chapters 10 and 11).

That those constraints could bite is illustrated by what has, for the moment, almost become the most popular "macroprudential" lever: setting and adjusting limits on how much people can borrow to buy a house or for other purposes relative to the value of the property or to their income (known, respectively, as *loan-to-value* and *loan-to-income ratios*).

Applying the Principles, it would be inappropriate for an independent agency (as opposed to the elected executive) to be able to set maximum loan-to-value (LTV) or loan-to-income (LTI) ratios for products available to households (and/or nonfinancial businesses). Such constraints could deprive some households (or such businesses) of opportunities even though they understood and were capable of meeting the obligation to repay due to, say, excellent prospects. As such, those measures would reduce liberty (on its liberal conception) and thus seem unsuitable for delegation to policy makers who do not have to seek reelection—unless they were the only available instrument for ensuring the resilience of the financial system, which they are not.[15]

An alternative approach, adopted by the Bank of England in 2014, would be to place a cap on the percentage of any lender's portfolio that could be accounted for by, say, high loan-to-value mortgages. This focuses on the resilience of the financial system itself, without venturing into laying down the law on the services and products available to households and businesses. One course seems to fit with insulated unelected power, the other does not. And it can probably deliver that without sacrificing the greater salience with the public of LTV and LTI limits compared to banks' capital requirements.

In a broadly similar vein, a central bank regulator should be constrained from getting into regional or sectoral policy. Plainly, there are sometimes particular hot spots in property and other markets, but that is not a concern to our Principles-compliant central bank regulator unless the resilience of the system as a whole is threatened. That is rarely the case. The public and politicians should not look to their central bank to cure housing bubbles in particular towns and districts, even though they could end in hardship for local people.

[15] This stricture would not apply to placing limits on the leverage provided to other financial intermediaries in the interest of maintaining the resilience of the system via, say, minimum margin requirements on derivatives transactions or minimum excess collateral requirements on secured loans (repos).

Fragmenting Power: A System of Specialist Committees

The Principles are also clear on internal structure. As argued in the previous chapter, there should be separate policy committees for each regime delegated to a central bank.

Like the monetary policy committee, the stability committee must meet regularly given a potential bias to inaction. Faced with uncertain long-term benefits but a risk of unpopularity, policy makers might incline toward delaying action until the resilience-eroding threats of exuberance or imbalances are widely perceived.[16] The solution is to make clear that *doing nothing is doing something.* That can be achieved by having the stability committee formally reset various core regulatory instruments at fixed intervals, with published minutes giving reasons for its decisions, including "no change."

That is, more or less, the postcrisis setup in the UK.[17] It is approximated in the euro area, with the ECB having separate monetary and microsupervisory committees, albeit with the former having a right to override the latter (and both being too big to be deliberative bodies).[18]

It is also approximated in the Fed's long-standing structure, with regulatory and monetary responsibilities split between the Federal Reserve Board and the Federal Open Market Committee (FOMC). In the spirit of the Principles, policy makers who are members only of the FOMC owe the public a duty not to sound as if the FOMC is (or should be) the "macroprudential" body or as if they have personally been delegated responsibility for stability by Congress when, in fact, they have

[16] This point was made eloquently by my old friend Nederlandsche Bank senior official Aerdt Houben at a conference held by CIGI with the Bank of Canada, the IMF, and the Peterson Institute in Ottawa in May 2016.

[17] The Bank of England has separate statutory committees responsible for micro- and macroprudential policy, essentially so that a majority on the latter are not infected by any lapses in micro-oversight and to draw on different types of technocratic skill (see below in main text). Reflecting proposals that George Blunden and I had each aired in the late 1970s, mid-1980s, early 1990s, and late 2000s, the micro body was initially established, on the French model, as a formal subsidiary in order, among other things, to give the external members a statutory role in internal organization given that some supervisory outputs are effected at desk level.

[18] The euro area's macroprudential structure is much more complicated, involving the Commission and others.

not. They *are* in a position, as FOMC members, to press the Board to act on risks to system resilience that they see as posing a threat to their monetary policy objective.

TRANSPARENCY AND ACCOUNTABILITY

The final vital preconditions for legitimacy that central banking stability regimes must satisfy are public debate and political accountability (Design Precepts 3 and 4). Here nothing short of a revolution is needed, but, thanks to innovations during the crisis, it might be under way.

Transparency for Operating Principles

If the watchword for microprudential supervision is adjudicatory and judgmental *fairness*, the counterpart for dynamic macroprudential policy is *systematic*. Both can be advanced through transparency around general policy and approach.

On the microsupervisory side, central banks must be fair in the sense of being consistent across different cases and over time. To that end, under Design Precept 3, as well as making clear how far they plan to rely on the enforcement of rules and how far on applying broad statutory standards via supervisory judgment, they should publish how they will assess requirements such as "prudence" in a way that furthers (and is limited to) the objective of system resilience.

On the macroprudential side, the policy committee must similarly publish an account of how it believes each of its instruments works; which is best suited to what kind of circumstances; and how it would choose between instruments when more than one might work. In the UK, legislation requires just that. In the US, although not required by law to do so, the Federal Reserve Board has published its framework for setting the countercyclical capital buffer and for countercyclical elements in the stress tests mandated by Dodd-Frank.[19]

[19] Regulatory Capital Rules: The Federal Reserve Board's Framework for Implementing the U.S. Basel III Countercyclical Capital Buffer, https://www.federalreserve.gov/newsevents/press-

The Problem of Monitoring Prudential Supervision

However worthwhile in exposing general policy to debate, those steps toward greater transparency would not scratch the surface of the prudential-supervision accountability problem. As noted in chapter 7, while *regulatory* outputs—rules and regulations—are obviously observable, historically the activities of prudential *supervisors* have been largely invisible, except to the individual regulated firms themselves. Neither *outputs* nor *outcomes* have been monitorable.

This is not an accident. Within the community of prudential supervisors, sensitivity to the social costs of firm failure long ago gave rise to a culture, a doctrine even, that their work must be confidential: that the world would not be safe if they revealed what they knew about firms' weaknesses or what remedial actions they were requiring or urging. Although those worries are understandable, they are, under the lights of the Principles, completely at odds with a parallel conviction of the regulatory community that prudential supervisors should be insulated from day-to-day politics.

Thus, even if a central bank (or other insulated) supervisor can itself monitor whether the system satisfies the resilience standard outlined earlier in the chapter, how can we, the people, and our elected representatives monitor their monitoring? Surely, if prudential supervision *must* be opaque, then it should be open to day-to-day political control.[20]

Fortunately, a solution might be in prospect. The enhanced regimes for resolving distressed firms in an orderly way can reduce the social costs of a firm's weakness becoming apparent, enabling supervisors to be braver about transparency. And, crucially, one of the US authorities' innovations during the 2008–2009 phase of the crisis has given supervisors something concrete and important to say.

---

releases/bcreg20160908b.htm. Policy statement on the scenario design framework for stress testing: https://www.federalreserve.gov/supervisionreg/dfa-stress-tests.

[20] This problem is recognized but, in my view, not solved in Amtenbrink and Lastra, "Securing Democratic Accountability."

Stress Testing: Finally, Something to Say in Public

Since the spring of 2009, the Federal Reserve has led the world in seeking to undertake *credible stress tests* of banks' capital adequacy. As well as being forward looking and focused on unlikely (tail) risks, the tests are conducted annually, concurrent for all firms above a certain size, systematic, and, by any previous standard of supervision, highly transparent.[21] They help supervisors assess system resilience and make adjudicatory judgments on the safety and soundness of individual firms, taking into account correlated exposures across intermediaries.

The Fed was followed by the ECB and the Bank of England when they took up their new prudential functions. Others will inevitably join the ranks of stress-testers in the coming years, with application to clearinghouses, dealers, and, perhaps, big asset management vehicles. As time passes, those various sectoral exercises can (and should) become joined up into macroprudential stress tests of the system as a whole.[22]

For our purposes, the big thing is that the regularity and transparency of the tests can transform public accountability for and public debate around prudential supervision, taking it toward what has become standard in the monetary policy world. Year by year, everyone will see the severity of the chosen stress scenarios as well as the firm-by-firm results. Legislators will be able to examine regulators on both, drawing on commentary from different parts of the financial system and, just as important, wider society. In time that will be informed by academic research on the effects on market discipline, the relative toughness of different jurisdictions' tests, how well they pinned down vulnerabilities before large losses were incurred, and so on.

At the level of high policy, this will help legislators think about the degree of resilience they want to require in the financial system, about how well the regime is working, where it needs reform, and where delegated responsibilities should be rejigged.

Separately, greater transparency, via stress testing, about the risk exposures and health of the system can help mitigate the risk of industry capture of regulators and supervisors. Stress testing forces a step change in transparency around the position of individual intermediaries—

[21] Transparency is not complete: notably, the regulator's own models are not published given the risk of gaming by the banks (Tarullo, "Departing Thoughts"), although that may change.

[22] Constancio, "Macroprudential Stress Tests."

provided, that is, that supervisors play it straight. Satisfying that condition could hardly be more important. It might be aided by each major jurisdiction's supervisors allowing in observers or participants from foreign authorities that have a stake in the system's resilience, and by independent reports on the integrity of each center's process. [23]

Finally, a regime of regular, highly publicized stress tests can help increase public awareness of prudential supervision. A perennial problem facing supervisors has been a lack of salience during "peacetime." That greatly troubled Bank of England governor Robin Leigh-Pemberton in the early 1990s. I well remember him urging his senior colleagues to try to identify ways of engaging with the public and the media on prudential supervision during the good times. He was concerned that the Bank's supervisory record was discussed publicly only following failures. He regarded those debates as necessary and proper, and in any case unavoidable. But he was frustrated that lapses and failures could never be weighed alongside achievements. Nobody knew what had gone well and, in particular, which firms had been turned around, avoiding public clatter and possible calamity (as the Midland Bank had during his period of office). That was a quarter of a century ago. Part of a solution might, finally, be at hand.

Pursuing transparent stress testing should, therefore, be a priority if the forces of "normative expectation" and the legitimacy-conferring benefits of public debate are to be realized. Supervision need no longer be a mystery—of interest and accessible to the public and their elected representatives only when something goes badly wrong. That would be unambiguously good for the legitimacy, and for the effectiveness, of any supervisory regime. It is close to essential if already powerful central banks are decently to hold onto their new responsibilities for stability.

Parliamentary Hearings

As highlighted in parts I–III, the imperative of transparency and public debate comes together in hearings before committees of the legislature. Here we must draw out an implication of the structure implied by

[23] Cecchetti and Tucker, "International Cooperation?" (While in office, I discussed inviting in materially interested observers with at least one overseas counterpart.)

the Principles for Delegation. For multiple-mission central banks, it is those members of the stability/regulatory committee serving only on that committee who are unambiguously impaled on their track record in maintaining the stability of the financial system as a whole. If and when the financial system does crack, those policy makers should be included among those summoned first to explain to legislators the failure of the central bank's stewardship. Such individual accountability is designed to ensure that they accept personal responsibility for the resilience of the system. It would mark a departure from overreliance on chair-centric testimony.

SUMMING UP: CENTRAL BANKS IN THE REGULATORY STATE

In this chapter, I have sketched how central banks should be constrained if they are part of the regulatory state as well as the fiscal state. Following the Principles for Delegation, this boils down to aligning the purpose of stability policy with the purpose of monetary policy, and making clear that the stability arm of a central bank must have an objective that is set by elected politicians and can be monitored by the public. The core of the answer is a standard of resilience pursued via (a) legislated standards for safety and soundness and (b) transparent stress testing.

Whatever its merits or demerits, however, the account in this chapter is unavoidably incomplete. Unlike monetary policy, a central bank can never control all of the policy instruments that affect stability: the "macroprudential moment" cannot license more or less every aspect of government policy affecting financial services being delegated to a single insulated institution. In consequence, the monetary authority has to be able to cooperate with other regulators, who themselves, therefore, need a clear statutory mandate for stability and the independence sufficient to make credible commitments. (That is precisely the issue around the SEC and other securities regulators first raised in chapter 7.)

More profoundly, the articulation of a central bank's place in the regulatory state cannot proceed independently of its place in the fiscal state. Concretely, which arm should move first to head off threats to stability—the financial stability committee or the monetary policy committee? Put another way, should a multiple-mission central bank lead with regulatory policy or with balance-sheet policy if it believes that the price of risk is so dangerously cheap that it is undermining the system's resilience? And should these functions be subject to different degrees of judicial scrutiny, as some argue?[24] Even to begin answering those questions, we need to see what constraints should apply to a central bank's balance-sheet operations and interventions.

[24] Lehmann, "Varying Standards."

22

Central Banking and the Fiscal State

BALANCE-SHEET POLICY AND THE FISCAL CARVE-OUT

> The Federal Reserve . . . is, in effect, acting as the world's largest financial intermediator. . . . Independence in a democratic society ultimately depends on . . . not be[ing] asked to do too much.
>
> —Paul Volcker, August 2013[1]

Perhaps the most charged area for central bankers and their political overseers is their role in what is known as *credit policy*: public policy designed directly to stimulate the supply of credit by private sector institutions to private sector borrowers and, perhaps, even to steer it toward particular sectors or regions.

As a matter of fact, this is where central banks have been most adventurous and innovative since 2007. As a matter of opinion, it is where they have faced the most questions. Marvin Goodfriend, formerly chief economist at the Federal Reserve Bank of Richmond, has argued that active involvement in credit policy undermines the "very idea of an independent central bank."[2]

Early in the crisis, some central banks, including the Fed and the Bank of England, acted as *market makers of last resort*, offering to buy private sector paper in order to sustain the liquidity of markets as private dealers withdrew due to capital constraints.

Later, they intervened in credit markets with more explicit and direct macroeconomic aims. Beginning in 2012, when economic recovery stalled, the Bank of England offered to lend for a four-year maturity against the security of portfolios of loans to businesses (and for a while mortgages) at an interest rate that was lower the more new loans

[1]Volcker, "Central Banking" and "Fed & Big Banking."

[2]Quote from personal recollection. The substantive point is made in Goodfriend, "Elusive Promise."

the counterparty firm extended. And after the Brexit referendum in 2016, it bought corporate bonds too. In the euro area, the ECB adopted a similar scheme, supplementing its regular auctions for loans (repos) against a wide range of credit securities. The Bank of Japan has been buying bonds and, indirectly, equities. And the Federal Reserve bought what are known as *agency mortgage-backed securities*, which since 2008 have been formally guaranteed by the federal government. Each of those operations was intended to stimulate spending in the economy by reducing the cost of credit in areas where risk premia would otherwise remain prohibitively high and/or where the central bank judged they would get a good macroeconomic bang for their buck.

So, in spasms of innovation, and with differences of detail, the advanced-economy central banks have all engaged in credit policy.

Putting to one side how well any of these operations worked, there are two big issues for legitimacy. First, allocating or steering credit to particular economic sectors or specific borrowers seems at odds with the Delegation Criteria since it involves choosing who to favor.[3] Second, outright purchases of risky bonds are just that: risky. If the risks crystallize, the taxpayer picks up any costs, if only through the central bank paying the Treasury lower dividends (known as *seigniorage*; broadly, the profits central banks make by financing interest-bearing assets through the creation of money).

As I write, this will not go away quickly. Even after purchases cease, it will take a long time for the portfolios of purchased securities to mature or be sold off, with private financing taking their place.

More profoundly, central banks now have choices unavailable in the past. Since the new millennium, many have moved to paying the policy rate of interest on bankers' reserves balances with them—the ECB and the Bank of England before the crisis, the Federal Reserve during the crisis. In doing so, they put behind them a couple of hundred years of not remunerating reserves: when I first floated this move at the Bank of England, the response of one of my closest colleagues was along the lines of "bloody hell." As a result, in addition to the regulatory tools discussed in the previous chapter, many central banks are, in principle, now in a position to make separate choices on their policy rate of

[3]For a (now former) Fed policy maker's concerns, see Plosser, "Limited Central Bank."

interest, the size of their balance sheet, and the composition of their asset portfolio. In theory, they could have a distinct target for each instrument: price stability, liquidity conditions, and credit conditions in whichever asset markets they choose to operate.

CENTRAL BANKING AS A COMANAGER OF THE STATE'S CONSOLIDATED BALANCE SHEET

To make sense of this, we need to step back. The best starting point is elemental, prior to objectives and questions of independence or legitimacy. It is to ask what a central bank *is*.

What Do Central Banks Do?

Many people would answer: the body that controls something called the money supply. That's getting close insofar as central banks can either directly control the creation of their own monetary liabilities or, alternatively, undertake to satisfy demand for their money, which emerges endogenously given, among other things, the interest rate they set to steer aggregate spending in the economy. But that story is still implicitly calling on an idea of central banking's purpose.

Instead, for this part of our inquiry it is useful to think of the central bank, more mechanically, as the marginal lender and/or borrower of overnight money (Francis Baring's monetary-system pivot); and as using that power to conduct financial operations that change the liability structure and, potentially, the asset structure of the state's consolidated balance sheet.

If a central bank buys (or lends against) only government paper, the structure of the state's consolidated liabilities is altered, with monetary liabilities substituted for longer-term debt obligations. If it purchases (or lends against) private sector paper, the state's consolidated balance sheet is enlarged, its asset portfolio changed, and its risk exposures affected. In either case, any net losses flow to the central treasury in the form of reduced seigniorage income, entailing either higher taxes or lower spending in the longer run (and conversely for net profits).

Taken in the round, the state's aggregate risks might not necessarily increase with such operations. If purchasing private sector assets helps revive spending in the economy, that might reduce the probability of the state making larger aggregate welfare payments and receiving lower taxes. But the form of the risk would change, and, because the driver of the risk transformation is central bank operations, the decision maker on the state's risk exposures would switch from elected fiscal policy makers to unelected central bankers.[4]

Seen in that light, the question is what degrees of freedom central banks should be granted to change the state's consolidated balance sheet, and to what ends.

A MINIMALIST CONCEPTION

A minimalist conception, articulated some years ago by Marvin Goodfriend among others, would restrict the proper scope of central bank interventions to open market operations (OMOs) that exchange monetary liabilities for short-term Treasury bills (in order to steer the overnight money market rate of interest). This model, which seeks historical authority in Federal Reserve debates of the early 1950s, has profound implications.[5]

The lender-of-last-resort (LOLR) function is restricted to accommodating shocks to the aggregate demand for central bank (base) money, and so plays no role in offsetting temporary problems in the distribution of reserves among banks in the private money markets. When the money markets are disfunctional, solvent banks simply go into bankruptcy if they cannot acquire reserves via the central bank's OMOs.[6]

At the effective lower bound for nominal interest rates, the only instrument available to the central bank would be to talk down expectations of the future path of the policy rate (what has become known as

[4]Central banks can, then, be placed within a broader class of quasi-fiscal institutions (Mackenzie and Stella, "Quasi-Fiscal Operations").

[5]William McChesney Martin succeeded in narrowing Fed operations to T-bills in the face of the opposition of New York Fed president Allan Sproul (Conti-Brown, *Power and Independence*, pp. 44–46). Within a decade, Martin's Fed had embarked on "Operation Twist," buying long-term Treasury bonds to reduce long-term financing costs, and allowing short-term rates to rise.

[6]Tucker, "Lender of Last Resort."

forward guidance).[7] All other interventions to stimulate aggregate demand—for example, the "quantitative easing" and "credit easing" of the postcrisis years—would fall to the "fiscal arm" of government. That—not a judgment on the merits of the minimal conception—is my main point: what is not within the realm of the central bank falls to elected policy makers, with the attendant problems of credible commitment and time inconsistency.

A MAXIMALIST CONCEPTION

At the other, maximalist end of the spectrum, the central bank would be given free rein to manage the consolidated balance sheet, which in theory would even include writing state-contingent options with different groups of households and firms. That would take central banks very close to *being* the fiscal authority, and cannot be squared with any mainstream ideas of central banking competencies in democracies.

So in one direction, the state's overall capabilities to maintain welfare shrivel, and in the other, its functions are, in effect, either seized by or abandoned to unelected central bankers.

If the dominant theme of parts II and III is the problem of vague objectives, we now see that, for central banks, a clear objective cannot suffice. Indeed, given their intrinsic operational capabilities, a clear objective makes it all the more important that, consistent with the first Design Precept, their delegated *powers* be clear, since otherwise they will be incentivized to do whatever is needed to deliver their mandate, however far that reaches into fiscal territory.

The Terms of Central Bank Independence: A Matter of Convention, Not Natural Law

Positive economics on the effectiveness of different instruments in mitigating economic problems cannot help with this, because it does not speak to which arm of the state should control which tools.[8] The un-

[7] *Effective* rather than *zero* lower bound because some central banks stopped at above zero due to the effects on banking-system credit supply of going down to zero and because, more recently, some have set negative marginal rates. I use the expression *zero lower constraint* to mean the low positive rate of interest at which a central bank faces a choice between the through-the-looking-glass world of negative interest rates and other unconventional measures.

[8] The focus is, thus, different from Bernanke, "Tools."

derlying problem appears to be the one at the center of this book: whether it is possible to balance the welfare advantages of credible commitment against the loss of majoritarian control.

While part II argues that central bank independence flows from the high-level separation of powers and is not just a matter of instrumental expedience, that does not demand more than the minimal conception of central bank operations outlined above. In the presence of fractional-reserve banking, however, we argued in chapter 20 that more is required because, as the issuer of an economy's final settlement asset (money), the central bank is unavoidably the lender of last resort. It will lend to individual (sound) private monetary institutions even where, strictly, there is no aggregate shortage of central bank money, because it would be madness to allow some banks to collapse simply because money markets have seized up or because other banks flush with cash will not lend to them. It is imperative to address severe problems in the distribution of central bank reserves because the social costs of (avoidable) bankruptcy are not negligible, even with the new resolution tools briefly discussed in previous chapters. In consequence, central bank balance sheets can never be the pristine thing that a purist minimal conception assumes.

Once that is admitted, the question is how to keep central banks on the "right side" of a blurred line between monetary policy and fiscal policy. The expression "right side" is in quotes because this is a matter of *convention*. It does not find its roots in natural law or some inalienable essence of central banking. We live in a world where, in a deep sense, there are not pure realms of "fiscal policy" and "monetary policy" but, rather, choices about how to separate what is controlled by, respectively, elected and unelected policy makers.

We therefore need general principles on central bank balance-sheet management to frame the options reasonably open to a democratic state when establishing *its* particular preferred convention for separating fiscal policy controlled by elected politicians from monetary policy controlled by an independent authority. The family of available options is constrained by principles for delegation to independent agencies more generally, including each polity's convention being open, comprehensible, and enforceable. What follows is where our particular Principles seem to lead for central banking.

THE FISCAL CARVE-OUT FOR CENTRAL BANKING

In chapter 12, it was argued that constitutionally grounded central banks need a *Fiscal Shield* to preserve the integrity of the delegation in the face of requests-cum-demands from government for monetary financing. We can now see that this needs to be combined with a *Fiscal Carve-Out* (FCO) that establishes the zone of constrained discretion, leaving them in control of their balance sheets within those bounds. For any independent central bank, an FCO exists already, however implicitly and fluidly, however wide or narrow. The Principles demand that it be as explicit as possible.[9]

A jurisdiction's Fiscal Carve-Out for its central bank needs to cover the following: the kind of assets it can lend against; the kind of assets it can buy, in what circumstances, and for which of its purposes; whether those operations are ever subject to consultation with the executive government or legislature; and how losses will be covered by the fiscal authority and communicated to the executive government and legislature.

In addressing each of those issues, the people's representatives must be realistic about what society might want a central bank to do in adversity. Where it wants to put something beyond bounds, the constraint should be in primary legislation, so that a change of course is visible and somewhat costly for the politicians to make.

This does not mean that either the legislature or the executive government must list or approve every security that the central bank may lend against or buy outright. A Fiscal Carve-Out might reasonably be cast in terms of general criteria (standards), leaving the detailed fleshing-out of the regime to the technical expertise of the central bank.

Within that broad framework, some concrete things can be said.

[9] Marvin Goodfriend first called for something like this as long ago as 1994 (Goodfriend, "Federal Reserve Credit Policy"). Marvin and I might draw the lines in slightly different places, but we agree on the need to draw lines and the significance of the high-level political economy issues, as we discussed during the mid-1990s.

Central Bank Capital Resources: A Political Economy Issue

First, the form of a central bank's "capital" resources is important. At one end of the spectrum, the fiscal authority could give a formal blanket indemnity against loss, but dictate the population of assets eligible in the central bank's operations and, thus at least indirectly, the scope and form of its market operations. At the other end of the spectrum, the central bank could be given a statement of purposes and permitted to offset losses against the seigniorage income due to the fiscal authority, with freedom to choose the form and scope of its operations. There are myriad points in between those poles, including central banks surrendering all the seigniorage, financing themselves instead from a levy on the banking system (the UK model), and case-by-case approval and indemnities for certain kinds of operation.

A society should know where its central bank regime lies on that spectrum, and recognize that its choice matters to insulation. Economists are fond of saying that central banks cannot go bust, but where local norms require positive net worth to be recorded in published accounts, recapitalization following losses would hand a big political lever to the executive and legislative branches.[10]

Constraints: Absolutes and Desirables

Beyond that, there are also some obvious constraints on any FCO.

The first and most important is that monetary independence should not be suspended or qualified other than via a formal legal instrument exercised transparently, and with the express consent of the legislature; and that government should not be able to command monetary financing, except via a legislative act.

Other desirable constraints are that central banks should have to (a) minimize risk to their capital, consistent with achieving their statutory

[10] For this reason, some years before the crisis I privately pressed for the Bank of England to have more equity capital. Financially, it would be a wash for government: Treasury, which owns the Bank, would inject more equity, and the Bank would invest in a portfolio of gilts. But the equity base should not be too large, since that could reduce risk discipline. My wish was that capital be set at a level that would cover a slice of losses incurred in tail events where the Bank's collateral haircuts proved insufficient. It would have reduced, but not eliminated, the need for government indemnities for some support operations.

objectives, and (b) minimize operations that, relative to normal economic conditions, favor or incentivize the allocation of resources to particular sectors, regions, individuals, or businesses.

Parsimony Given Statutory Objectives

For a given Fiscal Carve-Out, our third and fourth Design Precepts, taken together, make a further demand: that a central bank should itself publicly articulate how it plans to exercise its constrained discretion in ways that aid political accountability and public debate. This points to a principle of "instrument parsimony," by which I mean that, in any particular circumstances, they should conduct the most simple and straightforward set of permitted operations consistent with achieving their objectives.

The purpose here is to help the public and the legislature monitor what central banks are doing with their balance sheets. Easier, I suggest, for legislative overseers routinely to ask the central bank to explain why it has changed its short-term interest rate (and possibly, as discussed in the previous chapter, a macroprudential regulatory lever) than to have to make sense of why it is routinely intervening in a whole range of financial markets to influence term premia, liquidity premia, and credit-risk premia.

In practice, that entails a highly parsimonious approach when short-term interest rates are above the effective lower bound (ELB). But while this principle is particularly apposite for normal circumstances ("peacetime"), it should apply all the time.

Thus, while it was more than tolerable for central banks to become innovators during 2007–2009 as the circumstances had not been foreseen and there was an imperative of shielding the public from a repeat of the Great Depression, the sequential unrolling of multiple, experimental acronymed programs can and should be avoided if similar conditions arise again. Subject to where any particular jurisdiction decides that its Fiscal Carve-Out constraints should bind, central banks ought now to know enough to use the minimum number of such programs to meet the challenge presented by such conditions.[11] Those contingency programs should be articulated in advance (as discussed in the next chapter).

[11]For example, the Bank of England would not need to reinvent something like the March 2008–launched Special Liquidity Scheme (SLS), because since the autumn of 2008 it has been committed to lending, against a wide range of collateral, via a discount window facility and

GENERAL PRINCIPLES FOR CENTRAL BANK BALANCE-SHEET OPERATIONS

Summing up, I propose the following general principles to guide debates on central bank balance-sheet regimes, indicating in parentheses how they flow from our Principles for Delegation:

1. Each central bank should have clear purposes, powers, and constraints for its balance-sheet operations. The constraints comprise a Fiscal Carve-Out specifying the dividing line between independent central bankers and elected fiscal policy makers (*Delegation Criteria* and *Design Precept 1*).
2. Central banks should be protected by a *Fiscal Shield*, preventing elected governments from demanding monetary financing other than via legislative acts (*political insulation*).
3. The regime should be time consistent: central banks should not deny that they will do things that in fact they would do. So any formal constraints must be in primary legislation and incentives-compatible for lawmakers (*Delegation Criteria*).
4. Central bank balance-sheet operations should at all times be as parsimonious as possible consistent with achieving their objectives, in order to aid comprehensibility and accountability (*Design Precepts 3 and 4*).
5. Within the FCO constraints, central banks should minimize risk of loss consistent with achieving their statutory objectives (*Delegation Criteria*).
6. If they are permitted to operate in private sector paper, the selection of individual instruments should be as formulaic as possible, in order to avoid the central bank making detailed choices about the allocation of credit to borrowers in the real economy (*Delegation Criteria*).
7. Central banks should draw up and publish comprehensive contingency plans for the pursuit of their objectives within their mandate and, in particular, FCO constraints. Those plans should, so far as possible, preprogram any coordination with other parts of government that control material parts of the consolidated state balance

longer-term repos. The SLS was an innovation to plug a serious gap that, after late 2008, no longer existed in the Bank of England's standard published regime.

sheet (e.g., government debt managers), so that a back door is not opened to political control of policy intended to be delegated to the central bank (*Design Precept 5*).

While there is one further constraint to be added in the next chapter on emergencies, we already have enough to sketch what these general principles entail for various of the "unconventional" operations undertaken during or advocated in the years following the Great Financial Crisis. The discussion is structured around whether or not an operation entails transactions in risky securities, with liquidity reinsurance facilities deferred to the next chapter since they come into their own during disasters and emergencies.

APPLYING THE BALANCE-SHEET PRINCIPLES TO OPERATIONS IN DEFAULT-FREE GOVERNMENT INSTRUMENTS

This section, on default-free operations, covers quantitative easing (QE), "helicopter money," and operationalizing negative interest rates.[12] The running theme is around where cooperation or coordination with the fiscal authority might be needed.

Quantitative Easing and Government Debt Management

The most basic operation is *quantitative easing*, which involves the central bank buying long-term government bonds with the dual purpose of injecting money into the economy and lowering long-bond yields.

In terms of the state's consolidated balance sheet, QE is equivalent to a combination of two operations: (1) the central bank buys Treasury bills via a "minimalist" open market operation; (2) it then enters into another transaction that swaps the bills for longer-term bonds. The second leg has the economic substance of a government debt management operation. In consequence, the government's debt managers could offset some of the effects of the central bank's policy choices and actions by lengthening the maturity of its net issuance. Indeed, where their objective is to minimize debt-servicing costs over the medium-long run (chapter 7),

[12] For a more complete but preliminary review, see Tucker, "Political Economy."

they have a narrow incentive to do so in order to lock in the unusually cheap funding costs created by the central bank's operations. Remarkably, it seems that is just what happened in the United States.[13]

In the United Kingdom, the authorities recognized that coordination was needed. Before QE commenced in early 2009, the Bank of England and the Treasury published an exchange of letters through which finance minister Alistair Darling undertook that "the Government will not alter its issuance strategy as a result of asset transactions undertaken by the Bank of England for monetary policy purposes."[14]

The big point here is that once the composition of the state's consolidated (net) government/central bank balance sheet is being materially affected, in this case on the liabilities side, by the central bank's choice of what assets to operate in, a degree of explicit cooperation and coordination is unavoidable if overall policy is to be coherent.

This need not create a reflex alarm about encroachments on monetary independence, so long as it remains clear that the central bank is deciding the stance of monetary policy needed to achieve its objective.[15] Suspicions are more readily assuaged if the need for coordination with government has been countenanced and telegraphed in advance. In the UK, speeches to that end had been given by Bank policy makers a few years earlier.[16]

[13]This was documented by Harvard Kennedy School MPP candidate Joshua Rudolph and later elaborated in Greenwood, Hanson, Rudolph, and Summers, "Government Debt Management." The published version of the explanation given by discussants at the Brookings event are somewhat baffling unless Treasury had, prior to QE, publicly and formulaically committed to lengthen debt maturities.

[14]The letters between Mervyn King and Alistair Darling are dated February 17 and March 3, 2009.

[15]Mervyn King, Speech (2012).

[16]King, "Institutions of Monetary Policy," and Tucker, "Managing." Further, from the other side, the need for coordination was implicit in the UK debt management mandate introduced in the 1990s: "The debt management objective, originally established in 1995 following the 'Debt Management Review,' is: 'To minimise, over the long term, the costs of meeting the government's financing needs, taking into account risk, *while ensuring that debt management policy* is consistent with the aims of monetary policy.'" (My emphasis.) UK Treasury, Debt Management Report 2017–2018. Disclosure: I was one of the officials on the Bank side of the 1995 review.

Helicopter Money: Firmly into the Fiscal Realm

The maintained assumption of QE has been that the injection of excess central bank money into the economy will be maintained only so long as the economy is weak, which is to say that the central banks will sell bonds or let them run off as recovery takes hold. The first distinguishing feature of "helicopter money" is that the injection would be permanent. Its second distinguishing feature is that the money would be put into the hands of the people, as if dropped from helicopters, as Milton Friedman put it.[17]

Since that involves decisions on who should receive the money (all households, all taxpayers, all resident taxpayers, etc.) and on how much they should receive (the same lump sum for all, a flat percentage of income, or of wealth, etc.), it is abundantly clear that this is tax policy. For the central bank to take upon itself to choose would amount to an economic coup d'état. A formalized version, conferring a veneer of legitimacy, would be for legislation temporarily to bestow such power on the central bank—rather like the Romans electing a temporary dictator to help meet an emergency!—but surely today that would stretch legality's contribution to legitimacy.

Instead, the route most frequently canvassed is to split any such operation into two parts. An independent central bank would decide how much money to create in pursuit of its inflation target, and the fiscal authority would decide how to distribute/spend the money. Given the lessons of Central Europe's post–World War I history, however, it is hard to be confident that the central bank would retain the de facto autonomy to back out of the arrangement if after some years it had become a familiar part of the scene and an elected government was determined to continue.

Helicopter money is most prudently thought of as a leap to irresponsibility: suspending central bank independence in order to experiment with generating a surprise burst of inflation well beyond anything in the standard monetary policy mandate. For any economy in which government has the fiscal space to borrow more without becoming bankrupt, it would be odd to embark on that adventure before trying a more familiar debt-financed (fiscal) stimulus and reform of incentives to spend and invest. Anyway, it is not a decision for the central bank itself.

[17] Friedman, *Optimum Quantity of Money.*

Negative Interest Rates: The Political Economy of Wealth Transfers to Banks

Over recent years, some central banks—most notably the Bank of Japan, the Swiss National Bank, and the ECB—have stepped through the looking glass into a world of negative interest rates. A lot could be said about this, but its relevance to us is that some central banks set a negative rate on only the last few units of reserves, continuing to remunerate the general mass of reserves held by banks at a small positive rate or zero. Whatever its merits in terms of economic stimulus, which are contestable, in public finance terms it is a tax (or distributional) policy. It is equivalent to (1) a negative rate being paid by the central bank on all reserves; and (2) a transfer of resources from the government to banks that is equivalent to their having received a small positive rate on the bulk of their reserves. The second leg would, in other circumstances, generally be reserved to the elected fiscal authority, given that it redistributes public resources.

Under the Principles for Delegation, such a policy needs endorsement from elected politicians. That amounts to no more than saying that just as central banks needed to gain the approval of governments before they moved to paying interest on reserves, since that lifted a tax on banking, the same applies to a subsidy.

The moral of those three cases is that an independent central bank should not fear coordination with the fiscal authority so long as the monetary choices remain its own (constrained by its mandate), while not pretending that a measure is monetary in nature when it is not.

APPLYING THE BALANCE-SHEET PRINCIPLES TO PRIVATE SECTOR INSTRUMENTS

Things get more interesting when we turn to operations in risky instruments, such as market-maker-of-last-resort interventions and buying private securities to stimulate aggregate demand. Here the issues are less about coordination among the authorities, than about whether there are any absolute boundaries and what any permissive constraints might look like.

Secured Lending Is Much More Acceptable Than Purchases

The first thing to say is that, under our general principles for central bank operations, secured loans (*repos*) against baskets of diversified portfolios of private sector securities are preferable to outright purchases. Repos avoid important political economy hazards, as they leave the choice to invest in particular instruments in private hands and enable ongoing risk management by the central bank.[18]

For those reasons, if the usual banking counterparties are unable to participate in repo operations because they are distressed, rather than leap straight to outright purchases, it is preferable for the central bank temporarily to widen the population of intermediaries it will deal with (eligible counterparties). Since that would reduce their risks, doing so could stimulate wider demand for the type of securities in question, helping to sustain the functioning of private markets.

Nevertheless, there need to be constraints on offering soft terms on repo lending, which would amount to subsidizing counterparties and/or the issuers of the underlying paper. Central banks should, therefore, be transparent about how they set haircuts (the excess collateral required) and value securities, in order to enable democratic scrutiny (consistent with Design Precepts 3 and 4). The Bank of England tried to do that in 2010.[19]

Those various ways of getting central banks to stick to core notions of central banking are not available when it comes to outright purchases. Here the intermediate purpose matters: it might be to revive the liquidity of a market or, alternatively, to finance particular sectors on better terms than available in a stressed or atrophying market. We briefly discuss each.

Market Maker of Last Resort

The first type of intervention amounts to trying to repair the functioning of a fundamentally sound market afflicted by temporary problems that are severely impairing the performance of the economy or, more

[18] An outright purchase is a one-shot game, exposing the buyer to market and default risk. By contrast, under a standard repo, each day (or more frequently) the central bank can require additional collateral if their existing security has fallen in value; and it can require a different type of collateral if it no longer wants to lend against the original instruments.

[19] Breeden and Whisker, "Collateral," commissioned partly in response to Buiter, "Financial Crises."

narrowly, the transmission of monetary policy. This is best thought of as an extension of the LOLR function to capital markets: *market maker of last resort* (MMLR).[20] Whether and how central banks should play this role is likely to become more pressing if, as seems likely, capital markets gain importance relative to banks.

A fundamentally sound market might dry up suddenly for two reasons: market makers becoming capital constrained or unwarranted fears about the integrity of the underlying instruments. In either case, faced with a sudden wave of selling pressure, short-term traders might be unwilling to take the risk of ending up holding a large inventory if they each fear their peers will step back. This collective-action problem amounts to a market-maker run.

A market malfunction is a necessary but not a sufficient condition for an MMLR to step in. The authorities must also be satisfied (1) that a sudden closure of the market would be materially harmful to achieving their monetary policy objectives or to maintaining the resilience of the financial system as a whole; *and* (2) that there were not better solutions, such as lending secured to a wider class of market participants in order to help them enter the market as dealers.[21]

Where other options are not available, any MMLR intervention should be restricted to "systemically significant" markets and designed to be short-lived, with a catalytic goal: to revive the market in some way or to facilitate an orderly unwinding of positions. As with classic LOLR operations, the terms would need to mitigate moral hazard risk, with a bid-offer spread wider than that prevailing in normal conditions but narrower than the very wide spreads prevailing in the market crisis.[22]

Under the Principles for Delegation, those or any other rules of the game for MMLR operations should be determined and published in advance, so that there is a clear regime.

[20]Tucker, "Repertoire"; Buiter and Sibert, "Market Maker"; and Mehrling, *New Lombard Street.*

[21]I understand that Governor Carney has made a similar point.

[22]The Bank of England did that in its 2009 auctions for sterling corporate bonds by setting a ceiling price based partly on its assessment of fundamentals (Tucker, "Repertoire").

Pure Credit Policy: Steering Supply to Stimulate Aggregate Demand

What central bankers and economists call "credit policy" goes a lot further than MMLR operations.[23] The elemental question is why deliberately large outright purchases of risky paper might ever be contemplated.

While the obvious motive is to drive down the cost of credit in the capital markets, that would need to be over and above what could be delivered, directly or indirectly, by lowering the expected path of risk-free rates and by using basic QE to squeeze investors out of government paper into private securities. In other words, more regular central bank operations should be exhausted first. That suggests the following minimum substantive criteria before the use of credit policy options becomes a live issue:

- the monetary policy rate is at or very close to the effective lower bound and is expected to stay there;
- vanilla quantitative easing and guidance on the prospective path of the policy rate will not suffice or will entail even more unacceptable risks;
- repo operations in private sector paper will not suffice, even if eligible counterparties were extended beyond banks and maturities lengthened;
- in consequence, there is a serious risk of a deep and protracted recession that would create powerful disinflationary forces or even deflation becoming embedded in people's expectations.

Those are necessary, not sufficient, conditions. In the rare circumstances where they are satisfied, the ordinarily designated realms of the monetary policy maker and the fiscal authority would, in some sense, start to become coterminous. So political economy, or governance, criteria would also be needed—in advance. I suggest three constraints, designed to keep independent monetary policy makers as close to base as feasible.

First, any such operations should be booked to the central bank's balance sheet only if it has control (making independent decisions on amounts, terms, and timing), and they are clearly directed to achieving

[23] Hetzel, *Great Recession*, chapter 14.

its statutory purpose and objectives. Alternatively, independence should be explicitly suspended by government with the consent of the legislature. There should be no pretending that the central bank remains independent when the shots are being called elsewhere. (This follows from our Delegation Criteria.)

Second, having taken the plunge, and again constrained by the terms of the regime, the central bank should operate in as wide a class of paper as possible. Making allocative decisions could all too easily erode its legitimacy among businesses and households when economic peacetime is eventually restored. The Fed's purchases of mortgage-backed securities might not meet this test as, although within the law, they seem to favor household credit over business credit (except in circumstances where there is a specific malfunction in household mortgage markets). This is a problem of regime design. The relevant legislation permits purchases of government-guaranteed paper, but there are no federal government-guaranteed business loan securitizations. In terms of keeping the central bank away from subsidizing certain types of credit, it might be better if the statutory regime were either narrower or broader. (This also follows from our Delegation Criteria.)

Third, the basis of a central bank's pricing decisions should be transparent, so that it can be held accountable for any hidden subsidies that come to light later. If the legislature or elected executive government wants to grant hidden subsidies, they can do so under their own authorities. (This follows from Design Precept 4.)

Indeed, none of those preconditions and constraints on central bank action precludes the fiscal authority from setting up schemes to subsidize or direct the flow of credit. Broader fiscal action, on the initiative and under the control of elected policy makers, is the more natural step once monetary policy has run its course. We return to this massive issue in chapter 24.

Intervening in Capital Markets to Restrain Exuberance

Whereas any operations in credit markets undertaken for monetary policy purposes would be purchases intended to stimulate the economy when the standard interest rate is stuck at the effective lower bound, when it comes to financial stability it is sometimes sales, not purchases, that are contemplated. The objective would be to drive *up* the cost of credit in particular markets in order to lean against a stability-threatening boom.[24]

This returns us to the issue with which we closed the previous chapter. Given that a number of jurisdictions have given their authorities the power temporarily to raise capital (or other) regulatory requirements against sectoral exposures in stability-threatening conditions, the question arises whether it would be preferable, or at least legitimate, for central banks to seek to achieve the same effect by intervening directly in capital markets.

In political economy terms, this would have the apparent merit of locating the central bank's powers in its balance sheet, with transmission through market prices rather than through legally binding constraints on intermediaries or end borrowers.

There are two reasons for not taking this course. First, in order to be boom-time sellers, central banks would need to be steady purchasers in normal times in order to maintain sizable portfolios of the asset classes judged to be materially relevant to stability (e.g., mortgage and commercial real-estate bonds). But by adding to demand, that would tend to reduce the cost of credit and so would risk prompting overissuance, distorting the allocation of resources during economic peacetime. If central banks sought to avoid that by aiming to keep various market risk premia in line with economic fundamentals, we are back to the problem of how to monitor their success. (What's more, that objective would need to be suspended when, at the effective zero lower bound for interest rates, the central bank flipped to using QE to drive risk premia below their market level.)

More important in terms of this book's concerns, such operations cut across the previous chapter's line that a financial stability regime delegated to an IA should be dedicated to maintaining a desired degree of resilience in the financial system as a whole rather than managing the credit cycle or leaning against each and every market mispricing. That objective and our principle of parsimony for central bank balance-sheet

[24] For a proposal along these lines, see Benjamin Friedman, "Financial Crisis." A version appeared in the *Financial Times*: http://www.ft.com/intl/cms/s/0/47e50644-ea63-11e3-8dde-00144feabdc0.html#axzz45oZS59P3.

management drives a preference for deploying macroprudential regulatory tools, such as raising intermediaries' capital, collateral, or liquidity requirements, ahead of any direct intervention in markets. As such, central banks' participation in the regulatory state might be expected to reduce their incursion into the more politicized parts of the fiscal state.

PARSIMONY AND THE SIZE OF CENTRAL BANKS' BALANCE SHEETS

The principle of parsimony also helps resolve the question of the size of central bank balance sheets: in normal circumstances central banks should let the aggregate volume of reserves be determined by market demand rather than use it as an extra policy instrument. In other words, they should not routinely utilize the extra degree of freedom created by remunerating reserves, but should let banks choose what level of reserves to target given the monetary policy rate, liquidity requirements, risk of payment outflows, and other factors.

While constraining central banks during financial "peacetime," this would allow their balance sheets to expand when demand for reserves increased because of financial system strains or nervousness; and it would not preclude them from changing their operating systems when, stuck at the effective lower bound for interest rates, they shifted to using QE to increase the supply of base money. Those are virtues because they impose reasonably clear thresholds where, due to actual or incipient crisis, the central bank needs to resort to using more instruments to meet its statutory objectives.

What emerges from this chapter is, first, that healthy democracies might draw the lines differently but should be able to explain where their lines are and why. Why, for example, does the US confine the Fed to purchases of government paper when in Germany the stress is on avoiding precisely that? Second, any constraints should be credible or, more strongly, time consistent. Third, a regime might prudently incorporate a scale of graduated market interventions directed to pursuing unchanging (and monitorable) objectives in increasingly challenging conditions, with thresholds and constraints cast accordingly. There must, however, be a distinction between within-regime and out-of-regime operations, as will become clearer in the next chapter when we turn to lender-of-last-resort responsibilities—which at first seem to present a paradox.

23

Central Banks and the Emergency State

LESSONS FROM MILITARY/CIVILIAN RELATIONS FOR THE LENDER OF LAST RESORT

> The Fed has deviated from the classical model in so many ways as to make a mockery of the notion that it is a LOLR.
>
> —Thomas Humphrey, former adviser, Richmond Federal Reserve Bank[1]

> I could not in practice order the Bank to do what I wanted. Only the Bank of England can put the necessary funds into the banking system. . . . The fact that we had given the Bank independence had a downside as well as an upside.
>
> —Alistair Darling, UK finance minister 2007–2010[2]

The previous two chapters have addressed how central banks, from their place as the pivot of the money-credit system, a role that is essentially part of the services state, might find a legitimate place in the regulatory state and the fiscal state of mature democracies.[3] We now turn to more nuanced territory, which has been lurking in the background throughout.

A central issue in part II was whether the state's emergency powers can be squared with the principles of liberal democracy and, in particular, liberal conceptions of the rule of law.[4] In a way, we sidestepped it, by concluding that, however strong or weak the basis for the exercise of emergency powers by an elected government, independent agencies are

[1]Humphrey, "Lender of Last Resort," p. 333. For a different view, see Cline and Gagnon, "Lehman Died." As will become clear, my own general position is that decisions to bail out insolvent firms are *not* for central banks.

[2]Darling, *Back from the Brink*, p. 23.

[3]A wider discussion of their place in the services state would center on principled limits on their role as architects, engineers, and operators of the core financial-system infrastructure.

[4]Lazar, *States of Emergency*.

different. For them, the rules of the game have to bind more tightly, precisely because they do not carry the imprimatur of the ballot box. Thus our fifth Design Precept provided that it should be clear ex ante what happens, procedurally and/or substantively, when an IA reaches the boundaries of its mandate and powers and yet could, intrinsically, provide material help in addressing a disaster. This chapter explores whether that general principle can be sustained in central banking. As we saw in part III's brief encounter with the real world, some seasoned executive branch campaigners believe it cannot (chapter 16), but I differ.

Aside from the military, it is hard to think of a public agency for which this set of issues could be more relevant. To start with, one of the standard constraints over the exercise of emergency powers by executive government—the need for resources approved by the legislature—hardly applies to central banks. They can print money, and so can expand their balance sheet and asset portfolios without having to face the real-time checks applying to the enforcement of legal powers: they can just *do* things. Indeed, that is almost the point of central banks. They are an economy's final source of liquidity: its lender of last resort. In consequence, as we have said already, it is tempting for everyone—executive and legislative branches, commentators, the public—to look upon them as a financial US Cavalry. They are, in a nutshell, built to be *emergency institutions.*

But should they utilize that inherent capability? Should we risk their being, adapting the language of part II, the *economic sovereign*? Unlike the military, they are formally independent, insulated from day-to-day politics, and so cannot easily look for political authorization without compromising the point of their existence. That poses challenges as to just what they should and should not be allowed to do in a crisis: how far they should be allowed to write their own script and how they should be accountable ex post.

While, as we saw in the previous chapter, macroeconomic policy can pose those questions, they are particularly acute for the lender-of-last-resort function, since it can be called upon at a moment's notice and in extraordinarily complex circumstances. As we proceed, we need to distinguish between four broad stages of crisis escalation:

- Routine operations
- Disaster management operations that are plainly within-regime, and for which the IA has previously promulgated operating principles
- Disaster management operations that are within a central bank's legal competence but for which no operating principles have been promulgated and that prudently need political sanction given they would push beyond any reasonable political or public expectation when the regime was framed
- Disaster management operations that elected legislators could bring within the law *and* would not be at odds with the IA's purposes and/or violate the political values underpinning the Delegation Criteria

That general structure applies to macro policy interventions but is especially apposite for central banks in their guise as the LOLR. To begin with, then, what does society want from its LOLR?

CENTRAL BANKS AS LIQUIDITY REINSURERS REDUX: DESIGNING A REGIME

In earlier chapters, we have described an economy's central bank as its *liquidity reinsurer*—a sentiment Francis Baring first captured when he labeled the Bank of England the *dernier resort*. That being so, monetary authorities can do good by not waiting until the last moment or leaving their policy in doubt. In my preferred paraphrase (or rationalization) of Walter Bagehot's famous dictum:[5]

> Central banks should make clear that they stand ready to lend early and freely (i.e., without limit), to sound firms, against good collateral, and at rates higher than those prevailing in normal market conditions.

This, I repeat, is an integral part of a monetary economy with fractional-reserve banking (chapter 20). In principle, it brings two ben-

[5]My version generalizes from Bagehot's gold-standard context, which blurred the distinction between a country suffering a balance-of-payments crisis and an internal liquidity run on the banking system; and it emphasizes lending to sound firms only, which I believe is implicit in Bagehot (Tucker, "Repertoire").

efits. Ex ante, knowing that the LOLR is there, banks' short-term creditors should be less inclined to run. Ex post, if they do, the central bank's liquidity provision reduces the need for banks to resort to forced sales of assets, which would depress values, causing avoidable bankruptcies among households and firms and knocking the economy as a whole onto an inferior equilibrium growth path. In other words, the LOLR can in principle reduce both the probability and impact of runs. It helps to preserve stability in the face of unwarranted runs, and contains the spread of panic to *sound* firms in the face of warranted runs on other, fundamentally unsound firms. Its purpose is to deter and contain contagion.[6]

An Unresolved Debate

Needless to say, this regime is anything but uncontentious. Like all insurance regimes, it incorporates problems of moral hazard and adverse selection. The issues have been debated, often heatedly, for more than a century. When, in the 1860s, perhaps drawing on his experience in the family bank, Bagehot championed the Bank of England's overdue acceptance of its public responsibilities as LOLR, former governor Thomson Hankey retorted that he saw an implied promise of support as a threat to "any sound theory of banking."[7]

Following the recent financial crisis, this is all back in play. In 2010 the Dodd-Frank legislation trimmed the Fed's LOLR powers, followed in 2015 by a bipartisan proposal from Senator Elizabeth Warren and then senator David Vitter to tighten the constraints another notch or so. In the UK, by contrast, the Bank of England's liquidity reinsurance repertoire was transformationally expanded in late 2008; and, in case that wasn't enough, in 2012 the government took statutory powers to *make* the Bank act under certain conditions (see below).

These contrasting trajectories reflect a confused debate shaped by local contingencies. Central banks are celebrated and castigated in broadly equal measure for the actions they took (or did not take) to sta-

[6] The costs of contagion are the central theme of Scott, *Connectedness and Contagion*.

[7] Kynaston, *City of London*, p. 85.

bilize the financial system and wider economy when crisis broke in 2007 and spread through 2008. For every paean of praise for their innovations in injecting liquidity and keeping markets open (just), there is a chorus of reproof censuring central banks for breaching a crucial boundary between central banking and fiscal policy.

Substantively, probably the most serious accusation is that some central banks—including, it is alleged, the Federal Reserve—aided insolvent firms and that they stretched beyond their legal authority to do so.[8] Mario Draghi's ECB has been attacked for crossing an ordo-liberal line by using monetary operations as a form of state support.[9] By contrast, the Bank of England was castigated for initially being slow to act and overly cautious, for being too concerned about moral hazard. Whatever one's views of the substance, this transatlantic contrast is enough to make clear that what goes for orthodoxy in LOLR operations needs pinning down.

Indeed, assessed against our Design Precepts for *how* to delegate to an independent agency, the 2007/2008 crisis revealed problems on just about every front:

- boundaries for the LOLR function were often not clear (Design Precept 1);
- nor, before the heat of battle, were the principles that would guide central banks in exercising discretion (DP3);
- decisions were not always taken by committee (DP2);
- it was hard for elected representatives to monitor what was going on, partly due to the sheer speed, scale, and complexity of events, and partly because public disclosure could have exacerbated the crisis the monetary authorities were desperately trying to contain (DP4); and, finally,
- it was not always clear when and how central banks should seek and obtain political authority without compromising monetary independence (DP5).

[8] For example, Posner, "Legal Authority," arguing that the Fed stretched the law, saying that was essential, and advocating that it be given more crisis powers, with ex post accountability; and Selgin, "Last-Resort Lending," arguing the other side. My own concerns are recognized by Posner.

[9] Brunnermeier, James, and Landau, *Battle of Ideas*.

To be clear, in some jurisdictions there were applicable laws and/or codes agreed with government.[10] But they proved incomplete, to put it mildly.

Linked to these political economy problems, the events of 2007–2009 threw up a heap of substantive design issues. Notably, should central banks ever provide liquidity assistance to nonbanks? Should they promise to lend against a wide or narrow class of collateral? And how do we prevent LOLR assistance being a backdoor bailout?[11]

BACKWARD AND FORWARD: PUBLIC FACILITIES FROM EMERGENCY INSTITUTIONS

Here, then, is the tension flagged in chapter 19. On the one hand, this book is dedicated to arguing that central banks, the epitome of independent agencies designed to solve commitment problems, should be granted insulation from day-to-day politics only if their policy is systematic and transparent. On the other hand, as "emergency institutions" with a capacity to step in to prevent liquidity crises from destabilizing the economy as a whole, we observe a history of improvisation.

As we have seen, LOLR liquidity reinsurance faces problems of credible commitment that cut both ways. Will central banks keep their promise to lend into a liquidity crisis? But also, will central banks lend when they shouldn't, when the *underlying* problem is one of solvency rather than liquidity?

A jurisdiction can oscillate between the two. A century and a half after Governor Hankey's spat with Bagehot, UK Treasury secretary Alistair Darling found himself taking up the latter's cause, as the quote at the chapter head illustrates. But, ironically, his criticism of Governor Mervyn King for being slow to provide liquidity assistance in 2007 came only a decade or so after muttering Whitehall criticism of

[10] In the UK it was clear, under the terms of a published 1997 (refined 2006) memorandum of understanding with the Treasury, that the Bank of England needed executive government approval if it wished to go beyond its published regimes.

[11] A more detailed discussion of these and other issues can be found in Tucker, "Lender of Last Resort."

his predecessor, Eddie George, for being *too ready* to lend in the early 1990s to a swathe of liquidity-stricken small banks.

Perhaps reflecting those anxieties, a few years later when the incoming Labour government granted the Bank monetary independence, it also made "support operations" subject to approval by the chancellor of the exchequer. That risked drawing politics into even the most benign instances of bilateral liquidity provision, and early in his governorship Mervyn King supported my proposal that the crisis management Treasury/Bank memorandum of understanding be amended to the effect that political approval was needed only when the Bank was going beyond its "published facilities."[12]

The point is that in today's democracies the only way to combine effectiveness with legitimacy is transparency around the rules of the game. That is what a public liquidity assistance facility can provide. Central banks as "emergency institutions" become institutionalized.

If credible commitment and operating as an emergency institution can be reconciled in principle, getting from "in principle" to "in practice" requires, as part II argues, public deliberation and debate, so that the requisite degree of comprehension and support is established. That was lacking on both sides of the Atlantic before the crisis. Remarkable though it might seem given the origins and historical rites of passage of many central banks, the LOLR function largely disappeared from policy debates and the academic literature on monetary regimes.[13]

[12] At the time, those published facilities did not cover lending against collateral other than government bonds. On the early 1990s episode, in case I am misunderstood, I should record that the then deputy governor George's handling of the UK's small banks crisis was nothing short of a master class in crisis management. At much the same time, in the next-door office, Governor Robin Leigh-Pemberton headed off the threat of an even bigger crisis, drawing on strong support from Prime Minister John Major (see chapter 21). The second episode is covered in my eulogy at the memorial service for Lord Kingsdown (as he later became), available in the Bank of England archive.

[13] For the deep origins and hence nature of central banks, see Goodhart, *Evolution of Central Banks*, and Giannini, *Age of Central Banks*.

Rules versus Principles

Not completely, however. A generation ago, the late monetary historian Alan Meltzer called for *rules* for the LOLR.[14] This has been echoed by others on what might be called the constitutionalist, neoliberal Right.

The central thesis of this book is that a regime *is* needed, for reasons of instrumental efficiency and the intrinsic values of representative democracy. But I doubt that it could comprise mechanical rules requiring no interpretation or judgment (chapters 8 and 10). That is because, almost by definition, emergencies throw up problems that have not been foreseen or codified into institutional plans. The urgency and scale of problems that characterize a national (or international) emergency can call for innovation if the public is to be protected from avoidable harm, as in full-franchise democracies they demand and expect.

But nor should unelected independent agencies be given a free hand. As with monetary policy, we need a regime of *constrained discretion*, where the constraints are, consistent with our first and third Design Precepts, set out in a combination of legislation and a central bank's published *operating principles*.[15] Further, just as for other IA regimes, those constraints need to be widely debated, and the exercise of discretion needs to be capable of being reviewed ex post. At present, even in those jurisdictions that have some elements of an LOLR framework, they are rarely brought together in a coherent and digestible whole. That is unsatisfactory if independent central banking is to enjoy legitimacy, and so be sustainable.

Three things are needed: a substantive regime, a governance framework, and accountability mechanisms that do not undermine the purpose of the policy. Substantively, the regime must strike a consciously chosen balance among credibility, avoiding adverse selection problems, addressing moral hazard problems, and operating under a clear Fiscal Carve-Out within which the central bank can act on its own

[14] See concluding parts of Meltzer, "What's Wrong with the Fed?" Also, Laidler, "Central Banks as Lenders of Last Resort."

[15] In a recent paper (Calomiris et al., "Establishing Credible Rules"), Meltzer and his coauthors adopt essentially this approach, echoing Tucker, "Lender of Last Resort," but framed within the rhetoric of "rules" preferred on parts of the US Right.

authority but not venture beyond. The last of those is necessary to keep central bankers to central banking and, thus, to circumscribe their power.

SOME PRINCIPLES FOR AN INDEPENDENT LENDER OF LAST RESORT

Against that background, I would suggest that the following might lie at the core of an LOLR regime operated by an independent agency.

First, for the avoidance of doubt, it should be reaffirmed that central banks will act as the LOLR.[16] In today's democracies, that should become a legal responsibility rather than a matter of established practice. In which case, the central banks need a mandated purpose (Delegation Criteria and Design Precept 1). It should be to avoid or mitigate the social costs that flow from illiquid but fundamentally sound intermediaries failing in a disorderly way or rationing credit and other services (in order to serve the intermediaries' private interest in staying alive).

Once under such an obligation, as a general matter central banks would lose their discretion as to whether to activate their LOLR powers depending on their particular view of moral hazard costs. Instead, they would stand accountable for their assessment of the facts they confronted and the terms set on any assistance (Design Precept 4). They would also be incentivized to combat moral hazard through the ex ante terms and conditions of their lending facilities and through the regulatory regime. (As sketched in chapter 20's discussion of the Money-Credit Constitution, those could be linked if runnable liabilities had to be covered by assets eligible for discount at the central bank.)

Second, just as "no monetary financing" is integral to a securely independent monetary policy, a cardinal principle of an independent LOLR must be the following: *No lending to fundamentally insolvent firms* (Delegation Criteria).

Never again should major central banks find themselves unable to rebut accusations of "You bailed out firm X." Having good collateral is

[16] Tucker, "Repertoire."

necessary but, emphatically, not sufficient: it is possible to have negative net worth while still holding onto some undoubted assets.[17]

That is an eighth general principle for central bank balance-sheet management to add to the seven articulated in the previous chapter. It draws on history. At the very moment the Bank of England was putting into practice the principles that Bagehot would codify a decade later, it turned away Overend Gurney, one of the largest discount houses in mid-nineteenth-century London, on the grounds that it was unsound.[18]

Given recent advances in statutory regimes for resolving unsound firms without taxpayer solvency support, today's central banks have no reason to be more lax than their nineteenth-century predecessors. LOLR assistance is conceptually distinct from (and in practice can now truly avoid being) a bailout or rescue of fundamentally unsound firms. The breakthrough in resolution technology is nothing short of transformative for the LOLR, because they can say no when they should.[19] As legitimacy seekers, central bankers should begin every speech on LOLR with an explanation of their jurisdiction's resolution regime!

This shifts the uncertainty to how the central bank assesses solvency. Consistent with our third Design Precept, central banks need to publish a framework for how soundness/solvency will be assessed, which would have to be on a probabilistic basis. The problem is not different in kind from the uncertainties confronting observers in assessing the integrity and quality of the macroeconomic forecasts that underpin central banks' monetary policy decisions. Both are inherently forward looking, and so both can prove wrong ex post. In that spirit, central banks need internal processes for producing these assessments that match their monetary policy processes in formality, depth, and production-line organization.

Third, it should be accepted that a declared policy of lending against only a narrow class of very high quality collateral, whatever the circumstances, is not credible. Given the consequences for the economy of banking distress, ex post a central bank will lend (to a fundamentally sound firm) so long as it can get hold of decent collateral. But a central

[17]The "good collateral suffices" doctrine is a canard that central bankers espouse when apparently in self-destructive mode (Tucker, "Lender of Last Resort").

[18]Kynaston, *City of London*.

[19]Tucker, "Regulatory Reform" and "Resolution of Financial Institutions."

bank has no business lending against assets that it cannot understand, value, and manage (Delegation Criteria).[20]

Fourth, again in the interest of credibility, unless there exists an iron-clad legal bar, central banks should not rule out lending to solvent *nonbanks* on a *case-by-case* basis where stability would otherwise be seriously threatened.[21] But they should do so only after consultation with the executive branch of government, and should give a (suitably delayed or secret) account to the legislature.

There should, moreover, be ex post consequences for the management of any nonbank that ends up being so bank-like that it needs central bank liquidity assistance, since they will have engaged in socially costly regulatory arbitrage. In the same vein, other firms with similar business models should be forced to become banks or change so that they no longer run the risk of banking-like liquidity distress. After all, as British economist R. G. Hawtrey observed approaching a century ago, "Anyone who can borrow from the central bank can thereby procure legal tender money" (and, I would add, can therefore incur money-like liabilities and so should be regulated as a monetary institution).[22]

Fifth, within the statutory regime, central banks' decisions on how to exercise their constrained discretion to act as the LOLR should be made by a formal committee, with one person, one vote. While an elected president or prime minister might hold some personal powers, a central bank governor or chair should not, consistent with the republican element of the values underpinning the Principles (Design Precept 2, chapter 11).

Purpose and a Monitorable Mandate

What I am advocating amounts to the following conception of central banking LOLR facilities and operations:

- Liquidity assistance provided by the central bank to a borrower that is not fundamentally insolvent, with the purpose of

[20] Breeden and Whisker, "Collateral."

[21] Where the unqualified bar on such lending does exist, the polity's Money-Credit Constitution would prudently also bar liquidity transformation by or via nonbanks if it wishes to avoid the vortex.

[22] Hawtrey, "Genoa Resolutions," p. 292. More recently, Tarullo, "Shadow Banking."

- Avoiding the social costs that would follow from disorderly default or from distressed intermediaries withdrawing or heavily rationing services to the economy, or of
- Avoiding contagion to other intermediaries via direct or indirect channels that would be likely to lead to such social costs.

Incorporating a purpose within the definition of LOLR could enrich public debate and understanding. In the US, where there are various proposals for reforming the Fed's LOLR role, the debate is all about the pros and cons of various possible constraints, with the purpose barely mentioned. That is an odd way to frame, explain, and monitor public policy and at times risks moving the US to a regime that could end up harming the very people—the public—who the reformers most want to protect. LOLR is (or can be) about maintaining essential services during bad and hard times, not about bailing out equity holders, bond holders, or bosses of bust firms.

Nor, I might add, is it about the state providing liquidity insurance directly to households and regular businesses: central banks' place in the services state is elemental but also limited. Those suggesting that monetary authorities should use the new technology to enable everyone to bank with them—no longer the pivot of a tiered payments system but rather a direct provider of e-money services—will have to find an answer to the risk of their morphing into a state credit bank for everyone.[23]

What, though, of our first Design Precept? If an independent central bank is to make decisions on LOLR without political involvement, it demands a monitorable objective or standard. Unlike prophylactic regulation and supervision, which we have urged be directed at maintaining a quantified standard for system resilience, it seems harder to frame a monitorable objective for LOLR operations: how to tell whether or not they worked? We are, in fact, back to the problem of defining "financial instability" in a measurable way (chapter 21): how bad do the effects of liquidity stress need to be in order to warrant granting liquidity assistance? And even *if* we could specify that, how could we determine ex post whether an apparently successful intervention had been warranted because the threatened instability (as defined) was forestalled or, on the

[23] Tucker, "Central Banking in the Digital Age."

contrary, had been unnecessary because the threat of instability was, in truth, smaller than judged at the time?

The solution, I suggest, lies in moving away from an objective that proxies for welfare in some way (resilience, for prophylactic supervision) toward framing a definite responsibility of the LOLR to lend subject to being satisfied that the borrower and its collateral are eligible. Broad standards for eligibility would be set out in legislation and, following DP3, fleshed out by the central bank in its operating principles so as to produce a monitorable standard.

When the type of borrower or collateral is ineligible but the liquidity-stricken intermediary fundamentally sound, the central bank could also have a separate responsibility for reaching a view on whether the social costs (via the financial system) liable to be brought about by the intermediary's distress warrant its recommending to the elected executive branch that it be permitted to lend ("emergency assistance"). Under this setup, the formal discretionary decision on how bad is bad enough for the central bank to act beyond its published framework (but still within its legal powers), and whether to do so preemptively or only as incipient instability becomes obvious, would carry a majoritarian stamp.

That is an instance of the "special approvals" process discussed as part of the Design Precepts in chapter 6. The central bank would not escape having to judge whether its proposed intervention would work (and, especially, would not be counterproductive): if a trustee-type IA didn't believe those conditions were met, it should not lend even with political sanction. Thus, if emergency liquidity assistance to a particular firm is overt, it must be firmly expected either to dispel unwarranted panic or to provide a bridge to a solution to the borrower's fundamental problems.[24]

Where Do Things Stand?

Meanwhile, no jurisdiction that I know of has an LOLR regime that would pass all of those tests. Many do have some degrees of formality in place, however, and nearly all the major jurisdictions now make a

[24] This was the fatal flaw in the UK's initial liquidity support to Northern Rock in 2007.

distinction between regular liquidity reinsurance and emergency liquidity support that is subject to special procedures.

In the US, the assets the Federal Reserve may lend against are subject to statutory constraints, but no purpose is stated and it is not clear how the "no lending to fundamentally insolvent borrowers" is applied.[25] Following the Dodd-Frank Act, the Fed now has to get approval from the president, via the Treasury secretary, for any loans to nonbanks, and it can no longer create special facilities for individual firms. The former is perfectly consistent with the principles set out here, while the latter is likely to lead either to a socially costly mess or, as time passes, to imaginative applications of the statutory constraint.

In the euro area, a wide range of collateral has been eligible from the ECB's inception. It is unclear, however, just how much discretion either the ECB or national central banks have to lend to firms at, shall we say, the very edge of fundamental ill health.

In the UK, a full public Discount Window facility (and economically equivalent auctions) through which banks can borrow against a wide class of collateral waited until late 2008 but, in the most significant reforms for at least a century, now exists and has more recently been extended to various nonbank dealers that, in economic substance, are banks.[26] To lend outside that published framework, the Bank needs Treasury consent. Separately, since 2012 the executive government has had a statutory power to direct the Bank of England to provide assistance in the face of a very serious threat to stability. Following what Mervyn King described to me as, in I think almost perfectly recollected words, "the most important work we will ever do together," the government agreed to the following constraints on its directive power: any such lending would be undertaken as agent, booked in a special-purpose vehicle not on the Bank's balance sheet, indemnified by the government, and funded by the Bank rather than by the government only if the Monetary Policy Committee could control any consequent monetary expansion. Given that the government's concern was to ensure the Bank would lend when appropriate, they would have done much better to enact a statutory LOLR purpose for the Bank. In other words, they

[25] The objective in the 1913 act that created the Fed—of maintaining an "elastic currency"—does not provide much help.

[26] Bank of England, Development of Market Operations, sections II and V–VII.

should have relied on a (constrained) general responsibility to lend enshrined in law rather than case-specific political force.

Each of those three jurisdictional stories points toward the problem of casting the boundaries to an LOLR regime. Given that the contract, however carefully drawn up, is bound to prove incomplete and given that may have disastrous consequences, the question remains of what is to be done in true crises (as defined in chapter 6: disasters beyond formal powers, capabilities, and plans). Here we turn to lessons from one of the more established and seasoned pillars of unelected power: the military and their relationship with political principals.

CENTRAL BANKING IN EMERGENCIES: LESSONS FROM MILITARY/POLITICAL RELATIONS

When part I introduced the distinction between "pure agency" and "trustee" delegations, a sharp contrast was drawn between an independent central bank and the properly subordinate military (chapter 4). Now we are discovering that there is an important distinction between, on the one hand, normal circumstances, for which a regime of operational independence can be laid down by legislators, and, on the other hand, those emergencies or crises where central banks reach the limits of their script but could still come to the rescue.

In a crisis, at least three of the features identified as distinctive of military/political relations are shared by central bank/political relations. These are, first, the potential for confusion or even panic in the field (in financial markets and among the public) through conflicting communications about objectives and actions; second, the risk of strategic incoherence undermining the execution of crisis management efforts; and, third, leaders (generals or central bankers) who are facing new personal tests.[27] Jobs and economic output are not lives, but they are livelihoods and they matter greatly.

Moreover, a crisis can shift the legitimate boundary between politics and "administration." That too is apparent from war. The proper role of politics in war can vary greatly according to the nature and persistence

[27] Betts, "Civil-Military Relations," and Cohen, *Supreme Command*, pp. 8–9.

of the conflict: whether it is total war (as in World War II) or a more limited conflict in which the military has to engage with local people in a battle for hearts and minds or what Emile Simpson has called "armed politics" (as, for example, in Afghanistan).[28] Such vastly different circumstances drive the particular issues that are salient for the media and the public, affecting national morale and thus where politicians would ideally like to redraw the dividing line between control and delegated autonomy. Given the costs of uncertainty and of protagonists' energies being displaced from the real-world crisis to their own boundary dispute, this underlines the need for the nature of military/political relations in different combat scenarios to be as clear as possible ex ante. That requires structure, which is hard to get right, but no less important for that.[29]

There are broad lessons here for central bankers. As with the military, the circumstances warranting political input or decision can vary enormously. They might range from deciding to intervene fiscally to address a full-blown national emergency, through liaison with foreign counterparts, to helping regulators handle intense public upset at the failure of a bank, as occurred in the UK when the closure of BCCI in the early 1990s initially sparked accusations of racial bias. As with the military, there can be a need for technocrats to inject realism into political councils once crisis becomes unavoidable, with all that remains at stake being how to avoid descent into the deepest Circles of Hell. As with the military in coalition-based offensives, during an international financial crisis it can be vital to get across to the domestic public what authorities in other countries are doing, since their actions, however remote, might be directly relevant at home the day after tomorrow. And as Simpson, paraphrasing Clausewitz, has observed of the tension between ex ante high policy and the dynamics of war's violence, in an economic crisis policy must continuously command the authorities' choices but cannot fully control and so must adapt to the shifting demands imposed by the financial system's dynamics.[30]

[28] Simpson, *War*; especially chapter five, "Liberal Powers and Strategic Dialogue."

[29] It has been suggested that the UK could learn some lessons from the US in this area (de Waal, "Right People").

[30] Simpson, *War*, pp. 126–129.

Despite those structural similarities, there is a further twist when an independent central bank reaches the boundaries of its legal mandate and powers but crisis rages. Compared with the general case (chapters 11 and 16), those would likely be circumstances in which the functional purposes of the normally separated spheres of monetary policy, fiscal policy, government debt management, and regulatory policy have converged on the elemental need simply to keep the system, political as well as economic, afloat somehow or other. In other words, the ideal then might be to default to government by a "universal" central civil service under unitary political control (a solution beyond reach in some advanced-economy democracies). Whereas in normal conditions the very point of IA regimes is to establish and mark "territorial" boundaries, thereby making the system of government more resilient through enhanced delivery of public policy, precisely that separation of functions could, it seems, become a source of existential fragility during some types of crisis.

Arguably, that is what happened over 2007–2009, with the consequences still playing out years later in nationally distinct debates. While, as we have seen (chapters 2 and 16), the question ringing around Westminster was "Who in future will be in charge?" in the US the revelation that the Fed had cooperated with Treasury and market regulators sparked comment to the effect that their much vaunted independence was a bit of a sham.[31] In fact, it should hardly be controversial to say that a national financial and economic crisis requires all of the following:

- political objectives and high strategy;
- a "field marshal" to oversee the operational implementation (including adaptation to events) of the core of that strategy, and to signal when it needs updating; and
- mechanisms for cooperation and coordination among agencies, including IAs, holding specific powers conferred by the legislature and, where warranted, with other countries.

[31] For example, and bearing in mind that not all US "independent agencies" are independent, Bressman and Thompson, "Future of Agency Independence."

Depending on the nature of the response, the central banker can be the field marshal, disinterring part of the older tradition's know-how-oriented mind-set described in the introduction to part IV. It is well captured by Isaiah Berlin's account of the parallel universe of expert political judgment:[32]

> Integrating a vast amalgam of constantly changing, multicoloured, evanescent, perpetually overlapping data . . . [with] highly developed discrimination of what matters from the rest.

Whether or not they play that operationally strategic role on the field of battle, central bankers must be ready to cooperate with government and other agencies. The generation and, during prolonged turmoil, updating of objectives and high strategy should be, in the military terms quoted in chapter 4, as far as possible a matter of "equal dialogue but unequal authority."[33] That captures an important truth for central banks, subject to an equally important qualification.

In marked contrast to military/political relations, well-defined zones of monetary independence exist ex ante and should not be violated informally or surreptitiously. Subject to *overt* use of any statutory override powers or emergency legislation, an independent central bank remains autonomous for those decisions delegated to it by the legislature. That absolutely does not preclude discussion, cooperation, and, in particular, taking others' planned actions into account when deciding on the use of their own monetary and regulatory powers. As such, the set up allies effectiveness with democracy and the rule of law.

One of this book's core messages is that, in healthy democracies committed to remaining healthy, structure can and must help (fifth Design Precept). Thus, an economy's Money-Credit Constitution should incorporate substantive and procedural contingency arrangements that are as extensive as humanly possible, and are credible. That means clarifying the Fiscal Carve-Out, which needs

[32] Berlin, "Political Judgment." It is not a bad description of Eddie George in crisis management mode, and of both he and Alan Greenspan in conjunctural economics mode. Research suggests that, in certain circumstances, good decision making is eclectic and fox-like, "accept[ing] ambiguity and contradiction" (Tetlock, *Expert Political Judgment).*

[33] Betts, "Civil-Military Relations."

- to articulate a principled regime for emergency liquidity reinsurance beyond the routinely available facilities; and,
- *if* the people's elected representatives expressly wish, to make provision for interventions in broad credit markets when standard monetary transmission channels are severely impaired.

All that must be subject to the qualification of (a) *not* claiming that the monetary authority will never do something when in fact it will, and (b) not relaxing the bar on direct monetary financing of government and on liquidity assistance to irretrievably bust intermediaries. No doubt situations would still arise where even the appropriate processes had not been envisaged, but it is possible to push out the frontier at which pure procedural innovation takes over. As legitimacy seekers, it is desperately in central banks' interests to achieve this.

To the previous chapter's balance-sheet-management general principles and this chapter's LOLR principles, we must therefore add one more:

> Where it is not clear what would happen at the boundary of their normal powers, central banks should publicly urge elected politicians to make those boundaries absolutely binding or, alternatively, provide procedural clarity for how they would make decisions to adjust the boundaries in a crisis. Any such politically endorsed within-emergency extensions should be bindingly constrained by the purposes of the central bank and the imperative of not providing equity support.

Operational independence of independent central banks would be preserved within any new in-emergency boundaries set by the politicians, who would be constrained by the institution's formal ex ante purposes and their own accountability to the public. Where a central bank opposes the possibility of such in-emergency extensions, they must instead favor the initial set of constraints being completely binding.

In terms of our deep values, something very odd indeed would be going on if, instead of the course I prescribe, central bankers were to look to the courts to move public understanding of ambiguous boundary provisions. It should be elected politicians who decide whether to broaden the scope of their central bank's operational discretion in an emergency, not the judges. To repeat and apply a point from part II, one set of unelected high officials (the judges) cannot remedy the democratic deficit in another set of unelected officials (the central bankers).

This is the reasoned basis for the prescription in the introduction (chapter 1) that when the ECB innovated to save the euro area, it should have sought the blessing of the European Council. Even more elementally, it could have been an intergovernmental meeting of heads of government, since it was a moment for the members of the confederation to affirm whether they wished their Project to survive.[34]

Ex Post Accountability

Those are ex ante constraints. Ex post there is accountability to the legislature.

Here again there is a lesson from modern military history. It seems to be accepted that during the Vietnam War, the top brass dissembled and disguised from Congress their severe doubts, perhaps opposition to, President Lyndon Johnson's strategy, even when asked direct questions. Decades later, after initially stepping around the point, General Eric Shinseki took the opposite approach when he revealed to the Senate his views on broadly how many more soldiers would be needed on the ground to effect the administration's Iraq strategy. That, too, proved controversial.[35]

Reading across to central banking in emergencies, there is a similar risk of open and frank testimony during a crisis undermining operations intended to hold the economic system together. The same might occasionally go for revealing publicly certain threats to stability. In getting over this, lessons might, again, be learned from the world of security and intelligence, where briefings of legislative committees in-camera (in secret) are used in some jurisdictions to ensure accountability while protecting against perversely premature public transparency. I am not aware of such an arrangement for central banks and finance ministries anywhere in the advanced democracies, but it could be considered. Away from emergencies themselves, such hearings could also be used to enhance political oversight of prudential supervision of individual firms and of the system as a whole if the stress-test disclosures discussed in chapter 21 prove materially incomplete or opaque.

[34] Transparency International picked up this point (Braun, *Two Sides*).

[35] Bruce Ackerman's second 2010 Tanner Lecture on Human Values (Ackerman, *Decline and Fall*, footnote 29).

A small step in this direction has been taken in the UK. Angered not to have been informed at the time of the massive covert liquidity support provided to some UK banks in the autumn of 2008, the Treasury Select Committee and the Public Accounts Committee subsequently agreed with the Bank and Treasury that their chairs would be briefed on any similar covert operations in the future.

Summing up the lessons for central banking from the military sphere:

- *Before* crisis: Plan, both substance and procedures, and build realistic relationships between politicians and their likely field marshals.
- *In* crisis: Institute means for cooperation across agencies, with a division of labor that does not violate properly delegated statutory authorities and in particular IAs' insulation from direction, except via overt legal override.
- *Post*crisis: Ensure an account is given to legislators.

There should be as much serious interest in thinking about and establishing such regimes as there is in the delicate innards of the monetary policy regime.

The State of Play

As I write, jurisdictions vary in how far they approximate this book's broad prescriptions.

The ECB does not have anything approaching an ex ante accord with government on crisis management, plausibly because it has no finance ministry counterpart and because mistaken inferences about cooperation have been drawn from its deeply entrenched insulation.

Since 2013, the Bank of England's monetary policy remit has contained provisions to the effect that where unconventional interventions in specific markets or activities have implications for credit allocation or for risk, governance arrangements must be agreed with executive government.

In the US, the Treasury and the Federal Reserve issued a joint statement in 2009 on how they would cooperate in managing the crisis: broadly, that the Fed would avoid credit risk and credit allocation; that monetary stability should not be jeopardized by crisis measures; and that they would each urge Congress to introduce a comprehensive resolution regime for critical financial institutions. The late Anna Schwartz, coauthor with Milton Friedman of the seminal *Monetary History of the United States*, was one of very few people to take an interest in this important document. It has not been updated, even though it has since been overtaken by the 2010 Dodd-Frank legislation.[36]

So there is unfinished business here. With undemocratic liberalism in the people's sights, it would be sensible to articulate what happens when a central bank's limits are reached *before* they are breached. But would even that be enough?

[36]US Treasury, "Role of the Federal Reserve," and Schwartz, "Boundaries."

24

Overmighty Citizens After All?

THREATS AND RECONFIGURATIONS

Central bank independence had a specific justification. Monetary policy was thought to have major dynamic consistency issues and did not have much non-technical political content. In today's world where the dominant problem is too little not too much inflation the dynamic consistency argument loses its force. And the greater salience of exchange rate issues, fiscal monetary cooperation and credit allocation aspects of monetary policy draws it closer to policy normally delegated to democratic institutions. So at a minimum central bank independence needs reconsideration and it's possible that it can no longer be justified in its current form.

—Larry Summers, exchange with the author, 2017

If central bankers are the only game in town, I'm getting out of town!

—Mervyn King, at the Bank for International Settlements, 2013[1]

All we can do is ask simple questions and listen to your very erudite explanations. . . . What good is that sort of accountability to elected politicians?

—George Mudie, MP, to Mervyn King, House of Commons Treasury Committee hearing, June 28, 2011

The previous three chapters discussed substantive constraints, guided by the Principles for Delegation, necessary for the postcrisis central banks decently to find a place in, respectively, the regulatory state, the fiscal state, and the emergency state. Part of the solution is that each role

[1]Personal notes of Mervyn King's response to Raghuram Rajan ("Step in the Dark") during the first Andrew Crockett Memorial Lecture, June 2013.

must be framed, alongside monetary policy, as part of an economy's Money-Credit Constitution.

If simply armed with both regulatory and balance-sheet powers, a central bank in theory has numerous options when faced with some threats to monetary-system stability. If a credit and asset-price boom jeopardizes both the resilience of the banking system and price stability, it might in principle raise regulatory capital and/or liquidity requirements, apply stricter supervisory controls to those individual banking intermediaries that are especially vulnerable, increase the haircuts (excess collateral requirements) applied to its own operations in the particularly exuberant markets, increase interest rates, and so on. We have argued that it is important that the choice should not be biased in favor of balance-sheet policy over regulatory interventions, given the former's blurred boundary with fiscal policy.

Consistent with that precept, the principles for judicial review of democratically legitimate (Principles-compliant) IAs espoused in chapter 15 would leave the central bank broadly neutral. In particular, contrary to the likely effect of some prescriptions in this area, the central bank would not be incentivized to turn immediately to monetary policy measures simply because more intense judicial scrutiny would follow regulatory interventions. Instead, subject to the protection of liberal freedoms, each type of policy instrument would face the same broad standard of not being unreasonable or irrational.[2]

Rather than differential judicial standards driving things, the legislature's statutory regimes would do so. The effect of the Multiple-Mission Constraints would be that each separate policy committee would have to consider how, if at all, to use *its* specific powers in pursuit of *its* specific objective. The central bank's regulators could not look to monetary policy makers to relieve them of the responsibility for ensuring the system was resilient.

Nevertheless, in driving insulation from day-to-day politics, the central bank's monetary powers *are* special insofar as monetary independence is a corollary of the higher-level separation of powers (chapter 12). We turn finally, then, to the revival of a battery of arguments, initially encountered in the introduction (chapter 1), that monetary inde-

[2]This seems broadly consistent with Goldmann, "Adjudicating Economics?"

pendence was itself a false turn or, alternatively, that its moment has passed given the challenges facing economies following the Great Financial Crisis.

Even if the case for monetary independence emerges broadly intact, we should ask whether it leads inevitably to central banks being the "only game in town," with overreliance on them damaging the people's economic welfare. And while careful regime design can curb their hard power, we need to recognize that they might nevertheless emerge as overmighty citizens on account of their latent symbolic or *soft power*.[3] The first of those hazards points the way toward a need for renewed debate on fiscal regimes. On the second, this chapter and the book's conclusion draw lessons from judicial norms for how central bankers need to conduct themselves in our democratic constitutional republics in order for their formal political insulation to be sustainable.

All this leads up to the rather basic question, Who are the central bankers?

THE POLITICAL ECONOMY OF MONETARY POLICY AFTER THE CRISIS

Some critics have long maintained that a basic precondition for central bank independence (CBI)—its irrelevance to the long-run distribution of welfare—is a sham or smoke screen for an instrument of neoliberal ideology. In the wake of the Great Financial Crisis, the painfully slow and uneven recovery that followed, and the continuing power of private finance, those concerns have resurfaced. There are suggestions that monetary policy makers do make big distributional choices, that independence is no longer needed, and that narrowly focused interest-rate policy might even be perverse.

A Piece of Good News: Not Biased to Sacrifice Jobs

Before turning to those three challenges, there is, however, one highly positive thing to say about the postcrisis operation of monetary policy.

[3] Nye, *Future of Power*.

With credible regimes, it proved possible to provide monetary support to economies in distress without unleashing the inflation genie. As reported in chapter 1, some early critics of independence, particularly on the Left, believed that central bankers had asymmetric and unbalanced preferences: that they disliked above-target inflation more than they disliked below-target inflation, and so would sacrifice jobs to the altar of price stability. As it turned out, the anchoring of *medium-term* inflation expectations made it feasible for central banks to inject a truly massive stimulus to nominal demand in order to fend off the initial risk of the economy disappearing into the vortex of another Great Depression and, subsequently, to aid recovery.

It is hard to believe that monetary policy under the control of elected politicians could have held on to the credibility needed to permit anything like the amount of stimulus delivered. In the UK, with a watchful eye on medium-term inflation expectations, we maintained exceptional stimulus even while oil-price and other cost shocks temporarily pushed up headline inflation to over 5 percent during 2011. I hope that goes some way to assuage those who, in good faith, harbored concerns about central bankers being biased toward the welfare of particular interest groups. Whatever their private preferences, their democratically mandated legal duty was clear.

Distributional Effects versus Choices

That is not to say that there have not been distributional effects. There has been pronounced concern, perhaps especially in Germany and the UK, that quantitative and credit easing (QE)—prosaically, buying lots of government and private-issuer bonds—have created systematic winners and losers. By pushing up asset prices, the critics insist, QE has enriched the rich while making home ownership more of a stretch for the young; and by pushing down returns on savings, it has hurt those middling households and pensioners who are not remotely rich but who rely on an income from a lifetime of saving. Coming during a period of subdued growth and after years of static or declining median incomes in many advanced-economy democracies, this has seemed like taking a cake that was not growing much and redistributing it in favor of those who already had the biggest slices. Since democratic politics exists as the forum in which sectional interests get weighed and settled, the complaint—comprising the first of our three challenges—is that central bankers have wandered into, and found themselves stranded in, alien territory where they do not belong.

If they have (and are), this could violate the Delegation Criteria's proscription on insulated trustee agencies making big decisions on the distribution of welfare across groups and across time. To make sense of this, we have to call upon the distinction introduced in part I between distributional *choices* and *effects*.

There is no doubt that monetary policy can have, and has been having, distributional *effects*.[4] When a central bank raises interest rates to restrain demand, there is typically some cost to debtors and asset holders, and some uplift in the running return to savers. In normal circumstances, those effects are dominated for society as a whole by the benefits of maintaining sustainable growth; and, separately, they tend to be offset over time by the obverse effects that kick in during periods of easy monetary policy. The distinctive thing about the postcrisis period is that super-low nominal interest rates and asset purchases have gone on for years, so that some of the distributional effects have been more pronounced and long-lived. Given that the middle-income groups have a higher tendency to vote in elections than poorer people, and given anger that elements of the rich helped cause the crisis, it is hardly surprising that these effects prompted some disquiet.

For central bankers, the dominating concern, given their mandate, was to restore growth in aggregate incomes and jobs in order to bring inflation back toward target. With hindsight, however, they should have been more active in highlighting the costs of their policy.[5] Had they done so, it would have been clearer to the public and civil society that the political authorities had the means to mitigate some of the distribu-

[4] For similar analysis from a former colleague, see Bean, "Central Banking," which I read on the final day of writing this book.

[5] The Bank of England published a paper on distributional effects during 2012, in response to questions pressed by the House of Commons Treasury Select Committee. Central bankers are now devoting effort to explaining that monetary policy is not the main cause of inequality (e.g., Constancio, "Inequality") but, however necessary, that is a somewhat different point from the one in the main text.

tional consequences, and that a different mix of monetary and fiscal policy was worth considering (see below). In that sense, this becomes a topical example of the general issue posed in this book of how elected politicians should track the distributional effects of policies delegated to administrative agencies (chapters 7 and 16).

Nonneutrality: Hysteresis, Trade-Offs, and the Redundancy of CBI

The second, but most profound, challenge is directed at what might be the central tenet of monetary economics, partly underpinning the legitimacy of delegation-cum-insulation: that money is, in the jargon, neutral and even superneutral—in other words, that increasing the amount of money in the economy does not create more output and employment *in the long run*, and that increasing the growth rate of money simply translates into a higher steady-state rate of inflation (chapter 18). A group of social democrat political scientists and commentators has long challenged this, but failed to land a decisive evidence-based blow.[6] More recently, some very prominent US-based mainstream academic economists have begun to raise more nuanced points, arguing that monetary policy could (and should) be used to head off long-term damage from massive shocks to the economy.[7]

Their argument revives concern about what is known as *hysteresis*: the possibility that after the kind of body blow delivered by the 2008/2009 collapse, the economy will not of its own accord ever recover to its precrisis path and perhaps not even to its former growth rate. This amounts to saying that persistent weakness in spending in the economy (aggregate demand) can destroy productive capacity (aggregate supply) and underlying dynamism. As then Federal Reserve chair Janet Yellen put it before the 2016 US general election, the policy question becomes

[6] Forder, "Central Bank Independence," and McNamara, "Rational Fictions."

[7] Blanchard, Cerutti, and Summers, "Inflation and Activity." Also, in a world where central banks remunerate reserves at the policy rate of interest (chapter 22), some of the old arguments about the long-run neutrality of shifts in the money stock are not so straightforward. But technicalities aside, that does not provide a reason for thinking that the long-run performance of the economy could be improved by providing monetary stimulus to an economy already operating at capacity.

whether to run a "high-pressure economy" in an attempt to recover lost ground and forestall permanent deterioration.[8]

Whether to do so would have to be weighed against the social costs of risking higher inflation or of triggering a renewed wave of financial sector improvidence (see below). If, after all, it turned out that there happened to be little slack in the economy and that the pumped-up aggregate demand did not generate extra productive capacity, inflationary pressures would intensify in the short run. More important, longer-term inflation expectations might rise if persistent attempts to generate extra supply led markets and wage bargainers to the view that policy makers were minded to take asymmetric risks with inflation. The big question, which tends to be left hanging in the air, is who should make the decision whether to adopt a high-pressure policy. Could it be left to unelected technocrats?

At a higher level, debates about hysteresis shade into an argument, expressed in the quote from Larry Summers at the chapter head, that the circumstances in which central bank independence was useful are behind us. Here it is held, variously, that the inflation problem was a quirk, albeit a serious one, of the 1970s; that the battle against inflation is now *and enduringly* won; and that today's challenges of persistently low productivity growth and debt overhang could be met more effectively by having all macroeconomic policy instruments in one set of (political) hands, lifting artificial barriers to a joined-up monetary-fiscal strategy. An advocate might add that the political and even moral consequences of a world without growth are too grave for risks to be taken.[9] The moment for fastidious adherence to separate spheres has passed, they would say, perhaps adding for effect that this is manifest in the Bank of Japan's commitment to buy bonds on whatever scale is needed to hold down long-term yields as the economy recovers, placing it in the antechamber to debt monetization.

This is a big issue, amounting to whether there still exists sufficient consensus on the substantive merits of monetary independence to sustain it. The Principles for Delegation direct us to distinguish between,

[8] Yellen, "Macroeconomic Research."

[9] On the connection between growth and a society's moral qualities, see Benjamin Friedman, *Moral Consequences*. I have no sense that Ben Friedman opposes CBI.

on the one hand, elected legislators suspending CBI temporarily in order to deliver an inflationary shock through monetary financing of the deficit and, on the other hand, permanently delegating monetary policy to the elected executive. We have argued (chapter 12) that the latter would violate the separation of powers by putting the inflation tax in the hands of the executive branch; not an argument that depends on time inconsistency. Putting the central bank permanently under the control of the elected executive would, moreover, enable policy makers to steer credit or resources to particular groups, sectors, or regions without sanction from the legislature. And it would dilute government's capacity to commit to a systematic monetary policy. That is evident in some of the opposition to the main central banks' attempts since the Great Financial Crisis to get inflation back *up* to target, underlining that, as discussed in chapter 5, commitment problems go wider and deeper than the economists' beloved time inconsistency.[10] The risks to political stability and legitimacy from stagnant growth exist, therefore, alongside distinct risks from sidestepping our constitutionalist values and abandoning the value of commitment to agreed purposes. In the 1980s and 1990s, it probably did not matter much that, as chapter 18 recalled, different justifications for CBI commanded support in the core economics profession (time inconsistency) and among policy makers (political short-termism). Today, we should take the broader view of the commitment problem.

Welfare-wise, it would be perverse to give up CBI simply on the grounds that price stability is not sufficient to guarantee improving prosperity or to deliver financial stability, as it would be very odd if it were. In particular, it seems likely that the possibility of hysteresis persistently depleting economic capacity and dynamism has little or no bearing on whether the hazards of politically controlled monetary policy could reassert themselves at some point.[11] On that view, the monetary authority should have discretion to run a "high-pressure economy" only if medium- to long-term inflation expectations remain in line with the (explicit or implicit) target it has been given for inflation.

[10] Similar points, without the constitutionalist framing, are made in Bernanke, "Monetary Policy."

[11] For similar sentiments, see Granville, *Remembering Inflation*.

Any such conclusion has to rest, however, on a judgment that the social costs of an inflation bias or of politically motivated monetary policy are not worth inflicting upon people. Under the Principles, that is not a judgment for the central bankers themselves. If it did ever make sense temporarily to suspend monetary policy insulation, that should be an explicit, formal decision made by elected politicians.

Monetary Policy Undoes Itself: Risk Appetite and Debt

The third challenge to the current order of things is whether monetary policy can be counterproductive for broader monetary-system stability. After years of what seemed like denial, it is finally becoming accepted, if not yet a consensus, that monetary policy can and does affect risk taking in financial markets, and not always in healthy ways.

There has been increasing recognition that risk premia and risk appetite are affected by monetary policy—not only by those monetary operations, such as quantitative easing, that are designed to influence risk premia but also by regular interest-rate decisions. This might be so if very low interest rates, as prevailed during the early 2000s, push investors and traders to search for yield along the maturity spectrum and down the credit spectrum.[12] Alternatively, if asset-market volatility were dampened for protracted periods by monetary policy makers preferring to smooth the path of their policy rate, traders and investors might conclude the world is less risky than it is, with the perverse effect of making it more risky (jeopardizing the system's resilience).

Whatever the underlying forces, monetary policy could even start to look like part of the problem of boom-and-bust. That is essentially the position of the Bank for International Settlements (BIS), which argues that its members should place less weight on stabilizing "business cycle" fluctuations in jobs and activity, shifting their emphasis to managing a slower-moving "financial cycle." Were that so, the case

[12] Stein and Hanson, "Monetary Policy." First published as a Federal Reserve research paper in 2012, this revealed that persistently easy conventional monetary policy can lead to a reduction in term premia, the compensation investors demand for taking longer-term exposures. The result was replicated for the sterling yield curve, as reported in Tucker, "National Balance Sheets." Although not proven, this phenomenon might be driven by a search for yield by asset managers and intermediaries that are subject to nominal yield targets and/or relative performance objectives.

for independence would be weakened until and unless economists and central bankers have a deeper understanding of (a) how all this works, and (b) whether the new approach could be operationalized in ways amenable to legislators setting a monitorable objective that could be delegated consistently with democratic values (chapter 21)—for the moment leaving the central bankers' international headquarters looking like an unlikely (and no doubt inadvertent) ally of CBI's opponents.

The approach of this book is, instead, to place the burden of containing the social costs of misplaced exuberance on regulatory policies that set a robust standard of resilience for the financial system. If monetary policy can fuel imprudence, then multiple-mission central banks have incentives to be tough regulators (chapters 20 and 21).

That, it must be said, does not address broader concerns about the misallocation of resources, actual or incipient overindebtedness across the private sector and among governments, or the associated macroeconomic imbalances among countries.[13] The reason, quite simply, is that to attempt to do so would stretch the boundaries of central banking too far (as argued in chapter 21). But the effect is to reveal a deeper problem of "missing regimes" that, contrary to the atmosphere among policy makers after the Great Financial Crisis, was not cured by the "macroprudential moment" that for a while gripped the technocratic imagination.

In fact, there were and remain at least two other missing regimes if the social costs of the financial pathologies and frictions discussed in chapter 21 are to be mitigated: one for addressing those internal financial imbalances, including any excessive household indebtedness, that do not jeopardize monetary-system resilience; and one for managing national balance-sheet vulnerabilities that arise from the cumulative pattern of capital flows with the rest of the world (what might be called "whole economy macroprudential policy"). While it is for the elected executive part of government to ensure a proper review of the need for such rich macrostability regimes, there is nothing to stop central banks from drawing attention to the insufficiency of their own proper contributions.[14]

[13] Respectively, Turner, *Between Debt*, and King, *End of Alchemy*.
[14] Tucker, *Financial Stability Regimes*.

THE ONLY GAME IN TOWN: CENTRAL BANKING AS FALSE HOPE

Behind those various concerns and challenges lies a common theme: that we have become overly reliant on central banking. This has become a preoccupation of the central bankers themselves.

Giving the first Andrew Crockett Memorial Lecture in June 2013, Raghuram Rajan, the then recently appointed governor of the Reserve Bank of India, concluded by suggesting that central banks had "offered [themselves] as the only game in town." The assembled company of central bankers was not comfortable. Mervyn King got close to their feelings when he responded, "If central bankers are the only game in town, I'm getting out of town!" (which he literally was, retiring a few weeks later).[15]

That same weekend in Basel, the Bank for International Settlements' annual report set out at length why and how the true heavy lifting of sustainable economic recovery was, in fact, unavoidably in the hands of the governments, banks, households and firms whose balance sheets needed strengthening. Above all, supply side reform was needed to improve long-term growth prospects, increasing the spending power that easy monetary policy was bringing forward. By supporting near-term demand for goods and services, the central banks could create time for those fundamental adjustments and reforms to be effected, but could not do more. The BIS fretted that things would be even worse if that time was not grasped by governments and others because, perversely, central banking interventions seemed to suffice to get through immediate problems.

Even in countries with solid public finances and even when standard monetary policy reached the effective lower bound for short-term nominal interest rates, politicians declined to provide sustained discretionary short-term fiscal stimulus in the years after the worst of the Great Financial Crisis. So, as the BIS feared, the central banks were left as the only game in town. Coming on top of their sometimes controversial liquidity support operations during the first phase of the crisis, their macroeconomic interventions raised questions about independence.

[15] Rajan, "Step in the Dark," p. 12. Andrew Crockett was head of the Bank for International Settlements from 1994 to 2003. Among many other contributions to economic policy, he called in the early 2000s for a macroprudential approach to banking-system regulation.

For some, it reinforced preexisting doubts about whether CBI could ever be legitimate. For others, it ignited concerns that they had got too close to finance ministries, compromising invaluable independence.

In fact, the world was bumping into a costly strategic tension between central banks and elected policy makers. The former have legal mandates that impose constraints but also create obligations, whereas the latter are subject to few constraints but carry equally few legal obligations. In consequence, when short-term politics raises problems (what political scientists call *political transaction costs*) for elected governments and legislators acting to contain a crisis or bring about economic recovery, they can sit on their hands safe in the knowledge that their central bank will be obliged by its mandate to try (within the legal limits of its powers). Rajan had the right verb but the wrong mode. Central banks did not volunteer to be the only game in town, they were volunteered by governments (transitive, not intransitive, volunteering). The upshot can be a flawed mix of monetary, fiscal, and structural policies, creating avoidable risks in the world economy and financial system.

Central Banks Could Not Set Aside Their Legal Mandate

Notwithstanding those likely truths, however, it is a mistake to stipulate or imply that central banks should sit on their hands in order to induce governments to act. To do so would be to set aside their legal mandates from elected assemblies, flouting our democratic values and the rule of law. It is one thing for central banks to be the only game in town, but quite another for them to abrogate the sovereign power, taking it to themselves.

Constrained as they were, therefore, to do as much as they could within their powers, they ended up looking like something they are not: *the* macroeconomic policy makers. And they were left exposed to being held responsible for something they simply cannot deliver: prosperity.

That this has not caused a bigger political outcry among the people would be remarkable were it not for the precrisis orthodoxy that monetary policy could get us through any cyclical downturn and the practical success in escaping another Great Depression. In the short term, the only answer is for the community of central bankers to get back to a previous generation's mantra, repeated over and over again: Central banks can buy time but cannot enhance long-run prosperity. They can help the economy recover from disastrous recessions but cannot improve underlying growth dynamics. They can help bring spending forward but cannot create more long-term wealth. To channel the late Eddie George, stability is what central bankers exist to deliver, and stability is a necessary condition for the good things in life, but it is not remotely sufficient.[16]

Clarifying the Role of the Fiscal Authority in the Fiscal State

In the longer run, however, a deeper challenge has to be met.

While I have argued that it is possible to fix the democratic legitimacy of multiple-mission central banks, nothing I have offered cures the problematic strategic interaction between fiscal and monetary policy makers described above.

That is because I have focused on principles and democratic processes for drawing the boundary between unelected technocratic power and elected representative power. But in terms of effectiveness (welfare), it is hard to decide where the boundary should be by looking inside only one of the zones (that of the technocrats). It matters what is in the other zone and what incentives *its* occupants have to act. This is the *grand dilemma of central banking.*

In short, a Fiscal Constitution is needed, not just chapter 20's Money-Credit Constitution. It needs, among other things, to cover the role of the fiscal authority in macroeconomic stabilization when monetary policy is close to the effective lower bound and the economy faces deep recession; how the distributional effects of central banks' actions will be tracked; and, in the financial services sphere, whether a capital-of-last-resort policy will be in place for when all else has failed or whether a policy of "no bailouts" will be credibly absolute.[17]

[16] That is the theme of El-Erian, *Only Game in Town.*

[17] For example, DeLong and Summers, "Fiscal Policy in a Depressed Economy." On COLR, Tucker, "Repertoire," and Geithner, "Are We Safer?"

These questions are not small. For example, if the automatic stabilizers of the tax and welfare system were to be reset so as to kick in more strongly in really bad economic circumstances, it might be necessary for governments to operate with lower stocks of outstanding debt during normal times. Issues of this kind have tended to get much less attention than debates about optimal monetary policy.

What Central Bankers Can and Can't Do to Solve Their Own and Society's Problem

In other words, it is possible that a cost (negative externality) of central bank independence has been underinvestment in fiscal institutions (both research and practice).

We need society to reject the notion that central banks are the Only Game in Town, not because they failed but because it is not sustainable and violates our values. Even where central bankers themselves see this, as some surely do, they cannot do more than talk about it. They cannot play at being Plato's guardians. But, to reintroduce a point already made at a less strategic level, there is no reason on earth why they should not speak about the downsides to their policies and about their limited role in healing the economy.

This requires central bankers to pull off a tough act of communication, explaining what they cannot deliver rather than what others should do. The public should trust them for what they can do but not rely on them for what they cannot do. It means looking burdened by the current expectations they labor under. (As one wit put it, if they are the only game in town, God help us if they ever look as though they might be enjoying it.) And it means admitting ignorance of the deep forces that might be reshaping real-economy prospects.

OVERMIGHTY CITIZENS: CENTRAL BANKS IN A DEMOCRATIC SOCIETY

All that is made harder by the remarkable expansion in central banks' powers and responsibilities in the regulatory state. If central banks are not omniscient, why give them even more powers? We have spent this book articulating and, in part IV, applying principles to address this, the greatest *tractable* challenge to CBI.

Our solution revolves around well-defined regimes, with powers that are tied as narrowly as possible to the goal of monetary-system stability. That is needed to incentivize central bankers to seek esteem and prestige through results (chapter 5). Were they also to carry various of the responsibilities we ruled out in chapter 21 (e.g., competition policy, consumer protection), they would be so very powerful that simply holding office would instantly bestow on them whatever standing or fame they valued.

We should acknowledge, however, that risks remain even with central bankers that have tightly drawn responsibilities: today's top monetary officials can be world famous irrespective of their achievements. That reinforces the importance of effective political accountability (chapters 6, 9, 11, and 15).

Political Accountability

But lacking powers over central bank budgets, are legislators effectively impotent once they have set the rules of the game? This is not an idle question, as illustrated by the quotation at the chapter head from a Westminster committee hearing.

In June 2011, George Mudie, MP, then the senior Labour party member of the UK House of Commons Treasury Committee, pressed Mervyn King (and, briefly, me) on what, if anything, happened as a result of such hearings; could they really influence monetary policy? Our response was that so long as Parliament maintained the Bank's operational independence, month-by-month monetary policy decisions were for the Bank, but that parliamentarians had the power to change or abolish the regime. This is no less true of the Fed and most other national monetary authorities.

Here we see something important. It is not just that "independence" is still being negotiated, in a long process of becoming embedded into our societies. It means that it is a good thing that independence is debated, tossed around, criticized, applauded, tolerated, because those very debates are integral to the democratic legitimacy of IA regimes (chapter 11). That is the necessary ingredient for the people's representatives choosing to maintain independent central banks because they wish, on balance, to keep society strapped to the mast of a continuing commitment to monetary stability. Thus, far from retreating to safe spaces (chapter 1), monetary authorities need to expose their very existence to challenge.

Domestic Accountability and the Transnational Elite

Such debates and, where sustained, consensus go some way to address the concern that central banking has drifted into being, or always was, a vehicle serving the interests of a globalized metropolitan elite: policy by and for "Davos Man."

The sober version of that issue is that domestic democratic responsibility and accountability might in practice be closed off by the modalities of international policy making on the monetary system, symbolized by closed-door meetings at the central bankers' Basel Tower headquarters. That is exaggerated, however. The machinery for and acceptance of international policy cooperation exists only because domestic lawmakers permit and accept it. And, in the regulatory sphere, all stability policy is articulated in domestic laws, rules, and guidance, subject to local checks and balances.

Nevertheless, in the course of this book (chapters 12 and 15) we have advocated greater and more frequent transparency on the emerging ideas and plans of the international bodies and committees through which central banks cooperate. Among other things, they should actively seek out opportunities to testify domestically (and, in the EU, regionally) on international regulatory issues; call out politicians when they pretend not to know that domestic policy making draws or even relies on international cooperation; and make clear that the core standard for stability policy is set or blessed at the political level.

If only more could be done to ensure domestic awareness of international cooperation, more could also be done to insulate central bankers from the risk of capture by their private sector counterparts in the global financial elite. As well as staying away from cosmopolitan business gatherings that are not open to scrutiny, this might involve reinforcing the soft norms of their service. And for that, central bankers could usefully draw on the example of the judiciary.

LESSONS FROM THE JUDICIARY: APPOINTMENTS, TENURE, CONFLICTS

Like the central banks, the judiciary are subject to what one leading British constitutional commentator has called *explanatory accountability*, not sacrificial accountability: having to explain but without fear of being sacked.[18] Like the central banks, the highest courts decide cases in committees on the basis of individual "votes," acting under clear procedures and giving principles-based reasons for their decisions.[19]

Tenure

Unlike the central bankers, not only are the top judges appointed for longish terms, they actually serve out those terms, after which they typically retire into obscurity or, put another way, go into retirement proper. In the UK, the conditions of appointment preclude a retiring judge from returning to private practice, with the official guidance noting that retired judges might still be regarded by the public as representatives of the judicial community.[20] Here, practice across central banking might usefully shift.

Various problems arise. For example, terms might be long in principle but not in reality. In the UK, "external" members of the policy committees are not even appointed for long terms, but instead for only three years, renewable once. In the US, although appointed to long terms, Fed Board governors often in practice serve only a few years, which has inevitably led to what is commonly perceived as a chair-centric committee. It is hard to believe that this was intended by Congress when it gave governors terms of fourteen years but the chair a term of four years. It risks making a reality of "personnel is policy," contrary to the warrant

[18] Bogdanor, "Parliament and the Judiciary." Also, Judiciary of England and Wales, *Accountability of the Judiciary.*

[19] Paterson, *Final Judgment*; and for a comparison with central banking, Goodhart and Mead, "Central Banks."

[20] Judiciary of England and Wales, *Guide to Judicial Conduct*, chapter nine.

for insulation from day-to-day politics (chapter 5).[21] By contrast, no one expects a Supreme Court judge to step down after less than a handful of years.

Conversely, a lack of term limits can be problematic. They exist in the euro area and the UK but not in the US. It is widely thought that Alan Greenspan's eighteen and a half years as Fed chair was too long, for anyone. Ironically, given the justification for central bank independence, the problem arose due to an interesting twist on political short-termism: as Greenspan's stature grew, whenever the expiry of his four-year term approached, it was not in the president's short-term interest to do the right thing for the long-term health of the institution and the country. As his biographer puts it, when he was appointed for a fourth term, "[Greenspan] was thus being recruited to elevate the [president]"; and when the question of yet another term arose, the feeling was "the longer he stayed, the more reassuring his presence."[22] One possible solution would be a statutory limit on the cumulative length of service as chair: just as the US discovered was warranted for the office of president. Another (less robust) solution would be an age limit, as applies to top judges in the UK, although not in the US.

Conflicts of Interest

Finally, in contrast to the top judges, almost nowhere is high office on the central bank council seen as properly being a policy maker's last professional post. It might turn out that way sometimes, but it is not a norm. With many central banks accruing extensive prudential regulatory or supervisory functions, however, the weight of *independent* in "independent central bank" needs refreshing. Much care has been taken in insulating monetary policy makers and, I trust, macroprudential policy makers from short-term politics. Just as much care is now needed to ensure that central banks' prudential supervisors are similarly protected from the narrow interests of the community they regulate. They should

[21] In law, Fed governors may be removed only "for cause," whereas the legislation is silent on whether the president may change the chair midterm. The combination of short (four-year) terms for the chair and chair-led policy making is not a secure basis for credible commitment given the reappointment leverage hazard described in chapter 5.

[22] Mallaby, *Man Who Knew*, pp. 563–568 and 610.

not even face the possibility of *conflicts of interest*. In each jurisdiction, society needs to decide where it stands on this issue.

We could go further. Should top officials be allowed to vote in political elections? In the US, members of the Supreme Court *can* vote in congressional or presidential elections. In the UK, the position has changed. When, until 2005, the top judges were members of the House of Lords, they were subject to the bar on all members of the second chamber voting in general elections. Now they are barred from sitting in the second legislative chamber, underlining the separation of powers, but as a result are legally free to vote in elections.[23] I hope that they do not.

Interestingly, some military commanders from the past, notably World War II US general Omar Bradley (and I think, perhaps, George Marshall), held that they should not vote.[24] More than once during my decade in office I had the thought that I would not object to an informal norm that members of the Bank of England's Monetary Policy Committee would not vote. If top officials are to be insulated from politics, it is as well to reinforce, reciprocally, that they should not participate in party politics, even in the private recesses of their minds. A former president of England's Supreme Court said, "I am not even aware of the politics of my colleagues on the Court."[25] Nor, I am glad to say, did I know the politics of my tenured colleagues at the Bank of England.

Even where the deep values, interests, and preferences of individual policy makers are perforce kept at the door of the committee room by a clear mission and transparency, they should not expose the trust placed in them and their colleagues, as trustees, to perceptions that they stand for this or that rather than for the mandate. That means an absolute bar on outside activities with any public policy content, other than those ex officio roles entailed by their service. The US is more robust on that than the UK and the EU.

[23] Any members of the Supreme Court who are also members of the House of Lords legislative assembly are barred from voting on legislation in the House. Judges have been barred from sitting in the House of Commons since 1873.

[24] Ackerman, *Decline and Fall*. This was a late-nineteenth-century norm (Huntington, *Soldier and the State*, pp. 258–259).

[25] Phillip, "Judicial Independence and Accountability."

WHO ARE THE CENTRAL BANKERS?

Come what may, as central bankers exercise their great powers there will be continuing debate about who they are: not just about the chairs but, if the committee systems work as they should, also about their board colleagues who share the weighty responsibilities. That is to the good; a necessary condition for enduring legitimacy. Central banks may not (and should not) stand as high in the constitutional order as the judiciary (chapter 12), but the powers bestowed upon them are profound.

So, who are the central bankers? It is best expressed by who they are *not*.

Our central bankers are *not a priesthood*. Often deployed in critiques of central banking mystique or in genuflection to the incantations they still occasionally wheel out to keep markets on an even keel, the metaphor's resonance lies in its appeal to higher authority. As Hobbes observed, late-medieval priests and bishops saw themselves as beyond the control of political authority, owing their duty only to God (or the Pope). As latter-day priests, central bankers would owe a duty only to Stability; and, as carriers of that Truth, they would "detect . . . right in themselves."[26] If stability is a precondition for a democratic state, then wouldn't their higher duty be to do whatever they could to preserve stability and, so, the state itself? Our response to that is no. Mario Draghi's burden, as I perceive it, was that he is not serving a fully fledged democratic state, endowed with the powers to save itself without his organization's levitational aid to the monetary system.

Nor are the central bankers *philosopher kings, maestros, or celebrities*. That is in contrast, perhaps, to the Edwardian world of Montagu Norman. As painfully illustrated by the later Greenspan years, charisma and mystique do not suffice in the modern world.

Nor, more modestly, is the chair of a central bank board its *country's chief economist*, as I recall a governor of the Bank of England being described on television by a powerful and influential politician.[27] Rather,

[26] Holmes, *Passions and Constraint*, p. 90, which offers a striking interpretation of Hobbes's discussion of this issue.

[27] I understand that in Israel the central bank governor is formally chief economist to the government.

they head an independent agency operating with powers delegated by the legislature on the initiative or with the agreement of the executive government. They and their vote-carrying colleagues are not elected: they must work within clear democratic constraints and oversight.

Finally, the central bankers should exercise self-restraint, a point that has recurred through our inquiry and that we flesh out as we bring it to a close.

Conclusion

Unelected Democrats

CITIZENS IN SERVICE, NOT IN CHARGE

> I don't hate [him]. . . . I do love him, but the day that I say that I agree with him when I don't, is the day he must get rid of me because I am no use to him anymore.
>
> —Field Marshal Alan Brooke, Chief of the General Staff, after a row with Winston Churchill, Spring 1944[1]

> The Justices have their being near the political marketplace, in which the effects of their judgments are felt. . . . A number of controls are built into their craft, which they practice under the scrutiny of a profession whose expectations and approval must matter to them.
>
> —Alexander Bickel, *The Least Dangerous Branch*, 1962[2]

> Central bank governors require three qualities above all. A deep commitment to price stability. An ability to be clear and direct to politicians about the policies that are required to produce economic stability. And the ability to be unpopular when circumstances require.
>
> —Mervyn King at a retirement dinner for Jean-Claude Trichet, 2011[3]

Those three quotations—from the military, the law, and central banking—capture vital but nuanced distinctions in how the three pillars of modern unelected state power relate to politics and politicians. While pointing toward the specificity of norms of conduct and self-

[1]Quoted from the diaries of Joan Bright, War cabinet secretariat, in Roberts, *Masters and Commanders*, pp. 474–475. It is hard to imagine a better book about group decision making and strategy at the highest level.

[2]Bickel, *Least Dangerous Branch*, p. 197.

[3]Personal notes, quoted with the approval of Mervyn King.

restraint for the powerful, they also remind us that the ascendancy of independent central bankers is relatively recent.

This book was prompted by their accumulation of wide-ranging regulatory powers in the wake of the 2008/2009 financial crisis, meaning that the fiscal state and the regulatory state now overlap and so must satisfy common principles. It amounts to a series of reflections on how advanced-economy democratic societies could address the question of legitimacy presented by the prevalence of independent agencies, highly insulated from day-to-day politics, within the administrative state. Even for those who think only results matter, that question should be of concern because legitimacy provides insulation against corrosive discontent with the *system* of government following episodic policy failure (introduction to part II).

As diagnosis, the book's main conclusion is that politicians have erred badly in not determining or embracing principles for delegation-with-insulation and independent agency design. The people's tolerance for the inevitable disappointments and frustrations of government is greater when they can vote out their governors. Procedural constraints on independent agencies, while essential, do not suffice to fill the gap. Where a delegated policy regime lacks clear objectives, accountability has no anchor, drifting with the political tides. The book's prescription is that the Principles for Delegation (or something like them) should be adopted. In some ways, they blend three great traditions in modern state building: a Hamiltonian drive for efficiency, a Madisonian fragmentation of power, and a Jeffersonian voice for the people whose purposes should be served.

THE INEVITABILITY OF THE CHALLENGE

While some commentators, and perhaps some citizens, are outraged by the very existence of agencies that deploy discretionary powers, it would be extraordinary if the structure of governmental power stayed still. Conditions change, public expectations develop, and societal values (including legitimation norms) evolve. As recently as two hundred years ago, much of what today would be recognized as government was exercised in Britain by for-profit private sector bodies acting under parliamentary charters. Both the Bank of England and the East India Company started out that way. Even within what was formally reserved to the state, Westminster struggled with the standard agency problem of how to ensure that distant governors-general stuck to British policy.[4]

As representative democracy developed, through liberal reforms and a widening franchise, legitimation principles morphed to enable change without rupture in some countries (notably Britain), but not in others. As one American social scientist put it over half a century ago:[5]

> A crisis of legitimacy is a crisis of change, and therefore its roots, as a factor affecting the stability of democratic systems, must be sought in the character of change in modern society.

A maintained assumption of this book has been that our democracies are healthy and that, therefore, the question about IA regimes concerns derivative legitimacy. In fact, however, there has been an erosion of trust in the performance and promises of government, against a backdrop of widening disparities in income and wealth during a period of subdued economic growth, uncertainty about the future, and eroding social cohesion. As in the 1970s, describing current conditions as a "legitimacy crisis" would be hyperbolic: democratic elections continue to bring about orderly transfers of power, policy continues to be contested and challenged through legal means, and the decisions of courts are not resisted, suggesting once again that our system of government is more resilient than the standing of particular governments—one of the basic strengths of representative democracy. But during a period of momentous technological and geopolitical change, the tensions between populist and technocratic government are real nonetheless, and could become worse if highly persistent low growth renders improving prosperity a zero-sum game between households, regions, and nations. Overreliance on insulated technocracy would risk inviting the Party or the Leader to come to the rescue.

It does matter, then, that as the twentieth century proceeded, more policy areas were delegated to insulated agencies, perhaps in part, as I heard in Paris, to help repair trust in government. If the United States

[4] Bown, *Merchant Kings*.

[5] Lipset, "Some Social Requisites of Democracy," p. 87.

was the first full-franchise democracy to face the question of how to reconcile that with oversight by a democratically elected legislature, the challenge is now shared on the European side of the Atlantic, where the regulatory state has gradually displaced parts of the old services state.

Thus equipped with local powers, American and European independent agencies now meet their counterparts from Asia, Latin America, and Africa in international fora that frame, set, or implement global policy. Some of that is effected via treaty organizations whose policies, when they can be agreed, are binding on all nations that choose to remain members. In other areas, informal international agreements are given legal form and force back at home. The unelected policy makers gathering in those less formal settings *are* a transnational elite, nowhere more so than in central banking's Basel headquarters.

Through all this run two perennial questions. Does the structure of government work, helping the people to live good and free lives, with realistic hopes and opportunities? And for democratic countries, is government in touch with and properly shaped by the people's purposes so that the people's elected representatives can constrain, oversee, and reform their unelected governors?

That the details should change over time is hardly surprising. That our societies should have taken so little interest in debating and establishing principles for the new geometry of government *is* somewhat surprising. And if it were not surprising, it would be depressing—because surely we still believe that democratic governance has proved, for us, both the most flexible in maintaining the people's welfare and, perhaps most elementally, the best in history to date in gradually recognizing, mitigating, and containing wrongs done to the governed by their governors.

As we saw, Woodrow Wilson, writing toward the end of the nineteenth century just as the first (more or less) independent agencies were emerging in the US, sought to make these issues go away, holding that "administration is a field of business."[6] That always was, and remains, too narrow, too simple. It is also a field of power, and political power belongs with elected politicians. The British (and others, of course) learned that the hard way with the East India Company.

[6] Wilson, "Study of Administration," p. 209.

The proliferation of independent agencies throughout the advanced economies over recent decades *is* an issue. To be comfortable with our democracies, we need to pin down how they fit in to a country's constitutional arrangements and values. If ever that were in doubt, surely it is made clear by the exercise and accumulation of power by central banks—our modern epitome of insulated authority—during and following the Great Financial Crisis. For each society, the solution will have to meet the test of *incentives-values compatibility* if they are to find their way through the twin hazards of *populism* and *technocracy.*

IRONIES, MISCONCEPTIONS, AND RECONCILIATIONS

In some ways these issues revolve around the two familiar triangles that have structured thinking about the modern constitutional state. One, about functions and values, is democracy, the rule of law, and the efficient administration of government. The other, about institutional form, is the legislature, the judiciary, and the executive. On the face of it, they map onto each other rather neatly. But the emergence and development of the regulatory state has seemed to transform the familiar separation-of-powers structure established over the long eighteenth and nineteenth centuries, with the functions of executive government now divided between the people's elected representatives and unelected technocrats. Our concern, therefore, has been whether the institutional triangle has inadvertently—and, as it has seemed to some, unacceptably—become a square through the growth of the administrative state, severing an apparently simple link between law and democracy and presenting what might be a coequal fourth branch of government.

Certainly, we have seen how the mushrooming of the administrative state elicited evolution, and sometimes revolution, in public law across the advanced-economy democracies in attempts to keep proper checks on the exercise of delegated power. The legislature, too, has had to adjust to its own creations, developing processes and protocols for overseeing agencies via specialist committees. And the elected executive branch has needed to learn to coordinate across the multitude of government functions without violating the integrity of those agencies granted independence by the legislature.

In other words, structures, norms, and expectations have been adaptive, shaped not only by law but also by the changing demands and expectations of the public. Such, however, is the hold over us of the seventeenth- and eighteenth-century political theorists and founders of constitutional government that this latest phase of state evolution has not managed to escape persistent and principled discomfort.

That is for good reasons. But in the course of our exploration, we have bumped into more than a few ironies and misconceptions.

Ironies

The irony in attitudes to delegation is apparent on both sides of the Atlantic.

In the US, some find delegation to agencies deeply troubling, and arguably unconstitutional. But in many respects it is entirely in the spirit of the founding fathers. Madison especially wished to fragment power to avoid the tyranny of the majority, a despot in the White House, or what he and others of his generation referred to as *factions* (but today we call parties or interest groups). As the scale and reach of government has extended beyond probably the wildest dreams (or fears) of the founders and as presidential power exercised by unelected executive branch helpers has increased, structured delegation to agencies, under congressional scrutiny, can be viewed as in keeping with a desire, in the country's constitutional DNA, to fracture power. Seen in that light, the challenge becomes whether agency structure admits proper democratic design, oversight, and accountability.

That approach seems to some to miss the point. To quote David Schoenbrod, an eloquent critic of the administrative state,[7]

> the democracy-based argument is not the primary argument for the claim that the [US] Constitution forbids delegation, but rather one of the reasons why the Framers intended the Constitution to forbid delegation. It is the proponents of delegation who have placed the critical reliance on democracy. Seeking to change the subject by turning from formalism to instrumentalism, they claim that delegation should be constitutional because it does not undercut democracy.

[7] Schoenbrod, "Delegation and Democracy," p. 759.

One of Schoenbrod's core concerns—unduly vague statutory purposes and a paucity of legislated standards—would, on my account, similarly preoccupy democratic critiques of double delegation. The ground is, in my view, better advanced by making a point about the sustainability of the structure of government, given our deep values, than about how to construe ambiguous provisions of codified constitutions. As we discuss in part III, the greater formalism that many US critics of the administrative state espouse is, by comparison, more evident in English law, but that is not unconnected to the Westminster Parliament being an active legislature that can and does enact and reform the law.[8] In the US, Congress has fewer incentives to play that role, which perhaps explains why the men and women of the Supreme Court entrusted with constitutional guardianship have let pass so many vague delegations: formalism in US law might be incentives-*in*compatible. If "reflexivity" between public opinion and judicial doctrine is integral to the legitimacy of the constitutional court (chapter 4, note 12), then the argument for the restoration of a nondelegation doctrine for IAs needs to be won in the public forum in language people can understand.

Separately, I might be wrong, but I rather doubt whether many constitution-based criticisms of the administrative state would be assuaged if the democratic and constitutional right to amend the US Constitution was exercised to put the legality of an insulated regulatory state beyond doubt. I suspect that not a few deep critics would just prefer a smaller state. That is a perfectly reasonable point of view, of course—arguably one of the great longer-term domestic political issues for Western democracies—but it does not speak to democratic legitimacy.

The deep issue in the US is, we have suggested, whether incentives-values compatibility is within reach. Indeed, perhaps the greatest irony of all is that the calls for "no regulation without representation" obscure the brute fact that agencies can write legally binding rules and regulations only because they have been expressly authorized to do so by the people's elected representatives. How much freedom they have is largely in the hands of the legislators elected to represent the people.

On the other side of the Atlantic, the ironies are somewhat different. In the UK, the almost existential norm of accountable and responsible

[8] Atiyah and Summers, *Form and Substance.*

government could hardly fail to generate reservations about double delegation to unelected technocrats. While that was always somewhat at odds with the inherent capabilities of the Westminster system for shaping and overseeing delegated regimes, it is hard to exaggerate the turnaround. Today, the challenge is almost the reverse of the preoccupations of the 1980s: "operational independence" has been seized upon as something like a universal panacea for the quality of government. Successive UK governments declare war on the forest of quangos, only to stick with a policy of delegation. But they do so without clear principles for when, in what mode, and in what degree delegation-with-insulation is appropriate.

Continental ironies may be stated more briefly. In Germany, the Basic Law declares itself as solving the problem absolutely but does not necessarily solve it on the ground. In France, republican power is to be unified but is now dispersed. In the EU, the main controls over unelected regulators are in the hands of unelected commissioners and their unelected staff.

Misconceptions

Misconceptions are best illustrated by a truncated narrative of the efforts of US legal scholars to make sense of, and warrant, the administrative state, not least because pretty well all of the ideas still find adherents on the Western Atlantic.[9]

The early view, prevalent before the New Deal, that agencies were no more than a "transmission mechanism" for a fully fleshed-out congressional policy was plainly delusional. Some policy discretion *is* granted, and this view therefore obscured the need to ask *how much* discretion could decently be delegated. It probably drew on, and certainly persists today in, the German *Rechtsstaat* view of administration comprising a Weberian rationalist bureaucracy executing politically endorsed law (chapter 13).[10]

Nor was the New Dealers' elevation of "expertise" sustainable as a grounding principle. The modern manifestation of the case for Plato's

[9] Stewart, "Reformation of American Administrative Law."

[10] For the influence of German traditions in early-twentieth-century US thinking about administrative law, see Ernst, *Toqueville's Nightmare*, chapter 1 ("Freund and Frankfurter").

guardians, it risks opening the door to technocracy. Elected political decision makers can get the benefits of independent-expert advice without handing over the power to decide policy. In France, where the guardians of the Republic were traditionally found in a superelite bureaucracy under political control, they needed to reinvent themselves as AAI leaders without marginalizing politicians.

By the late 1960s, those theories of delegation had largely been superseded in the US by a "battle-of-interests" model, drawing on the broader theories of interest-group liberalism and participatory democracy flourishing during that period (chapter 11). This prompted US legislators and judges to require more consultation on draft rules and more exacting procedures for adjudication, and to grant a wide range of parties standing to contest actions and decisions via the courts. It suffered two defects. The battle might be seriously imbalanced, given uneven access to resources and the prevalence of policies where benefits (or costs) are concentrated but the counterpart costs (benefits) are dispersed across the general public. Even more critically, a conception of public policy as bargaining does not get us far when the ex post costs of failure, such as financial crises, are liable to render society as a whole poorer. Those are circumstances where the intergenerational public interest has to enter policy making somehow.

A fourth conception of the administrative state—presidential control—seems, at first sight, distinctly American, but it can be translated to other constitutional structures by saying that policy should always be delegated to the elected executive government. That very obviously misses the point of delegation to truly independent agencies: *credible commitment*. Unless the president's constitutional power is construed as being to advise but not control, this amounts, therefore, to advocating the abolition of trustee-type independent agencies altogether, which would be a violation of democratic values given the executive's strong incentives to get themselves (or their party) reelected by relaxing their pursuit of some settled public purposes (such as price stability).

This cannot be solved by shifting the whole burden of legitimation to a fifth conception: rule-of-law–inspired legal prohibitions on the arbitrary use of delegated power or "decision-making that is not rational, predictable or fair."[11] The time-inconsistency problems of an "inflation bias" or political regulation of infrastructure are rooted in phenomena that are entirely rational and predictable and, in that sense, fair. They result from lawful *misuses*, not illegal *abuses*, of power (chapter 10).

Reconciliations

Where does this leave us? Well, first, the "presidential control" view points us to the vital need to distinguish politically controlled agencies from truly insulated agencies. The warrant for delegation-with-some-ongoing-political-control is different, whether those levers are held by the elected executive or the legislature, from the warrant for delegation-with-insulation. Where commitment is desired, "checks and balances" must be applied ex ante through regime design, not through ongoing control by the elected branches or via policy adventures among members of the judicial branch.

Second, the successive US legitimation narratives tell a tale of the hazards of the schoolroom: the search for a monolithic theory that sweeps all before it. If, discarding that, we instead adopt a robustness approach to legitimacy (chapter 11), each of those American justificatory paradigms emerges as drawing on an important element of our democratic values: respectively, clear legislated purposes; expertise; consultation and public debate; majoritarian accountability; and fairness, reasonableness, and predictability.

The Principles for Delegation cover each of those elements, and more, for a world that combines market failure with government failure (chapter 3). As such, they attempt to find a way through the introduction's concern about an impending clash between populism and technocracy, between illiberal democracy and undemocratic liberalism. The answer lies in the rich history of the political traditions on which constitutional democracy draws. No single strand suffices.

Liberalism of all colors concerns itself with the freedom and rights of the individual. So if someone starts out with, at least formally, a "full set" of rights but does not make a success of their life's "project," the re-

[11] Bressman, "Beyond Accountability," p. 496.

sponse can seem to be "hard luck." The republican element in our politics reminds us, however, as recent elections illustrate, that those people can still exercise their political rights, and if there are enough of them, can change the course of politics via the ballot box.

In other words, the durability of a political regime focused on rights and efficiency (the usual contested terms of liberalism) turns not solely on judicial fortitude and technocratic prowess but on whether it can sustain broad support. Technocratic liberalism must be framed by republican democratic politics. Above all, this reminds us that, under representative democracy, the elected assembly acts as the focal point of public policy debates and, so, as the shaper and overseer of delegated power.

THE PRINCIPLES FOR DELEGATION TO INDEPENDENT AGENCIES

The Principles for Delegation address the importance of clarity around whether or not an agency should be independent and how to structure its insulation.

On *whether to delegate* to an independent agency, the key test is whether it can solve socially costly credible commitment problems without venturing into major choices on the distribution of wealth or society's values. That requires broadly settled preferences and a consensus that the policy regime will work, as reflected in public debate and, eventually, in cross-party convergence.

On *how* to delegate, the core Design Precepts are well-specified goals, responsibilities, and powers, coming from the legislature; clear, mandatory procedures for decision making; the articulation of operating principles for how discretion will be exercised, so that policy can be systematic and proportionate; transparency of outputs and outcomes sufficient to enable democratic oversight and informed public debate; and clear procedures for elected policy makers to determine whether a remit should be extended in an emergency.

Together, those principles more than genuflect to two broad pillars of modern constitutional democracy: "majoritarian" decisions on preferences and constraints on the abuse of power. But they go further than that. By harnessing IA policy makers to a monitorable objective, they seek to head off *misuses of power* by government, to offer an antidote to political or sectional capture, and to provide for ongoing public deliberation on ends and means. As such, the Principles seem to stack up under different conceptions of our politics—both liberal and republican, both competitive and deliberative (chapter 11).

The Principles as a Norm of Constitutional Democratic Governance

The Principles call upon politicians to step up to the plate when independent-agency regimes are debated and structured; and thereafter to be active overseers who recognize the central distinction between accountability for a regime's design and accountability for its stewardship. Members of the assembly play a special role in detecting instances of what I call *faux* independence, where the elected executive or private parties have suborned a body intended to be independent, as happened at the Fed in the 1970s (chapter 17).

Altogether, the import of this oversight role has grown as the administrative state has expanded. Ultimately, our trust as citizens is placed in our elected representatives. Relying on the judges to be the overseers amounts to the kind of democratic surrender almost guaranteed eventually to alienate the public. Achieving incentives-values compatibility is not easy, perhaps particularly in the United States, where the marginal lawmaker can all too frequently be an unelected judge or technocrat.

Given the imperatives that shape their world, politicians are unlikely to rise to what democracy's values demand of them in this part of the administrative state unless something like the Principles becomes embedded in our norms and conventions on the place of unelected power in democratic societies. That is true whether jurisdictions operate via legal or political constitutionalism (chapters 8, 12, and 13).

The Need for a Principles-Based Audit of the Administrative State

Although the introduction to this book raised the specter of our elected representatives being doomed to a life of tweeting, television studios, and fundraisers, that will come about only if they voluntarily vacate the ground that, in democratic societies, only they can occupy with legitimacy.

Now is hardly the moment for that. Alongside more high-profile priorities, this means their taking a close look at the mandates of today's IAs and at whether any parts of the administrative state are excessively or insufficiently insulated from day-to-day politics.

Where the lines are drawn is properly a matter for public debate, case by case. I doubt, however, whether many independent-agency regimes currently satisfy the Principles. The most serious problem would be where a policy area did not meet the conditions for delegation in the first place *and* the manner of the delegation was flawed.

A Summary of the Proposals

The concrete general proposals of this book, set out more fully in the appendix, can therefore be summarized as follows:

1. Democracies should have a clear and principled framework for cataloging agencies that are delegated discretionary powers but have different degrees of insulation from the day-to-day politics of the executive and legislative branches.
2. For those agencies that are highly insulated from both elected branches, democracies should articulate a clear set of principles or norms on whether and how they will structure the delegation.
3. Above all, such independent agencies should have clear, monitorable objectives and make policy in committees operating via one person, one vote for members with long, staggered terms (which they are expected to serve).
4. Independent agencies should have the power to issue legally binding rules only under a clear mandate to complete the job of the legislature over a period where legislators would likely not be able to sustain a consistent policy but wish to do so.
5. Such IA rules should not create criminal offenses, which in the interest of basic liberty is the inalienable job of the elected representative assembly.
6. Whether as parts of the regulatory, fiscal, or services state, IAs should not be given mandates that entail making big distributional choices or big value judgments on behalf of society, and their policy

choices should not interfere with individuals more than is warranted to achieve their statutory purpose.

7. Governments and legislatures should articulate in advance, and preferably in law, how (if at all) an independent agency's powers to intervene in an emergency would be extended, but any such extensions should not compromise the integrity and political insulation of its core mission.
8. The provisions of IA delegations should, in the usual course of things, be laid down in ordinary legislation, embedded through public support and usage.
9. These principles should be exposed to national public debate because the purpose of delegating to independent agencies is to make credible the achievement of purposes that enjoy wide and stable support among the public.
10. Being immensely powerful, and in many cases, unelected lawmakers, IA leaders should work under an ethic of self-restraint and should serve on IA policy boards toward the end of their professional careers, so that questions of postoffice conflicts of interest do not arise.
11. No healthy democracy should have more IA regimes than its legislature is capable of overseeing and keeping under review.

If those are our general proposals, the question with which we began this book can now be revisited: would the Principles suffice to guard against the central bankers becoming overmighty citizens?

THE CENTRAL BANKERS REDUX

The precrisis monetary authorities provided a model for truly independent agencies exercising, as former Fed chair Ben Bernanke put it nearly twenty years ago, constrained discretion. Indeed, before the Great Financial Crisis, they were frequently taken as an exemplar of efficient and effective delegation. Today, they risk being hoist on their own petard, having become a politically alluring solution to too many problems for comfort or, indeed, for their inherent capabilities. At times they have been presented as seeming to enjoy their unparalleled status, power, and prestige. But in fact, as they well know, they, like the rest of us, have a more tenuous grasp of what is going on in the economy than anyone ever expected.

In the course of this book, we have tried to get to the bottom of who they are and how they fit in.

"Custom" versus Regime-Based Central Banking

The book's stress on formal regimes is not intended to deny the importance of custom and practice in central banking. Once a central bank has undertaken a particular type of operation, there will be an expectation that it (and possibly its peers) could or, stronger, would do so again in broadly similar circumstances. Central bankers are, then, in the business of creating, refining, and sometimes overturning precedents. In other words, like common law judges, their choices and actions change the terms of trade within their (vast) sphere of influence and control. Just as our societies face a choice between how much of the law we wish to be made by judges and how much by elected legislatures, so we face a choice over whether we wish central banking doctrine and principles to remain latent in precedents filtered through a central banking mindset or, alternatively, to be transparent in ex ante regimes that are established by elected legislatures after due public debate and filled out by central banks.

The burden of this book is that, reflecting an evolution in legitimation standards during the latter part of the twentieth century and into the twenty-first, the effort needs to be tilted more toward the construction of regimes based on statute and published independent-agency operating principles. Whereas in Walter Bagehot's 1860s, precepts for the lender of last resort could be articulated by an outside commentator seeking to pin down what he thought useful in Bank of England practice, today that seems unlikely to be enough. In our full-franchise democracies, the location of the broad lines between the arenas of unelected and elected power cannot be determined by the unelected power holders themselves, whether central bankers or, via litigation, judges.

However unavoidable improvisation might be in the midst of crisis, it cannot today be sufficient for planning the future shape and uses of central bank capabilities if their independence is to be sustained and supported. Today, warranted predictability needs to be tied to normative expectations that have a democratic pedigree.

Against that background, we have argued the following points:

- "Price stability" is important to liberty (under both republican and liberal conceptions) because it amounts to protecting people from government imposing the inflation tax and leaves them able to pursue their goals free of that particular source of interference.
- If low and stable inflation is maintained, all sections of society can benefit from the saving on the government's *real* debt-serving costs.
- In a *fiat-money* system, central bank independence is necessary to preserve the higher-level separation of (fiscal) powers between legislature and executive government; given their electoral incentives, the core executive should not hold the power to apply an inflation tax, as that would mean it could avoid having to seek "supply" from the assembly of the people's elected representatives.
- Subject to credibility being maintained, independent central banks increase the state's capacity to smooth the economy's adjustment to nasty shocks, which entails their making choices that affect the shape and size of central government's consolidated (net) balance sheet.
- Further, with *fractional-reserve private banking* permitted, the central bank has an inalienable interest and unavoidable involvement in regulation and supervision to maintain the stability of the financial system because it is the economy's *liquidity reinsurer.*
- Therefore, central banks inevitably have a foot in each of the services state, the fiscal state, the regulatory state, and the emergency state.
- Central banks are responsible in one sphere, price stability, for producing a *public good* and in another, financial stability, for preserving the *common good* of system resilience in the face of private incentives that lead to its erosion.

In other words, it was the most tragic of false turns when fashion, sometimes within central banks themselves, dictated that their involvement in the financial system was not needed or esteemed. The pragmatic authority latent in being the pivot of the monetary system was worth something. We argue that, in today's world, the associated roles need to be formalized in order for this pillar of unelected power to be legitimate given our political values. In some ways, the postcrisis legislative reforms aim to do just that, attempting to catch up with underlying realities. But the effect is to concentrate a lot of power in the hands of central bankers. It should be no more than is needed to preserve broad *monetary-system stability.* Clear boundaries are needed.

Conventions for Central Bank Independence: A Money-Credit Constitution

Those boundaries do not draw themselves since to some extent they are matters of convention, determined in the light of each society's wider norms and conventions. Assuming, however, that some deep values are shared across constitutional democracies, the Principles for Delegation can help identify the family of options that might be feasible (incentives-values compatible). It is in that spirit that, in the course of part IV, precepts were suggested for central banks' role in prudential policy, liquidity reinsurance, and, to the extent that individual societies choose to permit it, credit policy.

Like the Principles themselves, this requires active public debate. It must also add up to a coherent whole. This is a *Money-Credit Constitution*, a politically embedded norm, which, at its most general, comprises an objective of broad monetary-system stability (coupling, say, an inflation target with a standard of resilience for the financial system); a Fiscal Carve-Out that recognizes that central banking has fiscal elements; and constraints on the structure and shape of private banking (and, suitably modified, other parts of the financial system). The objectives should be sufficiently clear to provide a shield against partisan or industry capture.

This is not cosmetic, as can be illustrated by the proposals (aired while I was writing this book) for central banks to raise their inflation targets to 4 percent and/or to embark on helicopter money (a permanent injection of central bank money designed to raise the price level and, thus, relieve an overhang of debt through a period of unexpectedly high inflation). Whatever their substantive merits and demerits in economics, both amount to imposing the inflation tax and so cross the line into what I judge our societies think of as Politics with a capital *P.* Consistent with that, under the Principles, neither is a decision that could decently be made by the unelected leaders of independent central banks. Put another way, even if technically their current statutes permit them to make such decisions, they would violate our democratic values and jeopardize their independence if they actually did so.

A Happy Conclusion: Not a Fourth Branch?

The argument has seemed to head toward a happy conclusion. Since chapter 4, we have stressed the profound difference between *trustee agencies*, responsible for an articulated policy regime delegated by elected legislators, and *guardian agencies* that have higher order responsibilities for underpinning the rule of law and democracy itself. In part II, we argue that the distinction goes to whether agencies make up part of a new "fourth branch" of government. Some electoral commissions might well do so. Independent regulatory agencies do not.

In the general run of things, nor do independent central banks. However important they might be to the well-being of our societies, they operate at a lower level than the three canonical branches. We are not talking about fundamental liberties or the state's overarching relationship with the people (chapter 8); nor about the preservation of democracy and the rule of law.

Where that is not so, as with the European Central Bank, it is because the normal high-level structure is incomplete, leaving the monetary technocrats adrift in the constitutional order of things, precariously perched as existential guarantors. Hence the legal and political dilemmas posed by the ECB's Sisyphus-like labors to preserve Europe's monetary union and the wider project it represents.

But away from Frankfurt, the nub of central bank accountability, as for other independent agencies, is whether legislators, listening to the people they represent, choose to keep, reform, or abolish their independence.

For that reason alone, central bankers are perforce in an ongoing conversation with society about what they are doing and why. As their powers accumulate, they need to broaden and deepen that debate and to ensure it is sustained even when economic peacetime returns: that was the burden of chapter 24. The central bankers need, continuously, to be *legitimacy seekers.* They need, put differently, to be *unelected democrats.*[12]

TOO GOOD TO BE TRUE: A NORM OF SELF-RESTRAINT

Putting it like that should make us pause, one final time. Even if, as I maintain, the Principles (or something like them) could usefully guide the design of decent mandates for IAs, it seems hard to believe that formal regimes and carefully framed values-compatible incentives will always suffice. They might do the job for central banks' hard power but not for their soft power. Given invisible but, when the public-political mood suits, barbed lines between politics and policy, there is an outstanding question about what central bankers can say and how they can say it. Something is missing.

Because central banks are so very powerful, there is a need for an *ethic of self-restraint*, underpinned by informal conventions and norms. But how should they know where the lines are? Here it is instructive to return to where we began in chapter 4: the strikingly different models provided by the military and the judiciary, the two more established pillars of unelected power.

The Three Unelected Pillars' Distinctive Relations with Elected Power

The quotations at the chapter head say it all. At one end of the spectrum stands the top military adviser and strategist. Clearly subordinate, but the bearer of great expertise and the carrier of venerable traditions (as Brooke was by both background and calling), the field marshal saw it as his duty sometimes to press and press, and at other moments doggedly to resist when he honestly believed that his political principal risked embarking on a course at odds with the government's war aims. The relationship between Churchill and Brooke was battering, intimate, for me utterly awe inspiring. With a personal style that could hardly have been

[12] An expression that emerged out of discussion some years ago with my former colleague Sebastian Walsh.

more different, Brooke's US counterpart, General George Marshall, was at times similarly unrelenting in his efforts to persuade President Roosevelt to do or refrain from doing something. Because, their personal greatness aside, that is what they could legitimately do—were duty bound to do—as subordinate advisers at one of civilization's existential moments. In lesser circumstances facing lesser men and women, no less is expected of their successors.

At the other end of the spectrum stands the top judge, a protector of our liberties. As Alexander Bickel nicely caught it, judges stand near the political marketplace but must not enter, for the simple reason that whatever is being discussed, debated, fought over in the political forum might end up in their court. Bickel's concern was how the judge should meet that hazard, advocating the "passive virtues" of small steps and a cautious approach to justiciability, leaving in the political forum what rightly belongs there. The same sentiment applies, arguably with even greater force, to how the judiciary conducts itself outside the courtroom. Of course, judges have opinions on public policy issues, but, rather than pressing their view in the manner of the concerned military commander, the judge cannot advise on any matter that is justiciable. This can be deeply frustrating for politicians, who want to make policy that will withstand challenge in the courts.[13]

Further, the judge must not be swayed by criticism or pressure. As former English master of the rolls Lord Denning put it:[14]

> We do not fear criticism, nor do we resent it. . . . Exposed as we are to the winds of criticism, nothing which is said by this person or that, nothing which is written by this pen or that, will deter us from doing what we believe is right.

That was nearly fifty years ago. Today, in a world with rather less deference toward even our finest institutions, judges do feel a need to explain their institution: what it is for and how it fits in. But the distance from politicians and the norm of being extraordinarily careful in their extrajudicial pronouncements survive, as they should.[15]

[13] There was a famous such episode in Britain in recent years, when Interior minister Charles Clarke sought a dialogue with the judges.

[14] Quoted in Dyson, "Criticising Judges."

[15] The tone of this is reflected in Judiciary of England and Wales, *Guide to Judicial Conduct.*

So where do our central bankers, the newcomers to this trinity of august power, fit into things? Well, we know that the waters they navigate can be treacherous. Just as US Supreme Court justice Ruth Bader Ginsburg attracted criticism for being drawn into a comment on a presidential candidate during the 2016 election, so former Federal Reserve chair Janet Yellen prompted some chatter when she dedicated a speech to inequality, and (then) governor Raghuram Rajan of the Reserve Bank of India raised eyebrows in speaking about the role of tolerance in society (taken by some to be a comment on intercommunity relations).[16] Closer to home territory, Jean-Claude Trichet spoke regularly about the importance to monetary stability of prudent public finances, but Mervyn King was criticized in some quarters when he offered a rare comment about British fiscal conditions in 2009. Mario Draghi is said to have occasionally irritated Europe's foremost politicians with calls for structural reform and fiscal stimulus.[17] Alan Greenspan offered one kind of master class in navigating politics but sometimes ventured into areas remote from his delegated mission.[18] "Steady Eddie" George offered a rather different kind, staying close to base.

Self-Restraint for Central Bankers

I would say this about self-restraint, and I think much of its essence is captured in the quotation at the chapter head from Mervyn King:

- Like the military but unlike the judiciary, the central bankers must be ready to advise in private on the wider government policies that are *necessary* for monetary-system stability.
- Unlike the military, precisely because they have job security, they must not obstinately press and press, while not equivocating in their advice.

[16] Respectively, Conti-Brown, *Power and Independence*, p. 50, and Kazmin, "India's Raghuram Rajan."

[17] For a carefully calibrated defense, see Pisani-Ferry, "Central Bank Advocacy." The argument turns partly on lack of expertise/authority elsewhere; partly on the *existential* LOLR having a duty to speak if, on its considered view, fatal vulnerabilities are neglected by elected politicians; and partly on a constraint of making general rather than specific prescriptions.

[18] Mallaby, *Man Who Knew*.

- Unlike the military, they can repeat this advice in public at their own initiative, but in doing so the intimate connection with their formal mandate must be explicit and able to withstand tough scrutiny.
- They cannot be in the business of offering their opinion, in private or public, on things they happen to know about or are interested in but do not rely on in fulfilling the trust placed in them by legislators.
- Like the judiciary, they must not be drawn into offering specific private advice or public remarks about things they will or might have to decide.
- Like the judiciary, as legitimacy seekers, they can (and, rationally, ought to) explain their institution to the public.
- Like the judiciary, they must be ready to take criticism.

To conclude, in taking up their role as trustees for monetary-system stability, central bankers lose their right to participate in the many other and broader issues confronting our societies. They gain an extraordinary platform but effectively surrender some of an ordinary citizen's rights of participation. They must be that rare breed of person who does not seek popularity today, but only the respect of their peers and of society as a whole for sticking to the job they were given by elected legislators. If personal gratification is involved, it is gratification so deferred that not all will live to see the verdict of history.

FINAL THOUGHTS

This book has revolved around Power, Welfare, Incentives, and Values. The central banks and other independent agencies can use their considerable power to enhance the people's welfare only if institutions are designed to create the right incentives. Since bad results from time to time are inevitable, those institutions will last only if they conform to our values. The proper sequence is revealed as Values-Incentives-Power-Welfare.

Perhaps the central message of this book, then, is that we, the people, are not faced with having to choose between Hamiltonian, Jeffersonian, or Madisonian conceptions of how independent central banks fit into politics. Yes, they carry centralized power (Hamilton), but the credibility that is their stock-in-trade depends on broad public discussion and acceptance (Jefferson), and their legitimacy depends on that together with the checks and balances provided by the three higher-level arms of the state (Madison). Because it relies on a sustained regime, credibility requires legitimacy, which in turn requires delegation via carefully constructed frameworks, ongoing oversight, and public debate. We can maintain a moderate version of the Enlightenment's project of disenchantment without embracing pseudoscience or surrendering republican democracy in favor of technocracy.

Overmighty Citizens?

Weighed in the scales of the great constitutional and political issues our democracies currently face, the concerns of this book hardly seem as momentous or pressing as gerrymandered legislative districts and resurgent money power in the United States, the future of Britain's federal union, how to deepen Europe's currency union while maintaining a broader free trade area, low voter turnout in regular elections, simmering popular discontent, and geopolitical reconfiguration. But the reemergence of unelected power *is* one of the defining features of modern governance. It has been on display, perhaps as never before, since 2007 as politicians chose to step back from the problems of restoring prosperity, largely leaving it to central bankers to revive and redesign the international economic and financial system.

We began, in the preface, with late-medieval England's problem of "overmighty subjects"—or perhaps it was as much an "undermighty king"—which led to the Plantagenets' drawn-out and disastrous Wars of the Roses. Today, some six hundred years later, we want functional, democratically elected, and accountable legislatures but definitely not unelected overmighty citizens. Fortunately, in modern democracies it is within our power to determine whether we end up with them. Imperatively, our societies must exercise that capability, on a principled basis, for us to remain who we are—who we managed to become.

APPENDIX

THE PRINCIPLES FOR DELEGATION TO INDEPENDENT AGENCIES INSULATED FROM DAY-TO-DAY POLITICS

This appendix gives a statement of the book's Principles for Delegation, updating the preliminary version of chapters 5 and 6 in light of parts II–IV.

DELEGATION CRITERIA

A public policy regime should be entrusted to an independent agency (IA) insulated from the day-to-day politics of both elected branches of government only after wide public debate and only if

1. The goal can be specified.
2. Society's preferences are reasonably stable and concern a major social cost.
3. There is a problem of credibly committing to a settled policy regime.
4. The policy instruments are confidently expected to work, and there exists a relevant community of experts outside the IA.
5. The IA will not have to make big choices on distributional trade-offs or society's values or that materially shift the distribution of political power.
6. The legislature has the capacity, through its committee system, properly to oversee each IA's stewardship and, separately, whether the regime is working adequately.
7. The society is capable of bestowing the esteem or prestige that can help bind the IA's policy makers to the mast of the regime's goal.

DESIGN PRECEPTS

1. Elected legislators should provide a statement of purpose, objectives, and powers, and a delineation of the regime's boundaries (*Purposes-Powers*). In particular,

    a. The objective or standard must be capable of being monitored.

    b. If there are multiple objectives, they should be lexicographic.

    c. Any statutorily mandated objective, standard, or prescribed instrument rule must be understood by legislators and broadly comprehensible to the public.

    d. An IA's rule making should not interfere with individual liberal rights more than necessary to achieve the legislated purpose and objective (proportionality).

    e. An IA should not be able to create or frame criminal laws or bring criminal prosecutions.

    f. Its sanctions should not include ruinous fines.

    g. Subject to the above, the agency's policy makers must be in control of the delegated policy instruments, and so must have statutory job security and not be subject to frequent political budgetary approvals (necessary conditions for insulation). Thus,

        i. any powers of *override* by elected politicians should be explicit in statute and, if exercised, should require transparency to the legislature and the public.

        ii. any provision for the IA to seek *special approval* for uses of powers outside emergencies (see DP5) should apply only where a political judgment is needed on whether a statutory regime's purpose can best be pursued by setting aside constraints framed as monitorable standards; it should be exercisable only in specific cases, and its use should be disclosed as soon as is safe to do so.

2. There should be clear prescriptions of who will exercise the delegated powers and of the procedures to be employed in delegating and exercising them (*Procedures*). In particular,

    a. The policy-making body should be deliberative, with a voting committee of equal members (one person, one vote).

    b. Terms of office should be long and staggered; and appointments should be subject to a dual key, so that a single elected politician cannot appoint a committee of allies.

c. Undue concentrations of power within agencies should be avoided.

d. The agency's processes must help deliver the values of the rule of law in agency rule making, adjudications, and other actions.

e. Within a rule-writing agency, the structure for determining (adjudicating) individual cases should have degrees of separation; and each distinct phase of policy making should have its own integrity.

3. The IA should publish principles for how it plans to exercise discretion within its boundaries (*Operating Principles*).
4. There should be sufficient transparency to enable the stewardship of the delegated policy maker and, separately, the design of the regime itself to be monitored and debated by elected representatives (*Transparency-Accountability*). In particular,

a. An independent agency should contribute to those public debates with information and research on how it evaluates the effectiveness of its instruments, and on the social costs of the ills it is mandated to mitigate.

b. An IA should publish data that enables ex post evaluation of its cost-benefit analysis and other forecasts, and more generally to enable independent research.

c. An IA involved in international policy standards should do what it can to ensure that plans and questions are properly exposed domestically.

5. There should be provisions determining what process is to be followed when the boundaries of the regime are reached during a disaster, including how democratic accountability works then (*Emergencies*). To be subject to the following constraints:

a. An IA should seek to consult key elected representatives before taking measures that, formally, are within its legal powers but were never remotely contemplated by legislators and the public.

b. Any decision to extend an IA's powers should be taken by the legislature or by the elected executive using delegated powers.

c. It should be completely clear whether the IA's powers are being reset for a period *with independence maintained* or are being both extended and subjected to case-by-case political review.

d. Where independence is maintained, no substantive extension or reset of powers granted by elected representatives shall be inconsistent with the purpose and objective of the regime or with any prior limits on the IA's powers intended to be absolutely binding in all circumstances, and so should not compromise the integrity and political insulation of the IA's core mission.

e. There shall be no de facto suspension of independence during a disaster or its aftermath without a formal legal measure transparent to the legislature and the public.

An IA should articulate extensive contingency plans for extraordinary measures that it could deploy using its standard set of powers and capabilities.

MULTIPLE-MISSION CONSTRAINTS

1. An independent agency should be given multiple missions only if (a) they are intrinsically connected, (b) each faces a problem of credible commitment and meets the other Delegation Criteria, and (c) it is judged that combining them under one roof will deliver materially better results.
2. Each mission should have its own objectives and constraints, consistent with the Design Precepts.
3. Each mission should be the responsibility of a distinct policy body within the agency, with a majority of members of each body serving on only that body and a minority serving on all of them.
4. Each of those policy committees should be fully informed on the debates and deliberations, as well as the actions, of the others.

SELF-RESTRAINT

Beyond the parameters of the formal regime, an ethic of self-restraint should be encouraged and fostered. Consistent with political insulation in their delegated field, IA policy makers should refrain from participating in the many other and broader issues confronting their societies.

ACKNOWLEDGMENTS

Producing a book is quite an endeavor. Working with a preliminary draft, Jennifer Goyder created the bibliography, sorted out the notes, and generally kept the text shipshape, and was a real pleasure to work with. My editor at Princeton, Sarah Caro, looked at the whole text and was an excellent source of advice; Jennifer McClain was a terrific copy editor; and Hannah Paul and the production and marketing teams were helpful and efficient. Many thanks to all of them and to their two anonymous reviewers.

The project has benefited enormously from the assistance of people across the world. It was an enormous treat and privilege to get to discuss my concerns with them. The list is long. I apologize to anyone I have omitted and thank those not listed here who have so generously helped with other projects.

In Cambridge, MA, I have been helped, at Harvard, by Eric Beerbohm, Dan Carpenter, John Coates, Richard Cooper, Chris Desan, Marty Feldstein, Jeff Frieden, Ben Friedman, Jacob Gersen, Robin Greenwood, Peter Hall, Olivier Hart, Howell Jackson, Louis Kaplow, Frank Michelman, Joe Nye, Richard Parker, Carmen Reinhart, Ken Rogoff, David Scharfstein, Hal Scott, Emile Simpson, Jeremy Stein, Cass Sunstein, Richard Tuck, Adrian Vermeule, and Richard Zeckhauser; and although we never met, I should mention Jenny Mansbridge, who e-introduced me to Philip Pettit. At MIT: Bengt Holmstrom, Athanasios Orphanides, and David Singer. Over the river: Vivien Schmidt (BU), Dan Coquillette (Boston College), and Alasdair Roberts (formerly Sussex).

At Yale, I was helped by Bruce Ackerman, Andrew Metrick, Nick Parillo, Roberta Romano, Susan Rose-Ackerman (who, amazingly, invited me to a conference on comparative administrative law). At Stanford: John Cochrane, Gary Cox, Darrel Duffie, James Fearon, Joe Grundfest, Margaret Levi, Paul Milgrom, Terry Moe, Josh Ober, John Taylor (who very kindly invited me), Barry Weingast, and, while he was visiting there, Alan Ryan. At Princeton: Alan Blinder, Markus Brunnermeier, Harold James, and Robert Keohane. At Chicago: Austan Goolsbee, Anil Kashyap (who invited me to visit), Randy Kroszner, Christian Leuz, Eric Posner, and Luigi Zingales. At Berkeley: Sean Gailmard and Anne O'Connell. At Brown: Mark Blyth, David Estlund, and Mark Suchman. At Columbia: Charlie Calomiris, Kate Judge, Perry Mehrling, Gillian Metzger, Sharyn O'Halloran, and Peter Strauss. At Georgetown: Kathleen McNamara and Henry Richardson. At Michigan: Elizabeth Anderson, Michael Barr, Daniel Crane, Scott Hershovitz, Bill Novak, and Charles Shipan. At NYU: Tony Bertelli, Ricky Revesz, Kim Schoenholz, Daniel Viehoff (when visiting at Yale), and Jeremy Waldron. At Philadelphia/Wharton: Cristina Bicchieri, Cary Coglianese, Peter Conti-Brown (who, as a recent first-time author, kindly helped with questions about the publishing process), and David Zaring. At Vanderbilt: David Lewis, Morgan Ricks, Ed Rubin, and Ganesh Sitaramen. Elsewhere in the US, I owe thanks to Joerg Bibow (Skidmore), Francesca Bignami (GWU), Joshua Cohen (Apple Uni), Marvin Goodfriend (Carnegie-Mellon), George Krause (Pittsburgh), Peter Lindseth (Connecticut), Anelise Riles (Cornell, not least for inviting me to a conference of sociologists and anthropologists on central banking), and Martin Rogoff (Maine).

Outside the US, I was helped at Cambridge by Mark Elliot, David Feldman, Petra Geraats, and David Runciman. At Oxford: Nick Barber, Paul Collier (who very kindly invited me to join annual conferences of central bank governors from Africa), Paul Craig, Christopher Decker, Richard Ekins, Timothy Endicott, and John Vickers. At LSE: Richard Baldwin, Tim Besley, Charles Goodhart, Christian List, Martin Lodge, Martin Loughlin, Ricardo Reiss, Cheryl Schonhardt Bailey, and Mark Thatcher. At Kings London: Jon Davis, Christel Koop, and Richard Whish. At ANU (where I was invited by Philip Pettit to give a lecture): John Braithwaite, Peter Cane, Bob Goodin, Therese Pearce Laanela, and John Uhr. Elsewhere: Thomas Gehring (Bamburg); Thobias Bach, Mark Hallerberg, and Kai Wegrich (Hertie, Berlin); Michelle Everson (Birkbeck); Tony Yates (Birmingham); Hermann Puender (Bucerius, Hamburg); Dominique Custos (Caen); Jon Stern (City); Madalina Busuioc (Exeter); Mathias Goldmann (Frankfurt Max Planck); Christoph Mollers and Matthias Ruffert (Humbolt); Thomas Perroud (Pantheon-

Arras, Paris II); Rosa Lastra (Queen Mary's); Matthew Flinders and Matthew Wood (Sheffield); Jeff King (UCL); Annetje Ottow (Utrecht); and Fabrizio Gilardi (Zurich).

A group of younger scholars have been more than helpful. At Harvard, I should single out Sam Chang (HLS), who was unfailing in deviling out my questions about the US system when I embarked on the project; Kyra Kaufman and Ed Stein (HLS), who read down material touching on US administrative law; Divya Kirti (Econ), who pointed me toward people and provided help whenever I needed it; and Vishal Chanani (Econ) who helped me understand some of the economics literature. Ann Klein, then a PhD student of Thomas Perroud's in Paris, very kindly translated part of a French Senate report on AAIs for me. Sara Dietz (Max Planck Institute and Ludwig Maximilian University, Munich) checked material on Germany. Remaining errors are my responsibility.

Thanks are also owed to think-tankers Lars Feld (Euken Institute, Freiburg), Peter Riddell PC, Jill Rutter and Miguel Coelho (UK Institute for Government), David Marsh (OMFIF), Graham Mather (European Policy Forum), David Wessel and Philip Wallach (Brookings), and Olivier Blanchard and Adam Posen (Peterson Institute); to lawyers Randy Guynn, Guy Morton, Michael Raffan, Philip Richards, Tom Richards, Gabe Rosenberg, Conrad Scott, Margaret Tahyar, and Benedikt Wolfers; and to writers David Kynaston, Sebastian Mallaby, Charles Moore, and Neville Shack.

Current and former policy makers and officials offered a special kind of perspective. The central bankers must come first, and I should list Scott Alverez, David Archer, Charlie Bean, Claudio Borio, Willem Buiter, Roger Clews, Benoit Coeure, Luis Urrutia Corral, Mathias Dewatripont, Guy Debelle, Dietrich Domanski, Andreas Dombret, Bill English, John Footman, Mike Gibson, Mick Grady, Andy Haldane, Aerdt Houben, Otmar Issing, Mike Joyce, Mervyn King, Don Kohn, Hans-Helmut Kotz, Nellie Liang, Jean-Pierre Landau, Thomas Laubach, Arnaud Mares, Sylie Matherat, Trish Moser, John Murray, Bill Nelson, Ed Nelson, Graham Nicholson, Pascual O'Dougherty Madrazo, Athanasios Orphanides, Guilermo Ortiz, Lucas Papademos, Franco Passacantando, Charlie Plosser, Vince Reinhart, Jose Maria Roldan, Larry Schembri, Hyun Shin, Masaaki Shirakawa, Francois Villeroy De Galhau, Kevin

Warsh, Jens Weidmann, Graeme Wheeler, and Paul Volcker. For some years, Stan Fischer and later Zeti Aziz invited me to join the meetings of the governors' group on governance at the Bank for International Settlements, which was useful for thinking through some of the issues presented by the recasting of the UK central banking architecture. Finally, although it now seems a long time ago, I remain very grateful to James Benford, Geoff Davies, and Sebastian Walsh for conversations before I retired from the Bank of England; and to my personal assistants in my final roles there, including Julia McKenzie and most especially Sandra Bannister.

Among central bankers who have passed away, the shadows of Eddie George and George Blunden, both of whom I miss deeply, hover around the book, perhaps no more so than at the very close where I single out carefully judged reserve and restraint as among the chief virtues for the unelected powers.

Very much among the living, former UK chancellors of the exchequer Lords Nigel Lawson and Norman Lamont were especially kind in refreshing my memory of events in the late 1980s/early 1990s, when I was private secretary to Governor Robin Leigh-Pemberton.

Public servants in many other walks of life were equally helpful. I should underline my thanks to, among the judiciary and their advisers, Lord Justice Sir Peter Gross (UK Court of Appeal), Douglas H. Ginsburg (a judge on, and former chair of, the DC Appeals Court), Bruno Lasserre (Conseil d'État and former head of the French competition authority), Maryvonne de Saint-Pulgent (Conseil d'État), Anissia Morel (maître des requêtes of the Conseil d'État), and John Sorabji. Among the military: General Sir Nick Carter. Among current and former UK regulators and agency heads: Andrew Bailey, David Currie, Ed Richards, Robert Steehman, Tim Tutton, Adair Turner, Sharon White, Andrew Whittaker, and Sam Woods.

Among Westminster parliamentarians and civil servants: Ed Balls, Terry Burns, Matt Hancock MP, Lord (John) McFall (former chair of the Commons Treasury Select Committee), Jesse Norman MP, Nick McPherson, and Tim Pitt.

In the official sector outside the UK, old friends and many new ones came to my aid. In France: Jean Pisani Ferry and David Viros. In Germany: Levin Holle, Petra Faber-Graw, and Jeromin Zettelmeyer. In the

Netherlands: Michiel Bijlsma. In the EU: Joaquin Almunia, Vittorio Di Bucci, Andrea Enria, Jonathan Faull, Sylvie Goulard, Steven Maijoor, and Christopher Tugendhat. In Australia: Wayne Byres and John Laker. In Canada: Julie Dickson and Mark Zelmer. Among US executive branch officials and regulators: Dick Berner, Vanessa Countryman, Bill Donaldson, Mark Flannery, Dan Gallagher, Tim Geithner, Gary Gensler, Bob Glauber, Bill Kovacic, Mike Krimminger, Mary Schapiro, and Christopher Smart. Among current or former staff in Congress: James Ahn and Jim Segal. Among international institutions: Ceyla Pazarbasioglu, Marc Quintyn, and Jose Vinals.

A few people are omitted from those lists because they have provided a special degree of intellectual and personal support. Among academics, I must single out Alberto Alesina, Philip Pettit, Paul Sagar, Andrei Shleifer, and Kevin Stack. I could hardly be more grateful to them. The enthusiasm of Philip for my project from its early stages made a massive difference. In places, the book is an exercise in Alesina meets Pettit and Waldron under the umbrella of David Beetham (whom I do not know at all) and the late Bernard Williams (whom I discussed with Paul and Kevin).

Larry Summers belongs both in that list and among those who made my transition to a new life, partly in Harvard, smooth and richly stimulating. Larry and I do not wholly agree on some of the biggest issues the book tackles, which has been a bonus as my debates with him have been especially enriching and enlightening. I am also enormously grateful to him for providing a perch in the Kennedy School's Mossavar-Rahmani Center for Business and Government, which, with John Haigh, he leads. Scott Leland has been a terrifically warm and helpful host there.

My time in Harvard, professional and social, is unimaginable without David Scharfstein, initially my sponsor at HBS, and Niall Ferguson, who first suggested the move at a juncture in my professional life.

Niall, Mark Blyth, and Luigi Zingales, occupying splendidly diverse points on the political spectrum, were true friends in sustaining me throughout the project, advising on book writing and publication, looking at draft project outlines, and offering unfailing encouragement. I dearly hope they think it was worth the trouble.

All that and even more goes for Steve Cecchetti, with whom I served at the Bank for International Settlements. Steve published one of the earlier pieces on postcrisis central banking and, from the outset, saw the point of my project and pushed me to pursue it. When, inevitably, I hit walls of incomprehension ("Why do you keep going on about democracy?"), his invariable response amounted to, that's why you have to do this. We debated by mail, phone, and over dinner many of the issues.

The only person to whom I am more grateful, as if that could be the right sentiment, is my wife, Sophie, whose love is a blessing, whose sense of the ridiculous is uplifting, and with whom sharing a life is a source of joy.

BIBLIOGRAPHY

Abrams, Burton A. "How Richard Nixon Pressured Arthur Burns: Evidence from the Nixon Tapes." *Journal of Economic Perspectives* 20, no. 4 (2006): 177–88.

Acemoglu, Daron. "Why Not a Political Coase Theorem? Social Conflict, Commitment and Politics." *Journal of Comparative Economics* 31 (2003): 620–52.

Acemoglu, Daron, Simon Johnson, Pablo Querubin, and James A. Robinson. "When Does Policy Reform Work? The Case of Central Bank Independence." Brookings Papers on Economic Activity, Spring 2008.

Ackerman, Bruce. *We the People: Foundations*. Cambridge, MA: Belknap Press of Harvard University Press, 1991.

———. "The New Separation of Powers." *Harvard Law Review* 113, no. 3 (2000).

———. *The Decline and Fall of the American Republic*. Second Tanner Lecture on Human Values. Cambridge, MA: Belknap Press of Harvard University Press, 2010.

Adler, Matthew D. "Justification, Legitimacy, and Administrative Governance." *Symposium: The Reformation of American Administrative Law* 3 (2005).

Akerlof, George A. "The Market for 'Lemons': Quality Uncertainty and the Market Mechanism." *Quarterly Journal of Economics* 84, no. 3 (1970): 488–500.

Alesina, Alberto, and Paola Giuliano. "Culture and Institutions." *Journal of Economic Literature* 53, no. 4 (2014): 898–944.

Alesina, Alberto, and Howard Rosenthal. "A Theory of Divided Government." *Econometrica* 64 (1996): 1311–41.

Alesina, Alberto, Nouriel Roubini, and Gerald D. Cohen. *Political Cycles and the Macroeconomy*. Cambridge, MA: MIT Press, 1997.

Alesina, Alberto, and L. H. Summers. "Central Bank Independence and Macroeconomic Performance: Some Comparative Evidence." *Journal of Money, Credit and Banking* 25, no. 2 (1993): 151–62.

Alesina, Alberto, and Guido Tabellini. "Bureaucrats or Politicians? Part I: A Single Policy Task." *American Economic Review* 97, no. 1 (2007): 169–79.

———. "Bureaucrats or Politicians? Part II: Multiple Policy Tasks." *Journal of Public Economics* 92 (2008): 426–47.

Alexy, Robert. "Constitutional Rights and Proportionality." *Journal for Constitutional Theory and Philosophy of Law, Revus (Online)* 22 (2014): 51–65.

Amato, Giuliano. *Antitrust and the Bounds of Power: The Dilemmas of Liberal Democracy in the History of the Market*. Oxford: Hart Publishing, 1997.

Amtenbrink, Fabian, and Rosa Lastra. "Securing Democratic Accountability of Financial Regulatory Agencies: A Theoretical Framework." In *Mitigating Risk in the Context of Safety and Security: How Relevant Is a Rational Approach?*, edited by R. V. Miller. Rotterdam: Erasmus School of Law & Research School for Safety and Security, 2008: 115–132.

Anderson, Elizabeth. "Critical Review of Amartya Sen, *Rationality and Freedom*." *Philosophical Review* 114, no. 2 (2005): 253–71.

———. "Democracy: Instrumental vs. Non-instrumental Value." In *Contemporary Debates in Political Philosophy*, edited by Thomas Christiano and John Christman. Chichester: Wiley-Blackwell, 2009.

Andoura, Sami, and Peter Timmerman. "Governance of the EU: The Reform Debate on European Agencies Reignited." European Policy Institutes Network, EPIN Working Paper, no. 19, October 2008.

Arneson, Richard J. "The Supposed Right to a Democratic Say." In *Contemporary Debates in Political Philosophy*, edited by Thomas Christiano and John Christman. Chichester: Wiley-Blackwell, 2009.

Arrow, Kenneth J. "A Difficulty in the Concept of Social Welfare." *Journal of Political Economy* 58, no. 4 (1950): 328–46.

Asimov, Michael. "Five Models of Administrative Ajudication." *American Journal of Comparative Law* 63 (2015), 3–32.

Atiyah, P. S., and R. S. Summers. *Form and Substance in Anglo-American Law*. Oxford: Clarendon Press, 1987.

Bach, Tobias, and Werner Jann. "Animals in the Administrative Zoo: Organizational Change and Agency Autonomy in Germany." *International Review of Administrative Sciences* 76, no. 3 (2010): 443–68.

Baeke, Pio, and Oliver Perschau. "The Law and Policy of Competition in Germany." In *Regulating Europe*, edited by Giandomenico Majone. London: Routledge, 1996.

Bagehot, Walter. *Lombard Street: A Description of the Money Market*. New York: John Wiley and Sons, Inc., 1999.

Balls, Ed, James Howat, and Anna Stansbury. "Central Bank Independence Revisited: After the Financial Crisis, What Should a Model Central Bank Look Like?" M-RCBG Associate Working Paper Series, no. 67, Harvard Kennedy School, November 2016.

Bank of England. "The Development of the Bank of England's Market Operations." October 2008.

———. "Prudential Supervision Authority: The Future Approach to Banking Supervision." May 2011.

Barber, N. W. "Prelude to the Separation of Powers." *Cambridge Law Journal* 60, no. 1 (2001): 59–88.

———. *The Constitutional State*. Oxford: Oxford University Press, 2010.

Baring, Francis. "Observations on the Establishment of the Bank of England. And on the Paper Circulation of the Country." 1797. Reprinted as chapter 1 of *The Lender of Last Resort*, edited by Forrest H. Cappie and Geoffrey Wood. London: Routledge, 2007.

Barkow, Rachel E. "Insulating Agencies: Avoiding Capture through Institutional Design." New York University Public Law and Legal Theory Working Papers, no. 240, 2010.

Barro, Robert J. "Rule of Law, Democracy, and Economic Performance." In *2000 Index of Economic Freedom*, edited by Gerald P. O'Driscoll, Kim R. Holmes, and Melanie Kirkpatrick. Washington, DC: Heritage Foundation.

Barro, Robert, and David B. Gordon. "Rules, Discretion and Reputation in a Model of Monetary Policy." *Journal of Monetary Economics* 12, no. 1 (1983): 101–21.

Basel Committee on Banking Supervision. *Core Principles for Effective Banking Supervision*, 2012.

Bean, Charles R. "Central Banking after the Great Recession." Wincott Lecture, November 28, 2017.

Beard, Mary. *SPQR: A History of Ancient Rome*. London: Profile Books, 2015.

Becker, Gary. "A Theory of Competition among Pressure Groups for Political Influence." *Quarterly Journal of Economics* 98, no. 3 (1983): 371–400.

Beetham, David. *The Legitimation of Power.* 2nd ed. Basingstoke: Palgrave Macmillan, 2013.

Bell, Daniel A. *The China Model: Political Meritocracy and the Limits of Democracy.* Princeton, NJ: Princeton University Press, 2015.

Bellamy, Richard. *Political Constitutionalism: A Republican Defence of the Constitutionality of Democracy.* Cambridge: Cambridge University Press, 2007.

———. "Constitutional Democracy." In *The Encyclopedia of Political Thought*, edited by Michael T. Gibbons, Dianna Coole, et al. Chichester: Wiley-Blackwell, 2014.

Berlin, Isiah. *Four Essays on Liberty.* Oxford: Oxford University Press, 1969.

———. "Political Judgment." In *The Sense of Reality: Studies in Ideas and their History.* London: Chatto & Windus, 1996.

Bernanke, Ben. "Central Bank Independence, Transparency, and Accountability." Speech given at the Institute for Monetary and Economic Studies International Conference, May 26, 2010. Bank of Japan.

———. "What Tools Does the Fed Have Left?" Parts 1–3, Hutchins Center (blog), Brookings Institution, 2016.

———. "Monetary Policy in a New Era." Peterson Institute for International Economics, October 2, 2017.

Bernhard, William. "A Political Explanation of Variations in Central Bank Independence." *American Political Science Review* 92, no. 2 (1998): 311–28.

———. *Banking on Reform: Political Parties and Central Bank Independence in the Industrial Democracies.* Ann Arbor: University of Michigan Press, 2002.

Bernhard, William, J. Lawrence Broz, and William Roberts Clark. "The Political Economy of Monetary Institutions." *International Organization* 56, no. 4 (2002): 1–31.

Bernstein, Marver H. *Regulating Business by Independent Commission.* Princeton, NJ: Princeton University Press, 1955.

Besley, Timothy. *Principled Agents: The Political Economy of Good Government.* Oxford: Oxford University Press, 2007.

Betts, Richard K. "Are American Civil-Military Relations Still a Problem?" Saltzman Working Paper, no. 1, September 2007.

Bibow, Joerg. "Keynes on Central Banking and the Structure of Monetary Policy." *History of Political Economy* 34, no. 4 (2002): 749–87.

———. "Reflections on the Current Fashion for Central Bank Independence." *Cambridge Journal of Economics* 28, no. 4 (2004): 549–76.

Bicchieri, Cristina. *Norms in the Wild.* Oxford: Oxford University Press, 2017.

Bickel, Alexander M. *The Least Dangerous Branch: The Supreme Court at the Bar of Politics.* 2nd ed. New Haven, CT: Yale University Press, 1986.

Bignami, Francesca. "Formal versus Functional Method in Comparative Constitutional Law." *Osgoode Hall Law Journal* 53, no. 2 (2016): 442–71.

———. "Regulation and the Courts: Judicial Review in Comparative Perspective." In *Comparative Law and Regulation: Understanding the Global Regulatory Process*, edited by Francesca Bignami and David Zaring. Cheltenham: Edward Elgar, 2016.

Binder, Sarah, and Mark Spindel. "Independence and Accountability: Congress and the Fed in a Polarized Era." Center for Effective Public Management, Brookings Institution, April 2016.

———. *The Myth of Independence: How Congress Governs the Federal Reserve*. Princeton, NJ: Princeton University Press, 2017.

Bingham, Tom. *The Business of Judging: Selected Essays and Speeches: 1985–1999*. Oxford: Oxford University Press, 2000.

———. *The Rule of Law*. London: Allen Lane, 2010.

Blanchard, Olivier, Eugenio Cerutti, and Lawrence H. Summers. "Inflation and Activity: Two Explorations and Their Monetary Policy Implications." Peterson Working Paper Series, no. WP15-19, Peterson Institute for International Economics, 2015.

Blinder, Alan S. "Is Government Too Political?" *Foreign Affairs*, November/December 1997.

———. *Central Banking in Theory and Practice*. Cambridge, MA: MIT Press, 1998.

———. "Central Bank Credibility: Why Do We Care? How Do We Build It?" *American Economic Review* 90, no. 5 (2000): 1421–31.

———. *The Quiet Revolution: Central Banking Goes Modern*. New Haven, CT: Yale University Press, 2004.

Blinder, A., M. Ermann, M. Fratzcher, J. de Haan, and D-J. Jansen. "Central Bank Communication and Monetary Policy: A Survey of Theory and Evidence." NBER Working Paper, no. 13932, April 2008.

Blunden, George. "Supervision and Central Banking." *Bank of England Quarterly Bulletin*, August 1987.

———. Julian Hodge Annual Lecture, 1990. Bank of England.

Bogdanor, Vernon. "Parliament and the Judiciary: The Problem of Accountability." Third Sunningdale Accountability Lecture, February 9, 2006.

Borio, Claudio, E. Kharroubi, C. Upper, and F. Zampolli. "Labour Reallocation and Productivity Dynamics: Financial Causes, Real Consequences." BIS Working Papers, no. 534, Bank for International Settlements, December 2015.

Bork, Robert. *The Antitrust Paradox: A Policy at War with Itself*. New York: Free Press, 1993.

Bourdieu, Pierre. "Social Space and Symbolic Power." *Sociological Theory* 7, no. 1 (1989): 14–25.

Bourdieu, Pierre, Loic D. Wacquant, and Samar Farage. "Rethinking the State: Genesis and Structure of the Bureaucratic Field." *Sociological Theory* 12, no. 1 (1994): 1–18.

Bovens, Mark. "Analysing and Assessing Accountability: A Conceptual Framework." *European Law Journal* 13, no. 4 (2007): 447–68.

Bown, Stephen R. *Merchant Kings: When Companies Ruled the World, 1600–1900*. New York: St. Martin's Press, 2009.

Braun, Benjamin. *Two Sides of the Same Coin? Independence and Accountability of the European Central Bank*. Transparency International EU, 2017.

Breeden, Sarah J., and R. Whisker. "Collateral Risk Management at the Bank of England." *Bank of England Quarterly Bulletin* Q2 (2010).

Bremer, Emily S. "The Unwritten Administrative Constitution." *Florida Law Review* 66, no. 3 (2015): 1215–73.

Brennan, Geoffrey, and James M. Buchanan. *The Reason of Rules: Constitutional Political Economy*. Cambridge: Cambridge University Press, 1985.

Bressman, Lisa Schultz. "Schechter Poultry at the Millennium: A Delegation Doctrine for the Administrative State." *Yale Law Journal* 109, no. 6 (2000): 1399–442.

———. "Disciplining Delegation after *Whitman v American Trucking Ass'ns.*" *Cornell Law Review* 87 (2002): 452–85.

———. "Beyond Accountability: Arbitrariness and Legitimacy in the Administrative State." *New York University Law Review* 78 (2003): 461–556.

Bressman, Lisa Schultz, and Robert B. Thompson. "The Future of Agency Independence." *Vanderbilt Law Review* 63, no. 3 (2010): 599–672.

Bressman, Lisa Schultz, and Michael P. Vandenburgh. "Inside the Administrative State: A Critical Look at the Practice of Presidential Control." *Michigan Law Review* 47 (2006).

Brooke, Henry (Lord Justice). "Judicial Independence: Its History in England and Wales." In *Fragile Bastion: Judicial Independence in the Nineties and Beyond*, Education Monograph no. 1, New South Wales Judicial Commission, 1997.

Brooks, Rosa. *How Everything Became War and the Military Became Everything: Tales from the Pentagon.* New York: Simon & Schuster, 2016.

Brownlow Committee. *Report of the Committee with Studies of Administrative Management in the Federal Government.* Washington, DC: US Government Printing Office, 1937.

Broz, J. Lawrence. "Political System Transparency and Monetary-Commitment Regimes." *International Organization* 56, no. 4 (2002): 861–87.

Brunnermeier, Markus K., Harold James, and Jean-Pierre Landau. *The Euro and the Battle of Ideas.* Princeton, NJ: Princeton University Press, 2016.

Buchanan, Allen. "Political Legitimacy and Democracy." *Ethics* 112, no. 4 (2002): 689–719.

Buchanan, Allen, and Robert O. Keohane. "The Legitimacy of Global Governance Institutions." *Ethics & International Affairs* 20, no. 4 (2006): 405–37.

Buchanan, James M. "The Constitutionalization of Money." *Cato Journal* 30, no. 2 (2010): 251–58.

Buchanan, James M., and Richard A. Musgrave. *Public Finance and Public Choice: Two Contrasting Visions of the State.* Cambridge, MA: MIT Press, 1999.

Buchanan, James M., and Gordon Tullock. *The Calculus of Consent: Logical Foundations of Constitutional Democracy.* Ann Arbor: University of Michigan Press, 1965.

Buiter, Willem. "Central Banks and Financial Crises." Federal Reserve Bank of Kansas City Jackson Hole Conference, 2008.

———. "Central Banks: Powerful, Political and Unaccountable?" Keynes Lecture in Economics 2014, *Journal of the British Academy* 2 (2014): 269–303.

Buiter, Willem, and Anne Sibert. "The Central Bank as Market Maker of Last Resort." Vox, *CEPR Policy Portal*, August 13, 2007.

Burke, Edmund. *The Works of the Right Honourable Edmund Burke.* London: Henry G. Bohn, 1854.

Burns, Arthur F. "The Anguish of Central Banking." 1979 Per Jacobsson Lecture, September 30, 1979. Per Jacobsson Foundation.

Busuioc, Madalina. "Accountability, Control and Independence: The Case of European Agencies." *European Law Journal* 15, no. 5 (2009): 599–615.

———. *European Agencies: Law and Practices of Accountability.* Oxford: Oxford University Press, 2013.

Cabinet Office (UK). *Public Bodies: A Guide for Departments*, and *Executive Agencies: A Guide for Departments.* 2006.

Calomiris, Charles W., Douglas Holtz-Flint, R. Glenn Hubbard, Allan H. Meltzer, and Hall Scott. "Establishing Credible Rules for Fed Emergency Lending." *Journal of Financial Economic Policy*, forthcoming.

Cama, G., and G. B. Pittaluga. "Central Banks and Democracy." *Rivista Internazionale di Scienze Sociali* CVII, no. 3 (1999): 235–77.

Cane, Peter. *Controlling Administrative Power: An Historical Comparison*. Cambridge: Cambridge University Press, 2016.

Capie, Forrest, Stanley Fischer et al., editors. *The Future of Central Banking: The Tercentenary Symposium of the Bank of England*. Cambridge: Cambridge University Press, 1994.

Carnwath, Robert (Lord). "Tribunal Justice: A New Start." *Public Law* 48, 2009.

———. "From Rationality to Proportionality in the Modern Law." Speech at the UCL-HKU Conference on Judicial Review in a Changing Society, April 14, 2014.

Carpenter, Daniel P. *The Forging of Bureaucratic Autonomy: Reputations, Networks, and Policy Innovation in Executive Agencies, 1862–1928*. Princeton, NJ: Princeton University Press, 2001.

Carpenter, Daniel, and David Moss, eds. *Preventing Regulatory Capture: Special-Interest Influence and How to Limit It*. New York: Cambridge University Press, 2014.

Carrigan, Christopher. *Structured to Fail? Regulatory Performance under Competing Mandates*. Cambridge: Cambridge University Press, 2017.

Cecchetti, Stephen G. "Why Central Banks Should Be Financial Supervisors." Vox Subprime Series, part 3. *CEPR Policy Portal*, November 30, 2007.

———. "Central Bank Independence: A Path Less Clear." Bank for International Settlements, 2013.

Cecchetti, Stephen G., and Kermit L. Schoenholtz. "Narrow Banking Won't Stop Bank Runs." *Money, Banking and Financial Markets* (blog), April 28, 2014.

Cecchetti, Stephen G., and Paul Tucker. "Is There Macro-Prudential Policy without International Cooperation?" In *Policy Challenges in a Diverging Global Economy*, Proceedings of the Asia Pacific Policy Conference, edited by R. Glick and M. Speigel. Federal Reserve Bank of San Francisco, November 2015.

Christiano, Thomas. *The Rule of the Many: Fundamental Issues in Democratic Theory*. Boulder, CO: Westview Press, 1996.

———. *The Constitution of Equality: Democratic Authority and Its Limits*. New York: Oxford University Press, 2008.

———. "Rational Deliberation amongst Experts and Citizens." In *Deliberative Systems: Deliberative Democracy at the Large Scale*, edited by John Parkinson and Jane Mansbridge. Cambridge: Cambridge University Press, 2012.

Christiano, Thomas, and John Christman. *Contemporary Debates in Political Philosophy*. Chichester: Wiley-Blackwell, 2009.

Chu, Vivian S., and Todd Garvey. "Executive Orders: Issuance, Modification, and Revocation." Congressional Research Service, April 16, 2014.

Chu, Vivian S., and Daniel T. Shedd. "Presidential Review of Independent Regulatory Commission Rulemaking: Legal Issues." Congressional Research Service, September 10, 2012.

Cline, William R., and Joseph E. Gagnon. "Lehman Died, Bagehot Lives: Why Did the Fed and Treasury Let a Major Wall Street Bank Fail?" Petersen Institute Policy Brief, September 2013.

Coase, Ronald. "Social Cost." *Journal of Law and Economics* 3 (1960): 1–44.

Cochrane, John H. "Toward a Run Free Financial System." April 16, 2014. http://papers.ssrn.com/sol3/papers.cfm?abstract_id=2425883.

Cohen, Elliot A. *Supreme Command: Soldiers, Statesmen, and Leadership in Wartime*. New York: Simon & Schuster, 2002.

Cohen, Joshua. "Deliberation and Democratic Legitimacy." In *The Good Polity: Normative Analysis of the State*, edited by Alan Hamlin and Philip Pettit. Oxford: Basil Blackwell, 1989.

Coicaud, Jean-Marc. *Legitimacy and Politics: A Contribution to the Study of Political Right and Political Responsibility*. Cambridge and New York: Cambridge University Press, 2002.

Coleman, Martin. "The Future of Section 60 of Competition Act 1998 Post-Brexit." Brexit Competition Law Working Group website, 2016.

Committee on Banking and Currency. *A Primer on Money*. US House of Representatives. Washington, DC, 1964.

Commonwealth (Latimer House). *Principles on the Accountability of and the Relationship between the Three Branches of Government*, agreed by Commonwealth Law Ministers and Heads of Government, 2003.

Conseil d'État. *Rapport Public 2001: Jurisprudence et Avis de 2000. Les Autorités Administratives Indépendantes*.

Constancio, Vitor. "Macro-prudential Stress Tests: A New Analytical Tool." *CEPR Policy Portal*, February 22, 2017.

———. "Inequality and Macroeconomic Policies." Speech given as ECB vice president, August 22, 2017.

Constant, Henri-Benjamin. "The Liberty of the Ancients Compared with That of the Moderns." In *The Political Writings of Benjamin Constant*, edited by Biancamaria Fontana. Cambridge: Cambridge University Press, 1988.

Conti-Brown, Peter. *The Power and Independence of the Federal Reserve*. Princeton, NJ: Princeton University Press, 2016.

Copelovitch, Mark S., and David Andrew Singer. "Financial Regulation, Monetary Policy, and Inflation in the Industrialized World." *Journal of Politics* 70, no. 3 (2008): 663–80.

Cox, Gary W., and M. D. McCubbins. "Political Structure and Economic Policy: The Institutional Determinants of Policy Outcomes." 1997. https://papers.ssrn.com/sol3/papers.cfm?abstract_id=1009999.

Craig, Paul. "Law, Fact and Discretion in the UK, EU and the USA." Paper delivered at Sciences Po, Paris, 2008.

———. *UK, EU and Global Administrative Law: Foundations and Challenges*. 2014 Hamlyn Lectures. Cambridge: Cambridge University Press, 2015.

Crane, Daniel A. "Rules versus Standards in Antitrust Adjudication." *Washington and Lee Law Review* 64 (2007).

Crowe, Christopher, and Ellen E. Mead. "The Evolution of Central Bank Governance around the World." *Journal of Economic Perspectives* 21, no. 4 (2007): 69–90.

Crozier, Michael J., Samuel P. Huntington, and Joji Watanuki. *The Crisis of Democracy: Report on the Governability of Democracies to the Trilateral Commission*. New York: New York University Press, 1975.

Currie, David. "Regulatory Capture: A Perspective from a Communications Regulator." In *Making Good Financial Regulation: Towards a Policy Response to Regulatory*

Capture, edited by Stefano Pagliari. International Centre for Financial Regulation. Guilford: Grosvenor House Publishing Ltd., 2012.

Custos, Dominique. "The 2015 French Code of Administrative Procedure: An Assessment." In *Comparative Administrative Law*, edited by Susan Rose-Ackerman and Peter Lindseth. 2nd ed. Cheltenham: Edward Elgar, 2017.

Dahl, Robert A. *Democracy and Its Critics*. New Haven, CT: Yale University Press, 1989.

———. *A Preface to Democratic Theory*. Expanded ed. Chicago: University of Chicago Press, 2006.

Dahrendorf, Ralf. "Politics in Industrial Society." In *The Modern Social Conflict: An Essay on the Politics of Liberty*. London: Weidenfeld and Nicolson, 1988.

Dal Bó, Ernesto. "Regulatory Capture: A Review." *Oxford Review of Economic Policy* 22, no. 2 (2006): 203–25.

Darling, Alistair. *Back from the Brink: 1000 Days at Number 11*. London: Atlantic Books, 2011.

Datla, Kirti, and Richard L. Revesz. "Deconstructing Independent Agencies (and Executive Agencies)." *Cornell Law Review* 98, no. 4 (2013): 769–844.

Davies, William. *The Limits of NeoLiberalism: Authority, Sovereignty and the Logic of Competition*. 2nd ed. Thousand Oaks, CA: SAGE Publications, 2017.

Debelle, Guy, and Stanley Fischer. "How Independent Should a Central Bank Be?" In *Goals, Guidelines and Constraints Facing Monetary Policymakers*, edited by J. C. Fuhrer, 195–221. Boston, MA: Federal Reserve Bank of Boston, 1994.

Decker, Christopher. *Modern Economic Regulation: An Introduction to Theory and Practice*. Cambridge: Cambridge University Press, 2015.

DeLong, J. Bradford, and Lawrence H. Summers. "Fiscal Policy in a Depressed Economy." *Brookings Papers on Economic Activity* (2012): 233–97.

DeMuth, Christopher. "Can the Administrative State Be Tamed." *Journal of Legal Analysis* 8, no. 1 (2016): 121–90.

de Waal, James. "Depending on the Right People: British Political-Military Relations 2001–2010." London: Chatham House, 2013.

Dewatripont, Mathias, Ian Jewitt, and Jean Tirole. "The Economics of Career Concerns, Part II: Application to Missions and Accountability of Government Agencies." *Review of Economic Studies* 66, no. 1 (1999): 199–217.

Dewey, John. *The Public and Its Problems*. Athens, OH: Swallow Press, 1954.

Diamond, Douglas W., and P. H. Dybvig. "Bank Runs, Deposit Insurance, and Liquidity." *Journal of Political Economy* 91, no. 3 (1983): 401–19.

Dicey, A. V. *Introduction to the Study of the Law of the Constitution*. London: Macmillan, 1982.

Doehler, Marian. "Institutional Choice and Bureaucratic Autonomy in Germany." *West European Politics* 25, no. 1 (2002): 101–24.

Dombret, Andreas. "What Is 'Good Regulation'?" Speech given at the Bundesbank "Banking Supervision in Dialogue?" Symposium, July 9, 2014.

———. "Banking Sector in Uncertain Times: A Challenge for Whom?" Keynote speech at British Bankers Association, Annual International Banking Conference, London, October 20, 2016.

Dorf, Michael C. "Putting the Democracy in Democracy and Distrust: The Coherentist Case for Representation Reinforcement." Cornell Faculty Working Papers, no. 73, 2004.

Dowd, Kevin. *Private Money: The Path to Monetary Stability.* Hobart Paper 112. London: Institute of Economic Affairs, 1988.

Doylan, Delia M. "Holding Democracy Hostage: Central Bank Autonomy and the Transition from Authoritarian Rule." *Politica y Goberno.* 5, no. 1 (1998).

———. *Defusing Democracy: Central Bank Autonomy and the Transition from Authoritarian Rule.* Ann Arbor: University of Michigan Press, 2001.

Drazen, Allan. "Central Bank Independence, Democracy, and Dollarization." *Journal of Applied Economics* 5, no. 1 (2002): 1–17.

Driffill, John. "Central Banks as Trustees Rather Than Agents." Unpublished paper, Southampton University, 1998.

Dryzek, John S., and Simon Niemeyer. "Reconciling Pluralism and Consensus as Political Ideals." *American Journal of Political Science* 50, no. 3 (2006): 634–49.

Dworkin, Ronald. *Freedom's Law: The Moral Reading of the American Constitution.* New York: Oxford University Press, 1986.

Dyson, John Anthony (Lord). "Criticising Judges: Fair Game or Off-Limits?" Third Annual Bailii Lecture, November 27, 2014.

Dyzenhaus, David. *The Constitution of Law: Legality in a Time of Emergency.* Cambridge: Cambridge University Press, 2006.

Econ Committee of the European Parliament. "Reaction to the Opinion of the Basel Committee on CRD4 (Capital Requirements Directive for Banks)." December 5, 2015.

Egeberg, Morten, and Jarie Trondol. "EU-Level Agencies: New Executive Centre Formation or Vehicles for National Control." *Journal of European Public Policy* 18, no. 6 (2011): 868–87.

Eggertsson, Gauti, and Eric Le Borgne. "A Political Agency Theory of Central Bank Independence." *Journal of Money, Credit and Banking* 42, no. 4 (June 2010): 647–77.

Eichengreen, Barry. *Globalizing Capital: A History of the International Monetary System.* Princeton, NJ: Princeton University Press, 1996.

Eichengreen, Barry, Mohamed El-Erian et al. "Rethinking Central Banking." Committee on International Economic Reform, Brookings Institution, September 2011.

El-Erian, Mohamed A. *The Only Game in Town: Central Banks, Instability, and Avoiding the Next Collapse.* New York: Penguin Random House, 2016.

Elgie, Robert. "Democratic Accountability and Central Bank Independence: Historical and Contemporary, National and European Perspectives." *West European Politics* 21, no. 3 (1998): 53–76.

———. "Semi-presidentialism: Concepts, Consequences and Contesting Explanations." *Political Studies Review* 2, no. 3 (2004): 314–30.

———. "Why Do Governments Delegate Authority to Quasi-Autonomous Agencies? The Case of Independent Administrative Authorities in France." *Governance* 19, no. 2 (2006): 207–27.

Elliot, Mark. "Ombudsmen, Tribunals, Inquiries: Re-fashioning Accountability beyond the Courts." Cambridge Legal Studies Research Papers, no. 21/20012, August 2012.

Elliot, Mark, and David Feldman, eds. *The Cambridge Companion to Public Law.* Cambridge: Cambridge University Press, 2015.

Elster, Jon. *Ulysses and the Sirens: Studies in Rationality and Irrationality.* Cambridge: Cambridge University Press, 1979.

Ely, John Hart. *Democracy and Distrust: A Theory of Judicial Review*. Cambridge, MA: Harvard University Press, 1980.

Endicott, Timothy. *Administrative Law*. 3rd ed. Oxford: Oxford University Press, 2015.

Epstein, David, and Sharyn O'Halloran. *Delegating Powers: A Transaction Cost Politics Approach to Policy Making under Separate Powers*. Cambridge: Cambridge University Press, 1999.

Epstein, Gerald. "Central Banks as Agents of Economic Development." Political Economy Research Institute Working Paper, no. 104, University of Massachusetts Amherst, September 2005.

Epstein, Richard A. "Why the Modern Administrative State Is Inconsistent with the Rule of Law." *NYU Journal of Law and Liberty* 3 (2008): 491–515.

Ernst, Daniel. *Toqueville's Nightmare: The Administrative State Emerges in America, 1900–1940*. New York: Oxford University Press, 2014.

Eskridge, William N., and John Ferejohn. "Super-Statutes." *Duke Law Journal* 50 (2001): 1215–76.

Estlund, David. *Democratic Authority*. Princeton, NJ: Princeton University Press, 2008.

———. "Jeremy Waldron on *Law and Disagreement*." *Philosophical Studies* 99 (2000): 111–28.

Farhi, Emmanuel, and Jean Tirole. "Collective Moral Hazard, Maturity Mismatch, and Systemic Bailouts." *American Economic Review* 102, no. 1 (2012): 60–93.

Fawcett, Edmund. *Liberalism: The Life of an Idea*. Princeton, NJ: Princeton University Press, 2014.

Feaver, Peter D. "Crisis as Shirking: An Agency Theory Explanation of the Souring of American Civil-Military Relations." *Armed Forces & Society* 24 (1998): 407–34.

Ferguson, Niall. *The Cash Nexus: Money and Power in the Modern World, 1700–2000*. New York: Penguin Books, 2002.

Fessenden, Helen. "1965: The Year the Fed and LBJ Clashed." Richmond Federal Reserve *Economic Focus* Third/Fourth Quarter (2016).

Field, Chris. "The Fourth Branch of Government: The Evolution of Integrity Agencies and Enhanced Government Accountability." Paper presented at the 2012 AIAL National Administrative Law Forum, Adelaide, Australia, July 19–20, 2012.

Fiorina, Morris P. "Legislative Choice of Regulatory Forms: Legal Process or Administrative Process?" *Public Choice* 39, no. 1 (1982): 33–71.

First, Henry, and Spencer Weber Waller. "Antitrust's Democratic Deficit." *Fordham Law Review* 81 (2013): 2543–2574.

Fischer, Stanley. "Rules versus Discretion in Monetary Policy." In *Handbook of Monetary Economics Volume II*, edited by B. M. Friedman and F. H. Hahn. Amsterdam: Elsevier Science Publishers, 1990.

———. "Modern Central Banking." In *The Future of Central Banking: The Tercentenary Symposium of the Bank of England*, edited by F. Capie, C. Goodhart, S. Fischer, and N. Schnadt. Cambridge: Cambridge University Press, 1994.

———. "The Washington Consensus." Part of a Petersen Institute retrospective on John Williamson's work, 2012.

Fisher, Irving. "100% Money and the Public Debt." *Economic Forum* April–June (1936): 406–20.

Fisher, Peter R. "Financial Stability and the Hemianopsia of Monetary Policy." *Business Economics* 51, no. 2 (2016): 68–70.

Flinders, Matthew. "Distributed Public Governance in Britain." *Public Administration* 82, no. 4 (2004): 883–909.

———. *Delegated Governance and the British State: Walking without Order*. Oxford: Oxford University Press, 2008.

Flinders, Matthew, and Matthew Wood. "When Politics Fails: Hyper-democracy and Hyper-depoliticization." *New Political Science* 37, no. 3 (2015): 363–81.

Fon, Vincy, and Francesco Parisi. "Judicial Precedents in Civil Law Systems: A Dynamic Analysis." *International Review of Law and Economics* 26 (2006): 519–35.

Forder, James. "Central Bank Independence and Credibility: Is There a Shred of Evidence?" *International Finance* 3, no. 1 (2000): 167–85.

———. "Why Is Central Bank Independence So Widely Approved?" *Journal of Economic Issues* 39, no. 4 (2005): 843–65.

Foucault, Michel. *The Birth of Biopolotics: Lectures at the College de France, 1978–1979*. Translated by Graham Burchell. Basingstoke: Palgrave MacMillan, 2008.

Freedman, John O. *Crisis and Legitimacy: The Administrative Process and American Government*. Cambridge and New York: Cambridge University Press, 1978.

French Senate. *A State within the State: Channeling the Proliferation of Independent Administrative Authorities in Order to Better Control Them*. Report of the French Senate Committee of Inquiry on the assessment and control of the creation, organization, activities, and management of independent administrative authorities, 2015.

Friedman, Benjamin M. *The Moral Consequences of Economic Growth*. New York: Vintage Books, 2006.

———. "Has the Financial Crisis Permanently Changed the Practice of Monetary Policy? Has It Changed the Theory of Monetary Policy?" *Manchester School* 83, no. 1 (2015).

Friedman, Milton. "Should There Be an Independent Monetary Authority?" In *In Search of a Monetary Constitution*, edited by Leland B. Yeager. Cambridge, MA: Harvard University Press, 1962.

———. "Statement, Testimony, and Comments" to US House of Representatives Banking and Currency Committee, March 3, 1964. In *The Federal Reserve System after Fifty Years*. US Congress House of Representatives, Committee on Banking and Currency, 1133–78. Washington, DC: US Government Printing Office.

———. *The Optimum Quantity of Money*. New Brunswick, NJ: Transaction Publishers, 1969.

———. "A Friedman Doctrine: The Social Responsibility of Business Is to Increase Its Profits." *New York Times*, September 13, 1970.

Friendly, Henry J. *The Federal Administrative Agencies: The Need for Better Definition of Standards*. Cambridge, MA: Harvard University Press, 1962.

Fukuyama, Francis. *The Origins of Political Order*. New York: Farrar, Straus and Giroux, 2011.

———. *Political Order and Political Decay*. New York: Farrar, Straus and Giroux, 2014.

Fuller, Lon L. *The Morality of Law*. Revised ed. New Haven, CT: Yale University Press, 1969.

Gailmard, Sean. "Accountability and Principal-Agent Models." In *The Oxford Handbook of Public Accountability*, edited by Mark Bovens, Robert E. Goodin, and Thomas Schillemans. New York: Oxford University Press, 2012.

Gates, Robert M. *Duty: Memoirs of a Secretary at War.* New York: Alfred A. Knopf, 2014.

Gehring, Thomas. "The Consequences of Delegation to Independent Agencies: Separation of Powers, Discursive Governance and the Regulation of Telecommunications in Germany." *European Journal of Political Research* 43, 2004: 677–98.

Geithner, Timothy F. *Stress Test: Reflections on Financial Crises.* New York: Broadway Books, 2015.

———. "Are We Safer? The Case for Updating Bagehot." 2016 Per Jacobsson Lecture, October 8, 2016. Per Jacobsson Foundation.

George, E. A. J. "The Pursuit of Financial Stability." Speech delivered November 18, 1993. *Bank of England Quarterly Bulletin*, February 1994.

———. Speech given at the TUC Congress in Blackpool, September 15, 1998. Bank of England.

———. "The Approach to Macroeconomic Management: How It Has Evolved." Per Jacobsson Lecture, June 29, 2008. Per Jacobsson Foundation.

Geraats, Petra M. "Central Bank Transparency." *Economic Journal* 112, no. 483 (2002): F532–F565.

———. "Monetary Policy Transparency." In *The Oxford Handbook of Economic and Institutional Transparency*, edited by Jens Forssbaeck and Lars Oxelheim. Oxford: Oxford University Press, 2014.

Gersen, Jacob E. "Designing Agencies." In *Research Handbook on Public Choice and Public Law*, edited by Daniel A. Farber and Anne Joseph O'Connell. Cheltenham: Edward Elgar, 2010.

Giannini, Curzio. *The Age of Central Banks.* Cheltenham: Edward Elgar, 2011.

Gilardi, Fabrizio. "The Same, But Different: Central Banks, Regulatory Agencies, and the Politics of Delegation to Independent Agencies." *Comparative European Politics* 5, no. 3 (2007): 303–27.

———. *Delegation in the Regulatory State: Independent Regulatory Agencies in Western Europe.* Cheltenham: Edward Elgar, 2008.

Ginsburg, Douglas H., and Steven Menashi. "Our Illiberal Administrative Law." *New York University Journal of Law & Liberty* 10, no. 2 (2016): 475–523.

Glaeser, Edward L., and Andrei Shleifer. "The Rise of the Regulatory State." NBER Working Paper, no. 8650, December 2001.

Goldmann, Matthias. "Adjudicating Economics? Central Bank Independence and the Appropriate Standard of Judicial Review." *German Law Journal* 15, no. 2 (2014): 266–80.

Goldsworthy, Jeffrey. *Parliamentary Sovereignty: Contemporary Debates.* Cambridge: Cambridge University Press, 2010.

Goodfriend, Marvin. "Why We Need an 'Accord' for Federal Reserve Credit Policy: A Note." *Journal of Money, Credit and Banking* 26, no. 3 (1994): 572–80.

———. "The Elusive Promise of Independent Central Banking." Institute for Monetary and Economic Studies, Bank of Japan, Tokyo, August 2012.

Goodhart, C. A. E. *Monetary Theory and Practice: The UK Experience.* London: Palgrave Macmillan, 1983.

———. *The Evolution of Central Banks.* Cambridge, MA: MIT Press, 1988.

———. "Game Theory for Central Bankers." *Journal of Economic Literature* 32 (1994): 101–14.

———. "The Changing Role of Central Banks." BIS Working Papers, no. 326, November 2010.

Goodhart, C. A. E., and Ellen Mead. "Central Banks and Supreme Courts: A Comparison of Monetary and Judicial Processes and Transparency." *Journal Moneda y Credito*, no. 218 (2004): 11–59.

Goodin, Robert E. "Institutions and Their Design." In *The Theory of Institutional Design*, edited by Goodin. Cambridge: Cambridge University Press, 1996.

Goodman, John B. "The Politics of Central Bank Independence." *Comparative Politics* 23, no. 3 (1991): 329–49.

Graber, Mark A. *A New Introduction to American Constitutionalism*. New York: Oxford University Press, 2013.

Granville, Brigitte. *Remembering Inflation*. Princeton, NJ: Princeton University Press, 2013.

Green, Leslie. *The Authority of the State*. Oxford: Oxford University Press, 1988.

Greenspan, Alan. "Transparency in Monetary Policy." Remarks at the Federal Reserve Bank of St. Louis, October 11, 2002.

Greenwald, Bruce, and Joseph Stiglitz. "Externalities in Economies with Imperfect Information and Incomplete Markets." *Quarterly Journal of Economics* 101, no. 2, 1986.

Greenwood, Robin, Samuel G. Hanson, Joshua S. Rudolph, and Lawrence H. Summers. "Government Debt Management at the Zero Lower Bound." Hutchins Center Working Papers, no. 5, September 30, 2014.

Greif, Avner. "The Impact of Administrative Power on Political and Economic Developments: Toward a Political Economy of Implementation." In *Institutions and Economic Performance*, ed. E. Helpman, 17–77. Cambridge, MA: Harvard University Press, 2008.

Greif, Avner, and Jared Rubin. "Endogenous Political Legitimacy: The English Reformation and the Institutional Foundation of Limited Government." Memo. Stanford University and Chapman University, 2017.

Gross, Peter (Lord Justice). "The Judicial Role Today." Queen Mary University, Law and Society Lecture, London, November 23, 2016.

Guimares, Rodrigo. "What Accounts for the Fall in UK Ten-Year Government Bond Yields?" *Bank of England Quarterly Bulletin* Q3 (2012).

Gutmann, Amy, and Dennis Thompson. *Democracy and Disagreement: Why Moral Conflict Cannot Be Avoided in Politics, and What Should Be Done about It*. Cambridge, MA: Belknap Press of Harvard University Press, 1998.

Habermas, Jürgen. *Legitimation Crisis*. Translated by Thomas McCarthy. Boston: Beacon Press, 1975.

———. *Between Facts and Norms: Contributions to a Discourse Theory of Law and Democracy*. Cambridge: Polity Press, 1996.

Halberstam, Daniel. "The Promise of Comparative Administrative Law: A Constitutional Perspective on Independent Agencies." In *Comparative Administrative Law*, edited by Susan Rose-Ackerman and Peter Lindseth. Cheltenham: Edward Elgar, 2010.

Hall, Edward. "Bernard Williams and the Basic Legitimation Demand: A Defence." *Political Studies* 63, no. 2 (2015): 466–80.

Hall, Peter A., and David Soskice, eds. *Varieties of Capitalism: The Institutional Foundations of Comparative Advantage*. New York: Oxford University Press, 2001.

Hallam-Eames, Lucy. "Echoes of the *Chevron* Doctrine in English Law." *Judicial Review* 15, no. 1 (2010): 81–84.

Hallerberg, Mark. "Veto Players and the Choice of Monetary Institutions." *International Organization* 56, no. 4 (2002): 775–802.

Hamilton, Alexander, James Madison, and John Jay. *The Federalist*. London: Phoenix Press, 2000.

Hamlin, Alan. "Contractarianism." In *International Encyclopedia of the Social & Behavioral Sciences*, edited by J. D. Wright. 2nd ed. New York: Elsevier, 2015.

Handke, Stefan. "A Problem of Chief and Indian—the Role of the Supervisory Authority BaFin and the Ministry of Finance in German Financial Policy." *Policy and Society* 31, no. 3 (2012): 237–47.

Hardin, Russell. "Institutional Commitment: Values or Incentives." In *Economics, Values and Organization*, edited by Avner Ben-Nur and Louis Putterman. New York: Cambridge University Press, 1998.

———. *Liberalism, Constitutionalism, and Democracy*. Oxford: Oxford University Press, 1999.

Harlow, Carol, and Richard Rawlings. *Law and Administration*. 3rd ed. Cambridge: Cambridge University Press, 2009.

Harris, Richard A., and Sidney M. Milkis. *The Politics of Regulatory Change: A Tale of Two Agencies*. 2nd ed. Oxford: Oxford University Press, 1996.

Hart, Henry Jr., and Albert Sacks. *The Legal Process: Basic Problems in the Making and Application of Law*. University Casebook Series. Westbury, NY: Foundation Press, 2006.

Hart, Oliver D. "Incomplete Contracts and the Theory of the Firm." *Journal of Law, Economics, & Organisation* 4, no. 1 (1988): 119–39.

Harvard Law Review Notes, "Independence, Congressional Weakness, and the Importance of Appointment: The Impact of Combining Budgetary Autonomy with Removal Protection." *Harvard Law Review* 125 (2012): 1822–43.

Hattersley, Roy. "Pragmatism Must Not Still Conscience." *Guardian*, May 14, 1997.

Hawtrey, R. G. "The Genoa Resolutions on Currency." *Economic Journal* 32, no. 127 (1922): 290–304.

Hayek, F. A. *The Political Ideal of the Rule of Law*. Cairo: National Bank of Egypt, 1955.

———. *The Constitution of Liberty*. Chicago: University of Chicago Press, 1960.

———. "Liberalism." In *New Studies in Philosophy, Politics, Economics, and the History of Ideas*. Chicago: University of Chicago Press, 1978.

———. *Denationalisation of Money: The Argument Refined*. 3rd ed. London: Institute of Economic Affairs, 1990.

———. *The Road to Serfdom*, edited by Bruce Caldwell. Chicago: University of Chicago Press, 1994.

Hegel, G.W.F. *Elements of the Philosophy of Right*. Cambridge: Cambridge University Press, 1991.

Herbert Smith Freehills. "Advocate General Wahl in Intel Appeal Opts for More Effects-Based Approach on Rebates and Proposes Annulment of General Court's Intel Judgment." *Legal Briefings*, October 20, 2016.

Hershovitz, Scott. "Legitimacy, Democracy, and Razian Authority." *Legal Theory* 9, no. 3 (2003): 201–20.

Hetzel, Robert L. *The Great Recession: Market Failure or Policy Failure? Studies in Macroeconomic History*. New York: Cambridge University Press, 2012.

Hetzel, Robert L., and Ralph F. Leach. "The Treasury-Fed Accord: A New Narrative Account." *Federal Reserve Bank of Richmond Economic Quarterly* 87, no. 1 (2001): 33–55.

———. "After the Accord: Reminiscences on the Birth of the Modern Fed." *Federal Reserve Bank of Richmond Economic Quarterly* 87, no. 1 (2001): 57–64.

Hohfeld, Wesley. *Fundamental Legal Conceptions as Applied in Judicial Reasoning*. New Haven, CT: Yale University Press, 1919.

Hollis, Martin. *Trust within Reason*. Cambridge: Cambridge University Press, 1998.

Holmes, Douglas R. *Economy of Words: Communicative Imperatives in Central Banks*. Chicago: University of Chicago Press, 2013.

Holmes, Stephen. *Passions and Constraint: On the Theory of Liberal Democracy*. Chicago: University of Chicago Press, 1995.

Holmstrom, Bengt. "Moral Hazard in Teams." *Bell Journal of Economics* 13, no. 2 (1982): 324–40.

Holmstrom, Bengt, and Paul Milgrom. "Multi-task Principal-Agent Analysis: Incentive Contracts, Asset Ownership and Job Design." *Journal of Law, Economics & Organisation* 7 (1991): 24–52.

Hood, Christopher. "A Public Management for All Seasons." *Public Administration* 69, no. 1 (1991): 3–19.

Horn, Murray. *The Political Economy of Public Administration: Institutional Choice in the Public Sector*. Cambridge: Cambridge University Press, 1995.

House of Commons Select Committee on Public Administration. "Who's Accountable? Relationships between Government and Arm's-Length Bodies." November 4, 2014.

———. "Quangos." Sixth Report, Session 1998–99.

Hovenkamp, Herbert J. "Distributive Justice and Consumer Welfare in Antitrust." August 3, 2011. https://ssrn.com/abstract=1873463.

Huber, John D. "Executive Decree Authority in France." In *Executive Decree Authority*, edited by John M. Carey and Matthew Soberg Shugart. Cambridge: Cambridge University Press, 1998.

Huber, John D., and Charles R. Shipan. *Deliberate Discretion? The Institutional Foundations of Bureaucratic Autonomy*. Cambridge: Cambridge University Press, 2002.

Hume, David. *A Treatise of Human Nature*, edited by L. A. Selby-Bigge and P. H. Nidditch. 2nd ed. Oxford: Clarendon Press, Oxford University Press, 1978.

Humphrey, Thomas M. "Lender of Last Resort: What It Is, Whence It Came, and Why the Fed Isn't It." *Cato Journal* 30, no. 2 (2010): 333–64.

Huntington, Samuel P. "The Marasmus of the ICC: The Commission, the Railroads, and the Public Interest." *Yale Law Journal* 61, no. 4 (1952): 467–509.

———. *The Soldier and the State: The Theory and Politics of Civil-Military Relations*. Cambridge, MA: Belknap Press of Harvard University Press, 1957.

———. "Conservatism as an Ideology." *American Political Science Review* 51, no. 2 (1957): 454–73.

Hurwicz, Leonid. "But Who Will Guard the Guardians?" Nobel Prize lecture, December 8, 2007.

Institute for Government. *Read Before Burning: Arm's-Length Government for a New Administration*. July 2010.

Institute for Policy Integrity. *Strengthening Regulatory Review: Recommendations for the Trump Administration from Former OIRA Leaders*. 2016.

Ip, Eric Chiyeung. "Building Constitutional Democracy on Oriental Foundations: An Anatomy of Sun Yat-Sen's Constitutionalism." *Historia Constitucional*, no. 9 (2008).

Issing, Otmar. "Hayek, Currency Competition and European Monetary Union." 1999 Annual Hayek Memorial Lecture, May 27, 1999. European Central Bank.

———. "Paradise Lost." Mayekawa Lecture, Institute for Monetary and Economic Studies, Tokyo, May 30, 2012. Bank of Japan.

James, Harold. *The End of Globalization: Lessons from the Great Depression*. Cambridge, MA: Harvard University Press, 2001.

Janowitz, Morris. "Military Elites and the Study of War." *Conflict Resolution* 1, no. 1 (1957): 9–18.

———. *The Professional Soldier: A Social and Political Portrait*. Glencoe, IL: Free Press, 1960.

Joyce, Michael A. S., Peter Lilholdt, and Steffan Sorensen. "Extracting Inflation Expectations and Inflation Risk Premia from the Term Structure: A Joint Model of the UK Nominal and Real Yield Curves." *Journal of Banking & Finance* 34, no. 2 (2010): 281–94.

Judge, Igor. *The Safest Shield: Lectures, Speeches and Essays*. Oxford: Hart Publishing, 2015.

———. "Ceding Power to the Executive: The Resurrection of Henry VIII." Paper delivered at King's College London, April 12, 2016.

Judiciary of England and Wales. "The Accountability of the Judiciary." October 2007.

———. *Guide to Judicial Conduct*. Published March 2013; amended July 2016.

Kaeding, Michael, and Kevin M. Stack. "Legislative Scrutiny? The Political Economy and Practice of Legislative Vetoes in the European Union." *Journal of Common Market Studies* 53, no. 6 (2015): 1268–84.

Kagan, Elena. "Presidential Administration." *Harvard Law Review* 114 (2001): 2246–85.

Kaplow, Louis. "On the (Ir)Relevance of Distribution and Labour Supply Distortion to Government Policy." *Journal of Economic Perspectives* 18, no. 4 (2004): 159–75.

———. "On the Choice of Welfare Standards in Competition Law." In *The Goals of Competition Policy*, edited by Daniel Zimmer, 3–26. Cheltenham: Edward Elgar, 2012.

Kashyap, Anil, Raghuram Rajan, and Jeremy Stein. "Banks as Liquidity Providers: An Explanation for the Coexistence of Lending and Deposit-Taking." *Journal of Finance* 57, no. 1 (2002): 33–73.

Kavanagh, Aileen. "Judicial Restraint in the Pursuit of Justice." *University of Toronto Law Journal* 60, no. 1 (2010): 23–40.

Kay, John. *Narrow Banking: The Reform of Banking*. Centre for the Study of Financial Innovation, September 2009.

Kazmin, Amy. "India's Raghuram Rajan Warns against Intolerance." *Financial Times*, November 1, 2015.

Keefer, Philip, and David Stasavage. "When Does Delegation Improve Credibility? Central Bank Independence and the Separation of Powers." Oxford Working Paper Series, no. 98-18, 1998.

Kelly, Terrence. "Unlocking the Iron Cage: Public Administration in the Deliberative Democracy of Juergen Habermas." *Administration & Society* 36, no. 1 (2004): 38–61.

Kelsen, Hans. "Foundations of Democracy." *Ethics* 66, no. 1, pt. 2: Foundations of Democracy (1955): 1–101.

Keohane, Robert O., and Joseph S. Nye Jr. "Transgovernmental Relations and International Organizations." *World Politics* 27, no. 1 (1974): 39–62.

Kessler, Jeremy K., and David E. Pozen. "Working Themselves Impure: A Life Cycle Theory of Legal Theories." *University of Chicago Law Review* 83 (2016): 1819–92.

Khademian, Anne M. *The SEC and Capital Markets Regulation: The Politics of Expertise*. Pittsburgh: University of Pittsburgh Press, 1992.

Khan, Lina. "New Tools to Promote Competition." *Democracy* 42 (2016).

King, Mervyn. "The Institutions of Monetary Policy—the Ely Lecture 2004." Speech given at the American Economic Association Annual Meeting, San Diego, January 12, 2004. Bank of England.

———. Speech given at the Lord Mayor's Banquet for Bankers and Merchants of the City of London at the Mansion House, June 17, 2009. Bank of England.

———. Speech given to the South Wales Chamber of Commerce at the Millennium Centre, Cardiff, October 23, 2012. Bank of England.

———. *The End of Alchemy: Money, Banking and the Future of the Global Economy*. London: Little Brown, 2016.

King, Michael. "Epistemic Communities and the Diffusion of Ideas: Central Bank Reform in the United Kingdom." *West European Politics* 28, no. 1 (2005): 94–123.

Kloppenberg, James T. *The Virtues of Liberalism*. New York: Oxford University Press, 2000.

Kohn, Don, and David Wessel. "Eight Ways to Improve the Fed's Accountability." Bloomberg, February 9, 2016.

Kotlikoff, Laurence J. *Jimmy Stewart Is Dead: Ending the World's Ongoing Financial Plague with Limited Purpose Banking*. Hoboken, NJ: John Wiley & Sons, Inc., 2010.

Kovacic, William E., and Carl Shapiro. "Antitrust Policy: A Century of Economic and Legal Thinking." *Journal of Economic Perspectives* 14, no. 1 (2000): 43–60.

Kraus, Bruce, and Connor Raso. "Rational Boundaries for SEC Cost-Benefit Analysis." *Yale Journal on Regulation* 30, no. 2 (2013): 289–342.

Krause, George A. *A Two-Way Street: The Institutional Dynamics of the Modern Administrative State*. Pittsburgh: University of Pittsburgh Press, 1999.

Krippner, Greta. *Capitalizing on Crisis: The Political Origins of the Rise of Finance*. Cambridge, MA: Harvard University Press, 2011.

Kruly, Charles. "Self-Funding and Agency Independence." *George Washington Law Review* 81 (2013): 1733–54.

Kydland, Finn E., and Edward C. Prescott. "Rules Rather Than Discretion: The Inconsistency of Optimal Plans." *Journal of Political Economy* 85, no. 3 (1977): 473–92.

Kynaston, David. *The City of London: A History*. London: Chatto & Windus, 2011.

Laidler, David. "Central Banks as Lenders of Last Resort—Trendy or Passé?" University of Western Ontario, Economic Policy Research Institute Working Papers, no. 20048, 2004.

Lamont, Norman. *In Office*. London: Little, Brown and Company, 1999.

Landis, James M. *The Administrative Process*. New Haven, CT: Yale University Press, 1938.

———. "Report on Regulatory Agencies to the President-Elect." December 1960.

Lastra, Rosa M. *International Financial and Monetary Law.* 2nd ed. Oxford: Oxford University Press, 2015.

Laws, John. *The Common Law Constitution* (Hamlyn Lectures). Cambridge: Cambridge University Press, 2014.

Lawson, Gary. "The Rise and Rise of the Administrative State." *Harvard Law Review* 107 (1994): 1231–54.

Lawson, Nigel. *The View from No. 11: Memoirs of a Tory Radical.* London: Bantam Press, 1992.

Lazar, Nomi C. "Must Exceptionalism Prove the Rule? An Angle on Emergency Government in the History of Political Thought." *Politics and Society* 34, no. 2 (2006) 245–75.

———. *States of Emergency in Liberal Democracy.* New York: Cambridge University Press, 2009.

Lehmann, Matthias. "Varying Standards of Judicial Review over Central Bank Actions." Forthcoming in the book of the European Central Bank's 2017 Legal Conference.

Lemos, Margaret H. "The Other Delegate: Judicially Administered Statutes and the Nondelegation Doctrine." *Southern California Law Review* 81 (2008): 405–76.

Leveson, Brian (Lord Justice). "Dicey Revisited: Separation of Powers for the 21st Century." Speech given at University of Liverpool Law School, November 2008.

Levi-Faur, David, and Sharon Gilad. "The Rise of the British Regulatory State: Transcending the Privatization Debate." *Comparative Politics* 37, no. 1 (2004): 105–24.

Lewis, David E. "Policy Durability and Agency Design." In *Living Legislation: Political Development and Contemporary American Politics*, edited by Jeffery A. Jenkins and Eric Patashnik. Chicago: University of Chicago Press, 2012.

———. *Presidents and the Politics of Agency Design: Political Insulation in the United States Government Bureaucracy, 1946–1997.* Palo Alto, CA: Stanford University Press, 2003.

Liang, Nellie, and Rochelle Edge. "New Financial Stability Governance Structures and Central Banks." Forthcoming in Proceedings of the Reserve Bank of Australia Conference, 2017.

Lijphart, Arend. *Patterns of Democracy: Government Forms and Performance in Thirty-Six Countries.* 2nd ed. New Haven, CT: Yale University Press, 2012.

Lilla, Mark. *The Reckless Mind: Intellectuals in Politics.* New York: New York Review of Books, 2016.

Lippmann, Walter. *The Phantom Public.* New Brunswick, NJ: Transaction Publishers, 1993.

Lipset, Seymour Martin. "Some Social Requisites of Democracy: Economic Development and Political Legitimacy." *American Political Science Review* 53, no. 1 (1959): 69–105.

Lipsey, Philip Y. "Democracy and Financial Crisis." Paper presented at the Annual Meeting of the International Political Economy Society, November 12, 2011.

List, Christian, and Philip Pettit. "Aggregating Sets of Judgments: An Impossibility Result." *Economics and Philosophy* 18, no. 1 (2002): 89–110.

Locke, John. *Two Treatises of Government*, edited by Peter Laslett. Revised ed. New York: Cambridge University Press, 1988.

Lohmann, Susanne. "Reputational versus Institutional Solutions to the Time-Consistency Problem in Monetary Policy." In *Positive Political Economy: Theory and Evidence*, edited by Sylvester C. W. Eijffinger and Harry P. Huizinga. Cambridge: Cambridge University Press, 1998.

———. "Why Do Institutions Matter? An Audience-Cost Theory of Institutional Commitment." *Governance* 16, no. 1 (2003): 95–110.

Loughlin, Martin. *The Idea of Public Law*. Oxford: Oxford University Press, 2003.

———. *Foundations of Public Law*. Oxford: Oxford University Press, 2010.

Lowe, Philip. "Consumer Welfare and Efficiency: New Guiding Principles of Competition Policy?" European Commission, 2007.

Lowi, Theodore J. *The End of Liberalism: The Second Republic of the United States*. 2nd ed. New York: W. W. Norton & Company, 1979.

Mackenzie, G. A., and Peter Stella. "Quasi-Fiscal Operations in Public Financial Institutions." IMF Occasional Paper no. 142. Washington, DC: IMF, 1996.

Mair, Peter. *Ruling the Void: The Hollowing Out of Western Democracy*. London: Verso, 2013.

Majone, Giandomenico, ed. *Regulating Europe*. London: Routledge, 1996.

———. "Temporal Consistency and Policy Credibility: Why Democracies Need Non-majoritarian Institutions." European University Institute, Working Paper RSC. No. 96/57, 1996.

———. "Two Logics of Delegation: Agency and Fiduciary Relations in EU Governance." *European Union Politics* 2, vol. 1 (2001): 103–21.

———. *Dilemmas of European Integration: The Ambiguities and Pitfalls of Integration by Stealth*. Oxford: Oxford University Press, 2005.

Mallaby, Sebastian. *The Man Who Knew: The Life and Times of Alan Greenspan*. New York: Penguin Press, 2016.

Mankiw, N. Gregory, and Ricardo Reiss. "Friedman's Presidential Address in the Evolution of Macroeconomic Thought." *Journal of Economic Perspectives* (forthcoming).

Manning, John F. "Separation of Powers as Ordinary Interpretation." *Harvard Law Review* 124 (2011): 1942–2040.

Mansbridge, Jane. "A 'Selection Model' of Political Representation." *Journal of Political Philosophy* 17, no. 4 (2009): 369–98.

Marsh, David. *The Bundesbank: The Bank That Rules Europe*. London: Heineman, 1992.

Martin, Wayne. "Forewarned and Four-Armed: Administrative Law Values and the Fourth Arm of Government." Whitmore Lecture, 2013.

———. "Reflections on a Fourth Branch of Government." Paper presented at Australasian Study of Parliament Group, 2013 Annual Conference.

Mashaw, Jerry L. *Creating the Administrative Constitution: The Lost One Hundred Years of American Administrative Law*. New Haven, CT: Yale University Press, 2012.

Maskin, Eric, and Jean Tirole. "The Politician and the Judge: Accountability in Government." *American Economic Review* 94, no. 4 (2004): 1034–54.

Mathews, Jud. "Proportionality Review in Administrative Law." In *Comparative Administrative Law*, edited by Susan Rose-Ackerman and Peter Lindseth. 2nd ed. Cheltenham: Edward Elgar, 2017.

Maxfield, Sylvia. *Gatekeepers of Growth: The International Political Economy of Central Banking in Developing Countries*. Princeton, NJ: Princeton University Press, 1997.

Mazower, Mark. *Governing the World: The History of an Idea*. London: Penguin Books, 2012.

McCallum, Bennett T. "Two Fallacies Concerning Central Bank Independence." *American Economic Review* 85, no. 2 (1995): 207–11.

McCarty, N., K. T. Poole, and H. Rosenthal. *Political Bubbles: Financial Crises and the Failure of American Democracy*. Princeton, NJ: Princeton University Press, 2013.

McCubbins, Mathew D. "Abdication or Delegation? Congress, the Bureaucracy, and the Delegation Dilemma." *Regulation* 22, no. 2 (1999): 30–37.

McCubbins, Mathew D., Roger G. Noll, and Barry R. Weingast. "Administrative Procedures as Instruments of Political Control." *Journal of Law, Economics and Organization* 3, no. 2 (1987): 243–77.

———. "Structure and Process, Politics and Policy: Administrative Arrangements and the Political Control of Agencies." *Virginia Law Review* 75, no. 2 (1989): 431–82.

McCubbins, Mathew D., and T. Schwartz. "Congressional Oversight Overlooked: Police Patrols versus Fire Alarms." *American Journal of Political Science* 28, no. 1 (1984): 165–79.

McNamara, Kathleen R. "Rational Fictions: Central Bank Independence and the Social Logic of Delegation." *West European Politics* 25, no. 1 (2002): 47–76.

Mehrling, Perry. *The New Lombard Street: How the Fed Became the Dealer of Last Resort*. Princeton, NJ: Princeton University Press, 2010.

Meltzer, Allan H. "What's Wrong with the Fed? What Would Restore Independence?" *Cato Journal* 33, no. 3 (2013): 401–16.

Metzger, Gillian E. "Through the Looking Glass to a Shared Reflection: The Evolving Relationship between Administrative Law and Financial Regulation." *Law and Contemporary Problems* 78 (2015): 129–56.

Meyer, Thomas (with Lewis Hainchman). *The Theory of Social Democracy*. Cambridge: Polity Press, 2007.

Middleton, Philip, David Marsh et al. "Challenges for Central Banks: Wider Powers, Greater Restraints." *Journal of Financial Perspectives*, OMFIF with Ernst & Young, 2013.

Miller, Gary J., and Andrew B. Whitford. *Above Politics: Bureaucratic Discretion and Credible Commitment*. New York: Cambridge University Press, 2016.

Miller, Geoffrey P. "Independent Agencies." *Supreme Court Review* (1986): 41–97.

Miller, Marcus, P. Weller, and L. Zhang. "Moral Hazard and the US Stock Market: Analyzing the 'Greenspan Put.'" *Economic Journal* 112, no. 478 (2002): C171–86.

Moe, Terry M. "Political Institutions: The Neglected Side of the Story." Special issue, *Journal of Law, Economics, and Organisation* 6 (1990): 213–54.

———. "Delegation, Control, and the Study of Bureaucracy." In *The Handbook of Organizational Economics*, edited by Robert Gibbons and John Roberts. Princeton, NJ: Princeton University Press, 2013.

Mollers, Christoph. *The Three Branches: A Comparative Mode of Separation of Powers*. Oxford: Oxford University Press, 2013.

Montesquieu, Baron. *The Spirit of the Laws*. Cambridge: Cambridge University Press, 1989.

Morris, Caroline, and Ryan Malone. "Regulations Review in the New Zealand Parliament." *Macquarie Law Journal* 4 (2004): 7–31.

Moser, Peter. "Checks and Balances, and the Supply of Central Bank Independence." *European Economic Review* 43, no. 8 (1996): 1569–93.

Mouffe, Chantal. "Deliberative Democracy or Agonistic Pluralism." Political Science Series, Institute for Advanced Studies, Vienna, December 2000.

Mounk, Yascha. "Illiberal Democracy or Undemocratic Liberalism?" *Project Syndicate*, June 9, 2016.

Mount, Ferdinand. *The New Few: Or a Very British Oligarchy*. New York: Simon & Schuster, 2012.

Muller, Jan-Werner. "The Triumph of What (If Anything?) Rethinking Political Ideologies and Political Institutions in Twentieth-Century Europe." *Journal of Political Ideologies* 14, no. 2 (2009): 211–26.

———. *Contesting Democracy: Political Ideas in Twentieth-Century Europe*. New Haven, CT: Yale University Press, 2011.

———. *What Is Populism?* Philadelphia: University of Pennsylvania Press, 2016.

Musgrave, Richard A. *The Theory of Public Finance*. New York: McGraw-Hill, 1959.

Myerson, Roger. "Fundamental Theory of Institutions: A Lecture in Honor of Leo Hurwicz." Hurwicz Lecture, presented at the North American Meetings of the Econometric Society, University of Minnesota, June 22, 2006.

———. "Perspectives on Mechanism Design in Economic Theory." Nobel Prize lecture, December 8, 2007.

Nichols, Tom. *The Death of Expertise: The Campaign against Established Knowledge and Why It Matters*. New York: Oxford University Press, 2017.

Nicolaides, Phedon, and Nadir Preziosi. "Discretion and Accountability: The ESMA Judgment and the Meroni Doctrine." Bruges European Economic Research Papers, no. 30, College of Europe, 2014.

Niskanen, William A. *Bureaucracy and Public Economics*. Expanded ed. Northampton, MA: Edward Elgar, 1994.

Norman, Jesse. *Edmund Burke: Philosopher, Politician, Prophet*. Glasgow: William Collins, 2013.

North, Douglas C., and Barry R. Weingast. "Constitutionalism and Commitment: The Evolution of Institutional Governing Public Choice in Seventeenth-Century England." *Journal of Economic History* 49, no. 4 (1989): 803–32.

Novak, William J. "A Revisionist History of Regulatory Capture." In *Preventing Regulatory Capture: Special-Interest Influence and How to Limit It*, edited by Daniel Carpenter and David Moss. Cambridge: Cambridge University Press, 2014.

Noyer, Christian. "A propos du statut et de l'indépendence des banques centrales." *Revue d'economie financiere* 22 (1992): 13–18.

Nye, Joseph S. Jr. *The Future of Power*. New York: Public Affairs, 2011.

Ober, Josiah. *Demopolis: Democracy before Liberalism in Theory and Practice*. Cambridge: Cambridge University Press, 2017.

OECD. *Distributed Public Governance: Agencies, Authorities and Other Government Bodies*, 2002.

———. *Being an Independent Regulator*. The Governance of Regulators. Paris: OECD Publishing, 2016.

Okun, Arthur M. *Equality and Efficiency: The Big Tradeoff*. Revised ed. Washington, DC: Brookings Institution Press, 2015.

Olson, Mancur. *The Logic of Collective Action: Public Goods and the Theory of Groups*. Cambridge, MA: Harvard University Press, 1971.

O'Neill, Onora. *A Question of Trust: The BBC Reith Lectures 2002*. Cambridge: Cambridge University Press, 2002.

———. "Perverting Trust." 2009 Ashby Lecture, Clare Hall, University of Cambridge, May 13, 2009.

Orphanides, Athanasios. "The Road to Price Stability." *American Economic Review* 96, no. 2 (2006): 178–181.

Ostrom, Elinor. *Governing the Commons: The Evolution of Institutions for Collective Action*. New York: Cambridge University Press, 1990.

Owen, Mackubin Thomas. *US Civil-Military Relations after 9/11: Renegotiating the Civil-Military Bargain*. New York: Continuum International Publishing Group, 2011.

Paterson, Alan. *Final Judgment: The Last Law Lords and the Supreme Court*. Oxford: Hart Publishing, 2013.

Paul, Ron. *End the Fed*. New York: Grand Central Publishing, 2009.

Peltzman, Samuel. "Towards a More General Theory of Regulation." NBER Working Paper, no. 133, 1976.

Peter, Fabienne. *Democratic Legitimacy*. New York: Routledge, 2009.

Pettit, Philip. "The Cunning of Trust." *Philosophy and Public Affairs* 24, no. 3 (summer 1995): 202–25.

———. "Depoliticizing Democracy." *Ratio Juris* 17, no. 1 (2004): 52–65.

———. "Varieties of Public Representation." In *Political Representation*, edited by Ian Shapiro, Susan C. Stokes, Elizabeth Jean Wood, and Alexander S. Kirschner. Cambridge: Cambridge University Press, 2010.

———. *On the People's Terms: A Republican Theory and Model of Democracy*. New York: Cambridge University Press, 2012.

———. *Just Freedom: A Moral Compass for a Complex World*. New York: W. W. Norton & Company, 2014.

Phillips, Nicholas (Lord). "The Art of the Possible: Statutory Interpretation and Human Rights." First Lord Alexander of Weedon Lecture, April 22, 2010.

———. "Judicial Independence and Accountability: A View from the Supreme Court." Speech delivered at the University College of London Constitution Unit, to launch its research project, "The Politics of Judicial Independence," February 8, 2011.

Phillips, Ronnie J. "The Chicago Plan and New Deal Banking Reform." Jerome Levy Economics Institute of Bard College Working Paper, no. 76, June 1992.

Pigou, Arthur C. *The Economics of Welfare*. London: Macmillan and Co., 1920.

Pincus, Steve. *1688: The First Modern Revolution*. New Haven, CT: Yale University Press, 2009.

Piraino, Thomas A. Jr. "Reconciling the Harvard and Chicago Schools: A New Antitrust Approach for the 21st Century." *Indiana Law Journal* 82, no. 2 (2007): 345–409.

Pisani-Ferry, Jean. "Central Bank Advocacy of Structural Reforms: Why and How?" ECB Forum on Central Banking, Sintra, May 2015.

Pitkin, Hanna F. *The Concept of Representation*. Berkeley: University of California Press, 1967.

Pitofsky, Robert. "The Political Content of Antitrust." *University of Pennsylvania Law Review* 137 (1979): 1051–75.

Plosser, Charles I. "A Limited Central Bank." *Cato Journal* 34, no. 2 (2014): 201–11.

Posen, Adam S. "Why Central Bank Independence Does Not Cause Low Inflation: There Is No Institutional Fix for Politics." In *Finance and the International Economy*, edited by R. O'Brien. Oxford: Oxford University Press, 1993.

———. "Do Better Institutions Make Better Policy?" *International Finance* 1, no. 1 (1998): 173–205.

———. "Declarations Are Not Enough: Financial Sector Sources of Central Bank Independence." *NBER Macroeconomic Annual* 10 (2005): 253–74.

Posner, Eric A. "What Legal Authority Does the Fed Need during a Financial Crisis?" University of Chicago Public Law Working Paper, no. 560, February 3, 2016.

Posner, Eric A., and Adrian Vermeule. "Interring the Nondelegation Doctrine." *University of Chicago Law Review* 69 (2002): 1721–62.

———. *The Executive Unbound: After the Madisonian Republic*. New York: Oxford University Press, 2010.

Posner, Richard A. "Taxation by Regulation." *Bell Journal of Economics and Management Science* 2, no. 1 (1971): 22–50.

Power, Michael. *The Audit Society: Rituals of Verification*. Oxford: Oxford University Press, 1999.

Pratt, John W., and Richard J. Zeckhauser. *Principals and Agents: The Structure of Business*. Boston, MA: Harvard Business Review Press, 1985.

Przeworski, Adam, Susan C. Stokes, and Bernard Manin, eds. *Democracy, Accountability and Representation*. Cambridge: Cambridge University Press, 1999.

Puender, Hermann. "Democratic Legitimation of Delegated Legislation: A Comparative View on the American, British and German Law." *International and Comparative Law Quarterly* 58 (2009): 353–78.

———. "German Administrative Procedure in Comparative Perspective: Observations on the Path to a Transnational *Ius Commune Proceduralis* in Administrative Law." *International Journal of Constitutional Law* 11, vol. 4 (2013): 940–61.

Quinn, Brian. "The Bank of England's Role in Prudential Supervision." *Bank of England Quarterly Bulletin* 33, no. 2 (1993).

Quintyn, Marc. "Independent Agencies: More Than a Cheap Copy of Independent Central Banks?" Washington, DC: IMF, 2007.

Rahman, K. Sabeel. "Domination, Democracy, and Constitutional Political Economy in the New Gilded Age: Towards a Fourth Wave of Legal Realism?" *Texas Law Review* 94 (2016): 1329–1358.

Rajan, Raghuram. *Fault Lines: How Hidden Fractures Still Threaten the World Economy*. Princeton, NJ: Princeton University Press, 2010.

———. "A Step in the Dark: Unconventional Monetary Policy after the Crisis." First Andrew Crockett Memorial Lecture at the Bank for International Settlements, June 23, 2013.

Ramraj, Victor V., ed. *Emergencies and the Limits of Legality*. Cambridge: Cambridge University Press, 2008.

Ranciere, Romain, Aaron Tornell, and Frank Westerman. "Systemic Crises and Growth." *Quarterly Journal of Economics* 123, no. 1 (2008): 359–406.

Rasmusen, Eric. "A Theory of Trustees, and Other Thoughts." 1998. https://papers.ssrn.com/sol3/papers.cfm?abstract_id=84388.

Rawls, John. *A Theory of Justice*. Oxford: Oxford University Press, 1973.

———. "The Idea of an Overlapping Consensus." *Oxford Journal of Legal Studies* 7, no. 1 (1987): 1–25.

———. *Political Liberalism*. New York: Columbia University Press, 1993.

Raz, Joseph. *The Authority of the Law: Essays on Law and Morality*. Oxford: Clarendon Press, 1979.

———. *The Morality of Freedom*. New York: Oxford University Press, 1986.

Richards, Tom. "Dogma in Telecoms, Cream for the CAT: 08-Numbers in the Supreme Court." *Competition Bulletin*, July 10, 2014.

Richardson, Henry. *Democratic Autonomy: Public Reasoning about the Ends of Policy*. New York: Oxford University Press, 2002.

Ricks, Thomas E. *The Generals: American Military Command from World War II to Today*. New York: Penguin Books, 2012.

Roberts, Alasdair. *The Logic of Discipline: Global Capitalism and the Architecture of Government*. New York: Oxford University Press, 2011.

Roberts, Andrew. *Masters and Commanders: How Roosevelt, Churchill, Marshall and Alanbrooke Won the War in the West*. London: Allen Lane, 2008.

Robinson, Lisa A., James K. Hammitt, and Richard Zeckhauser. "Attention to Distribution in U.S. Regulatory Analyses." *Review of Environmental Economics and Policy* 10, no. 2 (2016): 308–28.

Rodrik, Dani. *The Globalization Paradox: Why Global Markets, States, and Democracy Can't Coexist*. New York: Oxford University Press, 2011.

Rogoff, Kenneth. "The Optimal Degree of Commitment to an Intermediate Monetary Target." *Quarterly Journal of Economics* 100, no. 4 (1985): 1169–90.

Rohr, John A. *To Run a Constitution: The Legitimacy of the Administrative State*. Lawrence: University Press of Kansas, 1986.

Roll, Eric et al. *Independent and Accountable: A New Mandate for the Bank of England*. Report of an Independent Panel, CEPR, 1993.

Romano, Roberta. "Regulating in the Dark, and a Postscript Assessment of the Iron Law of Financial Regulation." *Hofstra Law Review* 43, no. 25 (2014): 25–93.

Rosanvallon, Pierre. *Democratic Legitimacy: Impartiality, Reflexivity, Proximity*. Translated by Arthur Goldhammer. Princeton, NJ: Princeton University Press, 2011.

Rose, Dinah, and Tom Richards. "Appeal and Review in the Competition Appeal Tribunal and High Court." *Judicial Review* 15, no. 3 (2010): 201–19.

Rose-Ackerman, Susan. "Judicial Review of Executive Policymaking in Advanced Democracies: Beyond Rights Review." *Yale Faculty Scholarship Series*, no. 4943 (2014).

———. "Citizens and Technocrats: An Essay on Trust, Public Participation, and Government Legitimacy." Paper presented at Yale Law School Faculty Workshop, November 2016.

Rose-Ackerman, Susan, and Thomas Perroud. "Policymaking and Public Law in France: Public Participation, Agency Independence, and Impact Assessment." *Columbia Journal of European Law* 19, no. 2 (2013): 223–310.

Rubin, Edward. "Hyperdepoliticization." *Wake Forest Law Review* 47, no. 3 (2012): 631–79.

Rudolph, Joshua S. "The Interaction between Government Debt Management and Monetary Policy: A Call to Develop a Debt-Maturity Framework for the Zero Lower Bound." Prepared for US Department of Treasury. Harvard Kennedy School, March 25, 2014.

Ruggie, John G. "International Regimes, Transactions, and Change: Embedded Liberalism in the Postwar Economic Order." *International Organization* 36, no. 2 (1982): 379–415.

Runciman, David. "The Paradox of Representation." *Journal of Political Philosophy* 15, no. 1 (2007): 93–114.

———. *The Confidence Trap: A History of Democracy in Crisis from World War I to the Present.* Princeton, NJ: Princeton University Press, 2013.

Rutter, Jill. "The Strange Case of Non-ministerial Departments." Institute for Government, 2013.

Ryan, Alan. *On Politics.* London: Penguin Books, 2012.

Sabl, Andrew. *Hume's Politics: Coordination and Crisis in the "History of England."* Princeton, NJ: Princeton University Press, 2012.

Sagar, Paul. "The State without Sovereignty: Authority and Obligation in Hume's Political Philosophy." *History of Political Thought* 37, no. 2 (2016): 271–305.

———. "Istvan Hont and Political Theory." Unpublished manuscript, 2016.

Sandel, Michael. *Democracy's Discontent.* Cambridge, MA: Belknap Press of Harvard University Press, 1996.

Scalia, Antonin. "The Rule of Law as a Law of Rules." *University of Chicago Law Review* 56, no. 4 (1989): 1175–88.

———. "Judicial Deference to Administrative Interpretations of Law." *Duke Law Journal*, no. 3 (1989).

Scharpf, Fritz W. *Governing in Europe: Effective and Democratic?* Oxford: Oxford University Press, 1999.

Scheuerman, William E. *Between the Norm and the Exception: The Frankfurt School and the Rule of Law.* Cambridge, MA: MIT Press, 1994.

Schlink, Bernhard. "Proportionality in Constitutional Law: Why Everywhere but Here?" *Duke Journal of Comparative & International Law* 22 (2012): 291–302.

Schmidt, Vivien A. "Democracy and Legitimacy in the European Union Revisited: Input, Output *and* 'Throughput.'" *Political Studies* 61, no. 1 (2013): 2–22.

Schmitter, Philippe C. "Still the Century of Corporatism?" *Review of Political Studies* 36, no. 1 (1974): 85–131.

Schoenbrod, David. *Power without Responsibility: How Congress Abuses the People through Delegation.* New Haven, CT: Yale University Press, 1993.

———. "Delegation and Democracy: A Reply to My Critics." *Cardozo Law Review* 20 (1999).

Schoenmaker, Dirk. *Governance of International Banking: The Financial Trilemma.* Oxford: Oxford University Press, 2013.

Schonhardt-Bailey, Cheryl. "Monetary Policy Oversight in Comparative Perspective: Britain and America during the Financial Crisis." Forthcoming in a book tentatively titled *Accountability, Oversight and Deliberation of Economic Policy in UK Parliamentary Committees.*

Schumpeter, Joseph A. *Capitalism, Socialism & Democracy.* London: Routledge, 1992.

Schwartz, Anna J. "Boundaries between the Fed and the Treasury." Paper presented to the Shadow Open Market Committee, May 8, 2009.

Scott, Colin. "Accountability and the Regulatory State." *Journal of Law and Society* 27, no. 1 (March 2000): 38–60.

Scott, Hal S. *Connectedness and Contagion: Protecting the Financial System from Panics*. Cambridge, MA: MIT Press, 2016.

Scruton, Roger. *The Meaning of Conservatism*. Basingstoke: Palgrave Macmillan, 1984.

Securities and Exchange Commission. *Current Guidance on Economic Analysis in SEC Rulemaking*. March 16, 2012.

———. "Operating Procedures for Economic Analysis to Implement the Current Guidance." Memo from Chair Mary Jo White, August 15, 2013.

Seidenfeld, Mark. "A Civic Republican Justification for the Bureaucratic State." *Harvard Law Review* 105, no. 7 (1992): 1511–76.

Selgin, George. "Posner on the Legality of the Fed's Last-Resort Lending." *Cato at Liberty* (blog), May 19, 2016.

Selin, Jennifer L. "What Makes an Agency Independent?" *American Journal of Political Science* 59, no. 4 (2015): 971–87.

Sen, Amartya. "Utilitarianism and Welfarism." *Journal of Philosophy* 76, no. 9 (1979): 463–89.

———. *Development as Freedom*. Oxford: Oxford University Press, 1999.

Shapiro, Martin. *Who Guards the Guardians? Judicial Control of Administration*. Athens: University of Georgia Press, 1988.

Shelby, Richard. "The Trouble with Dodd-Frank." Speech given at Harvard Law School, October 14, 2015.

Shepsle, Kenneth. *Analyzing Politics: Rationality, Behavior, and Institutions*. 2nd revised ed. New York: W. W. Norton & Company, 2010.

Shesol, Jeff. *Supreme Power: Franklin Roosevelt vs. the Supreme Court*. New York: W. W. Norton & Company, 2001.

Shirakawa, Masaaki. "Future of Central Banks and Central Banking." Bank of Japan, 2010.

Shleifer, Andrei. *The Failure of Judges and the Rise of Regulators*. Cambridge, MA: MIT Press, 2012.

Shorto, Russell. *Amsterdam: A History of the World's Most Liberal City*. New York: Doubleday, 2013.

Siegel, Jonathan R. "The REINS Act and the Struggle to Control Agency Rulemaking." *Legislation and Public Policy* 16 (2013): 131–85.

Silber, William L. *Volcker: The Triumph of Persistence*. New York: Bloomsbury Press, 2012.

Silverstein, Gordon. "Can Constitutional Democracies and Emergency Powers Coexist?" *Tulsa Law Review* 45 (2009): 619–29.

Simmons, A. John. *Justification and Legitimacy: Essays on Rights and Obligations*. Cambridge: Cambridge University Press, 2001.

Simmons, Beth A. "The Future of Central Bank Cooperation." Paper presented at the BIS Annual Research Conference, 2005.

Simons, Henry. "Rules versus Authorities in Monetary Policy." *Journal of Political Economy* 44, no. 1 (1936): 1–30.

Simpson, Emile. *War from the Ground Up: Twenty-First Century Combat as Politics*. London: C. Hurst & Co., 2012.

Sitaraman, Ganesh. "Foreign Hard Look Review." *Administrative Law Review* 66, no. 3 (2014): 489–563.

Skinner, Quentin. *Liberty before Liberalism*. Cambridge: Cambridge University Press, 1998.

Smith, Vera. *The Rationale of Central Banking and the Free Banking Alternative*. Indianapolis, IN: Liberty Fund Inc., 1990.

Sorabji, John. "The Constitutional Status of the Supreme Court of Justice of England and Wales and of the High Court Judiciary." In *Should the Civil Courts Be Unified?* A Report by Sir Henry Brooke. Judicial Office, August 2008. https://www.judiciary.gov.uk/wp-content/uploads/JCO/Documents/Speeches/brooke_report_ucc.pdf.

Stack, Kevin M. "Agency Independence after PCAOB." *Cardozo Law Review* 32, no. 6 (2011): 2391–420.

———. "An Administrative Jurisprudence: The Rule of Law in the Administrative State." *Columbia Law Review* 115, no. 7 (2015): 1985–2018.

———. "Purposivism in the Executive Branch: How Agencies Interpret Statutes." *Northwestern University Law Review* 109, no. 4 (2015): 871–932.

Stein, Jeremy, and Samuel Hanson. "Monetary Policy and Long-Term Real Rates." *Journal of Financial Economics* 115, no. 3 (2015): 429–48.

Stern, Jon. "The British Utility Regulation Model: Its Recent History and Future Prospects." CCPR Working Paper, no. 23, City University, London, 2014.

Stewart, Richard B. "The Reformation of American Administrative Law." *Harvard Law Review* 88, no. 8 (1975): 1669–813.

———. "Administrative Law in the Twenty-First Century." *New York University Law Review* 78, no. 2 (2003): 437–60.

Stigler, George J. "The Theory of Economic Regulation." *Bell Journal of Economics* 2, no. 1 (1971): 3–21.

Stiglitz, Joseph. "Central Banking in a Democratic Society." *De Economist* 146, no. 2 (1998): 199–226.

Stone Sweet, Alec. *Governing with Judges: Constitutional Politics in Europe*. New York: Oxford University Press, 2000.

———. "Constitutional Courts and Parliamentary Democracy." *West European Politics* 25, no. 1 (2002): 77–100.

Stone Sweet, Alec, and Mark Thatcher. "Theory and Practice of Delegation to Non-majoritarian Institutions." *West European Politics* 25, no. 1 (2002): 1–22.

Strauss, Peter L. "The Place of Agencies in Government: Separation of Powers and the Fourth Branch." *Columbia Law Review* 84, no. 3 (1984): 573–669.

———. "Rule-Making and the American Constitution." In *The Regulatory State: Constitutional Implications*, edited by Dawn Oliver, Tony Prosser, and Richard Rawlings. Oxford: Oxford University Press, 2010.

Stroud, Sarah. "Weakness of Will." In *The Stanford Encyclopedia of Philosophy*, edited by Edward N. Zalta. Spring 2014. https://plato.stanford.edu/archives/spr2014/entries/weakness-will/.

Suchman, Mark C. "Managing Legitimacy: Strategic and Institutional Approaches." *Academy of Management Review* 20, no. 3 (1995): 571–610.

Summers, Lawrence. "Price Stability: How Should Long-Term Monetary Policy Be Determined?" *Journal of Money, Credit and Banking* 23, no. 3, pt. 2: Price Stability (1991): 625–31.

Sumption, Jonathan (Lord). "The Limits of Law." Twenty-Seventh Sultan Azlan Shah Lecture, Kuala Lumpur, November 20, 2013.

Sunstein, Cass R. *After the Rights Revolution: Reconceiving the Regulatory State*. Cambridge, MA: Harvard University Press, 1990.

———. "Nondelegation Canons." *University of Chicago Law Review* 67, no. 2 (2000): 315–43.

Tamanaha, Brian Z. *On the Rule of Law: History, Politics, Theory*. Cambridge: Cambridge University Press, 2004.

Tarullo, Daniel K. "Shadow Banking and Systemic Risk Reduction." Board of Governors of the Federal Reserve System, November 22, 2013.

———. "Departing Thoughts." Remarks to the Federal Reserve Board of Governors, April 4, 2017.

Taylor, John B. "Discretion versus Policy Rules in Practice." *Carnegie-Rochester Conference Series on Public Policy* 39 (1993): 195–214.

———. "Legislating a Rule for Monetary Policy." *Cato Journal* 31, no. 3 (2011): 407–15.

Tetlock, Philip E. *Expert Political Judgment: How Good Is It? How Can We Know?* Princeton, NJ: Princeton University Press, 2005.

Tett, Gillian. *The Silo Effect*. London: Little, Brown, 2015.

Thatcher, Mark. "Delegation to Independent Regulatory Agencies: Pressures, Functions and Contextual Mediation." *West European Politics* 25, no. 1 (2002): 124–47.

Thornborough, Richard. "Overcriminalization and the Need for Legislative Reform." Testimony before the Subcommittee on Crime, Terrorism, and Homeland Security, House of Representatives Committee on the Judiciary, Wednesday, July 22, 2009.

Tirole, Jean. "The Internal Organisation of Government." *Oxford Economic Papers* 46, no. 1 (1994): 1–29.

Tollestrup, Jessica, and James V. Saturno. "The Congressional Appropriations Process: An Introduction." Congressional Research Service, November 14, 2014.

Tombs, Robert. *The English and Their History*. London: Allen Lane, 2015.

Trebilcock, Michael J., and Edward M. Iacobucci. "Designing Competition Law Institutions: Values, Structure and Mandate." *Loyola University Chicago Law Journal* 41, no. 3 (2010): 455–71.

Trichet, Jean-Claude. "Building Europe, Building Institutions." Acceptance speech for the 2011 Karlspreis in Aachen, June 2, 2011. European Central Bank.

Tsebelis, George. *Veto Players: How Political Institutions Work*. Princeton, NJ: Princeton University Press, 2002.

Tucker, Paul. "Managing the Central Bank's Balance Sheet: Where Monetary Policy Meets Financial Stability." *Bank of England Quarterly Bulletin* (Autumn 2004).

———. "Central Banking and Political Economy: The Example of the UK's Monetary Policy Committee." Speech given at the Inflation Targeting, Central Bank Independence and Transparency Conference, Cambridge, June 15, 2007. Bank of England.

———. Remarks at the *Turner Review* Conference, London, March 27, 2009. Bank of England.

———. "The Repertoire of Official Sector Interventions in the Financial System: Last Resort Lending, Market-Making, and Capital." Speech given at Bank of Japan Conference, May 27–28, 2009. Bank of England.

———. "National Balance Sheets and Macro Policy." Speech given at the Society of Business Economists' Annual Dinner, London, February 28, 2012. Bank of England.

———. "A New Regulatory Relationship: The Bank, the Financial System and the Wider Economy." Speech delivered at the Institute for Government, May 28, 2013. Bank of England.

———. "Regulatory Reform, Stability and Central Banking." Brookings Hutchins Center on Fiscal and Monetary Policy, 2014.

———. "Is There an Incipient Crisis in Securities Regulation?" Lecture at Princeton University, October 17, 2014.

———. "The Lender of Last Resort and Modern Central Banking: Principles and Reconstruction." BIS Papers, no. 79, Bank for International Settlements, 2014.

———. "The Resolution of Financial Institutions without Taxpayer Solvency Support: Seven Retrospective Clarifications and Elaborations." Paper presented at European Summer Symposium in Economic Theory, Gerzensee, Switzerland, July 3, 2014.

———. "Fundamental Challenges for Securities Regulation: A Political Economy Crisis in the Making?" Twenty-First SUERF Annual Lecture. In *Challenges in Securities Markets Regulation: Investor Protection and Corporate Governance,* edited by Pablo Gasós, Ernest Gnan, and Morten Balling. SUERF Study 2015/1. Madrid: SUERF, 2015.

———. "Can Monetary Policy Meet the Needs of Financial Stability? Remembering the FRB alongside the FOMC." *Business Economics* 51, no. 2 (2016): 71–75.

———. "The Political Economy of Central Bank Balance-Sheet Management." Columbia University, New York, May 5, 2016. https://www.newyorkfed.org/medialibrary/media/newsevents/events/markets/2016/frbny-columbiasipa-paultucker-paper.pdf.

———. *The Design and Governance of Financial Stability Regimes: A Common Resource Problem That Challenges Technical Know-How, Democratic Accountability and International Coordination.* CIGI Essays on International Finance, vol. 3. Waterloo, ON: CIGI, 2016.

———. "The Political Economy of Central Banking in the Digital Age." *SUERF Policy Notes*, no. 13, June 2017.

Turner, Adair. *Between Debt and the Devil: Money, Credit, and Fixing Global Finance.* Princeton, NJ: Princeton University Press, 2015.

Tutton, Tim. "The Future of Independent Economic Regulation in the UK." *European Policy Forum*, 2014.

Tyler, Tom. *Why People Obey the Law.* Princeton, NJ: Princeton University Press, 2006.

UK Department for Business, Innovation and Skills. *Principles for Economic Regulation.* 2011.

UK House of Lords Select Committee on Regulators. *UK Economic Regulators.* 2007.

UK Independent Commission on Banking. *Interim Report: Consultation on Reform Options,* April 2011.

UK Law Commission. "Criminal Liability in Regulatory Contexts." Consultation Paper no. 195. 2010.

United Nations. "Basic Principles on the Independence of the Judiciary." 1985.

Urbinati, Nadia. *Representative Democracy: Principles & Genealogy.* Chicago: University of Chicago Press, 2006.

US Department of Treasury. *Blueprint for a Modernized Financial Regulatory Structure.* March 2008.

———. "The Role of the Federal Reserve in Preserving Financial and Monetary Stability: Joint Statement by the Department of Treasury and the Federal Reserve." March 23, 2009.

Van Middelaar, Luuk. *The Passage to Europe: How a Continent Became a Union*. New Haven, CT: Yale University Press, 2013.

Verkuil, Paul R. "The Purposes and Limits of Independent Agencies." *Duke Law Journal* (1988): 257–79.

Vermeule, Adrian. "Super-Statutes." *New Republic*, October 26, 2010.

———. "No: Review of Philip Hamburger, Is Administrative Law Unlawful?" *Texas Law Review* 93 (2015).

———. *Law's Abnegation: From Law's Empire to the Administrative State*. Cambridge, MA: Harvard University Press, 2016.

Vibert, Frank. *The Rise of the Unelected: Democracy and the New Separation of Powers*. Cambridge: Cambridge University Press, 2007.

Vickers, John. "Competition Law and Economics: A Mid-Atlantic Viewpoint." eSapience Center for Competition Policy, 2007.

———. "Central Banks and Competition Authorities: Institutional Comparisons and New Concerns." BIS Working Papers, no. 331, Bank for International Settlements Annual Research Conference, 2010.

———. "Consequences of Brexit for Competition Law and Policy." Paper presented at *Oxford Review of Economic Policy*/British Academy Conference, December, 7, 2016.

Viehoff, Daniel. "Authority and Expertise." *Journal of Political Philosophy* 24, no. 2 (2016): 406–26.

Vile, M. J. C. *Constitutionalism and the Separation of Powers*. 2nd ed. Indianapolis: Liberty Fund, 1998.

Volcker, Paul. "Can We Survive Prosperity?" Federal Reserve Board, 1983.

———. "The Triumph of Central Banking?" Per Jacobsson Lecture, 1990. Per Jacobsson Foundation.

———. "Central Banking at a Crossroad." Remarks at the Economic Club of New York, May 29, 2013.

———. "The Fed & Big Banking at the Crossroads." *New York Review of Books*. August 15, 2013.

Wade, H. W. R., and C. F. Forsyth. *Administrative Law*. 10th ed. New York: Oxford University Press, 2009.

Waldron, Jeremy. *The Dignity of Legislation*. Cambridge: Cambridge University Press, 1999.

———. *Law and Disagreement*. New York: Oxford University Press, 1999.

———. "Is the Rule of Law an Essentially Contested Concept (in Florida)?" In the Wake of *Bush v. Gore*: Law, Legitimacy and Judicial Ethics. *Law and Philosophy* 21, no. 2 (2002): 137–64.

———. "The Core of the Case against Judicial Review." *Yale Law Journal* 115, no. 6 (2006): 1346–60.

———. "Separation of Powers or Division of Power?" New York University Public Law and Legal Theory Working Papers, no. 329, January 2012.

———. "*Political* Political Theory: An Inaugural Lecture." *Journal of Political Philosophy* 21, no. 1 (2013): 1–23.

———. "Separation of Powers in Thought and Practice." *Boston College Law Review* 54, no.2 (2013): 433–68.

———. "Accountability: Fundamental to Democracy." New York University Public Law and Legal Theory Working Papers, no. 462, August 2014.

Wallach, Philip. *To the Edge: Legality, Legitimacy, and the Response to the 2008 Financial Crisis*. Washington, DC: Brookings Institution Press, 2015.

———. "The Administrative State's Legitimacy Crisis." Center for Effective Public Management, Brookings Institution, April 2016.

Walsh, Carl E. "Optimal Contracts for Central Bankers." *American Economic Review* 85, no. 1 (1995): 150–67.

Warsh, Kevin. *Transparency and the Bank of England's Monetary Policy Committee*. Report to the Bank of England, December 2014.

Weber, Max. "Bureaucracy." In *Economy and Society: An Outline of Interpretive Sociology*, edited by G. Roth and C. Wittich. Berkeley: University of California Press, 1978.

———. *The Theory of Social and Economic Organisation*, edited by Talcot Parsons. New York: Free Press, 1947.

Weingast, Barry R. "The Congressional-Bureaucratic System: A Principal-Agent Perspective (with Applications to the SEC)." *Public Choice* 44, no. 1, Carnegie Papers on Political Economy (1984): 147–91.

Wheeler, Chris. "A Response to the 2013 Whitmore Lecture address." *Australian Law Journal* 88 (2014).

White, Mary Jo. "Enhancing Risk Monitoring and Regulatory Safeguards for the Asset Management Industry." December 11, 2014. Securities and Exchange Commission.

Williams, Bernard. *In the Beginning Was the Deed*, edited by Geoffrey Hawthorne. Princeton, NJ: Princeton University Press, 2005.

Williamson, John. "What Washington Means by Policy Reform?" Peterson Institute for International Economics, 1989.

Wilson, James Q. *Bureaucracy: What Government Agencies Do and Why They Do It*. New York: Basic Books, 1989.

Wilson, Woodrow. "The Study of Administration." *Political Science Quarterly* 2, no. 2 (1887): 197–222.

———. *The New Freedom: A Call for the Emancipation of the Generous Energies of a People*. Brooklyn, NY: Gray Rabbit Publications, 2011 [1913].

Wolf, Martin. *The Shifts and the Shocks: What We've Learned—and Have Still to Learn—from the Financial Crisis*. London: Allen Lane, 2014.

Wood, B. Dan, and Richard W. Waterman. "The Dynamics of Political Control of the Bureaucracy." *American Political Science Review* 85, no. 3 (1991): 801–28.

Woodford, Michael. "Principles and Public Policy Decisions: The Case of Monetary Policy." Paper presented at the Law, Economics, and Organization Workshop, Yale Law School, March 2008.

Woodward, Bob. *Maestro: Greenspan's Fed and the American Boom*. New York: Simon & Schuster, 2001.

Woolley, Peter J., and Albert R. Papa, eds. *American Politics: Core Argument/Current Controversy*. 2nd ed. Upper Saddle River, NJ: Prentice Hall, 2002.

Worsthorne, Peregrine. *In Defence of Aristocracy*. London: HarperCollins, 2004.

Wright, Tony. "The Politics of Accountability." In *The Cambridge Companion to Public Law*, edited by Mark Elliot and David Feldman. Cambridge: Cambridge University Press, 2015.

Yellen, Janet L. "Macroeconomic Research after the Crisis." Speech delivered at "The Elusive 'Great' Recovery: Causes and Implications for Future Business Cycle Dynamics" conference, October 14, 2016. Federal Reserve Bank of Boston.

Zingales, Luigi. "Towards a Political Theory of the Firm." Stigler Center New Working Paper Series, no. 10. University of Chicago, 2017.

Zolo, Danilo. *Democratic Complexity: A Realist Approach*. Cambridge: Polity Press, 1992.

INDEX